Lecture Notes in Computer Science　　13340

More information about this series at https://link.springer.com/bookseries/558

Xingming Sun · Xiaorui Zhang · Zhihua Xia ·
Elisa Bertino (Eds.)

Artificial Intelligence and Security

8th International Conference, ICAIS 2022
Qinghai, China, July 15–20, 2022
Proceedings, Part III

 Springer

Editors
Xingming Sun ⓘ
Nanjing University of Information Science
and Technology
Nanjing, China

Xiaorui Zhang ⓘ
Nanjing University of Information Science
and Technology
Nanjing, China

Zhihua Xia ⓘ
Jinan University
Guangzhou, China

Elisa Bertino
Purdue University
West Lafayette, IN, USA

ISSN 0302-9743   ISSN 1611-3349 (electronic)
Lecture Notes in Computer Science
ISBN 978-3-031-06790-7   ISBN 978-3-031-06791-4 (eBook)
https://doi.org/10.1007/978-3-031-06791-4

This Springer imprint is published by the registered company Springer Nature Switzerland AG
The registered company address is: Gewerbestrasse 11, 6330 Cham, Switzerland

Preface

The 8th International Conference on Artificial Intelligence and Security (ICAIS 2022), formerly called the International Conference on Cloud Computing and Security (ICCCS), was held during July 15–20, 2022, in Qinghai, China. Over the past seven years, ICAIS has become a leading conference for researchers and engineers to share their latest results of research, development, and applications in the fields of artificial intelligence and information security.

We used the Microsoft Conference Management Toolkit (CMT) system to manage the submission and review processes of ICAIS 2022. We received 1124 submissions from authors in 20 countries and regions, including the USA, Canada, the UK, Italy, Ireland, Japan, Russia, France, Australia, South Korea, South Africa, Iraq, Kazakhstan, Indonesia, Vietnam, Ghana, China, Taiwan, Macao, etc. The submissions cover the areas of artificial intelligence, big data, cloud computing and security, information hiding, IoT security, multimedia forensics, encryption and cybersecurity, and so on. We thank our Technical Program Committee (TPC) members and external reviewers for their efforts in reviewing papers and providing valuable comments to the authors. From the total of 1124 submissions, and based on at least three reviews per submission, the Program Chairs decided to accept 166 papers to be published in three LNCS volumes and 168 papers to be published in three CCIS volumes, yielding an acceptance rate of 30%. This volume of the conference proceedings contains all the regular, poster, and workshop papers.

The conference program was enriched by a series of keynote presentations, and the keynote speakers included Q.M. Jonathan Wu and Brij B. Gupta, amongst others. We thank them for their wonderful speeches.

There were 68 workshops organized in ICAIS 2022 which covered all the hot topics in artificial intelligence and security. We would like to take this moment to express our sincere appreciation for the contribution of all the workshop chairs and participants. We would like to extend our sincere thanks to all authors who submitted papers to ICAIS 2022 and to all TPC members. It was a truly great experience to work with such talented and hard-working researchers. We also appreciate the external reviewers for assisting the TPC members in their particular areas of expertise. Moreover, we want to thank our sponsors: ACM, ACM SIGWEB China, the University of Electronic Science and Technology of China, Qinghai Minzu University, Yuchi Blockchain Research Institute, Nanjing Normal University, Northeastern State University, New York University, Michigan State University, the University of Central Arkansas, Dublin City University,

Université Bretagne Sud, the National Nature Science Foundation of China, and Tech Science Press.

April 2022

Xingming Sun
Xiaorui Zhang
Zhihua Xia
Elisa Bertino

Organization

General Chairs

Yun Q. Shi	New Jersey Institute of Technology, USA
Weisheng Ma	Qinghai Minzu University, China
Mauro Barni	University of Siena, Italy
Ping Jiang	Southeast University, China
Elisa Bertino	Purdue University, USA
Xingming Sun	Nanjing University of Information Science and Technology, China

Technical Program Chairs

Aniello Castiglione	University of Salerno, Italy
Yunbiao Guo	China Information Technology Security Evaluation Center, China
Xiaorui Zhang	Engineering Research Center of Digital Forensics, Ministry of Education, China
Q. M. Jonathan Wu	University of Windsor, Canada
Shijie Zhou	University of Electronic Science and Technology of China, China

Publication Chair

Zhihua Xia	Jinan University, China

Publication Vice Chair

Ruohan Meng	Nanjing University of Information Science and Technology, China

Publicity Chair

Zhaoxia Yin	Anhui University, China

Workshop Chairs

Baowei Wang   Nanjing University of Information Science and
                               Technology, China
Lingyun Xiang   Changsha University of Science and Technology,
                               China

Organization Chairs

Genlin Ji   Nanjing Normal University, China
Jianguo Wei   Qinghai Minzu University and Tianjin University,
                               China
Xiaoyu Li   University of Electronic Science and Technology
                               of China, China
Zhangjie Fu   Nanjing University of Information Science and
                               Technology, China
Qilong Sun   Qinghai Minzu University, China

Technical Program Committee

Saeed Arif   University of Algeria, Algeria
Anthony Ayodele   University of Maryland Global Campus, USA
Zhifeng Bao   Royal Melbourne Institute of Technology,
                               Australia
Zhiping Cai   National University of Defense Technology,
                               China
Ning Cao   Qingdao Binhai University, China
Paolina Centonze   Iona College, USA
Chin-chen Chang   Feng Chia University, Taiwan, Republic of China
Han-Chieh Chao   National Dong Hwa University, Taiwan, Republic
                               of China
Bing Chen   Nanjing University of Aeronautics and
                               Astronautics, China
Hanhua Chen   Huazhong University of Science and Technology,
                               China
Xiaofeng Chen   Xidian University, China
Jieren Cheng   Hainan University, China
Lianhua Chi   IBM Research Center, Australia
Kim-Kwang Raymond Choo   University of Texas at San Antonio, USA
Ilyong Chung   Chosun University, South Korea
Martin Collier   Dublin City University, Ireland
Robert H. Deng   Singapore Management University, Singapore
Jintai Ding   University of Cincinnati, USA
Xinwen Fu   University of Central Florida, USA

Zhangjie Fu	Nanjing University of Information Science and Technology, China
Moncef Gabbouj	Tampere University of Technology, Finland
Ruili Geng	Spectral MD, USA
Song Guo	Hong Kong Polytechnic University, Hong Kong, China
Mohammad Mehedi Hassan	King Saud University, Saudi Arabia
Russell Higgs	University College Dublin, Ireland
Dinh Thai Hoang	University of Technology Sydney, Australia
Wien Hong	Nanfang College of Sun Yat-Sen University, China
Chih-Hsien Hsia	National Ilan University, Taiwan, Republic of China
Robert Hsu	Chung Hua University, Taiwan, Republic of China
Xinyi Huang	Fujian Normal University, China
Yongfeng Huang	Tsinghua University, China
Zhiqiu Huang	Nanjing University of Aeronautics and Astronautics, China
Patrick C. K. Hung	University of Ontario Institute of Technology, Canada
Farookh Hussain	University of Technology Sydney, Australia
Genlin Ji	Nanjing Normal University, China
Hai Jin	Huazhong University of Science and Technology, China
Sam Tak Wu Kwong	City University of Hong Kong, China
Chin-Feng Lai	Taiwan Cheng Kung University, Taiwan, Republic of China
Loukas Lazos	University of Arizona, USA
Sungyoung Lee	Kyung Hee University, South Korea
Hang Lei	University of Electronic Science and Technology of China, China
Chengcheng Li	University of Cincinnati, USA
Xiaoyu Li	University of Electronic Science and Technology of China, China
Feifei Li	Utah State University, USA
Jin Li	Guangzhou University, China
Jing Li	Rutgers University, USA
Kuan-Ching Li	Providence University, Taiwan, Republic of China
Peng Li	University of Aizu, Japan
Yangming Li	University of Washington, USA
Luming Liang	Uber Technology, USA
Haixiang Lin	Leiden University, The Netherlands

Xiaodong Lin   University of Ontario Institute of Technology,
                                   Canada
Zhenyi Lin   Verizon Wireless, USA
Alex Liu   Michigan State University, USA
Guangchi Liu   Stratifyd Inc., USA
Guohua Liu   Donghua University, China
Joseph Liu   Monash University, Australia
Quansheng Liu   University of South Brittany, France
Xiaodong Liu   Edinburgh Napier University, UK
Yuling Liu   Hunan University, China
Zhe Liu   Nanjing University of Aeronautics and
                                   Astronautics, China
Daniel Xiapu Luo   Hong Kong Polytechnic University, Hong Kong,
                                   China
Xiangyang Luo   Zhengzhou Science and Technology Institute,
                                   China
Tom Masino   TradeWeb LLC, USA
Nasir Memon   New York University, USA
Noel Murphy   Dublin City University, Ireland
Sangman Moh   Chosun University, South Korea
Yi Mu   University of Wollongong, Australia
Elie Naufal   Applied Deep Learning LLC, USA
Jiangqun Ni   Sun Yat-sen University, China
Rafal Niemiec   University of Information Technology and
                                   Management, Poland
Zemin Ning   Wellcome Trust Sanger Institute, UK
Shaozhang Niu   Beijing University of Posts and
                                   Telecommunications, China
Srikant Ojha   Sharda University, India
Jeff Z. Pan   University of Aberdeen, UK
Wei Pang   University of Aberdeen, UK
Chen Qian   University of California, Santa Cruz, USA
Zhenxing Qian   Fudan University, China
Chuan Qin   University of Shanghai for Science and
                                   Technology, China
Jiaohua Qin   Central South University of Forestry and
                                   Technology, China
Yanzhen Qu   Colorado Technical University, USA
Zhiguo Qu   Nanjing University of Information Science and
                                   Technology, China
Yongjun Ren   Nanjing University of Information Science and
                                   Technology, China
Arun Kumar Sangaiah   VIT University, India

Di Shang	Long Island University, USA
Victor S. Sheng	Texas Tech University, USA
Zheng-guo Sheng	University of Sussex, UK
Robert Simon Sherratt	University of Reading, UK
Yun Q. Shi	New Jersey Institute of Technology, USA
Frank Y. Shih	New Jersey Institute of Technology, USA
Guang Sun	Hunan University of Finance and Economics, China
Jianguo Sun	Harbin University of Engineering, China
Krzysztof Szczypiorski	Warsaw University of Technology, Poland
Tsuyoshi Takagi	Kyushu University, Japan
Shanyu Tang	University of West London, UK
Jing Tian	National University of Singapore, Singapore
Yoshito Tobe	Aoyang University, Japan
Cezhong Tong	Washington University in St. Louis, USA
Pengjun Wan	Illinois Institute of Technology, USA
Cai-Zhuang Wang	Ames Laboratory, USA
Ding Wang	Peking University, China
Guiling Wang	New Jersey Institute of Technology, USA
Honggang Wang	University of Massachusetts-Dartmouth, USA
Jian Wang	Nanjing University of Aeronautics and Astronautics, China
Jie Wang	University of Massachusetts Lowell, USA
Jin Wang	Changsha University of Science and Technology, China
Liangmin Wang	Jiangsu University, China
Ruili Wang	Massey University, New Zealand
Xiaojun Wang	Dublin City University, Ireland
Xiaokang Wang	St. Francis Xavier University, Canada
Zhaoxia Wang	Singapore Management University, Singapore
Jianguo Wei	Qinghai Minzu University and Tianjin University, China
Sheng Wen	Swinburne University of Technology, Australia
Jian Weng	Jinan University, China
Edward Wong	New York University, USA
Eric Wong	University of Texas at Dallas, USA
Shaoen Wu	Ball State University, USA
Shuangkui Xia	Beijing Institute of Electronics Technology and Application, China
Lingyun Xiang	Changsha University of Science and Technology, China
Yang Xiang	Deakin University, Australia

Yang Xiao	The University of Alabama, USA
Haoran Xie	The Education University of Hong Kong, China
Naixue Xiong	Northeastern State University, USA
Wei Qi Yan	Auckland University of Technology, New Zealand
Aimin Yang	Guangdong University of Technology, China
Ching-Nung Yang	National Dong Hwa University, Taiwan, Republic of China
Chunfang Yang	Zhengzhou Science and Technology Institute, China
Fan Yang	University of Maryland, USA
Guomin Yang	University of Wollongong, Australia
Qing Yang	University of North Texas, USA
Yimin Yang	Lakehead University, Canada
Ming Yin	Purdue University, USA
Shaodi You	Australian National University, Australia
Kun-Ming Yu	Chung Hua University, Taiwan, Republic of China
Shibin Zhang	Chengdu University of Information Technology, China
Weiming Zhang	University of Science and Technology of China, China
Xinpeng Zhang	Fudan University, China
Yan Zhang	Simula Research Laboratory, Norway
Yanchun Zhang	Victoria University, Australia
Yao Zhao	Beijing Jiaotong University, China
Desheng Zheng	Southwest Petroleum University, China
Qi Cui	Nanjing University of Information Science and Technology, China

Organization Committee

Tao Ye	Qinghai Minzu University, China
Xianyi Chen	Nanjing University of Information Science and Technology, China
Zilong Jin	Nanjing University of Information Science and Technology, China
Yiwei Li	Columbia University, USA
Yuling Liu	Hunan University, China
Zhiguo Qu	Nanjing University of Information Science and Technology, China
Huiyu Sun	New York University, USA
Le Sun	Nanjing University of Information Science and Technology, China
Jian Su	Nanjing University of Information Science and Technology, China

Qing Tian   Nanjing University of Information Science and
                              Technology, China
Qi Wang   Nanjing University of Information Science and
                              Technology, China
Lingyun Xiang   Changsha University of Science and Technology,
                              China
Zhihua Xia   Nanjing University of Information Science and
                              Technology, China
Lizhi Xiong   Nanjing University of Information Science and
                              Technology, China
Leiming Yan   Nanjing University of Information Science and
                              Technology, China
Li Yu   Nanjing University of Information Science and
                              Technology, China
Zhili Zhou   Nanjing University of Information Science and
                              Technology, China
Qi Cui   Nanjing University of Information Science and
                              Technology, China

Contents – Part III

A Data Reconciliation Model Based on QLDPC for Satellite-Ground
Quantum Key Distribution Network 271
*Wenting Zhou, Jie Liu, Bao Feng, Xiao Ye, Tianbing Zhang,
Yuxiang Bian, and Wenjie Liu*

Information Hiding

IoT Security

Encryption and Cybersecurity

Research on Offense and Defense of DDos Based on Evolutionary Game Theory

Tengteng Zhao[1], Wei Zhang[1], Xiaolong Li[1(✉)], Wenjing Wang[1], Xu Niu[1], and Hui Guo[2]

[1] Beijing Institute of Control and Electronics Technology, Muxidi North Street, Beijing 100038, China
lxl-777333@163.com

[2] State Key Laboratory of Networking and Switching Technology, Beijing University of Posts and Telecommunications, Beijing 100876, China

Abstract. While the advancement of network technology has brought convenience to people's lives, there are also potential threats. Cyberspace security is closely related to national security. DDos attacks exploit protocol vulnerabilities and use malicious traffic from multiple sources to attack networks and network services, have caused huge economic losses to users and service providers. Based on the evolutionary game theory, this paper models both the offense and defense of DDos, and studies the offense and defense of DDos from a micro perspective. Through the elaboration of the conflict of interest between the attackers and the defenders, the evolutionary game and simulation are carried out. The model and simulation results show that the attackers are more inclined to launch attacks, and the defenders' strategy choices are related to the cost of the active defense system.

Keywords: Network security · DDos attacks · Game theory · Evolutionary game theory

1 Introduction

With the rapid development of computer technology, informatization has widely penetrated into various fields. Nowadays, people's lives, studies and work rely more and more on computer technology. While the advancement of network technology has provided convenience to our lives, it has also caused certain threats. Some large but not strong cyberspace has gradually become the attack direction of some hostile forces, which may bring huge disasters to people, society, and even the country [1].

Distributed denial-of-service attack (DDOS attack) is a highly harmful and destructive attack method that has emerged in recent years [2]. It makes the military, national government agencies, enterprises and institutions face severe threats and challenges to network information security. DDOS attacks mostly use compromised computers on the Internet as "zombies" to initiate intensive "denial of service" requests to a specific target, so as to exhaust their network resources and system resources, making them unable to provide services to real users. Attackers use multiple servers to launch attacks and

X. Sun et al. (Eds.): ICAIS 2022, LNCS 13340, pp. 3–15, 2022.
https://doi.org/10.1007/978-3-031-06791-4_1

obtain expected benefits by maliciously brushing website traffic, mass spamming, and disrupting the services of commercial competitors [3, 4].

In reality, after the attacker initiates an DDos attack, the target system will detect the attack and adopt corresponding defense techniques to defend. At the same time, in order to achieve his own goals, the attacker will change attack method in order to further attack due to the intervention of the target system. The attacker and the defender confront each other, forming a cycle of offensive and defensive confrontation [5, 6]. In the process of network attack and defense, the result of the confrontation between the attacker and the defender determines the network status. There are similarities between game theory and offensive and defensive strategies. Combining game theory with network offense and defense can improve offensive and defensive capabilities. Facing the problem of DDOS attacks, establishing an offensive and defensive game model, and analyzing the strategies of the attacker and the defender, can make the game between the two parties reach an equilibrium. Combining game theory with DDOS attacks has laid the foundation for further research on network security [7–9].

However, the classic game assumes that the stakeholders are completely rational and have the overall information, which is inconsistent with the actual situation. While the dynamic game theory improves on the traditional game, considering the limitation of rationality, and regards the player's strategic choices as dynamic adjustment process [10].

By analyzing the strategies and conflicts of interest of the attacker and defender of DDOS, this paper constructs an evolutionary game model of DDOS offense and defense, weighs the strategies of both offense and defense, and optimizes the development trend through the dynamic evolution process.

2 Related Work

In recent years, many people have combined game theory with various technologies to give full play to the advantages of game theory. Liu et al. [11] used evolutionary game to establish a game model of data sharing for researchers under two mechanisms, trustless and trusted, and analyzed and compared the dynamic evolution mechanism of data sharing behaviors of researchers under these two mechanisms. Then a four-in-one driving strategy of "cost-data-trust-policy" was proposed, and "practice analysis" was carried out in combination with examples. Hewett et al. [12] established a dynamic game between the attacker and the manager of the security system, in which the interpretation of the game model was obtained by reverse induction. When the security protection system is attacked, according to solving the Nash equilibrium, defender can make accurate judgments and decisions in a timely manner. In the study of the spread of computer viruses, Zhang et al. [13] established a Markov game model. Ordinary computer users, network administrators, and attackers are three important players. According to the analysis of these three players and combining related algorithms, this paper obtained a method that can effectively organize the spread of the virus to prevent the spread of the virus from affecting computer users.

In addition, in order to effectively reduce security risks and make the best network defense decision with limited resources, Liu et al. [14] established a network attack and defense game model with limited resources, proposed an algorithm for attack and defense decision in the model, and designed a selection method. Finally, the applicability of the model is experimentally analyzed in the actual network attack and defense environment. In order to solve the problem that the defender analyzes the behavior of the attacker in the smart power grid, Li Jun et al. [15] put forward a Bayesian sequential game model, which solves the problem of the uncertainty of the attack method of the defender to the attacker. Through the calculation, the optimal strategies of both sides are obtained, which provides a reference for the security of the smart power grid. Pratyusa et al. [16] proposed a mobile target defense model based on complete information static game, which abstracts the optimal defense strategy into a balance between the security and availability of the target system. However, in the actual attack and defense process, due to the limited intelligence collection ability of the attackers and the defenders, and deliberately hiding their own information, the defense information mastered by the attackers is generally incomplete. Therefore, the model has the defect of insufficient accuracy in describing the actual attack and defense behaviors.

Many researchers at home and abroad have done a lot of research on DDoS attack and defense evaluation, and achieved some success. Reference [17] put forward a classification standard for evaluating the defense mechanism against DDoS attacks, and pointed out some standard parameters used in evaluating a defense mechanism, but there is a lack of specific experimental comparison. Reference [18] proposed an evaluation framework for DDoS Defense mechanism, but this method requires a strict assumption to clearly distinguish attack packets from legitimate packets, which is difficult to implement in actual network attack and defense confrontation. Reference [19] proposed a DDoS Defense Strategy Selection Algorithm based on multi-attribute decision-making, comprehensively considered various evaluation indexes, provided a reference for the selection of defense strategies, and verified the effectiveness of this method through experiments. In order to effectively evaluate DDoS attack and defense behaviors to defend against DDoS attacks, other studies combine DDoS attacks with game theory. Reference [20] put forward a performance evaluation method of DDoS attack and defense based on strategic game. This paper constructed the attack and defense strategy model based on game theory, defined the attack and defense utility function, and obtained the optimal attack and defense strategy by solving the mixed strategy Nash equilibrium. However, the above evaluation method only from the point of view of the change of the index value of the attack and defense results or the income of the attack and defense behavior to evaluate the DDoS defense strategy, which is more one-sided, belongs to the static evaluation, lack of consideration of the attack and defense process and lack of pertinence to the optimal defense measures.

In order to effectively evaluate the benefits of both the attacker and the defender, and to maximize the benefits, it is necessary to adjust the game strategy dynamically. Shi et al. [21] designed a DDoS attack and defense game model based on Q-learning, and proposed a model algorithm based on this model. When the defender uses the model, it can get higher benefits, thus proving the availability and effectiveness of the algorithm. Zhang et al. [22] based on the game nature of DDoS attack and defense behavior, used incomplete information static game theory to model DDoS attack and defense behavior. They put forward an evaluation method of DDoS defense mechanism based on incomplete information static game, and evaluated DDoS defense mechanism. Finally, simulation experiments were carried out with relevant simulation software, and the experimental results showed that the evaluation method is applicable and effective.

In summary, game theory and network security are compatible, the combination of this two is helpful to evaluate the security of network security, and the existing research has achieved good results in this area. In addition, compared with the static game, the dynamic adjustment game strategy can maximize the interests of both sides of the game. In the face of DDOS attacks, the use of dynamic adjustment game strategy has achieved better results. Therefore, this article combines evolutionary game with DDOS, which has certain research significance and research value.

3   Methodology

In the DDos attack and defense game, defenders need to consider whether to adopt active defense strategy, rather than passive defense based on firewall, attackers need to consider whether to attack a service. Attackers and defenders need to play games according to the benefits obtained by different strategies in the process of attack and defense in order to maximize the benefits.

3.1   Hypothesis of the Evolutionary Game Model

Hypothesis 1: Both attackers and defenders are bounded rational.

Hypothesis 2: Attackers and defenders can learn from each other and constantly improve their strategies by correcting mistakes, because they are bounded rational and it is difficult for them to choose the ideal strategy to maximize their own interests in the first place.

Hypothesis 3: The defender has two strategies: "active defense" and "passive defense". The probabilities of "active defense" and "passive defense" are $(0 \leq x \leq 1)$ and $1 - x$ respectively.

Hypothesis 4: Attackers have two strategies: "attack" and "do not attack". The probabilities of "attack" and "do not attack" are $y(0 \leq y \leq 1)$ and $1 - y$ respectively.

3.2   Evolutionary Game Between Attackers and Defenders

Based on the above problem description and the contradiction between the attackers and the defenders, we develop a large group-double population evolutionary game model.

The decision tree of the interest game model of both sides of attack and defense is shown in Fig. 1.

When the defender adopts the "active defense" strategy and the attacker adopts the "attack" strategy, the defender has to pay the cost of development and operation and maintenance of the defense system C_d. At the same time, when the defense system is deployed outside the service, the defender also has to pay for the performance loss C_l caused by the defense system. In addition, the defender gets the basic benefit R from the deployment of the service. Because the defense system can not completely resist the

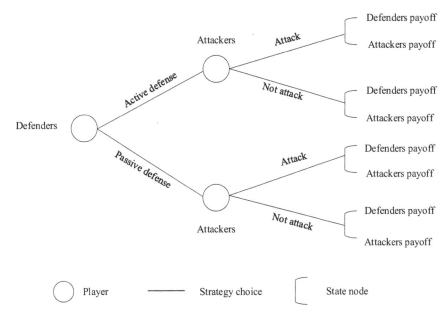

Fig. 1. A decision tree demonstrating the players' payoff.

attack of the attacker, it can only minimize the loss caused by the attack, so the defender also needs to pay the loss of the attack A_a.

When the defender adopts the "active defense" strategy and the attacker adopts the "do not attack" strategy, the defender needs to pay the cost of the development and operation of the defense system C_d and the performance loss caused by the defense system C_1, and get the basic benefit R of deploying the service.

When the defender adopts the "passive defense" strategy and the attacker adopts the "attack" strategy, the defender gets the basic benefit R of the deployment service, while the defender has to pay the loss caused by the attack A_p and the invisible loss of the user caused by the deterioration of the quality of service C_r.

When the defender adopts the "passive defense" strategy and the attacker adopts the "do not attack" strategy, the defender gets the basic benefit R of deploying the service.

When the attacker adopts the "do not attack" strategy, the attacker gains zero.

When the attacker adopts the "attack" strategy, and the defender adopts the "active defense" strategy, the benefit gained by the attacker is the benefit of the partial success of the attack A_a. If the defender successfully defends against the attack of the attacker, it will bring losses to the attacker. For example, if the defender discovers the servers that attacker used to launch DDos attacks, the defender will fix the bugs in this part of the servers, causing the attacker to lose control over these servers. Therefore, the attacker also needs to pay the loss of the successful defense of the defender C.

When the attacker adopts the "attack strategy" and the defender adopts the "passive defense" strategy, the benefit gained by the attacker is the benefit of a successful attack A_p.

The meaning of the parameters and the benefit matrix of both the attacker and the defender are shown in Table 1 and Table 2 respectively.

Table 1. Parameter definitions of evolutionary game model.

Parameters	Descriptions
R	Basic revenue from services
C_d	Defense system development operation and maintenance costs
C_l	Performance loss caused by defense systems
A_a	Losses incurred when the defender adopts a active defense strategy
A_p	Losses incurred when the defender adopts a passive defense strategy
C_r	The user invisible loss caused by the decline of service quality
C	Cost caused by an attacker being successfully defended

Table 2. Payoff matrix.

		Attackers	
		Attack	Do not attack
Defenders	Active defense	$R - C_d - C_l - A_a, A_a - C$	$R - C_d - C_l, 0$
	Passive defense	$R - A_p - C_r, A_p$	$R, 0$

3.3 Systematic Stability Analysis

π_{s1} represents the expected payoff of the defender when the defender chooses the "active defense" strategy, π_{s2} represents the expected payoff of the defender when the defender chooses the "passive defense" strategy, and $\overline{\pi_s}$ represents the average payoff of the defender. The benefits of all strategies are as follows:

$$\pi_{s1} = y(R - C_d - C_l - A_a) + (1 - y)(R - C_d - C_l) \tag{1}$$

$$\pi_{s2} = y(R - A_p - C_r) + (1 - y)R \tag{2}$$

$$\overline{\pi_s} = x\pi_{s1} + (1 - x)\pi_{s2} \tag{3}$$

Similarly, π_{a1} represents the expected payoff of the attacker when the attacker chooses the "attack" strategy, and π_{a2} represents the expected payoff of the attacker when the attacker chooses the "do not attack" strategy. And $\overline{\pi_a}$ represents the average payoff of the attacker. The benefits of all strategies are as follows:

$$\pi_{a1} = x(A_a - C) + (1 - x)A_p \tag{4}$$

$$\pi_{a2} = 0 \tag{5}$$

$$\overline{\pi_a} = y\pi_{a1} + (1 - y)\pi_{a2} \tag{6}$$

Accordingly, the replicator dynamics equations are:

$$F(x) = \frac{dx}{dt} = x(1 - x)[y(A_p + C_r - A_a) - (C_d + C_l)] \tag{7}$$

$$F(y) = \frac{dy}{dt} = y(1 - y)[x(A_a - C - A_p) + A_p] \tag{8}$$

Therefore, by combining Eq. (7) and Eq. (8) the replicated dynamic system is constructed, and local equilibrium points (LEP) can be obtained by letting Eq. (7) $= 0$ and Eq. (8) $= 0$. Then the five LEP are shown as follows: $(0, 0)$, $(0, 1)$, $(1, 0)$, $(1, 1)$, (x^*, y^*), $x^* \in [0, 1]$, $y^* \in [0, 1]$. $x^* = \frac{-A_p}{A_a - C - A_p}$, $y^* = \frac{C_d + C_l}{A_p + C_r - A_a}$. At the same time, these LEP are not necessarily the evolutionarily stable strategy (ESS), the stability of the LEP can be determined by the Jacobian matrix of the system, the Jacobian matrix is as follows:

$$J = \begin{bmatrix} \frac{\partial\left(\frac{dx}{dt}\right)}{\partial x} & \frac{\partial\left(\frac{dx}{dt}\right)}{\partial y} \\ \frac{\partial\left(\frac{dy}{dt}\right)}{\partial x} & \frac{\partial\left(\frac{dy}{dt}\right)}{\partial y} \end{bmatrix}$$
$$= \begin{bmatrix} (1 - 2x)[y(A_p + C_r - A_a) - (C_d + C_l)] & x(1 - x)(A_p + C_r - A_a) \\ y(1 - y)(A_a - C - A_p) & (1 - 2y)[x(A_a - C - A_p) + A_p] \end{bmatrix} \tag{9}$$

When the LEP of the replicated dynamic system meet condition tr < 0 and det > 0, the equilibrium point denotes the ESS. The results of det and tr for respective LEP are shown in Table 3.

In order to simplify the analysis, we first make some assumptions before the analysis: (1) $A_a < A_p$. Its practical significance is very clear. When the defender adopts the "active defense" strategy, the defender deploys the defense system in addition to the services provided to the user, and has a certain defense capability, so $A_a < A_p$. (2) $C_d + C_l > A_p$. The cost of development and operation and maintenance of the defense system C_d plus the performance loss C_l caused by the defense system is greater than the loss suffered by the defender when he was attacked when he adopted the "passive defense" strategy. In practice, the cost of developing and operating a DDos defense system is relatively high, but defense system will bring long-term benefits.

As shown in Table 3, in order to discuss the symbols of det$J$ and tr$J$ of different LEP, we should first discuss the symbols of $A_a - C$ and $A_p + C_r - A_a - C_d - C_l$, the results are shown in Table 4.

(1) Case 1: As shown in Table 4, Point D $(1, 1)$ is the ESS of the system, which means the defender adopt "active defense" strategy and the attacker adopt "attack" strategy. In this situation, the cost caused by the attack of the attacker to the defender is

Table 3. The results of det and tr for the LEP.

LEP	det J	tr J
A $(0, 0)$	$-A_p(C_d + C_l)$	$-(C_d + C_l) + A_p$
B $(0, 1)$	$-A_p(A_p + C_r - A_a - C_d - C_l)$	$C_r - A_a - C_d - C_l$
C $(1, 0)$	$(C_d + C_l)(A_a - C)$	$C_d + C_l + A_a - C$
D $(1, 1)$	$(A_p + C_r - A_a - C_d - C_l)(A_a - C)$	$C_d + C_l - A_p - C_r + C$
E (x^*, y^*)	$\dfrac{A_p(A_a-C)(C_d+C_l)(A_p+C_r-A_a-C_d-C_l)}{(A_a-C-A_p)(A_p+C_r-A_a)}$	0

Table 4. Evolutionary stability state under different cases.

Cases	LEP	det J	tr J	State
Case 1: $A_a - C > 0$ and $A_p + C_r - A_a - C_d - C_l > 0$	A $(0, 0)$	−	−	Unstable
	B $(0, 1)$	−	Uncertain	Saddle point
	C $(1, 0)$	+	+	Unstable
	D $(1, 1)$	+	−	ESS
	E (x^*, y^*)	−	0	Saddle point
Case 2: $A_a - C > 0$ and $A_p + C_r - A_a - C_d - C_l < 0$	A $(0, 0)$	−	−	Unstable
	B $(0, 1)$	+	−	ESS
	C $(1, 0)$	+	+	Unstable
	D $(1, 1)$	−	Uncertain	Saddle point
	E (x^*, y^*)	+	0	Saddle point
Case 3: $A_a - C < 0$ and $A_p + C_r - A_a - C_d - C_l > 0$	A $(0, 0)$	−	−	Unstable
	B $(0, 1)$	−	Uncertain	Saddle point
	C $(1, 0)$	−	Uncertain	Saddle point
	D $(1, 1)$	−	Uncertain	Saddle point
	E (x^*, y^*)	+	0	Saddle point
Case 4: $A_a - C < 0$ and $A_p + C_r - A_a - C_d - C_l < 0$	A $(0, 0)$	−	−	Unstable
	B $(0, 1)$	+	−	ESS
	C $(1, 0)$	−	Uncertain	Saddle point
	D $(1, 1)$	+	+	Unstable
	E (x^*, y^*)	−	0	Saddle point

greater than the cost caused by the active defense system to the attacker, therefore, attackers are more likely to launch attacks. At the same time, defenders are more inclined to adopt "active defense" strategy and build a defense system to reduce the loss of system services caused by attackers.

(2) Case 2: As shown in Table 4, Point B (0, 1) is the ESS of the system, which means the defender adopt "passive defense" strategy and the attacker adopt "attack" strategy. In this situation, the cost caused by the attack of the attacker to the defender is greater than the cost caused by the active defense system to the attacker, and the cost of building and running a defense system plus the loss of being attacked during active defense is less than the loss of being attacked when defender adopt "passive defense".

(3) Case 3: As shown in Table 4, there is no ESS in the system. In this situation, the system is in an unstable state and there is no optimal strategy for both sides of attacker and defender.

(4) Case 4: As shown in Table 4, Point B (0, 1) is the ESS of the system. In this situation, the cost caused by the attack of the attacker to the defender is less than the cost caused by the active defense system to the attacker, and the cost of building and running a defense system plus the loss of being attacked during active defense is less than the loss of being attacked when defender adopt "passive defense". As a result, defenders are more likely to adopt "passive defense" strategy.

4 System Simulation Analysis

Based on MATLAB, this paper simulates the dynamic evolution trajectories of DDos attack and defense system based on evolutionary game theory, in order to verify the accuracy of the model proposed in this paper, and make the dynamic evolution trend more clearly.

(1) In Case 1, we set $A_p = 15, C_d = 10, C_l = 2, A_a = 2, C_r = 3, C = 1$. In this case, the dynamic evolution trajectory of the system is shown in Fig. 2. At this time, the dynamic evolution trajectory of the system tends to D (1, 1), which is consistent with the model analysis.

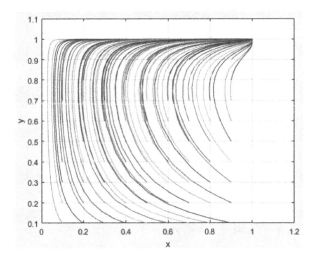

Fig. 2. Dynamic evolutionary path of case 1.

(2) In Case 2, we set $A_p = 10, C_d = 10, C_l = 2, A_a = 2, C_r = 3, C = 1$. In this case, the dynamic evolution trajectory of the system is shown in Fig. 3. At this time, the dynamic evolution trajectory of the system tends to B $(0, 1)$, which is consistent with the model analysis.

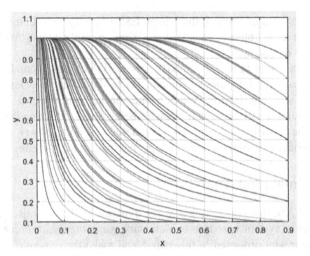

Fig. 3. Dynamic evolutionary path of case 2.

(3) In Case 3, we set $A_p = 15, C_d = 10, C_l = 2, A_a = 2, C_r = 3, C = 3$. In this case, there is no evolutionary stability strategy in the system. As shown in Fig. 4, which is consistent with the model analysis.

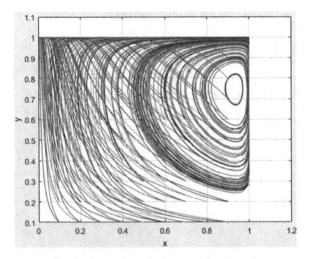

Fig. 4. Dynamic evolutionary path of case 3.

(4) In Case 4, we set $A_p = 10, C_d = 10, C_l = 2, A_a = 2, C_r = 3, C = 3$. In this case, the dynamic evolution trajectory of the system is shown in Fig. 5. At this time, the dynamic evolution trajectory of the system tends to B (0, 1), which is consistent with the model analysis.

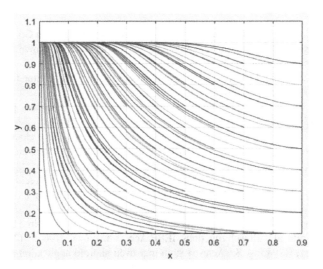

Fig. 5. Dynamic evolutionary path of case 4.

5 Conclusion

DDos attack is a kind of malicious attack which takes advantage of TCP/IP protocol defects or operating system vulnerabilities. The attacker attacks the targe system by controlling a large number of computers and combining them as an attack platform. As attackers, they aim to make the target system suffer the maximum loss, and the service providers, as the defenders, aim to provide the most stable service to legitimate users. In this paper, the evolutionary game model of attackers and defenders is established, and the attack and defense of DDos is studied from a microscopic point of view. Through the elaboration of the conflict of interest between the attackers and the defenders, the evolutionary game and simulation are carried out.

Analysis shows that attackers are more likely to launch attacks. Because the purpose of the attacker is to make the target system suffer the maximum loss, and only launching an attack will cause losses to the defenders. On the other hand, the strategy choice of the defender is related to the cost of the active defense system and other factors. If the cost of the development and operation of the defense system pluse the performance loss caused by the defense system is greater than the loss caused by the attack, the defenders are more likely to adopt the passive defense strategy, otherwise they are more inclined to adopt the active defense strategy. This is of guiding significance to the actual situation, if the current service is the core service and it will suffer greater losses after the attack, then the benefit of taking the active defense strategy is higher. In addition, improving the ability of DDos attack detection and defense will also promote defenders to adopt active defense strategies.

References

1. Tu, T., Liu, X., Song, L.: Understanding real-world concurrency bugs in Go. In: Proceedings of the Twenty-Fourth International Conference on Architectural Support for Programming Languages and Operating Systems, pp. 865–878 (2019)
2. Tu, T., Rao, L., Zhang, H.: Privacy-preserving outsourced auditing scheme for dynamic data storage in cloud. Secur. Commun. Netw. (2017)
3. Qin, B., Tu, T., Liu, Z.: Algorithmic profiling for real-world complexity problems. IEEE Trans. Softw. Eng. (2021)
4. Rao, L., Zhang, H., Tu, T.: Dynamic outsourced auditing services for cloud storage based on batch-leaves-authenticated Merkle hash tree. IEEE Trans. Serv. Comput. 13(3), 451–463 (2017)
5. Zhang, H., Qin, B., Tu, T.: An adaptive encryption-as-a-service architecture based on fog computing for real-time substation communications. IEEE Trans. Industr. Inf. 16(1), 658–668 (2019)
6. Qin, J., Zhang, H., Guo, J.: Vulnerability detection on android apps-inspired by case study on vulnerability related with web functions. IEEE Access 8, 106437–106451 (2020)
7. Qin, J., Zhang, H., Wang, S.: Acteve++: an improved android application automatic tester based on acteve. IEEE Access 7, 31358–31363 (2019)
8. Wang, S., Qin, S., Qin, J.: Ransomware-oriented detector for mobile devices based on behaviors. Appl. Sci. 11(14), 6557 (2021)
9. Wang, S., Qin, S., He, N.: KRRecover: an auto-recovery tool for hijacked devices and encrypted files by ransomwares on android. Symmetry 13(5), 861 (2021)
10. Artail, H., Safa, H., Sraj, M.: A hybrid honeypot framework for improving intrusion detection systems in protecting organizational networks. Comput. Secur. 25(4), 274–288 (2006)
11. Liu, X., Tong, Z., Shi, W.: A study on the evolutionary game of data sharing among researchers in the era of big data: a trust mechanism perspective. Intell. Theory Pract. 42(3), 92 (2019)
12. Hewett, R., Rudrapattana, S., Kijsanayothin, P.: Cyber-security analysis of smart grid SCADA systems with game models. In: Proceedings of the 9th Annual Cyber and Information Security Research Conference, pp. 109–112 (2014)
13. Zhang, Y., Tan, X., Cui, X.: Network security situation awareness approach based on Markov game model. J. Softw. 22(3), 495–508 (2011)
14. Liu, J., Liu, J., Lu, Y.: Optimal defense strategy selection method based on network attack and defense game model. Comput. Sci. 45(6), 117–123 (2018)
15. Jun, L., Li, T.: Cyber-physical security analysis of smart grids with bayesian sequential game models. Acta Automatica Sinica 45(1), 98–109 (2019)
16. Manadhata, P.K.: Game theoretic approaches to attack surface shifting. In: Moving Target Defense II, pp. 1–13. Springer, Cham (2013). https://doi.org/10.1007/978-1-4614-5416-8_1
17. Mölsä, J.V.E.: A taxonomy of criteria for evaluating defence mechanisms against flooding DoS Attacks. In: Blyth, A. (eds.) EC2ND 2005. Springer, London (2006). https://doi.org/10.1007/1-84628-352-3_2
18. Meadows, C.: A cost-based framework for analysis of denial of service in networks. J. Comput. Secur. 9(1–2), 143–164 (2001)

19. Huang, L., Feng, D., Lian, Y., Chen, K., Zhang, Y., et al.: A multi-attribute decision-based selection method for DDoS protection measures. J. Softw. **26**(7), 1742–1756 (2015)
20. Shi, P., Lian, Y.: Game-theoretical effectiveness evaluation of DDoS. In: Seventh International Conference on Networking, pp. 427–433 (2008)
21. Shi, Y., et al.: Q-learning based DDoS attack game model study. Comput. Sci. **41**(11), 203–226 (2014)
22. Zhang, S.: Research on the evaluation method of DDoS defense mechanism based on static game with incomplete information. J. Foshan Inst. Sci. Technol. Nat. Sci. Ed. **6**, 12–16 (2017)

A Method of Data Distribution and Traceability Based on Blockchain

Bin Gu[1], Yunfeng Zou[2(✉)], Dongyang Cai[1], and Huanyu Fan[2]

[1] State Grid Jiangsu Electric Power Co., Ltd., Jiangsu 210000, China
[2] State Grid Jiangsu Marketing Service Center (Metrology Center), Jiangsu 210000, China
13814099766@163.com

Abstract. In view of the privacy and particularity of power data, this paper proposes a traceability encryption data distribution method based on encryption technology in power system, including data distribution based on encryption technology in different storage modes and traceability mechanism suitable for different leak scenarios, so as to improve the traditional data distribution centralized degree, unclear rights allocation, low distribution efficiency and complex traceability conditions. This method uses league chain to construct block chain service, formulates different encrypted data forwarding schemes according to different storage modes of data files in the sender, adapts different data leakage traceability strategies according to different scenarios of data leakage in various forwarding schemes. A traceability, tamper-free, open and transparent shared traceability model is established. It ensures the safe transmission of power data and the traceability of data, and realizes the effective supervision of data sender and data receiver, so as to ensure the integrity of data distribution.

Keywords: Block chain · Encryption algorithm · Data distribution

1 Introduction

Data contains a large amount of high-value information, so it is necessary to ensure the security of data distribution process, the availability of data and the traceability of data leakage. Electric power data contains real electricity consumption data of residents and enterprises reflecting social life and production, which has a wide range of application scenarios and deep use value. In the power grid, each business department usually transmits the power data to the data console, and then the data console uniformly distributes it. With the deepening of power system informatization and power big data application, power data distribution is becoming more and more frequent, and the distribution scenarios are diverse. Under different distribution objects and distribution scenarios, the form of power data leakage is complex, and the leakage risk increases sharply. The safe distribution of power data and the traceability accountability after data leakage have become important security requirements.

X. Sun et al. (Eds.): ICAIS 2022, LNCS 13340, pp. 16–27, 2022.
https://doi.org/10.1007/978-3-031-06791-4_2

Blockchain technology [1] is a new distributed infrastructure and computing method that uses block chain data structure to verify and store data, uses distributed node consensus algorithm to generate and update data, uses cryptography to ensure the security of data transmission and access, and uses intelligent contract [2] composed of automatic script code to program and operate data. In terms of technical implementation, blockchain has the characteristics of transparency, traceability, non-tampering and trusted information sharing, so it can exactly solve the problem of trusted data transmission and sharing in various fields [3]. At the same time, blockchain can independently write smart contracts to realize the function of business logic, so blockchain technology will bring huge development to the whole Internet and even all walks of life in the future.

Encryption technology uses technical means to convert the plaintext data shared through insecure channels into ciphertext, and decrypts the ciphertext data after reaching the destination to prevent it from being stolen by a third party. Encryption consists of two elements: the algorithm and the key. An algorithm is the process of combining plain text (or comprehensible information) with a string of numbers (a key) to produce incomprehensible ciphertext. A key is a parameter used to encode and decode data. In the security and secrecy, the communication security of network can be ensured by proper key encryption technology and management mechanism. The cryptosystem of key encryption technology can be divided into symmetric key system and asymmetric key system. Accordingly, data encryption technology can be divided into two categories, namely symmetric encryption and asymmetric encryption. Symmetric Encryption is typically represented by Data Encryption Standard (DES) algorithm, while asymmetric Encryption is usually represented by Rivest Shamir Adleman (RSA) algorithm [4]. Symmetric encryption has the same encryption key and decryption key, while asymmetric encryption has different encryption key and decryption key. The encryption key can be made public while the decryption key needs to be kept secret.

The main purpose of this paper is to realize a data security sharing [2] and traceability strategy based on blockchain encryption technology [5, 6], so as to solve the situation of high degree of centralization of traditional data distribution, unclear authority allocation, low distribution efficiency and complex traceability conditions. The data sharing scheme based on blockchain technology implemented in this paper gives different data flow processes according to the differences of data file storage locations. At the same time, different traceability strategies are formulated corresponding to different data leakage scenarios in the data forwarding process, which effectively completes the supervision of data sender and receiver and improves the traceability efficiency. The author's main contributions are as follows:

(1) Based on block chain technology and domestic encryption algorithm, this paper designs a traceable and tamper-free data security distribution scheme for data transaction records. Data leakage can be effectively located on the premise of secure data distribution.
(2) Corresponding to the three data disclosure scenarios of attribute private key disclosure, encryption key disclosure and data unauthorized forwarding, feasible traceability schemes are proposed respectively.

2 Relation

At the policy level, governments around the world attach great importance to data sharing and data utilization in recent years, and constantly introduce various policies and regulations to promote the development of domestic and inter-regional data management and data sharing. On April 14, 2016, the EU approved the general data protection regulations and implemented them on May 25, 2018, replacing the EU data protection directive issued in 1995, the Regulation establishes a data protection framework from the aspects of personal data processing mode, user rights, obligations of all parties, product certification and regulatory measures. Its goal is to protect EU citizens from privacy and personal data disclosure. On March 23, 2018, in order to strengthen the control status of cross-border data in the United States, the president of the United States signed the explicit act on the legal use of overseas data, which addresses how the United States government can legally obtain foreign data and how foreign governments can legally obtain data within the United States.

In terms of encryption technology, In 1979, Shamir proposed the first secret sharing scheme, called (k, n) threshold scheme [7], whose core idea is that the secret data D to be shared is divided into N blocks, and the secret data can be reconstructed by any combination of k or more blocks. However, any $k-1$ block or any combination below $k-1$ blocks cannot obtain any information about data D. In 2010, Yu et al. realized fine-grained data sharing under the semi honest server model, but it can not realize flexible data sharing. Moreover, with the increase of the number of users, the complexity of creating files, user authorization and revocation will increase linearly, this makes the encryption key generation and users shall not apply to some specific application scenarios, such as mobile cloud environment. In 2010, Li et al. proposed a new access control framework to manage private health records in the cloud environment. The scheme uses ABE technology to encrypt private health records, divides the system into multiple security domains to reduce the complexity of key distribution, and supports flexible and on-demand user authority revocation. In 2015, Shao et al. proposed a data sharing scheme in mobile cloud environment based on attribute re encryption technology and transformation key technology, which allows data sharers to outsource some decryption permissions, but the offline computing cost of mobile users is very high. Most existing data sharing schemes are constructed using attribute-based encryption (ABE) [8, 9], but most of them do not consider or implement traceability. Therefore, Ahuja et al. proposed a traceable attribute-based signature encryption scheme (ABS) in 2016 to realize data sharing. In 2017, Sookhak et al. proposed a scheme to securely share private data between different vehicles in VANETs based on cloud environment [10]. The scheme is based on bilinear pairings and provides design ideas for data sharing schemes in many mobile cloud environments.

As for the data traceability tracking technology, the mainstream is the tracing based on log records [11]. The system log service provided by cloud service provider (CSP) [8] is used to extract data operation events from logs and realize data tracking. This approach is essentially system log analysis of the server, with the goal of extracting data operation records, and is now widely supported by most major cloud service providers such as Amazon. In the existing technology, most data sharing schemes are difficult to trace after data leakage, and the data tracing method inevitably introduces the assistance of CSP to generate operation records, which leads to the concern of users about the trust of CSP and the hidden trouble of insufficient traceability efficiency caused by excessive traceability evidence. Therefore, the characteristics of blockchain, such as transparency, traceability, non-tampering and trusted information sharing, can provide new ideas for solving the problem of trusted data transmission and traceability in various fields.

3 Risk Analysis, Workflow and Symbol Definition

3.1 Risk Analysis

General Form of Data Leakage. Use leaks. Such as operation error, printing, outgoing file, screen shooting and other ways to leak internal data.

Storage leaks. Data centers, servers, and databases were compromised and leaked; The former personnel copy the confidential information freely through mobile storage devices, or the former personnel export the confidential emails during their tenure; Data leakage caused by mobile terminal theft, loss or maintenance; Hacking attacks, etc.

Transmission leakage [12]. Tamper with, forge, and steal transmitted data by means of network monitoring and interception.

Risk Analysis of Data Distribution Process. There are various risks and challenges in the process of blockchain distribution. The types of risks and solutions are shown in Fig. 1.

Risk categories	Risk description	Solution
Data transmission risk	Data generated by business departments is stolen when uploaded to the data center through insecure channels	Utilize encryption algorithm and use the key or certificate issued by the company's unified cryptographic infrastructure to encrypt transmission to ensure its confidentiality
	Data provided by the data center is tampered when transmitted to various power institutions or users through insecure channels	Hashing algorithm is used to verify the message to ensure its integrity
Risk of illegal data forwarding	Data files may be directly forwarded to unauthorized personnel by business departments or data centers	The process of data forwarding by the business department is recorded on the blockchain. At the same time, the data information distributed by the data center is also recorded on the chain. According to the forwarding recorded in the blockchain, the responsible party can be traced
Risk of data leakage	Data files are illegally distributed directly from the business department without going through the blockchain or distributed off-chain by the data center	Watermark the data files to be forwarded, and judge the responsibility of the business department or the data center based on the watermark information of the leaked data files
Data Storage Risks	Business departments or data centers store data files in local or cloud servers	When storing important data, it should be encrypted and stored, and technical applications such as important data backup, access control, and security auditing should be implemented
Data use Risks	Unreasonable use of data on the recipient	You can sign a data use contract with the demander, and use desensitization, watermarking, auditing and other means to achieve differentiated protection in combination with data business scenarios

Fig. 1. Risk analysis and solutions in data distribution.

3.2 Working Process

The data security distribution process based on block chain is shown in Fig. 2.

(1) The data holder (business unit 1) packages and uploads the data to the data storer (Data Center) with encryption technology, and records the data transmission on the blockchain.

(2) The data depositor will encrypt the internal data and store it in the local or cloud server, broadcast the data summary to the blockchain network, and provide the data file information to the data user to select.

(3) Data users make data applications to the data depositor. The demand for confidential data shall be approved by the data holder who generate the data information and data auditor (Internet Department) before sharing, and the demand for detailed data shall be approved by the data auditor (Internet Department) before providing.

(4) The data store uses hashing and encryption algorithms to provide the shared data to the data user who requests it, and to link up the specific information of the transaction record.

(5) Once the data is illegally forwarded, the sender of the shared data can be found according to the transaction records of the blockchain. For data transmission without blockchain, watermark technology can be used to locate the disclosing party and complete the internal open traceability of data.

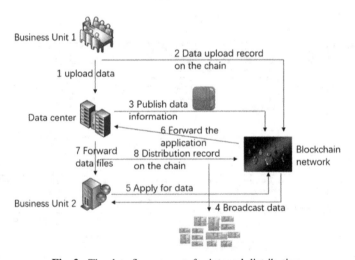

Fig. 2. The data flow process for internal distribution.

3.3 Symbol Definition

The symbols and descriptions used in this paper are shown in Table 1.

Table 1. Symbol and description.

Symbol	Description
Message	Data information broadcast by the data owner
M	Data file plaintext
C	Data file ciphertext
Content	Information displayed by the system to data users
Dataid	Number of data file
SKu	Data user's private key
Apply	Data applications sent by users
Addruser	The address of the data user in the blockchain
Request	Request forwarded by smart contract
Response	The sender's response to the receiver
EnattrbuteSKu	Encrypted attribute private key
EnSM4key	Encrypted SM4 key
Record	Transaction records recorded on the blockchain
Time	The time of the transaction
Dataown	Sender information in the transaction record
Datauser	Recipient information in the transaction record
Datamsg	Introduction to data files
Mhash	The hash value of the plaintext M
HSM4key	Hash value of SM4 key

4   Blockchain Based Data Distribution Scheme

The proposed blockchain-based data distribution scheme is shown in Fig. 3.

(1) The data owner (data center) broadcasts information about his own data files in the system. In this paper, when the data owner broadcasts the data file information to the block chain network, different data files are stored in different locations, and the data information released to the system is also different. Specifically,

    1) When data files are stored locally, we use SM4 symmetric cryptography algorithm to encrypt and store data files. The broadcast data information includes message<addressown\category\introduct\datahash\policy>.

    2) If the data file is stored in the cloud, the data owner completes the initialization based on attribute encryption before distributing the data, generates the public key and master private key [6], and formulates the access control policy, we use the public key generated by attribute encryption and the access control policy of the file to encrypt the data file M to generate a ciphertext

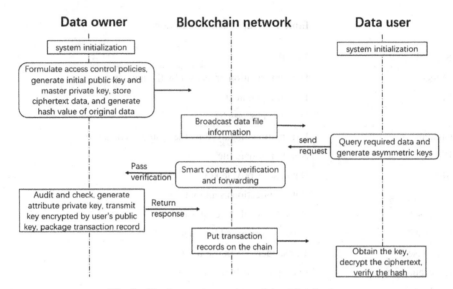

Fig. 3. The interactive process of data distribution.

C and upload it to the cloud server. The data messages broadcast included message<addressown\category\introduct\datahash\policy\addresscloud>.

Among them, addressown represents the address of the data owner in the blockchain network, the identity information in the data distribution, and the ownership of the data information; category represents the type of data information, which is used for data sorting and classification; introduct represents the introduction of data information, allowing data users to better understand the information content of data files. Data users can decide whether to apply for data according to category and introduct; datahash represents the original data hash value, which is used by the data user to hash the obtained data after decrypting the data, and then compare it with datahash to verify the integrity of the data; The policy represents the access control strategy formulated by the data owner, and the user who meets the strategy requests the smart contract to forward it; addresscloud represents the address information of the encrypted data file in the cloud storage server, and the data user can download the data ciphertext in the cloud server according to the address.

(2) When data users need to obtain data files, they query the system for the desired data file information and related access control permissions. Furthermore,

    1) Data users (external units or internal business departments) query data information, and the system displays data information content<addressown\category\introduct\datahash\policy\dataid>.

    2) In addition, if the data file is stored in the cloud, the data information content should also include the addresscloud field. The data user decides whether to

apply for a data file from the data owner based on the data file information, access strategy and own attributes.

(3) The data user satisfies the corresponding access authority and sends an access request to the smart contract. Furthermore,

    1) When a data user meets the corresponding access control authority and decides to apply for a data file, it must first locally generate a public and private key pair PKu, SKu based on domestically produced SM2 asymmetric encryption, and send an application Apply<dataid\addruser\PKu> to the system. Addruser represents the address of the data user in the blockchain, and is also the identity of the data user in data distribution; PKu is the public key of the data user.

    2) If attribute-based encryption is used, that is, the data file is stored in the cloud, PKu is used to encrypt the attribute private key of the data user generated by the data owner to ensure the privacy of private key transmission; If SM4 encryption is used, that is, the data file is stored locally, PKu is used to encrypt the symmetric key to ensure the reliability of key transmission.

(4) The smart contract determines that the data user meets the corresponding access rights, and then forwards the request to the data owner. Furthermore,

    1) The contracts in the system analyze the attributes of the data user, and determine whether the data user has permission to access it according to the access control strategy formulated by the data owner. If the user's authority is not enough, the contract may reject the user's request and forward the request <dataid\addruser\PKu> of the authorized user.

    2) If using attribute-based encryption, there should also be a userattrbute field, which represents the attributes of the data user. The data user attribute can be generated by the system according to the user's department, for the data owner to generate the attribute private key to decrypt the data file.

(5) The data owner transmits the encrypted data file and key information to the data user together. Furthermore,

    1) If the data file is stored in the cloud, the data owner will generate the corresponding attribute private key attrbuteSKu according to the attributes of the data user and the master private key after receiving the request sent by the contract. The attribute private key can be added with a random number according to the characteristics of the data user, so that it remains unique, and then the hashed value is also packaged in the transaction record for the traceability of the attribute private key leakage. After that, the data owner uses the received user public key PKu to encrypt the attribute private key [13] to obtain the encrypted attribute private key EnattrbuteSKu, and send response<HashattrbuteSKu\EnattrbuteSKu> to the data user, among them, HashattrbuteSKu represents the digest value obtained by the SM3 algorithm of the attribute private key, which is used to verify the authenticity of the attribute private key [14].

2) If the data file is stored locally, the response<HashSM4key, EnSM4key> and the encrypted data file need to be transmitted to the data user. Among them, HashSM4key represents the hashed SM4 key, which is used to verify transmission reliability, and EnSM4key represents the encrypted SM4 key.

3) At the same time, the system packs this transaction record for traceability query of data leakage. The transaction record includes record<time\dataown\datauser\datamsg\dataid\HashattrbuteSKu>.HashattrbuteSKu is used to trace the source of the leaked attribute private key. Considering that the blockchain is not suitable for storing large-capacity data [15], the record only contains the shortest information.

(6) The data user decrypts the received data file and compares the hash value of the data file in the broadcast after hashing. Furthermore,

1) The data user wants to download the data according to the response sent by the data owner. If the data file is stored in the cloud, the user needs to find the file storage address according to content<addresscloud> and download the data cipher text C, and then use the SM2 private key corresponding to Apply<PKu> in the attribute private key application to decrypt the encrypted attribute private key response<EnattrbuteSKu> get the attribute private key attrbuteSKu, use attrbuteSKu to hash operation to get HattrbuteSKu, compare with response<HashattrbuteSKu> to ensure that the attribute private key has not been tampered with, and then decrypt C with the attribute private key attrbuteSKu to obtain the plaintext M. Then perform SM3 hash operation on the plaintext to get Mhash, and compare Mhash with the hash value in content<datahash> to see if they are consistent [16].

2) If the data file is stored locally, the data owner will directly send the data ciphertext to the data user. The data user first uses the corresponding private key SKu in the Apply<PKu> to decrypt the SM4 key encrypted by PKu, The SM4 key is hashed to obtain the HSM4key, and to verify whether the key has been tampered with during the transmission process is to compare whether the HSM4key and the corresponding response<HashSM4key> are the same. The data user decrypts the transmitted encrypted data file C with the SM4 key to obtain the data plain text M. After hashing the plaintext M, compare it with content<datahash> to check its consistency.

(7) If the hash value is the same as the file hash value broadcast by the data owner, it proves that the received data file has not been tampered with and the transaction is successful. Specifically, if the hash value of the plaintext M after decryption is the same as the hash value in the data information, it proves that the complete target file is received and the transaction is successful.

(8) If the hash value is not the same as the file hash value of the initial broadcast, the integrity of the data file is destroyed and the transaction needs to be re-initiated. Specifically, if the hash value of the plaintext M after decryption is not the same as the hash value in the data information, it proves that the data has been tampered

with after unsafe transmission or the data information published by the data owner is inaccurate, and the data needs to be re-applied.

(9) Data leakage occurs in the system, and traceability queries are made based on the leaked information [17].

5 Data Tracing Schemes in Different Leak Scenarios

For different data leakage scenarios, Fig. 4 shows the corresponding traceability methods.

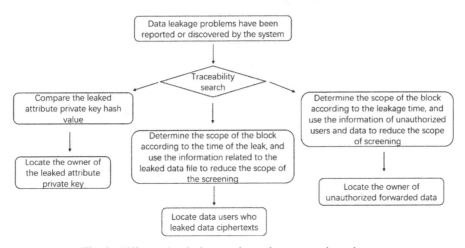

Fig. 4. Different data leak scenarios and source tracing schemes.

Scene1. For the data files stored on the cloud server, because there is a situation where the attribute private key [6] is deliberately leaked for profit, in this case, the attribute private key is generated by adding a random number to ensure its uniqueness, the leaked attribute private key can be hashed, and the corresponding data user can be found by comparing the hash value of the attribute private key in the transaction record in the blockchain.

In the process of data distribution, the data owner hashes the generated attribute private key, package it into the transaction record and finally store it in the blockchain. The time stamp of the block closest to the time when the leak occurs can be determined first by the time of leakage, and then compare one by one according to each record recorded in the block [18]. If the information of the partially leaked data file or the information of the data owner is determined, transaction records can be further screened through dataown and datamsg to reduce the scope of records to be tested and improve the efficiency of traceability and accountability.

Scene 2. If the attribute private key or the symmetric key encrypted with the public key of the data user is leaked, that is, EnattrbuteSKu or EnSM4key is leaked, the data user's private key SKu is used to perform an intensive test [19].

Specifically, from the time point when the leakage is determined, find the timestamp of the block closest to the leakage time and less than the leakage time, look forward from the block and try block by block. All data users contained in the transaction in the block try to decrypt the leaked EnattrbuteSKu or EnSM4key with their private key SKu. The user corresponding to the successfully decrypted private key is the responsible party. In particular, if the information of some data files has also been leaked and the types of data files or corresponding access control permissions are determined, it can be filtered by the data information and access permissions in transaction records. That is, the time is first used to determine the block scope of the corresponding record, and then further filter according to other known conditions to reduce the number of decryption attempts.

Scene 3. Unauthorized forwarding occurs [20, 21], where the data user does not have the appropriate permission to request the data file, but the data owner shares the data with other users over the blockchain network.

For this kind of situation, there are usually two possibilities. One is unauthorized forwarding when the business department transmits data to the data center; the other is unauthorized forwarding when the data center shares data with the business department that has data requirements. As with the above two scenarios, first determine the range of block records where unauthorized forwarding occurs based on the leak time, and query transaction records one by one. If you obtain the leaked data files and related unauthorized user information, you can further filter transactions based on the relevant information, reduce the scope of screening, and improve traceability efficiency.

6   Total

The author proposes a data distribution and traceability technology based on blockchain technology to construct a decentralized mode of power data distribution, realize the chaining of power distribution records, power data storage and power data security sharing. The security mechanism of asymmetric encryption key distribution, power data encryption transmission and power data integrity check is designed, and a traceable, tamper proof, open and transparent sharing model is established to realize effective supervision of data sender and data receiver. Compared with other security sharing schemes, data sharing has higher security factor and better traceability effect, providing more convenient service and more reliable network environment for users or departments to safely use power data. How to improve the speed of data sharing is one of the emphases of subsequent research.

Acknowledgement. Thanks to State Grid Jiangsu for supporting the data and funds to this project.

References

1. Liu, C.H.: The overview of blockchain technology foundation and application research. The Front. Soc. Sci. Technol. **2**(3), 13–17 (2017)

2. Ma, Z.F., Wang, X.C., Yang, J., Wang, L.Y., Zhao, W.Z.: Data Sharing Method and System Based on Blockchain. Beijing, China. (2004) https://xueshu.baidu.com/usercenter/paper/show?paperid=17270rm0nj570cb0431p0870ck349804&site=xueshu_se

3. Khonde, S.R., Ulagamuthalvi, V.: Blockchain: secured solution for signature transfer in distributed intrusion detection system. Comput. Syst. Sci. Eng. **40**(1), 37–51 (2022)

4. Song, Y. L.: Smart grid data security and privacy protection based on block technology. M.S. Dissertation, Xidian University, China (2020)

5. Zhao, H.X., Li, Y., Wang, J.W., Zhang, Y., Liu Z.Q.: Data Security Sharing System and Method Based on Blockchain Key Distribution. Guangdong, China. (2020) https://kns.cnki.net/kcms/detail/detail.aspx?FileName=CN111277412A&DbName=SCPD2020

6. Huang, B. W.: Research on application technology of data distribution service based on blockchain technology. M.S. Dissertation, Beijing University of Posts and Telecommunications, China (2020)

7. Li, Q.D., Zhou, Y.H.: Security decision analysis based on Shamir's (t, n) threshold key sharing scheme. Netw. Secur. Technol. Appl. (04), 23–26 (2012)

8. Shankar, K., Venkatraman, S.: A secure encrypted classified electronic healthcare data for public cloud environment. Intell. Autom. Soft Comput. **32**(2), 765–779 (2022)

9. Li, F., Liang, R.G., Li, X.C., He, Q.: Trusted data distribution based on blockchain and attribute. Small Microcomput. Syst. **42**(07), 1524–1531 (2021)

10. Jie, G., Bin, S., Ying, H., Fei, R.Y., Mehdi, S.: A survey on compressed sensing in vehicular infotainment systems. IEEE Commun. Surv. Tutor. **19**(4), 2662–2680 (2017)

11. Wei, Y.Z., Deng, Z.H., Guan, Y.R., Hu, Z.H.: A secure traceability method for scientific data based on blockchain and smart contracts. Mod. Intell. **41**(01), 32–38 (2021)

12. Alshambri, H.A., Alassery, F.: Securing fog computing for e-learning system using integration of two encryption algorithms. J. Cyber Secur. **3**(3), 149–166 (2021)

13. Jing, Y.R., Zhang, W.Q., Ge, L., Li, N.F., Shang, X.Y., Ye, Y.: Secure sharing method of network data transmission based on multi-layer encryption technology. E3S Web Conf. **252**, 01027 (2021)

14. Li, Z.D.: Research on data access control and privacy protection based on attribute encryption in cloud storage. Ph.D. Dissertation, Beijing University of Posts and Telecommunications, China (2020)

15. Xue, T.F.: Research on some problems of blockchain application. Ph.D. Dissertation, Beijing University of Posts and Telecommunications, China (2019)

16. Yang, L.: Design of robot data encryption transmission control system based on blockchain Technology. Comput. Meas. Control **29**(06), 119–122 (2021)

17. Hong, L.: Analysis of data traceability technology for blockchain. Inform. Syst. Eng. (11), 80–81 (2020)

18. Bragadeesh, S.A., Umamakeswari, A.: Secured vehicle life cycle tracking using blockchain and smart contract. Comput. Syst. Sci. Eng. **41**(1), 1–18 (2022)

19. Zhang, X.J.: Research on cryptographic technology against key disclosure. Ph.D. Dissertation, University of Electronic Science and Technology of China, China (2014)

20. Lu, X.H., Liu, P., Ke, Y., Zhang, H.: Network data security sharing system based on blockchain. Multimedia Tools Appl. **80**, 31887–31906 (2021)

21. El-mashad, S.Y., Yassen, A.M., Alsammak, A.K., Elhalawany, B.M.: Local features-based watermarking for image security in social media. Comput. Mater. Contin. **69**(3), 3857–3870 (2021)

Data Provenance in Large-Scale Distribution

Yunan Zhu[1], Wei Che[2], Chao Shan[1($\boxtimes$)], and Shen Zhao[2]

[1] State Grid Jiangsu Marketing Service Center (Metrology Center), Jiangsu 210000, China
1029121831@qq.com
[2] State Grid Jiangsu Electric Power Co., Ltd., Jiangsu 210000, China

Abstract. To meet the different needs in the digital age, many large companies adopt new technologies for big data processing and distributed infrastructure for collaborative data analysis. To ensure the safety and legal use of data, the company needs to record and track the use of data to establish a reasonable accountability and protection mechanism. In fact, the rapid growth of data scale and the complexity of the environment pose serious challenges to the realization of this goal. This paper proposes a new data provenance model and a method of quickly constructing provenance model according to provenance content, which improves the privacy protection in data provenance, simplifies the cumbersome provenance content, and improves the provenance efficiency in the case of large-scale distribution.

Keywords: Big data · Data provenance · Privacy protection · Provenance model

1 Introduction

Data provenance mainly refers to the ability to determine the provenance, history and lineage of a specific data product. In the first International Provenance and Annotation Workshop (IPAW), participants exchanged views on the concept of data provenance and reached a certain consensus. They put forward a relatively original data provenance model. After that, he University of Southampton and other organizations sorted out the exchange results of the meeting and published an article entitled "The Open Provenance Model" [1]. The model named OPM described in this paper has become the information exchange standard in the industry. OPM can be used directly by defining some formats and protocols according to the actual situation. However, the concept defined by the model is inappropriate, and the terminology and usage are vague.

In 2008, Sahoo et al. [2] proposed provenir data provenance model. The model refers to W3C standard to complete the logical description of the model, and considers the specific details of database and workflow. It has formed a relatively complete system in terms of model, storage and application, and has become the first complete data provenance management system. However, the definition of Prov is very detailed and complex [3], and the number of prov model is gradually increasing. Many implementations only focus on specific fields and are difficult to be applied to other fields [4].

X. Sun et al. (Eds.): ICAIS 2022, LNCS 13340, pp. 28–42, 2022.
https://doi.org/10.1007/978-3-031-06791-4_3

Wei et al. [5] proposed a data provenance model prov-m, which is compatible with the standard Prov model and complies with the latest provenance standard issued by W3C. Interoperability and optimization are considered in the background storage and implementation of prov-m provenance. However, prov-m considers the model design only from the perspective of application tools. It does not consider the problems such as privacy and complex provenance content that are easy to occur in data provenance.

Information technology—Data provenance descriptive model [6] proposes a data provenance model "ProVOC model", which defines three core types (data, activity and executive entity) and their relationships. Based on the original Prov, the model adds subcategories such as parameters and data sets, which can easily classify the provenance content. However, the provenance model itself has some vague definitions (such as executive entity, data set and data) and redundant component relationships (defined Association, ownership and contact between components). Based on the advantages of ProVOC, the provenance model in this paper improves the definition and relationship of model components.

At present, with the continuous growth of data scale, the corresponding content to be traced has become more and more complex [7], which increases the storage burden and reduces the provenance efficiency. The company's data inevitably involves the user's private data. A proper handling of these private data is not only the responsibility of the user, but also the requirement of the company itself. In the case of large-scale data provenance, the behavior of provenance records for each data modification and distribution will cause a lot of storage redundancy and reduce the provenance efficiency. This problem will become more obvious when using blockchain technology as the provenance data storage technology due to the low storage efficiency of blockchain and the visible content on the chain [8].

The main purpose of this paper is to solve the problems of privacy, complicated provenance content and low efficiency in large-scale data provenance. This paper proposes a provenance content filtering method based on data table frequency, and a provenance model to solve the privacy and low efficiency problem in large-scale data provenance. The main contributions are as follows

(1) Proposed a rank method based on table frequency, which can quickly filter the provenance content according to the provenance data.
(2) Based on the ProVOC model, this paper proposed a provenance model which improved the performance in protection of user privacy.
(3) In the case of large-scale distribution, this paper proposed a method of determining the index by features, which reduces the storage space and optimizes the storage efficiency through the use of the index.

2 Related Work

With more and more attention to data provenance, the international provenance and labeling Organization (IPAW) was officially established in 2006 to solve the problems of data provenance, document processing, data tracking and data labeling. After the establishment of IPAW, provenance standards were put on the agenda, resulting in a series of provenance challenges [9]. With the efforts of IPAW organizations and scholars, the open provenance model OPM1.00 [10] was promulgated in December 2007. OPM is mainly based on three entities, namely Artifact, Process and Agent, which are connected through casual relationship to express dependencies (such as used, was generated by, etc.). OPM expresses provenance information in the form of graph, including nodes and edges, and describes the query interface. The purpose of OPM is to define a developmental data model, which considering the interaction and the designers, inspectors and users of the model. The use and development of OPM has promoted the positive development of OPM provenance standard, but there are still some difficulties in using OPM model and provenance data [11], mainly including ① the fuzziness of some terms and usages, such as the concepts of account, profile and annotation. ② Improper conceptual design, such as time, properties and relationships.

W3C made significant modifications to OPM and published it as a provenance standard in 2013, named PROV [12]. PROV defines three core data types (Entity, Activity and Agent) and their relationships. Data relationships have attributes. One document integrates all data types, relationships and attributes. Aiming at the problems and difficulties faced by OPM model, PROV provides a set of definition documents to improve the interoperability of provenance information in heterogeneous environment, and brings OPM model into a new realm. PROV starts from the point of view of data modeling and considers the existing technical status in the field of information representation and data sharing. However, the definition document of PROV is too detailed and complex, and many studies often focus on specific fields. The implementation of PROV in specific fields is difficult to be applied to other fields.

Wei et al. [5] proposed a data provenance model PROV-M, which is compatible with the standard PROV model and complies with the latest provenance standard issued by W3C. PROV-M provenance framework is mainly composed of program interface (API) and configurable database for storing provenance information created according to prov standard. PROV-M deploys permanent data storage in the background, abides by the open architecture, and can easily make the existing software compatible with the future software tools. At the same time, interoperability and optimization are considered in the background storage and PROV-M implementation. PROV-M considers model design more from the perspective of application tools, ignoring some practical problems of data provenance, such as privacy, large-scale operation and so on.

ProVoc model [6] defines three core types (data, activity and execution entity) and their relationships. At the same time, a new component design (including data set, parameters, etc.) is carried out in the core type. It is more convenient to determine the general content of provenance according to the standard, but the criterion itself does not have a more specific and detailed design for practical problems, and there is no specific introduction to the method of provenance content component model.

Miao et al. [13] Based on OPM model and combined with the characteristics of index data provenance scene, designed a lightweight index data provenance expression model, which abstracted the index calculation process through four main relationships with three entity objects such as executor, calculation process and workpiece as the core. It provides guidance for the design and development of index data provenance management system and its preliminary application, and improves the transparency of index calculation process and the reliability of results. The definition of provenance content is not clear, which may be contrary to the enterprise standard.

Chen et al. [14] built the electric power WeChat official account network and used AARRR model to get information propagation path. First, it selects observable nodes based on the node tightness, then reduces the order of magnitude of the relationship network, calculates the information propagation activation time vector and the information propagation time approximate matrix vector using BFS algorithm. After that it establishes the information provenance estimation function according to the calculated information propagation activation time vector and the information propagation time approximate matrix vector, and estimate the information source nodes. Finally, the source of information on WeChat official account is realized. But this method is a provenance model for WeChat official account information, rather than information provenance to databases or platforms in enterprises.

Zhang et al. [15] aimed at the storage problem faced by light nodes in the blockchain data provenance system when verifying the provenance information, introduced a data structure Merkle mountain range (MMR) to optimize the dynamic addition performance of Merkle tree, and stored the complete block header on the blockchain into the MMR. An efficient and reliable verification method for provenance data is proposed, which reduces the size of the block containing the information required for verification. On this basis, a scheme of data provenance system based on blockchain is designed, which encapsulates the general modules required for data provenance and opens them to the provenance application through the interface. This scheme only needs a light node to store the information of the latest block, which can effectively verify whether the provenance information exists in the blockchain. But the scheme copied the provenance model of criterion [6] without improving the model according to the specific situation.

3 Workflow and Notation

Our workflow will quickly filter the existing database table content to obtain the component content required by the data provenance model. As shown in Fig. 1, the workflow starts with the contents of the database table, and a more reasonable set of data provenance columns is obtained through the screening and fusion of the column name set. Through the processing of privacy related data and the feature extraction [16] of some column names, the relevant content for privacy protection scenario and large-scale distribution scenario is obtained. Finally, the final data provenance content is formed according to the above content. The workflow is described below.

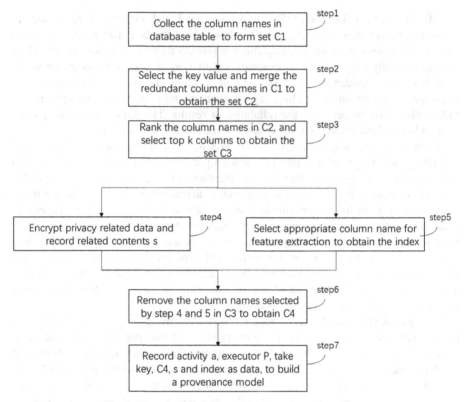

Fig. 1. The workflow of screening provenance content.

Table 1. Symbols and descriptions.

Symbols	Descriptions
c	set
key	key value
s	encrypt or hash results
$cname$	column name
$index$	index
a	activity
p	executor
k	number of columns selected in rank
h	encryption or hash function
$rank$	rank function

(*continued*)

Table 1. (*continued*)

Symbols	Descriptions
f	feature extraction function
combine	combine function
iskey	key value judgement function
privacylist	privacy related column list

(1) Collect the column names in database table to form set $C1$.
(2) Select the key value and merge the redundant column names in $C1$ to obtain the set $C2$.
(3) Rank the column names in $C2$, and select top k columns to obtain the set $C3$.
(4) Encrypt privacy related data and record related contents s.
(5) Select appropriate column name for feature extraction to obtain the index.
(6) Remove the column names selected by step 4 and 5 in $C3$ to obtain $C4$.
(7) Record activity a, executor p, take key, $C4$, s and $index$ as data, to build a provenance model.

In this paper, the symbols and their meanings we use are shown in Table 1.

4 Provenance Model

4.1 Our Model

We propose a data provenance model which consists of four levels of components. As shown in Table 2, the contents of each component are as follows.

The first level component includes three parts: activity, execution entity (or executor) and data. Activity: refers to the activity requiring data provenance. Executing entity: refers to the institution or person that generates the activity. Data: data content to be recorded for provenance. The activities and execution entities are no longer divided into subclass components, and only use one variable to store content, which can be directly used for retrieval.

The second level component includes two subclasses: parameter component and dataset component.

The third level component includes five subclasses. Three components belong to dataset which is privacy protection, active data and index. Others belong to parameters which is time parameters and space parameters. The time parameter is time stamp, which is used to specify the data distribution time and use time. The space parameter is the storage location of the data.

Table 2. Provenance model component

First level component	Second level component	Third level component	Fourth level component
Data	Dataset	Privacy protection	Encrypted data
			Encryption secret key
			Hash value
		Active data	
		Index	Continuous index
			Character index
	Parameter	Time parameters	
		Space parameters	
Activity			
Execution entity			

The forth level component includes five subclasses. Privacy protection includes three four level components, namely encrypted data, encryption secret key and hash value, which are used to save the results of encrypt privacy protection and hash processing [17]. The index includes two four level components: continuous index and character index, which are used for provenance records in the case of large-scale provenance and save storage space. When it comes to large-scale provenance, such as a batch of continuous files, there is no need to record the provenance of each file, just build the index according to the different provenance contents between files (such as file id), and only record the other same provenance contents once (such as storage location). When it comes to data provenance, you can find the provenance records according to the index.

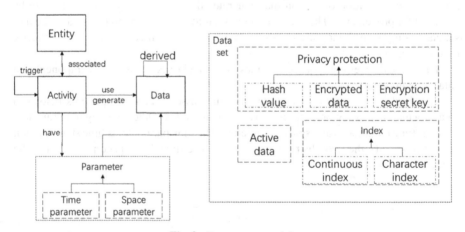

Fig. 2. Provenance model.

As shown in Fig. 2, each component has an association relationship. Executing entities execute activities, which are related to each other. Data used in activities. Data are generated in the activity. New activities may be generated in the activities. New data may be derived from the data. Activities have corresponding parameters, including time parameters and space parameters.

4.2 Fast Method to Build Provenance Model

Based on the above provenance model, we propose a method to quickly build a provenance model. When carrying out data provenance, the first problem to be faced is which data to select as the provenance content. If we choose all content as provenance data, we will face the complex database content in many companies. Moreover, the database content will increase with time, the provenance content should also be updated in time [18]. The manual method is not conducive to the iterative update of the provenance content in time. Therefore, we propose a method to determine the provenance content according to the database table key value and column name frequency, quickly screen the provenance content from the complex database table content, and construct the provenance model. The specific process has been described in Sect. 2 workflow and symbol definition. We supplement the details of this method here.

(1) Collect the column names in database table to form set $C1$.
(2) Select the key value and merge the redundant column names in $C1$ to obtain the set $C2$.
(3) Rank the column names in $C2$, and select top k columns to obtain the set $C3$.
(4) Encrypt privacy related data and record related contents s.
(5) Select appropriate column name for feature extraction to obtain the index.
(6) Remove the column names selected by step 4 and 5 in $C3$ to obtain $C4$.
(7) Record activity a, executor p, take key, $C4$, s and $index$ as data, to build a provenance model.

In step 2, select the key value key and combine the other column names to obtain the set $C2$. We first extract the key value as the provenance content. The key value in the database table is a natural and important provenance feature, which can be directly determined as a part of the provenance content. Column name combination is mainly aimed at the situation that different column names point to the same content, through whether the content is same to finish this process, reduce column name redundancy and improve provenance efficiency.

Algorithm 1. Fast algorithm for constructing provenance model.

Input: Column name set **c1**, Feature extraction function f, Encryption or hash function **h**, Rank function **rank**, Number of columns selected in rank **k**, Combine function **combine**, Key value judgment function **iskey**, Privacy related column list, **privacylist**, Feature extraction related column list **featurelist**.

Output: **key, c4, s, index**

 ① For **cname** in **c1**:
 ②   If **iskey**(**cname**) == True:
 ③   **key** += **cname**
 ④   **c1**.remove(**key**)
 ⑤   **c2** = **combine**(**c1**)
 ⑥   **c3** = **rank**(**k, c2**)
 ⑦ For **cname** in **c3**:
 ⑧   If **cname** in **privacylist**:
 ⑨   **s** += **h**(**cname**)
 ⑩   elif **cname** in **featurelist**:
 ⑪   **Index** += f(**cname**)
 ⑫   else:
 ⑬   **c4** += **cname**
 ⑭ return **key,c4,s,index**

In step 3, we rank the column names in set $C2$, and select top k columns to obtain the set $C3$. Obviously, the more the columns appears, and the more likely it is to play a role in provenance.

In step 4, encrypt privacy related data and record related contents s. When encryption is used, we record the encryption key and encrypted content. When hash is used, we record the hash value. This step is used to prevent privacy disclosure caused by provenance information disclosure.

In step 5, select the appropriate column name *cname* for feature extraction to obtain the *index*. Feature extraction builds different indexes according to the content type of column data. when the data content is continuous numbers, select the upper and lower bounds of numbers as the *index*. When the data content is discontinuous, such as a string, select the maximum matching string for indexing. The algorithm for quickly constructing provenance model is shown in Algorithm 1.

5   Implementation

5.1   Implementation on Electric Power System

To reflect the advantages of our method as much as possible, we select a set of database tables from the electric power system.

There is a huge amount of data in the electric power system. Taking Jiangsu Province in China as an example, the electric power system provides electric power resource for 46 million households, and there are 200000 repair data for only one service [19]. Such a huge amount and variety of services provided by the electric power system mean a huge database system and the complex database table content. It is unreasonable to directly take all types of data as the provenance content, so a fast and effective method is needed to filter the content.

Table 3. Database table example (1).

ORG_NO	CONS_NO	CONS_NAME	ELEC_ADDR	ELECTYPE_CODE	LINE_ID	TRADE_CODE	CONTRACTC_CAP
30408300***	3620128***	XX company	XX country, xx city, Jiangsu province	402	19520000	4710	315

Table 4. Database table example (2).

CONS_NO	CONS_NAME	ELEC_ADDR	ELECTYPE_CODE	LINE_ID	TRADE_CODE	VOLT_CODE	CONTRACTC _CAP
3620128***	XX company	XX country, xx city, Jiangsu province	402	19520000	4710	AC001**	315

Table 5. Database table example (3)

CONS_NO	CONS_NO	CONS_ADDR	PHONE_NUMBER	ELECTRICITY_CHANGES	FEE	ELECTYPE_CODE	COMPANY_CODE
3620128***	XX company	XX country, xx city, Jiangsu province	187********	19520000	423*	402	Z***

Electric power system has great reference value to other fields [20]. Therefore, it is inevitable to involve large-scale external data distribution and provenance. For example, the significance of electric power data to industrial production departments, especially large factories and other units is mainly to guide such institutions to optimize electric power consumption strategies, carry out green production and reduce enterprise operation costs. The most direct effect of electric power data on electric power seller is to improve enterprise benefits by analyzing data. Electricity consumption data can help the government analyze all aspects which related to the economic trend and people's daily life, such as industrial production, urban housing vacancy rate, and the impact of electricity price subsidy policies.

Electric power service is the artery of the national economy. Once the electric power data is tampered with, it will lead to extremely serious consequences [21]. Constructing a reasonable provenance process can not only help deal with the responsibility when the threat occurs, but also play a role of warning and protection in advance.

There are a lot of private information that should not be disclosed in electric power data, such as residents' address, telephone number, etc. Therefore, how to avoid the disclosure of residents' private information is an important provenance segment.

The workflow of fast provenance provided in this paper is shown in Fig. 1. Next, we will describe and show the specific steps using actual data. We use three actual database tables as method operation objects, as shown in Table 3, Table 4 and Table 5.

Step 1: collect the database table and collect the column name set $C1$. For step 1, the collected database tables are shown in Table 3, Table 4 and Table 5 to obtain a column name set $C1$.

Step 2: select the key and combine the other column names to obtain the set $C2$. For step 2, select the key value org_ NO、CONS_ No constitutes the key value set Key. Merge the remaining column names, as ELEC_ ADDR and CONS_ ADDR refers to the same content, and only ELEC_ ADDR remained, get $C2$.

In step 3, the column names in the set $C2$ are ranked by frequency, and the first k entries (here k is assumed to be 5) are selected to obtain the column name set $C3$. The provenance party can select a corresponding number of column names according to its own needs and storage requirements.

In step 4: encrypt or hash the privacy related data and record the related contents s. For those related to user privacy, such as phone_ Number, etc. are encrypted or hashed to obtain relevant contents s.

In step 5: select the appropriate column name *cname* for feature extraction to obtain the *index*. For step 5, when it is necessary to trace the data of a region (such as xx County in the table), select a part of string in column name ELEC_ADDR as index. In this example, we choose the string "xx Country, xx City, Jiangsu Province" as our index.

When you want to trace a batch of continuous transactions, select the column name TRADE_ CODE, record column name, transaction code, and code start value 4710 and code end value 4766. This step gets the content *index*.

In step 6, $C4$ is obtained by removing the column names selected in steps 4 and 5. For step 6, $C4$ is obtained by removing the column names selected in steps 4 and 5 in $C3$. For step 7, record activities such as meter charge calculation, executor xx electric power company, and take *key*, *C*4, s and *index* as data to build a provenance model as shown in Fig. 2.

5.2 Efficiency Analysis

We will analyze the efficiency improvement brought by our method from the perspective of database reading and provenance record storage.

The column name finally selected by the above method is divided into three parts: 1. Key value: ORG_NO and CONS_NO 2. High frequency column name: CONS_NAME, ELECTYPE_CODE, LINE_ID and TRADE_CODE 3. Index column name: ELEC_ADDR. When we build the index of ELEC_ADDR table items, we do not specify the detailed address (such as XX town or village), so we do not treat it as privacy protection content.

When we need to build provenance for a record, we select the required column data in each instance table. The data page size of the database is fixed and the storage records are limited. In large-scale reading and writing, the number of column names read in a row will affect the reading efficiency [22]. For Table 3, we only need to read six column names, which improves the efficiency by 33%. For Table 4, six column names are selected, and the efficiency is improved by 33%. For Table 5, we only select three column names, which improves the efficiency by 166%.

When storing provenance records, for 24 table items in Table 3, Table 4 and Table 5, only 7 of them need to be stored through our method, and the storage efficiency is improved by 243%.

6   Conclusions

To solve the shortcomings of existing provenance model in privacy protection and large-scale distribution, this paper proposed a provenance model based on ProVOC, which reduces the redundant affiliation and structure, and adds new components for the above problems. However, the real scene is often more complex than that in theory, and we can't consider all the cases of provenance content. Therefore, if applied to practice, some components of the model may be redundant and reduce the storage efficiency. If we can further carry out experiments in more scenarios, we believe that the model can be more efficient. Considering the possible complexity of provenance content in data provenance, a fast screening provenance content method based on column name frequency is proposed, which improves the provenance efficiency and reduces storage redundancy. We can think that frequency is positively correlated with importance, but it is less likely that they are linearly correlated. Therefore, the provenance method may still introduce some items with high frequency but may not be important for the provenance content. The accuracy of the automation method proposed by us is not enough to replace human experts. After the method is used, human experts may still need to select the appropriate provenance content from a small range of data items.

Acknowledgement. Thanks to State Grid Jiangsu for supporting the data and funds to this project.

References

1. Freire, J., Koop, D., Moreau, L.: Provenance and annotation of data and processes. Springer, Salt Lake City, UT, USA (2008)
2. Freire, J., Koop, D., Moreau, L. (eds.): IPAW 2008. LNCS, vol. 5272. Springer, Heidelberg (2008). https://doi.org/10.1007/978-3-540-89965-5
3. Kwasnikowska, N., Moreau, L., Van Den Bussche, J.: A formal account of the open provenance model. ACM Trans. Web **9**(2), 1–44 (2015). https://doi.org/10.1145/2734116
4. Yogesh, S., Groth, P., Moreau, L.: Special section: the third provenance challenge on using the open provenance model for interoperability. Future Gener. Comput. Syst. **27**(6), 737–742 (2011)
5. Wei, Y.Z., Deng, Z.H.: Design and implementation of provenance management based on Prov model. Inf. Stud.: Theor. Appl. **39**(11), 95–100 (2016)
6. Information technology Data provenance descriptive model: http://std.samr.gov.cn/gb/search/gbDetailed?id=71F772D82604D3A7E05397BE0A0AB82A (2021)
7. Yong, L.: A provenance-aware virtual sensor system using the open provenance model. In: ISCTS, pp. 330–339. IEEE (2010)
8. Marten, R., Spohrer, K.: A blockchain research framework. Bus. Inf. Syst. Eng. **59**(6), 385–409 (2017)
9. The provenance challenge wiki. https://openprovenance.org/provenance-challenge/Fourth ProvenanceChallenge.html (2021)
10. Moreau, L., et al.: The open provenance model core specification. Futur. Gener. Comput. Syst. **27**(6), 743–756 (2011)
11. Andreas, S.: The Provenance Store Proost for the Open Provenance Model. Springer, Heidelberg, Berlin, Germany (2012)
12. PROV-Overview: http://www.w3.org/TR/2013/NOTE-prov-overview-20130430 (2021)
13. Miu, X.P., Wu, Y., Kong, Q.B.: Research and design of index data provenance model for power grid enterprises. Power Syst. Big Data **24**(4), 70–77 (2021)
14. Chen, Q.R., Xu, J.N., Zhang, W.: Research on information tracing method of wechat official account based on aarrr mode. Microcomput. Appl. **37**(7), 97–99 (2021)
15. Zhang, X.W.: Trusted query method for data provenance based on blockchain. J. Appl. Sci. Electron. Inform. Eng. **39**(1), 42–54 (2021)
16. Ali, F.: Handling high dimensionality in ensemble learning for arrhythmia prediction. Intell. Autom. Soft Comput. **32**(3), 1729–1742 (2022)
17. Zhou, Y., Pan, L., Chen, R., Shao, W.: A novel image retrieval method with improved dcnn and hash. J. Inform. Hiding Priv. Prot. **2**(2), 77–86 (2020)
18. Rolf, F., et al.: The ecoinvent database: overview and methodological framework. The Int. J. Life Cycle Assess. **10**(1), 3–9 (2005)
19. 2020 Annual report on enterprise information disclosure: http://www.js.sgcc.com.cn/html/main/col2747/column_2747_1.html (2022)
20. Smida, A.: Gain enhancement of dielectric resonator antenna using electromagnetic bandgap structure. Comput. Mater. Contin. **71**(1), 1613–1623 (2022)
21. Uthathip, N., Bhasaputra, P., Pattaraprakorn, W.: Application of anfis model for thailand's electric vehicle consumption. Comput. Syst. Sci. Eng. **42**(1), 69–86 (2022)
22. Anchuen, P., Uthansakul, P., Uthansakul, M., Poochaya, S.: Fleet optimization of smart electric motorcycle system using deep reinforcement learning. Comput. Mater. Contin. **71**(1), 1925–1943 (2022)

A Vulnerability Detection Algorithm Based on Transformer Model

Fujin Hou[1], Kun Zhou[1], Longbin Li[2], Yuan Tian[2(✉)], Jie Li[2], and Jian Li[2]

[1] Shandong Hi-Speed Construction Management Group Co., Ltd., Jinan 250098, China
[2] Beijing University of Posts and Telecommunications, Beijing 100876, China
redrainiety@bupt.edu.cn

Abstract. In today's Internet background and the rapid development of computer science and technology, new software is born every day, whether it is on the computer or mobile phone and on the hardware. In order to meet people's various daily needs, developers need to continuously develop new software and firmware. The software development process requires the reuse of shared codes and the realization of the middle-station module codes. These reusable codes can save developers' development time and improve efficiency. The code of the middle-station model is highly complex, and the vulnerabilities hidden in it are not easy to be discovered. A large number of vulnerabilities are inevitably introduced, which leads to immeasurable losses in downstream task modules. In order to enable these middle-station codes to better serve downstream tasks and discover the vulnerabilities hidden in them in time, it is first necessary to extract the defined software method body from the source code. We build an abstract syntax tree for the method to form a statement set; then, the variable names, function names, and strings in the method are replaced. Each statement in the code is given a number to construct a node set. The dependency between functions and variables includes data dependency and control dependency extraction and the node set itself as the input feature of the model. This paper uses Transformer model to model the sequence information. Transformer model can make the information of each node in the sequence fully interact. Based on the Transformer model, this paper further attempts to add the attention structure to improve the probability of detecting vulnerabilities. In the final experimental results, the model can detect vulnerabilities in the code with an accuracy of 95.04% and a recall rate of 88.89%, which also proves that transformer can accurately detect vulnerabilities in the sequence.

Keywords: Vulnerability detection · Abstract syntax tree · Transformer · Attention

1 Introduction

Both firmware and software, there are inevitably some loopholes, and firmware should still be understood as a special software. As of the progress of integrated circuits, upgrading firmware has become easier and less dangerous. The difference between firmware programs and software programs has become smaller and smaller. Therefore, whether it is a bug in the software or the firmware, it is always a specific defect or omission in the software. These flaws and oversights will allow malicious attackers to perform a series of attacks, including stealing user privacy, privately controlling the running process of software, implanting Trojan horses, and destroying computer storage systems. With the development of mobile Internet and computer science and technology, the demand for software development is increasing. At the same time, with the development of the artificial intelligence industry, some hardware devices will also be implanted with specific software. For example, highway cameras will be embedded with some face recognition SDK (software development kit). As the demand for software development is increasing day by day, code reuse has become a function that developers urgently need to meet. In particular, the codes of some middle-station modules and the firmware can be directly shared by multiple hardware devices. The hidden vulnerabilities in these reused codes have brought great security threats and challenges to downstream programs. The vulnerabilities in the shared code may even cause the program crash of the entire line of business. Therefore, accurate and effective detection of hidden vulnerabilities in the code has become an important research topic in the software industry, firmware industry, and computer security field.

Traditional vulnerability detection methods include some manual search methods in the source code. These methods generally require technical personnel to have a lot of coding experience and vulnerability identification. This method will undoubtedly bring a very heavy burden to developers. In addition, other traditional methods can also formulate some fixed rules to detect vulnerabilities. However, as the software writing process is not static, fixed-rule inspections can no longer meet the needs of the current rapid development of software. At the same time, it will cause the company's economic losses due to missed inspections.

In recent years, thanks to the development of machine learning technology and deep learning technology, people can use these technologies for image recognition [1], machine translation [2]. It is precisely due to the powerful feature extraction technology of deep learning and high-dimensional space construction. Due to the effectiveness of the model, we can use these techniques to perform some classification [3] and regression tasks [4]. Seeing the achievements of deep learning technology in the field of NLP, some developers have already used this technology in the field of computer security. Especially the structure of Transformer [5] is efficient for sequence modeling. This paper uses Transformer to model the feature sequence. In addition, the information at each time step does not necessarily have a common function. This paper also employs the attention structure to describe the importance of each position in the sequence.

The main contributions of this paper are as follow:

1) We use abstract syntax tree modeling and analysis, relying on analysis technology, proposed a method that can extract source code features from software/firmware source code.
2) We use deep learning technology (transformer, attention) to model and analyze sequence features, and use static detection technology to detect vulnerabilities in the source code.

This paper will introduce related work in Sect. 2, experiment on the proposed method and code vulnerabilities in Sect. 3, analyze the experimental results in Sect. 4. Finally, in Sect. 5 summarizes and prospects.

2 Related Work

Before artificial intelligence was applied to the topic of vulnerability detection in the early days, there were some traditional detection methods. For example, by exploring the input space, also known as a certain degree of fuzzing, this method can be further divided into black box fuzzing [6] and gray box fuzzing [7]. This method is highly dependent on the input space. Exhaustive exploration cannot be applied to our middle-station multiplexing code module, the input of this module comes from multiple upstream inputs, and the detection efficiency is too low. In addition, there are some methods of fixing rules that we mentioned above. This method is relatively rigid and difficult to work around [8–13]. There are also some methods that analyze the internal state space of the program. This method relies on symbolic execution [14, 15]. The solver capacity of this method is limited, which is doomed to fail to meet a large number of detection requirements.

Artificial intelligence technology has developed rapidly in recent years, and its effectiveness has been verified in many fields, whether it is in the field of natural language processing [16–20] or the field of computer vision [21–25] and other areas [26–28], it has shown unparalleled performance. These work [16–25] promote the development of machine translation, text generation, target detection and character recognition. At the same time, due to the development of computing power, by building a large number of samples and expanding the model parameters, the accuracy of the model has been greatly improved [29]. In recent years, researchers have successively applied machine learning and deep learning techniques to the field of vulnerability detection. Harer et al. [30] use machine learning methods to train the source code and test the compiled code for vulnerability detection methods. Yamaguchi et al. [31] construct an abstract syntax tree for each method, and then use the bag-of-words model to perform latent semantic analysis. This method uses matrix singular value decomposition technology, which is mainly aimed at the structured pattern in the syntax tree. Russell et al. [32] used a tree model-random forest for vulnerability detection. After they abstracted the function into features, they used the random forest for discrimination. VulDeePecker [33] used deep learning technology for the first time in the field of vulnerability detection. This method can accurately locate the location of the vulnerability. That is to say, compared with traditional machine learning technology, deep learning can accurately locate the code location of the vulnerability. In addition, SySeVr [34] integrates deep learning technology, which can perform syntax, grammar, and vector analysis from the source code to detect various vulnerabilities.

3 Method

3.1 Overall Structure

The overall framework of the vulnerability detection method based on the transformer model in this paper is shown in Fig. 1.

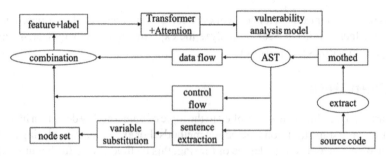

Fig. 1. Diagram of the overall process architecture of vulnerability detection.

First, we extract the method body from the source code to form a method set. Then we construct an abstract syntax tree for each method in the method set, and use the abstract syntax tree to extract the statements in the method to form a statement set. Following, we replace the custom variable names and functions in the statement set name and string, and assign an independent node number to each sentence, which forms a node set. We use data control flow analysis to extract the data dependency and control dependency between nodes. Then, the node set extracted from the method body, the data dependence relationship between the nodes and the control dependence relationship are combined into the feature representation corresponding to the method. The discretization coding technology is further processed into a high-dimensional discrete feature set, that is, the training sample. Finally, generate training samples for whether each sample contains a vulnerability label, use the transformer model as the baseline model, and then increase the importance of attention modeling time step and increase the accuracy of the vulnerability analysis model.

3.2 Node Set Generation

Abstract Syntax Tree. In the blow C++ code, the server will accept the connection request sent by the client. This paper uses the open-source tool ANTLR4 [35] to generate the abstract syntax tree, and now makes a simple analysis of the use of the open-source tool. Take the classic code shown in Fig. 2 with a buffer stack overflow vulnerability (CWE [36] G120: Buffer Copy without Checking Size of Input) as an example, we generated the abstract syntax tree for it, and then scanned the OSID code to view it.

In the blow C++ code, the server will accept the connection request sent by the client. The program code obtains the client's address information through the function gethostbyaddr. This address information will be copied by local variables, and then the client's host name, ip, port and other information output to the log file. However, there may be a large number of client request information, the number of these hostnames may exceed the memory size allocated by the variables corresponding to the local hostname. At this time, if you use the strcpy function to copy, it will cause oom (out of memory) exception, causing the buffer stack to overflow.

Generate Sentence Set. We extract sentences from the source code based on the generated abstract syntax tree. In this step, the control logic is deleted, forming a sentence set as shown in Fig. 3.

```
...
    struct hostent * clienthp;
    char hostname[MAX_LEN];
    //create server socket, bind to server address and listen on socket
    ...
    //accept client connections and process requests
    int count=0;
    for (count=0;count < MAX_CONNECTIONS; count++ ){
        int clientlen = sizeof(struct sockaddr_in);
        int clientsocket = accept(serversocket, (struct sockaddr * )& clientaddr, &clientlen);
        if (clientsocket > = 0 ) {
            clienthp = gethostbyaddr( ( char* )&clientaddr.sin_addr.s_addr,
                                sizeof(clientaddr.sin_addr.s_addr),AF_INET);
            strcpy(hostname, clienthp->h_name);
            logOutput("Acepted clientconnectionfrom host", hostname);
            //process client request
   .        ...
            close(clientsocket);
        }
    }
    close(serversocket);
...
```

Fig. 2. Buffer stack overflow code example.

Generate Node Set. Through the node type of the abstract syntax tree, we can select the variable name, function name and string defined by the programmer, different programmers may choose the variable name differently, such as the sum function sum (int a, int b), this Sometimes a programmer may define this function as sum (int num1, int num2). There may be tens of thousands of different variable names in the same method. In order to better analyze the vulnerability, we uniformly give custom variables defined as a designated identifier, which reduces the vocabulary size of variable names. For different variables in the same method, we use symbols like bid_1, bid_2, bid_3, ..., bid_n to distinguish them, and use node numbers to encode each sentence to form a node set, as shown in Fig. 4.

3.3 Data Dependence

In the process of program operation, data is a key link, and the flow of data is also the standard for us to build data dependencies. We use data flow analysis techniques. For example, bid_18 in n13 uses the variable bid_7, which forms n8→n13. The relationship between n13, which shows that the operation of n13 is affected by n8, and the key variable is bid_7. That is to say, the label attribute is bid_7, indicating that the unit variable that affects the data flow dependence is bid_7. The data dependency relationship between the formed nodes is shown in Fig. 5.

3.4 Control Dependence

Most of the control dependencies in the program are caused by if statements, which means that if the result of the if condition is True or False, there will be two execution modes. So

```
1.struct hostent * clienthp
2.char hostname[MAX_LEN]
3.int count=0
4.count=0
5.count < MAX_CONNECTIONS
6.count++
7.int clientlen=sizeof(struct sockaddr_in)
8.int clientsocket=accept(serversocket,(struct sockaddr * )
&
  clientaddr, &clientlen)
9.clientsocket > = 0
10.clienthp=gethostbyaddr((char* ) &
clientaddr.sin_addr.s_ad-
    dr, sizeof (clientaddr.sin_addr.s_addr), AF_INET)
11.strcpy(hostname, clienthp->h_name)
12.logOutput( "Accepted client connection from
host",hostname)
13.close(clientsocket)
14.close(serversocket)
```

Fig. 3. The result of the statement set generating.

```
n1 : struct hostent * bid_1
n2 : char bid_2 [bid_3]
n3 : int bid_4 = 0
n4 : bid_4 = 0
n5 : bid_4 < bid_5
n6 : bid_4++
n7 : int bid_6=sizeof(structsockaddr_in)
n8 : int bid_7=bid_8 (bid_9,(structsockaddr* ) &
    bid_11,& bid_6 )
n9 : bid_7 >= 0
n10 : bid_1 = bid_10((char * ) & bid_11.bid_12.bid_13,
      sizeof(bid_11.bid_12.bid_13),cib_14)
n11 : bid_15(bid_2,bid_1 -> bid_16)
n12 : bid_17("cstring_1", bid_2)
n13 : bid_18(bid_7)
n14 : bid_18(bid_9)
```

Fig. 4. The result of the node sets generating.

n2→n11	label:bid_2
n2→n12	label:bid_2
n4→n5	label:bid_4
n4→n6	label:bid_4
n6→n5	label:bid_4
n6→n6	label:bid_4
n8→n9	label:bid_7
n8→n13	label:bid_7
n10→n11	label:bid_1

Fig. 5. Data dependency between nodes.

that we use the control flow analysis technology to build the control dependency between nodes, as shown in Fig. 6. Among them, n9 is a judgment statement to determine whether the variable bid_7 is greater than or equal to 0, if it is greater than 0, it is True, jump to n6 for execution, otherwise it is False, and continue to execute n10.

```
n5→n7     label:True
n5→n14    label:False
n9→n6     label:False
n9→n10    label:True
```

Fig. 6. Control dependence between nodes.

3.5   Feature Encode

Feature Preprocessing. On the basis of node set, data dependence between nodes and control dependence between nodes, we segment each sentence. We segment the sentences with spaces as separators, and then token-encode each word, that is, give each word a unique code, for example, n1 corresponds to code 1, n2 corresponds to code 2. Each word will be mapping to its own encoding. Like NLP's processing of text sentences, we discarded sequences with a text length less than 15 because the amount of information in this part of the sequence is too small, and its proportion is small. Considering that the model may be insufficiently trained and will not have a large impact on the experimental results, it is discarded. In addition, some sentences are too long, and the length may reach three or four hundred. The proportion of this part of the sentence is not very high. In order to be able to align the length of the sentence, we will remove this part (more than three hundred in length). For the remaining sentences, we use padding technology to fill the sentences with a length of less than 300 with special coded characters. In our experiment, we use code 0 for tail padding, which makes all sentences reach 300 in length.

One-Hot Encode. We use one-hot to map each token in the sentence to the vector space. The token of a sentence has its own unique code. One-hot technology is a fixed-length code. The length is the total number of tokens. Each independent code will expand the entire vocabulary, and then the value of its corresponding index position set to 1, and the other to 0. This forms the discrete feature we defined. The advantages of discrete features are: 1). It introduces nonlinearity with the model, so that the training of the model will not overfit and easier to train; 2). it can solve the problem of inconsistent token feature lengths, and each feature uses the same length; 3).it can expand the characteristics. But one-hot encoding also has its own shortcomings. If the length of the entire vocabulary is too large, the one-hot vector formed will be too sparse. For example, our vocabulary has a total of 100,000 words, that is, the code length is 100,000, but only one position has a value of 1. This means that we need to spend a lot of space to store these sparse 0s, and at the same time results hard training. We introduced the embedding layer to densify the high-dimensional sparse features with low-dimensionality.

3.6 Embedding Layer

Embedding technology projects high-dimensional sparse discrete features to low-dimensional sparse discrete features. The specific operation is shown in Fig. 7. The arrows between one-hot matrix and embedding matrix means the finding mechanism. Its principle is that if the value of the k-th position of a certain token is 1, we go to the k-t row of the Embedding matrix and take the vector of this entire row as the embedding vector of this token. In Fig. 7, the embedding size is d, and v_1 donate the 1-th position value of the embedding vector.

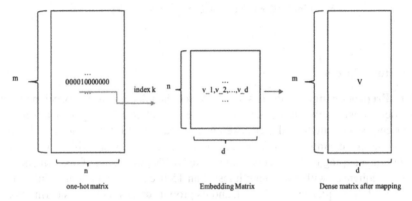

Fig. 7. Embedding look-up process.

3.7 Transformer

Transformer [5], is a technology that will be widely used in both the NLP field [16] and the CV field [37, 38]. The transformer model has powerful coding capabilities for sequences. It can use self-attention technology to make each position in the sentence cross each other, and it can use the multi-head attention mechanism to extract different aspects of information. It is a model with excellent sequence processing effects.

3.8 Attention Mechanism

The attention mechanism, like human attention, will give more weight to information in more critical locations. We know that when we see things in the outside world, the places we pay attention to are different. The attention mechanism is the same, which calculates the weights of different positions in the sentence and assigns different importance. In our work, we use scaled-dot product to calculate attention weight. We use the information of the last position as the guide information to calculate the weight of each position, and finally weight the information of each position to get the final vector.

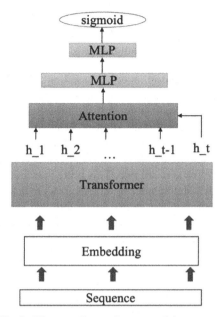

Fig. 8. The overall transformer model structures.

3.9 Model Structure

The overall structure of the model is shown in Fig. 8. After the sentence passes through the embedding layer, sentence vector enters the transformer structure, and then use the attention mechanism to calculate the weight of each position, and finally weights to get the final encoding vector. This final code vector will be sent to the MLP layers after the relu activation function, and then classified and estimated.

In the training sample, the label with loopholes is labeled to 1, and the label with no is labeled to 0. We use this label to calculate the cross-entropy loss function, and then train the model.

4 Experiments

In order to verify the model proposed in this paper, we selected 3 subsets as the data set on the Software Assurance reference Dataset (SaRD) [39] of the National Institute of Standards and Technology. All 3 subsets belong to stack buffer overflow, and is also the dataset used by the two other algorithms we compared. The experiments are all implemented in NVIDIA GeForce GTX 1080.

4.1 Dataset and Metrics

Dataset. The data set includes CWE-120 (Buffer Copy without Checking Size of Input), CWE-121 (Stack-based Buffer Overflow) and CWE-121 (Heap-based Buffer Overflow) 3 types of vulnerabilities. These three data sets include a total of 35374 methods, 13844 methods with loopholes, and 20618 methods without loopholes. In addition to these two methods, we also filtered out 912 unneeded methods. We divide the training set, the testing machine and the validation set, into 8:1:1.

Metrics. Our vulnerability detection model is based on a two-category classification model, the evaluation standard of the entire model is also a commonly used evaluation standard in the two-category classification. We use three score to evaluate the quality of the model. The first is precision rate. Another meaning of this score is that it can be checked accurately, which means the proportion of test samples predicted to be vulnerabilities and correct in the prediction to the total number of samples predicted to be vulnerabilities. Then there is the recall rate. This score is evaluated and checked, indicating the proportion of the total number of test samples predicted to be vulnerabilities and correctly predicted to the total number of vulnerabilities. The two score of precision and recall are contradictory, we have the F1-score to comprehensively consider these two indicators. The specific calculation formula is as follows:

$$precision = \frac{TP}{TP + FP} \tag{1}$$

$$recall = \frac{TP}{TP + FN} \tag{2}$$

$$F1 - score = \frac{2 \times precision \times recall}{precision + recall} \tag{3}$$

The definitions of TP, FP, TN, FN are shown in Table 1.

Table 1. Confusion matrix.

Actual predict	0	1
0	TN	FN
1	FP	TP

Experimental Parameters. We set up several sets of different parameters and optimizers on the basis of the previously extracted dataset. The specific parameter configuration and optimizer are shown in Table 2.

4.2 Experimental Results

The experimental results show that the accuracy rate and recall rate of the method proposed in this experiment have been improved to a certain extent as shown on Table 3. Among them, the maximum precision rate is 95.04%, and the maximum recall rate is 88.89%, which is greatly improved compared with the other two methods. Because the

Table 2. Model and training hyper-parameters settings in the experiment.

Parameters	Value
Learning rate	0.01,0.001,0.02
Batchsize	64,128,256
Embedding size	64,128,256
Head num	2,4,8
Transformer blocks	1,2,4

traditional prediction method uses source code API method extraction and API sequence extraction and quantified clustering. This leads to a certain degree of information omission, so the overall F1-score is not as good as the deep learning method.

The method proposed in this paper can efficiently and accurately extract vulnerabilities from the source code. These vulnerabilities are either implicit vulnerabilities or vulnerabilities that have been discovered by humans. This method can efficiently and accurately predict these vulnerabilities, not only can customize features according to needs, but give full play to the ability of deep learning models to model sparse features.

Table 3. Best experimental results of three experiments.

Model	Precision	Recall	F1-score
VulDeepecker	90.56%	83.72%	87.01%
AE-KNN	92.58%	87.44%	90.06%
Transformer	95.04%	88.89%	91.86%

5 Analysis of Valid Threads

This paper uses static program analysis technology to extract the characteristics of the source code, and on this basis uses the structure of transformer and attention to learn and predict system vulnerabilities. The modified method mainly uses the advanced modeling ideas of the deep learning model for this kind of sequence. From a large number of sequence features, it has a good ability to find and distinguish different vulnerabilities. If it can expand the training data set, it can steadily improve the effectiveness of the model.

In conclusion, in order to detect a large number of vulnerabilities hidden in software and firmware, this paper proposes to first extract the data dependence and control dependence between sentences from the source code, and then use it as a sparse feature representation. And on the basis of this sequence, the deep learning model of transformer and attention is used for training and experimental analysis. The experiment has achieved an F1-score of 91.86% on the three data sets CWE120, CWE121 and CWE122, which is better than the classic machine learning vulnerability detection model.

Acknowledgements. This work was supported by the National Natural Science Foundation of China under Grant 61472048. We also would like to thank the anonymous reviewers for their detailed review and valuable comments, which have enhanced the quality of this paper.

References

1. Szegedy, C., Ioffe, S., Vanhoucke, V.: Inception-v4, inception-resnet and the impact of residual connections on learning. In: Thirty-first AAAI Conference on Artificial Intelligence (2017)
2. Wei, Z., Shujian, H., Jun, X.: A reinforced generation of adversarial examples for neural machine translation. In: Proc. of the 58th Annual Meeting of the Association for Computational Linguistics, p. 34863497. ACL (2020)
3. Sitaula, C., Hossain, M.B.: Attention-based VGG-16 model for COVID-19 chest X-ray image classification. Appl. Intell. **51**(5), 2850–2863 (2020)
4. Xiankai, L., Ma, C., Ni, B., Yang, X., Reid, I., Yang, M.-H.: Deep regression tracking with shrinkage loss. In: Ferrari, V., Hebert, M., Sminchisescu, C., Weiss, Y. (eds.) Computer Vision – ECCV 2018. LNCS, vol. 11218, pp. 369–386. Springer, Cham (2018). https://doi.org/10.1007/978-3-030-01264-9_22
5. Vaswani, A., Shazeer, N., Parmar, N.: Attention is all you. In: Advances in neural information processing systems, pp. 5998–6008 (2017)
6. Zhao, M., Liu, P.: Empirical analysis and modeling of black-box mutational fuzzing. In: Caballero, J., Bodden, E., Athanasopoulos, E. (eds.) ESSoS 2016. LNCS, vol. 9639, pp. 173–189. Springer, Cham (2016). https://doi.org/10.1007/978-3-319-30806-7_11
7. Deng, J., Zhu, X., Xiao, X.: Fuzzing with optimized grammar-aware mutation strategies. IEEE Access **9**, 95061–95071 (2021)
8. Neuhaus, S., Zimmermann, T., Holler, C.: Predicting vulnerable software components. In: Proceedings of the 14th ACM Conference on Computer and Communications Security, pp. 529–540 (2007)
9. Yamaguchi, F., Golde, N., Arp, D.: Modeling and discovering vulnerabilities with code property graphs. In: 2014 IEEE Symposium on Security and Privacy, pp. 590–604 (2014)
10. Chandramohan, M., Xue, Y., Xu, Z.: Bingo: Cross-architecture cross-OS binary search. In: Proceedings of the 2016 24th ACM SIGSOFT International Symposium on Foundations of Software Engineering, pp. 678–689 (2016)
11. Xu, Z., Chen, B., Chandramohan, M.: Spain: security patch analysis for binaries towards understanding the pain and pills. In: ACM 39th International Conference on Software Engineering (ICSE), pp. 462–472 (2017)
12. Li, Z., Zou, D., Xu, S.: Vulpecker: An automated vulnerability detection system based on code similarity analysis. In: Proceedings of the 32nd Annual Conference on Computer Security Applications, pp. 201–213 (2016)
13. Kim, S., Woo, S., Lee, H.: Vuddy: A scalable approach for vulnerable code clone discovery. In: 2017 IEEE Symposium on Security and Privacy (SP), pp. 595–614 (2017)
14. Molnar, D.: Automated whitebox fuzz testing. In: Distributed System Security Symposium. DBLP (2011)
15. Babić, D., Martignoni, L., Mccamant, S.: Statically-directed dynamic automated test generation. In: Proceedings of the 2011 International Symposium on Software Testing and Analysis, pp. 12–22 (2011)
16. Devlin, J., Chang, M.W., Lee, K.: Pre-training of deep bidirectional transformers for language understanding. arXiv preprint arXiv:1810.04805 (2018)
17. Yang, L., Li, Y., Wang, J.: Sentiment analysis for E-commerce product reviews in Chinese based on sentiment lexicon and deep learning. IEEE Access **8**, 23522–23530 (2020)
18. Yadav, A., Vishwakarma, D.K.: Sentiment analysis using deep learning architectures: a review. Artif. Intell. Rev. **53**(6), 4335–4385 (2019). https://doi.org/10.1007/s10462-019-09794-5

19. Xu, G., Meng, Y., Qiu, X.: Sentiment analysis of comment texts based on BiLSTM. IEEE Access **7**, 51522–51532 (2019)

20. Xu, W., Zheng, S., He, L.: Segmented embedding of knowledge graphs. arXiv preprint arXiv: 2005.00856 (2020)

21. Huang, Z., Yu, Y., Xu, J.: Pf-net: Point fractal network for 3d point cloud. In: Proceedings of the IEEE/CVF Conference on Computer Vision and Pattern Recognition 2020, pp. 7662–7670 (2020)

22. Sengupta, S., Jayaram, V., Curless, B.: Background matting: the world is your green screen. In: Proceedings of the IEEE/CVF Conference on Computer Vision and Pattern Recognition 2020, pp. 2291–2300 (2020)

23. Xu, Q., Sun, X., Wu, C.Y.: Grid-gcn for fast and scalable point cloud learning. In: Proceedings of the IEEE/CVF Conference on Computer Vision and Pattern Recognition 2020, pp. 5661– 5670 (2020)

24. Tewari, A., Elgharib, M., Bharaj, G.: Rigging stylegan for 3d control over portrait images. In: Proceedings of the IEEE/CVF Conference on Computer Vision and Pattern Recognition 2020, pp. 6142–6151 (2020)

25. Chen, H., Wang, Y., Xu, C.: AdderNet: Do we really need multiplications in deep learning. In: Proceedings of the IEEE/CVF Conference on Computer Vision and Pattern Recognition 2020, pp. 1468–1477 (2020)

26. Anitha, G., Priya, S.B.: Vision based real time monitoring system for elderly fall event detection using deep learning. Comput. Syst. Sci. Eng. **42**(1), 87–103 (2022)

27. Sudha, V., Ganeshbabu, T.R.: A convolutional neural network classifier VGG-19 architecture for lesion detection and grading in diabetic retinopathy based on deep learning. Comput. Mater. Contin. **66**(1), 827–842 (2021)

28. Kalaivani, K., Chinnadurai, M.: A hybrid deep learning intrusion detection model for fog computing environment. Intell. Autom. Soft Comput. **30**(1), 1–15 (2021)

29. Brown, T.B., Mann, B., Ryder, N.: Language models are few-shot learners. arXiv preprint arXiv:2005.14165 (2020)

30. Harer, J.A., Kim, L.Y., Russell, R.L.: Automated software vulnerability detection with machine learning. arXiv preprint arXiv:1803.04497 (2018)

31. Yamaguchi, F., Lindner, F., Rieck, K.: Vulnerability extrapolation: assisted discovery of vulnerabilities using machine learning. In: Proceedings of the 5th USENIX Conference on Offensive technologies, p. 13 (2011)

32. Russell, R., Kim, L., Hamilton, L.: Automated vulnerability detection in source code using deep representation learning. In: 17th IEEE International Conference on Machine Learning and Applications (ICMLA), pp. 757–762 (2018)

33. Li, Z., Zou, D., Xu, S.: Vuldeepecker: A deep learning-based system for vulnerability detection. arXiv preprint arXiv:1801.01681 (2018)

34. Li, Z., Zou, D., Xu, S.: SySeVR: A framework for using deep learning to detect software vulnerabilities. IEEE Trans. Dependable Secure Comput. (2021, online). https://ieeexplore. ieee.org/document/9321538

35. ANTLR4: https://github.com/antlr/antlr4 (2021)

36. Common Weakness Enumeration: https://cwe.mitre.org (2021)

37. Graham, B., El-Nouby, A., Touvron, H.: LeViT: a Vision transformer in convnet's clothing for faster inference. arXiv preprint arXiv:2104.01136 (2021)

38. Touvron, H., Cord, M., Douze, M.: Training data-efficient image transformers & distillation through attention. In: International Conference on Machine Learning. PMLR 2021, pp. 10347–10357 (2021)

39. Software Assurance Reference Dataset of National Institute of Standards and Technology: https://samate.nist.gov/SARD (2017)

Research on Video Falsity Detection Based on Publisher and Publishing Environment Features

Xvhao Xiao[1], Xiaojun Li[1(✉)], Junping Yao[1], Shaochen Li[1], and Bilal Anwar[2]

[1] Xi'an Research Institute of High-Tech, Xi'an 710025, Shaanxi, China
`xi_anlxj@126.com`

[2] Department of Business Administration, University of Sahiwal, Punjab, Pakistan

Abstract. As one of the main ways of information dissemination, video is more popular among the public for its rich images and vivid audio. With the promotion of short videos in recent years, watching short videos has become one of people's daily habits, and therefore the harm of false videos is becoming more and more significant. In this paper, we study the falsity identification of videos through the characteristics of both video publishers and video publishing environment. The feature combinations of video publisher features and video environment features are studied to filter out the better feature sets; the filtered feature sets are fed into the joint video feature falsity detection model for training, and a falsity video detection model with high accuracy is derived. The experiments show that the joint publisher and environment feature model has significant advantages in terms of accuracy, precision and F1 score, and the experimental results have better recall rate. The research in this paper provides an effective technical means for video-based false information governance in cyberspace.

Keywords: Fake videos · Detection models · Video publisher characteristics · Video environment characteristics

1 Introduction

With the explosion of short videos, the impact of fake videos on society is also increasing. Fake videos usually appear in pursuit of high traffic, high profits or to satisfy the inner "thrill" of the publisher, or for the purpose of defamation and disturbing the public peace. In recent years, major internet platforms have begun to introduce relevant regulatory policies, for example, in 2018, FaceBook, Google, Microsoft and Twitter signed codes of conduct to tackle online disinformation. The crisis of trust in information dissemination brought about by the proliferation of fake videos and the consequent failure to successfully implement relevant policy measures has made the screening and governance of short video fakery urgent.

Fake videos are a type of false information that is spread in the form of videos. Disinformation is information that has a tendency to mislead. It can be false information that is illogical, or correct information that is logical but grafted onto other events.

X. Sun et al. (Eds.): ICAIS 2022, LNCS 13340, pp. 56–70, 2022.
https://doi.org/10.1007/978-3-031-06791-4_5

Since the release of false videos is usually purposeful, human factors and environmental influences can be used as one of the identifying features of false videos. In related disinformation studies, both the publisher of the information and the environmental information of the information can be used as features for information falsity testing. In this paper, we combine the existing publisher features and environmental features for false information detection, do further research on these features and apply them to the falsehood detection of videos, and finally construct a detection model for the joint features of video falsehood based on publisher features and environmental features.

The main contributions of this paper are: (1) to study the publisher features of false videos based on existing publisher features for information falsity detection; (2) to study the information features of false videos based on existing environment features for information falsity detection; (3) to construct a detection model for the joint features of video falsity based on publisher features and video environment features.

2 Related Work

Fake video is false information in the form of video dissemination of information, which is designed to spread misleading information to achieve the purpose desired by the publisher of the information, and to cause a certain social effect. Most current disinformation studies use content features, For example, Xu [1] et al. used texture features of face regions in videos to detect deepfake videos; Al-Adhaileh [2] et al. used bidirectional long-short term memory (BiLSTM) and convolutional neural network (CNN) to detect fake opinions. Khaled [3] et al. proposes a model architecture to detect fake news in the Arabic language by using only textual features; Alsubari [4] et al. used n-grams of comment texts and and sentiment scores given by commenters to detect fake reviews.

Disinformation is the intentional dissemination of information with the purpose of misleading or deceiving [5], and disinformation as defined by Floridi [6–8] and Fetzer [9] emphasizes the act of "intentional". According to "Jurisprudence", "intentional" is defined as the state of mind in which the actor knows that his or her behavior will cause socially harmful results and hopes or allows such results to happen. Therefore, the dissemination of false information has certain human factors and will produce certain social environment effects, so the characteristics of the information publisher and the characteristics of the environment where the information is located can also be used as the screening conditions for false information.

2.1 Research on the Identification of False Information Publishers

There are currently a variety of malicious behaviours on the Internet, such as users posting spam, spamming, nuisance advertising, malicious links, false comments, etc. The purpose of these actions is to achieve certain illegal and unlawful purposes or related commercial interests, which are a constant danger to people's daily lives.

Disinformation publishers spread misleading information with intentional psychology, so the features related to disinformation publishers can be used for information falsity screening. For example, Yusof [10] et al. extracted 16 publisher features, which were shown to be effective in detecting spam publishers. Shu [11] et al. used features in user profile files (e.g., age, political affiliation, whether they were authenticated, number of days registered, number of followers, etc.) to screen for fake news. helmstetter [12] et al. used the Twitter Hamdi [13] et al. combine user account features and user social graphs to detect fake information on Twitter. In addition, in the research of false video detection, Li [14] et al. proposed five features of false video publishers combined with Bayesian models for false video detection, and their falsity detection accuracy reached 70%.

2.2   Study of Disinformation Based on Environmental Characteristics

After the social platform to which the video message is posted is received by the recipient of the message, the recipient will have corresponding feedback information, which is defined in this paper as the environmental characteristics of the video, that is, the environmental characteristics of the message are the social effects generated around the message by the platform on which it is posted.

For example, in the study of false news screening, Shu [15] et al. used a position-based method to infer the authenticity of original news articles, which used features such as the amount of likes and dislikes of postings to discriminate. Wu [16] et al. analyzed the dissemination traces of tracked information disseminators to construct a diffusion network and proposed the TraceMiner method, and experimentally verified its classification of the falsity of news The effectiveness of the TraceMiner method was verified. In the study of false comment screening, Shu [17] et al. used RNN models to encode user comments and learn potential comment feature representations for false news identification detection. Ruan [18] et al. introduced geographic location features of accounts and proposed a GADM model for distinguishing false commenters from normal users. Mukherjee [19] et al. used the content of comments similarity, the burstiness of comments, the number of times a comment has been commented, and other features to construct a disinformation detection model. In rumour detection research, Guo [20] et al. proposed the HAS-BLSTM model for rumour detection in microblogs and Twitter, which combines rumour posts, their associated sub-events and posts to build hierarchical social attention networks for early rumour detection. Jang [21] et al. used news-related temporal features to detect fake news in Twitter. Ma [22] et al. introduced a time series model incorporating rumour-related social information features for Weibo rumour detection, where the social information features include the proportion of men and women involved in discussing the post, the average number of friends, the average number of followers, the average sentiment score of comments, and the average number of retweets over time of the post.

In summary, the indirect identification approach of assessing the credibility of the posting source first in the study of false information based on publisher features is less time-efficient than studies that use features directly for information falsehood identification. The publisher features are mostly used in conjunction with content features to detect false information, but the detection of information with "highly disguised" content is not satisfactory. The features selected for false information detection based on environmental features are difficult to extract in some scenarios, or rely more on temporal features.

In this paper, based on the above research on the effectiveness of publisher features and environment features in false information detection, the role of the two types of features in video-based false information detection is further investigated, and a joint publisher-environment feature set is proposed and used to construct a false video detection model.

3 Methodology Model

False videos are among the types of false information that are disseminated in the form of videos. However, whether the information is disseminated with misleading purpose in the form of video or in the form of text, the characteristics of the information publisher and the environmental effects generated by the information are similar. Therefore, this chapter will introduce the relevant characteristics of the information publisher, the environmental characteristics of the platform where the information is located and the detection model that will be used in this paper.

3.1 Publisher Characteristics of the Video

Based on such research, this paper extracts fourteen features for video publishers: number of followers(PF), number of fans(PFa), number of Likes(PL), number of plays(PP), number of reads(PR), number of contributions(PCon), number of channels(PCha), number of videos(PV), number of audios(PAu), number of columns(PCol), number of albums(PAl), Latest dynamic values(PLDV), follower-following ratio(PFFR) and average number of Likes(PAvL).

Eleven features are directly available: PF, PFa, PL, PP, PR, PCon, PCha, PV, PAu, PCol and PAl. PLDV, PFFR and PAvL are obtained by preprocessing the basic features.

(1) The latest dynamic values(PLDV) refers to the number of days between the time of the latest video posted by the video publisher and the reference time, which can reflect the current activity of the video publisher to a certain extent, as shown in Eq. 1.

$$User_{Act} = Time_{new} - Time_{Ref} \tag{1}$$

where $User_{Act}$ is PLDV of the video publisher. $Time_{new}$ is the time of the latest release of the video by the video publisher. $Time_{Ref}$ is the reference time. When $User_{Act}$ is negative, it means that the publisher's latest video release time is earlier than the reference time, and vice versa, it means that the publisher's latest video release time is later than the reference time. Obviously, the larger the value of $User_{Act}$ means the more active the information publisher is.

(2) The follower-following ratio(PFFR) refers to the ratio of the number of followers of the video publisher to the sum of the number of followers and fans, which can reflect the interaction between the video publisher itself and other users' feedback. If PFFR is too small, it means the number of other users the publisher follows is much larger than the number of fans; if PFFR is too large, it means the number of fans the publisher has is larger than the number of other users the publisher follows. PFFR is shown in Eq. 2.

$$Fol_F = \frac{FF_{Fans}}{FF_{Attention} + FF_{Fans}} \tag{2}$$

where, Fol_F indicates PFFR; FF_{Fans} indicates the number of fans gained by the video publisher; $FF_{Attention}$ indicates the number of followers of the video publisher.

(3) The average number of Likes(PAvL) refers to the ratio of the number of likes to the number of contributions received by the publisher since the creation of the account, which can reflect the quality of the information posted by the publisher, as shown in Eq. 3.

$$Like_{Ave} = \frac{Like_{Sum}}{Upload_{Sum}} \tag{3}$$

where $Like_{Ave}$ denotes PAvL; $Like_{Sum}$ denotes the total number of likes received by the publisher; $Upload_{Sum}$ denotes the total number of videos uploaded by the publisher since the account was created.

3.2 Environmental Characteristics of the Video

The video environment features are divided into two categories in this paper, the limited option feedback features and open descriptive feedback features of the video viewer. The limited option feedback features of video viewer are Likes, Coins, Favorites, Retweets and number of comments(EC); the open descriptive feedback features of video viewer are the comments of viewers.

The limited option feedback features in the video environment is a very convenient evaluation mechanism, which requires only a few clicks on the corresponding button to complete the video evaluation. Compared with textual feedback, video information recipients are more willing to participate in this kind of evaluation method, which is convenient and time-saving, so the limited option feedback features is one of the important environmental features.

The open descriptive feedback features in the environment features generally when the information receiver's emotion reaches a certain level, the receiver will make relevant textual comments about the video he or she is watching. And this category of features is a more detailed expression of user emotions. The open descriptive feedback features in this paper include the emotional polarity of comments(ESP), the number of modal particles of comments(EMP), and comment text length(ECTL).

(1) The emotional polarity of comments(ESP) is obtained using a sentiment lexicon based approach. Firstly, the comment text is preprocessed, that is, the comment text is divided into words and deactivated; secondly, the degree modifiers and sentiment words in the comment text are identified; finally, the degree modifiers and sentiment words are weighted, and the corresponding sentiment polarity of the comment is obtained by accumulation. As shown in Fig. 1.

ESP is calculated as shown in Eq. 4.

$$Sentiment = \sum_{i=1}^{5}(pw_i \times pws_i) + \sum_{i=1}^{5}(nw_i \times nws_i) \tag{4}$$

where $Sentiment$ denotes ESP, the number of positive words of degree i in pw_i comment; the rating of positive sentiment words of degree i in pws_i comment; the number of

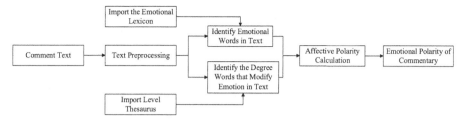

Fig. 1. Comment on the flow of emotional polarity calculation.

negative words of degree i in nw_i comment; the rating of negative sentiment words of degree i in nws_i comment.

(2) The number of modal particles of comments(EMP) is obtained by identifying the number of modal particles in the text information of the video comments, as shown in Eq. 5.

$$Tone_{Sum} = \sum_{i=1}^{n} tone(w_i) \tag{5}$$

where $Tone_{Sum}$ indicates EMP, $tone(w_i)$ determines whether the word is a modal particles, and w_i indicates the i word of the text.

(3) The comment text length(ECTL) is obtained by counting the comment words, as shown in Eq. 6.

$$Word_{Sum} = \sum w_i \tag{6}$$

where $Word_{Sum}$ denotes ECTL, and w_i denotes the i word of the text.

3.3 Model

Identifying whether the target video is a false video is a typical binary classification problem, neural networks are very suitable for binary classification problems, this paper uses convolutional neural networks to build a false video detection model, the detection model construction process is shown in Fig. 2.

First, fourteen publisher features and eight environment features of the video are extracted, and the traditional machine learning model is used for feature study to finally filter out the optimal feature combinations, and finally the selected feature combinations are sent to the convolutional neural network for training, which constitutes a joint feature detection model for video falsity based on publisher features and environment features.

The convolutional neural network consists of convolutional layers for feature extraction, and one convolutional layer contains several feature planes for its analysis, and the same feature plane shares weights, which reduces the connection between the layers of the network and also reduces the risk of overfitting. The convolutional computation uses a convolutional kernel with the corresponding input data for weighted summation, as shown in Eq. 7.

$$conv_{x,y} = \sum_{i}^{p*q} w_i v_i \tag{7}$$

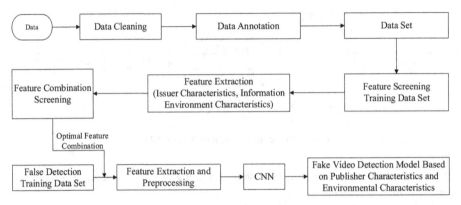

Fig. 2. False video detection model construction process.

The convolutional kernel is obtained by panning and scanning the input data, then using the activation function to form the feature plane of the corresponding layer, and finally sent to the next network layer. Due to the small size of the data input studied in this paper, the pooling layer used for dimensionality reduction is not used, but sent directly to the next convolutional layer until it is finally sent to the fully connected network layer for classification, and the video falsity detection results are obtained.

4 Experiment and Analysis

This chapter will present the experimental results and analysis of the information publisher feature group and environment feature group for video falsity detection, as well as the experimental results and analysis of the final filtered feature group for the joint feature detection model. Firstly, the experimental results and analysis of the information publisher feature group in false video detection are introduced; secondly, the experimental results and analysis of the environment feature group in false video detection are introduced; finally, the experimental results based on the information publisher features and environment features will be applied to the joint feature detection model for false videos.

4.1 Data Set

The dataset used in this study was independently collected and created by the research team and the dataset is a health video dataset. After data filtering and cleaning, the dataset contains a total of 700 video data, including 30 data items, including video number, URL, video title, video text content, number of video plays, and video time.

The latest dynamic value, follower ratio and average number of likes of the video publisher features are obtained by processing the basic features of the publisher, such as the video release time, number of followers and number of followers. The emotional polarity of comments, the number of words of tone of comments and the text length of comments in the environment features are obtained by processing the basic environment features, and the basic environment features such as number of likes, number of comments, number of coins, etc.

4.2   Video Falsity Test Based on Publisher Characteristics

Based on the fact that there are fourteen publisher features and all their combinations are 16,382, the effectiveness of publisher feature sets in video falsity detection is studied experimentally using three models: support vector machine (SVM), K-most-neighborly algorithm (KNN) and neural network.

Among them, PLDV takes January 1, 2021 as the reference time point, with negative values earlier than the reference time and positive values vice versa. Meanwhile, the video to be detected is not considered as the latest updated video, and if this publisher only released the video to be detected, the latest dynamic time is taken as January 1, 1900, which means PLDV is −44197. The top 15 items of the average accuracy of the three models are shown in Table 1.

From the experimental results shown in Table 3, the first 15 items with the highest average accuracy were all 69%. However, the fifth of them uses the least number of features to achieve the same accuracy rate as the other experimental groups, followed by the 14th, 12th and 13th experimental groups. The performance of each experimental group in SVM, KNN and artificial neural network is shown in Figs. 3, 4 and 5, in which the top 13 experimental groups in terms of average accuracy have 7 groups ranked top in KNN model in terms of accuracy and 3 groups ranked top in artificial neural network model in terms of accuracy.

Table 1. Experimental results of average accuracy of falsehood video detection based on publisher features.

No.	Feature groups	Average accuracy rate	Number of feature combinations
A1	('PL', 'PAvL', 'PR', 'PCon', 'PCha', 'PV', 'PAu', 'PCol')	0.69	8
A2	('PL', 'PAvL', 'PR', 'PCha', 'PV', 'PLDV')	0.69	6
A3	('PL', 'PR', 'PCon', 'PCha', 'PV', 'PLDV')	0.69	6
A4	('PL', 'PR', 'PCon', 'PCha', 'PAl', 'PLDV')	0.69	6
A5	('PF', 'PCol', 'PAl')	0.69	3
A6	('PFFR', 'PL', 'PAvL', 'PR', 'PCon', 'PCha', 'PV', 'PAu')	0.69	8
A7	('PFFR', 'PL', 'PAvL', 'PR', 'PCon', 'PCha', 'PV', 'PAl')	0.69	8
A8	('PL', 'PAvL', 'PR', 'PCon', 'PCha', 'PV', 'PAu', 'PAl')	0.69	8
A9	('PL', 'PAvL', 'PR', 'PCon', 'PCha', 'PV', 'PCol', 'PAl')	0.69	8

(continued)

Table 1. (*continued*)

No.	Feature groups	Average accuracy rate	Number of feature combinations
A10	('PL', 'PAvL', 'PR', 'PCha', 'PV', 'PAu', 'PCol', 'PAl')	0.69	8
A11	('PL', 'PR', 'PCon', 'PCha', 'PV', 'PAu', 'PCol', 'PAl')	0.69	8
A12	('PF', 'PFFR', 'PAu', 'PCol', 'PAl')	0.69	5
A13	('PFa', 'PL', 'PCha', 'PV', 'PLDV')	0.69	5
A14	('PF', 'PFa', 'PCha', 'PLDV')	0.69	4
A15	('PL', 'PR', 'PCon', 'PAu', 'PAl', 'PLDV')	0.69	6

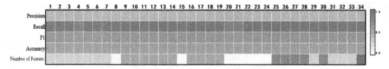

Fig. 3. Experimental results of publisher features in SVM model.

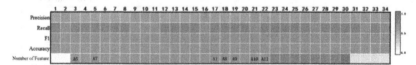

Fig. 4. Experimental results of publisher features in KNN model.

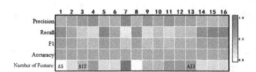

Fig. 5. Experimental results of publisher features in artificial neural network model.

As shown in Figs. 3, 4 and 5, where the number of feature combinations is made correlated and its value is between 0 and 1. Therefore the experimental group with fewer combinations (corresponding to lighter blocks of color) and higher accuracy (corresponding to darker blocks of color) is the optimal combination used to identify false videos. For example, in the SVM model, the 8th and 15th experimental groups have better feature combinations; in the KNN model, the 1st and 2nd experimental groups have better feature combinations; in the artificial neural network model, the 1st, 2nd and 8th experimental groups have better feature combinations. The detailed feature combinations and related experimental data are shown in Table 2.

Table 2. Data table of experimental results based on publisher characteristics.

No.	Combination of features	Precision	Recall	F1	Accuracy
SVM-8	('PF', 'PP', 'PCha')	0.66	0.97	0.78	0.73
SVM-15	('PFFR', 'PP', 'PCha')	0.66	0.97	0.78	0.73
KNN-1	('PAvL', 'PCha', 'PAu')	0.75	0.90	0.82	0.80
KNN-2	('PAvL', 'PCha', 'PCol')	0.78	0.83	0.81	0.80
ANN-1	('PP', 'PR', 'PCha')	0.68	0.83	0.75	0.72
ANN-2	('PP', 'PCha', 'PAu')	0.72	0.70	0.71	0.72
ANN-8	('PP', 'PCha', 'PCol')	0.65	0.80	0.72	0.68

Compared to the average accuracy, the combination of publisher features shown in Table 4 has more advantages in specific types of models, but does not have more stable generalizability compared to the average accuracy experimental group.

4.3 Video Falsity Testing Based on Environmental Features

Based on the fact that there are eight environmental features and all their combinations are 254, the effectiveness of environmental feature sets in video falsity detection is experimentally studied using three models: support vector machine (SVM), K-most-neighborly algorithm (KNN) and neural network. The top 8 average accuracies of the three models are shown in Table 3.

From the experimental results shown in Table 5, the average accuracy of the first 8 items in the experimental group ranged from 72% to 70%. Among them, the 1st and 2nd experimental groups have the highest average accuracy. The 3rd experimental group is the combination of features with the least number of features and the second highest average accuracy among the first 8 experimental groups.

The performance of each experimental group in SVM, KNN and artificial neural network is shown in Figs. 6, 7 and 8, where the top 8 experimental groups with average accuracy have better accuracy in SVM model, and 3 experimental groups each have higher accuracy in KNN model and artificial neural network model.

Table 3. Experimental results of the average accuracy of falsehood video detection based on environmental features.

No.	Feature groups	Average accuracy rate	Number of feature combinations
B1	('Likes', 'Coins', 'Favourite', 'EC', 'ESP', 'EMP')	0.72	6
B2	('Likes', 'Coins', 'Favourite', 'Retweets', 'ESP', 'RCTL', 'EMP')	0.72	7
B3	('Likes', 'Coins', 'Favourite', 'ESP', 'EMP')	0.71	5
B4	('Likes', 'Coins', 'Favourite', 'Retweets', 'EC', 'ESP', 'RCTL')	0.71	7
B5	('Likes', 'Coins', 'Favourite', 'RCTL', 'EMP')	0.71	5
B6	('Likes', 'Favourite', 'EC', 'ESP', 'RCTL')	0.71	5
B7	('Likes', 'Coins', 'Favourite', 'EC', 'RCTL')	0.71	5
B8	('Likes', 'Coins', 'Favourite', 'EC', 'EMP')	0.70	5

Fig. 6. Experimental results of environmental features in SVM model.

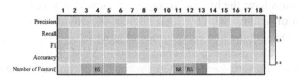

Fig. 7. Experimental results of environmental features in KNN model.

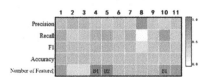

Fig. 8. Experimental results of environmental features in artificial neural network model.

Table 4. Data table of experimental results based on environmental characteristics.

No.	Combination of features	Precision	Recall	F1	Accuracy
SVM-2	('Likes', 'Favourite', 'EC')	0.88	0.77	0.82	0.83
SVM-3	('Likes', 'Coins', 'Favourite', 'Retweets')	0.92	0.73	0.81	0.83
SVM-4	('Likes', 'Favourite', 'EC', 'ESP')	0.85	0.77	0.81	0.82
SVM-5	('Likes', 'Favourite', 'EC', 'ECTL')	0.88	0.73	0.80	0.82
SVM-6	('Likes', 'Favourite', 'EC', 'EMP')	0.88	0.73	0.80	0.82
SVM-7	('Likes', 'Favourite', 'ESP', 'ECTL')	0.88	0.73	0.80	0.82
SVM-8	('Likes', 'Favourite', 'ECTL', 'EMP')	0.88	0.73	0.80	0.82
KNN-1	('Likes', 'Favourite', 'ESP', 'EMP')	0.69	0.80	0.74	0.72
KNN-2	('Likes', 'Favourite', 'EC', 'EMP')	0.70	0.70	0.70	0.70
KNN-7	('Likes', 'Favourite', 'ESP')	0.67	0.80	0.73	0.70
KNN-8	('Likes', 'Favourite', 'EMP')	0.68	0.77	0.72	0.70
ANN-2	('Favourite', 'Retweets', 'ESP', 'EMP')	0.76	0.63	0.69	0.72
ANN-3	('Favourite', 'ESP', 'ECTL', 'EMP')	0.74	0.67	0.70	0.72

As shown in Figs. 6, 7 and 8, where the number of feature combinations is made correlated and its value is between 0 and 1. Therefore, the experimental group with fewer combinations (corresponding to lighter color blocks) and higher accuracy (corresponding to darker color blocks) is the optimal combination for identifying false videos. For example, in the SVM-based model, the combination of features is better for the 2nd-8th experimental group; in the KNN-based model, the combination of features is better for the 1st, 2nd, 7th and 8th experimental groups; in the artificial neural network-based model, the combination of features is better for the 2nd and 3rd experimental groups. The detailed feature combinations and related experimental data are shown in Table 4.

Compared to the average accuracy, the combination of environmental features shown in Table 4 has more advantages in specific types of models, but does not have more stable generalizability compared to the average accuracy experimental group.

4.4 Experimental Results and Analysis

The experimental results of fake video detection based on publisher features and environment-based features show that the combination of A5 and B1 features is more effective in identifying fake videos compared to others. Except for the application of specific model scenarios, A5 and B1 are the combinations that use the least number of feature items and have the highest average accuracy, respectively, in terms of generally applicable feature selection. The publisher features and environment features selected with higher average accuracy are shown in Fig. 9.

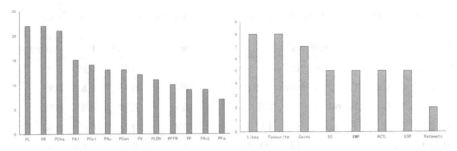

(left: publisher features; right: environment features)

Fig. 9. Feature usage.

Finally, a total of nine features, namely, PF, PCol, PAl, Likes, Coins, Favourite, EC, ESP and EMP, are sent to the convolutional neural network-based fake video detection model as a combination of joint features of publisher and information environment, and their experimental results are shown in Table 5.

Table 5. Comparison of experimental results.

	Accuracy	Precision	Recall	F1
Fake video detection model	0.88	0.82	0.9	0.86

Over experiments show that the joint feature detection model of video falsity based on publisher features and environment features has an accuracy of 88%. Compared with single-feature false video identification, the accuracy is improved. The simultaneous action of multiple features, the potential association between features and the learning ability of convolutional neural networks lead to an accuracy index of 82%. It outperforms most of the single-feature false video detection models in terms of accuracy and precision. In addition, the model outperforms the vast majority of comparison models in terms of recall rate, and the number of correctly identified falsehood videos accounts for 90% of the total number of falsehood videos to be predicted.

Meanwhile, after analyzing the experimental results with reference to real-world cases, we found that publishers of fake videos usually falsify the number of followers and activity in order to attract high traffic. Usually, they do not carefully divide the videos into columns or waste time posting meaningless pictures in order to seek "efficient" benefits. Fake video publishers usually have a bipolar tendency in following behavior, that is, they follow too many people at random to attract them to return, or they never use their illegal accounts for spreading fake videos to follow and interact. Analyzed from the perspective of the environment in which the fake videos are released, the number of likes, coins, favorites and comments harvested is usually also polarized because of the problematic content of the fake videos, that is, viewers will not interact positively with the content they hold suspicions about, or the fake video publishers will hire a large number of fake accounts to interact positively, thus leading to an abnormal number of likes, coins, favorites and comments in order to attract more users for the purpose of harvesting high traffic.

5 Conclusion

The text investigates publisher features and environment features of fake videos, and through extensive experiments and validation comparisons, the better feature groups are screened for use in fake video recognition applications. The experiments show that the accuracy of the filtered publisher feature set and environment feature set jointly fed into the convolutional neural network disinformation recognition model reaches 88%. Compared with the previous video falsity check using traditional machine learning with a single category of features, the recognition accuracy is improved. At the same time, it is further demonstrated that the publisher's own behavior and the environmental effects generated by the video are correlated with falsity.

The experiments in this paper use the same weights for nine features fed into the neural network training to obtain a better model for identifying falsity videos. The next step of the study is to investigate the role of publisher's own behavior and the environmental effects generated by the video in the falsity testing of the video, so as to further optimize the model and adjust the weights of the nine features to obtain a detection model with higher accuracy in identifying the falsity of the video.

References

1. Xu, B., Liu, J., Liang, J., Lu, W., Zhang, Y.: Deepfake videos detection based on texture features. Comp. Mater. Contin. **68**(1), 1375–1388 (2021)
2. Al-Adhaileh, M.H., Alsaade, F.W.: Detecting and analysing fake opinions using artificial intelligence algorithms. Intell. Auto. Soft Compu. **32**(1), 643–655 (2022)
3. Fouad, K.M., Sabbeh, S.F., Medhat, W.: Arabic fake news detection using deep learning. Comp. Mater. Contin. **71**(2), 3647–3665 (2022)
4. Alsubari, S.N., Deshmukh, S.N., Alqarni, A.A., Alsharif, N., Theyazn, H.: Data analytics for the identification of fake reviews using supervised learning. Comp. Mate. Contin. **70**(2), 3189–3204 (2022)
5. Fallis, D.: What is disinformation? Libr. Trends **63**(3), 401–426 (2015)
6. Floridi, L.: Brave: net. world: the internet as a disinformation superhighway. The Electronic Library **14**, 509–514 (1996)
7. Floridi, L.: Is semantic information meaningful data? Philos. Phenomenol. Res. **70**(2), 351–370 (2005)
8. Floridi: Semantic information and the correctness theory of truth. Erkenntnis **74**(2), 147–175 (2011)
9. Fetzer, J.: Disinformation: The use of false information. Mind. Mach. **14**, 231–240 (2004)
10. Yusof, Y., Sadoon, O.H.: Detecting video spammers in youtube social media. In: Proceedings of the International Conference on Computing and Informatics, pp. 228–234. IEEE (2017)
11. Shu, K., Zhou, X., Wang, S.: The role of user profiles for fake news detection. In: Proceedings of the 2019 IEEE/ACM international conference on advances in social networks analysis and mining, pp. 436–439 (2019)

12. Helmstetter, S., Paulheim, H.: Weakly supervised learning for fake news detection on twitter. In: IEEE/ACM International Conference on Advances in Social Networks Analysis and Mining (ASONAM), pp. 274–277 (2018)
13. Hamdi, T., Slimi, H., Bounhas, I.: A hybrid approach for fake news detection in twitter based on user features and graph embedding. In: Proceedings of the International conference on distributed computing and internet technology, pp. 266–280 (2020)
14. Li, X., Li, S., Li, J.: Detection of fake-video uploaders on social media using naive bayesian model with social cues. Sci. Rep. **1**, 16068 (2021)
15. Shu, K., Sliva, A., Wang, S.: Fake news detection on social media: A data mining perspective. ACM SIGKDD Explorations Newsl **19**, 22–36 (2017)
16. Wu, L., Liu, H.: Tracing fake-news footprints: characterizing social media messages by how they propagate. In: Proceedings of the eleventh ACM international conference on Web Search and Data Mining, pp. 637–645 (2018)
17. Shu, K., et al.: Defend: explainable fake news detection. In: Proceedings of the 25th ACM SIGKDD international conference on knowledge discovery & data mining, pp. 395–405 (2019)
18. Ruan, N., Deng, R., Su, C.: Gadm: manual fake review detection for o2o commercial platforms. Comput. Secur. **88**, 101657 (2020)
19. Mukherjee, A., Kumar, A., Liu, B.: Spotting opinion spammers using behavioral footprints. In: Proceedings of the 19th ACM SIGKDD international conference on Knowledge discovery and data mining, pp. 632–640. Association for Computing Machinery (2013)
20. Guo, H., Cao, J., Zhang, Y.: Rumor detection with hierarchical social attention network. In: Proceedings of the 27th ACM International Conference on Information and Knowledge Management, pp. 943–951 (2018)
21. Jang, Y., Park, C., Lee, D., Seo, Y.: Fake news detection on social media: a temporal-based approach. Comp. Mater. Contin. **69**(3), 3563–3579 (2021)
22. Ma, J., Gao, W., Wei, Z.: Detect rumors using time series of social context information on microblogging websites. In: Proceedings of the 24th ACM International on Conference on Information and Knowledge Management, pp. 1751–1754. Association for Computing Machinery (2015)

Intrusion Detection Model Based on KNN-AE-DNN

Hongtao Chen[1,2,3,4], Shuo Guo[1(✉)], Yanbo Shi[5], Weixuan Wei[1,2,3,4], and Kaidi Wang[6]

[1] College of Information Engineering, Shenyang University of Chemical Technology,
Shenyang 110142, China
10097947@qq.com

[2] Key Laboratory of Networked Control Systems, Chinese Academy of Sciences,
Shenyang 110016, China

[3] Shenyang Institute of Automation, Chinese Academy of Sciences, Shenyang 110016, China

[4] Institutes for Robotics and Intelligent Manufacturing, Chinese Academy of Sciences,
Shenyang 110169, China

[5] Shenyang Aircraft Corporation, Shenyang 110850, China

[6] Molarray Research, Toronto L4B3K1, Canada

Abstract. As an important aspect of industrial control security information, the field of intrusion detection has been plagued by the problems of high false positive rate, low detection rate, slow processing response and high data feature dimension of traditional intrusion detection algorithms. In order to solve these problems, an intrusion detection model KNN-AE-DNN based on K-NearestNeighbor (KNN), Dense Neural Network and auto encoder network (AE) is proposed. In view of the large number of industrial control system equipment and large amount of data, when extracting the type of industrial control attack, the data feature dimension is compressed to speed up the processing speed of the model. Firstly, the dimension is reduced through data preprocessing and AE self encoder, and the training data is input into KNN and DNN for model training. KNN is used as a preliminary identification and classification, and the results of the initial discrimination are input into DNN for secondary classification to obtain the final results. The experimental results on NSL-KDD dataset show that the intrusion model proposed in this paper shows good real-time performance and high detection rate.

Keywords: DNN · Auto encoder · Intrusion detection · NSL-KDD dataset

1 Introduction

The rapid development of the global Internet has rapidly promoted the process of the industrial information industry, gradually changing from the closed LAN to the fully open interconnection of all things, breaking the closure of the industrial control system, making the industrial network face a more serious traditional information security threat. Especially in the network security of industrial system, there are serious vulnerability risks in the current basic network due to the poor consideration of the security of the initial industrial protocol. Intrusion detection system (IDS) plays a key role in

© The Author(s), under exclusive license to Springer Nature Switzerland AG 2022
X. Sun et al. (Eds.): ICAIS 2022, LNCS 13340, pp. 71–83, 2022.
https://doi.org/10.1007/978-3-031-06791-4_6

protecting the information security of industrial system. The industrial system includes data acquisition system of various industrial control equipment, monitoring and control automation equipment system and monitoring management system. In recent years, due to the openness of industrial control system, there have been highly destructive Stuxnet virus and Ukrainian power grid attack. Intrusion detection system can extract and analyze the types of attacks from a large number of network traffic and log data, so as to judge the security status of the system.

Learn discrimination algorithms from supervised machines, such as k-nearest neighbor (KNN) and support vector machine (SVM) [1]. To deep learning algorithms, such as auto encoder (AE), supervised learning fully connected Dense Neural Network (DNN). Liao, YH et al. [2] generated configuration files for intrusion behaviors, matched the attack behaviors in the data set, and experimented with DARPA BSM audit data set. KNN algorithm can ensure low false positives and effectively detect intrusion detection attacks. Li, LX et al. [3] combined with the idea of density peak clustering (DPC), introduced density into KNN algorithm and proposed DPNN classifier. The classification performance on KDD CUP99 data set is better than that of SVM, KNN and other machine learning methods. Razon et al. [4] reduced the dimension of data sets by comparing AE and PCA methods, combined with multi machine learning methods to build classifiers, which can maintain high accuracy in two categories and multi categories. In the literature, a method combining stacked sparse denoising self encoder (SSDA) and softmax is proposed to improve the algorithm by reflecting the penalty term of attribute feature information on SSDA, The detection effect of the experiment is 4.7% higher than that of the original SSDA. Machine learning and deep learning methods [5] are directly used in intrusion detection, and the effect is not good. Therefore, we can consider processing according to the characteristics of different data, such as large amount of data and high-dimensional features. To sum up, the KNN-AE-DNN model is proposed in this paper. Firstly, the dimension of the data is reduced and filtered through AE, and the training data is sent to KNN algorithm for fast mass preprocessing, which has the problem of low accuracy; Then send the same data to DNN network for training, and complete intrusion detection in DNN network.

2   Related Theory

2.1   Auto-encoder

As an unsupervised fully connected neural network [6], self encoder network can be used to simplify data with higher dimension to data with lower dimension after feature extraction. The connection diagram of AE is shown in Fig. 1. It can be reduced to several dimensions by setting the number of nodes in the hidden layer in the middle of the network, and then adjusted according to the data retention integrity. The self encoder is composed of encoder and decoder. The former completes the abstract feature representation of samples, the latter completes the reconstruction of input samples, and completes iterative fine-tuning through gradient descent algorithm. 122 features were obtained from the preprocessed data set. The 122 features are used as the input of the self coding network, so the number of input nodes is set to 122, and then the three-layer hidden structure is used to reduce the dimension of the input data. The compression dimension is set to 10 dimensions by the trial value method, and the reconstructed data is decoded and restored by the decoding layer. Finally, the weights are continuously trained to minimize the error between the reconstructed item and the data before coding.

Algorithm steps:
Assume that X, W and b_e represents the weight and offset of the coding part. f represents a nonlinear activation function, such as relu or sigmoid. The self encoder encodes the samples through linear mapping and nonlinear mapping activation functions.

$$h = f(W * X + b_e) \tag{1}$$

Then, the decoder decodes and reconstructs the coding features and outputs:

$$X' = f(W' * h + b_d) \tag{2}$$

W' and b_d represents the weight and offset of the decoding part.

Finally, the mean square error method is used to measure the output and input errors, and the adaptive gradient descent algorithm of Adam is used to minimize the error after and before data coding.

$$L(X, X') = \frac{1}{2n} \sum_{i=1}^{n} (X_i' - X_i)^2 \tag{3}$$

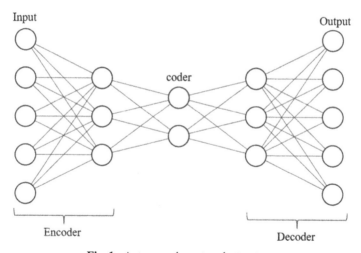

Fig. 1. Auto-encoder network structure.

2.2 Dense Neural Network

Fully connected network DNN [7] is one of the commonly used neural networks. It contains multiple hidden layers, in which all nodes between each two layers are connected

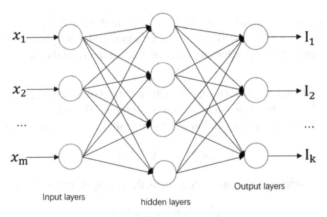

Fig. 2. DNN structure.

one by one. The structure is shown in Fig. 2. As a multi-layer perceptron, DNN has simple structure and convenient application.

In the fully connected neural network, any neuron in each layer will process and calculate the input data, and transfer the calculated result information to any neuron in the next layer. The weight and offset of the previous node are transferred to the next node [8]. The specific calculation formula is shown in (4):

$$z_j^i = w_j^i * X - b_j^i \tag{4}$$

$$f(Z_j^i) = \sigma(Z_j^i) \tag{5}$$

z_j^i represents the weighted result of the j node of layer i, w_j^i 和 b_d represents the connection weight and offset of the node of the previous layer to the node respectively, by the linear weighting of x, the weighting result is obtained, and then the result is input into the activation function σ, and get the output of node. The visual form of feedforward propagation of DNN neural network is expressed as formula (4) and formula (5).

The role of input layer neurons is to input the dimensionless data into the network without calculation and processing. The learning process of DNN is essentially to continuously adjust the connection weight and offset between neurons, so as to continuously approach the original results of training samples. The most commonly used algorithm is the error back propagation (BP) algorithm [9]. According to the gradient descent algorithm, the calculation expressions of weight and offset used in back propagation can be obtained, such as formula (6) and formula (7).

$$w_j^i = w_j^i - \eta \frac{\partial e}{\partial w_j^i} \tag{6}$$

$$b_j^i = b_j^i - \eta \frac{\partial e}{\partial b_j^i} \tag{7}$$

Activation functions include tanh function, sigmoid function and relu function [10]. Choosing different activation functions will have different convergence speed and training time in the same model. The simmoid function maps the input operation to 0~1,

The simmoid function maps the input operation to $-1{\sim}1$. Because tanh's input floats up and down around the origin, which is more in line with the characteristics of nonlinear monotonicity and good fault tolerance, tanh's performance is better than sigmoid, but when both of them encounter extreme data during training, it will lead to the function derivation approaching zero, so that the weight value cannot be updated, resulting in the disappearance of gradient, and the training of neural network cannot be completed. Relu compares the first two. As can be seen from function Fig. 3, while $x < 0$, the output value is 0, and when $x > 0$, the output value increases with x. Gradient calculation requires the cumulative multiplication of weight and activation function. As long as the output value is not 0 and the input data is usually greater than zero, the gradient will not disappear. And relu has faster convergence speed, so theoretically, it will perform better in the hidden layer. The images of the three activation functions are shown in Fig. 3.

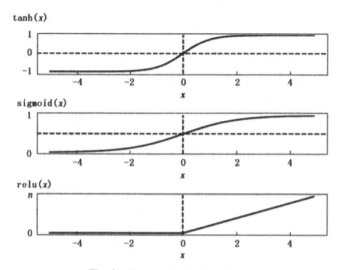

Fig. 3. Three activation functions.

In the selection of output function in the output layer, considering that the model uses one hot method to process the original data, and it is a multi classification task, the calculation results of each output point range in [0,1] and are closely related, while the application scenario of sigmoid function is mainly on the two classification problem, so softmax is selected as the output function in the experiment. The function expression is shown in formula (8).

$$f(z_i) = \frac{e^{z_i}}{\sum_{c=1}^{C} e^{z_C}} \tag{8}$$

3   KNN-AE-DNN Model Design

3.1   Design Ideas and Overall Framework

In order to solve the two problems caused by the high-dimensional data features of the data set to the detection model, which affect the extraction of effective data features, reduce the accuracy of training and increase the training time of the model, the following design ideas are given in this section.

The characteristics of NSL-KDD data reach 122 dimensions after preprocessing, which is the main reason for slowing down the training model and affecting the accuracy of the model. Therefore, it is necessary to reduce the dimension of the preprocessed high-dimensional data. There are several dimensionality reduction methods, such as PCA (principal components analysis) [11], AE. PCA algorithm maps the data in the data set from the original feature space to the orthogonal space sufficient to retain the feature components through base transformation. In the orthogonal space, a point in the data set can be found to be closest to the hyperplane. AE is an unsupervised neural network model, which does not need to label the data. By compressing the data dimension of the input data, comparing the data before and after compression coding, the parameters are continuously adjusted by the way of neural network back propagation, so that the output is the same as the input data as much as possible.

Because the data set [12] is encoded by one hot, resulting in many characteristic dimensions of the data, AE is used to reduce the dimension of the data. While training DNN, KNN is added to roughly classify the data, which can quickly classify a large number of positive and abnormal data, saving time for DNN network processing data. The more hidden layers of DNN will lead to poor real-time performance of data processing. The three methods are combined. Firstly, AE is used to reduce the dimension of the data, and then the training data is sent to KNN. KNN is used to screen the intrusion detection data that is easy to judge, which reduces the classification task of DNN and increases the real-time processing speed of DNN. Combined with the three, it can ensure high detection rate and good real-time performance.

The overall framework of the model proposed in this paper is shown in Fig. 4. The model is divided into three parts. The first part is to obtain data and preprocess data; The second part is the intrusion detection part of DNN neural network training model; The third part is the detection and classification module.

3.2   Data Preprocessing

The NSL-KDD data set [13] selected in this experiment is the optimized set improved by tavallaee and others on the basis of KDD CUP99 data set. The data volume of KDD CUP99 is about 5 million, including many duplicate data, which will cause poor detection results and too long training time. Compared with KDD CUP99, NSL-KDD has only 30000 data in training set and test set, which greatly reduces the training time. In contrast, the data of NSL-KDD is more refined, making the detection of the model more accurate. The NSL-KDD dataset contains 41 features and one label. The last column represents the number of times that the samples in this row are detected to be correctly classified

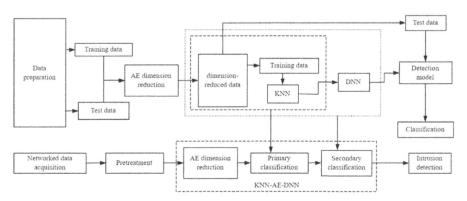

Fig. 4. Framework of the model.

Table 1. Attribute information of NSL-KDD data.

Attribute number	One-hot encoding
1–9	Basic characteristics of connection
10–22	Connected content characteristics
23–31	Time based traffic characteristics
32–41	Host based traffic characteristics
41	Label

in previous experiments. The higher the number of times, the easier it is to be classified. The specific information is shown in Table 1.

Preprocess the data set to obtain high-quality data set and further improve the performance of the model. It includes two parts: normalization of continuous data and coding of discrete values.

Data Normalization

In this paper, the normalization of the experimental part adopts the maximum and minimum standardization [14], and the specific expression is shown in formula (9). x_{min} is the maximum value of this dimension feature in all data, x_{max} is the maximum value of this dimension feature in all data x^* is normalized data.

$$x^* = \frac{x - x_{min}}{xmin_{max}} \tag{9}$$

Because the size of the numerical data in the data set is different, the normalization processing is carried out by formula (9), and the linear transformation is carried out on the original data to eliminate the influence of the dimension between the singular sample data on the data analysis results, so that the values are in the same order of magnitude. The normalized data can improve the accuracy and convergence speed of the model.

One-Hot Encoder

Single hot coding, n-bit status register is used to encode N states, and each state has its own independent register bit. For discrete type data in NSL-KDD data set, such as protocol_type in feature; The network service type (service) of the target host class has 70 service type data; Network connection status (flag), flag has 11 network connection status.

For example, protocol_ type has three values: TCP, UDP and ICMP. After one hot coding, TCP is 001; UDP is 010; ICMP is 100. Five classifications of the label of the sample, such as normal labeled 00001, probe labeled 00100, DOS labeled 00010, u2r labeled 01000, and r2l labeled 10000.

Division of Data Set

After preprocessing NSL-KDD data, the training model is randomly divided into 3 equal parts from 125973 training sets, 2/3 of which are trained and the rest are reserved for testing, as shown in Table 2.

Table 2. Partition of data sets.

Data set	Nor	Pro	Dos	U2r	R2l
Training set	44895	7771	30618	35	663
Test set	22448	3885	15309	17	332

4 Experiment and Data Analysis

4.1 Experimental Data and Experimental Environment

It can be seen from Sect. 3.2.3 that the NSL-KDD data set is used for the experimental data, and the label includes five categories: denial of service attack (Dos), scanning attack (probing), illegal local access of remote machine (R2l), unauthorized illegal access of ordinary users (U2r) and normal. The specific data types are shown in Table 3.

The experimental hardware environment is window10 operating system, the CPU is Intel i5-6300hq, the main frequency is 2.3 GHz, and the physical memory is 16.0 GB. The development language is python, and the neural network model is built by the open source framework keras.

4.2 Selection of Experimental Parameters

After normalizing the data, one hot coding is performed. After coding the service, the data dimension rises to 110. After coding the protocol_type and flag, the final data

Table 3. NSL-KDD Data distribution table.

Type		Train set	Test set
Normal		67 343	9 711
Attack	Dos	45 927	7 458
	U2e	52	200
	Probe	1 656	2 421
	R2l	995	2 754
Total		125 973	22 544

dimension rises to 122. In dealing with the five classification problem, the label obtains five-dimensional features through one hot coding, then the number of AE corresponding input nodes is 122, and the dimension is reduced to 10 dimensions, then the DNN input is 10 nodes and the output is 5 nodes. KNN parameter settings are shown in Table 5. The parameter settings of AE are shown in Table 6.

The trial value method is used to select the appropriate epoch for the model. Taking the 3 hidden layer network 10-50-40-20-5 as an example, the total number of epoch is 200. The iterative epoch and the corresponding cost loss are shown in Fig. 5.

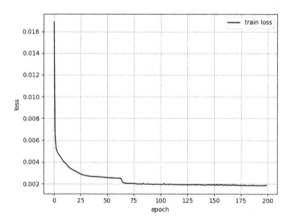

Fig. 5. Number of epoch and loss.

It can be observed from the figure that after 100 iterations, the loss cost decreases slightly between 50~75, and tends to be flat after 75~100. When selecting the number of iterations of epoch, if the number of iterations is too small, it will lead to insufficient training, and too many iterations may lead to over fitting. Therefore, based on the information on the graph, the selected number of iterations is 100.

For the selection of hidden layers of the network, the empirical trial value method is used to select different network structures with 2~4 hidden layers, which are divided into 10-20-5, 10-50-40-5 and 10-50-40-25-5. Experiments show that the overall detection rate is similar when the number of hidden layers is 3 and 4, but the detection rates of u2r and r2l in 4 hidden layers are lower than that in 3 hidden layers. The overall accuracy of 2 hidden layers is not as good as that of 3 hidden layers. Under comprehensive comparison, select the appropriate number of hidden layers as 3. After the epoch and network structure are determined, the specific parameters are shown in Table 4.

Table 4. DNN parameter setting.

Parameter	Value
Network structure	10-50-40-5
Activation function	ReLU, Softmax
Gradient descent	Adam
Learning rate	0.001
Batch size	256
Epoch	100

n_neighbors represents the number of adjacent points, which is obtained by recursive search method, and n_neighbors is set to 5. Algorithm: the algorithm used in the radius limited nearest neighbor method. There are three options, namely "auto", "ball_tree", "kd_tree" and "brute". KNN will make a trade-off among the above three algorithms and choose the best fitting algorithm. Metric is a distance measure of the proximity between test samples and training samples. There are three commonly used methods, namely "Minkowski", "Euclidean" and "Manhattan". n_jobs sets the number of parallel processing tasks, which is mainly used for parallel processing of multi-core CPUs to improve the running speed of the algorithm. The setting parameters of KNN are shown in Table 5.

Table 5. KNN parameter setting.

Parameter	Value
n_neighbors	5
Algorithm	auto
n_jobs	−1
Metric	Manhattan

The AE network structure is set as 122-80-40-10-40-80-122. The network is large on both sides, small in the middle and small in the middle. The parameter settings of AE are shown in Table 6, n_ components is the feature dimension after dimension reduction. The activation function is set to relu and sigmoid, and combined with adaptive gradient optimization algorithm Adam, the learning rate should be reduced to 0.001.

Table 6. AE parameter setting.

Parameter	Value
n_components	10
Activation function	ReLU, sigmoid
Gradient descent	Adam
Learning rate	0.001
Batch size	256

4.3 Experimental Result

This experiment is divided into two experiments. Experiment 1 mainly explores the real-time detection under two categories. The experiment mainly compares the binary prediction accuracy and training time of DT [15], CNN, AE-KNN and KNN-AE-DNN models. The specific experimental results are shown in the table below.

It can be seen from Table 7 that the accuracy rates of DT and CNN are the same, but the training time of CNN is much longer than that of DT, and the real-time detection performance is poor. DT has the advantage of fast training speed, but it is not as fast as AE-KNN and KNN-AE-DNN in prediction time, and its accuracy and detection rate are not as good as those after them. Compared with AE-KNN without KNN, KNN-AE-DNN improves the accuracy by 2% points and performs better in detection rate. The introduction of KNN has a slight impact on the training time, but can effectively improve the detection rate.

Table 7. Result of experiment 1.

Method	Accuracy/%	Detection rate/%	Train times/s	Forecast time/ms
DT	91.88	89.44	0.69	58.86
CNN	93.76	90.05	90.01	N/A
AE-KNN	95.05	94.42	38.3	21.05
KNN-AE-DNN	98.56	97.06	40.15	20.75

Experiment 2 mainly explores the real-time detection under the five categories of KNN-AE-DNN model. According to Table 8, KNN-AE-DNN's speed advantage in five categories is slightly inferior to DT, while DT and AE-KNN as a comparison have low overall accuracy and poor performance despite short training time. The training time of KNN-AE-DNN is about 3 s longer than that of AE-KNN, and the accuracy is improved by 3% points. It can be seen that the introduction of KNN can improve the accuracy without consuming a lot of time.

Table 8. Total result of experiment 2.

Method	Train times/s	Total accuracy/%
DT	0.69	89.48
CNN	92.04	91.64
AE-KNN	42.22	94.33
KNN-AE-DNN	43.14	97.38

It can be seen from Table 8 that KNN-AE-DNN lost data when KNN screened u2r with small sample size for the first time. In combination with Table 7 and Table 8, the overall detection rate of the two categories. of data is higher than that of the five categories, because in the two categories detection, the type probe is judged as u2r or r2l, which is judged to be correct, while in the five categories, it is considered to be wrong. From the results of the above two experiments, the overall detection rate of the intrusion detection model proposed in this paper is better than other methods, which proves the feasibility of the model on the whole. The specific results of five categories are shown in Table 9.

Table 9. Classification result of experiment 2.

Method	Evaluation	Normal	Dos	Probe	R2L	U2R
DT	Accuracy	94.01	89.44	0.69	58.86	50.20
	Detection rate	96.31	83.29	0.47	62.59	2.44
CNN	Accuracy	93.56	98.47	91.68	36.50	27.33
AE-KNN	Precision	88.41	96.32	97.57	82.35	70,23
	Detection rate	97.19	79.87	35.12	77.20	69.12
KNN-AE-DNN	Precision	91.12	92.12	96.88	87.22	75.23
	Detection rate	93.41	97.24	96.15	85.64	71.42

5 Conclusion

The intrusion detection model KNN-AE-DNN based on deep neural network proposed in this paper greatly improves the speed of training and detection on the basis of ensuring the accuracy. The dimension reduction of the model is completed by AE encoder. After the initial screening of KNN detection data, it is used as the input DNN for secondary judgment. The pre screening of KNN reduces the subsequent DNN work, effectively reduces the running time, and improves the overall training speed. The next step is to build a real network environment and collect real-time data for network intrusion detection.

Acknowledgments. This work is supported by the project: the national defense basic scientific research project "XX intelligent manufacturing XX technology" (jcky2020205b022).

References

1. Chitrakar, R., Huang, C.: Selection of candidate support vectors in incremental SVM for network intrusion detection. Comput. Secur. **45**(3), 231–241 (2014)
2. Liao, Y., Vemuri, V.R.: Use of k-nearest neighbor classifier for intrusion detection. Comput. Secur. **21**(5), 439–448 (2002)
3. Li, L., Zhang, H., Peng, H.: Nearest neighbors based density peaks approach to intrusion detection. Chaos, Solitons Fractals **110**, 33–40 (2018)
4. Abdulhammed, R., et al.: Features dimensionality reduction approaches for machine learning based network intrusion detection. Electronics **8**(3), 322 (2019)
5. Zhang, H., Shi, X., Guo, Y., Wang, Z., Yin, X.: More load, more differentiation-Let more flows finish before deadline in data center networks. Computer **127**, 352–367 (2017)
6. Hinton, G.E., Salakhutdinov, R.R.: Reducing the dimensionality of data with neural networks. Science **313**(5786), 504–507 (2006)
7. Hu, Y., Luo, D.Y.: Overview on deep learning. Trans. Intell. Sys. **14**(1), 1–19 (2019)
8. Yu, B.B., Wang, H.Z., Yan, B.Y.: Intrusion detection of industrial control system based on long short term memory. Inf. Control **47**(1), 54–59 (2018)
9. Mills, P.M., Zomaya, A.Y., Tadé, M.O.: Adaptive model-based control using neural networks. Int. J. Control **60**(6), 1163–1192 (1992)
10. Ding, S.: Research on the key technology of intrusion detection based on deep learning. M.S. Dissertation. Beijing Jiaotong University (2018)
11. Camacho, J., Ferrer, A.: Cross-validation in PCA models with the element-wise k-fold (ekf) algorithm: theoretical aspects. J. Chemom. **26**(7), 361–373 (2012)
12. Han, S., et al.: Log-based anomaly detection with robust feature extraction and online learning. IEEE Trans. Inf. Forensics Security **16**, 2300–2311 (2021)
13. Tavallaee, M., Bagheri, E., Lu, W.: A detailed analysis of the KDD CUP 99 data set. IEEE (2009)
14. Liu, X.: Study on data normalization in bp neural network. Mechani. Eng. Auto. **3**, 122–123 (2010)
15. Ding, L.B., Wu, Z.D., Su, J.L.: Intrusion detection method based on ensemble deep forests. Comput. Eng. **46**(3), 144–150 (2020)

A Framework for Unknown Traffic Identification Based on Neural Networks and Constraint Information

Lu Kang[1] , Qingbing Ji[1,2](✉), Lvlin Ni[1], and Jiaxin Li[3]

[1] Science and Technology On Communication Security Laboratory, Chengdu, China
jqbdxy@163.com
[2] School of Cybersecurity, Northwestern Polytechnical University, Xi'an, China
[3] School of Information Technology, Deakin University, Melbourne, Australia

Abstract. Nowadays, traffic identification is becoming increasingly important in network security. But in practice, we often encounter unknown traffic, in which we do not know its specific type, and makes it very difficult to manage and maintain network security. The ability to divide the mixed unknown traffic into multiple clusters, each of which contains only one type as far as possible, is a key point to tackle this problem. In this paper, we propose a framework for unknown traffic identification based on neural networks and constraint information to improve the clustering purity. The framework consists of two main innovations: (1) It uses neural network methods to reduce the dimensionality and select features of network traffic. (2) It analyzes the constraint information of traffic and uses this information to guide the process of identification. To verify the effectiveness of the framework in this paper, we make contrast experiments on two real-world packet traces respectively. Through our experimental results, we find that the maximum clustering purity of our framework in this paper can reach 96.10% on the traces of Internet Service Provider (ISP) and 91.89% on the public traces. Experimental results show that the proposed framework is more effective than Gaussian Mixture Model (GMM).

Keywords: Unknown traffic identification · Traffic classification · Neural networks · Constraint information

1 Introduction

With the rapid development of technologies on the Internet, hundreds of millions of network access points, devices, and network applications have generated massive amounts of network traffic. And the composition of network traffic has become more and more complex, a large amount of unknown traffic is mixed in the network. The unknown traffic refers to the traffic generated by unknown applications or services (i.e., zero-day applications), and it has never been covered by the identification system. These applications or services may be designed to evade network censorship by applying techniques such as dynamic ports to communicate. Due to privacy and economic concerns, more

X. Sun et al. (Eds.): ICAIS 2022, LNCS 13340, pp. 84–96, 2022.
https://doi.org/10.1007/978-3-031-06791-4_7

and more applications or services use private protocols for transmission. In addition, some malware also uses custom private protocols for data or command transmission, generating a large amount of unknown traffic [1].

This paper aims at the problem that unknown traffic accounts for a large proportion of network traffic, which makes it very difficult for network monitoring administration, and proposes a framework for unknown traffic identification based on neural networks and constraint information. There are generally three stages for close-grained unknown traffic identification: (1) Extracting unknown network traffic from mixed network traffic; (2) Dividing the traffic into multiple clusters according to type, and each of cluster contains only one type as far as possible; (3) Label each cluster, such as protocol, application, and other types [2]. In this paper, we focus on the second stage above.

In particular, according to the TCP/IP model, if some network flows are connecting to the same endpoint, and they share the same destination IP address, destination port, and protocols, these flows are typically handled by the same application process or network service behind. And extracting this information between network flows is obviously much easier than obtaining the service or application type. We extracted the constraint information to guide the identification of unknown traffic. In machine learning tasks, the ability of feature extraction is the key problem, we use autoencoder technology to reduce dimensionality and select features of network traffic after extracting features to improve clustering technology. To verify the effectiveness of our framework in this paper, we make contrast experiments on real-world datasets. And the experimental results show that the clustering purity rate of our framework can exceed 96% on the ISP traces and 91% on the public traces. The evaluation results demonstrate that the proposed framework obviously improves clustering purity.

2 Structure

This paper is organized as follows: Sect. 3 introduces the related works on unknown traffic identification; Then we introduce the unknown traffic identification framework based on neural networks and constraint information, including the schematic of the framework, deep autoencoder, and GMM with constraints in Sect. 4; Experimental results and discussions are given in Sect. 5; Finally, Sect. 6 concludes and summarizes this paper.

3 Related Works

There are four main categories of traffic identification methods, including port-based methods, payload-based methods, methods based on host behavior, and machine learning algorithms used in traffic classification [3]. However, due to the violation of port number assignments by more and more newly emerging applications, the port-based method has become increasingly inaccurate in recent years [4]. Payload-based methods are widely deployed in the industry today, which performs deep packet inspection (DPI) to either reconstruct and validate the application, protocol, sessions, or match protocol signatures against payload. Although payload-based methods are accurate, they require significant computing resources and specific knowledge of the target in advance. And the input data of methods based on host-behavior is log files, but in our scene, without log files.

The past decade has seen a lot of research on network traffic identification using machine learning techniques [5, 6]. Unknown traffic identification methods based on machine learning have gradually become an important research direction in the field of network security. Researchers based on the statistical features of network traffic, such as the number of packets, packet length, etc., then use machine learning algorithms to complete the identification of unknown traffic, such as K-means, GMM, DBSCAN, and other unsupervised learning methods.

Erman identified the unknown traffic using K-Means and DBSCAN algorithms, and the experimental results showed that both K-means and DBSCAN work very well [7]. To further improve the ability of identification, Liu et al. introduced log transform and feature selection methods to process the features, which more significantly improve the effectiveness of K-means in unknown traffic identification [8]. In [9], Zhang et al. based on Erman's idea, and aimed at zero-day traffic and parameter adaption problem, labeled unknown protocols with the same three-tuple (include the destination IP address/port and transport protocol) of flow, then divided the traffic into multiple clusters using semi-supervised learning methods based on the labeled information of protocols, and their experimental results showed that the effectiveness was better than C4.5, KNN, plain Bayesian, Bayesian networks and Erman's methods. There are others, including hierarchical clustering, Fuzzy C-means, and other algorithms that have been applied with unknown traffic identification. When using machine learning techniques to identify unknown traffic, extracting the features of the traffic is one of the keys to success. Moore et al. extracted statistical features of network traffic including maximum, minimum, average et al., 248 discriminators (i.e., features) per-flow were used [10]. In [11] Chen et al. used a neural network approach to extract the temporal and spatial features of the traffic, respectively. Wang et al. converted the network traffic into images and used the CNN model to extract features of the image to characterize the traffic [12]. In [13], Yang et al. used a neural network algorithm to extract the features of network traffic, then reduced the dimensionality and selected feature by autoencoder, the experimental results have shown that is better than the original method.

In this paper, based on previous research, we find that the observed traffic flows are not isolated. In the program, the system determines an IP flow through the IPv4 five-tuple, including source IP address/port, destination IP/port, and transport protocol. And if some network flows are connecting to the same endpoint, and they share the same destination IP address, destination port, and protocol, these flows are typically handled by the same application process or network service behind. Therefore, this paper obtains constraint information by the 3-tuple of flows and uses this information to guide the unknown traffic identification. Then, we train a multilayer neural network to reconstruct features, high-dimensional features can be converted to low-dimensional features, this process is better for classification and identification work [14]. In this paper, we use autoencoder to reduce dimensionality and select features of network traffic [15, 16], and propose a framework based on deep autoencoder and constraint information for unknown traffic identification.

4 The Framework for Unknown Traffic Identification

4.1 Structure of the Framework

Figure 1 shows the schematic of the framework proposed in this paper, which includes two main modules: feature extraction module and clustering module. In the feature extraction module, the input is statistical features of network traffic, and we use a deep auto-encoder to train a self-supervised deep neural network and learn higher-order features from unlabeled samples. In the clustering module, we extract the constraint information among network flows, then use the GMM algorithm with constraints to achieve the identification of unknown traffic.

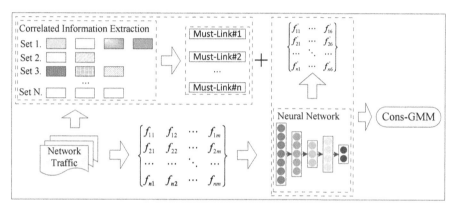

Fig. 1. The structure of framework.

4.2 Deep Autoencoder for Features Extraction

This section introduces the deep autoencoder in the feature extraction module, which can automatically train an unsupervised deep neural network model to extract features. Traditional identification models based on network traffic features are required to learn from the labeled training set. To further improve the model effectiveness, many researchers select features based on supervised learning, such as linear coefficient correlation, Lasso sparse selection, and so on[17]. But, in our scene, without labeled data, so supervised learning methods can't cover the identification of unknown network traffic. In this paper, we use a neural network, which has demonstrated feature learning capabilities and transform data with nonlinear mapping. The neural network maps the feature space from original to another as follow:

$$f_\theta : X \to Z$$

where Z is the target feature space, whose dimensionality is smaller than X. And θ is the parameter of the neural network, which can be learned automatically.

We use a deep neural network to implement automatic mapping of the original feature, which has multiple hidden layers and can train input features through nonlinear mapping. Due to without labeled data of features, we use a deep autoencoder to train and obtain higher-order features, which is an unsupervised neural network that consists of several multilayer autoencoders [18].

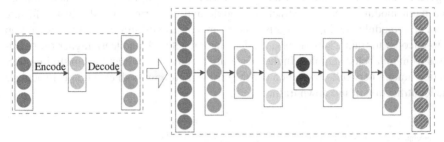

Fig. 2. The structure of autoencoder.

As shown in Fig. 2, an autoencoder is usually composed of an encoder and a decoder:

$$\psi : \alpha \rightarrow \beta$$

$$\phi : \beta \rightarrow \alpha$$

$$\psi, \phi = \arg \min_{\psi, \phi} ||\alpha - (\psi \circ \phi)\alpha||^2$$

where ψ is encoder, and ϕ is decoder.

In the stage of encoding, input $x \in R^d = \alpha$ is mapped to $z \in R^P = \beta$; In the stage of decoding, the autoencoder maps z to x', which is similar to x. This process can be computed as follows:

$$z = r_1\{W_1 x + b^1\}$$

$$x' = r_2\{W_2 z + b^2\}$$

where z is an implicit representation of x, r_1 and r_2 are activation function, such as Sigmoid, Rectified Linear Units (RELU), etc. W_1 and W_2 are the weights, b^1 and b^2 are the bias. In this paper, we use RELU as activation function.

The loss function in the training process can be defined as:

$$J(x, x') = \sum_{x \in D} L^P(x, x')$$

where L^P is the reconstruction errors, and we use the square of Euclidean norm: $||x - y||^2$. D is the dataset.

As shown in Fig. 2, the deep autoencoder is a multilayer deep neural network, and after training the autoencoder by greedy layer-wise training, all the encoders are connected in order, and then all decoders are combined in the opposite direction. When designing the deep network structure again, we set the middle layer as the minimum dimension, and this approach has been successfully applied in the field of speech recognition [19]. We finally obtained model which can map the original feature space to another, and get higher-order features.

4.3 GMM with Constraints

According to the TCP/IP model, traffic flows are not isolated, and there is some relationship between network flows. As shown in Fig. 3, in (1), Client#1 initiates three flows connected to the Dport#1 of Server#1 by different source port, but same application process or service behind. In Fig. 3 (2) Client#2, Client#3 and Client#4 initiate a flow connected to the Dport#2 of Server#2 respectively, they also share same application process or service. That means the information of type of application process or network service behind can be extracted by three-tuple (protocol, destination port, destination IP).

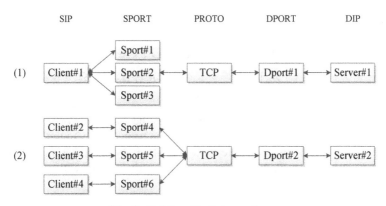

Fig. 3. Relationship between flows.

We introduce must-link constraints to express the constraint information between network flows. If two samples satisfy the must-link constraint, then they should be grouped into the same cluster when clustering.

Then, we present the GMM with constraints. A GMM refers to a linear combination of multiple gaussian distribution functions. Theoretically, a gaussian mixed model can fit any type of distribution and is usually used to solve the problem where data under the same set contains multiple different distributions. It is defined as:

$$p(x) = \sum_{k=1}^{K} \alpha_k \phi_k(x|\mu_k, \Sigma_k)$$

where x is a variable; α_k is the mixing coefficient of the k-th gaussian model, $\sum_{k=1}^{K} \alpha_k = 1 (0 \leq \alpha_k \leq 1)$. ϕ_k is the density function of the k-th gaussian model; (μ_k, Σ_k) is the distribution parameter of the k-th gaussian model.

In this paper, we apply the Expectation-Maximum (EM) algorithm to obtain maximum likelihood estimates of the GMM parameters [20]. Due to the constraint information, the search space for the maximum expectation of likelihood is restricted. Specifically, we assume that the equivalence sets are independent and identically distributed with respect to the mixing probabilities, and the flow instances within each set are generated by the data generation model based on the density parameters of the gaussian component.

Let $Y = \{y_1, y_2, ..., y_N\}$ denoted N observed unlabeled samples. $X = \{Y_1, Y_2, ..., Y_M\}$ denoted M equivalence sets. An equivalence set contains N_l data points $\{y_1^s, y_2^s, ..., y_{N_s}^s\}$, which satisfy the constraint information, and all data points in this set should be grouped into one cluster, $\sum_{s=1}^{M} N_s = N$. Let $\Upsilon = \{\gamma_1, \gamma_2, ..., \gamma_N\}$ denoted the source assignments of the respective data points ($\gamma_i \in \{1, 2, ..., K\}$), Υ_S denoted the source assignment of equivalence set X_S. Due to the constraint information, Υ can be divided into different data spaces according to the following formula:

$$\Omega = \{\Upsilon | (\gamma_1^s = ... = \gamma_{N_l}^s = \Upsilon_S), s = 1, ..., M\}$$

Therefore, the Q function can be computed as follow:

$$\begin{aligned} Q(\theta, \theta^*) &= E[\log p(Y, \Upsilon | \Upsilon \in \Omega, \theta) | Y, \Upsilon \in \Omega, \theta^*] \\ &= \sum_{\gamma \in \Omega} \log p(Y, \gamma | \gamma \in \Omega, \theta) P(\gamma | Y, \gamma \in \Omega, \theta^*) \end{aligned}$$

where θ^* is the estimated parameter currently, Ω is the data space of γ sliced by the constraint information, and θ is the new parameter to be iteratively optimized.

In the E-step of EM, we compute the expectation above. According to the data generation model, the log-likelihood for the complete data (Y, γ) with constraints can be computed as follow:

$$\begin{aligned} \log p(Y, \gamma | \gamma \in \Omega, \theta) &= \log p(\gamma | \gamma \in \Omega, \theta) p(Y | \gamma, \gamma \in \Omega, \theta) \\ &= \sum_{s=1}^{M} \log \alpha_{\Upsilon_s} + \sum_{s=1}^{M} \log p(Y_s | \Upsilon_s, \gamma \in \Omega, \theta) \end{aligned}$$

The marginal probability of the implied data can be calculated using the following formula:

$$\begin{aligned} P(\gamma | Y, \gamma \in \Omega, \theta^*) &= \frac{P(\gamma \in \Omega | Y, \gamma, \theta^*) P(\gamma | Y, \theta^*)}{P(\gamma \in \Omega | Y, \theta^*)} \\ &= \frac{\prod_{s=1}^{M} \zeta_{\Upsilon_s} P(\Upsilon_s | Y_s, \theta^*)}{\sum_{\Upsilon_1} \cdots \sum_{\Upsilon_M} \prod_{j=1}^{M} \zeta_{\Upsilon_j} P(\Upsilon_j | Y_j, \theta^*)} \end{aligned}$$

where ζ_{Υ_j} can be computed as follow:

$$\zeta_{\Upsilon_j} = \begin{cases} 1 & if \ \gamma_1^j = ... = \gamma_{N_j}^j \\ 0 & otherwise \end{cases}$$

Therefore, the Q function transforms into follow:

$$Q(\theta, \theta^*) = \sum_{s=1}^{M} \sum_{l=1}^{K} P(\Upsilon_s = l | Y_s, \gamma \in \Omega, \theta^*) \sum_{n=1}^{N_s} \log p_l(x_n^s | \theta_l)$$

$$+ \sum_{s=1}^{M} \sum_{l=1}^{K} P(\Upsilon_s = l | X_s, \gamma \in \Omega, \theta^*) N_s \log \alpha_l$$

The posterior probability of each equivalent set is:

$$P(\Upsilon_s = l | X_s, \gamma \in \Omega, \theta^*) \equiv P(\gamma_1^s = l, ..., \gamma_{N_s}^s | Y_s, \gamma \in \Omega, \theta^*)$$

$$= \frac{\prod_{n=1}^{N_s} [\alpha_l^* p_l(x_n^s | \theta_l^*)]}{\sum_{j=1}^{K} \prod_{n=1}^{N_s} [\alpha_j^* p_j(x_n^s | \theta_j^*)]}$$

In order to maximize $Q(\theta, \theta^*)$, we used the derivative-based approach and finally obtained the following results in the M-step with constraint information.

$$\mu_i = \frac{\sum_{s=1}^{M} P(i | Y_s, \gamma \in \Omega, \theta^*) \sum_{n=1}^{N_s} x_n^s}{\sum_{s=1}^{M} P(i | Y_s, \gamma \in \Omega, \theta^*) N_s}$$

$$\Sigma_i = \frac{\sum_{s=1}^{M} P(i | Y_s, y \in \Omega, \theta^*) \sum_{n=1}^{N_s} (x_n^s - \mu_i)(x_n^s - \mu_i)^T}{\sum_{s=1}^{M} P(i | Y_s, \gamma \in \Omega, \theta^*) N_s}$$

$$\alpha_i = \frac{1}{M} \sum_{s=1}^{M} P(l | Y_s, \gamma \in \Omega, \theta^*)$$

In summary, we first extract the constraint information, then guide the process of GMM. The GMM with constraints not only makes full use of constraint information, but also has excellent ability to discover unknown traffic types.

5 Experimental Methods and Results

5.1 Dataset

In this paper, two network traces, ISP and WIDE [21] traces, are used for our experimental study. The ISP traces were collected from the edge network of the work Internet environment for two hours per day between July 1 and 12, 2021; the public traces are all provided by the public traffic data repository maintained by the MAWI Working Group of the WIDE Project, and between 14:00 and 14:15 per day, from July 1 to July 20, 2021, total five hours, but these traffic IP addresses are anonymized and only part of the payload is retained. The following table shows the details of the composition of the dataset.

To validate the effectiveness of our proposed identification framework, we need to label the dataset. Because the payload of WIDE traces is incomplete, we use the port-based approach to label this dataset. For ISP trace, we use nDPI [22] which is a network open-source tool to identify and label this dataset. And in order to increase the confidence of results, we also use the port-based approach to review the identification results of nDPI. We selected the traffic corresponding to some common network protocols in all the data as the experimental data. The ISP traces contain BT, DNS, HTTP, ICMP, SSL, POP3, FTP, SMTP, and the WIDE traces contain DNS, HTTP, ICMP, SSL, IPsec, FTP, SMTP (Table 1).

Table 1. The traffic traces of dataset.

Trace from	Type	Data	Duration	Remarks
ISP	Edge	2021–07–01~2021–07–12	24 h	10:00~12:00 per day
WIDE	Backbone	2021–07–01~2021–07–20	5 h	14:00~14:15 per day

Then we use CICFlowMeter [23] to extract the statistical features of the dataset. CICFlowMeter is a network traffic flow generator and analyzer. It can be used to generate bidirectional flows, where the first packet determines the forward (source to destination) and backward (destination to source) directions, hence more than 80 statistical network traffic features such as Duration, Number of packets, Number of bytes, Length of packets, etc. can be calculated separately in the forward and backward directions. Some features are shown in Table 2.

Table 2. Some features and descriptions.

Feature type	Description
Packets	Number of packets transferred in bidirectional
Packet size	Packet size and Max, Min, Mean, standard deviation of packet size in bidirectional
Bytes	The volume of bytes transferred in bidirectional
Idle time	Sub-flow idle time and Max, Min, Mean, standard deviation of sub-flow idle time in bidirectional
Inter packet time	Inter packet time and Max, Min, Mean, standard deviation of packet time in bidirectional
Connection duration	Connection duration and Max, Min, Mean, standard deviation of duration in bidirectional

5.2 Dataset

In this paper, we use clustering purity to evaluate the effectiveness of our framework. Clustering purity is an external evaluation criterion of cluster quality. For cluster i, p_{ij} is the probability that samples in i belong to class j. The formula of p_{ij} is:

$$p_{ij} = \frac{m_{ij}}{m_i}$$

where m_i is the number of samples in cluster i and m_{ij} is the number of samples belonging to class j in i. The purity of cluster i is defined as:

$$P_i = \max(p_{ij})$$

So, the clustering purity can be computed as follow:

$$purity = \sum_{i=1}^{K} \frac{m_i}{m} p_i$$

where K is the number of clusters, and m is the number of all samples.

5.3 A Subsection Sample

To show the validity of the feature extraction method proposed in this paper, we used GMM to identify unknown traffic based on two feature sets: features generated by the method in this paper (PAPER-FEATURE) and CICFlowMeter (ORG-FEATURE). In the experiment, we take the number of clusters as the only input parameter, and the parameter ranges from ten to one hundred: $k = 10, ..., 50, ..., 100$. The following table gives the

Table 3. Clustering purity comparison of different features extraction methods

K	ISP		WIDE	
	ORG-FEATURE	PAPER-FEATURE	ORG-FEATURE	PAPER-FEATURE
10	44.51%	54.87%	47.43%	48.45%
20	58.31%	67.56%	63.54%	64.33%
30	69.18%	73.41%	68.23%	68.41%
40	72.85%	77.23%	75.20%	75.49%
50	75.25%	80.91%	76.78%	78.62%
60	78.23%	82.45%	77.29%	80.88%
70	78.94%	84.52%	77.87%	81.12%
80	78.78%	85.67%	78.04%	81.40%
90	79.03%	85.29%	77.48%	81.07%
100	78.86%	85.81%	77.58%	80.94%

purity of different feature processing methods on ISP and WIDE traces, respectively.Our target is to obtain higher purity at the lowest possible K value. As shown in Table 3, with the increase of K value, the clustering purity of this paper's method is almost always higher than the original features both on ISP and WIDE traces. This satisfies the original intention of our design.

And to illustrate the effect of constraint information in unknown traffic identification, we make two contrast experiments based on GMM and Cons-GMM using original features. Table 4 shows the experimental results. When the parameters are the same, Cons-GMM can always get the best results on both datasets. It means constraint information can improve purity in unknown traffic identification.

Table 4. The contrast experiments based on GMM and Cons-GMM using original features.

K	ISP		WIDE	
	GMM	Cons-GMM	GMM	Cons-GMM
10	44.51%	43.41%	47.43%	48.54%
20	58.31%	62.43%	63.54%	63.21%
30	69.18%	75.31%	68.23%	74.43%
40	72.85%	78.87%	75.20%	77.98%
50	75.25%	81.21%	76.78%	79.21%
60	78.23%	83.45%	77.29%	82.58%
70	78.94%	82.93%	77.87%	84.23%
80	78.78%	83.14%	78.04%	83.76%
90	79.03%	84.02%	77.48%	83.81%
100	78.86%	84.25%	77.58%	84.08%

Then, we make experiments based on the framework of this paper and traditional GMM, to show the validity of the framework. And the experimental results are given in Table 5, which shows that our framework is always better than GMM when the parameters are the same. On ISP traces, the clustering purity of our framework achieves over 96.10%. The maximum purity of our framework can reach 91.89% on WIDE traces, which is more than 7% higher than GMM. The framework of this paper is obviously superior to GMM.

Table 5. The experimental results based on the framework of this paper and traditional GMM.

K	ISP		WIDE	
	GMM	Paper	GMM	Paper
10	55.81%	41.89%	63.23%	38.45%
20	68.02%	71.25%	75.01%	77.28%
30	76.78%	82.87%	79.88%	83.77%
40	83.25%	89.45%	82.25%	89.26%
50	85.05%	92.34%	83.43%	90.34%
60	86.72%	94.57%	83.97%	91.57%
70	87.04%	95.77%	84.28%	91.71%
80	87.79%	95.89%	84.25%	91.89%
90	87.92%	96.05%	84.13%	91.76%
100	88.03%	96.10%	84.33%	91.80%

6 Conclusions

In this paper, we proposed a framework for unknown traffic identification based on autoencoder and constraint information. The framework extracts the statistical features of the network traffic, which is not affected by the encryption, it has strong universality. And usually, it's very difficult to get labels of traffic in the real world, but it is easy to get implicit information between the flows, and we extract constraint information from traffic to guide the identification of unknown traffic. In addition, our framework not only can cover protocols based on text, but also has the ability for binary protocols. In future work, we plan to further research the unknown traffic identification, we will focus on how to merge similar clusters, and determine the number of clusters automatically.

References

1. Chen, M., Wang, X., He, M., Jin, L., Javeed, K., Wang, X.: A network traffic classification model based on metric learning. Comp. Mater. Contin. **64**(2), 941–959 (2020)
2. Zhang, J., Chen, X., Xiang, Y., Zhou, W.: Zero-day traffic identification. In: International Symposium on Cyberspace Safety and Security, pp. 213–227. Springer, Cham (2013)
3. Cotton, M., Eggert, L., Touch, J.D., Westerlund, M., Cheshire, S.: Internet assigned numbers authority (iana) procedures for the management of the service name and transport protocol port number registry. RFC **6335**, 1–33 (2011)
4. Moore, A.W., Papagiannaki, K.: Toward the accurate identification of network applications. In: International Workshop on Passive and Active Network Measurement, pp. 41–54. Springer, Berlin, Heidelberg (2005)
5. Mao, J., Zhang, M., Chen, M., Chen, L., Xia, F.: Semisupervised encrypted traffic identification based on auxiliary classification generative adversarial network. Comput. Syst. Sci. Eng. **39**(3), 373–390 (2021)

6. Umair, M.B., Iqbal, Z., Bilal, M., Nebhen, J., Almohamad, T.A.: An efficient internet traffic classification system using deep learning for iot. Comp. Mater. Contin. **71**(1), 407–422 (2022)

7. Erman, J., Arlitt, M., Mahanti, A.: Traffic classification using clustering algorithms. In: Proceedings of the 2006 SIGCOMM workshop on Mining network data, pp. 281–286 (2006)

8. Liu, Y., Li, W., Li, Y.: Network traffic classification using k-means clustering. In: Second international multi-symposiums on computer and computational sciences (IMSCCS 2007), pp. 360–365. IEEE (2007)

9. Zhang, J., Chen, C., Xiang, Y., Zhou, W.: An effective network traffic classification method with unknown flow detection. IEEE Trans. Netw. Serv. Manage. **10**(2), 133–147 (2013)

10. Moore, A.W., Zuev, D.: Internet traffic classification using bayesian analysis techniques. In: Proceedings of the 2005 ACM SIGMETRICS international conference on Measurement and modeling of computer systems, pp. 50–60 (2005)

11. Ming-Hao, C., Yue-Fei, Z., Bin, L., Yi, Z., Ding, L.: Classification of application type of encrypted traffic based on attention-cnn. Computer Science **48**(4), 325–332 (2021)

12. Wang, W., Zhu, M., Zeng, X., Ye, X., Sheng, Y.: Malware traffic classification using convolutional neural network for representation learning. In: 2017 International Conference on Information Networking (ICOIN), pp. 712–717 (2017)

13. Yang, Y., Kang, C., Gou, G., Li, Z., Xiong, G.: TLS/SSL encrypted traffic classification with autoencoder and convolutional neural network. In: 2018 IEEE 20th International Conference on High Performance Computing and Communications; IEEE 16th International Conference on Smart City; IEEE 4th International Conference on Data Science and Systems (HPCC/SmartCity/DSS), pp. 362–369. IEEE (2018)

14. Ding, C., He, X.: Cluster structure of K-means clustering via principal component analysis. In: Pacific-Asia Conference on Knowledge Discovery and Data Mining. pp. 414–418. Springer, Berlin, Heidelberg (2004)

15. Chen, X., et al.: Variational lossy autoencoder. arXiv preprint arXiv:1611.02731 (2016)

16. Ng, J.D., Zhang, Z., Eyben, F., Schuller, B.: Autoencoder-based unsupervised domain adaptation for speech emotion recognition. IEEE Signal Process. Lett. **21**(9), 1068–1072 (2014)

17. Cui, H., Xu, S., Zhang, L., Roy, E.W., Horn, K.P.: Berthold: the key techniques and future vision of feature selection in machine learning. J. Beijing Univ. Posts Telecommu. Rev. **41**(1), 1–12 (2018)

18. Liou, C.Y., Cheng, W.C., Liou, J.W., Liou, D.R.: Autoencoder for words. Neurocomputing **139**(2), 84–96 (2014)

19. Yaman, S., Pelecanos, J.W., Sarikaya, R.: Bottleneck features for speaker recognition. In: Odyssey, vol. 12, pp. 105–1108 (2012)

20. Dempster, A.P., Laird, N.M., Rubin, D.B.: Maximum likelihood from incomplete data via the EM algorithm. J. Roy. Stat. Soc.: Ser. B (Methodol.) **39**(1), 1–122 (1997)

21. MAWI working group traffic archive. http://mawi.wide.ad.jp/mawi

22. Open source deep packet inspection software toolkit. https://github.com/ntop/nDPI

23. CICFlowMeter. https://www.unb.ca/cic/research/applications.html#CICFlowMeter

An Efficient Certificate-Based Encryption Scheme Without Random Oracles

Lan Guo[1], Yang Lu[1(✉)], Qing Miao[1], Guangao Zu[1], and Zhongqi Wang[2]

[1] School of Computer and Electronic Information, Nanjing Normal University,
Nanjing 210046, China
luyangnsd@163.com
[2] Graduate School of Science and Technology, University of Tsukuba Tsukuba,
Ibaraki 305-8577, Japan

Abstract. Certificate-based encryption combines traditional public key encryption and identity-based encryption while preserving their features. Compared with other public key cryptosystems, the advantage of certificate-based encryption are: (1) solving the problems of certificate revocation in traditional PKI and third-party queries about certificate status, (2) providing more efficient PKI that requires fewer infrastructures, (3) overcoming the key escrow problem inherent in the identity-based encryption. In this paper, we propose an efficient certificate-based encryption scheme which meets the chosen-ciphertext security under the complexity assumption of the truncated decision q-augmented bilinear Diffie-Hellman exponent problem and the decision 1-bilinear Diffie-Hellman inversion problem in the standard model. The proposed scheme requires computing only one bilinear pairing in the standard model, our scheme enjoys better performance, especially on the computation cost.

Keywords: Certificate-based encryption · Bilinear pairing · Chosen-ciphertext security · Standard model

1 Introduction

In Eurocrypt 2003, Gentry [1] introduced the concept of certificate-based encryption (CBE). In CBE, the function of implicit certificate mechanism is added to the traditional PKI and the certificate status can be updated periodically. As in a traditional PKI, in CBE, a CA is responsible for generating a certificate and sending updated certificate in each time period to the owner of the public key. In addition to the original functions of a traditional PKI certificate, a certificate in CBE add the partial decryption key. The sender does not need to obtain new information about the status of the certificate due to the implicit certificate provided by CBE, and the receiver can use his private key and the up-to-date certificate from his CA to decrypt the ciphertext. Problems in traditional PKI, such as certificate revocation and third-party queries about certificate status can be solved by introducing the concept of implicit certificate. Therefore, we can use CBE to construct an efficient PKI without requiring lots of infrastructures. Furthermore, there

© The Author(s), under exclusive license to Springer Nature Switzerland AG 2022
X. Sun et al. (Eds.): ICAIS 2022, LNCS 13340, pp. 97–107, 2022.
https://doi.org/10.1007/978-3-031-06791-4_8

is no key escrow problem (since the CA does not know the private keys of users) and key distribution problem (since the certificates need not be kept secret) in CBE.

In the original work [1], Gentry constructed the first CBE scheme in the random oracle [2, 3] from the BF-IBE scheme [4]. A subsequent paper by Yum and Lee [5] provided a formal equivalence theorem among IBE, certificateless public key encryption (CL-PKE) [6] and CBE, and showed that IBE implies both CBE and CL-PKE by giving a generic construction from IBE to those primitives. However, Galindo et al. [7] pointed out that the security of their generic constructions could be broken by a dishonest authority. In fact, due to the naive use of double encryption without further processing, these generic constructions have inherent flaws. In [8], Lu et al. solved this problem by using the Fujisaki-Okamoto conversions [9, 10] and gave a method to achieve generic CCA-secure CBE constructions in the random oracle model. In [11], Dodis and Katz proposed a generic mechanism to build multiple-encryption schemes from PKE and claimed the method they used can also be applied to IBE and PKE (instead of two PKEs) to build CBE schemes in standard model. However, their structure uses the encryption algorithms of IBE and PKE to encrypt messages in parallel, resulting in long ciphertext size. In 2005, Al-Riyami and Paterson [12] analyzed Gentry's CBE concept and fixed some problems in the original definition of the scheme and the security model of CBE. They also presented a generic conversion from CL-PKE to CBE and claimed that using the conversion can construct a secure CBE from any secure CL-PKE scheme. Kang and Park [13] found a flaw in their security proof, so Al-Riyami and Paterson's conversion was incorrect. Therefore, the derived CBE scheme by Al-Riyami and Paterson [12] is invalid. In [14], Yum and Lee proposed a separable implicit certificate revocation system called status CBE to reduce the burden of certificate issuers to revoke certificates. In the paper, they used a long-lived certificate to ensure the authenticity of a public key and a short-lived certificate to handle the certificate revocation problem. However, in [15], Park and Lee discovered that the status CBE scheme is insecure under the public key replacement attack. In 2006, Morillo and Ràfols [16] proposed the first concrete CBE scheme in the standard model from the Waters-IBE scheme [17] and the BB-IBE scheme [18]. In 2008, Galindo et al. [19] proposed an improved CBE scheme based on the CBE scheme in [16]. Liu and Zhou [20] also proposed a CBE scheme in the standard model from the Gentry-IBE scheme [21]. In 2009, Lu et al. [22] proposed a quite efficient CBE scheme in the random oracle model from the SK-IBE scheme [23, 24] which only one pairing needed to be repairing. Lately, Hwang et al. [25] proposed a lightweight certificate-based aggregate signature scheme to provide key insulation.Recently, with the rise of the Internet of Things and big data, the corresponding security issues have received extensive attention. In 2020, Li [26] presented a searchable encryption with access control on keywords in multi-user setting. Ali's scheme is to achieve authorized attribute-based encryption multi-keywords search through policy updating [27]. In 2021, Xu [28] used conjunctive searchable encryption to realizing private real-time detection. Then, Alameen [29] proposed a mechanism for repeated attribute optimization in big data encryption environment.

In this paper, we propose a quite efficient CBE scheme which can be proved to be chosen-ciphertext secure under the truncated decisional q-augmented bilinear Diffie-Hellman exponent (q-ABDHE) assumption [21] and the decisional 1-bilinear Diffie-Hellman inversion (1-BDHI) assumption [18] in the standard model. Our construction is based on Gentry-IBE scheme [21] and its variant proposed by Kiltz and Vahlis [30]. Only one bilinear pairing needed to be computed in the decryption algorithm in our scheme. Compared with the previous CBE schemes in the standard model, our scheme enjoys better performance, especially on the computation cost. What is worth mentioning is that our scheme also has performance comparable to the existing random-oracle based CBE schemes.

The rest of this paper is organized as follows: In Sect. 2, we briefly review some background definitions including certificated-based encryption, one-time authenticated encryption, bilinear map and hardness assumption that we need. In Sect. 3, we present a new efficient CBE scheme which is secure in the standard model. In Sect. 4, we make a comparison of our CBE scheme and the existing CBE schemes. The paper is concluded in Sect. 5.

2 Preliminaries

2.1 Certificate-Based Encryption

The following definition and security model for CBE are taken from [12] essentially, where the original definitions given in [1] were reconsidered.

Definition 1. A CBE scheme is defined by following five algorithms:

- *Setup* is a probabilistic algorithm taking a security parameter k as input. It returns CA's master-key *msk* and the public system parameters *params*. We assume that the descriptions of a finite message space *MSPC* and a finite ciphertext space *CSPC* are contained in the *params*. *params* is used to be an implicit input to the rest of the algorithms.
- *UserKeyGen* is a probabilistic algorithm that outputs a public and private key pair (*upk*, *usk*).
- *CertGen* is a deterministic certification algorithm that takes $<msk, \tau, id, upk>$ as input. It returns a certificate $Cert_{id,\tau}$ to the user. Here τ is used to identify a time period, while *id* contains other information needed to certify the user.
- *Encrypt* is a probabilistic algorithm taking $<\tau, id, upk, M>$ as input, where $M \in MSPC$. It returns a ciphertext $C \in CSPC$ for message M.
- *Decrypt* is a deterministic algorithm taking $<Cert_{id,\tau}, usk, C>$ as input in time period τ where *usk* is the user *id*'s private key. If decryption fails, it returns a special symbol $\perp$, else it returns message M.

Naturally, all these algorithms are need to satisfy the standard consistency constraint, that is $\forall M \in MSPC$, $Decrypt(Cert_{id,\tau}, usk, Encrypt(\tau, id, upk, M)) = M$, where $Cert_{id,\tau} = CertGen(msk, \tau, id, upk)$, and (*upk*, *usk*) is a valid key-pair generated by the algorithm *UserKeyGen*.

The chosen-ciphertext security for CBE (IND-CBE-CCA) is defined against two different types of adversaries:

- The Type I adversary $\mathcal{A}_1$ has no access to the master-key and acts as an uncertified client;
- The Type II adversary $\mathcal{A}_2$ acts as an honest-but-curious certifier who possesses the master-key *msk* and tries to attack a fixed client's public key.

Definition 2. A CBE scheme is said to be secure in the sense of IND-CBE-CCA if no polynomial-time adversary has non-negligible advantage in either IND-CBE-CCA Game 1 or IND-CBE-CCA Game 2 defined as follows:

IND-CBE-CCA Game 1: The challenger $\mathcal{C}$ runs Setup to generate *msk* and *params*, then gives *params* to the adversary $\mathcal{A}_1$ and keeps *msk* to itself.

- **Phase 1.** The adversary $\mathcal{A}_1$ adaptively makes request to certificate and decryption queries, $\mathcal{C}$ responses these queries as follows:

  - On certificate query $<\tau, id, upk, usk>$, $\mathcal{C}$ checks that (upk, usk) is a valid key-pair. If so, it runs CertGen on input $<msk, \tau, id, upk>$ to generate $Cert_{id,\tau}$; else it returns $\perp$.
  - On decryption query $<\tau, id, upk, usk, C>$, $\mathcal{C}$ checks whether the (upk, usk) is a valid key-pair. If so, it runs CertGen on input $<msk, \tau, id, upk>$ to obtain $Cert_{id,\tau}$ and outputs Decrypt($Cert_{id,\tau}, usk, C$); else it returns $\perp$.

- **Challenge.** On challenge query $<\tau^*, id^*, upk^*, usk^*, M_0, M_1>$, where $M_0, M_1 \in MSPC$ are of equal length, $\mathcal{C}$ checks that (upk^*, usk^*) is a valid key-pair and $<\tau^*, id^*, upk^*, usk^*>$ was not the subject of a certificate query in Phase 1. If so, the challenger flips a random coin $b \in \{0, 1\}$, and encrypts M_b using the challenge public key upk^* and returns the resulting ciphertext C^* to $\mathcal{A}_1$; else it returns $\perp$.
- **Phase 2.** As in phase 1, with the restriction that $<\tau^*, id^*, upk^*, usk^*, C^*>$ is not the subject of a decryption query and $<\tau^*, id^*, upk^*, usk^*>$ is not the subject of a certificate query.
- **Guess.** The adversary $\mathcal{A}_1$ outputs a guess $b' \in \{0, 1\}$ and wins the game if $b = b'$. $\mathcal{A}_1$'s advantage in this game is defined to be

$$Adv_{CBE,\mathcal{A}_1}^{CCA}(k) = |2\Pr[b = b'] - 1| \tag{1}$$

IND-CBE-CCA Game 2: $\mathcal{C}$ runs Setup to generate *msk* and *params*, and runs UserKeyGen to obtain a key-pair (upk^*, usk^*). It then gives *params*, *msk* and the challenge public key upk^* to $\mathcal{A}_2$.

- **Phase 1.** $\mathcal{A}_2$ issues a series of decryption queries of the form $<\tau, id, C>$. On this query, $\mathcal{C}$ runs CertGen on input $<msk, \tau, id, upk^*>$ to obtain $Cert_{id,\tau}$ and outputs Decrypt($Cert_{id,\tau}, usk^*, C$); else it returns $\perp$. These queries may be asked adaptively.

– **Challenge.** On challenge query $<\tau^*, id^*, M_0, M_1>$, where $M_0, M_1 \in MSPC$ are of equal length, $\mathcal{C}$ flips a random coin $b \in \{0,1\}$, encrypts M_b using the challenge public key upk^* and returns the resulting ciphertext C^* to $\mathcal{A}_2$; else it returns $\bot$.
– **Phase 2.** As in phase 1, with the restriction that $<\tau^*, id^*, C^*>$ is not the subject of a decryption query.
– **Guess.** $\mathcal{A}_2$ outputs a guess $b' \in \{0, 1\}$ and wins the game if $b = b'$. $\mathcal{A}_2$'s advantage in this game is defined to be

$$Adv^{CCA}_{CBE, \mathcal{A}_2}(k) = \left|2\Pr\left[b = b'\right] - 1\right| \qquad (2)$$

2.2 One Time Authenticated Encryption

A symmetric encryption scheme SE is specified by two algorithms (E, D). Encryption algorithm E takes a symmetric key $K \in \mathcal{K}(k)$ and a message M as input where k is a security parameter and $\mathcal{K}(k)$ is a key space, and returns a ciphertext $C = E_K(M)$. Decryption algorithm D takes $K \in \mathcal{K}(k)$ and a ciphertext C as input, and returns either a message $M = D_K(C)$ or the distinguished symbol $\bot$ denoting the invalid ciphertext.

An one time authenticated encryption scheme is a symmetric encryption scheme which not only satisfies the security of *ciphertext indistinguishability* (which requires that no adversary can efficiently distinguish between the encryptions of two messages they choose), but also satisfies the security of *ciphertext authenticity* (which requires that no adversary can efficiently generate a new valid ciphertext under some key when the selected message is encrypted under the same key) [25].

Definition 3. A symmetric encryption scheme SE = (E, D) satisfies the security of ciphertext indistinguishability if no adversary $\mathcal{A}$ in the following game has non-negligible advantage in the security parameter k:

– **Setup.** The challenger $\mathcal{C}$ chooses a random key $K \in \mathcal{K}(k)$.
– **Attack.** The adversary $\mathcal{A}$ interleaves a series of encryption queries and a challenge query, the challenger $\mathcal{C}$ handles these queries as follows:

- On encryption query $<M>$, $\mathcal{C}$ returns $C = E_K(M)$.
- On challenge query $<M_0, M_1>$, $\mathcal{C}$ picks a random bit $b \in \{0,1\}$, encrypts M_b under the key K and sends the resulting ciphertext C^* to $\mathcal{A}$.

– **Guess.** The adversary $\mathcal{A}$ outputs a guess $b' \in \{0, 1\}$ and wins the game if $b = b'$. $\mathcal{A}$'s advantage in this game is defined to be

$$Adv^{IND}_{SE, \mathcal{A}}(k) = \left|\Pr\left[b = b'\right] - 1/2\right| \qquad (3)$$

Definition 4. A symmetric encryption scheme SE = (E, D) has ciphertexts authenticity if no adversary $\mathcal{A}$ in the following game has non-negligible advantage in the security parameter k:

– **Setup.** The challenger $\mathcal{C}$ chooses a random key $K \in \mathcal{K}(k)$.

- **Attack.** The adversary $\mathcal{A}$ issues an encryption query $<M>$, and is then given in return $C = E_K(M)$. Following this, $\mathcal{A}$ outputs a ciphertext C^*. Adversary $\mathcal{A}$ wins the game if $C^* \neq C$ and $D_K(C^*) \neq \perp$. $\mathcal{A}$'s advantage in this game is defined to be

$$Adv_{SE,\mathcal{A}}^{AUTH}(k) = \Pr[C^* \neq C \wedge D_k(C^*) \neq \perp] \qquad (4)$$

Definition 5. A symmetric encryption scheme which is secure according to both Definition 3 and Definition 4 is said to be secure in the sense of *one time authenticated encryption* (or AE-OT).

In our CBE construction, we will use an abstract notion of AE-OT scheme as a building block. We refer the reader to [31–33] for the details about the concrete constructions of such schemes satisfying all required functionality and security.

2.3 Bilinear Map and Hardness Assumption

Let p be a large prime number, G and G_T denote two multiplicative cyclic groups of the same order p. A mapping $e: G \times G \to G_T$ is called a bilinear map if it satisfies the following properties:

- Bilinearity: $e(u^a, v^b) = e(u, v)^{ab}$ for all $u, v \in G$ and $a, b \in Z_p^*$.
- Non-degeneracy: $e(g, g) \neq 1$ for a random generator $g \in G$.
- Computablity: $e(u, v)$ can be efficiently computed for all $u, v \in G$.

The security of our CBE scheme is based on the truncated decision q-augmented bilinear Diffie-Hellman exponent (q-ABDHE) assumption [21] and the decision 1-bilinear Diffie-Hellman inversion (1-BDHI) assumption [18].

Let $q = q(k)$ be a polynomial. The truncated decision q-ABDHE problem is defined as follows: Given a tuple $(g, g^\alpha, ..., g^{\alpha^q}, g', g'^{\alpha^{q+2}}) \in G^{q+3}$ and an element $T \in G_T$ as input, where g and g' be generators of G and α be a random element in Z_p^*, decide whether $T = e(g, g')^{\alpha^{q+1}}$ or T is a random element in G_T.

Let $\mathcal{B}$ be a probabilistic algorithm that takes as input a random instance of the truncated decision q-ABDHE problem and outputs a bit $b \in \{0, 1\}$. The advantage of the algorithm $\mathcal{B}$ is defined to be

$$Adv_{\mathcal{B}}^{q-ABDHE}(k) = \left| \begin{array}{l} \Pr\left\{ \mathcal{B}(g, g^\alpha, ..., g^{\alpha^q}, g', g'^{\alpha^{q+2}}, e(g, g')^{\alpha^{q+1}}) = 1 \right\} - \\ \Pr\left\{ \mathcal{B}(g, g^\alpha, ..., g^{\alpha^q}, g', g'^{\alpha^{q+2}}, T) = 1 \right\} \end{array} \right| \qquad (5)$$

Definition 6. We say that the truncated decision (t, ε, q)-ABDHE assumption holds in (G, G_T) if no t-time algorithm has advantage at least ε over random guessing in solving the truncated decision q-ABDHE problem in (G, G_T).

The decision 1-BDHI problem is defined as follows: given a tuple $(g, g^\alpha) \in G^2$ and an element $T \in G_T$ as input, where α be a random element in Z_p^*, decide whether $T = e(g, g)^{1/\alpha}$ or T is a random element in G_T.

Let $\mathcal{B}$ be a probabilistic algorithm that takes as input a random instance of the decision 1-BDHI problem and outputs a bit $b \in \{0,1\}$. The advantage of $\mathcal{B}$ is defined to be

$$Adv_{\mathcal{B}}^{1-BDHI}(k) = \left| \Pr\left\{ \mathcal{B}(g, g^{\alpha}, e(g, g)^{1/\alpha}) = 1 \right\} - \Pr\left\{ \mathcal{B}(g, g^{\alpha}, T) = 1 \right\} \right| \quad (6)$$

Definition 7 We say that the decision $(t, \varepsilon, 1)$-BDHI assumption holds in (G, G_T) if no t-time algorithm has advantage at least ε over random guessing in solving the decision 1-BDHI problem in (G, G_T).

3 Construction

In this section, we propose a new efficient CBE scheme which is IND-CBE-CCA secure in the standard model. Our scheme is constructed from Gentry's IBE scheme [21] and its variant proposed by Kiltz and Vahlis [30]. Let G and G_T be two cyclic groups of prime order p and e: $G \times G \to G_T$ be a bilinear map. Let SE = (E, D) be a symmetric encryption scheme with key space = $\mathcal{K}G_T$. Our scheme is described as follows:

- *Setup*: This algorithm performs the following steps to setup the system:

  - Choose a generator $g \in G, \alpha, \beta_1, \beta_2 \in Z_p{}^*$, and computes $g_1 = g^{\alpha}, v_1 = e(g, g)^{\beta_1}$ and $v_2 = e(g, g)^{\beta_2}$ respectively;
  - Choose two collision-resistant hash functions H_1: $\{0, 1\}^* \times G^3 \to Z_p{}^*$ and H_2: $G \times G_T \to Z_p{}^*$;
  - Set the system public parameters $params = (g, g_1, h_1, h_2, H_1, H_2)$ and the certifier's master key $msk = (\alpha, \beta_1, \beta_2)$.

- *UserKeyGen*: This algorithm performs the following steps to produce a public/private key pair:

  - Choose two random elements $x_1, x_2 \in Z_p{}^*$ and set the private key as $usk = (x_1, x_2)$;
  - Compute the corresponding public key $upk = (g_1^{x_1}, g^{x_1}, g^{x_2})$.

- *CertGen*: To generate a certificate for the user with identity id and public key upk in the time period τ, This algorithm performs the following steps:

  - Randomly choose $s_1, s_2 \in Z_p{}^*$ and set $h = H_1(\tau, id, upk)$;
  - Compute the certificate $Cert_{id,\tau} = (s_1, d_1, s_2, d_2)$, where $d_1 = g^{(\beta_1 - s_1)/(\alpha - h)}$ and $d_2 = g^{(\beta_2 - s_2)/(\alpha - h)}$.

- *Encrypt*: To encrypt the message M for the user with identity id and public key $upk = (upk_1, upk_2, upk_3)$ in the time period τ, this algorithm performs the following steps:

  - Choose a random $r \in Z_p{}^*$ and compute $c_1 = (upk_1 \cdot upk_2{}^{-h})^r$ and $c_2 = e(g, g)^r$, where $h = H_1(\tau, id, upk)$;

- Compute $K = (v_1^t \cdot v_2 \cdot e(upk_3, g))^r$ and $c_3 = E_K(M)$, where $t = H_2(c_1, c_2)$;
- Output the ciphertext $C = (c_1, c_2, c_3)$. Note that encryption does not require computing any parings once $e(g, g)$ and $e(upk_3, g)$ have been pre-computed.

– *Decrypt*: To decrypt the ciphertext $C = (c_1, c_2, c_3)$ for the user with identity *id* using *id*'s private key $usk = (usk_1, usk_2)$ and certificate $Cert_{id,\tau} = (s_1, d_1, s_2, d_2)$ in the time period τ, this algorithm performs the following steps:

- Compute $K = e(c_1, d_1^t d_2)^{1/usk_1} \cdot c_2^{t \cdot s_1 + s_2 + usk_2}$, where $t = H_2(c_1, c_2)$;
- Compute $M/\perp = D_K(c_3)$ and output the message M or the failure symbol $\perp$.

The consistency of the above scheme is easy to check as we have:

$$
\begin{aligned}
K &= e(c_1, d_1^t d_2)^{1/usk_1} \cdot c_2^{t \cdot s_1 + s_2 + usk_2} \\
&= e((g_1^{x_1} \cdot g^{-hx_1})^r, (g^{\frac{\beta_1 - s_1}{\alpha - h}})^t \cdot g^{\frac{\beta_2 - s_2}{\alpha - h}})^{\frac{1}{x_1}} \cdot (e(g, g)^r)^{ts_1 + s_2 + x_2} \\
&= e(g^{r(\alpha - h)}, g^{\frac{t(\beta_1 - s_1) + \beta_2 - s_2}{\alpha - h}}) \cdot e(g, g)^{r(ts_1 + s_2 + x_2)} \\
&= e(g, g)^{r(t(\beta_1 - s_1) + \beta_2 - s_2)} \cdot e(g, g)^{r(ts_1 + s_2 + x_2)} \\
&= (v_1^t \cdot v_2 \cdot e(upk_3, g))^r
\end{aligned}
\tag{7}
$$

Next is our main result about the security of our CBE scheme.

Theorem 1. *The above CBE scheme is IND-CBE-CCA secure assuming that the truncated decision q-ABDHE assumption the decision 1-BDHI assumption holds in (G, G_T) and $SE = (E, D)$ is a one time authenticated encryption.*

Due to space constraints, the complete proof of the theorem is omitted in this paper, and will be written in the final version of this paper.

4 Performance Comparison

Table 1 displays a detailed efficiency comparison between our CBE scheme and other CBE schemes.

We consider four main operations: Pairing, Multi-exponentiation, and Exponentiation. Among these operations, despite the advancement of [34] implementation technology, the pairing operation is considered to be the most time-consuming. For simplicity, we denote these operations respectively by p (Pairing), m (Multi-exponentiation in G), and e (Exponentiation in G_T). As usual, all symmetric operations (the general cryptographic hash function, symmetric encryption, etc.) are ignored. However, the *maptopoint* hash function in Gentry03 scheme [1] is generally inefficient and slower than the general hash function. Hence, we also consider about such hashing operation in our comparison. Such operation denoted by h (Hashing to G). Furthermore, for the IND-CBE-CCA security, a one-time signature scheme or a combination of an encapsulation scheme and a message authentication code is needed in some CBE schemes. We use the (*Sign*,

Vfy) to represent the signing algorithm and the verification algorithm in the signature scheme, vk and σ to represent the verification key and the signature, com and dec to represent the public commitment string and the de-commitment string for the encapsulation scheme, and mac to represent the message authentication code in the ciphertext. Ciphertext expansion represents the difference between the ciphertext length and the message length. In ciphertext expansion comparison, the length of a string X is denoted by $|X|$. In [1] and [22], n should be at least 160 in order to obtain a reasonable security. Furthermore, "rom" means random oracle model while "standard" means standard model.

Table 1. Efficiency comparison of the proposed CBE scheme and other CBE schemes.

Scheme	Model	Encryption	Decryption	Ciphertext Expansion
Gentry03 [1]	rom	$2p + 1e + 1m + 2h$	$1p + 1m$	$|G|+n$
LLX09 [22]	rom	$2e + 2m$	$1p + 1e + 1m$	$|G|+n$
MR06 [16]	standard	$2e + 4m$	$3p + 3m$	$|dec|+3|G|+|com|+|mac|$
GMR08 [19]	standard	$2e + 5m + Sign$	$3p + 3m + Vfy$	$3|G|+|vk|+|\sigma|$
LZ08 [20]	standard	$7e + 2m$	$2p + 2e + 1m$	$2|G_T|+|G|$

From Table 1, we can see that our CBE scheme enjoys better performance, especially on the computation cost, when compared with the existing three standard-model CBE schemes in [16, 19, 20]. What is worth mentioning is that our scheme also offers performance competitive with other two random-oracle based CBE schemes in [1] and [22].

5 Conclusion

In this paper, we present a new CBE scheme which is IND-CBE-CCA secure under the truncated decision q-ABDHE assumption the decision 1-BDHI assumption in the standard model. Our scheme does not require computing any pairings in the encryption algorithm and needs to compute only one pairing in the decryption algorithm. When compared with the previous CBE schemes in the standard model, our CBE scheme has obvious advantage in the performance.

Acknowledgments. This work was supported in part by the National Natural Science Foundation of China under Grant No. 61772009, the Natural Science Foundation of Jiangsu Province under Grant No. BK20181304.

References

1. Gentry, C.: Certificate-based encryption and the certificate revocation problem. In: Biham, E. (eds) Advances in Cryptology—EUROCRYPT 2003. EUROCRYPT 2003. Lecture Notes

in Computer Science, vol. 2656. Springer, Berlin, Heidelberg. https://doi.org/10.1007/3-540-39200-9_17 (2003)

2. Bellare, M., Rogaway, P.: Random oracles are practical: a paradigm for designing efficient protocols. In: 1st ACM Conference on Communications and Computer Security, pp. 62–73. ACM, USA (1993)

3. Canetti, R., Goldreich, O., Halevi, S.: The random oracle methodology, revisited. In: STOC'98, pp. 209–218. ACM, Holland (1998)

4. Boneh, D., Franklin, M.: Identity-based encryption from the Weil Pairing. In: Kilian, J. (eds) Advances in Cryptology—CRYPTO 2001. CRYPTO 2001. Lecture Notes in Computer Science, vol. 2139. Springer, Berlin, Heidelberg. https://doi.org/10.1007/3-540-44647-8_13 (2001)

5. Yum, D.H., Lee, P.J.: Identity-based cryptography in public key management. In: Katsikas, S.K., Gritzalis, S., López, J. (eds) Public Key Infrastructure. EuroPKI 2004. Lecture Notes in Computer Science, vol. 3093. Springer, Berlin, Heidelberg. https://doi.org/10.1007/978-3-540-25980-0_6 (2004)

6. Al-Riyami, S.S., Paterson, K.G.: Certificateless public key cryptography. In: Laih, CS. (eds) Advances in Cryptology - ASIACRYPT 2003. ASIACRYPT 2003. Lecture Notes in Computer Science, vol. 2894. Springer, Berlin, Heidelberg. https://doi.org/10.1007/978-3-540-40061-5_29 (2003)

7. Galindo, D., Morillo, P., Ràfols, C.: Breaking Yum and Lee generic constructions of certificate-Less and certificate-based encryption schemes. In: Atzeni A.S., Lioy A. (eds.) EuroPKI 2006, vol. 4043, pp. 81–91. Springer, Heidelberg (2006)

8. Lu., Y., Li, J., Xiao, J.: Generic construction of certificate-based encryption. In: the 9th International Conference for Young Computer Scientists, pp. 1518–1594. IEEE, China (2008)

9. Fujisaki, E., Okamoto, T.: Secure integration of asymmetric and symmetric encryption schemes. J Cryptol **26**, 80–101 (2013)

10. Fujisaki, E., Okamoto, T.: How to enhance the security of public-key encryption at minimum cost. In: Public Key Cryptography-PKC'99, LNCS, vol. 1560, pp. 53–68. Springer, Heidelberg (1999)

11. Dodis, Y., Katz, J.: Chosen-ciphertext security of multiple encryption. In: Kilian J. (eds.) TCC 2005, LNCS, vol. 3378, pp. 188–209. Springer, Heidelberg (2005)

12. Al-Riyami, S.S., Paterson, K.G.: CBE from CL-PKE: a generic construction and efficient schemes. In: Vaudenay S. (eds.) PKC 2005, LNCS, vol. 3386, pp. 398–415. Springer, Heidelberg (2005)

13. Kang, B.G., Park, J.H.: Is it possible to have CBE from CL-PKE?. Cryptology ePrint Archive (2005)

14. Yum, D.H., Lee, P.J.: Separable implicit certificate revocation. In: Park C., Chee S. (eds.) 7th International Conference on Information Security and Cryptology, LNCS, vol. 3506, pp. 121–136. Springer, Heidelberg (2005)

15. Park, J.H., Lee, D.H.: On the security of status certificate-based encryption scheme. IEICE Trans. Fundamentals **E90A**(1), 303–304 (2007)

16. Morillo, P., Ràfols, C.: Certificate-based encryption without random oracles. Cryptology ePrint Archive (2006)

17. Waters, B.: Efficient identity-based encryption without random oracles. In: Cramer R. (eds.) Advances in Cryptology-Eurocrypt'2005, LNSC, vol. 3494, pp. 114-127. Springer, Heidelberg (2005)

18. Boneh, D., Boyen, X.: Efficient selective-ID secure identity based encryption without random oracles. In: Advances in Cryptology-Eurocrypt'04, LNCS, vol. 3027, pp. 223–238. Springer, Heidelberg (2004)

19. Galindo, D., Morillo, P., Ràfols, C.: Improved certificate-based encryption in the standard model. J. Syst. Softw. **81**(7), 1218–1226 (2008)

20. Liu, J. K., Zhou, J.: Efficient certificate-based encryption in the standard model. In: Visconti I. (eds.) SCN 2008, LNCS, vol. 5229, pp. 144–155. Springer, Heidelberg (2008)

21. Gentry, C.: Practical identity-based encryption without random oracles. In: Advances in Cryptology-EUROCRYPT'06, LNCS, vol. 4004, pp. 445–464. Springer, Heidelberg (2006)

22. Lu, Y., Li, J., Xiao, J.: Constructing efficient certificate-based encryption with paring. J. Comput. **4**(1), 19–26 (2009)

23. Sakai, R., Kasahara, M.: ID based cryptosystems with pairing on elliptic curve. Cryptology ePrint Archive (2003)

24. Chen, L.Q., Cheng, Z.H.: Security proof of Sakai-Kasahara's identity-based encryption scheme. In: Smart N.P. (eds.) Cryptography and Coding 2005, LNCS, vol. 3796, pp. 442–459. Springer, Heidelberg (2005)

25. Hwang, Y., Lee, I.: A lightweight certificate-based aggregate signature scheme providing key insulation. Comp. Mater. Contin. **69**(2), 1747–1764 (2021)

26. Li, L., Xu, C., Yu, X., Dou, B., Zuo, C.: Searchable encryption with access control on keywords in multi-user setting. Journal of Cyber Security **2**(1), 9–23 (2020)

27. Ali, M., Xu, C., Hussain, A.: Authorized attribute-based encryption multi-keywords search with policy updating. Journal of New Media **2**(1), 31–43 (2020)

28. Xu, C., Mei, L., Cheng, J., Zhao, Y., Zuo, C.: IoT services: realizing private real-time detection via authenticated conjunctive searchable encryption. Journal of Cyber Security **3**(1), 55–67 (2021)

29. Alameen, A.: Repeated attribute optimization for big data encryption. Comput. Syst. Sci. Eng. **40**(1), 53–64 (2022)

30. Kiltz, E., Vahlis, Y.: CCA2 secure IBE: standard model efficiency through authenticated symmetric encryption. In: Malkin T. (eds.) Cryptographer's Track at RSA Conference 2008, LNCS, vol. 4964, pp. 221–238. Springer, Heidelberg (2008)

31. Bellare, M., Namprempre, C.: Authenticated encryption: relations among notions and analysis of the generic composition paradigm. In: Okamoto T. (eds.) Advances in Cryptology-ASIACRYPT 2000, LNCS, vol. 1976, pp. 531–545. Springer, Heidelberg (2000)

32. Cramer, R., Shoup, V.: Design and analysis of practical public-key encryption schemes secure against adaptive chosen ciphertext attack. SIAM J. Comput. **33**(1), 167–226 (2003)

33. Rogaway, P., Bellare, M., Black, J., Krovetz, T.: OCB: a block-cipher mode of operation for efficient authenticated encryption. In: 8th ACM conference on Computer and Communications Security, pp. 196–205. ACM, USA (2001)

34. Barreto, P.S.L.M., Kim, H.Y., Lynn, B., Scott, M.: Efficient algorithms for pairing-based cryptosystems. In: Advances in Cryptology-CRYPTO 2002, LNCS, vol. 2442, pp. 354–368. Springer, Heidelberg (2002)

A Rational Hierarchical Quantum State Sharing Protocol

Huali Zhang[1] (ID), Bichen Che[1], Zhao Dou[1](✉), Hengji Li[2], Yu Yang[3], Xiubo Chen[1], and Jian Li[4]

[1] Information Security Center, State Key Laboratory of Networking and Switching Technology, Beijing University of Posts and Telecommunications, Beijing 100876, China
dou@bupt.edu.cn
[2] Quantum Technology Lab and Applied Mechanics Group, University of Milan, Milan, Italy
[3] School of Cyberspace Security, Beijing University of Posts and Telecommunications, Beijing 100876, China
[4] Information Security Center, School of Cyberspace Security, Beijing University of Posts and Telecommunications, Beijing 100876, China

Abstract. In this paper, we propose a rational hierarchical quantum state sharing protocol. First, the dealer shares an arbitrary two-particle entangled state with m high-power players and n low-power players through $(m + n + 1)$-particle cluster states. The high-power players and low-players have different authorities to reconstruct the quantum state. In detail, when a high-power player reconstructs the quantum state, he needs the help of the other high-power players and any low-power players; when a low-power player reconstructs the quantum, he needs the help of all the players. Then, in order to guarantee the fairness of the protocol, we make the players with different powers have the same possibility to be the player David who can reconstruct the quantum state shared by the dealer Alice, which means David is elected by all the rational players. Second, in the process of reconstructing the quantum state, when David is a high-power player, he does not need the help of all the low-power players. Under this circumstance, we analyze the game process and solve the bargaining equilibrium between David and the low-power players selected by David based on the Rubenstein bargaining model with incomplete information. Finally, our protocol achieves security, fairness, correctness, and strict Nash equilibrium, and conforms to the actual scenario.

Keywords: Hierarchical quantum state sharing · Bargaining model · Incomplete information · Strict Nash equilibrium · Fairness

X. Sun et al. (Eds.): ICAIS 2022, LNCS 13340, pp. 108–119, 2022.
https://doi.org/10.1007/978-3-031-06791-4_9

1 Introduction

1.1 A Subsection Sample

Quantum secure multiparty computation (QSMC) [1, 2] is an important branch of quantum cryptography. Because of its high security and communication efficiency, QSMC has a good application prospect in finance, military, and other fields. Quantum secret sharing (QSS) [3–5] is a fundamental method of QSMC. Especially, QSS for sharing quantum information is called quantum state sharing (QSTS). It can be divided into non-hierarchical QSTS (NQSTS) [6–10] and hierarchical QSTS (HQSTS) according to the players' power. In the latter, the players of different powers have different authorities to reconstruct the quantum state shared by the dealer Alice. Specifically, when a high-power player reconstructs the quantum state, he only needs the help of any low-power player and all the other high-power players; when a low-power player reconstructs the quantum state, he needs the help of all the other players. Since HQSTS is more general than NQSTS, it has been extensively studied. In 2010, Wang et al. [11] proposed the first HQSTS protocol. Later, a (2, 3) threshold [12] HQSTS protocol and a (m, n) threshold [13] HQSTS protocol were proposed. In 2013, Shukla et al. [14] studied a generalized approach for HQSTS protocol. Bai et al. [15] proposed a (3, 4)-hierarchy QSTS with an unknown eight-qubit cluster state [16]. In 2014, Xu et al. [17] implemented a (1, 2)-hierarchy QSTS protocol and a (m, n)-hierarchy QSTS protocol of an arbitrary two-particle entangled state. Zha et al. [18] proposed a HQSTS protocol by an eight-particle state in 2019. In 2021, Li et al. [19] designed HQSTS with the non-maximally entangled cluster state. With the emergence of rational secret sharing protocol [20–23], rational QSTS (RQSTS) protocol [24–27] is also explored. In the RQSTS protocol, the players are rational and execute their strategies aiming to maximize their own utilities. So far, most of the RQSTS effort is about NQSTS, almost nothing about HQSTS due to the players have different authorities to reconstruct the quantum state, so appropriate game models should be used to solve game equilibrium.

In this paper, we propose a rational hierarchical quantum state sharing protocol inspired by References [17, 24], and [26]. First, the dealer shares an arbitrary two-particle entangled state with the rational players based on $(m + n + 1)$-particle cluster states. The rational players are divided into high-power players and low-power players. Second, the shared quantum state is unknown to the dealer, so there are no copies of quantum information. Ultimately, only one player David can reconstruct the quantum state. And David is elected by all the players, guaranteeing the basic fairness requirement of the protocol. Besides, when a high-power player reconstructs the quantum state, he will bargain with several low-power players in order to obtain real information about their measurement results. Accordingly, the Rubenstein bargaining model is used to discuss the behavior of rational players in order to meet the actual application requirements. Finally, our protocol achieves security, fairness, correctness, and strict Nash equilibrium.

The rest paper is organized as follows. The quantum states related to our protocol are introduced in Sect. 2. In Sect. 3, we describe our RHQSTS protocol in detail. In Sect. 4, we discuss the Rubenstein bargaining model. Our protocol is analyzed in Sect. 5. Finally, the conclusion is discussed.

2 Preliminaries

2.1 Quantum States and Quantum Operators

Bell States. The Bell states are four specific two-particle maximally entangled quantum states [28, 29], shown as follows:

$$|\psi^{\pm}\rangle = \frac{1}{\sqrt{2}}(|01\rangle \pm |10\rangle), \quad |\phi^{\pm}\rangle = \frac{1}{\sqrt{2}}(|00\rangle \pm |11\rangle). \tag{1}$$

Four-Particle Cluster State

$$|\Psi\rangle_{1234} = \frac{1}{2}(|0000\rangle + |0011\rangle + |1100\rangle - |1111\rangle)_{1234} = \frac{1}{2}(|0\rangle|\varphi\rangle^0) + |1\rangle|\varphi\rangle^1))_{1234}, \tag{2}$$

where $|\varphi\rangle^0 = |000\rangle + |011\rangle$, $|\varphi\rangle^1 = |\varphi\rangle^1 = |100\rangle - |111\rangle$.

Some single qubits whose initial states are all $|0\rangle$ can be entangled with four-qubit cluster states by controlled-NOT operations, thus forming $(m + n + 1)$-particle cluster state is:

$$|\Psi\rangle_{012...m(m+1)...(m+n)} = \frac{1}{2}(|0\rangle|\varphi\rangle^0 + |1\rangle|\varphi\rangle^1)_{012...m(m+1)...(m+n)}, \tag{3}$$

where $|\varphi\rangle^0 = \left|\underbrace{0...0}_{m}\underbrace{0...0}_{n}\right\rangle + \left|\underbrace{0...0}_{m}\underbrace{1...1}_{n}\right\rangle$, $|\varphi\rangle^1 = \left|\underbrace{1...1}_{m}\underbrace{0...0}_{n}\right\rangle -$ $\left|\underbrace{1...1}_{m}\underbrace{1...1}_{n}\right\rangle$.

The Used Four-Particle Entangled State

$$|\Omega\rangle_{ABCD} = \frac{1}{\sqrt{2}}[|0000\rangle + |0110\rangle + |1001\rangle - |1111\rangle]_{ABCD}.$$
$$= \frac{1}{4}[|++\rangle(|00\rangle + |10\rangle + |01\rangle - |11\rangle) + |+-\rangle(|00\rangle - |10\rangle + |01\rangle + |11\rangle)$$
$$+ |-+\rangle(|00\rangle + |10\rangle - |01\rangle + |11\rangle) + |--\rangle(|00\rangle - |10\rangle - |01\rangle - |11\rangle)]_{ABCD}. \tag{4}$$

Pauli Operators. The Pauli operators represented by the computational basis are

$$U_0 = I = |0\rangle\langle0|+|1\rangle\langle1|, \ U_1 = Z = |0\rangle\langle0| - |1\rangle\langle1|,$$
$$U_2 = X = |0\rangle\langle1|+|1\rangle\langle0|, \ U_3 = iY = |0\rangle\langle1| - |1\rangle\langle0|. \tag{5}$$

Hadamard Gate

$$H = \frac{1}{\sqrt{2}}[(|0\rangle + |1\rangle)\langle0| + (|0\rangle - |1\rangle)\langle1|] = |+\rangle\langle0| + |-\rangle\langle1|,$$
$$H|0\rangle = \frac{1}{\sqrt{2}}(|0\rangle + |1\rangle) = |+\rangle, \ H|1\rangle = \frac{1}{\sqrt{2}}(|0\rangle - |1\rangle) = |-\rangle. \tag{6}$$

3   Rational Hierarchical Quantum State Sharing Protocol

In our protocol, there is a dealer Alice and $(m + n)$ rational players, who are m high-power players Bob$_i$ $(1 \le i \le m)$ and n low-power players Charlie$_j$ $(1 \le j \le n)$. Let David be the player who will reconstruct the two-particle entangled state $|\Phi\rangle_{xy}$ shared by Alice.

Alice determines the number of rounds $(r + w)$ based on the geometric distribution $\mathcal{G}(\gamma)$ and publishes it. The players know nothing about the revelation round r. The parameter γ is determined according to the players' utilities. The process of the protocol in the l-th $(1 \le l \le r + w)$ round are as follows.

3.1   Dealer's Protocol

[D-1] When $l \ne r$, Alice prepares $(m + n) |\Omega\rangle_{A_j B_j C_j D_j}$ $(1 \le j \le m + n)$ as in Eq. (4). If $1 \le j \le m, A_j B_j$ are sent to Bob$_j$; if $m+1 \le j \le m+n, A_j B_j$ are sent to Charlie$_{j-m}$. When $l = r$, Alice prepares $|\Psi\rangle_{a_0 a_1 a_2 \ldots a_m a_{m+1} \ldots a_{m+n}}$ and $|\Psi\rangle_{b_0 b_1 b_2 \ldots b_m b_{m+1} \ldots b_{m+n}}$ as in Eq. (3), then Alice sends the particles $a_j b_j$ and $a_{j+m} b_{j+m}$ to Bob$_j$ and Charlie$_j$, respectively.

[D-2] When $l \ne r$, Alice judged whether the players cheated through the measurement results published by them. Then Alice publishes the number of the cheating players, who are forbidden to participate in the protocol. The current round over and proceed with the next round. When $l = r$, if David pays the other players, Alice will perform the Bell states joint measurements on xa_0 and yb_0 respectively, then publish the measurement results. Otherwise, Alice aborts the protocol.

3.2   Player's Protocol

[P-1] Each player publishes an integer p_j $(0 \le p_j \le m + n - 1, \ 1 \le j \le m + n)$ at the same time. If any player does not publish it, he cannot participate in the protocol. Calculates the sum $k' = (\sum_{j=1}^{m+n} p_j) \mod (m + n)$.

[P-2] Let $k = k' + 1$, If $1 \le k \le m$, David is the high-power player Bob$_k$. Then the other high-power players perform X basis measurements on $a_j b_j$ $(1 \le j \le m, \ j \ne k)$ respectively and publish the measurement results. All the low-power players perform Z basis measurements on $a_j b_j$ $(m + 1 \le j \le m + n)$ respectively and publish the measurement results. If $m + 1 \le k \le m + n$, David is the low-power player Charlie$_{k-m}$. Then, the other players need to perform X basis measurements on $a_j b_j$ $(1 \le j \le m + n, \ j \ne k)$ respectively and publish the measurement results.

[P-3] When $l \ne r$, players who honestly participated in the protocol can continue. When $l = r$, if David is the high-power player Bob$_k$, he randomly elects several low-power players and bargains with them. Then David pays them. According to the measurement results, David performs unitary operations on $a_k b_k$. If David is a low-power player Charlie$_{k-m}$, he performs Hadamard operation and unitary operations on $a_{k-m} b_{k-m}$ according to the measurement results.

4   Rubenstein Bargaining Model with Incomplete Information

When David is a high-power player, he does not need the help of all the low-power players. Thus, David will bargain with them about the offer that he should pay [30].

4.1 Assumption

Assumption-1: The high-power player David is denoted by Bob_k, and any low-power player elected by David is denoted by $Charlie_j$. Bob_k's and $Charlie_j$'s fixed discounting factors are δ_B and δ_C respectively $(0 < \delta_B, \delta_C < 1)$. Here 0 represents extreme irritability and 1 represents extreme patience. Since they have different powers to reconstruct $|\Phi\rangle_{xy}$, there is $\delta_B > \delta_C$.

Assumption-2: Bob_k's offer range to $Charlie_j$ is $[B_{min}, B_{max}]$, and $Charlie_j$'s offer range is $[C_{min}, C_{max}]$. Both parties know $B_{min} \leq C_{min}$.

Assumption-3: $Charlie_j$ does not know Bob_k's highest offer B_{max}. $Charlie_j$ thinks that B_{max} is B_{max}^C. $Charlie_j$ does not know the size of B_{max} and B_{max}^C, while Bob_k does.

Assumption-4: Let $\Delta = B_{max} - C_{min}$, $\Delta^C = B_{max}^C - C_{min}$. According to the Harsanyi transformation [31], $Charlie_j$ does not know Bob_k's highest offer, but knows that Bob_k's offer is evenly distributed over $[0, \Delta^C]$. So the negotiation interval $[C_{min}, B_{max}]$ between Bob_k and $Charlie_j$ can be mapped to $[0, \Delta]$, and $[C_{min}, B_{max}^C]$ can be mapped to $[0, \Delta^C]$.

Assumption-5: Now consider that there are only three rounds in this bargaining model. Take the third round as the inverse point to deduce forward and solve the model. The utilities are as follows: In the first round: $Charlie_j$: $+(m-1)U_{b_{11}}]$; Bob_k: y_1. In the second round: $Charlie_j$: $\delta_C x_2$; Bob_k: $-mt_1 - xt_2)$. In the third round: $Charlie_j$: $\delta_C^2 x_3$; Bob_k: $\delta_B^2 y_3$.

4.2 Solution

In the third round, $Charlie_j$'s own offer is x_3. Although $Charlie_j$ does not know the size of Δ and Δ^C, he knows that Bob_k will choose to accept or reject depending on whether $\Delta \geq x_3$ holds. So $Charlie_j$ maximizes his expected utility

$$\max_{x_3} \delta_C^2 (p_{3a} \cdot x_3 + 0 \cdot p_{3r}), \tag{7}$$

where $p_{3a}(p_{3a} = P(\Delta \geq x_3) = (\Delta^C - x_3)/\Delta^C)$ and $p_{3r}(p_{3r} = 1 - p_{3a})$ are the probability that Bob accepts and rejects x_3, respectively. From Eq. (7), let $\dfrac{d \max_{x_3} \delta_C^2(x_3 - \frac{x_3^2}{\Delta^C})}{dx_3} = 0$,

x_3's optimal solution is $x_3^* = \frac{\Delta^C}{2}$. Bob_k's utility is $\delta_B^2 y_3 = \delta_B^2(\Delta - \frac{\Delta^C}{2})$. Finally, all $U_{Cooperating}^B(x)$ can know is $\Delta \geq \frac{\Delta^C}{2}$.

In the second round, Bob_k's offer to $Charlie_j$ is x_2. For $Charlie_j$, he does not know what Bob_k's highest offer is, so he simply rejects x_2. $Charlie_j$'s utility is $\delta_C x_2$.

In the first round, $Charlie_j$'s own offer is x_1. Bob_k's utility is $y_1 = \Delta - x_1$. The condition Bob_k can accept is his utility in this round exceeds in the third round:

$$\Delta - x_1 \geq \delta_B^2(\Delta - \frac{\Delta^C}{2}) \Rightarrow \Delta \geq \frac{2x_1 - \delta_B^2 \Delta^C}{2(1 - \delta_B^2)}. \tag{8}$$

If Eq. (8) holds, Bob_k chooses to accept x_1^*, otherwise reject x_1^*. For $Charlie_j$, he thinks what Bob_k can accept is

$$\Delta^C - x_1 \geq \delta_B^2(\Delta^C - \frac{\Delta^C}{2}) \Rightarrow \Delta^C \geq \frac{2x_1}{2 - \delta_B^2}. \tag{9}$$

With the increase of the number of rounds, the upper limit of Charlie$_j$'s own offer in each round gradually decreases, and both parties' utilities are gradually reduced due to δ_B, δ_C. So Charlie$_j$'s offer in the first round is the highest. From Eq. (9), Δ^C's optimal solution Charlie$_j$ guesses is

$$(\Delta^C)^* = \frac{2x_1}{2 - \delta_B^2}. \tag{10}$$

Charlie$_j$ wants to maximize his utility and meet Bob$_k$'s acceptance condition, then

$$\max_{x_1}(x_1 \cdot P_{1a} + \delta_C^2 x_3 \cdot P_{ra}) = \max_{x_1} \frac{x_1(2 - \delta_B^2)^2 + [\delta_C^2 - 2(2 - \delta_B^2)]x_1^2}{(2 - \delta_B^2)^2}, \tag{11}$$

where P_{1a} is the probability that Bob$_k$ accepts in the first round. $P_{ra}(P_{ra} = P_{1r} \cdot P_{3a} = \frac{x_1}{2 - \delta_B^2})$ is the probability that Bob$_k$ rejects in the first round and accepts in the third round. From Eq. (11), there is

$$x_1^* = \frac{(2 - \delta_B^2)^2}{2(4 - 2\delta_B^2 - \delta_C^2)}. \tag{12}$$

Then,

$$(\Delta^C)^* = \frac{2x_1^*}{2 - \delta_B^2} = \frac{2 - \delta_B^2}{4 - 2\delta_B^2 - \delta_C^2}, \; x_3^* = \frac{\Delta^C}{2} = \frac{2 - \delta_B^2}{2(4 - 2\delta_B^2 - \delta_C^2)} = \frac{x_1^*}{2 - \delta_B^2} < x_1^*. \tag{13}$$

Thus, we can have the following combination of strategies: In the first round, Charlie$_j$'s own offer is $x_1^* = \frac{(2 - \delta_B^2)^2}{2(4 - 2\delta_B^2 - \delta_C^2)} > 0$. From Eq. (8) and Eq. (9), if $\Delta \geq \frac{2x_1 - \delta_B^2 \Delta^C}{2(1 - \delta_B^2)} = \frac{2 - \delta_B^2}{4 - 2\delta_B^2 - \delta_C^2}$, Bob$_k$ accepts x_1^* and the negotiation ends. Then the bargaining equilibrium is

$$x_1^* = \frac{(2 - \delta_B^2)^2}{2(4 - 2\delta_B^2 - \delta_C^2)}, \; y_1^* = \Delta - \frac{(2 - \delta_B^2)^2}{2(4 - 2\delta_B^2 - \delta_C^2)}. \tag{14}$$

If x_1^* in the first round is rejected by Bob$_k$. Then $x_3^* = \frac{x_1^*}{2 - \delta_B^2} < x_1^*$ in the third round. If Δ satisfies $0 < x_3^* < \Delta$, then Bob$_k$ accepts, otherwise he still rejects.

When both parties can continue bargaining indefinitely, the bargaining equilibrium is that x_i^* satisfies $0 < x_i^* < \Delta$.

5 Analyses

In our protocol, when David is a low-power player, it is the same as rational NQSTS protocol. So we mainly analyze the protocol when David is a high-power player.

5.1 Utilities and Preferences

The Strategies of the Players
David (Bob_k):

a) d_{11}: Chooses to cooperate and pays the related players.
b) d_{21}: Chooses to cheat and refuses to pay.

Bob$_i$ ($1 \le i \le m$, $i \ne k$) (Charlie$_j$ ($1 \le j \le n$)):

a) b_{11} (c_{12}): Chooses to cooperate and publishes the correct measurement results.
b) b_{21} (c_{22}): Chooses to cheat and publishes the wrong measurement results, or remain silent.

The Utilities of the Players
David (Bob_k):

a) $U_{d_{11}}^+$: Successfully reconstructs $|\Phi\rangle_{xy}$.
b) $U_{d_{11}}$: Fails due to cheating by other players.
c) $U_{d_{21}}^-$: Fails due to own cheating.

Bob$_i$ ($1 \le i \le m$, $i \ne k$) (Charlie$_j$ ($1 \le j \le n$)):

a) $U_{b_{11}}^+$ ($U_{c_{12}}^+$): Successfully helps David.
b) $U_{b_{11}}$ ($U_{c_{12}}$): Fails to help David.
c) $U_{b_{21}}^-$ ($U_{c_{22}}^-$): His cheating is discovered by Alice.
d) $U_{b_{21}}$ ($U_{c_{22}}$): His cheating is not discovered by Alice.

For a rational player, he has the following preference: David: $U_{d_{11}}^+ > U_{d_{11}} > U_{d_{21}}^-$, Bob$_i$ ($1 \le i \le m$, $i \ne k$): $U_{b_{21}} > U_{b_{11}}^+ = U_{b_{11}} > U_{b_{21}}^-$, Charlie$_j$ ($1 \le j \le n$): $U_{c_{22}} > U_{c_{12}}^+ = U_{c_{12}} > U_{c_{22}}^-$.

For David, since David's actual utility is influenced by other players, $U_{d_{11}}^{+'}=U_{d_{11}} - mt_1 - xt_2$, where m and x ($1 \le x \le n$) are the numbers of high-power and low-power players who help David respectively, t_1 and t_2 are the corresponding David's offer to them. The players' goal is to obtain $|\Phi\rangle_{xy}$, so $U_{d_{11}}^{+'} > U_{b_{11}}^+$, $U_{d_{11}}^{+'} > U_{c_{12}}^+$. Besides, he will choose some low-power players to bargain. The low-power players do not know how many and which low-power players are elected by David. The highest offer, David can pay to each low-power player, is B_{max}. If David chooses x low-power players, there is an inequality $U_{d_{11}}^+ - mt_1 - xB_{max} \ge U_{d_{11}}$, then x satisfies $x \le \left\lfloor \dfrac{U_{d_{11}}^+ - mt_1 - U_{d_{11}}}{B_{max}} \right\rfloor \le n$.

For the other high-power players Bob$_i$, they can maximize their utilities by helping David. When Bob$_i$ chooses to cooperate, no matter whether David successfully reconstructs $|\Phi\rangle_{xy}$ or not, Bob's utility should not be affected by the other players, so $U_{b_{11}}^+ = U_{b_{11}}$. Obviously, the utility of successful cheating is the highest, then $U_{b_{21}} > U_{b_{11}}^+ = U_{b_{11}}$. Correspondingly, $U_{c_{22}} > U_{c_{12}}^+ = U_{c_{12}}$. The low-power and high-power players have different powers to reconstruct $|\Phi\rangle_{xy}$, so $U_{b_{11}}^+ > U_{c_{12}}^+$. Besides, all players' utilities of failing to cheat are the lowest and the same, then $U_{d_{21}}^- = U_{b_{21}}^- = U_{c_{22}}^-$.

5.2 Security

To ensure the security of the quantum channel, Alice will conduct a security test by inserting the decoy qubits into the qubits sent to the players. The players perform X or Z basis measurements by the location of the decoy particles announced by Alice. Alice compares the measurement results of the decoy qubits published by the players with the initial states of the decoy qubits. If the error rates are lower than the set threshold, the quantum channel is safe; otherwise, the communication ends. This detection method has been discussed in References [32, 33]. We mainly analyze protocol security from outside attacks and participants' attack [34].

Outside Attack. The common outside attacks are entanglement-measure attack and intercept-resend attack. Although the eavesdropper Eve intercepts the particles sent by the dealer to the players, he cannot steal any information about the quantum state shared by Alice. In our protocol, Alice ensures the quantum channel's security, if Eve attempts to steal secret information by the intercept-resend attack, this will result in the error rate exceeding the threshold and be detected by Alice.

Participants' Attack. For David, he may attempt to reconstruct $|\Phi\rangle_{xy}$ without the help of the other players. In fact, when David is a high-power player, he only knows the phase information about $|\Phi\rangle_{xy}$. When David is a low-power player, he knows nothing about $|\Phi\rangle_{xy}$. So David cannot reconstruct $|\Phi\rangle_{xy}$ by himself.

For the players who help David, they may attempt to reconstruct $|\Phi\rangle_{xy}$. Although they know their measurement results, they could not get David's quantum state because of the quantum no-cloning theorem. They naturally cannot reconstruct $|\Phi\rangle_{xy}$. If a dishonest player initiates the intercept-resend attack, he will be detected by Alice. Accordingly, our protocol achieves security.

5.3 Fairness

In our protocol, only David can reconstruct $|\Phi\rangle_{xy}$, but he is elected by all players rather than appointed by Alice [24]. This means that each player has the same probability $\frac{1}{m+n}$ of becoming David in each round. So David's election is fair to each player.

Theorem 1: If a player's utility from cooperating is higher than the utility from cheating, this protocol achieves fairness.

Proof: In this protocol, if a player deviates from the suggested strategy during the execution, the protocol will not be aborted. But the cheating player will not be able to continue participating in the protocol.

Take the example of a high-power player Bob$_i$ $(1 \le i \le m)$'s strategy and a low-power player Charlie$_j$ $(1 \le j \le n)$'s strategy in the l-th round, and the probability that this round is the revelation round is $\Pr(l = r)$ denoted by λ.

For Bob$_i$, when he cooperates, if $l = r$, his utility is $\frac{1}{m}(U_{d_{11}}^+ - mt_1 - xt_2) + \frac{m-1}{m}U_{b_{11}}$. If $l \ne r$, his utility is $\frac{1}{m}U_{d_{11}}^{+'} + \frac{m-1}{m}U_{b_{11}}^+$. When Bob$_i$ cheats, if $l = r$, his utility is $\frac{1}{m}(U_{d_{11}}^+ - mt_1 - xt_2) + \frac{m-1}{m}U_{b_{21}}$. If $l \ne r$, his utility is $\frac{1}{m}U_{d_{21}}^- + \frac{m-1}{m}U_{b_{21}}^-$. Thus, the expected utilities of Bob$_i$ cooperating and cheating are $U_{Cooperating}^B(x) = \frac{\lambda}{m}[(U_{d_{11}}^+ - mt_1 - xt_2) + (m-1)U_{b_{11}}] + \frac{1-\lambda}{m}[U_{d_{11}}^+ + (m-1)U_{b_{11}}^+]$ and $U_{Cheating}^B(x) = \frac{\lambda}{m}[(U_{d_{11}}^+ - mt_1 - xt_2) + (m-1)U_{b_{21}}] + \frac{1-\lambda}{m}[U_{d_{21}}^- + (m-1)U_{b_{21}}^-]$, respectively.

For Charlie$_j$, elected by David who is a high-power player, when Charlie$_j$ cooperates, if $l = r$, his utility is $\frac{x}{n}U_{c_{12}} + \frac{n-x}{n} \cdot 0$. If $l \ne r$, his utility is $\frac{x}{n}U_{c_{12}}^+ + \frac{n-x}{n} \cdot 0$. When Charlie$_j$ cheats, if $l = r$, his utility is $\frac{x}{n}U_{c_{22}} + \frac{n-x}{n} \cdot 0$. If $l \ne r$, his utility is $\frac{x}{n}U_{c_{22}}^- + \frac{n-x}{n} \cdot 0$. Thus, the expected utilities of Charlie$_j$ cooperating and cheating are $U_{Cooperating}^C = \frac{\lambda x}{n}U_{c_{12}} + \frac{(1-\lambda)x}{n}U_{c_{12}}^+$ and $U_{Cheating}^C = \frac{\lambda x}{n}U_{c_{22}} + \frac{(1-\lambda)x}{n}U_{c_{22}}^-$, respectively.

In order to ensure the fairness of the protocol, two inequalities $U_{Cooperating}^B(x) > U_{Cheating}^B(x)$ and $U_{Cooperating}^C > U_{Cheating}^C$ must hold. Because $U_{d_{11}}^{+'} > U_{b_{11}}$ and $U_{b_{11}} > U_{d_{21}}^-$, $U_{Cooperating}^B(x) > U_{Cheating}^B(x)$. For $U_{Cooperating}^C > U_{Cheating}^C$, there is $U_{c_{22}} > U_{c_{12}} > U_{c_{22}}^-$, then

$$\lambda < \frac{U_{c_{12}} - U_{c_{22}}^-}{U_{c_{22}} - U_{c_{22}}^-}. \qquad (15)$$

When Eq. (15) holds, our protocol achieves fairness.

5.4   Correctness

Theorem 2: If all players in this protocol are rational, the protocol can achieve correctness.

Proof: In our protocol, the players do not know the revelation round. Therefore, if a player sends the wrong measurement results or remains silent in one round, he cannot continue participating in the protocol. If David cheats in the revelation round, his utility is far lower than the utility he chooses to cooperate. Both David and the players who help David aim to maximize their utilities, so no player would be motivated to cheat, and David would successfully reconstruct $|\Phi\rangle_{xy}$. Therefore, our protocol achieves correctness.

5.5   Strict Nash Equilibrium

Theorem 3: If Eq. (15) holds, this protocol achieves strict Nash equilibrium.

Proof: In the game theory, if the protocol achieves strict Nash equilibrium, no matter what other players' strategies are, each player's utility cheating should be less than his utility cooperating.

In game theory, $\sigma = (\sigma_1, \ldots, \sigma_n)$ is the strategies of n players. The notations $\sigma_{-i} = (\sigma_1, \ldots, \sigma_{i-1}, \sigma_{i+1}, \ldots \sigma_n)$ and $(\sigma_i', \sigma_{-i}) = (\sigma_1, \ldots, \sigma_{i-1}, \sigma_i', \sigma_{i+1}, \ldots \sigma_n)$ are also used. The utility function u_i of each player P_i is defined over the set of possible outcomes for the game.

Then, in the l-th round, when any high-power player Bob$_i$ ($1 \le i \le m$) cooperates and follows the strategy σ_i, his utility is $u_i(\sigma) = U_{Cooperating}^B(x)$. When he cheats and executes the deviation strategy σ_i', his utility is $u_i(\sigma_i', \sigma_{-i}) = U_{Cheating}^B(x)$. Because $U_{d_{11}}^{+'} > U_{b_{11}}$ and $U_{b_{11}} > U_{d_{21}}^{-}$, $u_i(\sigma) > u_i(\sigma_i', \sigma_{-i})$.

When any low-power player Charlie$_j$ ($1 \le j \le n$) cooperates and follows the strategy σ_j, his utility is $u_j(\sigma) = U_{Cooperating}^C$. When he cheats and executes the deviation strategy σ_j', his utility is $u_j(\sigma_j', \sigma_{-j}) = U_{Cheating}^C$. When Eq. (15) holds, $u_j(\sigma) > u_j(\sigma_j', \sigma_{-j})$. So our protocol achieves the strict Nash equilibrium.

5.6 Comparison of Protocols

In the HQSTS protocol, there is no knowledge of game theory. In fact, the players should be thinking, i.e., rational. In other words, they should participate in the protocol with the intention of maximizing their own benefits. Besides, as the players have different authorities to reconstruct the quantum state, the high-power players may abuse their power, such as threatening the low-power players. Then, the low-power players may give up participating in the protocol for fear of damage to their own utilities, and eventually lead to failure. Therefore, we consider that the dealer is rational and design a rational RQSTS protocol. Ensure that every player honestly participates in the protocol, and the low-power players are not threatened by the high-power players. Accordingly, compared with other HQSTS protocols, our protocol is more in line with the actual situation.

All the RQSTS protocols that have been proposed are non-hierarchical, while our protocol is hierarchical. In our protocol, when different authorities of players reconstruct the quantum state shared by the dealer Alice, the game models are different. Especially, when David who will reconstruct the quantum state is a low-power player, there is no difference between the game process and rational NQSTS protocol. In contrast, when David is a high-power player, we use the Rubinstein bargaining model in game theory to analyze players' behavioral strategies. Our protocol also achieves the strict Nash equilibrium. Then, our protocol is more general.

6 Conclusion

In this paper, we proposed a RHQSTS protocol. An arbitrary two-particle entangled state is shared by $(m + n + 1)$-particle cluster states between the dealer and the players. The power of players to reconstruct $|\Phi\rangle_{xy}$ is no longer the same, and the players are divided into high-power players and low-power players. Besides, in order to ensure that each player reconstructs $|\Phi\rangle_{xy}$ with the same probability, David is elected by all players. When David is a high-power player, he does not need the help of all the low-power players. Thus, the high-power player will elect several low-power players. Both parties determine their respective utilities through bargaining. Since the players are rational, we discuss the players' behavior through the Rubinstein bargain model with incomplete information. Therefore, compared with the HQSTS protocol, our protocol is more in line with actual requirements. Finally, our protocol is proved to be secure, fair, correct, and achieve strict Nash equilibrium. Our protocol is helpful to promote the application of game theory in HQSTS protocol.

Funding Statement. This work is supported by the National Key R&D Program of China (Grant No. 2020YFB1805405), the Foundation of Guizhou Provincial Key Laboratory of Public Big Data (Grant No. 2019BDKFJJ014), the Fundamental Research Funds for the Central Universities (Grant No. 2020RC38) and NSFC (Grant Nos. 92046001, 61671087, 61962009, 61971021), the Fundamental Research Funds for Beijing Municipal Commission of Education, the Scientific Research Launch Funds of North China University of Technology, and Beijing Urban Governance Research Base of North China University of Technology.

References

1. Gianni, J., Qu, Z.: New quantum private comparison using hyperentangled ghz state. J. Quant. Comput. **3**(2), 45–54 (2021)
2. Sun, Y., Yan, L., Sun, Z., Zhang, S., Lu, J.: A novel semi-quantum private comparison scheme using bell entangle states. Comput. Mater. Continua **66**(3), 2385–2395 (2021)
3. Hillery, M., Bužek, V., Berthiaume, A.: Quantum secret sharing. Phys. Rev. A **59**(3), 1829 (1999)
4. Karlsson, A., Koashi, M., Imoto, N.: Quantum entanglement for secret sharing and secret splitting. Phys. Rev. A **59**(1), 162 (1999)
5. Cleve, R., Gottesman, D., Lo, H.K.: How to share a quantum secret. Phys. Rev. Lett. **83**(3), 648 (1999)
6. Li, Y., Zhang, K., Peng, K.: Multiparty secret sharing of quantum information based on entanglement swapping. Phys. Lett. A **324**(5), 420–424 (2004)
7. Lance, A.M., Symul, T., Bowen, W.P., et al.: Tripartite quantum state sharing. Phys. Rev. Lett. **92**(17), 77903 (2004)
8. Jiang, J.M., Dong, D.: Multi-party quantum state sharing via various probabilistic channels. Quant. Inf. Process. **12**(1), 237–249 (2013)
9. Cao, H., Ma, W.: Verifiable threshold quantum state sharing scheme. IEEE Access **6**, 10453–10457 (2018)
10. Song, X., Liu, Y., Xiao, M., et al.: A verifiable (t,n) threshold quantum state sharing scheme on IBM quantum cloud platform. Quantum Inf. Process. **19**(9), 1–21 (2020)
11. Wang, X.W., Xia, L.X., Wang, Z.Y., Zhang, D.Y.: Hierarchical quantum-information splitting. Opt. Commun. **283**(6), 1196–1199 (2010)
12. Wang, X.W., Zhang, D.Y., Tang, S.Q., Zhan, X.G., You, K.M.: Hierarchical quantum information splitting with six-photon cluster states. Int. J. Theor. Phys. **49**(11), 2691–2697 (2010)
13. Wang, X.W., Zhang, D.Y., Tang, S.Q., Xie, L.J.: Multiparty hierarchical quantum-information splitting. J. Phys. B: At. Mol. Opt. Phys. **44**(3), 035505 (2011)
14. Shukla, C., Pathak, A.: Hierarchical quantum communication. Phys. Lett. A **377**(19–20), 1337–1344 (2013)

15. Bai, M.Q., Mo, Z.W.: Hierarchical quantum information splitting with eight-qubit cluster states. Quant. Inf. Process. **12**(2), 1053–1064 (2013)
16. Yao, X.C., Wang, T.X., Chen, H.Z., et al.: Experimental demonstration of topological error correction. Nature **482**(7386), 489–494 (2012)
17. Xu, G., Wang, C., Yang, Y.-X.: Hierarchical quantum information splitting of an arbitrary two-qubit state via the cluster state. Quant. Inf. Process. **13**(1), 43–57 (2013)
18. Zha, X.W., Miao, N., Wang, H.F.: Hierarchical quantum information splitting of an arbitrary two-qubit using a single quantum resource. Int. J. Theor. Phys. **58**(8), 2428–2434 (2019)
19. Xu, G., Shan, R.T., Chen, X.B., Dong, M., Chen, Y.L.: Probabilistic and hierarchical quantum information splitting based on the non-maximally entangled cluster state. Comput. Mater. Continua **69**(1), 339–349 (2021)
20. Halpern, J., Teague, V.: Rational secret sharing and multiparty computation. In: Proceedings of the Thirty-Sixth Annual ACM Symposium on Theory of Computing, pp. 623–632. Association for Computing Machinery, New York (2004)
21. Kol, G., Naor, M.: Games for exchanging information. In: Proceedings of the Fortieth Annual ACM Symposium on Theory of Computing, pp. 423–432. Association for Computing Machinery, New York (2008)
22. De, S.J., Ruj, S.: Failure tolerant rational secret sharing. In: 2016 IEEE 30th International Conference on Advanced Information Networking and Applications (AINA), pp. 925–932. IEEE (2016)
23. Chen, Z., Tian, Y., Peng, C.: An incentive-compatible rational secret sharing scheme using blockchain and smart contract. Sci.China Inf. Sci. **64**(10), 1–21 (2021)
24. Maitra, A., De, S.J., Paul, G., Pal, A.K.: Proposal for quantum rational secret sharing. Phys. Rev. A **92**(2), 022305 (2015)
25. Qin, H., Tang, W.K., Tso, R.: Rational quantum secret sharing. Sci. Rep. **8**(1), 1–7 (2018)
26. Dou, Z., Xu, G., Chen, X.-B., Liu, X., Yang, Y.-X.: A secure rational quantum state sharing protocol. Sci. China Inf. Sci. **61**(2), 1–12 (2018)
27. Balasubramanian, P., Behera, B.K., Panigrahi, P.K.: Circuit implementation for rational quantum secure communication using IBM Q Experience beta platform
28. Khokhlov, D.L.: Interpretation of the entangled states. J. Quant. Comput. **2**(3), 147–150 (2020)
29. Li, Z.Z., Li, Z.C., Chen, X.B., Qu, Z., Wang, X., Pan, H.: A practical quantum network coding protocol based on non-maximally entangled state. Comput. Mater. Continua **68**(2), 2651–2663 (2021)
30. Rubinstein, A.: A bargaining model with incomplete information about time preferences. Econometrica: J. Economet. Soc. **53**(5), 1151–1172 (1985)
31. Harsanyi, J.C.: Games with incomplete information played by "Bayesian" players, I-III Part I. The basic model. Manag. Sci. **14**(3), 159–182 (1967)
32. Qin, L.R.: Research and simulation of hierarchical quantum information splitting protocol based on multi-particle state. M.S. Dissertation, Beijing University of Posts and Telecommunications, China (2019)
33. Bennett, C.H., Brassard, G.: Quantum cryptography: public key distribution and coin tossing. arXiv preprint arXiv:2003.06557 (2020)
34. Wen, Q.Y., Qin, S.J., Gao, F.: Cryptanalysis of quantum cryptographic protocols. J. Cryptol. Res. **1**(2), 200–210 (2014)

Blockchain-Based Efficient Incentive Mechanism in Crowdsensing

Qiulu Jiang[1,2], Wunan Wan[1,2(✉)], Zhi Qin[1,2], Jinquan Zhang[1,2], Hui Han[1,2], Shibin Zhang[1,2], and Jinyue Xia[3]

[1] School of Cybersecurity, Chengdu University of Information Technology, Chengdu 610225, China
nan_wwn@cuit.edu.cn
[2] Advanced Cryptography and System Security Key Laboratory of Sichuan Province, Chengdu 610255, China
[3] International Business Machines Corporation (IBM), New York, NY 10041-212, USA

Abstract. In recent years, with the popularization and widespread use of mobile smart devices, Crowdsensing has gradually become one of the current research hotspots. The incentive mechanism is an important issue in the research of Crowdsensing. The existing incentive mechanism usually relies on the bank-like trustworthy center, but the trustworthy center has the problem of system trust deficiency because of its opaque control and vulnerable to attack. Blockchain is decentralized, open, tamper-evident, and anonymous, which can be used as a solution to the trust deficit problem in Crowdsensing incentive mechanism. A blockchain-based incentive mechanism is proposed for Crowdsensing, which adopts a blockchain-secured distributed architecture, and the sensing users and data demanders participate in the sensing tasks as nodes in the blockchain. This incentive mechanism uses a reverse auction model to screen out irrational offer users and increase the execution efficiency of the sensing task. A Softmax regression algorithm is used to implement miners' verification of the quality grade of sensing data, and the value of data is calculated by the quality grade of user offers and data to encourage users to upload high quality and reliable data. Finally, the accuracy of the classification algorithm is compared through simulation experiments, and the security, efficiency and feasibility of the system are analyzed.

Keywords: Blockchain · Crowdsensing · Reverse auctions · Incentive mechanism · Classification algorithms

1 Introduction

Crowdsensing [1, 2] is a new model of data acquisition that combines the idea of crowdsourcing with the sensing capabilities of mobile devices, and is a manifestation of the Internet of Things. Crowdsensing refers to the formation of interactive, participatory sensing networks through ordinary users' existing mobile smart devices that perform specific sensing tasks and upload them to data-demanding groups, thereby helping professionals to collect data, analyze information and share knowledge.

© The Author(s), under exclusive license to Springer Nature Switzerland AG 2022
X. Sun et al. (Eds.): ICAIS 2022, LNCS 13340, pp. 120–132, 2022.
https://doi.org/10.1007/978-3-031-06791-4_10

The perception of data requires resources such as battery power, computing resources and data traffic from the participants' mobile devices, and in the process requires time and labor from the sensing users. Without appropriate rewards, participants are not interested in staying active in crowdsensing over time. Therefore, designing a reasonable incentive mechanism to motivate enough participants to participate in the sensing task and provide high quality and reliable sensing data is an important issue.

Currently, the main incentives in crowdsensing are reward payment incentives, entertainment game incentives, social relationship incentives and virtual point incentives. As a common incentive method in information networks [3–5], the issuance of reward payment incentives relies on trustworthy centers such as banks and government departments, but there are many problems with this method. Trusted centershave absolute control over the entire system, including the issuance of e-money and transaction data. The lack of transparency in the maintenance process, as well as its irregular operation and inadequate protection, has resulted in a lack of trust.

Blockchain technology can be used to solve the trust deficit problem caused by trusted third parties. However, during the research process of building secure distributed incentives based on blockchain, performance bottlenecks inherent to blockchain have been identified. For example, the transaction throughput of Bitcoin and Ether is about 7TPS and 15TPS respectively, and that of Hyperledger Fabric is no more than 2000TPS, which is much lower than that of existing databases [6]. The performance bottleneck of blockchain has become an important factor that hinders sensing users from participating in the task of crowdsensing. Therefore, in order to use the security and decentralization properties of blockchain in crowdsensing, it is necessary to consider improving its performance.

In response to the above problems, this paper proposes an efficient incentive mechanism based on blockchain in crowdsensing, in which blockchain technology and a reverse auction model are introduced to solve the security problems such as the lack of trust brought about by trusted third parties, and to improve the efficiency of the model.

The contribution of this paper is threefold:

- A blockchain-based distributed incentive mechanism is proposed to ensure the validity of sensing data while avoiding the security risks posed by trusted third parties.
- The incentive mechanism is designed using a reverse auction model. Screening out irrational offers by users making auction offers reduces the workload of miners in verifying data quality grades and increases the efficiency of performing a sensing task.
- Calculate the quality grade of sensing data using Softmax regression algorithm. The value of the data is calculated by the user offer and the quality grade of the data, and the compensation is distributed according to different data values to encourage users to upload data with higher value.

2 Background

2.1 Blockchain

In 2008 Satoshi Nakamoto introduced the concept of blockchain [7], a distributed shared digital ledger backed by cryptography and stored in chronological order.

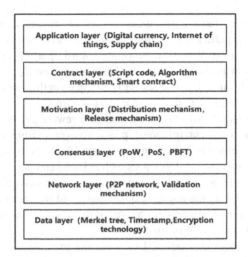

Fig. 1. Blockchain infrastructure model.

The infrastructure model of blockchain technology [8] is shown in Fig. 1. Generally speaking, a blockchain system consists of a data layer, a network layer, a consensus layer, an incentive layer, a contract layer and an application layer. The data layer encapsulates the underlying data blocks and related data encryption and timestamping technologies; the network layer includes distributed networking mechanisms and data validation mechanisms; the consensus layer mainly encapsulates various consensus algorithms of network nodes; the motivation layer mainly includes the issuance and distribution mechanisms of economic incentives; the contract layer mainly encapsulates various scripts, algorithms and smart contracts, which are the basis of the programmable features of the blockchain; The application layer encapsulates various application scenarios and cases of blockchain and provides programmable interfaces for users to customize, initiate and execute contracts.

2.2   Crowdsensing System Model

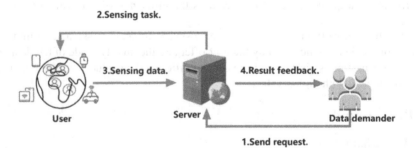

Fig. 2. Crowd sensing system architecture.

The system architecture model of crowdsensing is usually divided into three main parts [9, 10], namely the server, the data demander and the user.

The process of executing the tasks of the Groupware-aware system is shown in Fig. 2. First the server receives a service request from the data demander and broadcasts the demand to the user; the sensing and collection of information about the external environment by the user through sensors built into the mobile smart device; The server analyses and processes the collected data and finally hands over the processed data to the person who needs it.

2.3 Reverse Auction

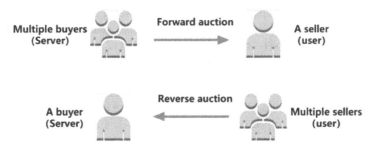

Fig. 3. Forward and reverse auctions.

Reverse auctions, also known as reduced auctions or Dutch auctions, are a different form of auction from traditional forward auctions where there are multiple buyers for one seller. As shown in Fig. 3, a reverse auction is an auction where there is one buyer and multiple potential sellers. In a traditional crowd-sensing system, the server is the buyer and the user are the sellers. In a traditional Crowdsensing system, the server is the buyer and the users are the sellers. The server issues a sensing task and the users quote the amount they want to be paid for completing the sensing task. In the end, the server selects the lowest bidder as the winner and pays them.

3   Related Work

In crowdsensing, incentive mechanism research is an important factor to promote its development. Only by ensuring the number of participants and data quality, and by promoting the efficient collaboration between organizers and participants to accomplish the purpose and maximize the benefits, can the further development of crowdsensing be promoted.

This system introduces blockchain technology to solve the problems of untrustworthiness and centralization in the incentive mechanism of crowdsensing. He [11] et al. proposed a blockchain-based real incentive mechanism for distributed P2P applications, which can meet the diverse needs of users in a dynamic distributed P2P environment. Li et al. [12] proposed a blockchain-based incentive framework CrowdBC for crowdsensing applications, CrowdBC focuses on the problems of privacy leakage, single point of failure, and high service costs, but does not give a specific payoff distribution scheme; Wang et al. [13] propose a blockchain-based distributed incentive mechanism based on crowdsensing applications, using EM algorithms to evaluate the quality of sensing data and issue payoffs according to different quality grades to encourage users to upload more high-quality data.

The reward payment incentive mainly uses game theoretic methods, the most prominent of which are auction models, including reverse auction, combination auction, multi-attribute auction, all-pay auction, two-way auction and VCG (Vickery-carlike-groves) auction. In addition, there are incentive approaches based on Stackelberg's game, among others [14]. J.S. Lee et al. [15] first applied reverse auctions in the economic field to the study of crowdsensing incentives, proposing a fixed-price randomized payment approach to ensure a high user participation rate while minimizing the payment cost. Krontiris et al. [16] use a multi-attribute auction mechanism in reverse auctions, which takes into account not only the user participation rate but also the quality of the sensing data, making the payment method more reasonable. Wen et al. [17–19] considered a location-sensitive crowdsensing task and used a reverse auction model to implement an incentive mechanism for high-quality data feedback. The use of reverse auctions can yield more desired profits than fixed prices. Therefore, in a crowdsensing incentive mechanism, the buyer dynamic bidding for the task used in the reverse auction can easily solve the problem of determining the price of the sensing task.

4   A Blockchain-Based Framework for Crowdsensing Incentives Mechanism

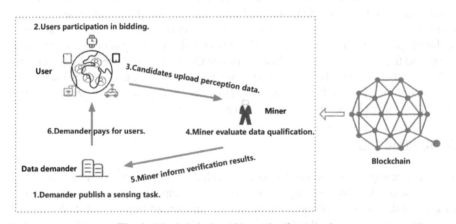

Fig. 4. Blockchain-based incentive framework.

- Data demander: physical crowdsources who are interested in data and are willing to offer incentives for doing so. Mostly enterprises (e. g. large internet companies such as Google, Amazon, Uber). They define the specifications and constraints of the sensing task.

- Miner: It calculates the quality grade and value of the sensing data, selects the sensing users involved in the sensing task and aggregates their results, and finally transmits the results back to the data demander.
- Sensing user: people who have the resources of a sensing mobile device and are willing to perform tasks in exchange for payment. These participants participate in the bidding based on the data collected by their own devices.

This paper uses blockchain technology and a reverse auction model to design an incentive mechanism that improves the efficiency of performing the entire sensing task while ensuring the overall welfare of the community. The case of one data demander and multiple sensing users is discussed here. The process is described in the Fig. 4: first, the data demander posts a sensing task, then the sensing user participates in a bid, and the miner selects the candidates to participate in this sensing task based on the sensing user's offer. The candidate uploads the sensing data to the miner, who verifies the quality grade of the sensing data. Afterwards, the miner estimates the value of the data by combining the user's offer and the quality grade of the sensing data, selects the candidate who offers the highest value of data as the winning bidder for this sensing task, and sends the validation results to the data demander. The data demander validates and pays the user r^*. The value of the sensing user uploaded data is used as the criterion for granting the reward, and a suitable reward r_{ui} is given. Thus, depending on the value of the sensing data $value_i$, users receive different sensing rewards.

4.1 Posting Sensing Tasks

The sensing user, the data demander, needs to complete registration and pay a deposit when entering the blockchain network. At this stage, the data demander publishes the sensing task. Firstly, the data demander signs the $Sig_{SK_{demand}}(CS - Task)$ for the sensing task with his private key SK_{demand} and then posts the signature on the blockchain network together with the sensing task announcement. The sensing task announcement includes information such as task type, task requirements, number threshold N, and quality announcement. In the quality announcement, the data demander gives a specific data quality rating indicator $y^{(j)} = \left\{ y_1^{(i)}, y_2^{(i)}, \ldots, y_k^{(i)} \right\}$ and a corresponding grade of payoff $R = \{r_1, r_2, \ldots, r_k\}$. The higher the grade of data, the higher the payoff, and the lower the grade, the lower the payoff. In addition, the data demander gives a deposit M based on the expected total remuneration and a task deadline.

4.2 Select the Winning Bidder

The system is based on a reverse auction design incentive mechanism, which is divided into two phases. In the first stage, the sensing user participates in an auction bid, and the miner selects the candidates to participate in this sensing task based on the user's offer; in the second stage, the candidates upload the sensing data to the miner, who calculates the quality grade of the sensing data. Finally, the miner calculates the value of the sensing data by the user's offer and the quality grade of the sensing data, and selects the winning bidder to participate in this sensing task based on the value of the data.

Select Candidate

This phase miners determine the eligibility of people to participate in the sensing task. The user reads the sensing task $CS - Task$ posted by the data demander and evaluates the sensing cost and decides whether to participate in the bidding. The actual benefits accruing to the user are:

$$profit_{ui} = r_{ui} - min_{ci} \tag{1}$$

The r_{ui} is the reward received by the user for participating in the sensing task and c_i is the total cost of the user's participation in the sensing task.

When $profit_{ui} > 0$, the sensing user participates in this sensing task as a bidder and makes an offer. This paper uses a reverse auction model, i.e. one buyer with multiple sellers. There are competitors for the sensing user to participate in the sensing task, so the user will offer as rationally as possible. The miner ranks the offers of the participating sensing task users from lowest to highest $P\{p_1, p_2, \ldots, p_n | p_1 < p_2 <, \ldots, < p_n, n > N\}$, where n is the number of bidders who want to participate in this sensing task and N is the number of data demanders required to participate in the sensing task. In order to ensure the overall social welfare, the number of bidders involved is required to be greater than the number of data demanders required for this sensing task, otherwise the sensing task is not performed. Since then, the first phase of selection has begun. In order to avoid situations such as bidders uploading data that does not meet the data demander's requirements, the miner selects the top n^* bidders in descending order of price as the winning candidate $P\{p_1, p_2, \ldots, p_{n*} | n > n^* > N\}$. The top n^* users selected, use the user's private key SK_{ui} to calculate the signature $Sig_{SK_{ui}}(Hash(Data_{ui}))$ of the sensing data as the voucher for redeeming the reward, and upload the voucher together with the sensing data $Data_{ui}$ after attaching it to the miner.

Calculating the Quality Grade of Sensing Data

After the winning candidate uploads the sensing data, the miner calculates the quality grade of the sensing data according to the constraints in the data demander's release announcement.

In this paper, we assume that the data demanders are large Internet companies such as Google, Amazon, Uber, etc. The sensing data can only be useful if it is uploaded to professionals. At the stage of publishing the sensing task, the data demander will give the criteria to determine the grade of the sensing data, i.e., the label $y^{(j)} = \left\{ y_1^{(i)}, y_2^{(i)}, \ldots, y_k^{(i)} \right\}$ that can be given to classify the sensing data. $y^{(j)}$ can take k different values, and k represents the classification of the sensing data into k grades.

$$y^{(j)} = \begin{bmatrix} y_1^{(i)} \\ y_2^{(i)} \\ \vdots \\ yk^{(i)} \end{bmatrix} \sim \left\{ \begin{bmatrix} 1 \\ 0 \\ \vdots \\ 0 \end{bmatrix}, \begin{bmatrix} 0 \\ 1 \\ \vdots \\ 0 \end{bmatrix}, \ldots, \begin{bmatrix} 0 \\ 0 \\ \vdots \\ 1 \end{bmatrix} \right\} \tag{2}$$

Therefore, this paper uses a classification algorithm from supervised learning to determine the quality grade of the sensing data. In practice, data demanders will maximize their interests by weighing the accuracy and complexity of classification criteria to classify multiple grades, so this paper chooses a generalized Softmax regression algorithm from logistic regression to achieve the need for supervised, multiple classifications when miners judge data grades.

In this paper, a continuous piece of sensing data is used as an example (e.g. audio data). For convenience, the audio data is divided into τ workload matrices $X = \{x_1, x_2, \ldots, x_\tau\}$. In step 1, $X = \{x_1, x_2, \ldots, x_\tau\}$ is put as input into a Softmax regression model to train and calculate the grade of the sensing data.

$$
\text{grade}_i = h_\theta(x^{(i)}) =
\begin{bmatrix}
P(y^{(i)} = 1 | x^{(i)}; \theta) \\
P(y^{(i)} = 2 | x^{(i)}; \theta) \\
\vdots \\
P(y^{(i)} = k | x^{(i)}; \theta)
\end{bmatrix}
= \frac{1}{\sum_{j=1}^{k} e^{\theta_j^T x(i)}}
\begin{bmatrix}
e^{\theta_1^T x(i)} \\
e^{\theta_2^T x(i)} \\
\vdots \\
e^{\theta_k^T x(i)}
\end{bmatrix}
\tag{3}
$$

where $\theta_1, \theta_2, \ldots, \theta_k \in R^{n+1}$ is a parameter of the linear regression model, $e^{\theta_j^T x^{(i)}} \geq 0$, and $\sum_{j=1}^{k} e^{\theta_j^T x^{(i)}} = 1 . p(y^{(i)} = \delta | x^{(i)}; \theta)$ represents the probability of each workload matrix $x^{(i)}$ being classified into δ grades.

In step 2, the cross-entropy method is used to determine the loss function of the Softmax regression model and to calculate the difference between the trained results of the model and the actual values.

$$
J(\theta) = -\frac{1}{m} \left[\sum_{i=1}^{m} \sum_{j=1}^{k} 1\{y^{(i)} = j\} \log \frac{e^{\theta_j^T x^{(i)}}}{\sum_{l=1}^{k} e^{\theta_l^T x^{(i)}}} \right]
\tag{4}
$$

In step 3, the parameters θ of the model are adjusted using the gradient descent method to reduce the gap between the results trained by the model and the actual values.

$$
\nabla_{\theta_j} J(\theta) = -\frac{1}{m} \sum_{i=1}^{m} \left[x^{(i)} \left(1\{y^{(i)} = j\} - P(y^{(i)} = j | x^{(i)}; \theta) \right) \right]
\tag{5}
$$

Step 4, update the parameter θ.

$$
\theta_j = \theta_j - \alpha \nabla_{\theta_j} J(\theta)
\tag{6}
$$

By continuously updating the parameters and substituting the updated parameters back into Eq. (3) to start a new round of training, the minimum value of the loss function $minJ(\theta^*)$ is finally found, at which point the parameter θ^* is the optimal parameter found by the Softmax model. Since then, substituting the parameter θ^* into Eq. (3) will result in the grade $h_{\theta^*}(x^{(i)})$ of this sensing data.

Calculating the Value of Sensing Data

After the miner verifies the quality grade of the sensing data, the value of each piece of data is calculated by selecting a price factor α and a data grade factor β based on the different requirements for price and data quality grade in the sensing task announcement posted by the data demander, taking into account the offers of the winning candidates and the quality grade of the sensing data provided.

$$value_i = \alpha p_i + \beta h_{\theta*}\left(x^{(i)}\right) \tag{7}$$

The p_i is the bidder's offer and $h_{\theta*}\left(x^{(i)}\right)$ is the sensing data quality grade.

Among the n^* candidates, the top N candidates are selected as the winning bidders for this perception task by ranking the $\{value | value_1 > value_2 > \ldots > value_{n*}\}$ of the winning bidders $value_i$ selected in the first stage from highest to lowest.

4.3 Remuneration Allocation

After the winning bidder is selected, the miner announces the winning bidder of this sensing task on the blockchain. It also encrypts the sensing data and the signature $Sig_{SK_{ui}}(Hash(Data_{ui}))$ of the sensing user with the public key PK_{demand} of the data demander who published the sensing task this time, and forwards it to the data demander. If the data demander can decrypt successfully with their own private key SK_{demand}, they have successfully obtained the sensing data and have successfully authenticated themselves.

It is assumed that the data demander is professional and rational. After acquiring the sensing data, the data demander tests the validity of the sensing data and verifies that the miner verifies the correctness of the sensing data grade. After the data demander has verified the completion of the verification, it issues a corresponding payment to the sensing user. At this point, the data demander uses the user's public key PK_{ui} to decode the signature. If the data demander succeeds in decoding the signature, it successfully authenticates the identity of the user u_i, and then gives the user the payment, otherwise no payment is given, thus completing the work of authenticating the user u_i. In addition, the data demander receives the ciphertext and calculates the digest of the plaintext, and compares the digest decrypted with the public key of the user u_i with the calculated digest, if it is consistent, the data has not been tampered with. This completes the authentication of the sensing data integrity and effectively prevents data tampering.

5 System Analysis

5.1 Safety Analysis

The system introduces blockchain technology in the crowdsensing application. Blockchain technology can be used to solve the problem of trust deficit caused by trusted third parties. Blockchain is traceable, trustless, decentralized, untamperable and anonymous. Using consensus mechanism, asymmetric encryption and blockchain structure, it can establish reliable trust relationship between unknown parties and realize information interaction between nodes. In the incentive mechanism designed by this system, the data demander releases the sensing task, the user uploads the sensing data, and the data demander gives the user remuneration, all of which are packaged and recorded in the blockchain, effectively solving the security problems such as the non-transparent operation process brought about by the intervention of trusted third parties. Miners act as sensing data grade verifiers in this system and select the sensing users who participate in the sensing tasks. As an uninterested party, the miner verifies the grade of the sensing data in a more trustworthy way than if it were verified by the server or self-checked by the sensing user.

5.2 Performance Analysis

Reverse Auction Model

The system considers the application scenario of one data demander and many potential sensing users, and uses a reverse auction model to design the incentive mechanism. In the first stage, through auction bidding, miners select the winning candidate based on the user's offer, eliminating irrational offers at this stage and ensuring the interests of the data demander. In the second stage, miners verify the quality grade of the sensing data uploaded by the winning candidate. The elimination of irrational bids in the first stage reduces the workload for miners to verify the quality grade of the sensing data in the second stage, which improves the efficiency of performing the sensing task. At the same time, the reduced workload of the miners means that the miners need to be paid less for the sensing tasks and the sensing users get paid more, increasing the incentive effect of the system.

Comparative Classifier Accuracy

The amount of crowdsensing data is huge and requires specialist equipment and researchers to make the most of the crowdsensing data, so it is important that the data demander can give specialist rating metrics for processing the sensing data for classification. Therefore, this paper uses a supervised learning-based classification algorithm to classify the grade of sensing data, and gives the user a corresponding payment according to the grade of sensing data estimated by the classification algorithm, which has an overwhelming advantage over the normal pricing mechanism with a uniform price for all users, and not only motivates the user to upload more usable sensing data, but also reduces the loss of benefits for the data demander.

The accuracy of the different classifiers was compared using the training and test sets respectively, and the results are shown in Fig. 5. The accuracy of a classifier is the ratio of the result of the classification algorithm in classifying a sample to the result of the true classification of the sample. The red solid line represents the accuracy of the training set and the green solid line represents the accuracy of the test set. the accuracy of the Softmax algorithm is approximately 0.93 for the training set and 0.86 for the test set. As can be seen from the figure, the Softmax regression algorithm has a certain guarantee of the accuracy of the sample classification results, so this system uses the Softmax regression algorithm for determining the quality grade of the sensing data.

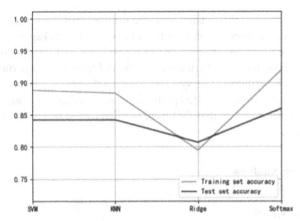

Fig. 5. Comparison of the accuracy of different classifiers

5.3 Simulation Results and Analysis

The incentive mechanism designed in this system is based on the reverse auction model. In the first stage, the sensing user offers a price and the miner selects a candidate based on the user's offer to enter the second stage; in the second stage, the miner verifies the quality grade of the sensing data uploaded by the candidate and then selects the winning bidder based on the candidate's offer and the quality grade of the sensing data. It appears that the focus and difficulty in implementing the incentive mechanism described in this system is to determine the sensing data quality grade so that the data demander can pay the user accordingly according to the different quality grades.

The simulation experiments to verify the quality grade of the sensing data are shown in Fig. 6. In the figure, the vertical coordinates represent the 3 different labels given by the data demander, representing each of the 3 different grades. The horizontal coordinate indicates the sample number. A piece of sensing data is divided into 50 samples $X = \{x_1, x_2, \ldots, x_{50}\}$, and each of these 50 samples is mapped to a different grade according to the label given by the data demander. The red dots represent the true classification results of the samples, while the green dots represent the results of classifying the samples using the Softmax regression algorithm. If the red dots overlap with the green, the Softmax regression algorithm classifies the sample in the same way as the true classification of the sample. Conversely, the classification result is inconsistent. The simulation results are shown in the figure, the input set of this sensing data is mapped in rank one, according to the rules, the miner classifies this sensing data as rank one, and the data demander should give this user the payoff of rank one.

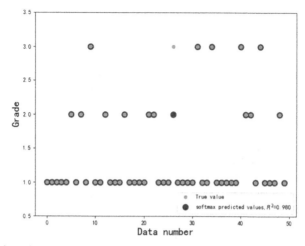

Fig. 6. Softmax regression algorithm calculates sensing data quality grades

6 Conclusion

This paper proposes a distributed architecture using blockchain security to solve the problem of the existence of a third-party transaction control center in the Crowdsensing incentive mechanism. In response to the inherent performance bottleneck of blockchain, a reverse auction model is introduced to reduce the workload of miners while increasing the incentive effect on users. Softmax regression algorithm is used to determine the quality grade of sensing data uploaded by users, which motivates users to upload high quality sensing data and ensures the benefits of data demanders. The accuracy and feasibility of the incentive mechanism are verified by simulation experiments. In future research, we will consider the contradiction between incentive and privacy, and introduce encryption technology to solve the problems of user identity privacy leakage and sensing data theft. We will also consider the cross-chain sensing data sharing problem to motivate more users to participate in data sharing and increase the utility of sensing data.

Acknowledgement. This work is supported by the Key Research and Development Project of Sichuan Province (No.2021YFSY0012, No. 2020YFG0307, No.2021YFG0332), the Key Research and Development Project of Cheng du (No. 2019-YF05–02028-GX), the Innovation Team of Quantum Security Communication of Sichuan Province (No.17TD0009), the Academic and Technical Leaders Training Funding Support Projects of Sichuan Province (No. 2016120080102643).

References

1. Liu, W., Yang, Y., Wang, E., Han, Z., Wang, X.: Prediction based user selection in time-sensitive mobile crowdsensing. In: 14th Annual IEEE International Conference on Sensing, Communication, and Networking (SECON), pp. 1–9 (2017)
2. Guo, B., Yu, Z., Zhang, D.: From participatory sensing to mobile crowd sensing. IEEE (2014)

3. Zhan, Y., Xia, Y., Zhang, J.: Incentive mechanism design in mobile opportunistic data collection with time sensitivity. IEEE Internet Things J. **5**, 246–256 (2018)
4. Islam, M.A., Mahmud, H., Ren, S.: A carbon-aware incentive mechanism for greening colocation data centers. IEEE Trans. Cloud Comput. **8**, pp. 1–1 (2017)
5. Rezai, A.A., Torki, L.: The impact of the electronic money development in the profitability of DBS banks of Singapore. In: 8th International Conference on e-Commerce in Developing Countries: With Focus on e-Trust, pp. 1–9 (2014)
6. Zhang, L., Liu, B.X., Zhang, R.Y.: Blockchain technology overview. Comput. Eng. **45**(5), 1–12 (2019)
7. Nakamoto, S.: Bitcoin: a peer-to-peer electronic cash system (2008)
8. Yuan, Y., Wang, F.Y.: Blockchain development status and outlook. Zidonghua Xuebao/Acta Autom. Sin. **42**(4), 481–494 (2016)
9. Peng, D., Wu, F., Chen, G.H.: Pay as how well you do: a quality based incentive mechanism for crowdsensing. In: ACM, pp.177–186 (2015)
10. Jin, H., Su, L., Ding, B.: Enabling privacy-preserving incentives for mobile crowd sensing systems. In: 2016 IEEE 36th International Conference on Distributed Computing Systems (ICDCS), pp. 344–353 (2016)
11. He, Y., Li, H., Cheng, X., Liu, Y., Yang, C., Sun, L.: A blockchain based truthful incentive mechanism for distributed p2p applications. IEEE Access **6**, 27324–27335 (2018)
12. Li, M., Weng, J., Yang, A.: CrowdBC: a blockchain-based decentralized framework for crowdsourcing. IEEE Trans. Parallel Distrib. Syst. **30**, 1251–1266 (2018)
13. Wang, J., Li, M., He, Y.: A blockchain based privacy-preserving incentive mechanism in crowdsensing applications. IEEE Access **6**, 17545–17556 (2018)
14. Wu, Y., Zeng, J.R., Peng, H.: Survey on incentive mechanisms for crowd sensing. J. Softw. **27**(8), 2025–2047 (2016)
15. Lee, J.S., Hoh, B.: Sell your experiences: a market mechanism based incentive for participatory sensing. In: 2010 IEEE International Conference on Pervasive Computing and Communications, pp. 60–68 (2010)
16. Kawajiri, R., Shimosaka, M., Kashima, H.: Steered crowdsensing: Incentive design towards quality-oriented place-centric crowdsensing. In: Proceedings of the 2014 ACM International Joint Conference on Pervasive and Ubiquitous Computing, pp. 691–701 (2014)
17. Wen, Y.: Quality-driven auction-based incentive mechanism for mobile crowd sensing. IEEE Trans. Veh. Technol. **64**, 4203–4214 (2015)
18. Dong, Z., Li, X.Y., Ma, H.: Budget-Feasible online incentive mechanisms for crowdsourcing tasks truthfully. IEEE/ACM Trans. Netw. **24**(2), 647–661 (2016)
19. Wu, H., Ma, H.: Quality-oriented incentive mechanism for video delivery in opportunistic networks. In: Proceeding of IEEE International Symposium on a World of Wireless, Mobile and Multimedia Networks, pp. 1–6 (2014)

BFAC-CS: A Blockchain-Based Fine-Grained Access Control Scheme for Complex Scenarios

Huailin Pu[1], Wunan Wan[1,2(✉)], Zhi Qin[1,2], Jinquan Zhang[1,2], Qiulu Jiang[1,2], Shibin Zhang[1,2], and Jinyue Xia[3]

[1] School of Cybersecurity, Chengdu University of Information Technology, Chengdu 610255, China
nan_wwn@cuit.edu.cn
[2] Advanced Cryptography and System Security Key Laboratory of Sichuan Province, Chengdu 610255, China
[3] International Business Machines Corporation (IBM), New York, New York 10041NY212, USA

Abstract. Blockchain technology is becoming increasingly mature and has a great deal of research in a variety of industries. Because of its characteristics such as unalterable, decentralized and unforgeable, it has become a general trend that blockchain technology becomes the infrastructure of various technologies. Therefore, there are many studies on the application of blockchain combined with access control technology. Role-based access control (RBAC), as an important tool of system information management, has become a security solution recognized by many enterprises, but in many complex scenarios, the roles in the system will be more redundant, and the permissions between roles are likely to conflict. In order to solve the problems of RBAC, which is difficult to control the roles in complex scenarios and the role explosion caused by frequent creation and revocation of roles, and to manage the access permissions more finely without losing the comprehensibility of the system, we propose BFAC-CS, a blockchain-based access control scheme combining RBAC and ABAC, using smart contracts as a means to implement its entire framework. We designed three contracts to manage user's role, attributes and permission. In this scheme, attributes are appended to user's role, so that in some complex scenarios, the creation and deletion of role will not be so frequent. Modifying the corresponding attributes of the role can achieve the purpose of changing the user's access permission, and the management of user's permission is more detailed. We used Solidity to write these smart contracts and deployed them on test network for testing, and evaluated the cost and security of the whole scheme.

Keywords: Blockchain · Access control · Role · Attribute · Smart contract

1   Introduction

As one of the most important resources in the Internet era, the control of information data is extremely important. The privacy and trustworthiness of data resources have always been a focus of great concern for all industries. The emergence of access control technology has solved the problem of access management of information data in various industries to a certain extent. Access control technology is used in almost all systems, including computer systems and non-computer systems, and it achieves access control to resources by identifying resources according to their characteristics, restricting them to one side, and restricting users to the other side with identity or other definitions related to the user who request access. Resources can only be accessed by the users who meet the access policy or requirements of the attribute restrictions. Traditional access control methods include discretionary access control (DAC) and mandatory access control (MAC), role-based access control (RBAC) [1], task-based access control (TBAC), attribute-based access control (ABAC) [2], etc.

Although the traditional access control technology has played a great role in solving the problem of management of access authority to resource, there are still many problems, such as single point of failure, low reliability, and difficulty in ensuring trustworthiness. In a centralized access control system, the access control server may be the bottleneck of the whole system, and once the access control server breaks down, the whole system will be affected, so a distributed system will provide a good solution. Blockchain is a peer-to-peer distributed system with a large number of peer nodes forming a network to jointly verify the information on blockchain. These decentralized, transparent, unalterable and unforgeable features provide a good solution for access control. There were research cases of blockchain combined with access control as early as 2017 [3], which were early solutions on Bitcoin and did not yet involve smart contract. In the subsequent studies, especially with the emergence of Ethereum and Hyperledger Fabric, possessing smart contracts makes the realization of access control technology on the blockchain closer to reality than Bitcoin blockchain.

1.1   Contributions

- We developed a fine-grained access control scheme based on Ethereum to implement RBAC combined with ABAC. It makes user's authority management more refined and flexible in complex scenarios, and makes smart contracts less expensive to execute.
- We wrote the code of the smart contracts and deployed it on test network for testing and analyzing the execution cost.

1.2   Structure

The structure of this paper is as follows: Sect. 2 makes a background introduction to blockchain and access control, Sect. 3 reviews related work, Sect. 4 describes the design of the whole system, Sect. 5 analyzes the security of the system, Sect. 6 is the implementation and performance evaluation of the system, and Sect. 7 concludes the paper.

2 Background

2.1 Blockchain

The earliest implementation form of blockchain technology is Bitcoin proposed by Satoshi Nakamoto [4], which is a representative work of the blockchain 1.0 era. Essentially, Blockchain is a peer-to-peer distributed database maintained by multiple peer nodes, which we call miners. A blockchain is formally composed of multiple blocks connected end to end in chronological order, each block contains a block header and a block body. The block header consists of the version number, previous block's hash value, Merkle root, timestamp, nonce value, and difficulty target, and the block body contains the information of the transaction, which exists in the form of hash values in the block. In the blockchain with proof-of-work as the consensus mechanism, the nonce value is computed by miners, a process known as mining. After the calculation is completed, miner will use the Merkle tree as the block body and add the block header to form a new block, and add it to the blockchain.

After more than a decade of development, great progress has been made in the field of blockchain technology, and a new generation of network architecture with blockchain technology as the core is under intensive construction. The incorporation of smart contract marks that blockchain has entered the 2.0 era and is mainly applied in the financial field. Ethereum is one of the most representative blockchain platforms. Subsequently, blockchain has been applied more widely, with a large number of applications in the fields of Internet of Things [5, 21, 22], healthcare [6, 23], and big data [7], surpassing the economic field and covering various industries, which is the blockchain 3.0 stage. Many excellent blockchain platforms have also emerged, such as Hyperledger Fabric, Ethereum, etc.

2.2 Access Control

Access control technology has been developed for many years and is used in almost all systems, because the management of information and resources is a problem faced by all industries, it is necessary to consider which resources can be accessed and which resources cannot be accessed. The core of access control technology is the rules for assigning permissions to access requesters, which are divided into various access control technologies according to different rules. This paper uses role-based access control and attribute-based access control.

Role-based access control was first proposed by Ravi Sandhu. In this access control mode, a role representing a certain permission is established between the user and the access permission. If a user is assigned a specific role, it means that the user has the corresponding privileges. For example, if a user is assigned the role of teacher, then he has the right to access the student's assignments.

Attribute-based access control defines access rules based on attributes such as subject attribute set (access subject), resource attribute set (access object), environment attribute and action attribute, and the access subject can have access rights only if the access policy and rules are satisfied. ABAC has high flexibility and more accurate control of rights, and the access rights of the access subject can be changed by simply changing the attribute values.

3 Related Work

There have been many research cases based on blockchain to implement access control technology. Aafaf Ouaddah et al. [8] developed FairAccess, one of the earliest applications of blockchain combined with access control. This scheme establishes a decentralized blockchain-based access control framework and creates a new type of transaction to grant, revoke access permission to user. After this, JASON PAUL CRUZ et al. [9] proposed a role-based access control system by means of smart contract and proposed a challenge-response protocol to verify the user's identity when he requests access permission. However, the problems about RBAC itself, such as role explosion, are not well resolved. Yuanyu Zhang et al. [10] proposed an ACL-based access control framework with smart contract to store ACLs, but since the object and contract are in a one-to-one responsible relationship, the execution cost of the contract is relatively high. This author also proposed a distributed smart city access control framework [11], which implements access control with smart contract. Yepeng Ding et al. [12] proposed Bloccess, a fine-grained access control framework with permission blockchain technology, which provides a solution for implementing trusted access control in distributed untrustworthy environment. Sheng Gao et al. [13] proposed TrustAccess, a blockchain-based trusted secure access control system, and designed a HP-CP-ABE ciphertext policy and attribute hiding scheme based on CP-ABE. Priyanka Kamboj et al. [14] proposed an RBAC model to manage role assignment in organizations, completed the model implementation with blockchain smart contract, and designed a threat and security model to resist attacks. Qiliang Yang et al. [15] developed a non-interactive, attribute-based access control scheme that aims to protect the privacy of data requester's attributes and data holder's attributes and access policies. Sheng Ding et al. [16] proposed an attribute-based access control scheme for the Internet of Things that leverages the benefits of blockchain to solve the problem of traditional access control technology such as single point of failure, and simplify the management of access. Hao Chen et al. [17] proposed a task attribute-based blockchain access control technique for IoT that combines task-based and attribute-based access control techniques and is able to dynamically assign privileges to users.

4 BFAC-CS Scheme

In this section, we elaborate on the proposed system of the access control scheme in complex environments. The system is divided into five parts: user (U), role manager (RM), attribute manager (AM), permission manager (PM) and resource (R). U, RM, AM and PM each have a pair of keys (i.e., private key and public key), an Ethereum address, and an externally owned account (EOA). We take the hospital scenario as an example, but it is not limited to this, but also includes other more complex scenarios. The user, as the access requester, who includes all kinds of people in the hospital. We specify the user's general function by applying for a role from RM, and then applies for the role's corresponding attributes from the AM to specify the user's permission within his responsibilities. Resource include data such as patient's medical records. Blockchain is used here as the deployment environment for smart contract to ensure that information such as user's role and attributes are unalterable and credible, and to complete the verification of access policies. If the user wants to access the resource, then he needs to pass PM's inspection. It should be noted that the resource is not stored on the blockchain. The blockchain only manages the role and role's attributes, as well as the user's access permission check for resource, and grants the user access permission according to the access policy.

4.1 System Model

In order to conveniently express the user's role, attribute and permission status, we make the following definitions.

- $U = \{u_1, u_2, u_3, \ldots, u_n\}$, U denotes the set of user, $u_i(i \in (0,1,\ldots,n))$ denotes a single user.
- $C = \{c_1, c_2, c_3, \ldots, c_n\}$, C denotes the set of role, $c_i(i \in (0,1,\ldots,n))$ denotes a single role.
- $CAttr = \{c_i | cattr_1, cattr_2, cattr_3, \ldots, cattr_n\}$, CAttr denotes the attributes set corresponding to c_i, $cattr_i$ denotes a single role attribute.
- $R = \{r_1, r_1, r_1, \ldots, r_n\}$, R denotes the set of resource objects, $r_i(i \in (0,1,2,\ldots,n))$ denotes a single resource object.
- $RAttr = \{r_i | rattr_1, rattr_2, rattr_3, \ldots, rattr_n\}$, RAttr denotes the attributes set corresponding to r_i, $rattr_i$ denotes a single resource attribute.
- $u_i = \{c_i | cattr_1, cattr_2, cattr_3, \ldots, cattr_j\}$, $j \in n$, u_i represents a user who is assigned a role and the role is also assigned the corresponding attributes.

User. The user is the resource access requester of this system. He uses his address (u_i address) to request a role from RM and an attribute from PM to get access to the corresponding resource.

Role Manager. RM uses its EOA to deploy the role management contract, after deployment the contract will have a contract address through which external parties can call some methods of the contract. RM is responsible for the assignment, deletion and state transition of user's role.

Attribute Manager. Similar to RM, he uses an external account to deploy the attribute management contract and acts as the sole executor of some methods, and is responsible for the assignment and change of the corresponding attribute of the role.

Permission Manager. When a user requests access to a resource, PM is responsible for checking whether the user's role and attributes meet the access policy of the accessed resource, that is, whether the attributes of both parties match, and if they do, granting the user access permission.

Resource. The resource is the object to be accessed, and its own attributes will be uploaded to the blockchain. For example, in the example mentioned above, the patient's medical record information will be the resource to be accessed, then the patient can be uniquely identified with attributes such as inpatient department, department, floor number and ward number, which can also be used as an access policy to control access permission.

The structure of the whole system is shown below (see Fig. 1).

1. *Apply-1*: u_i requests a role from RM. *Issue-1*: RM assigns a role to u_i. $u_i = \{c_i\}$.
2. *Apply-2*: u_i requests attributes corresponding to role of u_i from AM. *Issue-2*: AM assigns attributes to u_i, $u_i = \{c_i|cattr_1,cattr_2,cattr_3,...,cattr_j\}, j \in n$.
3. User requests access to resource from PM, to obtain access to the specified resource.
4. *Check*: PM judges whether the user is qualified to access such resources according to his role, and if so, then judges the following Eq. (1) holds according to the attributes of his role and resource object.

$$\{cattr_1, cattr_2, cattr_3, \ldots, cattr_n\} = \{rattr_1, rattr_2, rattr_3, \ldots, rattr_n\} \quad (1)$$

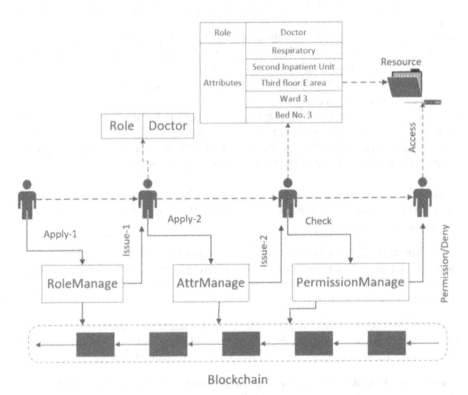

Fig. 1. System architecture.

In complex scenarios, we need to control access permission to the point where they can be flexibly changed, and the fine granularity of this system is reflected in the precision control of user's access permission. In the previous role-based access control schemes, a role determines the scope of user's access permission, while in our proposed scheme (see Fig. 2), the scope of user's access permission is accurate to a small part of a certain type of permission. This has both the advantages of role-based schemes and attribute-based schemes.

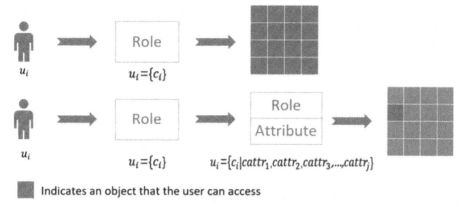

Indicates an object that the user can access

Fig. 2. Permission changes.

4.2 Smart Contract

In order to manage user's information, assign role to user, and assign attributes to role, we designed three smart contracts, including Role Management Smart Contract (RMAC), for managing roles for users, Attribute Management Smart Contract (AMSC), for managing attributes for users, Permission Manage Smart Contract (PMSC), for checking users' permissions.

Role Management Smart Contract. This contract is responsible for granting (addUser), removing (removeUser) role to user and changing the status of user (changeStatus), and these functions can only be executed by RM. We use the Ethereum address as a unique identifier for user. If the user is a doctor, then giving him the role of doctor will give him the general privileges and responsibilities of a doctor, and further privileges need to be determined by the role's attributes. The role can be regarded as a resident attribute of a user.

addUser(u_i.address, u_i.role, u_i.name): This function first checks whether the user applying for the role already exists in the blockchain, if not, it uses the user's address on Ethereum to identify the user, and records the basic information of the user, including the user name, and assigns the role to the user, and then uploads this information to the blockchain.

removeUser(u_i.address): This function checks whether the user exists according to his address, if so, the user will be removed from the user list directly, and the user's role and attributes will also be removed.

changeStatus(u_i.address, u_i.status): If we don't want to delete the user directly but deactivate the user, then this function will change the user's status from active to inactive, and the role and attribute information of the user in inactive will lose its validity but will still be kept in the blockchain. We only need to change the user's status when we enable the user's function and permission again.

Attribute Management Smart Contract. When a user is assigned a certain role, AM can assign corresponding attributes to the user according to the user's role through this contract. The contract includes attribute assignment (addAttr) and attribute change (changeAttr), and they can only be executed by AM. For example, we can assign attributes such as department, inpatient department ID, ward ID and bed ID to the role of doctor, and we can assign attributes such as floor ID and partition ID to the role of general staff, so that we can be more detailed in the management of staff authority.

addAttr(u_i.address, u_i.attributes): Based on the user's address, AM can know user's role. If the user's role is doctor, then only the relevant attributes of doctor can be assigned to him. The user's attributes are determined by parameters of this function.

changeAttr(u_i.address, u_i.attributes): This function is responsible for the change of user's attributes.

Permission Management Contract. PMSC is responsible for user's permission check. There is only one function – check.

check(u_i.address): It first check the user's role, then compare the user's attributes with the attributes of the resource object, if it matches, the check will be passed and the user will be granted access to the resource. For example, if a user in the hospital wants to access patient's information, the first thing to do is to check whether the user's role is a doctor, then proceed to the next step of attribute detection, assuming that the attributes of the doctor are {respiratory department, first inpatient unit, ward 1, bed 2}, then the doctor can access the patient's information with the same attributes {respiratory department, first inpatient unit, ward 1, bed 2}.

5 Security Analysis

5.1 Ultra Vires Attack Resistant

In traditional access control technology, taking role-based access control as an example, after a user is assigned a role, he gets access permission to a resource corresponding to his role. However, this permission may contain permission other than the resource requested by the user. Malicious users can exploit this vulnerability. In our solution, the user's attributes control the user's access permission to an accurate range, so it can resist ultra vires attack.

5.2 Collusion Attack Resistant

Complicity attack means that, in the system, none of the attributes of two users can satisfy the access policy of a certain resource, while their attributes union can satisfy it, then they can unite to request access permission. In the scheme, the user's role can only determine the category of resources he can access, which is a broad range of permissions, but the specific access objects are still determined by his attributes, and these attributes can only be modified by the attribute manager. Once these attributes are uploaded to blockchain, so the collusion of malicious users cannot share attributes to satisfy the access policy during permission detection.

6 Implementation and Performance Analysis

To test our proposed scheme, we used Remix [18] as the IDE to develop our smart contracts and set up Truffle [19] and Ganache [20] on Ubuntu 20.04 (virtual machine) as test environment. Truffle mainly provides us with a method to deploy and invoke smart contracts on test network (see Fig. 3).

```
truffle(development)> instance.addUser(accounts[1],"nurse","alice",{from:account
s[0]})
{
  tx: '0xec5a5984e8de68b956388acc18ab72cf174a45fad14a0a450ccec426820ed9bb',
  receipt: {
    transactionHash: '0xec5a5984e8de68b956388acc18ab72cf174a45fad14a0a450ccec426
820ed9bb',
    transactionIndex: 0,
    blockHash: '0x8967cb78e96298563d20e44eefb8cf492845fed1dfb6c8da6aa173be5bd3e7
c3',
    blockNumber: 3,
    from: '0x595f12c53c490ddf742b368f90f4008d89511e10',
    to: '0xc7ec0232ae1bf3453a1b8652c719339673bf3fda',
    gasUsed: 130940,
    cumulativeGasUsed: 130940,
    contractAddress: null,
    logs: [],
    status: true,
```

Fig. 3. Calling smart contracts in Truffle.

When the methods of smart contract are executed on Ethereum, if the contract states are changed, the execution process will consume gas. Gas is a unit of measurement in Ethereum network as a price for consuming computing power. Gas consumption is related to gas unit price and gas usage. Transaction fee Fees = Gas Used * Gas price. The maximum gas consumed by transaction is limited by the gas limit in the network, and gas price is usually variable, and can be set by the user himself. The unit price is too low, and the time for processing transactions will often be prolonged. In this test network, we set the gas price to 1000000000, which is 1gwei, 1gwei is equal to 0.000000001eth. The implementation costs of our scheme are shown in Table 1.

Table 1. Smart contract execution cost consumption.

Functions	Gas fee	Tx cost (Ether)
Contract creation	2444780	0.002445
addUser	130940	0.000130
removeUser	22945	0.000023
changeStatus	14533	0.000015
addAttr	31167	0.000031
changeAttr	31101	0.000031
CHECK	29512	0,000030

Because the user's permission may change frequently in complex scenarios. In our proposed scheme, changing permissions is an attribute change. In the previous role-based access control solution, this is equal to the cost of role removal plus the cost of role addition. We tested the gas consumption for handling user permission changes in this scenario and made the relevant calculations. The gas consumption is shown in Table 2.

Table 2. Gas consumption of different schemes.

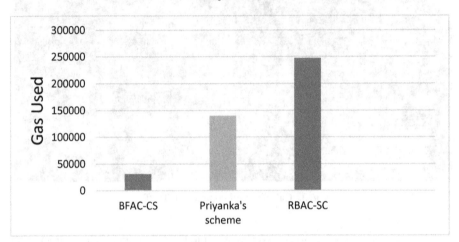

7 Conclusion

We propose an access control scheme combining role and attribute on the blockchain, which aims to provide a fine-grained access control scheme for complex scenarios. It regards role as a resident attribute of user, that is, the role generally is not changed, and changes in permission is more related to changes in user's attributes. This provides a good idea for access control technology in complex scenarios. Not only the control of permissions is more refined, but the cost of implementation is also reduced. We have successfully written smart contracts and deployed them in the test network, but the solution and contract design are not yet perfect, and we still need to supplement our scheme and the code of smart contracts.

Acknowledgement. This work is supported by the Key Research and Development Project of Sichuan Province (No.2021YFSY0012, No. 2020YFG0307, No.2021YFG0332), the Key Research and Development Project of Chengdu (No. 2019-YF05–02028-GX), the Innovation Team of Quantum Security Communication of Sichuan Province (No.17TD0009), the Academic and Technical Leaders Training Funding Support Projects of Sichuan Province (No.2016120080102643).

References

1. Sandhu, R.S., Coyne, E.J., Feinstein, H.L., Youman, C.E.: Role-based access control models. Computer **29**(2), 38–47 (1996)
2. Hu, V.C., Kuhn, D.R., Ferraiolo, D.F., Voas, J.: Attribute-based access control. Computer **48**(2), 85–88 (2015)
3. Maesa, D., Mori, P., Ricci, L.: Blockchain Based Access Control. Springer, Cham Springer, Cham (2017)
4. Nakamoto, S.: Bitcoin. https://bitcoin.org/bitcoin.pdf (2009)
5. Dlimi, Z., Ezzati, A., Alla, S.B.: A lightweight blockchain for IoT in smart city (IoT-SmartChain). Comput. Mater. Contin. **69**(2), 2687–2703 (2021)
6. Jaishankar, B., Vishwakarma, S., Mohan, P., Kumar, A., Patel, I.: Blockchain for securing healthcare data using squirrel search optimization algorithm. Intell. Autom. Soft Comput. **32**(3), 1815–1829 (2022)
7. Xu, C.: Making big data open in edges: a resource-efficient blockchain-based approach. IEEE Trans. Parallel Distrib. Syst. **30**, 870–882 (2019)
8. Ouaddah, A., Elkalam, A.A., Ouahman, A.: A: FairAccess: a new blockchain-based access control framework for the Internet of things. Security Comm. Networks **9**, 5943–5964 (2016)
9. Cruz, J.P., Kaji, Y., Yanai, N.: RBAC-SC: role-based access control using smart contract. IEEE Access **6**, 12240–12251 (2018)
10. Zhang, Y., Kasahara, S., Shen, Y., Jiang, X., Wan, J.: Smart contract-based access control for the internet of things. IEEE Internet Things J. **6**(2), 1594–1605 (2019)
11. Zhang, Y., Yutaka, M., Sasabe, M., Kasahara, S.: Attribute-based access control for smart cities: a smart-contract-driven framework. IEEE Internet Things J. **8**(8), 6372–6384 (2021)
12. Ding, Y., Sato, H.: Bloccess: Towards Fine-grained access control using blockchain in a distributed untrustworthy environment. In: 2020 8th IEEE International Conference on Mobile Cloud Computing, Services, and Engineering (MobileCloud), pp. 17–22 (2020)
13. Gao, S., Piao, G., Zhu, J., Ma, X., Ma, J.: TrustAccess: a trustworthy secure ciphertext-policy and attribute hiding access control scheme based on blockchain. IEEE Trans. Veh. Technol. **69**, 5784–5798 (2020)
14. Kamboj, P., Khare, S., Pal, S.: User authentication using Blockchain based smart contract in role-based access control. Peer Peer Network. Appl. **14**(5), 2961–2976 (2021). https://doi.org/10.1007/s12083-021-01150-1
15. Yang, Q., Zhang, M., Zhou, Y., Wang, T., Xia, Z., Yang, B.: A non-interactive attribute-based access control scheme by blockchain for IoT. Electronics **10**(15), 1855 (2021)
16. Ding, S., Cao, J., Li, C., Fan, K., Li, H.: A novel attribute-based access control scheme using blockchain for IoT. IEEE Access **7**, 38431–38441 (2019)
17. Chen, H., Wan, W., Xia, J., Zhang, S., Fan, X.: Task-attribute-based access control scheme for IoT via blockchain. Comput. Mater. Contin. **65**(3), 2441–2453 (2020)
18. Remix: The Ethereum IDE. https://remix.ethereum.org.lastaccessed (2022)
19. Truffle: The smart contract development framework. https://www.trufflesuite.com (2022)
20. Ganache: The Ethereum development test tool. https://www.trufflesuite.com/ganache (2022)
21. Yan, H., Liu, Y., Qiu, S., Hu, S., Zhang, W.: Towards public integrity audition for cloud-IoT data based on blockchain. Comput. Syst. Sci. Eng. **41**(3), 1129–1142 (2022)
22. Malathi, D., Ponnusamy, V., Saravanan, S., Deepa, D., Ahanger, T.A.: A design framework for smart ration shop using blockchain and IoT technologies. Intell. Autom. Soft Comput. **32**(1), 605–619 (2022)
23. Almagrabi, A.O., Ali, R., Alghazzawi, D., Albarakati, A., Khurshaid, T.: Blockchain-as-a-utility for next-generation healthcare internet of things. Comput. Mater. Contin. **68**(1), 359–376 (2021)

Thoughts on the Application of Low-Interactive Honeypot Based on Raspberry Pi in Public Security Actual Combat, LIHRP

Jing Shi[1,2,3,4(✉)], Mingyang Chen[1,2,3,4], and Jiazheng Jiao[1,2,3,4]

[1] Jiangsu Police Institute, Nanjing 210000, China
813963697@qq.com
[2] Department of Computer Information and Cyber Security, Jiangsu Police Institute, Nanjing 210031, People's Republic of China
[3] Jiangsu Province Electronic Data Forensics and Analysis Engineering Research Center, Nanjing 210031, People's Republic of China
[4] Key Laboratory of Digital Forensics of Jiangsu Provincial Public Security Department, Nanjing 210031, People's Republic of China

Abstract. With development of the network, more and more information elements have been integrated into people's daily life. However, the seriousness of the network security problem has become increasingly apparent, too. By analyzing the characteristics of honeypot and raspberry pi, this paper will introduce how to build a honeypot on raspberry pi and the difference between it and building on PC, demonstrate cyber attacks on honeypots, put forward some ideas of broadening the data collecting range of low interaction honeypot and the thoughts on practical application to establish a mobile network attack data collecting microcenter, which will be used in public network security or private network security monitoring or alarm.

Keywords: Network security · Raspberry pi · Honeypot · Data acquisition

1 Opening Words

In recent years, with the development of network and computer, more and more information elements have been integrated into people's daily life. As to the promotion of informatization and the wide popularization of network, the problem of network security is becoming more and more serious. As of December 2020, the number of Internet users in China has reached 989 million. In the past seven years, the national public security organs have solved 405,000 online criminal cases and arrested 590,000 criminal suspects. In these cases, cyber attacks only account for a small part, but the losses caused by them are far from comparable to ordinary criminal cases. "Without cyber security, there would be no national security, no stable operation of the economy and society, and the interests of the general public would hardly be guaranteed," President Xi stressed. It is urgent to prevent and solve the network security problem of network attack.

X. Sun et al. (Eds.): ICAIS 2022, LNCS 13340, pp. 144–156, 2022.
https://doi.org/10.1007/978-3-031-06791-4_12

The continuous development of the rise of the network attack technology, security threats in the form of new emerging are in the continued evolution, and the defense technology can't keep up with the change of the security threat in time. The offense and defense are obviously not at the same starting line, how to effectively prevent and prevent blocking network attack have become an important field of study. Honeypot is such an active defense technology proposed by defenders to reverse this asymmetry [1].

Today, from the perspective of security applications, based on the practical problems effectively prevent the attack on the network, we make the following understanding to honeypot, including introduction, the tutorials to build the basis of environment, the display of attacks on the building demonstration and log interpretation, how to broaden the scope of data acquisition through different network connection way and thoughts on practicial applicants five aspects.

2 Introduction of Basic Information About Relevant Technologies

2.1 Raspberry Pi

First, we introduce raspberry pi, which is the carrier of this experiment. Raspberry pi development platform is a widely used processor platform at present. It is an ARM-based micro computer motherboard, which is only the size of a credit card, but it has all the basic functions of a computer, so it is also called 'card computer'. The raspberry pi uses SD/MicroSD cards as memory drives, and has 1/2/4 USB ports and a 10/100 Eth ernet port around the card's motherboard.

In the early days, there were only A and B two types of raspberry pi. The main differences between them were the size of internal memory and the number of ports that could be connected. Later, B+ type, 2B type, 3B type, red version, 3B+ type, 4B type came, its overall CPU calculation power, pin number, port number, power consumption, including design appearance, have been improved to a certain extent.

Raspberry pi 4B (4G) is used in this experiment. The computing power and environment of raspberry pi 4B are sufficient to support the experiment and part of the ideas made in this paper.

2.2 Honeypot Technology

Honeypot is defined as a kind of security resource, it has no business use, its value is to attract attackers to use it illegally [2]. Honeypot technology is sentially a technology to deceive the attacker. It can issue disguised system services, such as Web, database, etc., to lure the attacker to attack, record the attack source and attack behavior, give re al-time warning of the hidden security risks and intrusion behaviors in the network, an d buy time for the security administrator to deal with them. Thus, the attack behavior can be captured, prevented in real time, and analyzed after the event to understand the tools and methods used by the attacker, predict the attack intention and motivation, and enhance the security defense capability of the actual system through technical and management methods.

Honeypots can be divided into low-interaction honeypots and high-interaction honeypots according to their interaction modes. High-interaction honeypots provide real services, operating systems or applications that can capture a large amount of information, but they have high risks and are difficult to deploy and maintain. High interaction honeypot can capture quantitative information about attack through simulated TCP/IP protocol stack and vulnerability, which is easy to deploy and has low risk. Of course, in addition to low interaction and high interaction, there are some honeypots with fewer functions between the two, which have some characteristics of the two. We will call them medium interaction honeypots habitually.

In China, there are many honeypots that are relatively popular in application.

Honeypot security products are also widely used in local area network security of companies, enterprises and families. There are several honeypots as following (Table 1):

Table 1. Brief introduction to several honeypots.

Name	Introduction	Whether open source	High interaction/low interaction	Is there a visual interface
Pentbox	Runs on systems that support the Ruby language	Yes	Low	No
Hfish	Based on the development of Golang cross-platform multi-functional active inducement open source honeypot framework system	Yes	High	Yes
T-pot	Docker container-based integration of many honeypot programs for different applications of the system	Yes	High	Yes
Dionaea	A program that runs on Linus	Yes	Low	Yes
Kippo	SSH honeypot, can execute some Linus instructions	Yes	Between high interaction and low interaction	No
DiTing	Commercial honeypot	No	High	Yes
ChuangYu	Commercial honeypot	No	High	Yes

3   Environment Building

There are two honeypots used in this experiment, namely Pentbox and Hfish. They are chosen mainly because their characteristics. Pentbox honeypot is a low interaction honeypot, no visual interface, unable to realize the automatic classifying of log, collecting data ability is relatively limited, while Hfish honeypot, on the contrary, is quite maturer in the field of application, therefore, this article choose Hfish honeypot as control group to explore the function expansion of Pentbox honey pot.

3.1   Build Pentbox Honey Pot

Pentbox is a security suite that includes a number of tools to streamline penetration testing, allowing you to open your host port and listen for incoming connection requests from outside. Written in Ruby for GNU/Linux, it also supports Windows, McOS, and any other system with Ruby installed.

The construction of Pentbox honeypot fully reflects the characteristics of low- inter-action honeypot, and the construction process of Pentbox honeypot is basically the same as that of raspberry Pie, which can be realized by virtual machine during the construction of host.

After opening the instruction page, we can directly download the compressed package and input 'wget http://downloads.sourceforge.net/project/pentbox18realised/pentbox-1.8.tar.gz'.

Then, to decompress the compressed package, enter 'tar zxvf pentbox-1.8.tar.gz'.

Fig. 1. The result of running the instruction.

When Fig. 1 is displayed, it represents decompression success.

Enter 'sudo./pentbox.rb' to run pentbox. (Note: Not all raspberry pi operations require root privileges, and raspberry pi(4B) will automatically block external "access" in some cases, similar to the host opening a firewall.) (Fig. 2)

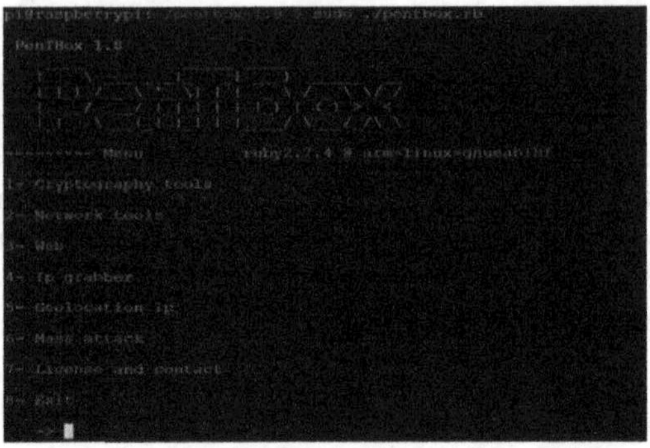

Fig. 2. Pentbox options.

Select 2-network tools -> 3- Honeypot -> 1- Fast Auto Configuration

HONEYPOT ACTIVATED ON PORT 80 (2021-11-23 14:58:32 +0800)

Fig. 3. Honeypot interface.

When Fig. 3 is displayed, it represents decompression success.

3.2 Build Hfish Honey Pot

HFish is a cross-platform multi-functional active inducer open source honeypot framework system developed based on Golang, which can realize the records of hacker attack and realize independent protection. It also supports HTTP(S) honeypot. SSH honeypot, SFTP honeypot, Redis honeypot, Mysql honeypot, FTP5 honeypot, Telnet honeypot, dark web honeypot and so on. In addition, it also provides API interface, users can expand honeypot module (WEB, PC, APP). It uses Golang + SQLite development, which means users can quickly deploy a set of Hfish honeypots on Win + Mac + Linux.

Compared with Pentbox honey pot, building Hfish may face some problems, such as port conflict and mirror pulling. Specific Hfish deployment questions can be found at the Hfish project address on Github (https://github.com/hacklcx/HFish/) or project official address (https://hub.docker.com/r/imdevops/hfish) In order to facilitate construction, 'docker pull' is used to pull the image.

3.3 Download the Docker

Raspberry pi and PC download Doceker in different ways. If using raspberry pi, firstly download pip, through 'pip install' download docker. The best way to PC is to enter 'apt install docker. io -y' on the VIRTUAL machine. Of course, you can also directly download the specific in Windows for reference (https://docs.docker.com/toolbox/ove rview/).

3.4   Pull the Mirror and Enter 'Docker Pull Imdevops/hfish'

Then use following command directly to start the honeypot container 'docker run -d --name hfish -p 21:21 -p 22:22 -p 23:23 -p 69:69 -p 3306:3306 -p 5900:5900 -p 6379:6379 -p 8080:8080 -p 8081:8081 -p 8989:8989 -p 9000:9000 -p 9001:9001 -p 9200:9200 -p 11211:11211 --restart = always imdevops/hfish:latest' like Fig. 4.

Fig. 4. Operation process.

Numbers 21, 22, and 23 correspond to port numbers of different protocols. For example, 21 corresponds to FTP and 22 corresponds to SSH. For that Hfish supports multiple protocols and loads multiple protocols, there are so many kinds of honeypots supported by Hfish. Of course, this is also the place where port conflict problems occur. You can choose whether to open the port conflict according to the situation. 3. After completing the previous step, you can access the Web service through port 9000 and see that the default world map is ready (the map is blank when it has not scan any source of attack data):

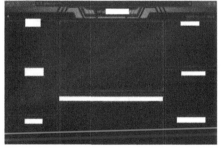

Fig. 5. Hfish interface 1.   **Fig. 6.** Hfish interface 2.

When Figs. 5 and 6 are displayed, it means that Hfish is set up.

4   Attack Demonstration and Log Analysis

4.1 Hfish Attack Demonstration and Log

The operations performed through VM are shown as follows:

First enter its login page and find it is a website built on wordpress. Enter several accounts randomly and then check whether it can be captured in the background.

Obviously, according to Figs. 7 and 8, the background captured several accounts and passwords of the test. It can be seen from the list that the attack type is phishing.

Fig. 7. Record 1 on fishing.

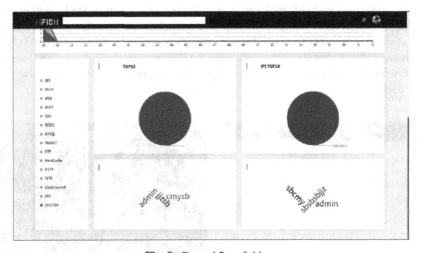

Fig. 8. Record 2 on fishing.

Then we log in the website, SQL injection test, also detected in the background (Figs. 9 and 10).

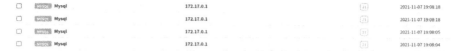

Fig. 9. Record 1 on SQL.

Then find a mysql dictionary and try to explode mysql and succeed, too.

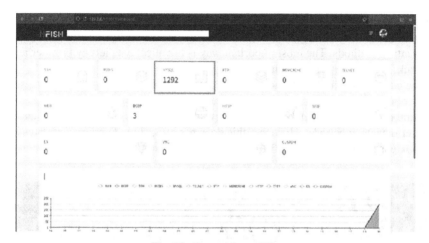

Fig. 10. Record 2 on SQL.

Finally, take a look at the data analysis of honeypot platform.

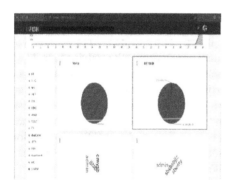

Fig. 11. Record 1 on attacks.

Fig. 12. Record 2 on attacks.

From the data analysis of Hfish platform, Figs. 11 and 12, we can see the chart of the proportion of various attacks. The data left by attacks can be automatically classified, and most of them come from MySQL explosion. At the same time of the attack, the global situation map will automatically report the address of the attacker's IP. Moreover, the honeypot records the account numbers and passwords used by hackers as they inject, revealing more and more of their behavior and attack habits as they gloat. The specific content recorded by each attack can be seen from the hook list, and the visual interface provides good readability, which fully reflects the advantages of high interaction honeypot.

4.2 Pentbox Attack Demonstration and Log

Pentbox Attack Demonstration and Log Analysis

Compared with Hfish honeypot, Pentbox honeypot has fewer functions and can collect fewer attack methods. The most important way is to collect data left by browser access or attack. We did the Pentbox attack demo on raspberry pi.

We can directly access the address of Pentbox honey pot by using the browser of another host.

Pentbox may be blocked because the firewall of the host is not closed or because the browser detects page risks. However, this does not affect how Pentbox generates logs. Pentbox generates logs as Fig. 13.

Fig. 13. Attack logs.

We generally describe this log, the first line: attack hint! From 192.168.43.31 (attack time), where the attack time is the time when the raspberry PI deploying the honeypot was attacked; The second line tells us that the other party is doing the activity over HTTP; The third line is raspberry PI's IP address; The fourth line is the network status of both parties. Keep-alive indicates that the other party is still connected. At this time, we can counter attack or block in some ways. The fifth line adds' upgrade- insecure -Requests: 1 'to the HTTP request. The server will return "Content-security- policy: The upgrade-insecure-requests header tells the browser that you can upgrade all HTTP connections to HTTPS for your site. Sometimes this line, such as cache- ontrol: max-age = 1, means that the content is immediately considered stale (and must be fetched again) and the log will be fetched again; The sixth line is the system and software used by the other party, here we use Win10 (64-bit), Chrome browser; The seventh line is the data types that can be recorded, such as the other party's listed file browsing or uploading data, which can achieve certain feedback; The eighth line is not displayed in most cases and is shown here for purposes: preview; The ninth line is that the encoding type supports GZIP and DEFLATE;

The tenth line shows the language used by the host, which is displayed as Chinese.

Then, we Ping the honeypot IP with the host CMD. Even if the Ping succeeds and the data is exchanged, Pentbox honeypot does not respond.

Pentbox Honey Pot to Achieve the Idea of Log Storage

Pentbox honeypot is written in Ruby, a relatively simple language supported by Linux, Windows, MacOS and other systems.

Pentbox honey itself does not have the function of log storage, so it needs the operation of changing the source program. Like Pycharm, VS C++ and other language compilers, you can open the file to view the code by right clicking the corresponding language file. You can also do the same operation through Ruby language compiler to open Pentbox source program and store the output data in TXT file under the output line of response to attack. Through this way, you can realize simple storage of data log.

In addition, Screen scanning software such as Screen Scraper Studio and Boxsoft Screen OCR can be used for fixed point scanning of Pentbox honeypots on the Screen so that when the honeypots are accessed, the data log generated can be automatically recognized and stored. The disadvantage is that an external screen is required. However, using data scanning software to monitor honeypot monitoring area may realize automatic log storage without screen.

5 The Idea of Broadening the Data Collecting Range of Low Interaction Honeypot

Low interaction honeypot's data collecting ability, compared with high interaction honeypot, is disadvantaged in the width and the types of data. This links to the reason for designing them. Low interaction honeypot mostly only acts as a basic information collection, like relatively low-level characters and attack alarm. But how to occupy more information through low interaction honeypot under the limited condition, it is still a problem worth thinking. To solve this problem, this paper puts forward several ideas based on the research of some scholars.

5.1 Mixed Honeypot

Unlike high interaction honeypots, low interaction honeypots with static configuration are not disguised, so they are easier to be discovered and avoided by attackers. In addition, the low interaction honeypot can only capture some directional and quantitative data. If attackers have a counter attack consciousness of attacker data collection, the low interaction honeypots may not work as well as expection, but a good high interaction honeypot can just make up for these disadvantages. That's why we propose a method of using hybrid honeypot [7]. The honeypot system is made of a large number of low interaction honeypots and one or a few high interaction honeypots. Low interaction honeypots expand the data collection range of high interaction honeypots, while high interaction honeypots improve the processing services such as camouflage, log analysis and data classification for low interaction honeypots.

The system would make the high interaction honeypot dynamically specify and configure the attributes of the low-interaction honeypot according to the scanning results and use the high interaction honeypot to virtual host [3] to deceive the attackers. In addition, considering the shortcomings of the low interaction honeypot in capturing data, if the virtual low interaction honeypot can interact with packets of the other party, the low-interaction honeypot will directly interact with each other. If not, certain measures will be taken to forward the request of the attacker. The system uses Redirect technology to forward some access traffic to a high-interaction honeypot for deep and multi-faceted environment simulation to further obtain interactive information [4].

5.2 Cloud Honeypot

Cloud server is the cloud host that we say, like virtual machine, VPS and other similar technonlgy. With the development of technology, cloud server is gradually becoming popular, which has been applied in many network fields. On the one hand, cloud server is similar to virtual machine and provides stronger computing power, which can provide important foundation for low interaction honeypots' integration and data log-storage analysis. On the other hand, the development trend of cloud server is also a promotion to the development of static honeypot (low interaction honeypot), making it develop towards dynamic honeypot [5] and private cloud honeypot [7].

5.3 Broadened Honeypot

Broadened honeypot here mainly refers to broadening its data collecting range. Generally, low interaction honeypot can collect data on the same LAN, namely the same network segment, and tends to provide private security problems and provide active defense function. In terms of application, the broadened honeypot can increase the scope of honeypot data collection by changing the network connection mode under certain conditions, what makes it more inclined to actively collect data. There are two ideas about the concrete realization of the broadened honeypot.

First, as honeypots need to interact through network segments, can virtual networks and virtual switches [8] be used to collect data across servers and hosts (namely Bridging) or use a technology similar to virtual honeypots to install low interaction honeypots as the bottom layer at one or some ports for monitoring?

Second, we may achieve our aim through the establishment of open hot spot. We are not unfamiliar with hot spot. Most mobile phones now have hot spot function. To some extent, hot spot is equivalent to a small mobile local area network. In the same hot spot, different devices can also interact with each other through network segments, which opens up an idea for us, whether it is possible to monitor the network in the mobile area by building a large open hotspot plus flow control equipment could be something to think about. Most low interaction honeypots can collect attack data made by zombie hosts and record data when their hosts automatically connect to open hotspots.

6 Thoughts on the Practical Application of Low Interaction Honeypot

With the promotion of the big data strategy of the public security bureau, strengthening the intelligence security guarantee ability of the big data of the public security bureau has become an important part. In the normative technical document of big data of public security – general technical framework of big data security of public security "attack trapping" (deception defense technology, namely honeypot technology) is also included as an indicator. The direction of action is also relatively obvious. Here, I think about some public security application of the low interactive honeypot built on raspberry pi.

6.1 Detecting Basic Network Attacks

As an active security defense strategy, honeypot technology was initially applied to assist intrusion detection technology to find attackers and malicious codes in the network [1]. Similarly, through using honeypots built in raspberry pie or based on raspberry pie as a sub port which set within a larger flow rate and relative important local area network (LAN) and the final summary data to the center of high interaction honeypot (like the hybrid honeypot) or cloud platform (namely cloud honeypot), the public security organ can also realize the flow of the important network protection.

The Internet is a very large whole, it is very difficult to achieve overall protection because it's time-consuming and laborious, so we need to adopt the protection of key methods. For that all the attack weaknesses and attack objects displayed by low-interactive honeypots for attackers are not real product systems, the risk is low. As a result, we can deploy a large number of low-interaction honeypots as the main body to establish a honeypot network. In addition, with the portability of raspberry pi, it can meet the requirements of moving the honeypot port based on traffic changes. Therefore, it can be relatively bold to realize simultaneous monitoring of internal and external networks through appropriate network configuration, so as to prevent basic network attacks.

6.2 Learning Network Defence Through Honeypot

Through the honeypot construction, honeypot collection of information analysis, interpretation, we can learn to understand the study of network and network security issues, improve the overall network security application literacy and cultivate new police team to meet the needs of the times.

If we can, we certainly don't want to see cyber attacks and other activities that disrupts social security, but it's hard to come it true. Therefore, public security officers should also keep pace with the times, learning related network defense technology.

The characteristics of low interaction honeypot to collect information, low risk and low cost, provide network police with valuable opportunities to learn and deal with network attacks. At the same time, in accordance with the provisions of the case, the public security network police can easily carry the honey pot through the raspberry pi to learn network knowledge or in certain circumstances, such as there are limited facilities, we can connect the raspberry pi to a computer or two raspberry pi connect with each other for data comparison. Combined with other more professional honeypot technology, network police can realize more timely detection of potential attacks and respond to them in advance. Through learning the attackers' attack skills and the code they used to achieve "with the enemy to defeat the enemy". Moreover, through honeypot, we can collect many users' personal network information. Learning technology and knowledge related to honeypot can improve our understanding of network law and exercise our secret awareness.

6.3 Delay the Cyber Attack by Deploying a Large Number of Low-Interaction Honeypots

When protecting important networks, public security organs may make use of the characteristics of low interaction honeypots occupying low resource to create multiple nodes as the initial defense line to confuse attackers when they are scanning and detecting to delay their discovery of protected objects so that protectors can have enough time to carry out more effective prevention measures. Multiple nodes can be created using one IP address corresponding to multiple terminals, or terminals can be created using multiple virtual IP addresses. In addition, the honeypot terminal can return basic data, so we can process and analyze the basic data by developing our own programs to extract the concerned information or increase the alarm function.

7 The End

In recent years, research on raspberry pi and honeypot has never stopped, from the initial static honeypot to virtual honeypot to dynamic honeypot based on cloud server, etc. Its function has al so changed from the original auxiliary invasive monitoring to the extension to assist in all aspects of network security. With the joint efforts of several generations, wo have changed the work against the unequal situation in attack and defense and made important contributions to maintaining network security.

At the end of the article, I would like to thank all hardworking networkers for their contribution in the field of network security. In addition, there is no conflict of interest between the authors and the public website tutorials cited in this article, the researcher claims no conflicts of interests and we deeply appreciate the selfless researchers who made the tutorials public.

References

1. Zhuge, J., Tang, Y., Han, X., Duan, H.: Honeypot technology research and application. J. Softw. **24**(4), 825–842 (2013)
2. Spitzner, L.: Honeypots: Tracking Hackers. Addison-Wesley Longman Publishing Co., Inc., Boston (2002)
3. Su, Y.: Internet attack feature extraction and security defense based on virtual honeypot technology. J. Chongqing Univ. Sci. Technol. **23**(05) (2021)
4. Li, Z.: Design and Implementation of Network Security Defense System Based on Honeypot Technology. Master of Engineering Thesis, Southeast University (2019)
5. Wang, S.: Dynamic Honeypot Design and Implementation in Cloud Environment. Master of Engineering Thesis, Southeast University (2019)
6. Wu, J.: New Hybrid Honeypot System Based on Open Stack. Master of Engineering Thesis, Xidian University (2014)
7. Li, Z.: Research and Construct the Virtual Network of Hybrid Desktop Cloud Server. Master Dissertation. South China University of Technology (2015)

Multi-objective Dual-Route Planning Algorithm for Grid Communication Network

Xiaojun Gou[✉], Shunhui Luo, and Liang Xiao

State Grid Info-Telecom Great Power Science and Technology Co., Ltd., Beijing 102211, China
820029136@qq.com

Abstract. In order to adapt to the construction of the new generation power system, it is urgent to make use of various controllable resources to build a new generation of comprehensive defense system of power grid security. In this paper, we aim to design a multi-objective dual-route planning algorithm for grid communication network. Firstly, we consider the network structure, site level and service load in the node and link risk model. On this basis, we calculate the overall risk equilibrium value of the network. Moreover, we also take into account the QoS performance to formulate the highly reliable dual-route planning problem with the optimization target of the network overall risk equilibrium value and the end-to-end communication delay. Then, we propose the multi-objective dual-route planning optimization algorithm to solve the problem. Simulation results show that the proposed algorithm has advance in terms of the balance of network risk and the performance of QoS.

Keywords: Route planning · Balance of network risk · Grid communication network

1 Introduction

With the implementation of various ultra-high voltage, new energy sources such as wind, solar and tidal energy is connected to the grid [1]. Correspondingly, the capacity of power grid disaster tolerance and its own stable operation degree need to be improved [2]. In order to adapt to the construction of the new generation power system, it is urgent to make use of various controllable resources to build a new generation of comprehensive defense system of power grid security. It mainly realizes the functions of voltage, frequency emergency control, rapid isolation of faults and chain faults, real-time monitoring and early warning, high-precision synchronous recording [3].

In the current network, the dual routing configuration is realized mainly by establishing the route path between the source and destination node pairs that do not intersect or approximately does not intersect [4]. At the same time, one of the dual-path pairs is set as a working route according to the business requirements, and the other is used as an alternate route to achieve continuous transmission through routing after network failure [5]. Compared with the single route setup, the dual-route configuration is of great significance to improve the reliability of service transmission and the stable operation of

X. Sun et al. (Eds.): ICAIS 2022, LNCS 13340, pp. 157–170, 2022.
https://doi.org/10.1007/978-3-031-06791-4_13

the system [6]. However, because the power service has the characteristics of aggregating from the low voltage level station to the high voltage level station or dispatch center site, the dual-route configuration algorithm in the current network may cause the service carrying over-aggregation on some communication links [7]. At the same time, the current dual-routing algorithm does not take enough account of the performance of hosting service. In order to reduce the risk of network operation, ensure the reliable transmission of power service, ensure the balanced distribution of service in the network, design a good performance [8]. How to meet the requirements of the dual-route planning scheme is the main problem to be solved in the paper.

In the related works, the dual route optimization design scheme in substation is analyzed. Considering the importance of power service, network average risk and network risk equilibrium, the shortest path algorithm for each service is proposed to calculate the required path [9]. The Min-Max algorithm is proposed to choose the network risk equilibrium value of the smallest route [10]. However, the selected route can't guarantee global optimization, and the algorithm can't ensure the overall network performance. In [11], the authors build a dual-route optimization model with the average risk and risk equilibrium of the network as the goal. They use the genetic algorithm (GA) to solve the model, but the proposed method lacks consideration to the voltage level and performance index of the substation where the nodes are located in the power communication network.

In the paper, we aim to design a dual-route planning scheme for grid communication network that takes into account the balance of network risk and the performance guarantee of QoS. First of all, we clarify the network topology and communication requirements, according to the network structure, site level and business carrying situation and other factors. Then we give the node and link risk model, and calculate the overall risk equilibrium value of the network. At the same time, taking into account of the QoS performance, the highly reliable dual-route planning problem is modeled as the optimization target of the network overall risk equilibrium value and the end-to-end communication delay. The multi-objective optimization algorithm is used to solve the problem, and the goal of the overall dual-route planning solution is realized.

2   System Model and Problem Formulation

As shown in Fig. 1, we construct a directionless graph $G = (V,E)$ to represent the communication network. Here, V represents a collection of nodes, representing communications devices deployed in power plants and sites. E is a collection of edges that represent communication channels. n and m represent the element cardinality in collections V and E, respectively, i.e. $n = |V|$, $m = |E|$. The adjacency matrix between network nodes is a 0–1 matrix $X = [x_{ij}]$. Here, $x_{ij} = 1$ indicates that there exists an edge between the nodes v_i, v_j. Suppose that $S = \{s_1, s_2, \ldots, s_k, \ldots\}$ denotes the collection of services in the network that need to be configured for dual routing. Here, s_k represents the kth business in the collection S and each service is represented as a binary group $s_k(v_k^s, v_k^d)$, where v_k^s, v_k^d represent the source and host node and $v_k^s, v_k^d \in V$. The route of the service s_k can be represented as $p(k) = (v_s(k), e_{s,f}(k), \ldots, v_i(k), e_{i,t}(k), \ldots, e_{x,d}(k), v_d(k))$. Assuming that the variable P is the business route collection and $p(k) \in P$.

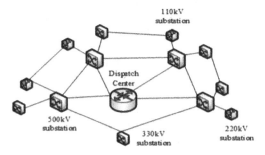

Fig. 1. Network topology of the grid communication.

Based on the network risk, we model and analyze the dual routing planning of services. In order to avoid the problem of imbalanced network risk caused by business aggregation, we define the concepts of the node risk model, the link risk model and the equilibrium network risk, which are described below.

2.1 The Node Risk Model

Node risk is the impact of a communication node failure [12]. To calculate the node risk, we consider the probability of node failure, node importance and the carried services. The calculation of node failure probability is not complicated, we can use $P_i^v = C_i^v/T$ by collecting historical data in the network management system. Here, C_i^v represents the number of failures for any node within the time period T. v_i in practice, T is often a year, a month, or a week.

The failure of the node can spread across the network through adjacent nodes or links, and then continuously cracks network performance. The failure of the typical node causes all the connected communication links to be unavailable. It is assumed that the fault affects propagation along the shortest path. Intuitively, nodes with larger degrees or nodes that are more critical in the network play a greater role in failure propagation, and the more important nodes are. The greater the number of node degrees, the stronger the node connectivity, which corresponds to a wider range of fault propagation after the failure occurs. In addition, node betweenness is the global characteristics of node importance and impact in complex networks. The more critical the position of the node in the network, the more important the node is. A larger node betweenness indicates that the failure will affect network performance more quickly. In this paper, we introduce the node degree-betweenness (DB) correlation index, which is defined as follows.

$$\alpha_i^v = a_i^v (b_i^v)^\theta \tag{1}$$

Here, α_i^v is the DB of the node v_i. b_i^v is the degree of the node v_i. θ is the adjustment coefficient. a_i^v indicates the betweenness of the node v_i, which is shown as follows.

$$a_i^v = \sum_{s,d \in V, s \neq d} \frac{A_{s,d}^{v_i}}{A_{s,d}} \tag{2}$$

Here, $A_{s,d}^{v_i}$ represents the number of shortest paths passing through the node v_i between the node s and the node d. $A_{s,d}$ denotes the number of shortest paths between the node s and the node d.

Different from the general communication network, different levels of sites have different roles in the power communication network [13]. The power communication network has the same lauding structure as the power grid. Various communication equipment, such as switches and routers, are deployed in substations or dispatch centers with different voltage levels. Therefore, we use the substation point importance where the node is located to approximate the importance of the node. The substation point importance is related to the site voltage level and site size, in general, the higher the site voltage level, the higher the control level [14]. For example, it is generally considered that the 500 kV substation point is more important than the 220 kV substation point, so the greater the business traffic carried by the communication equipment in the site, the higher the importance of the corresponding node. In particular, communication devices located in the dispatch center are the most important in the network. It should be pointed out that the coupling relationship between communication network equipment and physical power grid substation points is not included in this study, in order to reduce the complexity of the problem, this paper assumes that the two are one-in-one mapping. Suppose there are μ different voltage level values in the network and a collection of voltage values can be denoted as $U = \{\sigma_1, \sigma_2, \ldots, \sigma_u\}$, such as 66 kV, 110 kV, 220 kV, 500 kV, and so on. The different voltage values are standardized by the min-max method.

$$\sigma_i^v = \frac{\sigma_i - \sigma_{min}}{\sigma_{max} - \sigma_{min}}, \forall v_i \in V, \sigma_i \in U \qquad (3)$$

Here, σ_i^v is the normalized voltage value of the node v_i. σ_i is the actual voltage value of the node v_i. σ_{max} and σ_{min} are the maximum and minimum voltage value of the set U, respectively. The importance degree of node is calculated as follows.

$$N_i^v = \omega_1 \sigma_i^v + \omega_2 a_i^v \qquad (4)$$

Here, N_i^v represents the importance degree of the node v_i. ω_1 and ω_2 are the weight coefficients for the DB indicator respectively and $\omega_1 + \omega_2 = 1$. In addition, the service load of the node also affects the size of the node's importance degree. That is, the more kinds of services that are hosted on the node, the larger impact caused by a node failure. Thus, the importance degree of node is calculated as follows.

$$N_i^v = \sum_{s_k \in S_i^v} P_i^v N_i^v, v_i \in p_s(k), S_i^v \in S \qquad (5)$$

Here, the node v_i belongs to the route of the service s_k. S_i^v denotes the service collection hosted by the node v_i.

2.2 The Link Risk Model

Compared to communication nodes, most communication lines are exposed to relatively harsh environments. As a result, communication links are more likely to fail than nodes. Similar to the aforementioned node risk model, link risk is the impact of a communication link failure that is related to the probability of link failure, link importance, and load on the link. The link risk is calculated as follows.

$$D_{ij}^e = \sum_{s_k \in S_{ij}^E} N_{ij}^E P_{ij}^E, e_{ij} \in p(k), S_{ij}^E \in S \tag{6}$$

Here, $D_{ij}^e e_{ij}$ is the value of the link risk. N_{ij}^E and P_{ij}^E represent the probability of failure and importance degree of the link that is passing through the path $p(k)$ of the service s_k, respectively. S_{ij}^E is a collection of services on the link e_{ij}. Link importance is related to betweenness and voltage level. The importance degree of the link is calculated as follows.

$$N_{ij}^E = \omega_3 \sigma_{ij}^E + \omega_4 a_{ij}^E, e_{ij} \in E \tag{7}$$

Here, σ_{ij}^E and a_{ij}^E denote the voltage level and the betweenness of the link e_{ij}, respectively. ω_3 and ω_4 is the weight factor and $\omega_3 + \omega_4 = 1$. The link betweenness a_{ij}^E is calculated as follows.

$$a_{ij}^E = \sum_{l,f \in V, l \neq f} \frac{A_{l,f}^{e_{ij}}}{A_{l,f}}, e_{ij} \in E \tag{8}$$

Here, $A_{l,f}$ is the number of shortest paths through the node pair (l,f) in the network. $A_{l,f}^{e_{ij}}$ denotes the number of shortest paths through the node pair (l,f) and the link e_{ij}.

2.3 The Equilibrium Value of Network Risk

There is no clear calculation in the relevant research to characterize the balance degree of service distribution in the network. To reasonably evaluate the equilibrium of service distribution, we introduce standard deviations to measure the equilibrium of network risk. It consists of the equilibrium value of node risk and the equilibrium value of link risk. The smaller the standard deviation, the more evenly distributed the service is. Then, we calculate the equilibrium value of network risk, as shown below.

$$D_{avg}^G = \frac{1}{m} \sum_{v_i \in p(k)} D_i^v + \frac{1}{n} \sum_{e_{ij} \in p(k)} D_{ij}^e \tag{9}$$

$$D_B = \frac{1}{m+n} \sum_{v_i, e_{ij} \in p(k)} ((D_{ij}^e - D_{avg}^G)^2 + (D_i^v - D_{avg}^G)^2)^{\frac{1}{2}} \tag{10}$$

Here, D_{avg}^G and D_B are the average and equilibrium values for network risk, respectively. m and n are the number of nodes and links in the network, respectively.

2.4 The End-to-End Delay

Considering the high reliability of communication network transmission, we don't take into account the impact of other QoS indicators such as packet loss rate and error rate. According to the queuing theory, the end-to-end delay includes send delay, queue delay, processing delay and propagation delay on each switch. Because processing delay is related to algorithm complexity and hardware device performance, this part of delay is set to a fixed value. In addition, the switch is responsible for forwarding information and is not involved in data processing. Therefore, it makes sense to ignore processing delays on the switch. We calculate the end-to-end communication delay for the service s_k on the route $p(k)$, as shown follows.

$$T_s^p(k) = M \times T_{avg} + \frac{1}{c} \sum\nolimits_{s_k \in S} L_{ij} x_{ij}^{k,p}, \; v_i, v_j \in p(k) \tag{11}$$

Here, c is a constant, which represents data traveling rate through the fiber. $x_{ij}^{k,p}$ denote the decision variable, which is defined as follows. M is the number of switches on the route $p(k)$. T_{avg} is the average forwarding delay for the queuing through the switch. L_{ij} is the length of the link between neighboring nodes v_i, v_j on the route $p(k)$.

$$x_{ij}^{k,p} = \begin{cases} 1, \; \textit{if the route } p(k) \text{ of the service } s_k \text{ through nodes } v_i, v_j \\ 0, \; \textit{others} \end{cases} \tag{12}$$

Based on the mentioned above, the total communication delay for all services is calculated as follows.

$$T_{total}(p(k)) = \sum\nolimits_{p(k) \in P} T_s^p(k), \; s_k \in S \tag{13}$$

2.5 Constraints

The routing planning problem formulated in this paper should also include the following constraints.

Constraint 1: Route Uniqueness. A unique routing path needs to be assigned to each service in the network. Define y_{rk} as a binary variable and R as the number of candidate paths for the service s_k. If $p(k)$ is the route path for the service s_k, then $y_{rk} = 1$. Otherwise, $y_{rk} = 0$.

$$\sum\nolimits_{r=1}^{R} y_{rk} = 1, \; s_k \in S \tag{14}$$

Constraint 2: Path Ringless. Each route should satisfy the ringless constraint, i.e.

$$\sum\nolimits_{v_i \in V, e_{ij} \in E} x_{ij}^{k,p} \le 1 \tag{15}$$

Constraint 3: Link Bandwidth Limitation. In a preconfigured dual-route plan, it is assumed that the business in Safe Zone I has dedicated protection on the alternate route. To ensure rapid recovery after a failure and prevent network congestion, all services should allocate less bandwidth resources than the link bandwidth threshold. The constraint is represented as follows.

$$\sum\nolimits_{k=1}^{|S|} x_{ij}^{k,p} z_{ij}^e(k) \le Z, e_{ij} \in p(k), S_{ij}^E \in S \tag{16}$$

Here, $z_{ij}^e(k)$ is the bandwidth requirements for the service s_k. $|S|$ is the total number of services. Z is the reserved link bandwidth.

Constraint 4: Two-way Intersection Limitation. The two-route path should be physically independent. However, in a particular network topology, we may not be able to find a dual-route path that completely does not intersect. To meet the requirement of service, we need to search for services with work paths and alternate paths that are as dissected as possible. To do this, we introduce a two-way minimum intersection. First, we describe the intersection of paths, which refers to the number of public nodes and links on the two paths except the original and destination nodes. The two-way minimum intersection refers to two paths with the least common elements. Assumed $p_w(k)$ is the working path and $p_b(k)$ is an alternate path. The Two-way intersection $\delta(k)$ and the minimum value are calculated below, respectively.

$$\delta(k) = p_w(k) \cap p_b(k), p_w(k), p_b(k) \in P \tag{17}$$

$$min\delta(k) = argmax_{s_k \in S}(\delta(k)) \leq \varphi \tag{18}$$

Based on the above analysis, we optimize routing planning decisions with the goal of minimizing total business communication latency and network risk balance to ensure the real-time and balanced distribution of network risks in routing planning schemes. Then, we represent the objective function as follows.

$$minf(\overline{p(k)}) = min[T_{total}(\overline{p(k)}), D_B(\overline{p(k)})] \tag{19}$$

Here, $f(\overline{p(k)})$ is a vector consisting of two target functions and the optimal solution is a one-dimensional column vector consisting of k elements, *i.e.* $\overline{p(k)}^* = [p(1)^*, p(1)^*, \ldots, p(k)^*]$.

The optimization problem proposed can be expressed as follows.

$$minf(\overline{p(k)}) \tag{20}$$

$$s.t.C1 : 0 \leq T_s^p(k) \leq T_0 \tag{21}$$

$$C2 : argmax_{s_k \in S}(\delta(k)) \leq \varphi \tag{22}$$

$$C3 : \sum_{r=1}^{R} y_{rk} = 1, s_k \in S \tag{23}$$

$$C4 : \sum_{v_i \in V, e_{ij} \in E} x_{ij}^{k,p} \leq 1 \tag{24}$$

$$C5 : \sum_{k=1}^{|S|} x_{ij}^{k,p} z_{ij}^e(k) \leq Z, e_{ij} \in p(k), S_{ij}^E \in S \tag{25}$$

3 Multi-objective Optimization Algorithm for Dual Routing Planning

In this paper, we formulate a typical nonlinear multi-objective joint optimization problem. The problem has been proven to be an NP problem. As for the problem, there are two strategies to obtain the solution. First, regardless of the relationship between objective functions, the multi-objective optimization problem is transformed into a single-objective optimization problem by the standardization process, and then solved by using heuristic algorithm [15]. The second is to solve the solution through a special multi-target optimization algorithm. The first solution strategy applies when there is no correlation between the target functions. If each target function in the multi-objective optimization problem has different meanings and quantitative outlines, and the target functions are interdependent and compete with each other, that is, the optimization of one objective function often comes at the expense of the degradation of another objective function, it is more suitable to adopt the second solution strategy at this time. In the system model, if the total traffic delay of the business is reduced, it indicates that the business is more inclined to travel through the shorter routing path, which leads to the concentration of the business on some links and the increase of the overall network risk equilibrium value, so there is a conflicting relationship between the two objective functions, which is obviously more suitable for the second solution idea.

Multi-objective optimization algorithms include particle group algorithm, genetic algorithm, ant group algorithm and fast non-dominant sorting genetic algorithm with elite strategy [16]. Among them, the genetic algorithm is a random search algorithm designed by drawing on the law of survival and survival evolution followed by biological evolution in nature, which does not limit the specific areas of the problem in the process of solving, does not rely on specific gradient information in the search, does not require the target function to be continuous and guidable, has a strong global search ability, and because of its excellent global optimal solution performance, it is widely used in the traditional search algorithm difficult to solve large-scale, non-linear combination optimization problem. NSGAII algorithm in the traditional genetic algorithm selection, cross and variation on the basis of operators, the introduction of rapid non-dominant sorting and elite strategy, because of the better performance in the benchmark problem and practical application, is widely used in multi-objective optimization problem solving, which is one of the reasons for this paper to use the NSGA II progressive model solution.

3.1 Chromosome Encoding and Decoding

In NSGA II, chromosome coding and decoding will directly affect algorithmic performance. In order to improve the efficiency of compilation and solution and realize the unified routing planning for all services, we use a fixed-length integer coding method. Here, each chromosome represents a routing plan. Each chromosome has several separate chromosome fragments. Each chromosome fragment corresponds to a business path, and the length of the chromosome fragment depends on the number of network nodes. Therefore, we need to number the network nodes and then randomly generate the gene bits based on the number of network nodes. From the above coding process, it can be seen that the length of each chromosome is the product of the number of network nodes and the number of services.

In the decoding process, we use location-based priority decoding. We specify the source point as the first node on the path. Then, based on the relationship between nodes in the network topology adjacency matrix, we select the node with a high priority, i.e., a large location index, as the next hop node. Then we repeat the process until the business destination node. For ease of understanding, let's illustrate it below with examples. As shown in Fig. 2(a), in a 7-node network, we assume that two services $s_1(v_1,v_2)$ need to plan a dual route path. Figure 2(b) shows an example of a randomly generated chromosome. The first node v_1 of the route for the service s_1 has three adjacent points v_2,v_3,v_7, respectively. They correspond to location priorities of 2, 3, 7. Based on the above encoding, we determine the second node v_7 on the path. Similarly, the three adjacent points v_3,v_4,v_6 correspond to location priorities of 5, 6, 2. Therefore, the next hop node of v_7 is v_4. v_4 is the end node, and the process of decoding is complete. It is important to note that to avoid routing loops, the decoding process specifies that each node has a path and can only occur once.

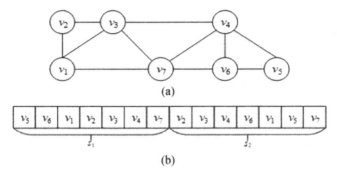

Fig. 2. (a) Network topology. (b) Chromosome encoding and decoding.

3.2 Selection, Crossover and Variation Operator

The selection operator is the process of selecting good individuals to form new populations with a certain probability from the old population, and we use the binary tournament method and elite strategy to realize the selection operation. In the variant operator, the mutant chromosome is selected according to the set probability of variation and the position of the two genes in the same chromosome fragment is exchanged to achieve population diversity. Unlike other intelligent optimization algorithms, cross operators are important operations to produce new individuals in population, and determining the cross position and exception handling after intersection is the key to designing cross operators. Common cross-algorithms include single-point intersection, two-point intersection, multi-point intersection, local matching cross and loop cross, etc.

4 Simulation and Analysis

In this paper, we use MATLAB R2019a to carry out simulation experiments in 14-node NSFnet. There are 21 edges in the NSFnet, with an average network node level of 3, as shown in Fig. 3.

The number on the network node is the node number, and the link-side number represents the link length. 80% of the services takes the 500 kV site and dispatch center as the

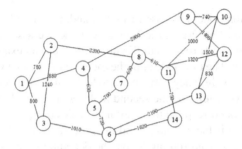

Fig. 3. Network topology.

source or destination node, and no more than 3 hop nodes are the other communication node. The source and destination nodes of the remaining 20% of the services are randomly selected from node set *V*. To further compare the performance of the algorithm, the algorithm proposed in this chapter is compared with the following routing algorithm containing the LRGB algorithm [17], the GA-Based algorithm [18], which is shown in Table 1 below.

Table 1. Simulation parameters settings.

Simulation parameters	Representations/values
Node 11 in NSFnet	Dispatch center
Node 6 in NSFnet	500 kV substation
Node 1,5,8,10 in NSFnet	330 kV substation
Node 13 in NSFnet	110 kV substation
Node 2,3,4,7,9,12,14 in NSFnet	220 kV substation
Population size	100
Maximum number of evolutions	500
Probability of variation	0.05

We mainly count idle links and links that carry 3 or more services. Figure 4 shows the service and link correspondence in the main route for different algorithms. For the proposed algorithm, the number of idle links that do not carry business is 3, the number of links carrying 3 or more services is 1, and the proportion of total links is 16%. For GA-Based algorithm, the number of links hosted by 3 or more services is 3, and the number of idle links is 6, accounting for 36% of the total link. For LRGB algorithm, the number of links hosted by 3 or more services is 5, the number of idle links is 11, and the proportion of total links is 64%. From the above comparison, the three algorithms mentioned in this paper correspond to the link obviously did not appear load concentration. The experimental results of the algorithm proposed in this paper are obviously better than those of the other two algorithms. In addition, the LRGB compliance link has significant business aggregation and the worst business distribution balance.

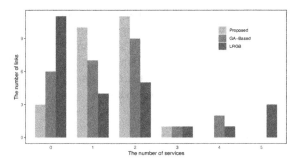

Fig. 4. The service and link correspondence in the main route for different algorithms.

Figure 5 shows the service and link correspondence in the alternate route for different algorithms. It can be seen that in the GA-Based algorithm, the number of idle links is 4 and the number of business links carrying 3 or more is 2, accounting for 24% of the total number of links. In the proposed algorithm, the number of links carrying 3 or more services is 1 and the number of idle links is 3, which accounts for 16% of the total number of links. In general, for the alternate route, the proposed algorithm is slightly better than the GA-Based algorithm, because the proposed algorithm aims at minimizing network risk equilibrium while it ensures the network risk equilibrium under the premise of ensuring the delay of communication and the GA-Based algorithm only takes into account the delay and network risk equilibrium factors. In the LRGB algorithm, there are 11 idle links, and 5 links carry 3 or more services, accounting for 64% of the total number of links. The reason is that the LRGB algorithm uses the suboptimal shortest path as the alternate path for the business. Thus, the service distribution is the worst balanced in the three scenarios.

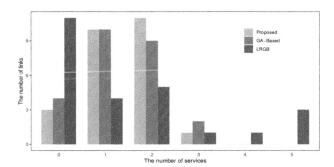

Fig. 5. The service and link correspondence in the alternate route for different algorithms.

Figure 6 shows the network risk balance corresponding to the main and alternate route planning of the service under different scenarios. As for the main routing plan, the network risk equilibrium value of the proposed algorithm decreases by 8.24% and 29.3% than GA-Based algorithm and LRGB algorithm, respectively. As for the alternative routing plan, the network risk equilibrium value of the proposed algorithm decreases by 4.95% and 57.48% than GA-Based algorithm and LRGB algorithm, respectively. Both the comparisons show the effectiveness of routing optimization in this paper. In addition, the network risk equilibrium value corresponding to business master routing planning is higher than that of standby routing planning. The reason is to prioritize the minimum latency of total business traffic when determining the master route plan. Alternative routing is the scenario of selecting the lowest equilibrium value of network risk from the pareto-front, subject to performance and constraints.

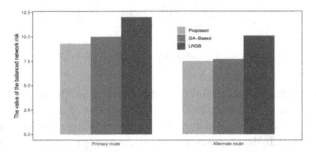

Fig. 6. The network risk balance for the main and alternate route planning of the service.

Figure 7 compares the communication delay corresponding to the main and alternate route planning under different algorithms. As for the main route planning, the communication delay of the proposed algorithm and LRGB algorithm is 68.655 ms and 64.830 ms, respectively. The two values are similar and both are lower than the communication delay of the GA-Based algorithm. As for the alternative routing scheme, the communication delay of the three algorithms is obviously increased due to the constraints such as path intersection, delay and link resources. In addition, the communication delay of the proposed algorithm is still lower than that based on the GA-Based algorithm.

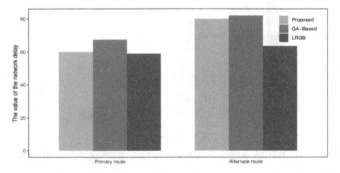

Fig. 7. The communication delay for the main and alternate route planning of the service.

5   Conclusion

In wireless sensor networks, it is an important issue to use node energy rationally and extend the life of the network. This paper proposes a wireless sensor network node protection routing algorithm based on clustering ant colony strategy. Considering that in the existing clustering wireless sensor network routing protocol, sensor nodes close to the sink often takes on too many transmission tasks. Too fast energy consumption leads to premature death. Our solution first clusters sensor nodes. We believe that clusters with a large number of nodes in the cluster or clusters close to the sink have greater communication pressure. Therefore, we select multiple cluster head nodes for clusters with high communication pressure to share the communication pressure. In the inter-cluster routing stage, we optimize the visibility in the ant colony algorithm to amplify the influence of the remaining energy factors of the nodes close to the receiver on the path selection. Experiments show that the algorithm can effectively delay the death of nodes and extend the life of wireless sensor networks.

Acknowledgement. This paper was supported by Collaborative Innovation in Energy and Material Applications.

References

1. Deepak, S.P., Mukeshkrishnan, M.B.: Secured route selection using E-ACO in underwater wireless sensor networks. Intell. Autom. Soft Comput. **32**(2), 963–978 (2022)
2. Abu-Shareha, A.A.: Integrated random early detection for congestion control at the router buffer. Comput. Syst. Sci. Eng. **40**(2), 719–734 (2022)
3. Puthige, I., Bansal, K., Bindra, C., Kapur, M., Singh, D.: Safest route detection via danger index calculation and k-means clustering. Comput. Mater. Contin. **69**(2), 2761–2777 (2021)
4. Hussain, D., Khan, M.A., Abbas, S., Naqvi, R.A., Mushtaq, M.F.: Enabling smart cities with cognition based intelligent route decision in vehicles empowered with deep extreme learning machine. Comput. Mater. Contin. **66**(1), 141–156 (2021)
5. Duhayyim, M.A., Obayya, M., Al-Wesabi, F.N., Hilal, A.M., Rizwanullah, M.: Energy aware data collection with route planning for 6G enabled UAV communication. Comput. Mater. Continu. **71**(1), 825–842 (2022)
6. Casellas, R., Vilalta, R., Martínez, R., Muñoz, R.: Highly available SDN control of flexi- grid networks with network function virtualization-enabled replication. J. Opt. Commun. Netw. **9**(2), 207–215 (2017)
7. Gharavi, H., Hu, B.: Multigate communication network for smart grid. In: Proceedings of the IEEE, vol. 99, no. 6, pp. 1028–1045 (2011)
8. Yin, S.: Shared-protection survivable multipath scheme in flexible-grid optical networks against multiple failures. J. Lightwave Technol. **35**(2), 201–211 (2017)
9. Khan, A.W., Abdullah, A.H., Razzaque, M.A., Bangash, J.I.: VGDRA: a virtual grid-based dynamic routes adjustment scheme for mobile sink-based wireless sensor networks. IEEE Sens. J. **15**(1), 526–534 (2015)
10. Hasan, M.M., Mouftah, H.T.: Optimization of trust node assignment for securing routes in smart grid SCADA networks. IEEE Syst. J. **13**(2), 1505–1513 (2019)
11. Zhao, P., Yu, P., Ji, C., Feng, L., Li, W.: A routing optimization method based on risk prediction for communication services in smart grid. In: 2016 12th International Conference on Network and Service Management (CNSM), pp. 377–382 (2016)

12. Zhao, P., Chen, X., Yu, P., Li, W., Qiu, X., Guo, S.: Risk assessment and optimization for key services in smart grid communication network. In: 2017 IFIP/IEEE Symposium on Integrated Network and Service Management, pp. 600–603 (2017)
13. Jamshed, M.A., Héliot, F., Brown, T.W.C.: A survey on electromagnetic risk assessment and evaluation mechanism for future wireless communication systems. IEEE J. Electromagn. RF Microw. Med. Biol. 4(1), 24–36 (2020)
14. Babuscia, A., Cheung, K.: Statistical risk estimation for communication system design. IEEE Syst. J. 7(1), 125–136 (2013)
15. Xie, J., Xiao, S., Liang, Y., Wang, L., Fang, J.: A throughput-aware joint vehicle route and access network selection approach based on SMDP. China Commun. 17(5), 243–265 (2020)
16. Sarro, F., Ferrucci, F., Harman, M., Manna, A., Ren, J.: Adaptive multi-objective evolutionary algorithms for overtime planning in software projects. IEEE Trans. Softw. Eng. 43(10), 898–917 (2017)
17. Zhang, M., Wang, N., He, Z., Yang, Z., Guan, Y.: Bi-objective vehicle routing for hazardous materials transportation with actual load dependent risks and considering the risk of each vehicle. IEEE Trans. Eng. Manage. 66(3), 429–442 (2019)
18. More, S., Naik, U.L.: Optimization driven Multipath Routing for the video transmission. In: the VANET. 2018 IEEE Global Conference on Wireless Computing and Networking (GCWCN), pp. 6–10 (2018)

Blockchain Cross-Chain Research Based on Verifiable Ring Signatures

Zhe Li[1], Zhiwei Sheng[1,2(✉)], Wunan Wan[1,2], Shibin Zhang[1,2], Zhi Qin[1,2], Jinquan Zhang[1,2], and Jinyue Xia[3]

[1] School of Cybersecurity, Chengdu University of Information Technology, Chengdu 610225, China
shengziwei@cuit.edu.cn

[2] Advanced Cryptography and System Security Key Laboratory of Sichuan Province, Chengdu 610255, China

[3] International Business Machines Corporation (IBM), New York, NY 10041, USA

Abstract. Along with the spurt of blockchain technology, the problem of blockchain's closedness is getting more attention, leading to cross-chain technology. Cross-chain technology solves the problem that blockchains cannot be interconnected and opens up the value circulation between blockchains. With the development of blockchain technology, cross-chain technology is getting more and more attention. This paper introduces the development of blockchain cross-chain technology and the mainstream schemes of cross-chain, such as hash locking, notary model, side-chain relay, distributed secret key, etc. Since there is a situation of who initiates who has the advantage in the cross-chain solution without introducing a third party, therefore, this paper proposes a new smart contract lock cross-chain solution based on ring signature ambiguity and verifiable ring signature that can remove ring signature ambiguity after announcing some secret information, which can satisfy the situation of ensuring fair and just value exchange between chains without third-party participation.

Keywords: Blockchain · Cross-chain · Verifiable ring signatures · Smart contracts

1 Introduction

Bitcoin: A Peer-to-Peer Electronic Cash System is a paper published on November 1, 2018, by a person calling himself Satoshi Nakamot on the "metzdowd.com" cryptography mailing list. Com first proposed a distributed, decentralized, electronic cash system that does not require mutual trust [1]. The first 50 bitcoins were harvested in a way called "mining", which meant the introduction of the bitcoin financial system. The Bitcoin cryptocurrency was built on blockchain technology and was the first blockchain application to be recognized and practically used by the public. It was later discovered that the blockchain technology extracted from Bitcoin is applied in digital currency. Still, it can also make non-trustworthy parties carry out trustworthy value transfer in an environment without a trustworthy intermediary. The distributed ledger ensures that the data is not modified or damaged, the availability, reliability, and integrity of the data is high. The HASH function makes the data verifiable, even if some nodes are offline or under attack the system still the system is highly resilient and has a natural backup of data [2].

With the rapid development of blockchain technology, various private chains, public chains, and federated chains have emerged, and various blockchain applications are also increasing, such as blockchain e-healthcare system [3], negotiation of user behaviour system using blockchain [4], blockchain combination of Internet of Things [5], and blockchain-based risk assessment system [6]. and each blockchain is an independent value island. As the current blockchain projects are based on different usage scenarios and design ideas, the structure system, smart contract system, user privacy protection, underlying design, throughput, and many other technologies of each blockchain have their own characteristics, leading to the growth of a large number of heterogeneous blockchains, resulting in the interconnection of chains with high barriers. Since 2018, a large amount of capital has flooded into the blockchain, and various blockchain projects have blossomed, and the industry has announced that the blockchain has entered the blockchain 3.0 era while making 2018 the "first year of public chain". The consensus mechanism is considered as the soul of blockchain, but with the increasing number of chains leading to the conversion of value between chains, cross-chain technology has also become the key of the blockchain 3.0 era [7].

In this paper, we design a cross-chain solution for blockchain contract lock based on a verifiable ring signature. It realizes asset value exchange between blockchains that can deploy smart contracts without a third party so that blockchains can operate with each other, thus solving the closed situation of value silos between blockchains. Thus, the blockchain network changes from information transfer to value conversion network.

2 Blockchain Cross-Chain Technology

2.1 Status of Cross-Chain Technology Research

Cross-chaining is the process of transferring the value from one blockchain to another by breaking the barriers between the chains through technical means. The value owned in one blockchain is transformed into the value in another chain, and the circulation of value between chains is further realized through this value transformation [8]. Cross-chaining essentially does not change the total value of the blockchain itself but is only an exchange of value between different users on the chain [9]. Cross-chaining is not just about sending messages between chains, not just to ensure stable delivery of messages from one chain to another, but to ensure synchronization when data changes between chains and ledgers on the chain to avoid the loss of value the double-spending problem. So cross-chaining is to flow the value between different blockchains under the condition that the value is conserved between chains. From the birth of blockchain in 2009, at the early stage of blockchain development, blockchain technology is mainly developed in a single chain, and the upgrading and optimization of blockchain are only carried out on a single chain. When the developers of a single chain disagree on the development direction of blockchain, the only thing that can be done is to carry out a hard fork of blockchain in order to continue to promote the development of single-chain. Otherwise, they can only start from scratch to carry out a new blockchain design. Since 2012, Bitcoin applications have been overly constrained by the need to add six blocks to a single block in the backlog, the small block size, and the functional limitations of smart contracts. To solve the problem of collaborative interaction between different blockchains, the InterLedger protocol was proposed by Ripple Labs in 2012 [10]. The concept of the atomic swap was proposed by Herlihy in 2013, where atomic swap suggests that a cross-chain transaction does not have a third state throughout the swap, only success or failure [11]. The cross-chain approach of hash locking through the concept of the atomic swap was proposed and became the mainstream cross-chain approach at the same time. With the rapid development of new blockchains such as ethereum and litecoin, the development of bitcoin was accelerated, and the concept of side-chain was first proposed by Blockstream in 2014, using two-way peg [12] with anchored side-chain to make the value flow in the main chain and side-chain at some exchange rate. In 2015, hash locking was used in the lightning network to improve the efficiency of bitcoin transactions [13]. 2016 saw the development of relay cross-chain platforms, and bitcoin used the BTC-Relay relay cross-chain approach to complete the bitcoin to ethereum cross-chain. Still, this solution is a one-way communication from bitcoin to ethereum. 2017 saw the gradual emergence of cross-chain infrastructure platforms. The aim is to build a foundation platform that is compatible with all blockchain applications.

2.2 Cross-Chain Technology Classification

Cross-chain technology is usually discussed in two cases, one is homogeneous blockchain, and the other is heterogeneous blockchain. Homogeneous blockchains have the same interface, block generation rules, block structure, verification logic, smart contracts, etc. So cross-chaining between homogeneous blockchains has easy operability [14], and it is easier to complete cross-chaining operations. For cross-chain between heterogeneous blockchains, cross-chain interaction between heterogeneous blockchains is more complex and challenging to operate because of having different data layers, network layer, consensus layer, contract layer, and application layer [15]. For example, the processing mechanism in Bitcoin is UTXO, the processing mechanism in EtherHub is the accountability mechanism, and the processing mechanism in Hyperledger Fabric is the way of chain code. So in heterogeneous blockchains usually need to join the third party to perform cross-chain operations. There are four types of mainstream cross-chain mechanisms: hash locking, notary model, distributed private key control, and side-chain relaying [16].

Hash locking was first applied to Bitcoin's Lightning Network, which relies on the irreversibility and low-collision nature of hash functions combined with the delayed nature of transaction posting in blockchains as a cross-chain mechanism. Hash locking is usually used in blockchains with programmable smart contracts, such as Bitcoin, Ether, and Fabric. Hash locking can well achieve cross-chain atomicity between chains and can realize the exchange operation of assets between chains without relying on third parties, i.e., the total assets owned on each blockchain do not change, only the change of asset ownership, and cannot transfer the assets on one chain to another [17].

The notary model is a way to introduce a third party trusted by both parties as an intermediary to assist in completing inter-chain asset transfers when neither party can be trusted. The notary model uses a set of trusted nodes selected by both parties as to the trusted third party, and this trusted third party is called a notary. The notary uses a consensus algorithm to reach a proof of consensus to track and verify the events on one chain and prove the authenticity of the events to the other chain. Since the notary model does not need to consider the complex work of different structures between chains, consensus algorithms, and block-out mechanisms, it makes the cross-chain interoperability between chains easier. It is now the most widely used cross-chain approach.

Distributed private key control is similar to the notary model. Still, the user maintains control over the owned assets, except that the distributed storage is used to store the user's private key, which avoids the centralization problem of the notary model to some extent. Distributed private key control uses distributed nodes to manage the user's private key and maps the assets on the original chain to cross-chains to achieve interconnection of assets on different blockchains. By splitting the ownership and usage rights of user assets, the usage rights of assets are reasonably mapped to the cross-chain system to achieve the purpose of cross-chain. The Fusion project uses distributed private key control.

The side chain in the side-chain relay model is a concept relative to the main chain, a blockchain that operates independently relative to the main chain but depends on the main chain in its operation. One of the most critical technologies is the two-way-peg. There are four ways to implement the two-way-peg: single hosting mode, joint anchoring mode, drive chain mode, and SPV anchoring mode. In the single hosting model, a cross-chain participant sends assets to a third party for escrow, and the escrow party trades the escrow assets in the side-chain to the other party's side-chain account. The federated anchoring model selects a group of notaries to form a federation to become a third-party custodian and uses multiple signature technologies to avoid a single point of danger. The Drive Chain model was first proposed by Paul, the founder of Bitcoin Hivemind. Notaries are represented by a transaction processing node in the drive chain, which locks and unlocks assets and submits asset lock proposals initiated by other chains to the block through the transaction processing node. SPV (simple payment verification) was first mentioned in the Bitcoin White Paper to verify the existence of data in the blockchain in light client applications by downloading only the block header information without obtaining the complete blockchain data. Verification. BTCRelay is a classic relay project that can verify information on another chain without a third party by initiating a mint transaction on the side chain and verifying the SPV with details from the main chain.

3   Verifiable Ring Signature Cross-Chain Technology Model

3.1   Cross-Chain Model

The cross-chain model of this solution is shown in Fig. 1, in which the assets are locked by means of contract locks on two programmable blockchains, and a pair of verifiable ring signatures are signed on the assets. The value circulation on the two blockchains is carried out by unlocking the assets, ensuring the fairness and security of both sides of the transaction. It is based on the cross-chain operation of atomic operation, only the success or failure of asset exchange exists, and there is no third case.

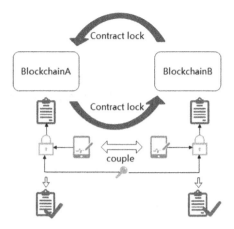

Fig. 1. Cross-chain model.

3.2 Verifiable Ring Signature

Ring signature is an anonymous signature scheme first proposed by Rivest et al. in the paper [18]. The signer performs the signing operation by selecting n signature members, including himself, to form the ring members of the ring signature and using the public keys of $n-1$ ring members other than himself without relying on others. The verifier can verify the signature and determine whether it is one of the n ring members but cannot determine which ring member the real signer is. This unconditional anonymity can well protect the signer's identity from being traced. This unconditional anonymity protects the signer's identity from being traced. The ring signature hides the real signer from the ring members so that the signer cannot prove that he is the real signer but can only verify that the signature comes from one of the ring members.

In order to solve the problem that the signer of a ring signature can verify the identity of his signer voluntarily, Lv et al. proposed the verifiable ring signature scheme for the first time in the paper [19]. The verifiable ring signature scheme consists of three parts: ring-sign, ring-verify, and ring-check.

Ring-Sign: A ring-sign is a ring $U = \{U_1, U_2, \ldots U_n\}$ consisting of a given n ring members, each member of the ring has a public-private key pair (Pk_i, Sk_i), $i = 1, 2, \ldots n$, the actual signer $U_s (1 \leq s \leq n)$. Where the input is the message to be signed M, all the public keys of the ring members Pk_i, $i = 1, 2, \ldots n$ and the private key of the actual signer is Sk_s; Output ring signature $\sigma = Rsign(M, Pk_1 \ldots Pk_n, Sk_s)$ of ring member U_s to sign message M.

Ring-Verify: The message M to be verified, the ring signature σ, and all public keys Pk_i, $i = 1, 2, \ldots n$ in the ring members are used as input, and the output is Y or N, $Y/N = Rverify(M, \sigma, Pk_1 \ldots Pk_n)$.

Ring-Check: The ring-check consists of the message M, its signature σ, and the published secret message *Keystone* as input, and the output is the real ring signature member $U_s U_s = Rcheck(M, \sigma, Keystone)$.

3.3 Concurrent Signature

In the RSA public key system, choose two suitable large prime numbers p and q to compute $n = p \times q$, compute the Euler function $\varphi(n) = (p-1)(q-1)$, choose an integer e $1 < e < \varphi(n)$, $\gcd(\varphi(n), e) = 1$ and compute $d \times e \equiv 1 \mod \varphi(n)$ to find d, so take the public key $PK_i = (n_i, e_i)$ and the private key $SK_i = (d, n)$.

$F_i(x) = x^{e_i}(\mathrm{mod}\, n_i)$ is a one-way threshold permutation, and the inverse permutation F_i^{-1} is known only to the A_i corresponding to it. E_k is the symmetric encryption algorithm. Define the function $C_{k,v}(y_1, y_2) = E_k(y_1 \oplus E_k(y_2))$, M is the message to be signed, and H is the hash function of the L bit output.

Signature algorithm: Compute $k = H(M)$, choose a random initial value v, choose a random *keystone* and compute $x_b = H(keystone)$, assuming that the participants include Alice and Bob, and Alice is the initiator of the protocol. Compute $y_b = F_b(x_b)$, bring y_b into the equation $C_{k,v}(y_a, y_b) = E_k(y_a \oplus E_k(y_b)) = v$, and find y_a $x_a = F_a^{-1}(y_a)$ and represent the signature as a quintet $\sigma = (PK_a, PK_b, v, x_a, x_b)$.

Validation algorithm: Verify the possession of the binary $(M, \sigma) = (M, (PK_a, PK_b, v, x_a, x_b))$, computing $y_a = F_a(x_a)$, $y_b = F_b(x_b)$, $k = H(M)$. Bring y_a, y_b, k, into the equation $C_{k,v}(y_a, y_b) = E_k(y_a \oplus E_k(y_b)) = v$, and if the signature is correct, then one can conclude that the signer is one of Alice or Bob, but due to the ambiguity of the ring signature, no one can conclude which of the two performed the signature.

Identification algorithm: After Alice discloses the secret message keystone, for $x_i = H(keystone)$, for x_a, x_b are not equal to x_i, then verify that *keystone* is a false value. Otherwise, there must be a value between x_a, x_b and x_i match, then at this time the public key PK_i matching with x_i is the public key of this signature receiver, and vice versa another public key is the initiator's public key. By announcing *keystone*, the ambiguity of the ring signature can be removed, and thus the signature can be validated.

3.4 Cross-Chain Contract Deployment

Smart contracts are a set of digital promises, first proposed by Szabo in 1995 [20]. Smart contracts do not yet have an accepted definition on the blockchain. From a narrow perspective, smart contracts can be seen as applications for asset management that run on a blockchain distributed ledger with pre-defined rules that can encapsulate validation and complete information exchange or value transfer. The smart contract is decentralized in nature. Ethereum is a public blockchain platform with smart contract, which can be Turing-complete on Ether and processed by EVM (Ethereum virtual machine). Hyperledger Fabric is an open-source modular federated chain blockchain platform, in which smart contracts are collectively called chaincode, which is the bearer of business logic and can be used in multiple languages, such as Go, Java, Python, etc. EOS is a distributed design public chain blockchain platform and is used for business scenarios. Smart contract of EOS is an application registered and executed in the nodes of the EOSIO blockchain, and the contract content is stored in the distributed ledger through contract specific functions. Ledger for storage.

Chaincode is located between the application layer of the whole blockchain architecture and the bottom layer of the blockchain. The process is shown in Fig. 2. Before deploying chaincode to Fabric, you need to set up the Fabric blockchain network environment and download the Fabric binaries, corresponding docker image, and configuration files. You need to download the Fabric binaries, corresponding docker image, and configuration file. Batch start the fabric image through docker-compose to compose the network environment. In Fabric network, it mainly needs to generate node MSP identity, genesis block file, channel file, sorting node file, and peer node configuration file. After the environment is deployed, we need to install Chaincode for each peer in the Fabric network to execute and endorse transactions, and then instantiate Chaincode in the channel. The process of packaging, compressing, serializing, decompressing, and compiling the chaincode is mainly included. Each chaincode must implement the TransactionContextInterface interface to read or modify the ledger. Blockchain operations can be performed by writing applications through the Fabric SDK.

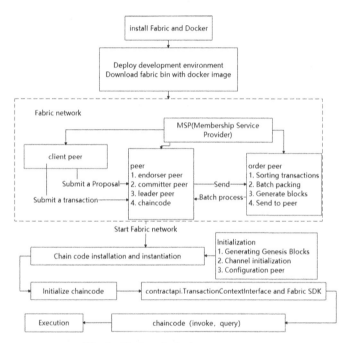

Fig. 2. Chaincode deployment process.

3.5 Cross-Chain Chaincode Interface Design

Since Fabric is a blockchain without assets, we first need to make the users in Fabric network with personal account assets, so we need to write the chain code of account assets to implement basic account functions for users. accountCC (Account Chaincode) is used to implement user account functions, and the account structure is shown in Table 1. The AccountCC interface is shown in Table 2.

Table 1. Account data structure.

Account Data Structure		
type Account struct {		
Address	string	// Account Address
Amount	uint64	// Account Asset Balance
Passwd	string	// Account Password
Sequence	uint64	// Account serial number
Type	int	// 0:MidAccount ;1:General Account
TransferTo	[2]string	// Midaccount transfer address
}		

For the assets on blockchain, use a locking contract to anchor the assets to the intermediate account for the duration of the transaction and transfer the assets through a smart contract when the transaction between the two parties is reached. So we write locking contract chain code LockCC (LockChaincode) to lock assets to intermediate accounts. the data structure of LockCC is shown in Table 3. The LockCC chaincode interface is shown in Table 4.

Table 2. AccountCC interface.

Interface	Description
fun InitAccount(args)	Initialize account data
fun CreateAccount(args)	Create a general account
fun CreateMidAccount(args)	Create intermediate accounts
fun Transfer(args)	Asset transfer
fun Query(args)	Account asset inquiry

Table 3. Lock data structure.

Lock Data Structure		
type Lock struct {		
Sender	string	// Sender Address
Receiver	string	// Receiver Adress
Amount	uint64	//Locked Asset
ConSign	string	// Concurrent Signature
TimeLock	int64	// Automatic return of assets after timeout
LockAddress	string	// Locked intermediate account addresses
State	State	//0:Locked;1: Signed;2:Refund
}		

Table 4. LockCC Interface.

Interface	Description
fun CreateMidAccount(args)	Invoke AccountCC create MidAccount
fun CreateConSign(args)	Add concurrent signature
fun Withdraw(args)	Withdraw asset
fun Refund(args)	Refund asset
fun Query(args)	Query locked information

3.6 Cross-Chain Transaction Process

1. Through the fuzziness of the verifiable ring signature to enable both sides to exchange contracts can be verified at the same time, but the fuzziness of the ring signature leads to the contract between the two sides does not take effect, only when the secret information keystone is published well, the signature fuzziness of both sides disappears at the same time, making it possible for both sides to exchange assets on different blockchains at the same time without the need of a third party. The specific process is shown in Fig. 3, and the cross-chain transaction process is as follows.

2. Alice wants to exchange tokens of value V on blockchain A for Bob's equivalent tokens on blockchain B. Through offline negotiation, she generates a contract message $M_1 = (U_A, U_b, V)$, U_A to exchange tokens of value V with U_b. She uses the digital signature algorithm RSA to sign M_1. First, she performs a hash operation $h_1 = H(M_1)$ on M_1 and uses Alice's private key Sk_A to encrypt h_1 to obtain $s_1 = Sk_A(h_1)$. M_1, Pk_A, s_1 will be packaged as $pkg_1(M_1, Pk_A, s_1)$ and sent it to Bob.

3. Bob receives pkg_1 from Alice and uses Alice's public key Pk_A to verify the signature s_1, $M_1' = Pk_A(s_1)$. If verification fails, the offer is rejected. $M_1' = M_1$ Verification is successful, and Bob agrees to the token swap. Call AccountCC to create an intermediate locked account. Call LockCC to lock V to the lock address $Lockadd_b$ on the intermediate account return blockchain B and sign it simultaneously $\sigma = (PK_a, PK_b, v, x_a, x_b)$, $s_2 = Lockadd_b$. Select a secret message *keystone* and hash it to get $x_b = H(keystone)$, pack the s_2, x_b to get $pkg_2(s_2, x_b)$, then use Bob's private key Sk_B to encrypt the hash of pkg_2 to get $s_3 = Sk_B(H(pkg_2))$, randomly select a new secret key k to encrypt pkg_2 symmetrically to get $s_4 = E_k(pkg_2)$, use Alice's The public key Pk_A of Alice is used to encrypt k to get the digital envelope $dig_1 = Pk_A(k_2)$, and finally s_3, dig_1, s_4 is packaged as $pkg_3(s_3, dig, s_4)$ and sent to Alice.

4. Alice receives pkg_3 from Bob, Alice uses Bob's public key Pk_B to decrypt ciphertext s_3 to get $pkg_2' = Pk_B(s_3)$, then uses Alice's private key Sk_A to decrypt digital envelope dig to get session secret key $k = Sk_A(dig)$, uses k to decrypt ciphertext s_4 to get pkg_2 and hashes it $pkg_2'' = H(D_{k_2}(s_4))$. If pkg_2' matches pkg_2'', the protocol continues, otherwise it terminates immediately. Alice calls the AccountCC chaincode on blockchain A to create an intermediate account and the LockCC chaincode

to create a locking contract. Locked contract address $Lockadd_a$ on blockchain A and make $x'_a = x_b$ and sign it simultaneously $\sigma' = (PK_a, PK_b, v', x'_a, x'_b)$ will be passed to Bob in the same way as in step 2, but the message does not include x_b in step 2.

5. Bob receives Alice's pkg_4 and gets Alice's locked contract $Lockadd_a$ on blockchainA. At this time, Bob queries the locked contract on blockchainA and verifies the signature operation, that is, $x'_a = x_b$ verifies it, and Bob publishes *keystone*. With the publication of *keystone* the two signatures remove the ambiguity of the ring signature so the operation of getting assets can be carried out. At this point, Bob goes to blockchainA and calls lockCC chaincode to get the assets on blockchainA.

6. Alice receives the *keystone* announced by Bob to go to blockchainB to call lockCC chaincode to get the assets on blockchainB.

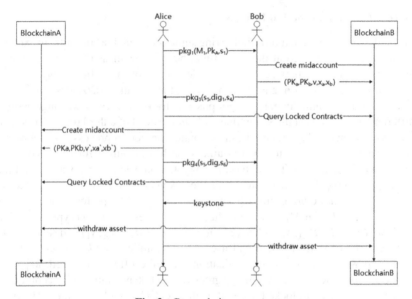

Fig. 3. Cross-chain processes.

3.7 Security Analysis

This scheme is based on the ambiguity of ring signature, which can be satisfied with the ambiguity and unforgeability of ring signature in the case of ideal symmetric encryption algorithm E.

Since this scheme uses a ring signature to lock the cross-chain contract, that is, anyone can verify the authenticity of the signature and can know that the signature is signed by both parties of the cross-chain transaction, but cannot know who is the initiator and who is the receiver, at this time the contract is not effective, and only after the secret information keystone is published, the initiator and receiver can be associated with the corresponding public key so as to lift the ring signature's ambiguity, then the two cross-chain contracts take effect at the same time, and both parties can retrieve assets in the chain. At the end of this scheme, Bob can choose not to publish the keystone, but Bob needs to go to blockchainA to get the assets through the keystone. At this time, even if Bob does not publish the keystone, Alice can still get the keystone, which satisfies the most basic fairness of the cross-chain contract, and there will not be a situation where one party takes the assets and the other party loses. This satisfies the most basic fairness of cross-chain contracts, and there will be no situation where one party takes the assets, and the other loses.

4 Analysis of Experimental Result

By building two Hyperledger Fabric federated chains, each blockchain consists of two peer nodes, one order node, and one ca node. Create accounts for Alice and Bob on each blockchain, and initialize each account with 500 assets. A complete cross-chain request is made by Alice to initiate a cross-chain request transaction until Alice and Bob complete the exchange of 10 assets at the same time. During the testing process, the time required is counted in steps of 5 cross-chain requests each time they are initiated. As shown in Table 5, the overall system is running on a standalone host with Ubuntu 20.04 LTS using zsh, Docker v19.03.8, docker-compose v1.25.0, Go v1.16.2, Hyperledger Fabric v2.1.0, Node v10.19.0, host configuration is, inter(R) Core i7-9700k, RAM-32 GB, VMware Workstation 15.5.1 installed in the host and running on 64bit-Windows 10 pro system.

Table 5. Running environment.

Name	Version
Operating System	Ubuntu 20.04 LTS
Shell	Zsh
CPU	inter(R) Core i7-9700k
RAM	32 GB
Hyperledger-fabric	v2.2.0LTS
Docker	v19.03.8
Docker-compose	v1.25.0
Go	v1.16.2
NodeJS	v10.19.0

As can be seen in Fig. 4, this solution can process roughly 70 complete cross-chain transactions per second. The analysis shows that the bottleneck of system processing is mainly in the ordering node of Hyperledger Fabric because the ordering node is mainly used to pack the transactions of each node into blocks and distribute them, but since the whole system is running on a standalone host, the docker container is used to simulate each node, and the whole host maintains four peer nodes and two order nodes, the ordering node occupies high resources in terms of CPU usage order nodes, the sorting nodes take up higher resources in terms of CPU occupancy, and the network latency is negligible because it is running on a single machine. So hardware conditions may have a greater impact on cross-chain transactions.

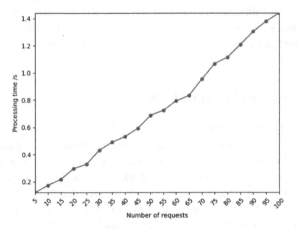

Fig. 4. Cross-chain throughput.

5 Conclusion

In the era of blockchain 3.0, the importance of cross-chain technology is particularly prominent. Only the development of cross-chain technology can promote blockchain interconnection and break value silos. Due to the blossoming of existing blockchain technologies, cross-chain technology is not yet mature, and the existing cross-chain technologies have different research directions and different application scenarios. Still, the future is destined to be a situation of interconnection and coexistence of multiple chains. Therefore, cross-chain technology still needs continuous research and exploration. This paper constructs a cross-chain solution with simultaneous effect by means of contract lock based on the ambiguity of ring signature, so that the users on the chain can complete the value exchange between chains only under the operation of smart contracts without the intervention of third parties, thus achieving the purpose of cross-chain. At the same time, this solution is dependent on smart contracts, and cross-chain interoperability can only be accomplished on blockchains where smart contracts can be deployed, and there is still much room for optimization in terms of efficiency and throughput, which is hoped to be improved in the future research process.

Acknowledgement. This work is supported by the Key Research and Development Project of Sichuan Province (No. 2021YFSY0012, No. 2020YFG0307, No. 2021YFG0332), the National Natural Science Foundation of China (No. 62076042), the Science and Technology Innovation Project of Sichuan (No. 2020017), the Key Research and Development Project of Chengdu (No. 2019-YF05-02028-GX), the Innovation Team of Quantum Security Communication of Sichuan

Province (No.17TD0009), the Academic and Technical Leaders Training Funding Support Projects of Sichuan Province (No. 2016120080102643).

References

1. Nakamoto, S., Bitcoin, A.: A peer-to-peer electronic cash system. Bitcoin (2008). https://bit coin.org/bitcoin
2. Shao, Q.F., Jin, C.Q., Zhang, Z., Qian, W.N., Zhou, A.Y.: Blockchain, architecture and research progress. Chin. J. Comput. **41**, 969–988 (2018)
3. Peng, X., Zhang, J., Zhang, S., Wan, W., Chen, H., Xia, J.: A secure signcryption scheme for electronic health records sharing in blockchain. Comput. Syst. Sci. Eng. **37**, 265–281 (2021)
4. Yang, M., Zhang, S., Zhao, Y., Wang, Q.: Dynamic negotiation of user behaviour via blockchain technology in federated system. Int. J. Comput. Sci. Eng. **22**, 74–83 (2020)
5. Chen, H., et al.: Task-attribute-based access control scheme for IoT via blockchain. Comput. Mater. Contin. **65**, 2441–2453 (2020)
6. Zhao, Y., Zhang, S., Yang, M., He, P., Wang, Q.: Research on architecture of risk assessment system based on block chain. Comput. Mater. Contin. **61**, 677–686 (2019)
7. Xu, Z., Zhou, X.: Survey on crosschain technology. Appl. Res. Comput. **38**, 341–346 (2021)
8. Lu, A., Zhao, K., Yang, J., Wang, F.: Research on cross-chain technology of blockchain. Netinfo Secur. **19**, 83–90 (2019)
9. Zhao, G., Guo, S., Zhang, S., Hui, W.: Analysis of cross-chain technology of blockchain. Chin. J. Internet Things **4**, 35 (2020)
10. Hope-Bailie, A., Thomas, S.: Interledger: creating a standard for payments. In: Proceedings of the 25th International Conference Companion on World Wide Web, pp. 281–282 (2016)
11. Yie, A., Casallas, R., Deridder, D., Wagelaar, D.: Realizing model transformation chain interoperability. Softw. Syst. Model. **11**, 55–75 (2012)
12. Asgaonkar, A., Krishnamachari, B.: Solving the buyer and seller's dilemma: a dual-deposit escrow smart contract for provably cheat-proof delivery and payment for a digital good without a trusted mediator. In: 2019 IEEE International Conference on Blockchain and Cryptocurrency (ICBC), pp. 262–267. IEEE (2019)
13. Poon, J., Dryja, T.: The bitcoin lightning network: scalable off-chain instant payments (2016)
14. Wei, A.: An improved cross-chain technology of blockchain. Cybersp. Secur. **10**, 40–45 (2019)
15. Xie, J., Li, Z., Jin, J.: Cross chain mechanism based on Spark blockchain. J. Comput. Appl. **42**, 519 (2021)
16. Zhang, S., Qin, B., Zheng, H.: Research on the protocol of multiple cross-chains based on the hash lock. Cybersp. Secur. **9**, 57–62 (2018)
17. Li, F., Li, Z., Zhao, H.: Research on the progress in cross-chain technology of blockchains. Ruan Jian Xue Bao/J. Softw. **30**, 1649–1660 (2019)
18. Rivest, R.L., Shamir, A., Tauman, Y.: How to leak a secret. In: Boyd, C. (ed.) ASIACRYPT 2001. LNCS, vol. 2248, pp. 552–565. Springer, Heidelberg (2001). https://doi.org/10.1007/3-540-45682-1_32
19. Lv, J., Wang, X.: Verifiable ring signature. In: Proceedings of DMS 2003-the 9th International Conference on Distributed Multimedia Systems, pp. 663–667 (2003)
20. Szabo, N.: Formalizing and securing relationships on public networks. First Monday (1997)

A Routing Algorithm for Node Protection in Wireless Sensor Network Based on Clustering Ant Colony Strategy

Xiao Feng[✉], Yuanzheng Wang, Tengfei Dong, Yingxia Liao, Yixin Zhang, and Yi Lin

State Grid Information Telecommunication Group Co., Ltd., Beijing 102211, China
1009156962@qq.com

Abstract. Thanks to the rapid development of wireless communication and electronic technology, wireless sensor networks have been increasingly used in military, medical and other fields. Because of the characteristics of wireless sensor networks, traditional network routing protocols are not applicable in wireless sensor networks. In recent research, many wireless sensor network routing algorithms have been proposed. Among these algorithms, the cluster routing algorithm performs well, but the cluster routing algorithm often has the problem that some nodes die prematurely due to too many communication tasks. Ant colony optimization algorithm can effectively solve the combinatorial optimization problem with NP-Hard characteristics, and is widely used in routing algorithms. Therefore, we propose a node protection routing algorithm for wireless sensor network based on clustering ant colony strategy (NPAWSN). This algorithm optimizes the clustering process, selects multiple cluster head nodes for clusters with high communication pressure, and at the same time, designs a new path probability selection model for ant movement, which fully considers the remaining energy of cluster head nodes close to the sink, effectively alleviating the problem of premature death of some nodes due to too many transmission tasks. The algorithm considers the sensor energy, communication efficiency and other factors. The use of adaptive ant colony algorithm improves the convergence speed and maintains the high performance of the routing algorithm.

Keywords: Clustering · Ant colony optimize · Routing algorithm

1 Introduction

The wireless sensor network includes a large number of sensor nodes with perceptual capabilities, and a wireless network composed of self-organization among nodes. Sensors monitor the physical or environmental conditions in different locations. Wireless sensor networks were initially used in military applications such as battlefield monitoring and received extensive attention and developed rapidly. Nowadays, wireless sensor networks are used in many civilian fields, such as environmental and ecological monitoring, health monitoring, home automation, and traffic control. As shown in Fig. 1, a typical wireless sensor network system architecture includes distributed wireless sensor nodes (groups), receiver-transmitter convergence nodes, Internet or communication satellites, and task management nodes.

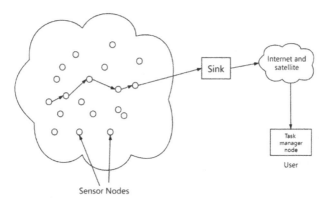

Fig. 1. Wireless sensor network.

The wireless sensor network routing protocol is responsible for forwarding data from the sensor node to the sink. Different from traditional wireless networks, sensor nodes in wireless sensor networks are usually powered by batteries and have limited energy. After the energy of sensor nodes is exhausted, some or all of their working capabilities will be lost. Therefore, the energy consumption of sensor nodes needs to be considered when designing routing protocols to extend the lifetime of wireless sensor networks. At the same time, sensor nodes can only obtain local topology information, and it is necessary to design efficient routing algorithms based on local topology information.

Therefore, unlike routing protocols in traditional networks, routing protocols suitable for wireless sensor networks need to maintain transmission efficiency as much as possible while ensuring low node consumption.

The ant colony algorithm is a heuristic algorithm. People found that the ant colony can always find the shortest path from the ant nest to the food source when foraging. Inspired by this, the Italian scholar M. Dorigo, V. Maniezzo and A. Colorni proposed a new type of intelligent optimization algorithm, the ant system, in the early 1990s. The algorithm was first used to solve the traveling salesman problem, and the algorithm showed good performance on this problem. Ants will release pheromone on the path they pass during their foraging. Since the ants that choose a shorter path return to the ant nest earlier, there are more pheromones on the shorter path than on the long path, which will increase the number of ants on the shorter path. The probability of the path forms a positive feedback mechanism. In the end, most ants will choose a segment path. Ant colony algorithm is widely used in path planning, network routing and other problems because it can be used to solve complex optimization problems.

This paper proposes a wireless sensor network node protection routing algorithm based on clustering ant colony strategy. The contributions of this paper are as follows: 1. A clustering algorithm is proposed, which allocates multiple cluster heads to clusters with high communication pressure, thereby alleviating the communication pressure of cluster heads. 2. A new model of path probability selection for ant movement is designed. The remaining energy in the area close to the sink has a greater impact on node selection, avoiding death of some nodes due to excessive communication tasks and excessive energy consumption.

2 Related Work

In recent years, research on wireless sensor networks has developed rapidly, and many routing protocols have been proposed. Hierarchical routing algorithms perform well in wireless sensor networks. In hierarchical routing protocols, the network is usually divided into clusters. The nodes in the cluster are divided into cluster-head nodes and non-cluster-head nodes. The non-cluster-head nodes transmit data to the cluster-head node, and the cluster-head node communicates with the receiver, and is responsible for aggregating and forwarding the data of the nodes in the cluster. The clustering routing protocol is mainly divided into distributed and centralized. Among them, the centralized algorithm requires the global topology of the network, which in some cases cannot be achieved or requires a large cost, so we focus on the distributed algorithm. Distributed algorithms are mainly based on the idea of splitting or clustering. [1] proposed the LEACH algorithm, the first cluster routing protocol proposed. The algorithm randomly selects cluster heads, and then the cluster head nodes broadcast the message that they become cluster heads. Non-cluster head nodes decide to join according to the strength of the broadcast signal. cluster. In the data transmission phase, the non-cluster head node sends the message to the cluster head node and then sends it to the sensor after aggregation. In [2], LEACH algorithm is optimized to generate uneven cluster heads. [3] proposed a clustering algorithm based on geographic location.

Ant colony algorithm is an effective algorithm to solve routing optimization. Some existing wireless sensor network routing protocols are based on ant colony algorithm. Ant colony algorithm was first proposed in [4]. Ant colony algorithm is a swarm intelligence algorithm that solves complex optimization problems through the cooperation of ants. [5] reviewed the application of ant colony algorithm in network routing. [6] proposed to extend the life of the network based on finding the maximum number of disjoint connection coverage that satisfies the sensor coverage and the network connection. [7] proposed a routing protocol based on the minimum spanning tree ant colony algorithm. [8] uses three kinds of pheromone to realize the ant colony optimization algorithm.

On the basis of the above algorithm, our algorithm optimizes the clustering process, designs a new path probability selection model for ants movement, and uses an adaptive ant colony algorithm. The algorithm effectively prolongs the life of the network in wireless sensor networks, while meeting the requirements of low transmission consumption and high transmission efficiency, and the convergence speed is higher than that of traditional ant colony algorithm-based wireless sensor network routing protocols.

3 System Model and Problem Formulation

3.1 System Model

Consider a wireless sensor network containing n sensor nodes, where v_i represents the i node. The set of nodes is $V = (v_1, v_2, \ldots, v_n)$. Assuming the sensors and sink no longer move after deployment, it can be considered that the sensor nodes are distributed in a rectangular area and the sink are located outside the rectangular area. The specific location of the nodes is unknown, and the distance between the nodes can be calculated by the received signal strength. Suppose the communication radius of the wireless sensor node is R_0, and the initial energy is C.

3.2 Energy Consumption Model

Suppose that node a sends k bit data to node b at a distance of d. According to the secondary fading model and the multipath fading model, its energy consumption is as follows:

$$E_{send}(k, d) = \begin{cases} k \times E_{elec} + k \times \varepsilon_{fs} \times d^2, d < d_0 \\ k \times E_{elec} + k \times \varepsilon_{mp} \times d^4, d > d_0 \end{cases} \tag{1}$$

In the formula (1), d_0 represents a threshold, ε_{fs} and ε_{mp} represent the power amplification coefficients corresponding to different distances between nodes, and E_{elec} represents the energy consumed by processing each bit of data in the node. It can be seen that when the distance between nodes is greater than d_0, the energy consumption of communication between nodes is greatly increased. Therefore, communication behaviors between nodes with a distance greater than d_0 should be avoided as much as possible. In our scheme, single-hop communication is used for intra-cluster node communication. When the cluster head node is far away from the receiver node, multi-hop communication is used to reduce energy consumption.

4 Routing Algorithm for Node protection in Wireless Sensor Network based on Clustering ant Colony Strategy

4.1 Cluster Head Selection

The hierarchical routing protocol has the following advantages:

1. Data from non-cluster head nodes is forwarded via the cluster head node, reducing long-distance wireless communication.
2. It is conducive to the application of distributed algorithms and is more suitable for large-scale networks.
3. Has good scalability.
4. The cluster head node aggregates the data of the nodes in the cluster, can merge and compress the data before forwarding, reducing the amount of data transmitted in the network.

In the scheme of this article, we first divide the clusters according to the topology of the network itself, and then select the cluster heads in the divided clusters. We use the modularity-based clustering algorithm to obtain stable cluster divisions [10–15].

According to the above algorithm to get the result of cluster division, we need to select the cluster head for each cluster. In the clustering routing protocol, the cluster head node close to the sink not only has to transmit the data in the cluster, but also forward the data from the cluster head node farther away, which causes greater communication pressure. This may cause the node to run out of energy prematurely and die, thereby affecting the life of the wireless sensor network. At the same time, the cluster head node needs to aggregate and transmit the data of the nodes in the cluster. When the number of nodes in the cluster where the cluster head is located is large, the transmission pressure of the cluster head node will increase. Based on the above analysis, we propose an adaptive cluster head selection scheme. The main idea of the scheme is to increase the number of cluster heads in the cluster appropriately according to the communication pressure of the cluster. Suppose that the sensor nodes are divided into N clusters after the clustering is completed. C_i represents the i cluster, and M_i represents the number of nodes in the i cluster. We first use the receiver as the source node for a round of flooding to obtain the distance between the sensor node i and the sink The number of hops h_i, the average number of hops H_i from the i cluster node to the sink is

$$H_i = \frac{\sum_{j \in C_i} h_j}{M_i} \tag{2}$$

We use the following formula to measure the communication pressure of the cluster

$$P_i = \alpha \times M_i + \beta \times H_i \tag{3}$$

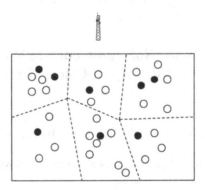

Fig. 2. A result of clustering.

In the formula (3), M_i represents the number of nodes in the cluster. α and β are constants, and their value reflects the influence of the number of nodes in the cluster and the average distance between the nodes in the cluster and the sink on the communication pressure. This scheme sorts the communication pressures of each cluster, and allocates two cluster head nodes to the clusters with greater communication pressure, which account for the total number of clusters $\frac{1}{3}$. For one example, a result of clustering is shown in Fig. 2.

4.2 Node Protection Routing Between Clusters Based on Ant Colony Algorithm

In the basic ant colony optimization algorithm, the transition probability function of the data packet from node v_i to node v_j can be expressed as

$$p_{ij}^k(t) = \frac{\tau_{ij}^\alpha(t)\eta_{ij}^\beta(t)}{\sum_{\mu \in V_{allow}} \tau_{i\mu}^\alpha(t)\eta_{i\mu}^\beta(t)} \tag{4}$$

V_{allow} represents the set of next hop candidate nodes, $p_{ij}^k(t)$ is the probability of ant k transferring from cluster head node i to cluster head node j, $\tau_{ij}(t)$ is time t The pheromone level between cluster head node i and cluster head node j, the update rule of pheromone is

$$\tau_{ij} \leftarrow \rho\tau_{ij} + \Delta\tau_{ij} \tag{5}$$

$$\Delta\tau_{ij} = \sum_{k=1}^{m} \Delta\tau_{ij}^k \tag{6}$$

$$\Delta\tau_{ij}^k = \frac{Q}{L_k} \tag{7}$$

ρ represents the volatilization coefficient of pheromone, τ_{ij}^k represents the pheromone left by the k ant on the path from i to j, and $\Delta\tau_{ij}$ represents the information on the path from i to j in the simulation of this round of ant colony algorithm Prime increase. Q is a parameter, and L_k is the length of the path traversed by ant k in the simulation of this round of ant colony algorithm. It can be seen that the longer the path the ant travels, the smaller the pheromone increment imposed by the ant on the path.

$\eta_{ij}(t)$ represents visibility. In traditional routing algorithms based on ant colony algorithm, visibility is expressed as

$$\eta_{ij}(t) = \frac{1}{C - E(V_j)} \tag{8}$$

C represents the initial energy of the node, $E(V_j)$ represents the remaining energy of the current node. The energy consumed by the node will affect the visibility. The visibility value of node j that has consumed more energy is smaller, leading to the next round in the stimulation of ant colony algorithm, the probability of ants selecting node j is reduced.

$$\eta_{ij}(t) = \frac{1}{H_j[C - E(V_j)]} \tag{9}$$

In the algorithm proposed in this paper, we improve the visibility expression. H_j reflects the distance between the cluster head node j and the sink to a certain extent. The analysis shows that the impact of the energy consumed by the node on visibility will be amplified at the cluster head node that is less distant from the sink. In the next round of ant colony algorithm simulation, in the area close to the sink, nodes with higher residual energy have a greater probability of being selected.

α and β are the parameters that need to be set, α reflects the influence of pheromone on the transition probability, β reflects the influence of visibility on the transition probability.

Ant colony algorithm has problems such as slow convergence speed and easy to fall into local extreme value. In order to solve the above problems, we add self-adaptability to the algorithm by adjusting the pheromone volatilization coefficient ρ. When the value of ρ is small, the global search ability of the ant colony algorithm is improved, but the convergence speed is slower. When the value of ρ is large, the searched path has a greater probability of being selected again, and the convergence speed is accelerated, but the overall situation of the algorithm is sacrificed search ability. Use the algorithm in [9] to adaptively change the value of ρ. The initial value of ρ is set to $\rho(t_0) = 1$. When the optimal value obtained by the algorithm does not change in N cycles, ρ is updated to

$$\rho(t) = \begin{cases} 0.95\rho(t-1) & if\ 0.95\rho(t-1) >= \rho_{min} \\ \rho_{min} & else \end{cases} \qquad (10)$$

ρ_{min} represents the minimum value of ρ to prevent the convergence speed of the algorithm from being reduced because ρ is too small.

The steps of node protection routing between clusters based on ant colony algorithm are as follows:

Step 1: Initialize the settings.

Step 2: Place m identical ants on the source node.

Step 3: Ant k at node i selects the next hop node according to formula (4).

Step 4: When all m ants reach the target node or after timeout, find the best path of all ants. If the best path of the current round is the same as the best path before N rounds, update ρ according to formula (10).

Step 5: Perform pheromone update according to formula (5).

Step 6: The algorithm does not reach the termination condition, go to step 2, otherwise go to step 7.

Step 7: Output the optimal solution.

5   Evaluation Analysis

In order to test the performance of the algorithm, we use the NS-2 network simulation tool for simulation. In the experiment, the wireless sensor network contains 150 randomly distributed sensor nodes. The sensor node distribution area can be approximated as a 50 m × 50 m rectangle. The initial energy of each sensor node is 0.5 J, and the sink energy is unlimited. According to the energy consumption model mentioned above, the power consumption of the transmitting and receiving circuit is $E_{elec} = 50$ nJ.bit. When the distance d between the two communicating parties is less than the threshold. d_0, the power consumption of the amplifying circuit is $\varepsilon_{fs} = 10$ pJ/bit/m^2. When the distance d between the communication parties is greater than the threshold d_0, the power consumption of the amplifying circuit is $\varepsilon_{mp} = 0.0013$ pJ/bit/m^4. Each node sends a data packet with a size of 2000 bit in each round. Compare the algorithm proposed in this article with LEACH and HEED algorithms.

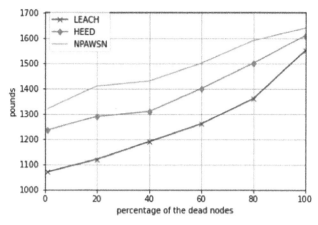

Fig. 3. The lifetime of the network when different proportions of nodes die.

As shown in Fig. 3. we fixed the sensor and receiver nodes. After starting the simulation, when 1%, 20%, 40%, 60%, 80%, 100% of the nodes died, we recorded LEACH, HEED, and the sensor nodes and receivers of the NPAWSN algorithm proposed in this article. The results of the communication rounds of the device nodes are shown in the figure. It can be seen that compared with LEACH and HEED algorithms, the NPAWSN proposed in this paper has a greater improvement in network life, and its advantages are more obvious under the standards of different dead node ratios.

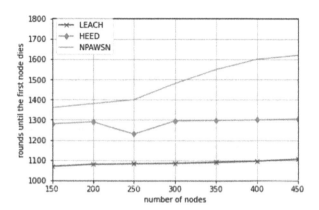

Fig. 4. The lifetime of the network when the number of nodes increases.

As shown in Fig. 4, we fixed the sensor and receiver nodes, and after starting the simulation, we recorded the life of the network as the number of sensor nodes increased (using the death of the first sensor node as the standard), and the results are shown in the figure. It can be seen that compared with LEACH and HEED algorithms, the NPAWSN proposed in this paper can delay the death time of the first node under different network scales, and as the network scale increases, its effect becomes more obvious and effectively improves the network lifespan.

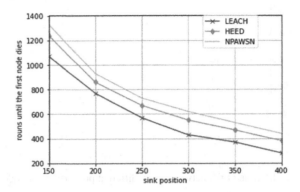

Fig. 5. Network lifetime until the first node dies.

As shown in Fig. 5, we fix the sensor node, move the sink node away from the sensor distribution area gradually, and record the life of the network as the position of the receiver node changes (take the death of the first node as the standard), and the result is shown in the Fig. 4. It can be seen that when the distance between the sink node and the sensor node area is the same, using the NPAWSN algorithm proposed in this paper can increase the life of the network compared to LEACH and HEED algorithms. As the distance increases, this advantage still exists.

6   Conclusion

In wireless sensor networks, it is an important issue to use node energy rationally and extend the life of the network. This paper proposes a wireless sensor network node protection routing algorithm based on clustering ant colony strategy. Considering that in the existing clustering wireless sensor network routing protocol, sensor nodes close to the sink often takes on too many transmission tasks. Too fast energy consumption leads to premature death. Our solution first clusters sensor nodes. We believe that clusters with a large number of nodes in the cluster or clusters close to the sink have greater communication pressure. So we select multiple cluster head nodes for clusters with high communication pressure to share the communication pressure. In the inter-cluster routing stage, we optimize the visibility in the ant colony algorithm to amplify the influence of the remaining energy factors of the nodes close to the receiver on the path selection. Experiments show that the algorithm can effectively delay the death of nodes and extend the life of wireless sensor networks.

Acknowledgement. This paper was supported by collaborative innovation in energy and material applications.

References

1. Heinzelman, W.R., Chandrakasan, A., Balakrishnan, H.: Energy-efficient communication protocol for wireless microsensor networks. In: Proceedings of the 33rd Annual Hawaii International Conference on System Sciences, vol. 2, p. 10 (2000)
2. Younis, O., Fahmy, S.: Distributed clustering in ad-hoc sensor networks: a hybrid, energy-efficient approach. In: Joint Conference of the IEEE Computer & Communications Societies. IEEE (2004)
3. Smaragdakis, G., Matta, I., Bestavros, A.: SEP: a stable election protocol for clustered heterogeneous wireless sensor networks. In: Second international workshop on sensor and actor network protocols and applications (SANPA 2004), vol. 3 (2013)
4. Dorigo, M., Birattari, M., Stutzle, T.: Ant colony optimization. IEEE Comput. Intell. Mag. 1(4), 28–39 (2006)
5. Sim, K.M., Weng, H.S.: Ant colony optimization for routing and load-balancing: survey and new directions. IEEE Trans. Syst. Man Cybern. Part A Syst. Hum. 33, 560–572 (2003)
6. Ying, L.: An ant colony optimization approach for maximizing the lifetime of heterogeneous wireless sensor networks. IEEE Trans. Syst. Man Cybern. Part C (Appl. Rev.) 42, 408–420 (2012)
7. Wang, P.D., Tang, G.Y., Li, Y., Yang, X.X.: Improved ant colony algorithm for traveling salesman problems. In: 2012 24th Chinese Control and Decision Conference (CCDC), pp. 660–664. IEEE (2012)
8. Lee, J.W., Choi, B.S., Lee, J.: Energy-efficient coverage of wireless sensor networks using ant colony optimization with three types of pheromones. IEEE Trans. Industr. Inf. 7(3), 419–427 (2011)
9. Wang, Y., Xie, J.: An adaptive ant colony algorithm and its simulation research. J. Syst. Simul. 01, 31–33 (2002)
10. Newman, M.: Fast algorithm for detecting community structure in networks. Phys. Rev. E Stat. Nonlin. Soft Matter Phys. 6, 66133 (2004)
11. Kocher, I.S.: An experimental simulation of addressing auto-configuration issues for wireless sensor networks. Comput. Mater. Contin. 71(2), 3821–3838 (2022)
12. Rajab, A.: Fault tolerance techniques for multi-hop clustering in wireless sensor networks. Intell. Autom. Soft Comput. 32(3), 1743–1761 (2022)
13. Chinnaraju, G., Nithyanandam, S.: Grey hole attack detection and prevention methods in wireless sensor networks. Comput. Syst. Sci. Eng. 42(1), 373–386 (2022)
14. Fouad, K.M., Salim, O.M.: Hybrid sensor selection technique for lifetime extension of wireless sensor networks. Comput. Mater. Contin. 70(3), 4965–4985 (2022)
15. Alajlan, A.M.: Multi-step detection of simplex and duplex wormhole attacks over wireless sensor networks. Comput. Mater. Contin. 70(3), 4241–4259 (2022)

Deep Learning Network Intrusion Detection Based on Network Traffic

Hanyang Wang[1], Sirui Zhou[1], Honglei Li[1], Juan Hu[1], Xinran Du[1], Jinghui Zhou[2], Yunlong He[2], Fa Fu[1(✉)], and Houqun Yang[1(✉)]

[1] Hainan University, Haikou 570228, China
{fufa,yhq}@hainanu.edu.cn
[2] Hainan Century Network Security Information Technology Co., Ltd., Haikou, China

Abstract. Network intrusion detection is an important protection tool after firewall, and intrusion detection algorithm is the core of intrusion detection system. The purpose of studying intrusion detection algorithm is to improve the detection rate of abnormal attacks and reduce the false positive rate. Deep learning is the first mock exam to deal with network data traffic. It does not make full use of the unique characteristics of network data when solving classification problems, and often shows the drawback of not fully summarizing the characteristics and limited generalization ability of specific data sets. The fusion of convolutional neural network and long-term and short-term memory network can fully extract the effective features of intrusion samples by mining the spatio-temporal features of all aspects of network data flow, especially the sequence of feature sequences retained by LSTM, which makes intrusion detection more accurate in classifying normal data and four kinds of abnormal data, Experiments show that CNN-LSTM model is more accurate and has excellent performance on UNSW-NB15 data set and NLS-KDD 99 data set.

Keywords: Intrusion detection · Convolutional neural network · Long-short cycle memory network

1 Introduction

The rise of cloud computing, big data and the Internet of things has led to the rapid construction of global information networks. The dense data transmission in information network links has made the network the target of attackers; through the network, we can realize rapid data interaction and sharing, but also make the information system more vulnerable to intrusion and attack. Ac-cording to the Internet security threat report released by China's national Internet emergency department, the number of terminals infected with Trojan horses or bot-net malware in China was nearly 1.15 million in March 2021; The number of tampered websites is 12947, including 61 tampered government websites; The number of websites implanted with backdoors is 1872, including 15 government websites [1].

X. Sun et al. (Eds.): ICAIS 2022, LNCS 13340, pp. 194–207, 2022.
https://doi.org/10.1007/978-3-031-06791-4_16

The application of machine learning method in intrusion detection system has a long history. For example, Pervez et al. Proposed a filtering algorithm based on support vector machine (SVM) [2]; Shapoorifard et al. Proposed a KNN-ACO method based on KNN [3]; Ingre and bhupendra et al. Proposed an intrusion detection meth-od based on decision tree [4]. In recent years, the research and application of deep learning have also developed rapidly. Remarkable achievements have been made in the fields of speech recognition, image recognition and face recognition. It also shows significant performance in network anomaly detection [5]. Its performance and ex-perimental results are better than traditional machine learning methods [6].

2 Background

2.1 Intrusion Detection Systems

The most commonly used classification standard of intrusion detection system is based on the similarity and difference of data sources and different exception handling methods. It is divided into host based intrusion detection system [7] and network-based intrusion detection system, misuse based intrusion detection system and anomaly based intrusion detection system [8]. Hybrid intrusion detection system combines the advantages of host based and network-based intrusion detection system, avoids these two methods, and forms a complete and comprehensive intrusion detection system. This paper mainly studies the intrusion detection system based on network anomaly.

2.2 Intrusion Detection Techniques

With the update speed of attacker attack methods becoming faster and faster, network attacks show new characteristics of complexity, flexibility and intelligence. Traditional intrusion detection technology has some problems, such as high false positive rate, poor generalization ability, poor timeliness and so on [9]. As the core embodiment of artificial intelligence, machine learning is simply regarded as a set of algorithms to optimize system performance to a certain extent through empirical data collection [10]. In recent years, deep learning technology has shown stronger performance advantages than traditional machine learning methods in the field of speech and image recognition. Artificial neural network has become a research hotspot in this field because of its high autonomous learning ability.

2.3 Neural Network Model

Convolutional neural network has superior feature extraction ability; In the face of multi-dimensional network traffic data, we can fully mine the relationship between the features and improve the feature extraction and recognition accuracy of the model. Convolutional neural network model needs less parameters, lower complexity and less time overhead. In addition, CNN may understand some more complex features of modern network attacks, which are difficult to be captured by other neural network models. Finally, CNN can better classify network attack samples, so that IDSS can potentially detect innovative attacks with characteristics similar to known attacks [11].

The long-term and short-term memory model (LSTM) is a special recurrent neural network (RNN) model [12]. LSTM is suitable for processing time series data with long-term dependence. Literature [13] uses LSMT network for network security data processing, and achieves relatively high anomaly detection accuracy. The processing process of LSTM model is as follows: firstly, the feature sequence set is input to the input layer, the gating unit of LSTM extracts the feature sequence of the input layer, and solves the problem of long-term dependence by adding three gating designs [14].

2.4 Related Works

Sheraz Naseer et al. [15] explore the applicability of deep learning methods in anomaly-based intrusion detection systems to develop anomaly detection models using deep CNNs, LSTMs, and multiple types of autoencoders. The technical feasibility and efficiency of deep learning models including convolutional neural networks, autoencoders and recurrent neural networks are verified in the study by comparing traditional MLIDS models.

Fahimeh Farahnakian et al. [16] proposed a deep learning model based on anomalies and using deep autoencoders (DAE), which aims to avoid overfitting and local optimum problems in deep learning models. MAJJED AL-QATF [17] et al. proposed an SAE-based STL framework for feature learning and dimensionality reduction based on a self-learning framework for good data representation. The method outperforms the traditional NSL-KDD classification algorithm and most previous methods in terms of binary and multi classification. O. Almomani [18] proposed a hybrid model of network IDS based on hybrid bionic meta heuristic algorithm to detect generic attacks. In this paper, bionic meta heuristic algorithms are mixed with each other to reduce the number of selected functions of network IDs; General attacks are detected by using support vector machine (SVM) C45 (j48) decision tree and random forest (RF) classifier. N.O. Aljehane [19] proposed a depth stack automatic encoder with parameter adjustment based on deep learning (DL) and called it PT-DSAE for IDS in CPS. The author carried out a series of experiments using the data from sensor based CPS. The experimental results verify the superior performance of the applied data in the comparison method.

Wang Qian et al. [20] proposed an image enhancement based convolutional neural network (ID-IE-CNN) fusion detection algorithm, and the proposed model outperformed the comparative algorithm on the KDDCup99 dataset for both binary and multiclassification tasks. The performance of the model proposed in the article is significantly better than the comparison algorithms for the task of binary classification and multiclassification. Yan Ruiyuan et al. [21] proposed an intrusion detection method based on Focal Loss and convolutional neural network in the face of the challenges brought by unbalanced datasets for intrusion detection models; the research method proposed in the paper tries to overcome the pressure caused by data imbalance from the perspective of improving the loss function, and after experiments show that the proposed method can overcome this problem well.

Considering that the detection performance of convolutional neural networks is closely related to the initial weights, thresholds, network structure parameters, optimizers and the number of neurons in the convolutional and fully connected layers, Minsheng Tan et al. [22] optimized LeNet5 in their study by using genetic algorithm operations such as selection, crossover and variation to obtain optimal initial weights, thresholds, network structure parameters, optimizers and the number of neurons in the fully connected layer. After the improvement the accuracy and detection rate of the model for intrusion data detection have been significantly improved and the false alarm rate has been significantly reduced. M. Chen [23], the author combines metric learning with convolutional neural network (CNN) and proposes a new network traffic classification model, called arcmargin, which makes the CNN model more discriminative; Experiments show that arcmargin model not only has good performance in network traffic classification task, but also can cluster unknown data classes in open set task.

To address the problem that existing models do not extract enough information about the characteristics of network data traffic, Yifei Wang et al. [24] propose an intrusion detection model based on internal and external convolutional networks, taking into account both the internal characteristics of the traffic and the interaction information carried out on the external network side, which improves the accuracy of the intrusion detection model and reduces the false alarm rate; time-consuming experiments on the DARPA 1998 dataset show that the proposed model has better timeliness than most baseline models. In their study, B. Almaslukh et al. [25] in this paper, aiming at the security of wireless sensor networks, studied the transformation of the original features of entity embedding into a more powerful representation, which can make more accurate detection; The experimental results show that its recognition accuracy is higher than some models based on traditional machine learning (ML) methods or deep learning.

Considering the simultaneous temporal and spatial characteristics of network traffic data, Wanya Wang et al. build a deep hierarchical network model [26] by combining convolutional neural networks with bidirectional long-short make memory networks to fully learn the spatial and temporal characteristics of the data. In their study, Xingjian Zhang et al. [27] proposed an intrusion detection model based on convolutional neural networks and gated recurrent units. The model introduces a residual network to extract the spatial features of the traffic data by using a convolutional kernel to shrink or expand the dimensions of the input information, and GRU is used to learn the temporal features of the traffic data; the experimental results show that the accuracy of the ResNet-GRU-based model is slightly improved compared with the CNN-GRU-based model, and the running time is significantly reduced. At the same time, the ResNet-GRU-based model solves the problem of overfitting during training of the CNN-GRU-based model.

X.D. Hao [28] Aiming at the problem that the massive high-dimensional data in cloud computing network has a negative impact on anomaly detection, and improving the accuracy of intrusion detection, a dual LSTM method based on attention mechanism is proposed in this paper. The results on KDD cup 99 dataset show that the model has high detection accuracy and low false positive rate, and Huiwen Lin et al. [29] used back-propagation ID3 decision tree combined with LeNet-5 model for the design of intrusion detection algorithm in their study. The study used behavioral feature selection, image matrix trans-formation, and weight comparison to classify network threats; the experimental results show that when the data traffic increases, the classification of the model for multi-classification tasks there is a significant improvement in the precision.

3 Model Design

3.1 Introduction to the Dataset

The NSL-KDD dataset is usually used together with the KDDCUP99 dataset [30] to evaluate the effectiveness of the model. However, for the current network threat environment, these data sets cannot fully reflect network traffic and modern low occupancy attacks. Therefore, the UNSW-NB15 [31] data set is introduced. The original network packets of the USW-NB15 dataset were created by the XAI PrimestRoT tool of the Canberra network range Laboratory of the University of New South Wales to produce a mixture of real modern normal activities and synthetic contemporary attack behaviors. The dataset has nine types of attacks.

3.2 Data Set Pre-processing

The first is the division of the training set and the test set. In this experiment, the validation set will be left for evaluation, and 15% of the training set is divided to act as the validation set. Next is the pre-processing of the experimental data, through the introduction of the dataset above, it can be found that both datasets contain character-based features, so firstly, the character features need to be converted into numerical features; secondly, the features in the dataset are classified into two attributes: continuous and discrete, so the dataset needs to be normalized.

(1) Numerical

In the dataset, protocol_tpye, service and state are character-based features, where protocol_type contains 3 protocol types, service contains 70 network service types and flag contains 11 network connection types, and these are converted into numbers with different values in turn. For example, the three protocol types of protocol_type feature are TCP, UDP and ICMP, which are converted to values of "0", "1" and "2" respectively."

(2) Data normalization

After numerical processing of the intrusion detection data individual features take large differences, if not normalized, when using the backpropagation algorithm is easy to cause gradient dispersion, that is, with the backpropagation, the magnitude of the gradient will continue to decrease, making the intrusion detection model learning weights and queues slow down the rate of increase, so that the complex features of the data set cannot be well extracted to achieve deep learning, and thus in The data pre-processing stage requires normalization of the intrusion detection data. In this paper, the z-score standardization method is used to compress the data to $[-1, 1]$, as shown in Eq.

$$m_i' = \frac{m_i - \overline{m}}{x} \tag{1}$$

m_i' is the data value of a feature after normalization of the data sample; mi is the data value of a feature before normalization of the data sample; $\overline{m}$ is the average data value of a feature before normalization of the data sample.

(3) Unique heat code

When the feature values appear in the learning task are not all continuous values, for categorical variables when the variables need to be converted to numeric, which is conducive to improving the efficiency of the model, but if directly converted to numeric, the model will default to the features as continuous variables, which will affect the efficiency of the model and affect the weight of the same feature in the sample, so the one-hot encoding is used for feature conversion. In this paper, the labels are converted into one-hot encoding.

3.3 Intrusion Detection Model Design

The flowchart of the proposed intrusion detection model is shown in Fig. 1, which combines the advantages of CNN spatial feature extraction and LSTM temporal feature extraction. In the model, a convolutional layer with small convolutional kernels is firstly used to extract local features of the input vector, such as protocol type and IP information, and secondly a larger convolutional kernel is used to analyze the relationship between two parts that are far apart, such as information about the payload in a packet. After the convolutional operation, the output feature map is passed to the pooling layer for feature selection and information filtering, replacing the result of a single point in the feature map with the feature map statistics of its neighboring regions, preserving the effective features while achieving feature map dimensionality reduction to avoid the overfitting phenomenon. After the processing of the convolutional neural network, the CNN part outputs a high-dimensional packet vector to the LSTM part. In part s, the overall process

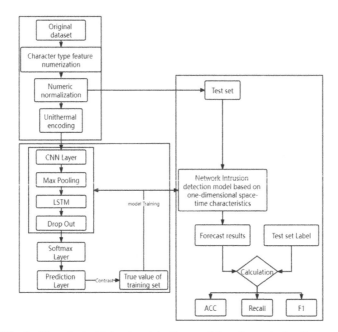

Fig. 1. Flowchart of intrusion detection model as shown in the diagram.

processes the high-dimensional packet vector into a vector representing the probability of each classification, and finally the final result is output by the softmax layer. The main functions of the LSTM network in this process are: the first step determines which information the model will discard from a set of cells, the second step decides which information needs to be updated, and the third step determines which parts of the cell state are derived.

The architectural setup of the proposed CNN-LSTM model in this paper is shown in Fig. 2. Table 1 shows the list of model training hyperparameters the initialization methods of both the CNN layer and the fully connected layer use the enlightenment method proposed by Kaiming He, which helps to speed up the convergence of the model. The model optimizer uses the Adam method, which has faster convergence speed and stability.

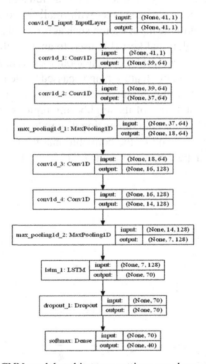

Fig. 2. The CNN model architecture settings are shown in the figure.

Table 1. CNN-LSTM model training hyperparameters.

CNN layer Kaiming	Full connection layer Kaiming	Optimizer Adam	learning rate 0.001
Loss function MSE	Number of training rounds 35	Drop rate 0.5	Batch size 128

4 Experimental Result

4.1 Simulation Experiments

The hardware environment used for the experiments: AMD Ryzen 5 4600H with Radeon Graphics 3.00 GHz, NVIDIA GeForce GTX 1650 with 16G video memory software environment: Win64-bit operating system, programming language bit Python3.6, deep keras with TensorFlow The software environment is: Win64 bit operating system, programming language bit Python3.6, deep learning platform using TensorFlow keras.

4.2 Experimental Data

(1) Model parameter settings

After preprocessing the dataset, 41 * 1 one-dimensional text data is obtained as the input to the intrusion detection model, so the input layer dimension 41 * 1, and the data samples are labeled with a total of 39 attack categories and NORMAL normal traffic categories. The unique thermal coding is applied to 40 categories of labels and transformed into 40-dimensional vectors, so the output layer is set to 40.

(2) Model evaluation indicators

a. Confusion matrix

The confusion matrix, also known as the error matrix, is used as an evaluation metric for accuracy evaluation [33] and is usually represented in the form of an n × n matrix [32]. By displaying the accuracy of classification results inside a confusion matrix, the classification results are compared with the actual measured values. The horizontal coordinate represents the predicted result for the test set samples, the vertical coordinate is the true label of the test set samples, and the diagonal data is the predicted result equal to the true label.

b. Accuracy (ACC), DR, F1 score, FPR

Accuracy (ACC), Recall, and F1 score are common metrics for machine learning to describe the performance of a model and are described by the formula

$$Acc = \frac{TP + FN}{TP + TN + FP + FN} \tag{2}$$

$$DR = \frac{TP}{TP + FN} \tag{3}$$

$$Precision = \frac{TP}{TP + FN} \tag{4}$$

$$F1 = \frac{2 * \text{Precision} * \text{Recall}}{\text{Precision} + \text{Recal}} \qquad (5)$$

$$FPR = \frac{TP}{TP + FN} \qquad (6)$$

where ACC denotes the accuracy of the model, TP represents the number of correctly identified target flows, TN represents the number of correctly identified.

TP represents the number of correctly identified target flows, TN represents the number of correctly identified other flows, FP represents the number of incorrectly identified target flows, and FN represents the number of unidentified target flows. FN represents the number of unidentified target flows.

4.3   Experimental Results and Analysis

Performance Analysis of Classification

Multiple classifiers in intrusion detection models are able to predict the attack category for each sample record. To effectively illustrate why CNN + LSTM is used as the original model for intrusion detection in this paper, experimental results as well as conclusions are drawn by using multiple comparison experiments on multiple datasets. The results of the runs on two datasets, NSL-KDD and UNSW-NB, are used to compare the advantages of CNN-LSTM to be compared with other machine learning models and other neural network models in extracting temporal and spatial features.

Table 2 shows the AC, Recall and F1-score performance of the model for binary classification on the NSL-KDD dataset and the comparison with other algorithms. Compared with traditional machine learning algorithms, the deep learning model has greater advantages and higher detection accuracy in resolving network anomalies. The CNN-LSTM algorithm outperforms other algorithms in terms of accuracy and has better classification results. The above experimental results can verify that CNN-LSTM has a higher detection rate in solving network anomalies.

Table 2. Performance comparison table (second classification).

Model	Accuracy rate %	Precision rate %	Recall%
Naive Bayes	74.40%	70.50%	76.10%
SVM	73%	70.30%	72.50%
DNN	73%	52.24%	72.63%
CNN	74.00%	84.80%	74.00%
CNN + LSTM	76%	86.68%	76.23%

Performance Analysis of the Model on the UNSW-NB15 Dataset
In order to study the generalization ability of the model in this paper, the newer dataset UNSW-NB15 was selected to set up the comparison experiment, the number of samples of the training set used in the experiment was about 100,000, and the test machine was 0.15 of them. the dataset was input into the CNN network after the preprocessing operation, and a feature vector was extracted by the CNN network, and then it was fed into the LSTM network model before, according to the network intrusion traffic characteristics, a total of 10 classifications were performed, and the final output layer of the network used softmax to obtain the classification results. The Batch Normalization mechanism was introduced in several of the network layers, thus ensuring that the input values of the neural network remain homogeneously distributed, and the Drop Out algorithm was used in the hidden layer, with the algorithm deactivation rate adjusted and set to 0.5, thus preventing the joint action of the feature detectors and making the model not too dependent on local features. The comparison experiments used the more widely used CNN, DNN, GRN, and CNN + GRN algorithms as comparisons. As can be seen from Fig. 3 and Middle and Fig. 4, the CNN + LSTM model stabilizes the loss value area after more than 70 iterations, and the final accuracy value reaches 0.91, which is higher than other typical models. And compared with CNN, algorithms such as CNN + GRN have faster convergence speed and higher accuracy rate. These show that the model is significantly better than CNN, GRN, CNN + GRN and other algorithms in the intrusion detection experiments. It has stronger detection capability.

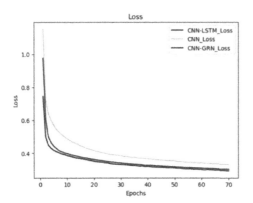

Fig. 3. Model loss comparison

Figure 5 shows the confusion matrix generated by the CNN-LSTM model for intrusion detection on the test set samples. The number on the diagonal line is the number of correct detections for the attack type corresponding to the test set, and the number of false detections on the remaining coordinates. Considering this multi-classification problem, the probability that the fourth type of attack is misidentified as the fifth type of attack is higher, and a smaller fraction of the fifth type of attack is also misidentified as the fourth type of attack. So for category 4 and 5 attacks have a higher misidentification rate. Category 2 and 8 have a certain impact on the misidentification because of the small

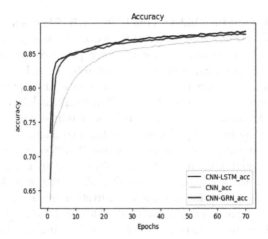

Fig. 4. Model accuracy comparison

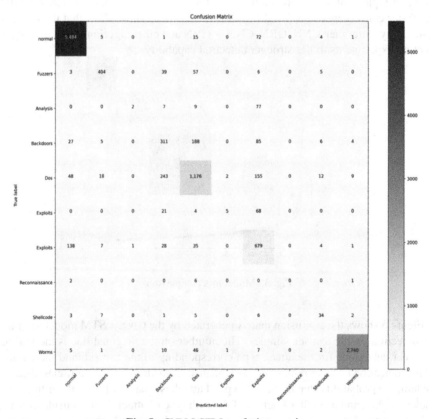

Fig. 5. CNN-LSTM confusion matrix

number of samples. To achieve better results, it is still not enough to start from the algorithm level alone, but also need to start from the data level to complete further sampling of this type of attacks. Other than that, all other categories achieved high classification results.

Table 3. Performance comparison table (multi classification).

Model	ACC	DR	FPR	F1
CNN	86.2%	84.52%	0.03%	83.21%
DNN	85.3%	84.04%	0.0315%	82.01%
SimpleRNN	83.5%	82.64%	0.0332%	82.66%
GRN	82.8%	81.53%	0.0331%	83.02%
CNN + GRN	89.7%	87.17%	0.02973%	86.56%
CNN + SimpleRNN	89.3%	87.44%	0.02963%	87.04%
CNN + LSTM	91.8%	87.57%	0.02801%	87.22%

From Table 3, we can see that the CNN + LSTM model in this paper, has obvious advantages over other models. Where DR is the ratio of the number of correctly classified normal samples to the number of actual normal samples, and FAP is the ratio of the number of incorrectly classified negative samples to the number of total negative samples. While the accuracy and F1 scores were improved, neither the DR (check-all rate), nor the FPR (false alarm rate) had an impact and were also improved to some extent.

5 Conclusion

For the traditional intrusion detection focusing on alarm logs, the detection accuracy ground in large-scale complex network environment, the system overhead, this paper proposes a hybrid algorithm based on convolutional neural network and long and short time memory network, extracting temporal space features from network traffic, analyzing the network attacks implied in the traffic, on the basis of CNN extraction of spatial features, fully explore the structure between the attack packet The temporal features of the data flow are extracted and fused by LSTM algorithm. The experimental results show that the overall accuracy of the algorithm in this paper reaches 91.82. Compared with other algorithms, the algorithm in this paper obtains higher accuracy in most cases, while maintaining a lower false alarm rate, effectively improving the accuracy of the traffic-based intrusion detection algorithm. Although the model performs well in the comparison experiments, the overfitting phenomenon of the model caused by too many network layers still needs to be paid attention to in future work; adversarial training of the model using adversarial samples of network traffic data can be considered to improve the robustness of the model. In addition, the obvious data imbalance in the dataset is also the focus of the next research, whether to add feature selection in the data. In addition, the obvious data imbalance in the dataset is also the focus of the next research, whether to add feature selection in the data pre-processing process is also worth thinking about. Deep learning in cyberspace has a long-term development prospect, and the team will explore relentlessly to pursue a more accurate, robust and simple model.

Funding Statement. This work was supported by Hainan Provincial Natural Science Foundation of China (620RC559), Education Teaching Reform of Hainan University (hdjy2117) and Research Project on Education Teaching Reform in Hainan Higher Education Institutions (Hnjg2021-25).

Conflicts of Interest. The authors declare that they have no conflicts of interest to report regarding the present study.

References

1. Internet security threat report. National Internet Emergency Response Center, China (2021). https://www.cert.org.cn/publish/main/upload/File/CNCERTreport202103(3).pdf
2. Pervez, M.S., Farid, D.M.: Feature selection and intrusion classification in NSL-KDD cup 99 dataset employing SVMs. In: International Conference on Software, Knowledge, Information Management and Applications. IEEE (2015)
3. Shapoorifard, H., Shamsinejad, P.: Intrusion detection using a novel hybrid method incorporating an improved KNN. Int. J. Comput. Appl. **173**, 1 (2017)
4. Ingre, B., Yadav, A., Soni, A.K.: Decision tree based intrusion detection system for NSL-KDD dataset. In: Satapathy, S., Joshi, A. (eds.) Information and Communication Technology for Intelligent Systems (ICTIS 2017) - Volume 2. ICTIS 2017. Smart Innovation, Systems and Technologies, vol. 84. Springer, Cham (2018). https://doi.org/10.1007/978-3-319-63645-0_23
5. Li, G., et al.: Deep learning algorithms for cyber security applications: a survey. J. Comput. Secur. **29**(5), 447–471 (2021)
6. Gan, L.J., Kong, L., Ma, Y.J.: College Computer Basic Tutorial, vol. 08, p. 152. Chongqing University Press (2017)
7. Xu, W.: Research on the application of machine learning in intrusion detection technology. Donghua University (2021)
8. Zhang, Q.: Research on network intrusion detection based on deep learning model. Tianjin University of Technology (2021)
9. Dou, L.: Rumination on the application of machine learning in network security. Netw. Secur. Technol. Appl. **2021**(06), 40–42 (2021)
10. Yu, N.: A novel selection method of network intrusion optimal route detection based on Naive Bayesian. Int. J. Appl. Decis. Sci. **11**(1), 1–1 (2018)
11. Ho, S., Al Jufout, S., Dajani, K.: A novel intrusion detection model for detecting known and innovative cyberattacks using convolutional neural network. IEEE Open J. Comput. Soc. **2**, 14–25 (2021)
12. Zeng, X.: Anomalous traffic detection method based on improved RNN and density clustering. Beijing University of Posts and Telecommunications (2019)
13. Liang, Y., Zu, X.: Research on intrusion detection model based on LSTM network. Digit. User **24**(35), 12 (2018)
14. Feng, J.: Research on network intrusion detection algorithm based on convolutional neural network. Shanxi University (2020)
15. Naseer, S., Saleem, Y., Khalid, S.: Enhanced network anomaly detection based on deep neural networks. IEEE Access **6**, 48231–48246 (2018)

16. Farahnakian, F., Heikkonen, J.: A deep auto-encoder based approach for intrusion detection system. In: 2018 20th International Conference on Advanced Communication Technology (ICACT) (2018)

17. Al-Qatf, M., Lasheng, Y., Al-Habib, M., et al.: Deep learning approach combining sparse autoencoder with SVM for network intrusion detection. IEEE Access **6**, 52843–52856 (2018)

18. Almomani, O.: A hybrid model using bio-inspired metaheuristic algorithms for network intrusion detection system. Comput. Mater. Contin. **68**(1), 409–429 (2021)

19. Aljehane, N.O.: A secure intrusion detection system in cyberphysical systems using a parameter-tuned deep-stacked autoencoder. Comput. Mater. Contin. **68**(3), 3915–3929 (2021)

20. Wang, Q., Zhao, W., Ren, J.: Intrusion detection algorithm based on image enhanced convolutional neural network. J. Intell. Fuzzy Syst. **41**(1), 2183–2194 (2021)

21. Yan, R., Zhang, L.: Intrusion detection based on Focal Loss and convolutional neural network. Comput. Mod. **01**, 65–69 (2021)

22. Tan, M.S., Peng, M., Ding, L., Wu, G.: Application of genetic-based CNN optimization method in intrusion detection. Comput. Simul. **38**(02), 416–421 (2021)

23. Chen, M., Wang, X., He, M., Jin, L., Javeed, K., Wang, X.: A network traffic classification model based on metric learning. Comput. Mater. Contin. **64**(2), 941–959 (2020)

24. Wang, Y., Mo, S., Wu, W., Fan, S., Xiao, D.: Network intrusion detection based on internal and external convolutional networks. J. Beijing Univ. Posts Telecommun. **44**(05), 94–100 (2021). https://doi.org/10.13190/j.jbupt.2021-007

25. Almaslukh, B.: Deep learning and entity embedding-based intrusion detection model for wireless sensor networks. Comput. Mater. Contin. **69**(1), 1343–1360 (2021)

26. Wang, W.: Design and implementation of network intrusion detection algorithm based on convolutional neural network. Harbin Institute of Technology (2021)

27. Zhang, X.: Research on network intrusion detection based on CNN-GRU and ResNet. Tianjin University of Technology (2021)

28. Hao, X.D., Zhou, J.M., Shen, X.Q., Yang, Y.: A novel intrusion detection algorithm based on long short term memory network. J. Quantum Comput. **2**(2), 97–104 (2020)

29. Lin, W.H.: Behaviour classification of cyber attacks using convolutional neural networks. J. Comput. Sci. **32**(1), 65–82 (2021)

30. Arora, I.S., Bhatia, G.K.: Comparative analysis of classification algorithms on KDD'99 data set. Int. J. Comput. Netw. Inf. Secur. (IJCNIS) **8**(9), 34–40 (2016)

31. Moustafa, N., Slay, J.: UNSW-NB15: a comprehensive dataset for network intrusion detection systems (UNSW-NB15 network dataset). In: 2015 Military Communications and Information Systems Conference (MilCIS), pp. 1–6 (2015)

32. Hongmin, C., Qingxiang, W.: Research on intrusion detection technology based on deep learning. Netw. Secur. Technol. Appl. **11**, 62–64 (2017)

33. Yang, Y.R., Song, R.J., Hu, G.Q.: CNN-ELM-based intrusion detection. Comput. Eng. Des. **40**(12), 3382–3387 (2019)

A Survey of Consensus Mechanism Based on Reputation Model

Yuanshen Li[1,3], Jieren Cheng[2,3(✉)], Hui Li[4], Yuming Yuan[4], and Victor S. Sheng[5]

[1] School of Cyberspace Security (School of Cryptology), Hainan University, Haikou 570228, China
[2] School of Compute Science and Technology, Hainan University, Haikou 570228, China
[3] Hainan Blockchain Technology Engineering Research Center, Hainan University, Haikou 570228, China
412800149@qq.com
[4] Hainan Huochain Technology Co. Ltd., Haikou 570100, China
[5] Department of Computer Science, Texas Tech University, 79409 Texas, USA

Abstract. The reputation models may be used to evaluate the reputation of blockchain nodes, and the consensus mechanisms can use the reputation models to quantify the credibility or dependability of nodes. The consensus mechanisms and the reputation models have been coupled by researchers with the goal of improving the performance and security of consensus mechanisms. We summarized the consensus mechanism based on the reputation model (reputation consensus) in this paper. To begin, we've classified the many types of reputation consensuses and explained the benefits of each one. Second, we suggest a new performance assessment criterion for reputation consensuses based on the experimental section of the literatures, and we evaluate the performance of current reputation consensuses using the provided performance evaluation criterion. After that, we ran a statistical investigation on the security of reputation consensuses. Finally, we summed up the reputation consensuses in order to better grasp present research issues and future research directions.

Keywords: Reputation consensus · Classification · Performance evaluation · Security

1 Introduction

1.1 Blockchain and Consensus Mechanism

With the publication of Satoshi Nakamoto's article "Bitcoin: A Peer-to-Peer Electronic Cash System" [1] in 2008, blockchain entered the minds of academics all over the world. Blockchain [2,3] is a strong distributed ledger system that can be shared around the globe [4]. All blockchain transactions are carefully recorded in blocks, which are linked in chronological order by hash [5]. Traceability and

© The Author(s), under exclusive license to Springer Nature Switzerland AG 2022
X. Sun et al. (Eds.): ICAIS 2022, LNCS 13340, pp. 208–221, 2022.
https://doi.org/10.1007/978-3-031-06791-4_17

tamper resistance are two properties of blockchain [6]. Blockchain is being used in a growing number of industries, including finance [7], the Internet of Things [8,9], data traceability [10], and so on [11]. Figure 1 depicts the blockchain architecture.

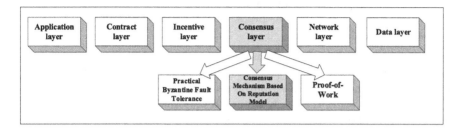

Fig. 1. Structure of blockchain.

The consensus mechanism is one of the blockchain's essential technologies, and its objective is to keep the blockchain view consistent [12]. The blockchain system is made up of numerous nodes, all of which must agree on the block's content [13]. Because the nodes in the blockchain system are self-interested and subjective [14], some nodes will dynamically choose low-risk and high-yield action strategies, and there are even malicious nodes looking for, attacking, and exploiting blockchain vulnerabilities in order to gain illegal benefits and jeopardize block chain security. When certain nodes do not perform as expected, the consensus mechanism ensures that other nodes can still achieve a consensus [15].

1.2 Advantages of Reputation Consensus

The reputation model is a paradigm for establishing trust between parties who interact, and it can be used to effectively build trust between different entities [16]. The primary idea is to assess different users depending on how well they complete jobs, and then to grade them fully based on several factors to provide reputation scores [17]. Users can choose whether or not they trust based on the reputation score [18]. In addition, the reputation model has a corrective effect. Good behaviors will be encouraged by positive reputation incentives and negative reputation punishments [19].

The combination of a reputation model and a consensus mechanism may maintain the trust state of nodes in a blockchain network and assess the trust degree of each consensus node, improving the consensus mechanism's safety and dependability, and thereby improving blockchain credibility [20]. The following three advantages will result from combining the two: (1) Evaluate node trustworthiness and screen out a batch of dependable nodes based on trustworthiness; (2) Punish malicious nodes to minimize the rate of blockchain network node evildoing; (3) Improve blockchain security and resist network attacks on the blockchain.

The following are the key contributions of this article:

(1) A classification method is proposed for the consensus mechanism based on the reputation model;
(2) A new performance evaluation index is proposed for the consensus mechanism based on the reputation model;
(3) The security of the consensus mechanism based on the reputation model is analyzed and discussed.

The following is how the rest of the article is structured: Sect. 2 classifies reputation consensuses; Sect. 3 proposes performance evaluation indicators for the reputation consensuses based on literature analysis, and evaluates the reputation consensus using the newly proposed performance evaluation indicators; Sect. 4 analyzes and discusses the security of the reputation consensus; Finally, Sect. 5 summarizes and looks forward to the reputation consensus.

2 Classification of Consensus Mechanisms Based on Reputation Models

We categorize reputation consensus into four groups based on the sorts of incentives provided: token rewards, conceptual incentives, dual incentives, and no incentives.

2.1 Token Incentive

The reputation consensuses that provide token incentives will reward blockchain network nodes based on the completion of tasks after they complete them, So as to increase the positivity of the nodes. The reputation model is mainly to evaluate the reputation of blockchain nodes, so as to select nodes with high reputation values. Liu [21] proposed a consensus mechanism for reputation proof. The node with the highest reputation value is responsible for generating blocks, other nodes are responsible for validating blocks, and new block rewards are distributed according to the reputation ratio. Kang [22] designed a reputation-based consensus for the miner collusion problem. Nodes with high reputation value may be selected as backup miners, who can verify and audit blocks to prevent active miners from colluding with each other. Guan [23] proposed a reputation-based consensus mechanism for proof of equity. The selection of the accounting node is related to the reputation value of the node. The reputation value is calculated by reference items such as default rate and arbitration success rate. Yu [24] obtained its reputation value by analyzing and calculating the comprehensive ability of the node. Only when the reputation value between nodes exceeds 2/3 of the consensus group can a consensus be reached, Miners can only obtain token rewards if they dig out a key block and confirm it. Qiao [25] proposed a reputation consensus. The consensus scores each node based on its performance and historical reputation, and the power of a node is related to its reputation value. Qin [26] proposed a consensus algorithm for reputation proof. When the number of malicious nodes is less than 1/2, it can ensure the security of the blockchain system.

2.2 Concept Incentives

The so-called conceptual incentive is to use reputation as a reward, and the consensus mechanism increases or decreases the reputation score based on the completion of tasks by the blockchain nodes. Through conceptual rewards, the reputation value of blockchain nodes will dynamically increase and decrease, and blockchain nodes with higher reputation values will also have higher authority. This can increase the activity of the blockchain system. Gai [27] proposed a reputation-based consensus protocol, which can ensure the reliability and integrity of transaction results and provide reputation incentives to blockchain nodes. Ke [28] proposed a reputation fusion method to reach a consensus. Nodes with high reputation not only have more rights, but also are easier to be selected for consensus. Wang [29] proposed a secure and fast reputation consensus. The block generation speed of the node is related to the reputation value. Sidharth [30] proposed a reputation-based consensus scheme for node dishonesty and collusion. It will punishe dishonest nodes. Sun [31] designed a kind of RTChin, which can influence the consensus behavior of blockchain nodes through reputation incentives. Nodes with high reputation value are more likely to be selected as trading partners. Zhao [32] proposed a reputation-based blockchain consensus mechanism. It is able to dynamically assign roles and permissions to nodes reputation based on their values. Xuan [33] proposed a secure and low-cost reputation-based edge computing consensus model, and introduced a node replacement mechanism to improve the fault tolerance of the consensus mechanism. Besfort [34] proposed a new reputation consensus mechanism, which ranks nodes based on the content of reputation-related aspects. Those with high trust will be selected as the block creator nodes. In addition, nodes with good performance will be given reputation rewards. Lei [35] proposed a Byzantine fault-tolerant reputation consensus. It combines the reputation model to evaluate the behavior of , and the reputation value affects the size of the power. Chen [36] proposed a consensus mechanism based on a reputation model and voting. The master node is elected through the node reputation value to ensure its reliability. If the node successfully generates a valid block, the system will reward it with reputation. Zhang [37] proposed a "reputation proof" consensus algorithm, which improves the credibility of the network environment by screening credible nodes, and then reaches a credible consensus.

2.3 Double Incentive

The reputation consensuses that provides dual incentives will give tokens and conceptual rewards based on the completion of tasks by blockchain nodes. Double incentives can enable blockchain nodes to obtain both reputation and tokens. This can ensure that the reputation of the blockchain nodes can maintain dynamic growth and decrease while also obtaining real tokens, so as to combine the advantages of the two types. Marcela [38] proposed a reputation consensus. The consensus will randomly select a group of judges to monitor blockchain nodes and update their reputation scores. Nodes with low reputation values will be blocked from accessing the blockchain. Wang [39] proposed a reputation consensus. By designing the reward and punishment factor in the income payment function of reputation, nodes are encouraged to participate in network collaboration in a good way. Hu [40] improved the traditional DPoS consensus mechanism and added a reputation model. By evaluating the behavior of blockchain nodes, dividing them into different states and selecting high-quality nodes as consensus nodes, the blockchain nodes that complete the task well will receive tokens and reputation rewards. Han [41] proposed a consensus mechanism based on reputation proof, which quantifies whether the node is beneficial to the system by evaluating the reputation of the node. Nodes that actively perform the agreement will receive a mixed incentive of fees and reputation. Abdo [42] proposed a consensus mechanism based on proof of reputation, which deducts deposit and reputation for nodes with malicious behavior. Only when the remaining balance of the node is higher than the threshold can participate in the consensus. Abdo [43] proposed a reputation-based permissionless consensus mechanism. For actively working nodes, the deposit will be refunded and the reputation will be improved. For nodes with malicious behavior, the deposit and reputation value will be deducted. This strategy can prevent nodes from causing uncontrolled damage. Sun [44] proposed a hybrid consensus based on reputation to solve the problem of transaction security and efficiency. The reputation value of the node is obtained by evaluating the past and current transaction behavior of the node. He reputation value of the node will be recorded in the reputation system and fed back to the new In a round of consensus.

2.4   No Incentive

The reputation consensuses that does not provide incentives generally evaluates the blockchain nodes based on their task completion, and selects blockchain nodes with high reputation values as the consensus nodes. After these nodes complete the corresponding tasks, they will not be rewarded accordingly, thereby reducing the burden of reputation consensus. Amrendra [45] proposed a reputation consensus for the cumbersome management of land boarding transactions, which is more efficient than traditional consensus mechanisms. Tong [46] designed a consensus mechanism based on PeerTrust for the operator's reputation problem. The consensus dynamically adjusts nodes according to the reputation value, reducing the message and influence generated by malicious nodes. Leila [47] proposed a consensus mechanism for proof of credibility in response to the large energy consumption of the PoW consensus mechanism. The node reputation value can affect the size of the workload. Zhou [48] proposed a consensus mechanism based on reputation proof, which selects nodes according to the level of reputation value, which solves the scalability problem of traditional methods. Alex [49] introduced a reputation module in the consensus mechanism, ranked nodes according to the results of the consensus mechanism, and determined whether they could be selected as members based on the reputation of the node. Sun [50] proposed a consensus mechanism with dynamic reputation and designed an evaluation standard that combines equity voting and reputation to improve the reliability and security of nodes. Gao [51] designed a consensus mechanism based on the EigenTrust model. It is a multi-stage consensus mechanism that evaluates the reputation value of nodes through transactions between nodes and selects nodes with high reputation values as the consensus group. Huang [52] proposed a reputation consensus for IoT devices. In this consensus, the computational complexity of blockchain nodes is related to the reputation value, and at the same time it can improve system security and efficiency. Huang [53] proposed a reputation-based consensus mechanism for IoT devices. The reputation value will change dynamically according to the node behavior, and the calculation difficulty of the node is related to its reputation value. Zhang [54] proposed a reputation proof consensus mechanism for edge network nodes. The consensus divides reputation into personal reputation and global reputation, enabling nodes to evaluate the credibility of each other Li [55] proposed a reputation-based PBFT consensus mechanism. The consensus can dynamically add or delete nodes according to the reputation value. Xu [56] proposed an efficient reputation Byzantine consensus mechanism, which can reduce network overhead by selecting nodes with high reputation value to join the consensus. Wei [57] proposed a Trust-PBFT consensus mechanism, which determines whether they are eligible to join the consensus by evaluating the reputation of nodes, which effectively improves the fault tolerance and scalability of the consensus mechanism. Oladotun [58] proposed a reputation-based consensus mechanism, which manages the node reputation value by adding a side chain connected to the main chain. Cai [59] proposed a dynamic reputation consensus mechanism for energy industry. The monitoring node divides the nodes into consensus nodes and auxiliary nodes according to the reputation value of other nodes, and dynamically updates nodes with low reputation values. Anjana [60] proposed a low-cost and lightweight reputation consensus. The administrator will keep a list of trusted relay cluster heads to better select trusted nodes. Thuat [61] proposed a reputation-based delegation proof consensus mechanism. The reputation of a node determines the weight of its vote. Tang [62] added a reputation mechanism to the consensus mechanism, and evaluated nodes through the reputation mechanism, which can delete faulty nodes in time and improve the robustness of the blockchain system.

By dividing the reputation consensus into four major categories, the blockchain system can better choose according to needs. In the dozens of documents mentioned above, the reputation consensuses that provide token incentives can meet the real needs of nodes and improve the enthusiasm of nodes. The reputation consensuses that provide conceptual incentives can dynamically change the reputation value and authority of nodes, thereby ensuring the activity of the blockchain system. The reputation consensuses that provide double incentives can not only meet the real-life monetary needs of blockchain nodes, but also dynamically change the reputation value, thereby ensuring the activeness and positivity of the blockchain system. Incentive-free reputation consensuses can reduce the burden of the consensus mechanism and improve the efficiency of consensuses.

3 Analysis of Evaluation Indicators of Reputation Consensus Performance

With the development of blockchain technology, the consensus mechanisms, which is the most important thing, are also constantly improving [63]. More and more consensus mechanisms have been studied [64], and reputation consensus have also been favored by more and more researchers. Wan [65] proposed to evaluate the performance of the consensus mechanism in four dimensions, thereby presenting the different advantages and disadvantages of different consensus mechanisms. Seyed [66] investigated and studied the performance of the consensus mechanism, and explained and evaluated it in terms of throughput and block generation time. However, these performance evaluations are not only for the reputation consensus, they can't accurately evaluate the reputation consensus. Therefore, it's necessary to have a performance evaluation index for reputation consensus to accurately evaluate them.

Throughput: the number of transactions per second. Good consensus mechanisms will have a high throughput. The calculation formula is shown in (1):

$$T_{tps} = \frac{T_{SUM}}{\Delta t} \tag{1}$$

where T_{tps} represents throughput, Δt represents the time to generate T_{SUM} blocks, T_{SUM} represents the number of blocks generated in Δt time.

Fault tolerance: Blockchain nodes occasionally fail or generate malicious behavior. At this time, consensus mechanisms are required to still reach consensus.

Safety: Due to the self-interested nature of blockchain nodes, certain blockchain nodes may engage in malicious behavior on the blockchain system in order to get more rewards. The security of the consensus mechanisms have a lot to do with the security of the blockchain. As a result, a security study of the reputation consensuses is required.

Resource consumption: When blockchain nodes perform consensus work, they need to consume certain resources to reach a consensus. By evaluating the performance of blockchain resource consumption, a batch of low-cost reputation consensuses can be selected.

Consensus efficiency: The time required to reach a consensus between blockchain nodes, from the time a node initiates a consensus to the time it takes for all nodes to reach a consensus.

Difficulty of block generation: Block generation difficulty refers to the difficulty for miner nodes to calculate a block. Since in some reputation consensuses, the nodes' reputation value will affect the difficulty of their block generation.

Reputation performance: Reputation performance is a unique evaluation standard for reputation consensus. Since the reputation consensus will perform a series of operations such as reputation evaluation on each node through the reputation model, and the reputation performance is an evaluation of these series of operations. Part of the literature will conduct an experimental or theoretical comprehensive analysis of the reputation consensus in the article in the experimental part, so as to get the performance of the reputation model in the consensus mechanism.

The performance evaluation table of the reputation consensus is shown in Table 1.

Table 1. Reputation consensus performance evaluation Table.

Schemes	Throughput	Fault tolerance	Safety	Resource consumption	Consensus efficiency	Difficulty of block generation	Reputation performance
[14,33,35,36,42,45,47]			✓				✓
[15,21–23]			✓			✓	✓
[16,40,53]			✓	✓			✓
[17,51]	✓	✓	✓		✓		✓
[18]			✓	✓			
[19]					✓		
[20]	✓		✓	✓	✓	✓	
[24]	✓	✓	✓		✓	✓	✓
[25]	✓	✓		✓	✓	✓	
[26,32]			✓		✓	✓	✓
[27]			✓				
[28]	✓	✓				✓	✓
[29]	✓				✓		
[30]	✓	✓			✓		
[31]		✓	✓				✓
[34]			✓				
[37]	✓		✓				
[38]				✓	✓	✓	✓
[39,50]		✓					✓
[41,46]			✓		✓		✓
[43]			✓	✓		✓	
[44]		✓			✓		✓
[48]	✓	✓		✓			✓
[49]	✓				✓		✓
[52]	✓			✓			✓
[54]	✓					✓	✓
[55]				✓			
[56]		✓			✓		
[57]		✓					
[58]	✓	✓					✓

4   Security Analysis of Reputation Consensus

With the increasing value of Bitcoin and other virtual currencies, blockchain technology has also seen more and more attacks, and the frequent occurrence of security incidents has also caused huge economic losses [67]. These security problems may be caused by internal nodes or external entities [68]. By combining reputation consensus with consensus mechanism, they can resist some network attacks. This section provides a statistical analysis of the attacks that reputation consensuses can defend against. As shown in Fig. 2.

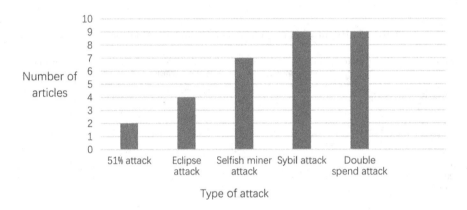

Fig. 2. Statistics on reputation consensus to resist cyber attacks.

Partial reputation consensuses can reduce the reputation value of malicious nodes [36] to increase the computational cost or introduce a competition cycle [37] to resist %51 attacks [69]. Some reputation consensus can randomly select consensus nodes and leaders [29] or prevent attackers from isolating multiple consensus nodes at the same time [22,56] to defend against Eclipse attacks [70]. There is also a part of reputation consensus to reduce selfish miner attacks [71] through the way of deposits, expulsion of nodes [36,39], group cooperation [56], random selection of consensus nodes [29], or division of labor between mining and publishing blocks [40]. Partial reputation consensus resists Sybil attacks [72] through reputation values [19,40] or random selection of consensus nodes [37,47]. Partial reputation consensus resists double-spending attacks [73] by maintaining blockchain consistency [22,29,36,39,40] or controlling mining difficulty through reputation value [27,50,51].

5   Conclusion

The reputation consensuses are an important branch of the consensus mechanismes. By evaluating the behavior of the nodes, the reputation value is obtained, then a batch of honest nodes can be screened out. Reputation consensuses have received extensive attention from researchers and practitioners, but the combination of reputation model and consensus mechanism still has many limitations, such as fairness and applicability.

From the work reviewed here, we have observed the advantages and disadvantages of most reputation consensuses operations, as well as their security. We believe that this research can be helpful to related researchers and hope that it can promote the development of reputation consensus and help readers analyze current and future reputation consensus.

Acknowledgements. This work was supported by National Natural Science Foundation of China (Grant No. 62162022 and 62162024), Key Projects in Hainan Province (Grant ZDYF2021GXJS003 and Grant ZDYF2020040), the Major science and technology project of Hainan Province(Grant No. ZDKJ2020012).

References

1. Nakamoto, S.: Bitcoin: a peer-to-peer electronic cash system. Decentralized Bus. Rev. 21260 (2008)
2. Sanka, A.I., Cheung, R.C.: A systematic review of blockchain scalability: issues, solutions, analysis and future research. J. Netw. Comput. Appl. **195**, 103232 (2021)
3. Jamil, F., Qayyum, F., Alhelaly, S., Javed, F., Muthanna, A.: Intelligent microservice based on blockchain for healthcare applications. CMC-Comput. Mater. Contin **69**, 2513–2530 (2021)
4. Huang, J., Tan, L., Li, W., Yu, K.: Ron-enhanced blockchain propagation mechanism for edge-enabled smart cities. J. Inf. Sec. Appli. **61**, 102936 (2021)
5. Alam, S., et al.: Blockchain-based initiatives: current state and challenges. Comput. Netw. **198**, 108395 (2021)
6. Hong, G.W., Kim, J.W., Chang, H.: Blockchain technology based information classification management service. CMC-Comput. Mater. Continua **67**, 1489–1501 (2021)
7. Mazzoni, M., Corradi, A., di Nicola, V.: Performance evaluation of permissioned blockchains for financial applications the consensys quorum case study. Blockchain Res. Appli. **3**(1), 100026 (2021)
8. Bera, B., Vangala, A., Das, A.K., Lorenz, P., Khan, M.K.: Private blockchain-envisioned drones-assisted authentication scheme in IOT-enabled agricultural environment. Computer Stan. Interfaces **80**, 103567 (2022)
9. Pavithran, D., Al-Karaki, J.N., Shaalan, K.: Edge-based blockchain architecture for event-driven IOT using hierarchical identity based encryption. Inf. Proc. Manage. **58**(3), 102528 (2021)
10. Centobelli, P., Cerchione, R., Vecchio, P.D., Oropallo, E., Secundo, G.: Blockchain technology for bridging trust, traceability and transparency in circular supply chain. Inf. Manage. 103508 (2021)
11. Zhang, L., Peng, M., Wang, W., Su, Y., Kim, S.: Secure and efficient data storage and sharing scheme based on double blockchain. CMC Tech, Sci. Press **66**(1), 499–515 (2020)
12. Bouraga, S.: A taxonomy of blockchain consensus protocols: a survey and classification framework. Expert Syst. Appl. **168**, 114384 (2021)
13. Aslam, T., et al.: Blockchain based enhanced ERP transaction integrity architecture and poet consensus. CMC-Comput. Mater. Continua **70**(1), 1089–1109 (2022)

14. Liu, J., Sun, X., Song, K.: A food traceability framework based on permissioned blockchain. J. Cybersecurity **2**(2), 107 (2020)
15. Ferdous, M.S., Chowdhury, M.J.M., Hoque, M.A.: A survey of consensus algorithms in public blockchain systems for crypto-currencies. J. Netw. Comput. Appl. **182**, 103035 (2021)
16. Cheng, J., Yang, Y., Tang, X., Xiong, N., Zhang, Y., Lei, F.: Generative adversarial networks: a literature review. KSII Trans. Inter. Inf. Syst. **14**(12), 4625–4647 (2020)
17. Almasoud, A.S., Hussain, F.K., Hussain, O.K.: Smart contracts for blockchain-based reputation systems: a systematic literature review. J. Netw. Comput. Appl. **170**, 102814 (2020)
18. Braga, D.D.S., Niemann, M., Hellingrath, B., Neto, F.B.D.L.: Survey on computational trust and reputation models. ACM Comput. Surv. **51**(5), 1–40 (2018)
19. Hendrikx, F., Bubendorfer, K., Chard, R.: Reputation systems: a survey and taxonomy. J. Parallel Distrib. Comput. **75**, 184–197 (2015)
20. Cheng, J., Liu, J., Xu, X., Xia, D., Liu, L., Sheng, V.S.: A review of Chinese named entity recognition. KSII Trans Inter. In. Syst. (TIIS) **15**(6), 2012–2030 (2021)
21. Zhuang, Q., Liu, Y., Chen, L., Ai, Z.: Proof of reputation: A reputation-based consensus protocol for blockchain based systems. In: Proceedings of the 2019 International Electronics Communication Conference, IECC 2019, pp. 131–138. Association for Computing Machinery, New York (2019)
22. Kang, J., Xiong, Z., Niyato, D., Ye, D., Kim, D.I., Zhao, J.: Toward secure blockchain-enabled internet of vehicles: optimizing consensus management using reputation and contract theory. IEEE Trans. Veh. Technol. **68**(3), 2906–2920 (2019)
23. Guan, Z., Lu, X., Yang, W., Wu, L., Wang, N., Zhang, Z.: Achieving efficient and privacy-preserving energy trading based on blockchain and ABE in smart grid. J. Parallel Distrib. Comput. **147**, 34–45 (2021)
24. Yu, J., Kozhaya, D., Decouchant, J., Esteves-Verissimo, P.: Repucoin: your reputation is your power. IEEE Trans. Comput. **68**(8), 1225–1237 (2019)
25. Qiao, G., Leng, S., Chai, H., Asadi, A., Zhang, Y.: Blockchain empowered resource trading in mobile edge computing and networks. In: ICC 2019–2019 IEEE International Conference on Communications, ICC, pp. 1–6 (2019)
26. Qin, D., Wang, C., Jiang, Y.: RPchain: a blockchain-based academic social networking service for credible reputation building. In: Chen, S., Wang, H., Zhang, L.-J. (eds.) ICBC 2018. LNCS, vol. 10974, pp. 183–198. Springer, Cham (2018). https://doi.org/10.1007/978-3-319-94478-4_13
27. Gai, F., Wang, B., Deng, W., Peng, W.: Proof of reputation: a reputation-based consensus protocol for peer-to-peer network. In: Pei, J., Manolopoulos, Y., Sadiq, S., Li, J. (eds.) DASFAA 2018. LNCS, vol. 10828, pp. 666–681. Springer, Cham (2018). https://doi.org/10.1007/978-3-319-91458-9_41
28. Wang, K., et al.: A trusted consensus fusion scheme for decentralized collaborated learning in massive IOT domain. Inf. Fusion **72**, 100–109 (2021)
29. Wang, E.K., Sun, R., Chen, C.M., Liang, Z., Kumari, S., Khurram Khan, M.: Proof of x-repute blockchain consensus protocol for IOT systems. Comput. Secur. **95**, 101871 (2020)
30. Shyamsukha, S., Bhattacharya, P., Patel, F., Tanwar, S., Gupta, R., Pricop, E.: Porf: Proof-of-reputation-based consensus scheme for fair transaction ordering. In: 2021 13th International Conference on Electronics, Computers and Artificial Intelligence, ECAI, pp. 1–6 (2021)

31. Sun, Y., Xue, R., Zhang, R., Su, Q., Gao, S.: Rtchain: a reputation system with transaction and consensus incentives for e-commerce blockchain. ACM Trans. Internet Technol. **21**(1), 1–24 (2020)
32. Zhao, Q., Sun, Y., Zhang, P.: Design of trust blockchain consensus protocol based on node role classification. In: 2019 IEEE International Conference on Service Operations and Logistics, and Informatics, SOLI, pp. 104–109 (2019)
33. Xuan, S., et al.: Ecbcm: a prestige-based edge computing blockchain security consensus model. Trans. Emerg. Telecommun. Technol. **32**(6), e4015 (2021)
34. Shala, B., Trick, U., Lehmann, A., Ghita, B., Shiaeles, S.: Novel trust consensus protocol and blockchain-based trust evaluation system for m2m application services. Internet of Things **7**, 100058 (2019)
35. Lei, K., Zhang, Q., Xu, L., Qi, Z.: Reputation-based byzantine fault-tolerance for consortium blockchain. In: 2018 IEEE 24th International Conference on Parallel and Distributed Systems, ICPADS, pp. 604–611 (2018)
36. Chen, J., Zhang, X., Shangguan, P.: Improved PBFT algorithm based on reputation and voting mechanism. J. Phys. Conf. Ser. **1486**(3), 032023 (2020)
37. Xiaohui, Z., Xianghua, M.: A reputation-based approach using consortium blockchain for cyber threat intelligence sharing (2021). arXiv preprint, arXiv:2107.06662
38. de Oliveira, M.T., Reis, L.H., Medeiros, D.S., Carrano, R.C., Olabarriaga, S.D., Mattos, D.M.: Blockchain reputation-based consensus: a scalable and resilient mechanism for distributed mistrusting applications. Comput. Netw. **179**, 107367 (2020)
39. Wang, E.K., Liang, Z., Chen, C.M., Kumari, S., Khan, M.K.: Porx: a reputation incentive scheme for blockchain consensus of IOT. Futur. Gener. Comput. Syst. **102**, 140–151 (2020)
40. Hu, Q., Yan, B., Han, Y., Yu, J.: An improved delegated proof of stake consensus algorithm. In: Procedia Computer Science **187**, 341–346 (2021), 2020 International Conference on Identification, Information and Knowledge in the Internet of Things, IIKI 2020
41. Han, X., Yuan, Y., Wang, F.Y.: A fair blockchain based on proof of credit. IEEE Trans. Comput. Soc. Syst. **6**(5), 922–931 (2019)
42. Bou Abdo, J., El Sibai, R., Demerjian, J.: Permissionless proof-of-reputation-x: a hybrid reputation-based consensus algorithm for permissionless blockchains. Trans. Emerg. Telecommun. Technol. **32**(1), e4148 (2021)
43. Bou Abdo, J., El Sibai, R., Kambhampaty, K., Demerjian, J.: Permissionless reputation-based consensus algorithm for blockchain. Internet Technol. Lett. **3**(3), e151 (2020), ITL-19-0118.R2
44. Sun, Y., Zhang, R., Xue, R., Su, Q., Li, P.: A reputation based hybrid consensus for e-commerce blockchain. In: Ku, W.-S., Kanemasa, Y., Serhani, M.A., Zhang, L.-J. (eds.) ICWS 2020. LNCS, vol. 12406, pp. 1–16. Springer, Cham (2020). https://doi.org/10.1007/978-3-030-59618-7_1
45. Yadav, A.S., Agrawal, S., Kushwaha, D.S.: Distributed ledger technology-based land transaction system with trusted nodes consensus mechanism. J. King Saud Univ. Comput. Inf. Sci. **34**(5) (2021)
46. Tong, W., Dong, X., Shen, Y., Zheng, J.: Bc-ran: cloud radio access network enabled by blockchain for 5g. Comput. Commun. **162**, 179–186 (2020)
47. Bahri, L., Girdzijauskas, S.: When trust saves energy: a reference framework for proof of trust (pot) blockchains. In: Companion Proceedings of the the Web Conference WWW 2018, International World Wide Web Conferences Steering Committee, Republic and Canton of Geneva, CHE, pp. 1165–1169 (2018)

48. Zou, J., Ye, B., Qu, L., Wang, Y., Orgun, M.A., Li, L.: A proof-of-trust consensus protocol for enhancing accountability in crowdsourcing services. IEEE Trans. Serv. Comput. **12**(3), 429–445 (2019)
49. Biryukov, A., Feher, D.: Recon: sybil-resistant consensus from reputation. Pervasive Mob. Comput. **61**, 101109 (2020)
50. Sun, Y., Yan, B., Yao, Y., Yu, J.: Dt-dpos: A delegated proof of stake consensus algorithm with dynamic trust. In: Procedia Computer Science, vol. 187, 371–376 (2021), 2020 International Conference on Identification, Information and Knowledge in the Internet of Things, IIKI 2020
51. Gao, S., Yu, T., Zhu, J., Cai, W.: T-PBFT: an eigentrust-based practical byzantine fault tolerance consensus algorithm. China Commun. **16**(12), 111–123 (2019)
52. Huang, J., Kong, L., Chen, G., Wu, M.Y., Liu, X., Zeng, P.: Towards secure industrial IOT: blockchain system with credit-based consensus mechanism. IEEE Trans. Industr. Inf. **15**(6), 3680–3689 (2019)
53. Huang, J., Kong, L., Chen, G., Cheng, L., Wu, K., Liu, X.: B-IOT: Blockchain driven internet of things with credit-based consensus mechanism. In: 2019 IEEE 39th International Conference on Distributed Computing Systems, ICDCS, pp. 1348–1357 (2019)
54. Zhang, J., Huang, Y., Ye, F., Yang, Y.: A novel proof-of-reputation consensus for storage allocation in edge blockchain systems. In: 2021 IEEE/ACM 29th International Symposium on Quality of Service, IWQOS, pp. 1–10 (2021)
55. Jun-Qing, L.I., Xin, Y.S., Song, C.Q., Zhou, H., Wang, T.J., Deng, H.W.: Reputation-based dynamic authorization pbft consensus mechanism. Comput. Eng. Softw. (2019)
56. Yuan, X., Luo, F., Haider, M.Z., Chen, Z., Li, Y.: Efficient byzantine consensus mechanism based on reputation in IOT blockchain. In: Wireless Communications and Mobile Computing 2021 (2021)
57. Tong, W., Dong, X., Zheng, J.: Trust-PBFT: a peertrust-based practical byzantine consensus algorithm. In: 2019 International Conference on Networking and Network Applications, NaNA, pp. 344–349. IEEE (2019)
58. Aluko, O., Kolonin, A.: Proof-of-reputation: an alternative consensus mechanism for blockchain systems. Int. J. Netw. Secur. Appli. (IJNSA) **13**, 23–40 (2021)
59. Cai, W., Jiang, W., Xie, K., Zhu, Y., Liu, Y., Shen, T.: Dynamic reputation-based consensus mechanism: real-time transactions for energy blockchain. Int. J. Distrib. Sens. Netw. **16**(3), 1550147720907335 (2020)
60. Prabhakar, A., Anjali, T.: Tcon - a lightweight trust-dependent consensus framework for blockchain. In: 2019 11th International Conference on Communication Systems Networks, COMSNETS, pp. 1–6 (2019)
61. Do, T., Nguyen, T., Pham, H.: Delegated proof of reputation: a novel blockchain consensus. In: Proceedings of the 2019 International Electronics Communication Conference, IECC 2019, pp. 90–98. Association for Computing Machinery, New York (2019)
62. Tang, H., Sun, Y., Ouyang, J.: Excellent practical byzantine fault tolerance. J. Cybersecurity **2**(4), 167–182 (2020)
63. Lei, F., Cheng, J., Yang, Y., Tang, X., Sheng, V.S., Huang, C.: Improving heterogeneous network knowledge transfer based on the principle of generative adversarial. Electronics **10**(13), 1525 (2021)
64. Tang, X., Tu, W., Li, K., Cheng, J.: Dffnet: an IOT-perceptive dual feature fusion network for general real-time semantic segmentation. Inf. Sci. **565**, 326–343 (2021)

65. Wan, S., Li, M., Liu, G., Wang, C.: Recent advances in consensus protocols for blockchain: a survey. Wireless Netw. **26**(8), 5579–5593 (2019). https://doi.org/10.1007/s11276-019-02195-0
66. Bamakan, S.M.H., Motavali, A., Babaei Bondarti, A.: A survey of blockchain consensus algorithms performance evaluation criteria. Expert Syst. Appli. **154**, 113385 (2020)
67. Zhang, Q., Zhou, C., Tian, Y.C., Xiong, N., Qin, Y., Hu, B.: A fuzzy probability bayesian network approach for dynamic cybersecurity risk assessment in industrial control systems. IEEE Trans. Industr. Inf. **14**(6), 2497–2506 (2018)
68. Bhushan, B., Sinha, P., Sagayam, K.M., Andrew, J.: Untangling blockchain technology: a survey on state of the art, security threats, privacy services, applications and future research directions. Comput. Electr. Eng. **90**, 106897 (2021)
69. Li, X., Jiang, P., Chen, T., Luo, X., Wen, Q.: A survey on the security of blockchain systems. Futur. Gener. Comput. Syst. **107**, 841–853 (2020)
70. Heilman, E., Kendler, A., Zohar, A., Goldberg, S.: Eclipse attacks on Bitcoin's Peer-to-Peer network. In: 24th USENIX Security Symposium, USENIX Security 2015, pp. 129–144. USENIX Association, Washington, August 2015
71. Joshi, A.P., Han, M., Wang, Y.: A survey on security and privacy issues of blockchain technology. Math. Found. Comput. **1**(2), 121–147 (2018)
72. Platt, M., McBurney, P.: Sybil attacks on identity-augmented proof-of-stake. Comput. Netw. **199**, 108424 (2021)
73. Karame, G.O., Androulaki, E., Roeschlin, M., Gervais, A., Čapkun, S.: Misbehavior in bitcoin: a study of double-spending and accountability. ACM Trans. Inf. Syst. Secur. **18**(1), 1–32 (2015)

A Survey on Ethereum Illicit Detection

Meng Li[1,2,3(✉)]

[1] Basic Course Teaching and Research Department, Jiangsu Police Institute,
Nanjing 210031, People's Republic of China
1101055828@qq.com
[2] Jiangsu Province Electronic Data Forensics and Analysis Engineering Research Center,
Nanjing 210031, People's Republic of China
[3] Key Laboratory of Digital Forensics of Jiangsu Provincial Public Security Department,
Nanjing 210031, People's Republic of China

Abstract. In recent years, blockchain technology has developed rapidly and has been widely used in finance, healthcare, and energy. As the 2.0 version of the blockchain, Ethereum has been seen as the mainstream smart contract development and operation platform, which attracted the attention of criminals. Many Ethereum financial crimes have occurred from time to time, making the Ethereum trading environment facing serious security problems. The safety supervision of the blockchain cannot be delayed. Among them, the detection and early warning of illicit transactions has become the top priority. Traditional machine learning, graph embedding, deep learning and other machine learning methods have all been used for illicit detection. The paper introduces a comprehensive investigation of illicit detection on Ethereum using machine learning technology, it has two sides: one is from the perspective of Ethereum transaction data, using general detection methods; the other is for specific types of illicit transactions detection (Including Ponzi schemes and honeypot contracts). For each transaction type, summarized relevant research ideas, model establishment and evaluation effects. Finally, the paper analyzes the general trend of the current Ethereum illicit detection research, and looks forward to the future research directions and challenges.

Keywords: Ethereum · Illicit detection · Machine learning · Network supervision

1 Introduction

In 2009, Satoshi Nakamoto proposed a protocol that enables users to transfer value without witnesses: Bitcoin [38]. It uses workload consensus to ensure the immutability of public ledgers and is the 1.0 version of the blockchain. As blockchain 2.0, Ethereum adds the function of building and deploying smart contracts. Smart contracts allow trusted transactions to be executed without the intervention of a third party. They are also irreversible and fully traceable. Users can participate in Ethereum currency transactions as anonymous. This provides a living environment for malicious transactions. Criminals can use smart contracts to construct scams to steal user currency. Once the smart contract

X. Sun et al. (Eds.): ICAIS 2022, LNCS 13340, pp. 222–232, 2022.
https://doi.org/10.1007/978-3-031-06791-4_18

is executed, it cannot be stopped artificially unless the user's ether is emptied or the conditions for stopping execution are met. Therefore, the research on the safety supervision of Ethereum is imminent.

All the history of Ethereum ownership and transfer, as well as the deployment and interaction of smart contracts, can be found on the public ledger called the Ethereum blockchain. This provides us with material for studying the anonymity and security of Ethereum. Researchers have achieved many research results in the security and performance of the blockchain [1–15, 40–44]. The author found that the research on the security of Ethereum is generally divided into two categories: the security of smart contract code and the security of Ethereum transactions. The first category is aimed at smart contract code vulnerabilities in normal transactions, researching vulnerabilities in the code and various attack methods against vulnerabilities, aiming to automatically detect vulnerabilities in the smart contract code, and repair the contract before the code is executed, without giving hackers Can take advantage of this opportunity [16–22]. The second category is aimed at illicit transactions on Ethereum. It mainly studies the characteristics of illicit transactions including network fraud, and aims to discover various transaction traps of criminals and raise alarms. Among the more common ones are honeypot contracts and Ponzi schemes.

There have been many papers on the vulnerability detection model of Ethereum, but almost no one has summarized the illicit transaction detection model on Ethereum. Therefore, this paper will focus on the Ethereum transaction network and focus on the use of data mining. Technical illicit transaction detection research, summarizing the research results obtained from the data perspective. The contributions of this paper are as follows:

(1) Classification and overview of the current research results in detecting illicit transactions on Ethereum.
(2) Through comparison, suggestions are made on the selection and application of data mining methods related to illicit detection of Ethereum.
(3) Discuss the trends and challenges of illicit detection on Ethereum.

This paper will summarize and analyze the illicit detection problems on Ethereum from two perspectives. On the one hand, starting from the perspective of Ethereum transaction data, observing the behavioral characteristics in the transaction process, using general detection methods to identify abnormal data, it is mainly divided into two machine learning models: unsupervised learning and supervised learning; on the other hand, it is targeted at specific Types of illicit transactions, such as Ponzi schemes and honeypot contracts, extract relevant features based on marked transaction data, and conduct targeted detection and research.

The rest of this paper is organized as follows. In Sect. 2, we review the general detection techniques for illicit transactions. The Sect. 3 focuses on the analysis and evaluation of specific illicit transaction detection models, and gives a summary and refinement of the methods. In Sect. 4, the consideration on the trends and challenges of illicit transaction detection will be given. Finally, we conclude this paper in Sect. 5.

2 General Detection Technology for Illicit Transactions

Under normal circumstances, in the course of a transaction, the occurrence of an abnormality means that the nature of the transaction is different from the normal transaction, which often includes illicit transactions disguised as normal legal transactions. Therefore, the detection of abnormal transactions is very necessary. Universal detection technology is an anomaly detection technology that is not designed for any specific type of illicit transaction, which means that these technologies can detect different types of anomalies at the same time or lay a solid foundation for them. Basically, these technologies use two modes of supervised machine learning and unsupervised machine learning, so they can be divided into two categories: unsupervised learning models and supervised learning models. The following will discuss from these two perspectives.

2.1 Unsupervised Learning

Please note that the first paragraph of a section or subsection is not indented. The first paragraphs that follows a table, figure, equation etc. does not have an indent, either.

Subsequent paragraphs, however, are indented.

The main idea of unsupervised learning is to cluster transaction data sets into clusters based on the similarity and connectivity of transaction characteristics. At this time, "abnormal points" outside the clusters can be regarded as illicit transactions. The key point is whether the selected clustering algorithm can reasonably divide the data set, and whether the "abnormal points" obtained are really illicit transactions. O'Kane [13] and Morishima [10] both use K-means clustering algorithm for clustering, but there is a flaw: the number of clusters needs to be set manually, and different numbers of clusters often get different abnormal points, so It is not conducive to our detection of truly illicit transactions. Sun et al. [1] considered the radiation effects of known malicious users and judged potential Ethereum malicious users based on the vector space distance of user nodes. After forming the marked set $A = \{a_1, a_2, \cdots, a_n\}$, for each marked node $a_i = (i = 1, 2, \cdots, n)$, select the nearest neighboring node to form a new set A_i, at this time, the nodes contained in the intersection of all sets are regarded as potential malicious users. Baek et al. [23] combined unsupervised learning and supervised learning, used unsupervised learning expectation maximization (EM) algorithm to design the features of the wallet, and then used random forest (RF) for anomaly detection.

2.2 Supervised Learning

Supervised learning models generally study labeled illicit user information, and extract relevant features from them for detection model training. Farrugia et al. [7] first collected the transaction history and account attributes of the Ethereum community, and then trained the XGBoost classifier to detect illicit accounts, and found that the first three features that have the greatest impact on the final model output were determined as the "first and last Time difference between one (minutes)", "Total Ether balance" and "Minimum value received". Sachan et al. [24] studied the feasibility of using metadata such as the domain name (DN) associated with the account in the blockchain, and determined whether the account should be marked as malicious; at the same time, it compared unsupervised and supervised machine learning algorithms. It is found that the decision tree performs best in terms of the balance accuracy of the data set. Poursafaei et al. [25] use logistic regression, support vector machines, random forests, and other integration methods (such as Stacking and AdaBoost classifiers) variants to form a malicious entity detection model in the Ethereum blockchain network. The integrated method showed high performance, with an average F1 score of 0.996. Ibrahim et al. [6] aimed at the detection of Ethereum fraud, and compared the effects of three machine learning algorithms: Decision Tree Algorithm, Random Forest Algorithm and K-nearest neighbors Algorithm (KNN). Finally, a detection model based on random forest was established and a good detection effect was achieved. Agarwal et al. [25] introduced time features and judged whether it is malicious or benign according to changes in account behavior. At the same time, it uses supervised machine learning models (ExtraTreesClassifier has the best detection effect) and unsupervised machine learning models (such as K-Means). Detection, it is found that combined with the analysis of the behavior change of the account, more malicious behaviors can be identified.

Based on the above research results, this paper finds that the supervised learning model shows better performance in illicit detection, which may be due to the existence of labeled data that is beneficial to the correction and training of model parameters. In the supervised learning model, paying attention to the changes in transaction behavior in the time dimension can extract more representative features, while machine learning algorithms such as decision trees and random forests can also establish highly accurate detection models to achieve anti-malware Accurate detection of behavior.

3 Special Detection Technology for Illicit Transactions

Due to the complexity of Ethereum and the lack of supervision, the increasing popularity of blockchain transaction contracts has attracted a lot of fraud. According to the latest data from the blockchain analysis group Chainalysis, cryptographic fraud hidden in blockchain transactions caused losses of US\$4.3 billion in 2019, based solely on Reported encryption fraud. Fraud mainly includes three main fraud methods: Ponzi scheme and honeypot contract, which we will discuss separately below.

3.1 Ponzi Scheme

A Ponzi scheme is an investment scam that uses funds from new investors to pay returns to existing investors. The U.S. Securities and Exchange Commission (SEC) authoritative definition of a Ponzi scheme is as follows:

Definition 1 (Ponzi scheme) [39] A Ponzi scheme is a type of investment fraud that involves paying so-called returns to existing investors from funds provided by new investors. Organizers of Ponzi schemes often solicit new investors by promising to invest funds in opportunities that claim to generate high returns with little or no risk. With little or no legal gains, the Ponzi scheme requires a continuous flow of funds from new investors to continue. Ponzi schemes will inevitably collapse, most often when recruiting new investors becomes difficult or when a large number of investors demand the return of their funds.

The traditional Ponzi scheme can be terminated artificially, and its organizers can disappear at any time with the money. But in the Ethereum smart contract, the scam organizer can write the Ponzi scheme into the code of the smart contract, and once it is executed, it cannot be terminated artificially unless the preset conditions in the smart contract code are met. This requires us to establish a suitable detection model based on the characteristics of the Ponzi scheme smart contract, which can be detected and terminated before the scam is run. Since the number of illicit transactions is like a drop in the bucket compared to the transaction volume on the Ethereum blockchain, whether it is possible to extract representative features, whether it can overcome the problem of imbalances, and whether it can improve the accuracy of the model is the focus of our attention.

As shown in Table 1, Bartoletti et al. [33] analyzed the behavior of Ponzi scheme smart contracts on Ethereum, and used a similar heuristic method to summarize the 4 requirements for satisfying Ponzi scheme, highlighting the characteristics of Ponzi scheme behavior. For example, high Gini coefficient. In 2018, Chen et al. [26] proposed a method to detect Ponzi schemes on the blockchain using data mining and machine learning methods. At the same time, extract the operating code characteristics and transaction behavior characteristics of the smart contract, and then build the XGBoost-based classification model Account, Opcode and Account+Opcode to detect Ponzi schemes. Experimental results show that the best performance comes from the Account+Opcode model, with an accuracy of 94% and a recall rate of 81%. Furthermore, Chen et al. [27] established the Random Forest model to detect smart Ponzi schemes and obtained higher accuracy. Jung et al. [29] extended the selection of behavioral features and used different machine learning algorithms to obtain a classification model with better detection results. In contrast to the previous methods based on gradient boosting algorithm in machine learning, Fan et al. [30] use the idea of ordered boosting to train the PonziTect model, in which the ordered target statistics approach can directly deal with category features and avoid prediction shift caused by target leakage. They also use a data augmentation method to solve the problem of imbalanced dataset in order to improve the quality and performance of model.

If the formation of the Ponzi transaction smart contract can be detected in an instant, it is possible to achieve zero loss. At this time, since there is no transaction behavior, the transaction data cannot be relied on, and only the contract code information can be used as the basis for analysis. Sun et al. [28] introduced a behavior forest to capture the dynamic behavior of smart contracts in the interaction process, which makes it possible to detect Ponzi transactions early. BIAN et al. [31] used the bytecode and ABI of the contract for detection and analysis, which improved the limitations caused by only using the contract source code. After the features are visualized, SE-CapsNet is used to detect the Ponzi scheme in Ethereum, and the detection results are better than other detection methods.

Category imbalance is also the focus of research. Wang et al. [32] used oversampling technology we propose a Ponzi Scheme detection method via oversampling-based Long Short-Term Memory for smart contracts (or PSD-OL) in this paper to fill in the sample features of Ponzi scheme smart contracts data. Train the LSTM model by learning from the feature data for future Ponzi scheme detection. Zhang et al. [34] chose Smote+Tomek

Table 1. Ponzi scheme detection model.

Time	Author	Methods	Classification model	Feature extracted	Precision	Recall
2018	Chen et al. [26]	Data mining, machine learning	XGBoost	Account features, code features	94%	81%
2019	Chen et al. [27]	Data mining, machine learning	Random Forest	Account features, code features	95%	69%
2020	Sun et al. [28]	Machine learning	Behavior forest	code features	94.6%	93%
2019	Jung et al. [29]	machine learning	J48, Random Forest, Stochastic Gradient Descent	Account features, code features	98%	94%
2020	Fan et al. [30]	Data mining, machine learning	PonziTect model with n-gram opcodes	code features	98%	97%
2020	BIAN et al. [31]	Deep learning	SE-CapsNet	code features	97.79%	98.98%
2021	Wang et al. [32]	Neural Network	oversampling-based Long Short-Term Memory Network	Account features, code features	97%	96%

to improve the LightGBM method, which is a method to deal with imbalanced data sets. Experimental results show that the proposed method surpasses the state-of-the-art methods in terms of recall, accuracy, AUC and time efficiency.

Summarizing the above research findings, in the Ponzi scheme detection model, the model based on machine learning can almost achieve an accuracy of more than 95%, which proves the effectiveness and scientific nature of machine learning. However, because the methods used in the data collection stage and the feature extraction stage are different, there is a slight difference between the accuracy rate and the recall rate. From the perspective of model accuracy, the models constructed by Jung et al. [29] and Fan et al. [30] have the highest accuracy, reaching 98%, among which Jung et al. [29] emphasizes the selection of behavior characteristics; Fan et al. [30] focused on the problem of class imbalance and improved it; and in terms of recall rate, the model of BIAN et al. [31] reached the highest 98.98%, and they discovered that the contract includes source code More data information included for early detection of Ponzi schemes. Therefore, in the data collection stage, we need to pay attention to the problem of class imbalance and use methods such as data enhancement to improve the accuracy of the model; in feature extraction, pay attention to time factors, pay attention to behavior changes, and focus on mining more and more representative features, To achieve a higher recall rate. At the same time, the deep learning model, as a popular mathematical model in recent years, can also be considered for Ethereum detection.

3.2 Honeypot Contract

In the past few years, attackers took the initiative to find vulnerabilities in smart contracts for attacks. Recently, a new, more subtle method seems to be emerging, where attackers no longer search for vulnerable contracts. Instead, they try to lure victims into the trap by deploying seemingly fragile contracts that contain hidden traps. This new type of contract is often called a honeypot.

Definition 2 (Honeypot) A honeypot is a smart contract that pretends to leak its funds to an arbitrary user (victim), provided that the user sends additional funds to it. However, the funds provided by the user will be trapped and at most the honeypot creator (attacker) will be able to retrieve them.

The difficulty of honeypot detection research lies in that, on the one hand, this is a new type of illicit activity, the amount of labeled data that can be studied is too small, the imbalance problem is more serious than that of the Ponzi scheme, and it is difficult to extract representative features; on the other hand,, Facing a smart contract with loopholes, is it a real loophole or a trap? People are often difficult to distinguish, and once they are shot, they fall into a trap, and there is a situation in which cleverness turns out to be mistaken. This requires us to start from the logical chain of smart contracts and explore clues.

Torres et al. [35] conducted a systematic analysis of honeypot smart contracts for the first time by investigating the popularity, behavior and impact of honeypot smart contracts on the Ethereum blockchain. They adopted a symbolic execution method, defined a heuristic method for automatically detecting honeypot contracts, and analyzed honeypot contracts from the perspective of behavior, diversity, and activity. The constructed HONEYBADGER detector can effectively detect wild honeypots with a very low false alarm rate.

Camino et al. [36] introduced machine learning methods to study the detection of honeypot contracts. Feature extraction is a very important part of machine learning. Camino adds transaction aggregation features, such as the number of transactions and corresponding averages, and other contract features, creating all possibilities among contract creators, contracts, transaction senders, and other participants. Partition of the capital flow situation, and then build the XGBoost model and train it. Finally, a detection model was successfully established, and two previously unknown honeypot contract technologies were discovered.

Since the establishment of the above detection model requires the participation of transaction characteristics, it is difficult to remind users before the scam occurs. Chen et al. [37] only extracts the features of the contract bytecode and builds a machine learning model based on N-gram features and LightGBM to detect honeypot contracts, which can issue an early warning at the moment the contract is deployed. The experimental results show that the model with unigram+bigram features has an F1 value of 93% and an AUC value of 99% for the binary classification of honeypot contract recognition.

At present, there are very few researches on the detection of honeypot contracts, and there are only three research results. Therefore, in the future, further research can be carried out in this direction to find more labeled contracts, extract contract features, optimize detection models, and improve detection accuracy.

4 Trends and Challenges

The source code of the smart contract may be hidden. In fact, only bytecode is required to implement smart contracts on the Ethereum blockchain. There are now more than one million smart contracts running on Ethereum, but fewer than four thousand have source code. This means that Ethereum not only hides the contract creator, but also hides the logic of potential illicit transactions. This raises many questions: What types of illicit transactions are there on Ethereum? What are their characteristics? How to test smoothly?

4.1 Trends

The information that can be extracted on Ethereum mainly includes two major blocks: the bytecode of the smart contract and the transaction data generated when the smart contract interacts with the environment. Therefore, the research mainly starts from these two points. As soon as the transaction starts, the smart contract will run automatically and cannot be terminated due to the wishes of a certain party. Therefore, in order to reduce losses, we need pre-defense, that is, we can detect and issue an early warning before the illicit transaction starts. At this point, it is particularly important to be able to extract key information from the smart contract bytecode. Among many machine learning algorithms, the graph embedding algorithm can effectively reduce the data dimension of the transaction network, convert the large-scale sparse high-dimensional one-hot node vector into a dense low-dimensional node vector, and achieve accurate research on multi-dimensional data. The illicit transaction data feature extraction showed good performance. Therefore, the graph embedding algorithm has gradually entered the attention of researchers in the near future, and has been used in many applications.

Another key issue is the problem of class imbalance. Ethereum transaction volume is growing explosively, most of which are normal transactions and serve our daily lives. Illicit transactions are only a very small part of them, which are often difficult to find, and there are many new illicit forms that are hiding in. The existing labeled illicit transaction data set and the normal transaction data set have the problem of data imbalance, and it is necessary to find a suitable sampling method to improve the classification effect of the model. The main methods are data enhancement method, over-sampling method, Smooth+Tomek method, double sampling method, etc. Among them, the Smooth+Tomek method can handle imbalanced data sets and performs well. In the process of model training, an ordered target statistical method can also be used to directly process category features, so as to achieve a high degree of fit effect.

4.2 Trends

(1) Real-time transaction data collection. Ethereum generates transactions all the time. The transaction network is not solidified, but is constantly updated over time illicit transactions are also happening. So how to collect transaction data in real time, and use new data to continuously update training detection models and achieve early warning is the key node.

(2) High-accuracy model establishment. Nowadays, machine learning algorithms are constantly being developed. Combining topology knowledge, probability theory knowledge, and graph network knowledge will derive more new and more efficient machine learning models, which are worthy of your attention and research.

(3) Development of detection platform for illicit transactions. Nowadays, there have been many researches on the detection model of illicit transactions on Ethereum, but almost no real application on the Ethereum platform. How to apply the trained detection model to the Ethereum environmental supervision, so that the detection technology really serves Ethereum users are also worthy of our consideration and future challenges.

5   Conclusion

This paper comprehensively investigates the detection models of illicit transactions and accounts on Ethereum. Mainly from two perspectives: On the one hand, from the perspective of Ethereum transaction data, analyze the characteristics of transaction behaviors in the time and space dimensions, and identify abnormal transaction behaviors. This type of method is universal; on the other hand, it is aimed at specific illicit transactions. Transaction types (mainly including Ponzi schemes, honeypot contracts, etc.) are tested. For each type of scam, summarize the researchers' research ideas, model establishment and evaluation effects. Finally, a comparative analysis of the current status of illicit detection research on Ethereum, and prospects for future research directions and challenges.

Acknowledgement. The work is supported by 2020 Scientific Research Project of Jiangsu Police Academy: Blockchain supervision technology research (2020SJYZR02) and 2021 General Project of Philosophy and Social Science Research in Jiangsu Universities: Research on the Construction of Social Credit System Based on Blockchain (2021SJA0497).

References

1. Sun, H., Ruan, N., Liu, H.: Ethereum analysis via node clustering. In: Liu, J.K., Huang, X. (eds.) NSS 2019. LNCS, vol. 11928, pp. 114–129. Springer, Cham (2019). https://doi.org/10.1007/978-3-030-36938-5_7

2. Chen, T., Cao, R., Li, T.: SODA: A generic online detection framework for smart contracts. In: Network and Distributed System Security Symposium (2020)

3. Chen, T., et al.: An Adaptive gas cost mechanism for ethereum to defend against under-priced dos attacks. In: Liu, J.K., Samarati, P. (eds.) ISPEC 2017. LNCS, vol. 10701, pp. 3–24. Springer, Cham (2017). https://doi.org/10.1007/978-3-319-72359-4_1

4. Liang, G., Wang, Q., Xin, J.: Overview of mobile edge computing resource allocation. J. Inf. Secur. **6**(03), 227–256 (2021)
5. Chen, T., Zhang, Y., Li, Z.: TokenScope: automatically detecting inconsistent behaviors of cryptocurrency tokens in Ethereum. In: Proceedings of the 2019 ACM SIGSAC Conference on Computer and Communications Security, pp. 1503–1520 (2019)
6. Ibrahim, R.F., Elian, A.M., Ababneh, M.: Illicit account detection in the Ethereum blockchain using machine learning. In: 2021 International Conference on Information Technology (ICIT), pp. 488–493 (2021)
7. Farrugia, S., Ellul, J., Azzopardi, G.: Detection of illicit accounts over the Ethereum blockchain. Expert Syst. Appl. **150**, 113318 (2020)
8. Wu, L., Wu, S., Zhou, Y., et al.: EthScope: a transaction-centric security analytics framework to detect malicious smart contracts on ethereum. arXiv:2005.08278 (2020)
9. Liu, X., Tang, Z., Li, P.: A graph learning based approach for identity inference in DApp platform blockchain. IEEE Trans. Emerg. Top. Comput. (2020). https://doi.org/10.1109/TETC. 2020.3027309
10. Kalejahi, B.K., Eminov, R., Guliyev, A.: Using blockchain technology in mobile network to create decentralized home location registry (HLR). Comput. Syst. Sci. Eng. **39**(2), 287–296 (2021)
11. Hu, T., Liu, X., Chen, T.: Transaction-based classification and detection approach for Ethereum smart contract. Inf. Process. Manage. **58**(2), 102462 (2021)
12. Sai, K., Tipper, D.: Disincentivizing double spend attacks across interoperable blockchains. In: 2019 First IEEE International Conference on Trust, Privacy and Security in Intelligent Systems and Applications, pp. 36–45 (2019)
13. O'kane, E.: Detecting patterns in the Ethereum transactional data using unsupervised learning. Trinity College, Dublin, Ireland (2018)
14. Gao, Z., Jiang, L., Xia, X.: Checking smart contracts with structural code embedding. IEEE Trans. Softw. Eng. (2020). https://doi.org/10.1109/TSE.2020.2971482
15. Signorini, M., Pontecorvi, M., Kanoun, W., et al.: BAD: blockchain anomaly detection. arXiv: 1807.03833 (2018)
16. Grech, N., Kong, M., Jurisevic, A.: MadMax: surviving out-of-gas conditions in Ethereum smart contracts. In: Proceedings of the ACM on Programming Languages 2 (OOPSLA), pp. 1–27 (2018)
17. Ashizawa, N., Yanai, N., Cruz, J.P.: Learning contract-wide code representations for vulnerability detection on Ethereum smart contracts. IEICE Technical Report, vol. 120, no. 411, pp. 273–280 (2021)
18. Praitheeshan, P., Pan, L., Yu, J., et al.: Security analysis methods on Ethereum smart contract vulnerabilities: a survey. arXiv:1908.08605 (2019)
19. Samreen, N.F., Alalfi, M.H.: SmartScan: an approach to detect denial of service vulnerability in Ethereum smart contracts. arXiv:2105.02852 (2021)
20. Liu, C., Liu, H., Cao, Z.: ReGuard: finding reentrancy bugs in smart contracts. In: 2018 IEEE/ACM 40th International Conference on Software Engineering: Companion (ICSE-Companion), pp. 65–68 (2018)
21. Huang, Y., Bian, Y., Li, R.: Smart contract security: a software lifecycle perspective. IEEE Access **7**, 150184–150202 (2019)
22. Sayeed, S., Marco-Gisbert, H., Caira, T.: Smart contract: attacks and protections. IEEE Access **8**, 24416–24427 (2020)
23. Baek, H., Oh, J., Kim, C.Y.: A model for detecting cryptocurrency transactions with discernible purpose. In: 2019 Eleventh International Conference on Ubiquitous and Future Networks (ICUFN), pp. 713–717 (2019)
24. Sachan, R.K., Agarwal, R., Shukla, S.K.: Identifying malicious accounts in blockchains using domain names and associated temporal properties. arXiv:2106.13420 (2021)

25. Poursafaei, F., Hamad, G.B., Zilic, Z.: Detecting malicious Ethereum entities via application of machine learning classification. In: 2020 2nd Conference on Blockchain Research & Applications for Innovative Networks and Services (BRAINS), pp. 120–127 (2020)
26. Chen, W., Zheng, Z., Cui, J.: Detecting Ponzi schemes on Ethereum: Towards healthier blockchain technology. In: Proceedings of the 2018 World Wide Web Conference, pp. 1409–1418 (2018)
27. Chen, W., Zheng, Z., Ngai, E.C.: Exploiting blockchain data to detect smart Ponzi schemes on ethereum. IEEE Access 7, 37575–37586 (2019)
28. Sun, W., Xu, G., Yang, Z.: Early Detection of smart Ponzi scheme contracts based on behavior forest similarity. In: 2020 IEEE 20th International Conference on Software Quality, Reliability and Security (QRS), pp. 297–309 (2020)
29. Jung, E., Tilly, L., Gehani, M.A.: Data mining-based Ethereum fraud detection. In: 2019 IEEE International Conference on Blockchain (Blockchain), pp. 266–273 (2019)
30. Fan, S., Fu, S., Xu, H.: Expose your mask: smart Ponzi schemes detection on blockchain. In: 2020 International Joint Conference on Neural Networks (IJCNN), pp. 1–7 (2020)
31. Bian, L., Zhang, L., Zhao, K.: Image-based scam detection method using an attention capsule network. IEEE Access 9, 33654–33665 (2021)
32. Wang, L., Cheng, H., Zheng, Z., et al.: Ponzi scheme detection via oversampling-based Long Short-Term Memory for smart contracts. Knowl.-Based Syst. 228, 107312 (2021)
33. Bartoletti, M., Carta, S., Cimoli, T.: Dissecting Ponzi schemes on Ethereum: identification, analysis, and impact. Futur. Gener. Comput. Syst. 102, 259–277 (2020)
34. Zhang, Y., Yu, W., Li, Z.: Detecting Ethereum Ponzi schemes based on improved lightGBM algorithm. IEEE Trans. Comput. Soc. Syst. (2021). https://doi.org/10.1109/TCSS.2021.3088145
35. Torres, C.F., Steichen, M.: The art of the scam: demystifying honeypots in ethereum smart contracts. In: 28th {USENIX} security symposium ({USENIX} security 19), pp. 1591–1607 (2019)
36. Camino, R., Torres, C.F., Baden, M.: A data science approach for detecting honeypots in ethereum. In: 2020 IEEE International Conference on Blockchain and Cryptocurrency (ICBC), pp. 1–9 (2020)
37. Chen, W., Guo, X., Chen, Z., et al.: Honeypot contract risk warning on ethereum smart contracts. In: 2020 IEEE International Conference on Joint Cloud Computing, pp. 1–8. IEEE (2020)
38. Nakamoto, S.B.: A peer-to-peer electronic cash system (2008)
39. Marie, V., Tyler, M., Marie, V., et al.: Analyzing the bitcoin Ponzi scheme ecosystem. In: International Conference on Financial Cryptography and Data Security; Workshop on Bitcoin and Blockchain Research; Workshop on Advances in Secure Electronic Voting Schemes; Workshop on Trusted Smart Contracts. Computer Science, University of New Mexico, Albuquerque, USA; Tandy School of Computer Science, The University of Tulsa, Tulsa, USA (2018)
40. Sahu, P., Singh, S.K., Singh, K.A.: Blockchain based secure solution for cloud storage: a model for synchronizing Industry 4.0 and IIoT. J. Cyber Secur. 3(2), 107–115 (2021)
41. Khonde, S.R., Ulagamuthalvi, V.: Blockchain: secured solution for signature transfer in distributed intrusion detection system. Comput. Syst. Sci. Eng. 40(1), 37–51 (2022)
42. Wang, P., Susilo, W.: Data security storage model of the internet of things based on blockchain. Comput. Syst. Sci. Eng. 36(1), 213–224 (2021)
43. Devi, I., Karpagam, G.: Energy-aware scheduling for tasks with target-time in blockchain based data centres. Comput. Syst. Sci. Eng. 40(2), 405–419 (2022)
44. Aslam, T., Maqbool, A., Akhtar, M., Mirza, A., Khan, M.A.: Blockchain based enhanced ERP transaction integrity architecture and poet consensus. Comput. Mater. Contin. 70(1), 1089–1109 (2022)

Detect Adversarial Examples by Using Feature Autoencoder

Hongwei Ye[1,2], Xiaozhang Liu[1(✉)], Anli Yan[1], Lang Li[1], and Xiulai Li[1,3]

[1] Hainan University, Haikou 570228, China
lxzh@hainanu.edu.cn
[2] School of Electronic and Information Engineering, Heyuan Polytechnic, Heyuan 517000, China
[3] Hainan Hairui Zhong Chuang Technology Co. Ltd., Haikou 570228, China

Abstract. The existence of adversarial samples seriously threatens the security of various deep learning models. Therefore, the detection of adversarial examples is a very important work. Motivated by the comparison with feature maps of adversarial examples and normal examples, we designed an autoencoder to detect the adversarial examples using the feature maps. The feature autoencoder has been evaluated to detect FGSM, DeepFool, JSMA and C&W attacks on CIFAR-10 datasets. The experimental results showed that feature-level detector can detect state-of-art attacks more effectively than at the pixel-level.

Keywords: Adversarial example · Adversarial attack · Feature autoencoder · Adversarial detection

1 Introduction

In speech recognition and computer vision, deep learning neural networks have a wide range of applications [1–3]. Unfortunately, it has been demonstrated that imperceptible perturbations added to clean images can induce the deep neural learning network to make incorrect predictions, though the perturbation is imperceptible to human eyes. Szegedy et al. found that applying an imperceptible perturbation to an image can cause misclassification and the same perturbation can make a different network which is trained on a different subset of the datasets to misclassify the same input data [4], which was the earliest work related to attacks against deep neural network image classifiers [5]. Since then, there have been many different types of adversarial attacks on deep learning in computer vision. Fast gradient sign method (FGSM) is an efficient adversarial example generation method [6]. Jacobian-based Saliency Map Attack (JSMA) introduced a novel class of algorithms to craft adversarial samples based on a precise understanding of the mapping between inputs and outputs of the networks [7]. The DeepFool algorithm can efficiently compute perturbations to fool the deep learning networks and quantify the robustness of the classifiers reliably [8]. Carlini and Wagner's Attack (CW) introduced three new attack algorithms that are successful on distilled and undistilled

X. Sun et al. (Eds.): ICAIS 2022, LNCS 13340, pp. 233–242, 2022.
https://doi.org/10.1007/978-3-031-06791-4_19

neural networks, which are more effective than the previous adversarial example generation method [9]. Moosavi-Dezfooli et al. proposed a method for generating adversarial example which is called universal adversarial perturbations. The universal perturbations have a remarkable generalization property, which can fool new images with high probability [10]. In the driverless car system which uses DNN to identify traffic signs, the attackers will make the "stop" sign to be classified as "speed limit" sign [11]. The misclassification of the driverless car system will threaten personal safety of drivers and pedestrians. Therefore, in the application scenarios of deep learning, the detection of adversarial examples is a very important work.

To detect those adversarial perturbations, ZhitaoGong et al. build a simple binary classifier separating the adversarial examples from the clean data with high accuracy in their experiments [12]. Naveed Akhtar et al. made a Perturbation Rectifying Network (PRN) as a preprocess layer for a target model to detect adversarial examples [13]. Hendrycks et al. used PCA whiten coefficient variance as a threshold for detecting adversarial images [14]. Grosse et al. used two statistical metrics, the MMD and the energy distance, to detect the adversarial examples [15]. In this way, they showed that statistical properties of adversarial examples are essential to adversarial examples detector. However, those above detect methods all used the adversarial examples in the training data, which requires a large number of adversarial examples to train the detector [16].

To address this problem, we propose an autoencoder method based on feature maps to detect adversarial examples. Due to adversarial examples will make excessive reconstruction error than clean images, the autoencoder training only uses clean images, which enables the autoencoder to be used to detect adversarial examples. Compared with the conventional autoencoder methods, we base our autoencoder on feature maps.

2 Proposed Approach

Generally, the detector is a binary classifier that detects whether the input is an adversarial sample. In order to train the classifier to distinguish between clean and adversarial examples, it needs different types of adversarial samples which are generated by various generation algorithms. On the other hand, if we need to detect adversarial samples that have not been trained before, we must generate this adversarial sample and train the classifier again. Otherwise, the classifier cannot detect this type of adversarial sample. This is the fundamental limitation of the detector training. To avoid the limitation of the detector which mentioned above, our implementation use an autoencoder as the detector. An autoencoder is a neural network that is trained to attempt to copy its input to its output [17]. An encoder used to represent the input x to a low dimension h and the decoder that learns to reconstruct g which is the input from the low dimension. For example, an autoencoder has an encoder f and decoder g, ϕ is the nonlinear transformation function, where W and b is the weight and bias of the neural network.

$$\mathbf{f} = \phi(\mathbf{W}_{xh}x + \mathbf{b}_{xh}) \tag{1}$$

$$\mathbf{g} = \phi(\mathbf{W}_{hx}h + \mathbf{b}_{hx}) \tag{2}$$

The training objective for the autoencoder model is to minimize the reconstruction error $\mathbf{r} = \|\mathbf{x} - \mathbf{g}\|_p$, which is difference between the input and the output. It is sufficient to use L_1 and L_2 when calculating reconstruction errors, autoencoder primarily based anomaly detection is a deviation anomaly detection approach using semi-supervised learning. It makes use of the reconstruction error as the anomaly score, if data points with excessive reconstruction error, these data will be regarded to be anomalies. Algorithm 1 shows the anomaly detection using reconstruction errors of autoencoders, θ and ε is the parameters in encoder and decoder, respectively.

Algorithm 1 anomaly detection algorithm using feature autoencoder

---

Input: normal examples feature dataset $\mathbf{x}$, adversarial examples feature dataset $\mathbf{y}$, threshold α
Output: reconstruction error $\mathbf{r}$
1: $\theta, \varepsilon \leftarrow$ train a autoencoder using the normal examples feature dataset $\mathbf{x}$
2: **for** $i = 1; i \leq n; i + +$ **do**
3:     $\mathbf{r}^{(i)} = \| \mathbf{x}^{(i)} - \mathbf{g}_\varepsilon\left(\mathbf{f}_\theta(\mathbf{x}^{(i)})\right) \|$
4:     **if** $\mathbf{r}^{(i)} > \alpha$ **then**
5:         $\mathbf{x}^{(i)}$ is an adversarial example
6:     **else**
7:         $\mathbf{x}^{(i)}$ is a normal example
8:     **end if**
9: **end for**

In general, an autoencoder training using the clean images, and adversarial examples will make excessive reconstruction errors, but the difference is smaller than that using the feature maps as the training dataset. Imperceptible perturbations were added to the original image, which lead to dramatically misleading in the DNN model. Figure 1 shows the sum feature maps of the "block5_pool" layer of VGG-16 applied on a clean image and on its adversarial examples, which indicate that the adversarial perturbations, while small in the origin pixel space, caused a clear contrast in the feature maps of the model. The adversarial image was incorrectly identified as "American_Staffordshire_terrier" with 70.23% confidence, but the true label is "bull_mastiff" with 97.37% confidence. The detailed difference is shown in the Fig. 2, the red box indicates that there is 80% difference between the normal feature maps and the adversarial feature maps in "block5_pool" layer in VGG-16. Motivated by this observation, we can improve the autoencoder anomaly detection by using this feature maps. The detector is implemented as an autoencoder which is only trained by the normal examples. Both normal and adversarial examples feature maps of the classifier model are fed to it, if the reconstruction error is larger than the threshold α, the input image is a normal example, else is an adversarial example.

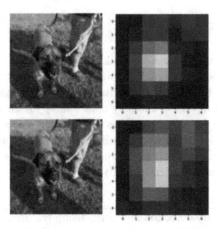

Fig. 1. The sum feature maps of an adversarial image in the "block5_pool" layer in VGG-16.

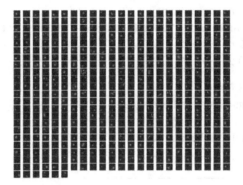

Fig. 2. The 80% difference between the normal feature maps and the adversarial feature maps of the "block5_pool" layer in VGG-16.

3   Experiments

3.1   Reconstruction Error Operations

We experiment with four different types of loss function and a combination of them in our reconstruction error operations. In MAE and MSE loss function, to find a min reconstruction error in data training. Meanwhile, our goal is to find a latent-space Ø such that the distribution of images $\hat{p}$ is as close as possible to the empirical distribution of our input data p. To achieve this, we can use Kullback-Leibler (KL) divergence and Jensen-Shannon (JSKL) divergence to minimize the distance between p and $\hat{p}$. The Kullback-Leibler (KL) divergence of p and $\hat{p}$, denoted $D_{KL}(p\|\hat{p})$, is a measure of the information lost when p is used to approximate $\hat{p}$, where $Q = \frac{1}{2}(p + \hat{p})$. We use different combinations of the loss function to get the optimal parameters of the autoencoder. For example, the reconstruction error were calculated by KL as show in Fig. 3.

$$MAE = \frac{1}{N} \sum_{i=1}^{N} \| \mathbf{x}^{(i)} - \mathbf{g}_\varepsilon \left(\mathbf{f}_\theta \left(\mathbf{x}^{(i)} \right) \right) \| \tag{3}$$

$$MSE = \frac{1}{N} \sum_{i=1}^{N} \| \mathbf{x}^{(i)} - \mathbf{g}_\varepsilon \left(\mathbf{f}_\theta \left(\mathbf{x}^{(i)} \right) \right) \|_2 \tag{4}$$

$$KL = D_{KL}\left(p\|\hat{p}\right) = \sum_{i}^{N} p(i) log \frac{p(i)}{\hat{p}(i)} \tag{5}$$

$$JSKL = \tfrac{1}{2} D_{KL}(p\|Q) + \tfrac{1}{2} D_{KL}\left(\hat{p}\|Q\right) \tag{6}$$

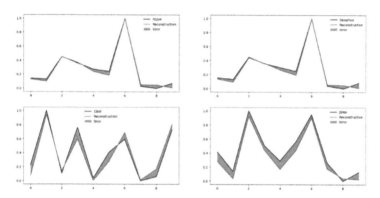

Fig. 3. Reconstruction error were calculated using KL in four types of attacks.

3.2 Architectures

Table 1 shows the architecture of the autoencoder in the pixel-level and feature-level respectively. For example, in the encoder compresses processing of pixel-level autoencoder, the $32 \times 32 \times 3$ input image is fed to Conv 3×3, stride $= 1$, feature maps $= 32$, 'same' convolution; and then Conv 3×3, stride $= 1$, feature maps $= 16$, 'same' convolution. The last layer's activation function is Sigmoid(). Meanwhile, the classifier architecture of CIFAR-10 is VGG-16.

3.3 Generate Adversarial Examples

Our experiment is built on Adversarial Robustness Toolbox (ART) with TensorFlow [18], with NVIDIA Tesla P100 16G.The adversarial examples is shown in Fig. 4, which are generated by the four adversarial attacks mentioned in Sect. 1. For example, the first row is the adversarial example generate by FGSM, all the examples were misclassified by the classifier model VGG-16 (Table 2).

Table 1. Architecture of the autoencoder.

Pixel-level		Feature-level	
Conv2D.ReLU	32,(3,3)	Dense.ReLU	32
Conv2D.ReLU	16,(3,3)	Dense.ReLU	16
Conv2D.ReLU	8,(3,3)	Dense.ReLU	8
Encoder		Encoder	
Conv2DTranspose	8,(3,3)	Dense.ReLU	16
Conv2DTranspose	16,(3,3)	Dense.ReLU	32
Conv2D	3,(3,3)	Dense	10
Sigmoid()		Sigmoid()	

Table 2. Accuracy of the different attack with different perturbation.

Attacks	Accuracy	
	High perturbation	Small perturbation
No Attack	88.31%	88.31%
FGSM	10.74%	74.50%
DeepFool	9.30%	15.19%
C&W	11.67%	80.85%
JSMA	1.53%	1.55%

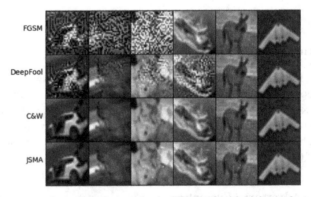

Fig. 4. Four types of adversarial examples in CIFAR-10 with high attack success rate.

3.4 Detection Evaluation

Datasets used for our experiment are CIFAR-10 dataset [19], the CIFAR-10 dataset consists of 60000 32 × 32 color images in 10 classes, with 6000 images in each class. There are 50000 training images and 10000 test images in the CIFAR-10 dataset. The training data are 50000 normal images and the 10000 normal test data using to evaluate the autoencoder. We use min max scaling to make the input data to be within 0 and 1 in pixel-level and feature-level detection, threshold α is defined based on the mean of training loss. Our experiments are performed on 20000 images which combine 10000 test images with 10000 adversarial examples were generated by four types attacks using ART. At first, we use these 10000 adversarial examples were classified by the VGG-16 network to obtain their true labels, then the same data were fed to the network to get the feature maps.

Table 3. The results of autoencoder detector in adversarial examples with high perturbation using pixel-level detector.

Loss	Attacks	Accuracy	Precision	Recall	F1_score
MAE	FGSM	0.7179	0.6127	1.0	0.7598
	DeepFool	0.6784	0.6018	0.8593	0.7079
	C&W	0.5609	0.5023	0.5935	0.5441
	JSMA	0.5536	0.4954	0.5936	0.5400
MSE	FGSM	0.7473	0.6385	1.0	0.7794
	DeepFool	0.7028	0.6282	0.8443	0.7204
	C&W	0.5714	0.5140	0.5440	0.5286
	JSMA	0.5841	0.5256	0.5980	0.5595

In order to compare with the ability of detecting adversarial examples between high perturbations and small perturbations, we evaluate 2 types of adversarial examples. The evaluate results is shown in Tables 3 and 4. It is clearly shown that detection at feature-level performs better than at pixel-level on 3 types of attacks: DeepFool, C&W and JSMA. For example, although piexl-level detection better than feature-level on FGSM in many cases, the results is caused by high perturbation. As we can see in Fig. 4, the adversarial examples crafted by FGSM with high perturbation in the first three columns, which can lead to the reconstruction error larger than 3 types of attack, it is easier to detect in pixel-level detection. But in feature-level detection using MSE+JSKL makes better result than pixel-level in 4 types of attacks. It can be seen from Table 5 that feature-level detector perform better than pixel-level detector in the adversarial examples with small perturbations.

Table 4. The results of autoencoder detector in adversarial examples with high perturbation using feature-level detector.

Loss	Attacks	Accuracy	Precision	Recall	F1_score
MAE+JSKL	FGSM	0.6793	0.6149	0.7530	0.6770
	DeepFool	0.7302	0.6492	0.8881	0.7476
	C&W	0.7354	0.6483	0.8760	0.7451
	JSMA	0.8154	0.7274	0.9998	0.8422
MSE+JSKL	FGSM	0.7302	0.6728	0.7699	0.7180
	DeepFool	0.7577	0.6933	0.8353	0.7577
	C&W	0.7496	0.6856	0.7995	0.7382
	JSMA	0.8601	0.7796	0.9981	0.8754

Table 5. The results of autoencoder detector in adversarial examples with small perturbation.

Detector	Loss	Attacks	Accuracy	Precision	Recall	F1_score
Pixel-level	MAE	FGSM	0.5124	0.1111	0.4035	0.1742
		DeepFool	0.6444	0.5530	0.8416	0.6674
		C&W	0.5200	0.0850	0.4110	0.1409
		JSMA	0.4770	0.0948	0.5222	0.1605
Feature-level	MSE+JSKL	FGSM	0.7258	0.2855	0.7659	0.4159
		DeepFool	0.7136	0.6368	0.7555	0.6910
		C&W	0.8004	0.3051	0.8491	0.4489
		JSMA	0.8635	0.7848	0.9957	0.8778

We also establish detector evaluation metrics in Area Under the Receiver Operating Characteristic curve (AU-ROC) [20]. ROC curves typically feature true positive rate on the Y axis, and false positive rate on the X axis, a larger area under the curve (AUC) is usually better. Figures 1 and 2 shows the ROC curves for each individual attacks using feature-level detector in Adv-1 and Adv-2 respectively, Figs. 3 and 4 shows the ROC curves for each individual attacks using pixel-level detector in Adv-1 and Adv-2, it is clearly that the feature-level detector is able to most easily handle the 4 types attacks than that in pixel-level detector, especially in the JSMA attack the AUC is up to 0.96 (Figs. 5 and 6).

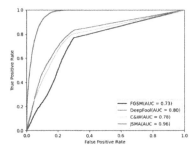
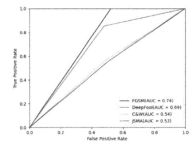

Fig. 5. ROC curves for the different attack types with high perturbation, the left using feature-level detector and the right using pixel-level detector.

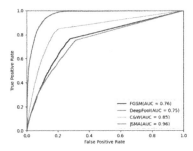
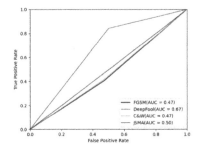

Fig. 6. ROC curves for the different attack types with small perturbation, the left using feature-level detector and the right using pixel-level detector.

4 Conclusion

Motivated by the compare with feature maps of adversarial examples and clean images, we designed an autoencoder to detect the adversarial examples using the feature maps, which come from the classifier model. The feature autoencoder has been evaluated to detect FGSM, DeepFool, JSMA and C&W attacks on CIFAR-10 datasets. The experimental results showed that feature-level detector can detect state-of-art attacks more effectively than at the pixel-level. Though the adversarial examples with small perturbations, the feature-level detector still perform better than pixel-level. It has high accuracy but low precision, in our future work we will improve the precision of detecting adversarial examples with small perturbations.

Acknowledgement. This work is supported by the Project of Educational Commission of Guangdong Province of China (2018GKTSCX114), Key Research and Development Program of Hainan Province (Grant No. ZDYF2020033), Young Talents' Science and Technology Innovation Project of Hainan Association for Science and Technology (Grant No. QCXM202007), Hainan Provincial Natural Science Foundation of China (Grant No. 621RC612), Hainan Provincial Natural Science Foundation of China (Grant No. 2019RC107).

Conflicts of Interest. The authors declare that they have no conflicts of interest to report regarding the present study.

References

1. Hinton, G., Deng, L., Yu, D.: Deep neural networks for acoustic modeling in speech recognition: the shared views of four research groups. IEEE Signal Process. Mag. **29**, 82–97 (2012)
2. Alex, K., Ilya, S., Hg, E.: Imagenet classification with deep convolutional neural networks. In: Proceedings of NIPS, IEEE, Neural Information Processing System Foundation, pp. 1097–1105 (2012)
3. Liu, W., Wang, Z., Liu, X., Zeng, N., Liu, Y., Alsaadi, F.: A survey of deep neural network architectures and their applications. Neurocomputing **234**, 11–26 (2016)
4. Szegedy, C., Zaremba, W., Goodfellow, I.: Intriguing properties of neural networks. arXiv: 1312.6199 (2013)
5. Xu, H., et al.: Adversarial attacks and defenses in images, graphs and text: a review. IEEE Signal Process. Mag. **17**, 151–178 (2020)
6. Goodfellow, I.J., Shlens, J., Szegedy, C.: Explaining and harnessing adversarial examples. arXiv:1412.6572 (2014)
7. Papernot, N., Mcdaniel, P., Jha, S., Fredrikson, M., Celik, Z.B., Swami, A.: The limitations of deep learning in adversarial settings. In: IEEE European Symposium on Security & Privacy (2015)
8. Moosavi-Dezfooli, S.M., Fawzi, A., Frossard, P.: DeepFool: a simple and accurate method to fool deep neural networks. arXiv:1511.04599 (2015)
9. Carlini, N., Wagner, D.: Towards evaluating the robustness of neural networks. arXiv:1608.04644 (2016)
10. Moosavi-Dezfooli, S.M., Fawzi, A., Fawzi, O., Frossard, P.: Universal adversarial perturbations. In: 2017 IEEE Conference on Computer Vision and Pattern Recognition (CVPR), pp.86–94 (2017)
11. Gu, T., Dolan-Gavitt, B., Garg, S.: Identifying vulnerabilities in the machine learning model supply chain (2017)
12. Gong, Z., Wang, W., Ku, W.S.: Adversarial and clean data are not twins. arXiv:1704.04960 (2017)
13. Akhtar, N., Liu, J., Mian, A.: Defense against universal adversarial perturbations. arXiv:1711.05929 (2017)
14. Hendrycks, D., Gimpel, K.: Early methods for detecting adversarial images. arXiv:1608.00530 (2016)
15. Grosse, K., Manoharan, P., Papernot, N., et al.: On the (statistical) detection of adversarial examples. arXiv:1702.06280 (2017)
16. Lee, S., Kim, N.R., Cho, Y., Choi, J.Y., Kim, S., et al.: Adversarial detection with gaussian process regression-based detector. KSII Trans. Internet Inf. Syst. **13**, 4285–4299 (2019)
17. Goodfellow, I., Bengio, Y., Courville, A.: Deep learning. MIT Press, New York (2016). http://www.deeplearningbook.org
18. IBM, Welcome to the adversarial robustness toolbox (2019). https://adversarial-robustness-toolbox.readthedocs.io/en/stable/
19. Krizhevsky, A., Nair, V., Hinton, G.: CIFAR-10 and CIFAR-100 datasets (2009). https://www.cs.toronto.edu/~kriz/cifar.html
20. Davis, J., Goadrich, M.: The relationship between precision-recall and ROC curves. In: Proceedings of the 23rd International Conference on Machine Learning, vol. 6. ACM (2006)

Effect of Language Mixture on Speaker Verification: An Investigation with Amharic, English, and Mandarin Chinese

Firew Tadele⬤, Jianguo Wei[(✉)], Kiyoshi Honda, Ruiteng Zhang, and Wenhao Yang

College of Intelligence and Computing, Tianjin University, Tianjin 300000, China
`frewt2020@tju.edu.cn`

Abstract. Speaker verification (SV) tasks with low-resource language corpora naturally face technical difficulties and often require language mixture processing. In this paper, the LibriSpeech ASR corpus, the AISHELL-I Mandarin Speech corpus, and the Yegna2021 corpus were used for training the x-vector model. The Yegna2021 is a bilingual speech corpus consisting of Amharic and English languages. We designed and collected the Yegna2021 corpus to facilitate SV experimentation. Over 200 native Ethiopian speakers who are bilingual in both languages have participated in the creation of the corpus. To the best of our knowledge, this is the first study of SV systems in Amharic language. This study proposes that improving SV performance degradation, caused by language mismatch between training and testing utterances, requires not only combining two or more languages for training, but also considering the phonetic similarities and differences between languages that impact on obtaining better SV performance. The varied effects of language combinations have been examined on Mandarin Chinese, Amharic, and English languages. In this paper, we investigate the impact of language mismatches between training and testing on SV performance using only the Yegna2021 corpus. The experimental results show that a language variability between training and testing utterances significantly degrades SV performance (between 6.5% to 9.0%). The combination of Amharic and Mandarin yields better SV performance than English and Mandarin, achieving an Equal error rate (EER) of 8.3% as compared to 9.8%, with relative performance degradation of 17.1%. To verify these results, we paired Mandarin with data from the LibriSpeech, and the result shows 18.2% relative performance degradation, with an EER of 9.9% for English and Mandarin.

Keywords: Amharic language · Speaker verification · Low-resource language · Yegna2021 corpus · Language Mixture

1 Introduction

Speaker verification (SV) is an essential biometric recognition technology that has gained popularity in various applications such as access control, banking, forensic work, and personalization. SV has improved greatly in performance throughout the years of research

X. Sun et al. (Eds.): ICAIS 2022, LNCS 13340, pp. 243–256, 2022.
https://doi.org/10.1007/978-3-031-06791-4_20

and is now being employed in real-world applications [1, 2]. Despite such a major achievement, current speaker verification systems often suffer from performance degradation due to various factors [3]. Environment, recording, channel conditions, speaker traits (e.g., dialect/accent, stress, speaking style), and spoken language can be considered as irregular dimensions in the acoustic space. Also, a mismatch between training and testing datasets in any of these acoustic dimensions results in performance degradation in speaker recognition applications [4].

SV applications can be categorized into text-dependent and text-independent. In text-dependent systems, the same set of utterances are used for training and testing, and language may not be important for text-dependent verification. In text-independent systems, on the other hand, different utterances are used for testing, implying that text-independent verification does not require fixed input voice content, and it is more flexible but their accuracy is considerably lower than that of comparable text-dependent systems because of the constraint of the phonetic variability between training and testing sets [5, 6]. This study is dealt with text-independent speaker verification performance in case of language mismatch between training and testing sets.

Half of the world's population is bilingual, and people frequently switch between their first and second languages while speaking [7]. For instance, according to a source at the Ethiopian Embassy in China, 15,000–20,000 Ethiopians are living all across China, many of whom speak both Mandarin Chinese and Amharic. When he/she uses speaker recognition systems, one likely enrolls in Mandarin Chinese and tests in Amharic, or vice versa. Language discrepancy is a particular case of mismatch that degrades SV performance. Language mismatch falls into two scenarios: (i) the speaker verification system is trained with data in one language, but operates in other languages, and (ii) the enrollment data is in one language, but the test data is in a second language. These two types of mismatches could be mixed, that is, the training, enrolment, and testing are in three different languages [3, 8].

Since the past a few years, researchers have worked on speaker verification applications in bilingual and multilingual environments, where speaker models may be trained with recordings in one language but testing is performed in another [37]. Those trials show performance degradation in language-mismatched conditions. In [10], to alleviate this problem of language changes in test utterances, speaker models were trained with utterances from two languages combined (English and Cantonese). In other works, such as [11], the model trained using data from two languages (English & Farsi) is outperformed by the model trained using samples from English language alone. However, in these approaches, the impact of phonetic property of languages to combine on the performance of speaker verification systems has been less attended, and the authors did not investigate whether phonetic similarity or difference in languages or other reasons gives rise to performance variation in the speaker verification system. Therefore, this study proposes that improving SV performance degradation, caused by language mismatch between training and testing utterances, requires not only combining two or more languages for training, but also considering the phonetic similarities and differences between world's languages that impact on obtaining better SV performance. In order to prove this, we formulated a null hypothesis, H0: to improve SV performance requires not only combining two or more languages for training the model, but also considering phonetic similarities and differences across languages.

In this paper, the first Amharic and English bilingual speech corpus, called Yegna2021, was designed and collected to facilitate such studies. The full set of experiments is based on a recently proposed speaker model known as the x-vector [12]. The x-vector is based on time-delay neural network (TDNN) architecture that computes speaker embeddings from variable-length acoustic segments [8]. This model is trained by the speech data from the Yegna2021 bilingual corpus, the LibriSpeech, and the AISHELL-I Mandarin Chinese Speech corpus.

The paper is organized as follows: Sect. 2 describes the Yegna2021 bilingual speech corpus. Section 3 describes the experimental setup and results. Section 4 provide theoretical justifications for the experiment results. Finally, the paper is concluded in Sect. 5.

2   The Yegna2021 Bilingual Speech Corpus

In developing countries such as Ethiopia, bilingual speech resources are limited for studying the impact of language on voice technology, speaker recognition, and ASR application. The Amharic speech corpus in [36], was created for speech recognition studies, and it lacks bilingual speakers as well as sufficient number of speakers, making it difficult to use for systematically studying language variability in speaker recognition. Collecting standardized and annotated corpora is one of the most difficult and expensive processes. Amharic is the national language of Ethiopia. It belongs to the Semitic language family [14]. Low-resource languages may have a few or all of the following aspects; lack of linguistic expertise, less web resources, lack of transcribed speech data, lack of digital phonetical dictionaries, etc. [13]. According to this definition, Amharic is a language with limited resources and less technological support, making it difficult to create digital text and audio corpora. In fact, no existing data resources could meet the requirements of our experimental work, and thus we decided to create our own bilingual dataset called "Yegna2021" as a key contribution.

Yegna2021 is the first bilingual speech dataset that consists of Amharic and English languages, and it is built for studying cross-lingual speaker verification. The speech signals were collected using a smartphone from bilingual Ethiopian speakers. Each speech utterance varies in length and was recorded at a 16-kHz sample rate and 16-bits resolution. The utterances were also recorded in a single or double session in a closed sound room, mostly in the evening or at night, but this does not imply that all data are noise-free. The Yegna2021 dataset contains a total of 207 speakers, and the number of male and female speakers was approximately balanced. For each speaker, we prepared a different set of utterances in both languages to read aloud while recording. The utterances are standard and most frequently used Amharic or English strings to make this dataset suitable for studying language mismatch. About 80% of the speakers are between the ages of 19 to 48, and the full name, gender, age, native language, and birthplace of each speaker are recorded as meta-data. Each speech utterance has a unique ID that is compatible with speaker recognition and ASR engines such as Kaldi [15]. The attributes of designing the dataset are summarized in Table 1.

Table 1. Description of Yegna2021 dataset.

Attribute	Detail
# of speakers	207 (120 Male/87 Female)
Speakers' status	Students (high school, preparatory, undergraduate, and doctorate students)
No. of sessions	1 or 2
Data type and format	speech signal, wav
Sampling rate	16 kHz
Sampling format	16-bit, mono
Type of speech	read sentences
Channel	Smartphone
Languages	Amharic, English
Microphones	mobile device mic
Recording Mob app	AVR X, mobile app recorder
Acoustic environment	living room, lab environment

2.1 Building the Yegna2021 Bilingual Speech Corpus

Amharic is the official working language of the Federal Democratic Republic of Ethiopia. English, on the other hand, is used as a medium of instruction and communication in educational institutions, as well as a working language in governmental and non-governmental organizations in Ethiopia. Experimenting on these two languages is thus more useful for studying cross-lingual speaker verification.

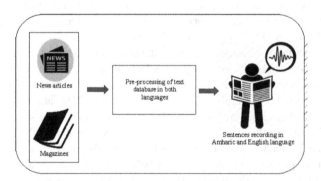

Fig. 1. Overall process of text and speech collection

Text data was collected from a variety of domains, including newspapers (አዲስ አድማስ, አዲስ ዘመን, ሪፖርተር, ነጋሪት ጋዜጣ), news articles (Ethiopian News Agency, Global Voices, CNN, BCC), and magazines, to cover all of the Amharic and English languages. Spelling correction and punctuation mark normalization are examples of document pre-processing. We prepared a different set of utterances in both languages for each speaker to read while recording. Approximately one million words from each language have been collected. Figure 1 depicts the overall procedure for collecting text data and recording speech.

3   Experiments and Findings

This section presents experimental procedures and results. A series of experiments was conducted using our bilingual corpus and publicly available datasets. As previously mentioned, these experiments enabled us to investigate what are the factors behind language combinations for improving the text-independent speaker verification performance, which was hampered by the language discrepancy in training and testing utterances.

3.1   Training Data Details

Our experimental work incorporated speech sounds from the LibriSpeech ASR English corpus, our bilingual (Amharic and English) speech corpus, and AISHELL-I Mandarin Chinese Speech corpus to train the Kaldi Voxceleb x-vector model.

Both LibriSpeech ASR corpus and AISHELL-I corpus are publicly available datasets, and both are discussed in detail in [16, 17]. The LibriSpeech ASR corpus has approximately 100 h of clean speech data; we selected 187 speakers from this training set, each with 50 utterances (a total of 9350 utterances). Also, we selected 30 speakers from AISHELL-I, with each of the speakers having 100 utterances ($30 \times 100 = 3000$ utterances in total). Similarly, for the testing set, 1000 utterances are chosen from 20 speakers in the LibriSpeech ASR corpus, and 1200 utterances are chosen from 12 speakers in the AISHELL-I testing set. These two datasets were used as materials to train and test the model and fulfill the requirements for our experimental work.

Yegna2021 dataset was used as the primary training data, and it was split into training and testing subsets. The training set contains 80% of the total data, while the rest is used for testing separately in both languages, with no speaker overlap. To be more specific, the Yegna2021 dataset contains a total of 20,700 utterances from 207 bilingual speakers. This total amount of the training set for each language contains 9350 utterances from 187 speakers, while the testing set for each language contains 1000 utterances from 20 speakers. The statistics of the three training sets are shown in Table 2.

Table 2. Statistics of the training sets.

Dataset	# of speakers	# of utterances
Yegna2021 (Amharic and English corpus)	187	18,700 (each language 9350)
LibriSpeech ASR corpus (English)	187	9350
AISHELL Mandarin Chinese Speech corpus	30	3000

3.2 Experimental Setup

The full set of experiments is based on a recently proposed speaker model known as the x-vector. In this experiment, for the acoustic feature processing, we utilized the Mel-frequency cepstral coefficients (MFCC) as the acoustic features. MFCC considers individual emotional sensitivity when determining which frequencies are optimal for speech and speaker recognition [9]. The x-vector system uses 23-dimensional MFCC features as input with the window length: 25-ms, frameshift: 10-ms. An energy-based Voice Activity Detection (VAD) is performed to remove silent frames from the input utterances. Finally, we applied cepstral mean and variance normalization (CMVN) and removed the record which is less than 3 s before moving to the training step. To extract speaker representations, the x-vector system is proven to be very successful in a variety of speaker recognition tasks [8] and is well described in [12]. The entire x-vector system is trained with the Kaldi toolkit [15], using the Kaldi Voxceleb v2 recipe [18]. TDNN computes speaker embeddings from variable-length acoustic segments. The network consists of layers that operate on speech frames, i.e., a statistic pooling layer that aggregates over the frame-level representations, additional layers that operate at the segment level, and finally a softmax output layer. The embeddings are extracted after the statistics pooling layers. After extracting the speaker embeddings, LDA and PLDA are employed as the back-end. The embeddings are centered, and the dimensionality is reduced to 150 using LDA. After dimensionality reduction, PLDA was used to compare pairs of speaker embeddings and generate the verification scores.

3.3 Evaluation Metrics

The results are reported in terms of the standard Equal Error Rate (EER) and minimum Detection Cost Function (minDCF(p-target = 0.01)). EER measures the value at which the false-reject (miss) rate equals the false-accept (false-alarm) rate, and minDCF (p-target = 0.01) is defined as a weighted sum of false-reject and false-accept error probabilities.

3.4 Speaker Verification Experimental Results

Experiment 1
Speaker verification (SV) performance was investigated in our first experiment, which examines the effects of language mismatches between training and testing utterances. As part of this experiment, Amharic and English are used as target languages both from the Yegna2021 bilingual dataset. Section 3.1 contains a detailed description of the Yegna2021 training data. For each test, the number of trials is 28,406. Existing SV systems often suffer from performance degradation if there is any language mismatch across model training, speaker enrollment, and testing [8, 10, 11]. Cross-language testings are implemented in our experiment, and the result also shows that the language mismatch between training and testing leads to a significant degradation in SV performance. The experimental results are shown in Table 3.

Table 3. SV performance of training and testing cases with language mismatch.

			Testing languages			
			Amharic		English	
			EER %	minDCF	EER %	minDCF
Training language	Exp. 1	**Amharic**	**5.922**	**0.5422**	6.457	0.6894
	Exp. 2	**English**	7.082	0.6285	**6.424**	**0.6897**

From Table 3, we observe that SV results for training in Amharic (exp.1) show a relative performance degradation of 9.0%, from EER of 5.9% (with Amharic testing data) to 6.5% (with English testing data). For training in English (exp.2), the performance degrades from EER of 6.4% (with English testing data) to 7.1% (with Amharic testing data), which is 10.2% of relative performance degradation.

Experiment 2

In the second set of experiments, we investigate if the performance of SV can be improved by training the x-vector model with all utterances mixed from the Yegna2021 (Amharic and English) bilingual dataset. As we mentioned in Sect. 3.1, the Yegna2021 dataset contains a total of 18,700 utterances in a training set, with each language containing 9350 utterances to train the model. The PLDA classifiers are also trained with all utterances combined from both languages. The number of trials in both experiments is 28,406. It is found in the result that combining utterances and training the speaker model can significantly improve the performance from degradation caused by the language mismatch in speaker verification. The experimental result is shown in Table 4.

Table 4. Comparison of Amharic and English.

		Testing languages			
		Amharic		English	
		EER %	minDCF	EER %	minDCF
Training language	**Amharic+English**	**5.224**	**0.4879**	**5.784**	**0.6117**

In Table 4, it can be seen that the EER in the mismatched condition is relatively improved when compared to previous cross-lingual testing results in Table 3. Since combining utterances increased training data, the model improved verification performance by 35.5% when testing in Amharic and 11.7% when testing in English. Based on the results, training models using utterances from both languages can effectively fill the performance degradation gap due to language mismatch.

Experiment 3

Previous studies in [10, 11] have shown that language combination can significantly reduce performance degradation caused by language mismatch, and our experimental results in Table 4 also show that SV performance can be improved significantly when the model is trained with combined languages (Amharic and English). Based on these results, we investigate the impact of language combination SV performance.

For these experiments, the x-vector model was trained using the AISHELL-I Mandarin Chinese speech corpus as constant training data. This means that we combined the AISHELL-I speech corpus with Yegna2021 bilingual corpus and as well as with the LibriSpeech ASR corpus separately. We conducted three sets of experiments; the first is the Amharic system (Exp. 1), which combines the Amharic language from the Yegna2021 dataset with the Mandarin Chinese language. The Yegna2021 dataset, as mentioned in Sect. 3.1, contains 9350 Amharic utterances from 187 speakers and the AISHELL-I contains 3000 Mandarin Chinese utterances from 30 speakers. Then the model was trained using a total of 12,350 utterances from both languages (Amharic and Mandarin), and the PLDA classifiers were also trained using all utterances from both languages. A total of 345,458 trials were created in all experiments. The second experiment is on the English system (Exp. 2), and we combined the English language from the Yegna2021 dataset with the Mandarin Chinese language. All experimental results are depicted in Table 5.

Table 5. Comparison of SV performance between the Amharic and English systems.

			Testing language	
			Mandarin	
			EER %	minDCF
Training language	Exp. 1	**Amharic+Mandarin**	**8.348**	**0.8012**
	Exp. 2	**English (Yegna2021)+Mandarin**	9.781	0.8510
	Exp. 3	**English (LibriSpeech)+Mandarin**	9.872	0.8247

From Table 5, we find some interesting observations. We can see that the EERs in the Amharic system (exp. 1) yields better SV performance than the English system (Exp. 2). When everything else in the training set remains constant and only the spoken language varies, the performance of the SV degraded by 17.1%, from EER of 8.3% to 9.8%. To confirm these results, we combined the English language from LibriSpeech ASR corpus with the Mandarin Chinese language in the third experiment. The results show that the Amharic system (Exp. 1) still outperforms the English system (Exp. 3).

4   Phonetics of Languages and Speaker Recognition Performance

This study investigated the impact of language mismatches between training and testing on speaker verification performance, and the results showed that language combination significantly improves performance degradation caused by language mismatch and suggested that their phonetics similarities and differences result in SV performance variations.

According to our experimental results, the two-language combination for training produced better SV performance. In this section, we discuss the phonetic similarity of Amharic and Mandarin Chinese languages as a possible factor for enhanced SV performance. In automatic speaker recognition, the phonetic nature of the training and testing utterances is important and this has been the focus of the research. The studies in [19–22] conclude that phonetic segmental properties have a significant contribution to overall recognition performance.

To provide theoretical justifications for our experiment results, we formulate the following comparative analysis of the speech sound system of the three languages based on the segmental properties and syllable structure, and we speculate that this comparative analysis gives an interpretation to the results of speaker verification performance. Despite a large number of speakers, the phonetic similarities and differences in Amharic and Mandarin Chinese have not previously been studied. Therefore, to accomplish the analysis of the two sound systems, we used data from different references about Amharic and Mandarin Chinese, and the examples were randomly selected from the datasets used in our experiment. The focus on the comparison is three-fold as shown below.

1. Locating the same vowel sound, having the same articulation, in Amharic and Mandarin Chinese sound systems.
2. Contrasting whether there are differences in the frequency of occurrence of consonants in the three languages depending on whether they are in the onset or the coda.
3. Contrasting the total voiced segments of the three languages using closed-syllable sequences (CVC).

4.1 Classification of Vowel Sounds in Amharic and Mandarin Chinese

Vowels carry the major part of static speaker characteristics because those sounds reflect resonance of the whole vocal tract. This section aims at exploring the degree of phonetic similarity between Amharic and Mandarin Chinese vowels in terms of articulatory features. Amharic language has a non-Latin syllabic script called "Fidel" or "Abugida" [14]. The scripts are more or less orthographic representations of the phonemes in the language. It has 32 consonants and 7 vowels, which comprises a complete set of sounds for Amharic language [23]. Mandarin language, spoken in the form of Standard Chinese, is the official language for both mainland China and Taiwan. Pinyin can be regarded as the 'alphabet' of Mandarin Chinese. It consists of 21 consonants and 7 singled vowels [24]. As Chinese is a tonal language, each character pronounced in a different tone will give a different meaning. For this study, we are concerned with the isolated segmental unit (vowels) of Mandarin, leaving aside the suprasegmental component (tone) (Table 6).

Table 6. Amharic and Mandarin Chinese vowels map.

Tongue Position	Front			Centre		Back	
	Mandarin		Amh	Mandarin	Amh	Mandarin	Amh
	Un-rounded	Rounded	Un-rounded	Unrounded		Rounded	
High/closed	i	y	i		ɨ	u	u
Mid	e		e	ə	ə	o	o
Low/open				a	a		

4.2 Syllable Structure

The phonetic similarity of two languages is characterized not only by their segmental properties but also by their phonotactic properties, including permissible segment combinations and syllable shapes [25]. Our analyses show that not only do Amharic and Mandarin Chinese have similar vowel articulation, but also the two languages have some significant similarities in terms of phoneme combination.

The way the sounds are combined in speech differs between languages. Comparing Amharic, Mandarin Chinese, and English syllable structures reveals some similarities and differences in how each language uses syllables to form words. Several linguists studied the syllable structures of Amharic language and came up with different structures. According to the studies in [26, 27] the possible syllabic structures in Amharic are V, VC, VCC, CV, CVC, and CVCC. As for Mandarin, twelve syllable structures can be observed [28]. As a comparison, English allows a wider variety of syllable types than that of Amharic and Mandarin Chinese syllables when forming a word. The syllable structures of the three languages are summarized in Table 7; similar syllable structures are marked (+) while those that are different are marked (–).

Table 7. Syllable structure contrast between Amharic, Mandarin Chinese and English (Amh = $C_{0-1} V_1 C_{0-2}$, MC = $C_{0-1} V_{1-2} C_{0-2}$ and English = $C_{0-3} V_1 C_{0-4}$).

Syllable Structure	Amharic	Mandarin	English
V	+	+	+
VC	+	+	+
VCC	+	+	+
CV	+	+	+
CCV	-	-	+
CCCV	-	-	+
CVC	+	+	+
CVCC	+	+	+
CVCCC	-	-	+
CVCCCC	-	-	+

From Table 7, when comparing Amharic and English languages, it is natural to highlight that Amharic language prohibits the presence of more than one consonant (CC: V) in an onset/beginning of a word, and also Amharic language prohibits the presence of more than two consonants (V: CCC) in a coda/end of a word [29], according to the properties of syllable formation. In Table 7, there are also similar syllabic properties for Mandarin Chinese, which varies from English. Before the nuclear vowel, Mandarin Chinese allows CG- but not CC-, whereas English allows both CG- and CC-, where G is a "glide", which is a prenuclear vowel in Mandarin [28]. Similarly, Mandarin Chinese only allows final consonants ([–n] and [–ŋ]) after the nuclear vowel, whereas English allows many more consonants [28, 30]. To be more specific, the syllable types permitted by Amharic and Mandarin Chinese languages appear to be limited to one consonant at the beginning of the word and two consonant clusters at the end of the syllable. In other words, the heavy consonant clusters (e.g., CCCVCCC) as in English do not occur in Amharic and Mandarin Chinese languages.

By looking at this contrast, it is obvious that Amharic and Mandarin Chinese share common syllable properties, whereas English shows a tendency to allow more consonant sounds at the end and beginning of words. Based on this analysis, we can summarize that Amharic is more phonetically related to Mandarin Chinese than to English and that their combination of utterances can produce more vowel sounds than consonant sounds, which could be a factor for improved SV performance in our combinatorial training.

4.3 Production of Voiced Segments

As previously noted, voiced segments in speech sounds reflect resonance of the whole vocal tract and thus signal individual vocal characteristics. In this section, we compare vowel duration between the three languages as a factor that may contribute to improving SV performance. In many languages of the world, some vowels are characterized by shorter durations than other vowels. The English language contains 24 consonants and 11 vowels [31, 32] and the vowels are classified into four categories, according to durational and phonological features. The four vowels /ɪ/, / ɛ /, / ʌ /, and / ʊ / are traditionally described as 'short' vowels, and they are characterized by the shortest mean duration, and the other seven vowels are referred to as long vowels. According to the studies in [33–35] none of the short vowels, /ɪ/, / ɛ /, / ʌ /, and /ʊ/ can appear in open syllables, indicating that these vowels have a higher tendency to appear in closed syllables as in [bit /bɪt/], [bet /bɛt/], [bud /bʌd/], and [foot /fʊt/]. In each of these words, the vowel length is shorter than the remaining English long vowels as in [beat /biːt/], [bait /beɪt/], [bad /bæd/], and [boot /buːt/]. When comparing the three languages based on their closed syllable structure, English has a shorter nucleus length than the other two languages and tends to reduce the frequency of occurrence of the phonemes /a/, /e/, and /o/, which are used for effective speaker discrimination [22]. In Mandarin, the consonants that appear at the end of syllables are the two nasal consonants: /n/ and / ŋ / [30]. Thus, Mandarin Chinese finals (i.e., nucleus and coda in a syllable) are all voiced having vowels with various lengths with or without a nasal coda. This syllable pattern reveals uniquely long voiced segments possibly with long syllable durations. This observation supports a conjecture: the more abundant the voiced frames in a unit time, the more robust the clues to enhance SV performance. As evidenced by our third experimental results, the combination of Amharic and Mandarin Chinese achieves better SV performance than English and Mandarin Chinese, with an EER of 8.3% compared to 9.8%.

5 Conclusions

In this paper, we investigated the impact of language mismatches between training and testing on speaker verification performance, as well as the impact of phonetic spaces in languages to combine on SV performance. We combined languages of a different nature to improve speaker verification performance, which was hampered by the language mismatch in training and testing utterances. For this study, we introduced the first bilingual speech dataset, Yegna2021, and used other two popular publicly available datasets LibriSpeech ASR corpus, and the AISHELL-I Mandarin Chinese speech corpus for training the x-vector model. The experimental results show that the linguistic combination significantly improves performance degradation caused by language mismatch between training and testing utterances, and we found that the SV showed performance variations in the case of language combinatorial training. Our hypothesis was not rejected based on the result obtained from an experiment. Employing the knowledge of phonetics could be one of the solutions to explore underlying factors to advance machine-based speech technology. In the future, we will extend this work to include other Ethiopian languages. We will also investigate various techniques for improving speaker verification performance.

Acknowledgements. Thanks to the National Key R&D Program of China (No. 2020YFC 2004103), National Natural Science Foundation of China (No. 61876131, U1936102), and Basic Research Project of Qinghai Science and Technology Program (No. 2021-ZJ-609).

References

1. Reynolds, D.A.: An overview of automatic speaker recognition technology. In: 2002 IEEE International Conference on Acoustics, Speech, and Signal Processing, vol. 4, pp. 4072–4072 (2002)
2. Campbell, J.P.: Speaker recognition: a tutorial. Proc. IEEE **85**(9), 1437–1462 (1997)
3. Li, L., Wang, D., Rozi, A., Zheng, T.F.: Cross-lingual speaker verification with deep feature learning. In: 2017 Asia-Pacific Signal and Information Processing Association Annual Summit and Conference (APSIPA ASC), pp. 1040–1044 (2017)
4. Akbacak, M., Hansen, J.H.: Language normalization for bilingual speaker recognition systems. In: 2007 IEEE International Conference on Acoustics, Speech and Signal Processing-ICASSP 2007, vol. 4, p. 257 (2007)
5. Qing, X.K., Chen, K.: On use of GMM for multilingual speaker verification: an empirical study. In: Proceedings of ISCSLP, pp. 263–266 (2000)
6. Zhang, S.X., Chen, Z., Zhao, Y., Li, J., Gong, Y.: End-to-end attention based text-dependent speaker verification. In: 2016 IEEE Spoken Language Technology Workshop (SLT), pp. 171–178 (2016)
7. Nawaz, S., et al.: Cross-modal speaker verification and recognition: a multilingual perspective. In: Proceedings of the IEEE/CVF Conference on Computer Vision and Pattern Recognition, pp. 1682–1691 (2021)

8. Xia, W., Huang, J., Hansen, J.H.: Cross-lingual text-independent speaker verification using unsupervised adversarial discriminative domain adaptation. In: ICASSP 2019–2019 IEEE International Conference on Acoustics, Speech and Signal Processing (ICASSP), pp. 5816–5820 (2019)

9. Padmini, P., Paramasivam, C., Lal, G.J., Alharbi, S., Bhowmick, K.: Age-based automatic voice conversion using blood relation for voice impaired. Comput. Mater. Continua **70**(2), 4027–4051 (2022)

10. Ma, B., Meng, H.: English-Chinese bilingual text-independent speaker verification. In: 2004 IEEE International Conference on Acoustics, Speech, and Signal Processing, vol. 5 (2004)

11. Vaheb, A., Choobbasti, A.J., Najafabadi, S.H.E.M., Safavi, S.: Investigating language variability on the performance of speaker verification systems. In: Karpov, A., Jokisch, O., Potapova, R. (eds.) SPECOM 2018. LNCS (LNAI), vol. 11096, pp. 718–727. Springer, Cham (2018). https://doi.org/10.1007/978-3-319-99579-3_73

12. Snyder, D., Garcia-Romero, D., Sell, G., Povey, D., Khudanpur, S.: X-vectors: robust DNN embeddings for speaker recognition. In: 2018 IEEE International Conference on Acoustics, Speech and Signal Processing (ICASSP), pp. 5329–5333 (2018)

13. Changrampadi, M.H., Shahina, A., Narayanan, M.B., Khan, A.N.: End-to-end speech recognition of Tamil language. Intell. Autom. Soft Comput. **32**(2), 1309–1323 (2022)

14. Shiferaw, M.: Syllable-based text-to-speech synthesis (TTS) for Amharic. Addis Ababa, Ethiopia (2012)

15. Povey, D., et al.: The Kaldi speech recognition toolkit. In: IEEE 2011 Workshop on Automatic Speech Recognition and Understanding, CONF. IEEE Signal Processing Society (2011)

16. Panayotov, V., Chen, G., Povey, D., Khudanpur, S.: LibriSpeech: an ASR corpus based on public domain audio books. In: 2015 IEEE International Conference on Acoustics, Speech and Signal Processing (ICASSP), pp. 5206–5210 (2015)

17. Bu, H., Du, J., Na, X., Wu, B., Zheng, H.: Aishell-1: an open-source mandarin speech corpus and a speech recognition baseline. In: International Coordinating Committee on Speech Databases and Speech I/O Systems and Assessment (O-COCOSDA), pp. 1–5 (2017)

18. Snyder, D., et al.: Kaldi VoxCeleb x-vector recipe (2018). https://github.com/kaldi-asr/kaldi/tree/master/egs/voxceleb/v2

19. Antal, M., Toderean, G.: Speaker recognition and broad phonetic groups. SPPRA, pp. 155–159 (2006)

20. Fakotakis, N., Sirigos, J.: A high performance text independent speaker recognition system based on vowel spotting and neural nets. In: 1996 IEEE International Conference on Acoustics, Speech, and Signal Processing Conference Proceedings, vol. 2, pp. 661–664 (1996)

21. Paliwal, K.K.: Effectiveness of different vowel sounds in automatic speaker identification. J. Phon. **12**, 17–21 (1984)

22. Gopal, S., Padmavathi, S.: Speaker verification on English Language using phonemes. In: 2016 International Conference on Electrical, Electronics, and Optimization Techniques (ICEEOT), pp. 1520–1224 (2016)

23. Yimam, B.: Yeamarigna sewasew (Amharic version). Addis Ababa, Ethiopia, EMPDA (1986)

24. Sukarto, A.R., Wikarti, E., Renata, S.: Moira: contrastive analysis between Chinese and Indonesian phonology and implementation on conversation class. Int. J. Cult. Art Stud. **3**(1), 1–14 (2019)

25. Bradlow, A., Clopper, C., Smiljanic, R., Walter, M.A.: A perceptual phonetic similarity space for languages: evidence from five native language listener groups. Speech Commun. **52**(11), 930–942 (2010)

26. Getahun, A.: ዘመናዊ የአማርኛ ሰዋስው በቀላል አቀራረብ(Modern Amharic Grammar in a Simple Approach) Addis Ababa, Ethiopia (2010)

27. Seyoum, M.: The syllable structure and syllabification in Amharic, Masters of philosophy in general linguistic thesis. Trondheim, Norway (2001)

28. Třísková, H.: The structure of the mandarin syllable: why, when and how to teach it. Archivorientální **79**(1), 99–134 (2011)

29. Baye, Y.: Phonological features of the Amharic variety of South Wallo. Oslo Stud. Lang. **8**(1), 9–30 (2016)

30. Duanmu, S., Kim, H.Y., Stiennon, N.: 1 Stress and Syllable Structure in English: Approaches to Phonological Variations (2005)

31. Peterson, G.E., Barney, H.L.: Control methods used in a study of the vowels. J. Acoust. Soc. Am. **24**, 175–184 (1951)

32. Chen, Y., Robb, M., Gilbert, H., Lerman, J.: Vowel production by Mandarin speakers of English. Clin. Linguist. Phon. **15**(6), 427–440 (2001)

33. Ladefoged, P., Johnson, K.: A course in phonetics. Cengage learning (2014)

34. Umeda, N.: Vowel duration in American English. J. Acoust. Soc. Am. **58**, 434–479 (1975)

35. House, A.S.: On vowel duration in English. J. Acoust. Soc. Am. **33**(9), 1174–1178 (1961)

36. Abate, S.T., Menzel, W., Tafila, B.: An Amharic speech corpus for large vocabulary continuous speech recognition. In: Ninth European Conference on Speech Communication and Technology (2005)

37. Auckenthaler, R., Carey, M.J., Mason, J.S.: Language dependency in text-independent speaker verification. In: 2001 IEEE International Conference on Acoustics, Speech, and Signal Processing. Proceedings (Cat. No. 01CH37221) vol. 1, pp. 441–444 (2001)

A WGAN-Based Method for Generating Malicious Domain Training Data

Kaixin Zhang[✉] [iD], Bing Huang [iD], Yunfeng Wu [iD], Chuchu Chai, Jiufa Zhang [iD], and Zhengjing Bao

The 6th Research Institute of China Electronics Corporation (CEC), Beijing, China
2352628732@qq.com

Abstract. Domain Generation Algorithm (DGA) is a common method used by malware to generate a large number of domains on a regular basis. These domains can be used for malicious purposes such as botnet construction and data leakage. DGA malicious domain names, not only in number, but also in types, are a major challenge for malicious domain detection technology. The current detection methods based on artificial rules and detection algorithms based on machine learning are not effective due to the inability to obtain the latest DGA malicious domain data set in time. In this paper, a new encoding method is proposed to construct the encoder and decoder, combined with an improved version of the Generative Adversarial Network—Wasserstein Generative Adversarial Networks (WGAN), which uses a variety of known real DGA malicious domain family data to predict and generate DGA variant training samples. And through classifier training and performance evaluation of the effectiveness of domain names generated by the malicious domain name generator, it is proved that the data generated by this method can as a real DGA sample and provide a large amount of training data for the future DGA domain detector.

Keywords: DGA · Malicious domain name · Training sample · WGAN

1 Introduction

Domain Name System (DNS), as an important infrastructure of the Internet, undertakes network services that map domain names and IP addresses to each other. However, DNS does not detect services that rely on it, and the availability and user-friendliness of firewalls and intrusion detection devices will make it difficult to completely filter out DNS traffic, creating opportunities for DNS attacks. DNS services are abused for various malicious activities. For example, when malicious programs infect the host, The attacker can then directly control the infected host by connecting to command and control(C&C) servers. C&C servers acts as an interface between the attacker and the infected host. Attackers often write their own registered malicious domain names into malicious programs, and then malicious programs use domain name resolution to obtain the C&C's IP address for connection and communication. The use of DNS in malicious behavior maintains the robustness of malicious networks. Therefore, these malicious

© The Author(s), under exclusive license to Springer Nature Switzerland AG 2022
X. Sun et al. (Eds.): ICAIS 2022, LNCS 13340, pp. 257–270, 2022.
https://doi.org/10.1007/978-3-031-06791-4_21

programs often access the C&C server through malicious domain names instead of the server's IP address. In order to avoid the detection of domain name blacklist, DGA is widely used. Because DGA can generate thousands of malicious domain names. The attacker selects dozens or hundreds of domain names to register to cover the domain name of the real C&C server, because the DGA algorithm is difficult to reverse, which making it impossible for network security administrators to block all malicious domain names. Malicious domain names have become an important means of botnet and Trojan virus attacks, so the detection of malicious domain names has always been one of the research hotspots in the field of network security.

This paper analyzes the statistical characteristics and N-gram model characteristics of each malicious domain family in DGA, combined with WGAN, a generation confrontation network in deep neural networks, to predict and generate DGA domain names, and design experiments to verify the effectiveness of the generated malicious domain names. To prove that the generated results can provide effective and sufficient training samples for the construction of malicious domain detector models.

2   Related Work

Researchers at home and abroad have carried out many related researches on malicious domain detection. According to the detection technology and research objects used, this paper divides the existing malicious domain detection methods into two categories: DNS flow characteristics and text characteristics of domain names.

2.1   Malicious Domain Detection Based on DNS Flow

Malicious domain name detection based on DNS flow mainly analyzes DNS flow data, summarizes various information contained therein, finds the connection between DNS data and request intent, extracts characteristic values, and establishes a domain name detection classifier.

Initially, researchers manually extract features. Passerini analysed domain name registration time, registrar, address, A record, TTL value and other DNS data information to detect malicious domain names. This type of detection method has a simple principle and can quickly detect domain names in the network, but the robustness of this method is very weak. And it is manifested as changes in the network environment and attack algorithms. In order to maintain the effectiveness of the detector, the system is set the threshold value of the network will also change accordingly, so it will require continuous maintenance by professionals, and it will not be able to meet the defense needs in a timely manner under the high-speed network.

Subsequently, researchers began to use machine learning algorithms to detect malicious domain names. By using classification and clustering models, they trained a large amount of DNS flow data to learn and summarize the flow characteristics of malicious domain names. Zhao et al. proposed a malicious domain name detection algorithm based on lexical analysis and feature quantification. This algorithm first calculates the edit distance between the domain name to be tested and the blacklisted domain name with determined attributes, and initially classifies the domain name to be detected as clearly malicious or potential Malicious, and then use N-gram to calculate the reputation value of malicious domain names, and judge the maliciousness of potential malicious domain names based on the reputation value. The effectiveness of this method is verified on public data. For rapidly changing domain names, Cui Jia and others combined three domain detection technologies, including black-and-white list filters, DNS record resolvers, and feature classification-based detectors, to construct a new malicious domain detection framework, which has good completeness.

The malicious domain name detection method based on machine learning solves the problem of the poor adaptability of the domain name detector that manually sets the threshold to a certain extent, and can adjust the data sample to increase the detection accuracy of the model.

2.2 Malicious Domain Detection Based on Text Characteristics of Domain Names

The self-learning ability of deep neural networks not only avoids manual feature extraction, but also is superior to traditional machine learning technology in terms of accuracy. The current malicious domain name detection based on domain text character features mainly uses deep learning neural network algorithms, and Mainly focus on two neural networks, recurrent neural network (RNN) and convolutional neural network (CNN).

Long short-term memory network (LSTM) can handle sequence tasks excellently, and domain names can be regarded as character sequences. Some researchers use Bi-LSTM (bidirectional long short-term memory) to achieve character sequence encoding and preliminary feature extraction, combined with multi-head attention mechanism Perform deep feature extraction. The main feature of Convolutional Neural Network (CNN) is that it can process input grid data. Saxe et al. proposed a CNN-based classifier, which became the NYU model. This classifier takes generic short characters as input and Check whether they are malicious, short characters can be URL, file path or registry key. Subsequent studies are improvements on these two types of neural networks. Vinayakumar et al. compared the performance of RNN, CNN, especially hybrid networks, on DGA domain detection. The results show that deep learning methods has a good performance, but recent studies have shown that it is vulnerable to adversarial attacks. At the same time, the detection effect for different types of malicious domain name variants is unstable.

In summary, a major difficulty in malicious domain detection is that the emerging new types of malicious domains reduce the effectiveness of current well-performing detectors, and the network adaptability is poor. The model trained on a limited data set is better for the new DGA The variant is a bit blind. In [9], Anderson et al. used the concept of generative adversarial networks to build a DGA based on deep learning—DeepDGA, which aims to intentionally bypass detectors based on deep learning. In a series of confrontation rounds, the generator model outputs domain names that are increasingly difficult to detect. In turn, the detector model updates its parameters to compensate for the domain generated by the confrontation. A hypothesis was verified: the training set can be augmented with the domain generated by the confrontation, so as to strengthen other machine learning models for the DGA that has not yet been observed.

1. Different from [9] using Alexa one million domains for training, this paper uses known real malicious DGA families for training to generate training data, such as,

emotet, rovnix, tinba, Ramnit, etc., to generate the data learns the characteristics of the domain name data of each major family of DGA, as a training sample of the DGA detector, can make the model stable in the detection of different types of domain name variant attacks;

2. Different from [10], this paper uses it in the training data. The generated confrontation network model is WGAN (Wasserstein GAN). WGAN mainly improves GAN from the perspective of loss function. After the loss function is improved, WGAN can get good performance results even on the fully-linked layer;

3. This paper uses a broader classification model to classify and test the generated domain name samples. The main idea is that when using the real DGA malicious domain name and the classification model trained by the Alexa legal domain name, the data generated by the malicious domain name model can be basically successfully marked as malicious. The domain name can prove the effectiveness of the generated data as a malicious domain name training sample;

4. The structure of the encoder and decoder has the characteristics of simplifying and being close to the original data, so as to maintain the characteristics of the original data to the greatest extent.

3 Wasserstein GAN

Generative Adversarial Network (GAN) is a deep learning model and one of the most promising methods for unsupervised learning on complex distributions in recent years. Since it was proposed by Ian Goodfellow in 2014, it has received extensive attention and research, and has achieved rapid development in just a few years, and has achieved remarkable results in many application scenarios, in the field of computer vision (CV) Take the task of face generation in, as an example, the face images generated by GAN have achieved great improvements in resolution, authenticity, and diversity, as can be seen in Goodfellow's tweets in 2019.

3.1 GAN

The idea of the GAN model is to produce a fairly good output through the mutual game learning of two modules in the framework: the generative model (G) and the discriminant model (D). The corresponding GAN neural network model is shown in Fig. 1.

P_r Represents the true sample distribution, P_z Represents random input distribution. When GAN training is used for data generation, it is assumed that there are real data x(classified as 1) and generated data $G(z)$ (classified as 0). For D, the optimal result is to distinguish x as many as possible as 1, and $G(z)$ as much as possible, there is a loss function of D as (1), and the learning process of D is to increase the loss function.

$$\text{loss}_D(x, z) = \log D(x) + \log(1 - D(G(z))) \qquad (1)$$

For G, the training process is to let D discriminate $G(z)$ as many 1 as possible, there is a loss function of G as (2), and the learning process of G is to reduce the loss function.

$$\text{loss}_G(x, z) = \log(1 - D(G(z))) \qquad (2)$$

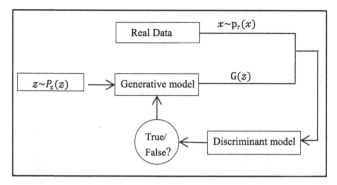

Fig. 1. Schematic diagram of GAN network model

GAN expresses this confrontation process as (3):

$$\min_G \max_D V(G, D) = E_{X \sim P_r}\left[\log D(x)\right] + E_{z \sim P_{z(z)}}\left[\log(1 - D(G(z)))\right] \qquad (3)$$

After multiple rounds of competition in training, G and D finally reach a distribution model that balances and approximates the real data, which is the biggest advantage and characteristic of GAN neural network.

3.2 WGAN

However, GAN has training difficulties, the gradient is unstable, and the imbalance of the diversity and accuracy penalties leads to the mode collapse problem.

In [8], the authors gives the reason for the instability of GAN training, that is, JS divergence is not suitable for measuring the distance between the distributions with disjoint parts, and thus gives the key points for improvement. In [2], Starting from this point of improvement, the authors using Wasserstein distance measures the distance between the generated data distribution and the real data distribution, which theoretically solves the problems of training instability and model collapse, and the diversity of generated results is richer.

The advantage of Wasserstein distance over KL divergence and JS divergence is that even if the two distributions do not overlap. If it is defined as the loss of the generator, a meaningful gradient can be generated to update the generator, so that the generation distribution is pulled to the true distribution.

In the training process, D should be maximized as much as possible, while G should be approximately minimized. Due to the excellent nature of Wasserstein distance, there is no need to worry about the disappearance of the generator gradient.

4   The Training Data Generation Model

Domain names are mainly divided into host names, top-level domains, and second-level domains in structure. DGA domain names are mostly composed of a series of random characters generated by some DGA algorithms as host names and existing top-level domains. The top-level domains of most DGA families are relatively fixed. For example, the Emotet family can have 96 new domain names each time. The top-level domain only uses "eu." Therefore, the implementation of this malicious domain name generator only considers the host name.

Before constructing the neural network structure, the domain name text needs to be encoded and converted into a neural network trainable digital vector. And the resulting tensor output by the generator needs to be decoded into a text domain name. The module that completes this function is an encoder and a decoder. Therefore, the DGA malicious domain name training data generation model based on WGAN mainly includes three parts: domain name encoder/decoder, generation network, and discrimination network.

4.1 Domain Name Encoder/Decoder

Under normal circumstances, the characters of a domain name include: 26 English letters, 0–9, and "-" a total of 63 characters. Because the ASCII codes of these 63 characters are not continuous, the generated characters will not be in these 63 characters. Therefore, a new encoding method using the ASCII code of these 63 characters to be re-encoded into a continuous interval [1,63] is proposed, as in the following Table 1.

In this paper, the domain name vector length is defined as 30. If the length is not enough, it is filled with "0". After the above encoding process, the domain name text is converted into a vector a, $a = [a_0, a_1, \ldots, a_i, \ldots, a_{29}]$, $a_i \in [0, 63]$. In order to make the learning of the network more efficient, each element in the digital vector of the domain name is further mapped to the [0,1] interval, by dividing each element in the original vector a by 63, and the result will keep eight decimal places after the decimal point. The implementation process of the encoder takes a malicious domain name "pjmdtihjbfv.eu" of the emotet family as an example, as shown in the following Fig. 2.

After being encoded by the encoder, the character domain name is converted into WGAN training data, which is converted into a tensor d through TensorFlow, $d = [d_0, d_1, \ldots, d_i, \ldots, d_{29}]$, $d_i \in [0, 1]$.

The function of the decoder is to convert the tensor output by the generator into domain name characters. Knowing the operating principle of the encoder, the decoder is the reverse conversion of the encoding process. Output of the generator should be a one-dimensional tensor d^* which will be converted to a^*, $d_i^* \in [0, 1] a_i^* \in [0, 63]$, $d^* = [d_0^*, d_1^*, \ldots, d_i^*, \ldots, d_{29}^*]$, $a^* = [a_0^*, a_1^*, \ldots, a_i^*, \ldots, a_{29}^*]$, The mapping formula is (4):

$$a^* = [a_0^*, a_1^*, \ldots, a_i^*, \ldots, a_{29}^*]$$
$$[\mathrm{round}(d_0^* * 63), \ldots, \mathrm{round}(d_i^* * 63), \ldots, \mathrm{round}(d_{29}^* * 63)] \tag{4}$$

The next step is to map each element a_i^* in the obtained vector a^* from the new code to the ASCAII code, and obtain the corresponding character through the ASCAII code. The mapping table is as following Table 2.

Table 1. Encoder implement from ASCII to New Code.

Character	New Code	Re-encoded method
0–9	1–10	(ASCII)-47
a–z	11–36	(ASCII)-86
A–Z	37–62	(ASCII)-28
"-"	63	(ASCII) + 18

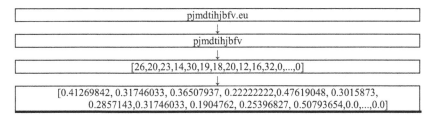

Fig. 2. Encoder coding process of "pjmdtihjbfv.eu"

Table 2. Decoder implement from New Code to ASCII.

a_i^*	ASCAII code	Character
1–10	$a_i^* + 47$	0–9
11–36	$a_i^* + 86$	A–z
37–62	$a_i^* + 28$	A–Z
63	$a_i^* - 18$	"-"

4.2 Structure of the Generate Network

The generative network is a four-layer fully connected layer, including an input layer, a hidden layer and an output layer. The input layer data is 100-dimensional random noise, the two hidden layers, the number of nodes are 100 and 128 respectively, the activation function adopts the ReLU function, and the number of nodes in the output layer is 30, which is the domain name vector dimension. Considering that the domain name vector elements are in the interval [0, 1], so the activation function of the output layer adopts the sigmoid function. The optimization function used in training is RMSProp, which is proved to be more stable in training in [2].

4.3 Structure of the Discrimination Network

The discriminant network is a four-layer fully connected layer, including an input layer, a hidden layer, and an output layer. The input layer data is 30-dimensional real data or generated data. The number of nodes in two hidden layers is 100 and 128, the activation function adopts the ReLU function, and the number of nodes in the output layer is 1. The discriminator in WGAN is to approximate the Wasserstein distance, which is a regression task, so the sigmoid function should not be set in the output layer, and the optimization function used during training is RMSProp.

DGA malicious domain training data generation model is shown in Fig. 3.

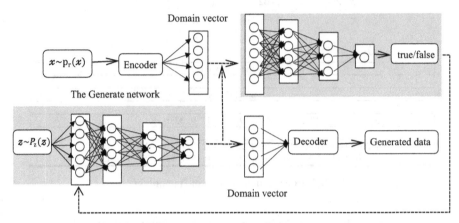

Fig. 3. DGA malicious domain name training data generation model.

5   Experiment and Result Analysis

5.1   Experiment Environment

The experimental environment of this paper mainly includes two parts: experimental platform and environment configuration. The detailed information is shown in Table 3.

Table 3. Experimental platform and environment configuration.

Experiment platform	Environment configuration
Operating System	Window10
CPU	Intel Corei7-10700 2.90 GHz
RAM	16 GB
Programming language	Python3.5
Deep learning framework	TensorFlow 2.3.1
Machine learning platform	Weka 3.8.5

5.2 Data Set

The data set is divided into three parts: 400,000 samples containing 11 real malicious domain names of the DGA family as shown in Table 4. Alexa ranked top 20,000 negative samples and real DGA randomly selected 20,000 positive samples, Alexa ranked top 1,000 negative samples and generated 1,000 positive samples similar to DGA.

After selecting and dividing the above data set, you need to preprocess it before selecting features: split the domain name, intercept the host name of the domain name, remove the top-level domain and possible second-level domains, third-level domains, etc., and perform data encoding and normalization on the processed domain name text, convert it into the input tensor of the WGAN network through the data standard reading format in TensorFlow.

Table 4. Composition of samples of real DGA malicious domain names.

DGA family	Number	Length	Instance
Emotet	50000	Fixed16	grdawgrcwegpjaoo.eu
Rovnix	50000	Fixed18	Abyfq71wc3ai12wseh.com
Tinba	50000	Fixed12	oykjietwrmlw.ru
Pykspa_v1	50000	[6–15]	agadss.biz
Simda	30000	Variable	puvecyq.info
Flubot	30000	Fixed15	bsgejiagbavgavk.cn
Ramnit	20000	[8–19]	jrkaxdlkvhgsiyknhw.com
Ranbyus	20000	Fixed14	nslxbdyiofityx.com
Virut	30000	Fixed6	yvvioe.com
Necurs	30000	[7–21]	wiyqgyiwgm.ga
Shiotob	40000	[10–15]	qq3adkdlzbcq43u.com

5.3 Design of Verification Experiment

In this paper, after the DGA malicious domain name training data generation model outputs the generated domain name data, the classifier proves the validity of these data. The experimental design is as follows:

The Acquisition of the Generated Domain Name Data. This section inputs the preprocessed samples of 11 real malicious domain names of DGA family into the generation model for training and producing the generated domain name data. The network training is set to 10,000 times. Output once every 100 training, and each output contains 100 the generated domain name data produced by the current generation network. At the same time, the output form of the generator generated data is a tensor. So, the decoder should convert the output tensor into the corresponding domain name character data.

Feature Selection. The feature part mainly uses statistical features, including the length of the domain name, the entropy of the character distribution in the domain name, the proportion of vowels, the proportion of unique characters, and the frequency of n-grams (n = 2,3,4,5,6). As shown in Fig. 4, The Alexa sample and the DGA sample have a certain degree of difference in the distribution of the three features including the length of the domain name character, the information entropy of the domain name.

The Classification of Negative Samples Positive Samples. Use the features to classify the sample set using a variety of classification algorithms on the Weka platform, and save the classification model to provide tools for verifying the effectiveness of the generated results.

Validation Verification of the Generated Domain Name Data. Classify the top 1000 negative samples ranked by Alexa and 1000 positive samples similar to DGA on the multiple classification models obtained, check the classification results, If the classification result is good, it proves that the generated DGA data has the characteristics of real DGA data, which proves the validity of the generated domain name data.

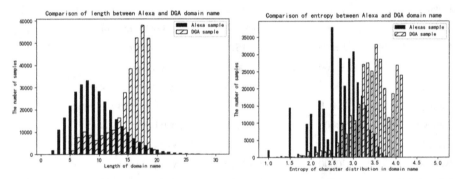

Fig. 4. The distribution of positive/negative samples in domain character length, information entropy.

5.4 Experimental Results and Analysis

Display of Domain Name Data Generated in Different Rounds. In order to obtain the learning results of the WGAN generation model for different confrontation rounds, the experimental design outputs the learning results of the current generation model after every 100 rounds of learning, so as to perform tracking output. The tracking output results are shown in Fig. 5. They are samples of domain name data generated in the confrontation rounds 500–600, 5000–5100, and 9900–10000 and real DGA malicious domain data.

Analysis of the Generated Domain Name Data. The real data in Fig. 5 is the preprocessed characters of the domain name randomly selected from the data set containing

.....REAL DGA.........
tpryjbuddibj
ilxhrgfxklmnhw
lmxddtmnimdyx
Rjryqmlljkyw
pkgnghwlllem
Jrjhvfnnilmn
iermso
ierwlueoya
Pjmdtihjbfvrumym
iesdfeiq
iesjuyeoya
iesqrwiugkeq
ietsaueoya
Iettia
... ...

the generated domain name data

in 9900 ~ 10000 round

aHay
nwegpjlkvejqlszfEdcBv
hwgikcky
lwfhnjtxov5kto
cq8fidt7BjctE
5teogcmepqdoglf
... ...

the generated domain name data

in 500 ~600 round

etkoheolhd8f765j6311
9wemh45klailcuts6813
Bpe12kiflen9clbc5331
ac8g96dglbhjgnafspjd34
9qmpvlq8gfhecbdhd662
Excvgoffochggau8c752
... ...

the generated domain name data

in 5000 ~5100 round

mlollrwrklnqrtra66
8audcKM6
fhmkmtDldiekpDr942
9eygdMMm4h88
iismnxGnbrgrtGq6
dfederAga87fflf32
... ...

Fig. 5. Real samples and the generated domain name data in different rounds of confrontation

11 DGA family, which is the real data distribution that WGAN needs to learn, and it is against Round 500–600 part of the generated data, the length of the data generated at this time is not much different, in the data generated in the 5000–5100 part of the confrontation round, you can see that the data length has changed, indicating that the learning ability of WGAN has improved, The data generated during the confrontation round 9900–10000 is more similar to the real data, most of which can be used as domain names.

As shown in Fig. 6, After the WGAN confrontation training, the frequency distribution of the DGA sample generated by the large sample fluctuates around the average frequency of the real DGA 0.0185. Therefore, from the perspective of the distribution characteristics of the character length, it shows that the generated similar DGA samples and the real DGA samples already have a certain similarity.

The Result of Classification Verification. The classifier selects Naive Bayes, J48, KNN, and Bagging in Weka 3.8.5. According to the design of the classification verification test, first use the second data set to train each classification model, The performance evaluation indicators for each classification model include the total number of samples, correct rate, error rate, F-measure, and ROC area; the training results of the classifier are shown in Table 5. Load the third data set to each classification model for classification verification. The evaluation indicators include correct classification, misclassification, Kappa coefficient, and total number of samples. The classifier verification results are shown in Table 5.

Analysis of the Result of Classification Verification. From the training results in Table 5, the classification effect of Naive Bayes is better than the other three classifiers,

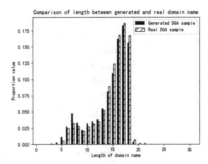

Fig. 6. The character length distribution of domain names in generated and real DGA samples.

so it can be said that Features selected by the experiment are effective for classification of positive and negative samples. In Table 6, the negative sample of the generated domain name data and the positive sample of Alexa are used as the input of each of the above classification models, and each classification model gives the predicted classification, so as to obtain the number of correct classifications, the number of incorrect classifications and other data, from the table The verification result in Table 6 shows that when the classification features are the same, the classification model can better distinguish between negative samples and Alexa positive samples, indicating that the generated domain name data already has some of the characteristics of the real DGA sample.

Table 5. The training results of creating multiple classification models.

Classifier	Number	Correct rate	Error rate	F-measure	ROC
Naive Bayes	40000	99.30%	0.70%	0.993	0.998
J48	40000	98.60%	1.40%	0.986	0.996
KNN	40000	96.24%	3.76%	0.962	0.982
Bagging	40000	98.31%	1.69%	0.983	0.995

Table 6. Validation results of multiple classification models.

Classifier	Number	Positive samples		Negative samples		Kappa
		Correct	Error	Correct	Error	
Naive Bayes	2000	941	59	955	45	0.896
J48	2000	947	53	955	45	0.902
KNN	2000	964	36	924	76	0.888
Bagging	2000	931	69	955	45	0.886

6 Conclusion

The data collection of malicious domain name recognition is one of the important tasks in the detection of malicious domain names in the field of network security.

This paper attempts to apply the generation of confrontation networks to network security to generate malicious DGA domain name character data sets, which solved the problem of insufficient training data for malicious domain name recognition and initially verified the feasibility of this method. In the experiment, the ASCII code of DGA domain name characters is used for simple re-encoding and data normalization, and at the same time, the network can directly learn the characteristics of the original data. Next, we can further study and improve the design of the encoder, which can preserve the correlation between characters in the process of converting characters to vectors, thereby improving the quality of the generated domain name data.

In recent years, more DGA algorithms are trying dictionary-based malicious domain names, and these malicious domain names are more "like" real domain names, such as the "middleapple.net" generated by Suppobox DGA. The conventional domain name detection is based on the significant difference between of DGA domain names and the real domain names, so Malicious domains of Suppobox cannot be detected effectively. For the detection of such DGA malicious domain names, we can use the generative adversarial network model to learn the characteristics of real domain names, and generate data sets of fake domain name which similar to real domain names as training data sets, so that the DGA malicious domain name detector can effectively detect this type of DGA. The application of the theory and technology of deep learning makes the detection and recognition methods more intelligent, with the ability of self-learning and self-adaptation. The application of GAN in the generation of malicious domain name training data provides new ideas for solving the problems of deep learning-based detection models that lack the ability to recognize newly emerging DGA variant domain names and lack sufficient malicious domain name training data.

References

1. Passerini, E., Paleari, R., Martignoni, L., Bruschi, D.: FluXOR: detecting and monitoring fast-flux service networks. In: Zamboni, D. (ed.) DIMVA 2008. LNCS, vol. 5137, pp. 186–206. Springer, Heidelberg (2008). https://doi.org/10.1007/978-3-540-70542-0_10
2. Martin, A., Soumith, C., Léon, B.: Wasserstein GAN. In: Thirty-Fourth International Conference on Machine Learning, vol. 70, pp. 214–223 (2017)
3. Koh, J.J., Rhodes, B.: Inline detection of domain generation algorithms with context-sensitive word embeddings. In: 2018 IEEE International Conference on Big Data (Big Data), pp. 2966–2971. IEEE (2018)
4. Zhao, H., Chang, Z., Wang, W., Zeng, X.: Malicious domain names detection algorithm based on lexical analysis and feature quantification. IEEE Access 7, 128990–128999 (2019)
5. Cui, J., Shi, L., Li, J., Liu, Z.: An efficient framework for malicious domain name detection. J. Beijing Inst. Technol. 39, 64–67 (2019)
6. Vinayakumar, R., Soman, K.P., Poomachandran, P., et al.: Evaluating deep leaning approaches to characterize and classify the DGAs at scale. J. Intell. Fuzzy Syst. 34, 1265–1276 (2018)
7. Arjovsky, M., Bottou, L.: Towards principled methods for training generative adversarial networks. arXiv:1701.04862 (2017)

8. Anderson, H.S., Woodbridge, J., Filar, B.: DeepDGA: adversarially-tuned domain generation and detection. In: Artificial Intelligence and Security 2016, pp.13–21. ACM 2016, Vienna, Austria (2016)

9. Yuan, C., Qian, L., Hui, Z., Ting, Z.: Training data generation of malicious domain names based on generative adversarial networks. Appl. Res. Comput. **36**(05), 1540–1545 (2019)

10. Kim, Y., Jernite, Y., Sontag, D., Rush, A.M.: Character-aware neural language models. In: Thirtieth AAAI Conference on Artificial Intelligence, pp. 2741–2749. AAAI Press, Phoenix, AZ, USA (2016)

11. Satoh, A., Fukuda, Y., Kitagata, G., Nakamura, Y.: A word-level analytical approach for identifying malicious domain names caused by dictionary-based DGA malware. Electronics **10**(9), 1039 (2021)

12. Yury, Z., Issa, K., Ting, Y., Marc, D.: A survey on malicious domains detection through DNS data analysis. ACM Comput. Surv. **51**(4), 1–36 (2018)

13. Tan, H., Zhou, L., Wang, G., Zhang, Z.: Instability analysis and processing technology of generative confrontation network. Sci. China Inf. Sci. **51**(04), 602–617 (2021)

14. Luo, C., Tan, Z., Min, G., Gan, J., Shi, W., Tian, Z.: A novel web attack detection system for internet of things via ensemble classification. IEEE Trans. Industr. Inf. **17**(8), 5810–5818 (2021)

15. Khan, M.A., Kim, Y.: Deep learning-based hybrid intelligent intrusion detection system. Comput. Mater. Continua **68**(1), 671–687 (2021)

16. David, D.S., Anam, M., Kaliappan, C., Arun, S., Sharma, D.K.: Cloud security service for identifying unauthorized user behaviour. Comput. Mater. Continua **70**(2), 2581–2600 (2022)

17. He, H., Zhao, Z., Luo, W., Zhang, J.: Community detection in aviation network based on k-means and complex network. Comput. Syst. Sci. Eng. **39**(2), 251–264 (2021)

18. Deng, B., Ran, Z., Chen, J., Zheng, D., Yang, Q.: Adversarial examples generation algorithm through DCGAN. Intell. Autom. Soft Comput. **30**(3), 889–898 (2021)

A Data Reconciliation Model Based on QLDPC for Satellite-Ground Quantum Key Distribution Network

Wenting Zhou[1], Jie Liu[1], Bao Feng[2], Xiao Ye[1], Tianbing Zhang[2], Yuxiang Bian[2], and Wenjie Liu[3(✉)]

[1] State Grid Xinjiang Electric Power Information and Telecommunication Co., Ltd., Wulumuqi 830000, China
[2] NRGD Quantum CTEK, LTD., Nanjing 211000, China
[3] School of Computer and Software,
Nanjing University of Information Science and Technology, Nanjing 210044, China
wenjie1@163.com

Abstract. In the satellite-ground quantum key distribution network for electric IoT, the transmitted data may have errors caused by the external environment and equipment. In order to ensure the correctness and consistency of the transmitted data, we propose a data reconciliation model based on quantum low density parity check (QLDPC) code for satellite-ground quantum key distribution network. We perform the check operator of QLDPC on the obtained raw keys, and use belief propagation algorithm and ordered statistics decoding technology to implement error correction. Compared with MET-LDPC and Turbo code, our model based on QLDPC has higher error correction efficiency with the increase of bit error rate.

Keywords: QLDPC · Data reconciliation · Satellite-ground quantum key distribution network

1 Introduction

BB84 protocol [1] is the first quantum key distribution (QKD) protocol, which mainly uses different forms of single photons to randomly encode. And the first entangled state protocol is proposed in 1991, referred to as the E91 protocol for short [2]. After that, six-state protocol [3], DPS protocol [4], SARG04 protocol [5] and LM05 proto-col [6] are proposed later, making QKD develop rapidly. At present, QKD has been in the practical application [7].

With the development of quantum key distribution technology, researchers began to study how to construct quantum key distribution network [23]. For the distribution of quantum keys between satellites and the ground, the communication process will be affected by many factors such as weather systems, eavesdroppers, and even measurement equipment, etc. These factors will cause that the key sequence obtained by two parties after key distribution is not the same. In order to make the shared key consistent, both parties in communication need to post-process the original key, i.e., data reconciliation. Many data reconciliation models use low-density parity-check code (LDPC) [8], Polar code [9], Turbo code [10], etc.

On the other hand, the earliest quantum error correction scheme is proposed by Shor in 1995 [11]. The code comprehensively utilizes the characteristics of three-qubit phase reversal code and single-bit reversal code, to realize error detection and correction operations for any single-qubit error. Calderbank, Shor and Steane proposed a systematic construction scheme of quantum error correction codes [12,13]. This scheme uses classical binary codes with self-dual properties to construct quantum codes, called CSS codes. In the same year, Gottesman introduced group theory into the field of quantum error correction and proposed a stabilizer code [14]. One attracted great attention is the use of low-density parity-check code (LDPC) to construct quantum codes [15]. For example, MacKay et al. used CSS code to propose four kinds of quantum LDPC (QLDPC) code based on a special cyclic sparse sequence [16]. Based on the entanglement-assisted quantum code, Hsieh et al. constructed an entangled-assisted quantum LDPC code by classic quasi-cyclic (QC) LDPC code, which only needs one pre-entangled bit pair and avoids the disadvantage of four rings in traditional quantum code.

However, compared with classic LDPC codes, there is no mature decoder that can be applied to all quantum LDPC codes. A recent study by Grospellier et al. [17] showed that combining small set-flip (SSF) decoder with classic belief propagation (BP) algorithm can improve its performance. This two-stage BP+SSF decoder is not only suitable for a wider range of random QLDPC codes than a single SSF decoder, but also exhibits a higher code threshold. In this paper, we use two-stage quantum decoder, which combines BP with a post-processing technique known as ordered statistics decoding (OSD) [18]. The decoder can be general for all QLDPC codes that can be constructed from the hypergraph product. And based on this QLPDC, we pro-pose a new key error correction model in QKD network. Comparing with MET-LDPC and Turbo code, our proposed model based on QLDPC has higher error correction efficiency, when the bit error grows.

The structure of this paper is as follows: Sect. 2 presents some preliminary knowledge about low-density parity-check code. In Sect. 3, we present the data reconciliation model based on QLDPC code for satellite-ground quantum key distribution network. Section 4 is devoted to compare our model with some existing ones based on MET-LDPC and Turbo. We summarize this paper in Sect. 5.

2   Low Density Parity Check Code

Low density parity check codes mainly use check matrix to correct data errors, which was proposed by Robert Gallager in 1961 [15]. The check matrix is generally an $m \times n$ matrix, where each row represents a check node, and each column corresponds to an information node of the code word. We take the following 4×6 matrix H as an example.

$$H = \begin{bmatrix} 1 & 1 & 0 & 0 & 0 & 1 \\ 0 & 1 & 0 & 1 & 1 & 0 \\ 1 & 0 & 1 & 0 & 1 & 0 \\ 0 & 0 & 1 & 1 & 0 & 1 \end{bmatrix} \tag{1}$$

Then, in matrix H, the row weight is 3 and the column weight is 2. And we find that the elements in the code word v and the elements in the check node c satisfy the following relationship:

$$\begin{cases} c_1 = v_1 + v_2 + v_6 \\ c_2 = v_2 + v_4 + v_5 \\ c_3 = v_1 + v_3 + v_6 \\ c_4 = v_3 + v_4 + v_6 \end{cases} \tag{2}$$

In the LDPC error correction process, the Belief Propagation (BP) algorithm is based on soft decision algorithm, which can maximize the error correction ability of the error correction code. The BP algorithm process is as follows:

Algorithm 1. Belief Propagation Algorithm [15]

---

1. Initialize the binary channel based on channel characteristics and preset node information:
$L^0(q_{ij}) = \ln \frac{p_i(c_i = 0 | y_i)}{p_i(c_i = 1 | y_i)}$
2. Calculate the soft information value for each check node $i \in R_i/j$ (the lth iteration):
$L^l(r_{ij}) = 2\tanh^{-1} \left\{ \Pi_{i \in R_i/j} \tanh(\frac{1}{2} L(q_{ij})) \right\}$
3. Calculate the soft information value for each information node $j \in c_i \backslash j$:
$L^l(q_{ij}) = L^0(q_{ij}) + \sum_{j \in c_i \backslash j} L(r_{ji})$
4. Calculate the posterior probability for all information node,
$L^l(q_i) = L(q_{ij}) + \sum_{j \in c_i} L^l(r_{ij})$
5. Hard judgment on all information node,
$\begin{cases} L^l(q_i) < 0 : z_i = 1 \\ L^l(q_i) > 0 : z_i = 0 \end{cases}$
6. If $Hz_i = 0$, the decoding is successful; otherwise goto step 2.

---

3 Data Reconciliation Model Based on QLDPC for Satellite-Ground Quantum Key Distribution Network

3.1 Quantum Low Density Parity Check Code

To construct error correction operator, Pauli matrices are usually choosen to derive a family of LDPC stabilizer codes based on finite geometries. Let $P = \{I, X, Z, Y\}$, and each Pauli operator is defined as below:

$$I = \begin{bmatrix} 1 & 0 \\ 0 & 1 \end{bmatrix}, X = \begin{bmatrix} 0 & 1 \\ 1 & 0 \end{bmatrix}, Z = \begin{bmatrix} 1 & 0 \\ 0 & -1 \end{bmatrix}, Y = \begin{bmatrix} 0 & -i \\ i & 0 \end{bmatrix} \tag{3}$$

where each operator is mapped to a vector of length 2: $I \rightarrow (0,0)$, $X \rightarrow (1,0)$, $Z \rightarrow (0,1)$, and $Y \rightarrow (1,1)$.

Suppose a stabilizer group S generated by a set $\{S_1, S_2, \cdots, S_n\}$, where each error operator S_i is generated by a tensor product of n Pauli matrices:

$$S_i = P_1 \otimes P_2 \otimes \cdots \otimes P_n, P_i \in P \tag{4}$$

S_i can be seen as a binary vector of length $2n$ in the form of $s_i = (x, z)$, where the length of x and z is n, representing the X and Z-Pauli operator position, respectively.

Suppose a quantum error correction code Q is a mapping from the k-qubit quantum state $|\psi\rangle$ to the entangled n-qubit code word state $|\psi\rangle_L$. The quantum code word $|\psi\rangle_L \in Q$ satisfies all the conditions of $S_i|\psi\rangle_L = |\psi\rangle_L$.

Generally, a quantum parity check matrix can be defined as a matrix in the form of $H_{CSS} = \begin{bmatrix} H_Z & 0 \\ 0 & H_X \end{bmatrix}$, and in which each row corresponds to a code stabilizer in the binary representation. For the requirement of the stabilizers commute, $H_Z \cdot H_X^T = 0$. Note that, the matrix H_X and H_Z is constructed by replacing every nonzero element in matrix H_G with Pauli matrices X and Z, respectively. The matrix H_G is defined as below [19]:

$$H_G = \begin{cases} [H_1^T H_2^T \cdots H_n^T | 1] . for \, add \, n \\ [H_1^T H_2^T \cdots H_n^T | 1 \, T] . for \, even \, n \end{cases} \tag{5}$$

Suppose that a Pauli error is $E \rightarrow e_Q = (x, z)$, then the quantum syndrome is defined as below:

$$S_Q = (S_X, S_Z) = (H_Z \cdot x, H_X \cdot z) \tag{6}$$

It can be seen from the above that the CSS code can be used to detect bit reversal (X-errors) and reverse conversion (Z-errors) through two classic codes $C(H_Z)$ and $C(H_X)$, respectively. For (n, k, d) QLDPC code, the symmetric product $HGP(C_H)$ of its C_H is calculated as below:

$$H_X = (H \otimes I_n | I_m \otimes H^T) \tag{7}$$

$$H_Z = (I_n \otimes H | H^T \otimes I_m) \tag{8}$$

The quantum code parameters of $HGP(H)$ are $(n^2 + m^2, k^2 + (k^T)^2, \min(d, d^T))$, where k^T is the number of logical qubits and d^T is the distance of the transpose code.

3.2   Data Reconciliation Model Based on QLDPC

Suppose that the raw keys K_A and K_B, owned by Alice and Bob respectively after the key distribution, and the check matrix H has been shared. The error correction process of QLDPC is shown as below.

Step 1. Alice uses the check matrix H to generate an operator $H = \begin{bmatrix} H_Z & 0 \\ 0 & H_X \end{bmatrix}$, and get the feature vector state $|S_A\rangle = H|K_A\rangle$ for her key K_A, and measure $|S_A\rangle$ to get S_A. And Alice send this information S_A to Bob.

Step 2. Bob performs a similar operation to get $|S_B\rangle = H|K_B\rangle$, and compares S_B with the received S_A. If they are the same, the keys of the two are the same. If they are different, they need to be iteratively decoded through BP+OSD algorithm (which is shown as below).

Step 3. Judging whether $H_{S,T} \cdot e_{S,T}$ is equal to is used to determine whether the decoding is successful, and if successful, the QLDPC decoding is completed. Otherwise, iterate decoding again.

Step 4. When the decoding is completed, Alice and Bob check each decoded keys and re-move the different parts.

In the BP decoding phase of data reconciliation model based on QLDPC, in order to solve the quantum degeneracy problem, many attempts have been made to modify or supplement the BP algorithm. So far, the most successful method is to apply a post-processing algorithm called an ordered statistic decoder (OSD). OSD was originally designed by Fossosier and Lin [20] to reduce the error layer in classical LDPC codes. It was originally applied in quantum settings by Panteleev and Kalachev [21] and proved that it is an amazingly effective decoder for random QLDPC codes. Nnote that in the following, in order to simplify the notation, we describe the application of OSD post-processing to a classic decoding problem $s = H \cdot e$. The process we outlined also applies to H_X and H_Z components that decode CSS code. The steps of BP+OSD decoder is as below.

Algorithm 2. BP+OSD Decoder [19]

---

1. Use the BP soft decision vector $p_i(e)$ to obtain a sorted list of bit index O_{BP}.
2. Sort the columns of the parity check matrix H to $H_{O_{BP}}$ according to O_{BP}.
3. Select the first $RANK(H)$ linearly independent column of $H_{O_{BP}}$ as the most probable basis set S.
4. Calculate the OSD-0 solution at the base position by matrix inversion
$e_S = H_S^{-1} \cdot s$
5. OSD-0 solution for all bits is $e_{S,T} = (e_S, e_T) = (e_S, 0)$, where the OSD-0 solution will always satisfy the syndrome equation $H_{S,T} \cdot e_{S,T} = s$.
6. Map the OSD-0 solution to the original bit ordering $e_{S,T} \rightarrow e_{OSD-0}$.

3.3   Satellite-Ground Quantum Key Distribution Network with Data Reconciliation Model

With the continuous maturity of quantum key distribution technology, a quantum key distribution network model composed of many single-QKD channels has been continuously proposed. The basic structure of the satellite-to-earth QKD network is shown in Fig. 1. Suppose Alice and Bob want to share common key by this QKD network.

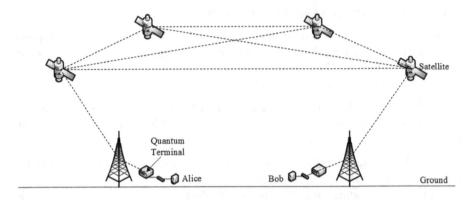

Fig. 1. The structure of satellite-ground quantum key distribution network.

The quantum terminal in Fig. 1 serves as an important part (as shown in Fig. 2). Firstly, its QKD module can receive and send quantum keys. When it receives quantum keys, its control layer can perform data reconciliation to correct keys with an-other quantum terminal through quantum channel. Finally, its application layer can control the entire terminal by classic computers.

4   Performance Evaluation

We will compare the error correction efficiency of the data reconciliation based on QLDPC, MET-LDPC (Multiedges type LDPC [22]) and Turbo code through simulation. The error correction efficiency depends on the ratio of the bit error rate before error correction and the bit error rate after error correction:

$$ECE = \frac{100\% - BER_a}{100\% - BER_b} \tag{9}$$

where ECE is the error correction efficiency, BER_a and BER_b represents the bit error rate after and before error correction, respectively. The comparison result is shown in Fig. 3.

From Fig. 3, we can see that our proposed QLDPC code is relatively low error correction efficiency, when the bit error is between 0.01 and 0.030. At a small bit error rate, QLDPC may cause errors due to the measurement, which makes the efficiency lower than that of classic error correction codes. But, the overall trend of QLDPC is upward. When the bit error is bigger than 0.035, the error correction efficiency is approximate to the Turbo code. After that, its efficiency has begun to outperform the other two codes. Although the error correction efficiencies of MET-LDPC and Turbo code are also on the rise when bit error rate grow up, QLDPC can handle more data bits, which is directly reflected in the error correction efficiency.

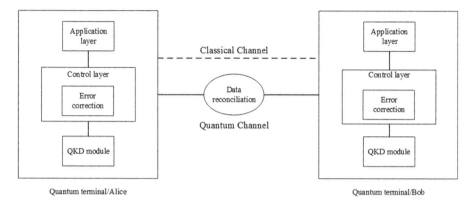

Fig. 2. The process of data connection between two quantum terminals (Alice and Bob).

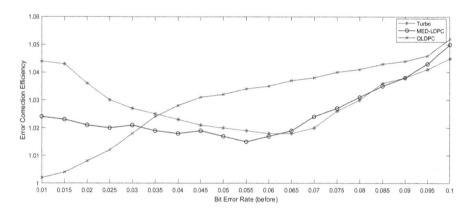

Fig. 3. Error correction efficiency of QLDPC, MET-LDPC, Cascade and Turbo code.

5   Conclusion

In this paper, we proposed a data reconciliation model based on QLDPC for satellite-ground quantum key distribution network. Firstly, we propose a new quantum LDPC based on BP and OSD decoder algorithm. And we construct the data reconciliation model with QLDPC. Finally, the model is embedded in our proposed satellite-to-earth quantum key distribution network environment. Through simulation, comparing with other codes: MET-LDPC and Turbo, our proposed model has higher error correction efficiency, when the bit error grows.

Acknowledgements. The authors would like to thank the anonymous reviewers and editor for their comments that improved the quality of this paper. This work is support by Scientific Project of Xinjiang Electric Power Co., Ltd. of SGCC under Grant No. SGXJXT00JFJS2000097.

References

1. Bennett, C.H., Brassard, G.: An update on quantum cryptography. In: Blakley, G.R., Chaum, D. (eds.) CRYPTO 1984. LNCS, vol. 196, pp. 475–480. Springer, Heidelberg (1985). https://doi.org/10.1007/3-540-39568-7_39

2. Ekert, A.K.: Quantum cryptography based on Bell's theorem. Phys. Rev. Lett. **67**(6), 661 (1991)

3. Bruß, D.: Optimal eavesdropping in quantum cryptography with six states. Phys. Rev. Lett. **81**(14), 3018 (1998)

4. Inoue, K., Waks, E., Yamamoto, Y.: Quantum cryptography protocols robust against photon number splitting attacks for weak laser pulse implementations. Phys. Rev. Lett. **92**(5), 057901 (2004)

5. Scarani, V., Acin, A., Ribordy, G., Gisin, N.: Differential phase shift quantum key distribution. Phys. Rev. Lett. **89**(3), 037902 (2002)

6. Lucamarini, M., Mancini, S.: Secure deterministic communication without entanglement. Phys. Rev. Lett. **94**(14), 140501 (2005)

7. Boaron, A., et al.: Secure quantum key distribution over 421 km of optical fiber. Phys. Rev. Lett. **121**(19), 190502 (2018)

8. Guo, L., Ran, Q., Jin, D., Huang, D.: QKD iterative information reconciliation based on LDPC codes. Int. J. Theor. Phys. **59**(6), 1–13 (2020)

9. Lee, S., Park, J., Heo, J.: Improved reconciliation with polar codes in quantum key distribution (2018). arXiv:1805.05046

10. Ben Ismail, D.K., Karadimas, P., Epiphaniou, G., Al-Khateeb, H.M.: Error reconciliation with turbo codes for secret key generation in vehicular AD hoc networks. In: Arai, K., Kapoor, S., Bhatia, R. (eds.) SAI 2018. AISC, vol. 857, pp. 696–704. Springer, Cham (2019). https://doi.org/10.1007/978-3-030-01177-2_51

11. Shor, P.W.: Scheme for reducing decoherence in quantum computer memory. Phys. Rev. A **52**(4), R2493 (1995)

12. Calderbank, A.R., Shor, P.W.: Good quantum error-correcting codes exist. Phys. Rev. A **54**(2), 1098 (1996)

13. Steane, A.M.: Simple quantum error-correcting codes. Phys. Rev. A **54**(6), 4741 (1996)

14. Gottesman, D.: Stabilizer codes and quantum error correction. California Institute of Technology (1997)

15. Gallager, R.: Low-density parity-check codes. IRE Trans. Inf. Theory **8**(1), 21–28 (1962)

16. MacKay, D.J.C., Mitchison, G., McFadden, P.L.: Sparse-graph codes for quantum error correction. IEEE Trans. Inf. Theory **50**(10), 2315–2330 (2004)

17. Babar, Z., Botsinis, P., Alanis, D., Ng, S.X., Hanzo, L.: Construction of quantum LDPC codes from classical row-circulant QC-LDPCs. IEEE Commun. Lett. **20**(1), 9–12 (2015)

18. Grospellier, A., Grouès, L., Krishna, A., Leverrier, A.: Combining hard and soft decoders for hypergraph product codes. Quantum **5**, 432 (2021)

19. Roffe, J., White, D.R., Burton, S., Campbell, E.T.: Decoding across the quantum LDPC code landscape (2020). arXiv:2005.07016

20. Fossorier, M.P.C., Lin, S.: Soft-decision decoding of linear block codes based on ordered statistics. IEEE Trans. Inf. Theory **41**(5), 1379–1396 (1995)

21. Panteleev, P., Kalachev, G.: Degenerate quantum LDPC codes with good finite length performance (2019). arXiv:1904.02703

22. Richardson, T., Urbanke, R.: Multi-edge type LDPC codes. In: Workshop honoring, Prof. Bob McEliece on his 60th birthday, California Institute of Technology, Pasadena, California. Springer (2002)
23. Liao, S.K., et al.: Satellite-to-ground quantum key distribution. Nature **549**(7670), 43–47 (2017)

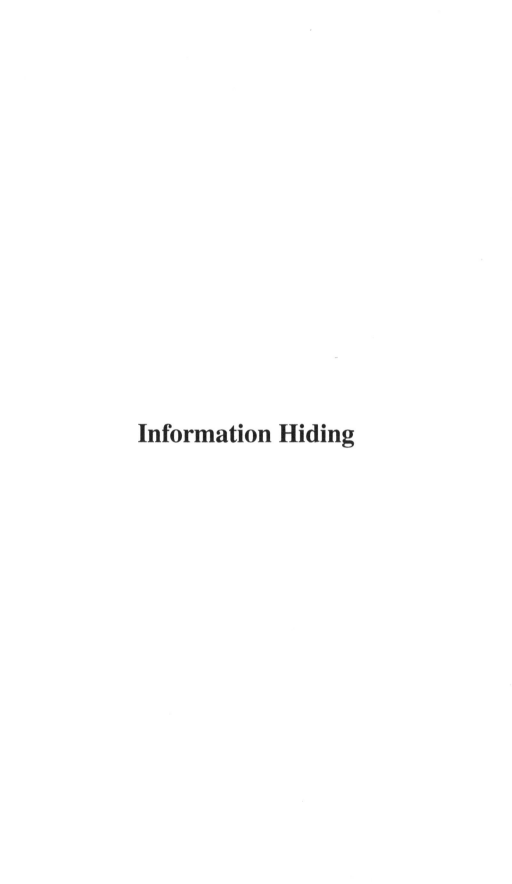

Information Hiding

Noise Simulation-Based Deep Optical Watermarking

Feng Wang[1] , Hang Zhou[2] , Han Fang[3] , Weiming Zhang[1](✉),
and Nenghai Yu[1]

[1] University of Science and Technology of China, Hefei, China
zhangwm@ustc.edu.cn
[2] Simon Fraser University, Vancouver, Canada
[3] National University of Singapore, Singapore, Singapore

Abstract. Digital watermarking is an important branch of information hiding, which effectively guarantees the robustness of embedded watermarks in distorted channels. To embed the watermark into the host carrier, traditional watermarking schemes often require the modification of the carrier. However, in some cases, the modification of the carrier is not allowed such as paintings in museums. To address such limitation, we utilize optical watermarking to embed the watermark into the host carrier. Optical watermarking refers to a technique that encodes the watermark into the visible light irradiating the object, where the watermark can be further extracted by the camera photography process. To realize transparency and robustness of the watermark, we propose a color-decomposition-based watermarking pattern generation algorithm which satisfies human visual system (HVS) characteristics, a camera shooting simulation algorithm which accurately produces the dataset for training, and a decoding network which can realize loss-less decoding of the embedded watermark. Various experiments demonstrate the superiority of our method and reveal the broad applicability of the proposed technique.

Keywords: Noise simulation · Optical watermarking · Human visual system

1 Introduction

Information hiding [1] refers to the technique of hiding secret information in the publicly available media so that people cannot be aware of its existence. As an important branch of information hiding, digital watermarking [2–4] can serve as a way to protect copyright or realize information transmission. The most important property of watermarking schemes is robustness, which directly influences the protection ability and transmission accuracy. To realize robustness, traditional schemes often embed the watermark into the stable coefficients of the carrier [5–8].

Although it is possible to achieve sufficient robustness with little perturbation, in some cases, even slight disturbance to the carrier is not allowed. For example, any damage is prohibited for the paintings displayed in the museum. Since paintings cannot be converted into electronic signals and cannot be modified, traditional watermarking

X. Sun et al. (Eds.): ICAIS 2022, LNCS 13340, pp. 283–298, 2022.
https://doi.org/10.1007/978-3-031-06791-4_23

techniques fail to be applied to the case. To address such limitation, we utilize the optical watermarking techniques [9–16] which can effectively realize the content-independent embedding. Optical watermarking refers to a technique that encodes the watermark signal into the visible light and projects the light onto the real object. With such a process, the object is unnecessary to be modified. At the extraction side, we use a camera to capture the irradiated object and decode the watermark by some image processing operations. Therefore, the content-independence and robustness can be both achieved.

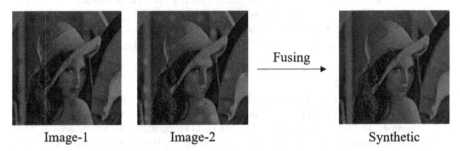

Image-1   Image-2   Synthetic

Fig. 1. Visual fusing. Both images containing the pattern are fused to a clean image by human eyes.

Previous optical watermarking schemes often utilize the well-designed pattern to represent the watermark signal. The pattern should contain two important properties: transparency and robustness. Transparency refers to the visual quality after projecting the pattern onto the object, and robustness represents the extraction accuracy of captured images. However, there is an inherent contradiction between the two properties. So, how to guarantee robustness and visual quality at the same time is an unsolved problem worthy of further exploration.

To better balance transparency and robustness, we propose a novel noise simulation-based deep optical watermarking scheme. For transparency, we carefully study the human visual system (HVS) characteristics and propose a color-decomposition-based [16–19] watermarking pattern generation algorithm. Generally, it is based on the observation that human eyes will fuse two images into one if the two images are refreshed in a high frequency (no less than 60 Hz). Therefore, by alternatively projecting two complementary watermarked frames, human eyes can only see the synthetic frame. As shown in Fig. 1, some circular blocks are neatly arranged in the both images on the left. But human eyes would see the third image (HVS fuses the both images and composes the third image). Unlike HVS, the shutter speed of modern cameras is much higher and instead captures the decomposed frame that contains the pattern, making robustness possible. Moreover, we design a deep neural network at the extraction side to decode the watermark from the captured image. Given the assumption that the object surface is a flat 2D image, we generate the training dataset by simulating the projecting-shooting process, which achieves an approximate mapping from the generated pattern and the carrier image to the captured image.

In summary, our main contributions are three-fold:

- We propose a novel deep optical watermarking system that not only ensures the high visual quality but also realizes the strong robustness.
- To improve the extraction accuracy, we propose a generic noise-aware channel simulation model for the projecting-shooting process to create effective training data.
- Various experiment results demonstrate the superiority of our method compared with baseline methods and reveal broad application prospects of the proposed technique.

2   Related Work

2.1   Optical Watermarking

A series of works of optical watermarking have been presented [10–16] in the past few years, which can be divided into two categories: spatial-based methods and temporal-based methods.

For the first category, Uehira et al. [10] proposed to employ brightness-modulated light to embed invisible watermarking into objects. In [11], orthogonal transforms such Walsh-Hadamard Transform (WHT) and Discrete Cosine Transform (DCT) are utilized to generate the watermarking pattern. Uehira et al. [12] proposed the color difference-based modulation to represent the watermark and embed messages into the color difference signal Cb of Luminance, Chroma-blue and Chroma-red (YCbCr) signal to resist JPEG compression. However, the generated watermark patterns with these methods are often with poor visual quality and are obvious in human eyes.

As for the temporal-based methods, Unno et al. [13–16] proposed to introduce time modulation for better invisibility. In these schemes, two complementary watermarked images are generated and alternately displayed on a projector with a sufficient frequency. Although transparency is better, the message must be extracted via the video. Therefore, when facing the one-photo-capturing extraction, the watermarking scheme cannot be applied.

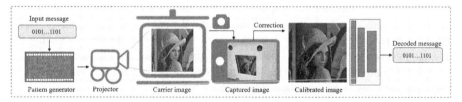

Fig. 2. The framework of optical watermarking system. First, the message is encoded into two patterns modulated positively and negatively. Second, the pattern scream is displayed temporally by the projector on the real object at 60 Hz. Third, a user takes a photo that contains the optical watermarking. Fourth, the captured image is transformed into a canonical image after perspective transformation. Finally, the calibrated image is fed into the following extracting network and the message hidden in the image is extracted.

2.2 Visual Illumination Model

Human Vision System. Human eyes can perceive changes in external light intensity such as flicker over time, but they cannot perceive flickering beyond a certain frequency, which is called flicker fusion threshold. The lowest frequency that causes flicker fusion is dubbed critical flicker frequency (CFF). CFF is generally considered to be about 60 Hz under most circumstances [20]. That is, when the flicker frequency is no less than 60 Hz, human eyes may not be able to observe the change. Besides, most projectors are designed to refresh at more than 60 Hz frequency to avoid visible flicker like screen devices [21]. Moreover, modern cameras can often capture the flicker since its shutter is shorter than the flicker cycle. With 60 Hz projectors, we can realize invisibility in eyes but recordable in camera.

Intrinsic Image Decomposition. The constituent elements of a natural image's appearance mainly include the illumination, shape and material [22]. As the Retinex theory shown in [23, 24], the image can be decomposed as the pixel-wise product of the illumination and the albedo, plus the specular component accounting for highlights due to viewpoint:

$$I(x, y) = S(x, y) \odot R(x, y) + C(x, y) \tag{1}$$

where $I(x, y)$ is the observed intensity at pixel (x, y), $S(x, y)$ is the illumination intensity, $R(x, y)$ is the albedo and $C(x, y)$ is the specular term. In the optical watermarking system, the captured image, the carrier image and the watermark pattern satisfy the aforementioned relationship. So based on the above equation, we could achieve a mapping from the carrier image and watermark to the captured image.

3 Method

In this section, we elaborate the proposed optical watermarking system. Figure 2 shows the basic framework, which consists of three parts: the pattern generator, the projector and the watermark extractor. The pattern generator is responsible for modulating the message into two complementary patterns. And the projector can alternatively project both patterns onto the carrier image. The final extractor can extract the watermark after correcting the image into the canonical image.

3.1 Pattern Generator

As a very important process, pattern generation determines the transparency of the watermarking. Projecting-shooting channel distortions are non-differential and the pattern is independent of the carrier, so we can't employ a deep learning-based method to generate an optimal pattern. Based on previous pattern generation algorithms [25, 26] and HVS, we propose a color-decomposition based watermarking pattern generation algorithm. For a message sequence of length L, we first reshape the sequence into a binary matrix with height h and width w (zeroing the part of $h \times w$). Based on the spatial arrangement of messages, we employ a block of size $b \times b$ to represent 1-bit message so that the whole pattern size is $(b*h) \times (b*w)$. Formally, the 1-bit block can be generated by:

$$B(x, y) = \begin{cases} 1 - \left(\frac{D(x,y)}{\frac{b}{3}}\right)^2, & \text{if } D(x, y) \leq b/3 \\ 0, & \text{otherwise} \end{cases} \tag{2}$$

where $D(x, y)$ indicates the distance between (x, y) and the center of the block:

$$D(x, y) = \sqrt{\left(x - \frac{b}{2}\right)^2 + \left(y - \frac{b}{2}\right)^2} \tag{3}$$

and (x, y) indicates the pixel coordinates of the image block. Considering the HVS is less sensitive to the red and blue components than the green component, we hide 1-bit message m into these two components and create two complementary templates $(+, -)$ for m:

$$B_{\pm}(r, g, b) = \begin{cases} [\beta \pm \alpha * B, \beta, \beta], & \text{if } m = 0 \\ [\beta, \beta, \beta \mp \alpha * B], & \text{otherwise} \end{cases} \tag{4}$$

where α controls the embedding intensity and $\alpha + \beta = 1$ for normalization. The generation of the whole pattern is by arranging each small block in the spatial order of the message matrix. After all the messages are embedded, we can generate two patterns, denoted by P_+ and P_-.

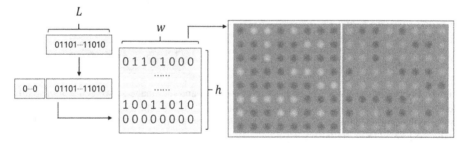

Fig. 3. Pattern generation. The sequence of bits of length L is resized to a binary matrix with height h and width w after zeroing the part of $w \times h - L$. Then the two patterns are modulated by the matrix positively and negatively.

3.2 Projector

The watermark embedding process is carried out by a projector, which alternatively projects the generated two complementary patterns with 60 Hz onto the object. Considering that the 60 Hz flicker is not perceptible to human eyes but recordable for cameras, both the transparency and the recorded ability can be satisfied. Practically, we often limit the projected pattern to tightly fit the carrier image for better performance.

3.3 Watermark Extractor

Perspective Correction. After captured, the captured image should be further perspectively corrected and fed into the decoding network. The correction process can be described as: after capturing the projected image by the camera, we detect the watermarking region and warp the region back to a rectangular image. We add a black border around the projected region and use the method in [27] to automatically locate 4 vertices of $V_1(x_1, y_1)$, $V_2(x_2, y_2)$, $V_3(x_3, y_3)$ and $V_4(x_4, y_4)$ as shown in Fig. 4. Then we set the transformation:

$$\begin{cases} x' = \frac{a_1 x + b_1 y + c_1}{a_0 x + b_0 y + 1}, \\ y' = \frac{a_2 x + b_2 y + c_2}{a_0 x + b_0 y + 1}. \end{cases} \tag{5}$$

(x', y') is the corresponding coordinate to these 4 vertices $V_1'\left(x_1', y_1'\right)$, $V_2'\left(x_2', y_2'\right)$, $V_3'\left(x_3', y_3'\right)$ and $V_4'\left(x_4', y_4'\right)$. Based on the equation, we can get 8 equations and solve them to obtain the value of eight variables. After that, we can form a stable mapping from the captured image to the calibrated image. Then the corrected image is cropped and resized to the input image size of the decoder network.

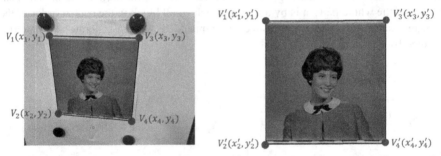

Fig. 4. *Correction process.* We add a black border around the image so we can automatically detect the marked four vertices. Then we can subsequently acquire the mapping from the captured image to the calibrated image. Note that the additional dots are magnets which are responsible for fixing the printed image to the board.

Simulated Dataset Generation. Since the final watermarking extraction is carried out by the decoding network, we need generate enough training data. Considering it is very complicated in time and effort to acquire real photo data, so instead, we propose an algorithm to simulate the distortions in the projecting-shooting process, as shown in Fig. 5. Assuming the projected object is a 2D plane with a wide variety of textures, the distortions in the actual physical process of projecting-shooting can be divided into three parts: The projecting color distortion, the synthesis distortion and the capturing distortion.

Projecting Color Distortion: Given the assumption that the projected pattern is spatially aligned with the carrier-image, we can approximate the projecting color distortions by the pattern fusion and Gamma adjustment. Due to the shutter exposure effect, the captured image might consist of a part of the pattern P_+ and a part of pattern P_-, and the ratio is determined by the exposure time t_+ and t_-. Besides, the color of the projected P is quite different from its original status due to the hardware difference, so we utilize the Gamma adjustment with γ_1 to make an approximation. The whole simulation can be formulated by:

$$P(x, y) = \left[P_+(x, y) * t_+ + P_-(x, y) * t_- \right]^{\gamma_1} \tag{6}$$

where we set $t_+ + t_- = 1$ for normalization.

Synthesis Distortion: Since the embedding process is carried out by the projecting operation, the synthesis distortions mainly come from the lighting environment. Specifically, as mentioned above, the watermarking image is influenced by the projecting pattern $P(x, y)$, the carrier image $R(x, y$, the ambient illumination I_A and specular reflection I_C:

$$I(x, y) = (P(x, y) + I_A) \odot R(x, y) + I_C \tag{7}$$

where we assume I_A and I_C are constants over the entire image.

Capturing Distortion: Tancik et al. [28] proposed StegaStamp, which applied a set of differentiable image perturbations to simulate the print-shooting distortions during training. Similarly, we conclude the capturing process as four types of distortions: color manipulation, Gaussian noise, defocus blurring and JPEG compression.

As for color manipulation, there is an inherent difference between the captured image with its original color because of the sensor sampling operation. To better simulate such perturbations, we propose to utilize contrast adjustment, brightness shifting, hue shifting and Gamma adjustment on the watermarking image. We affine histogram rescaling $mx+n$ to achieve brightness shifting and contrast adjustment. For hue shifting, a random color offset s is added to each channel of RGB. Non-linear mismatching exists during shooting so we bring in Gamma adjustment with γ_2 to make an approximation.

In the camera shooting process, cameras may not fully focus on the target area, which will result in the defocus blurring distortion. To simulate the defocus blurring distortion, we perform a 5×5-sized Gaussian blurring operation on the image.

Due to the hardware components and the capturing environments, there are always different noises in the camera shooting process. Therefore, we directly employ Gaussian noise model with the standard deviation σ to represent the noise distortion that occurred during capturing.

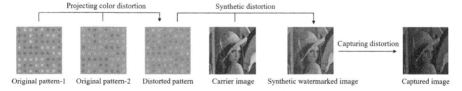

Fig. 5. Noise-aware channel simulation. First, original two patterns generate the distorted pattern under the influence of the projecting color distortion. Second, the synthetic watermarking image is synthesized by the distorted pattern and the carrier image. Finally, the captured image is generated from the synthetic watermarked image after capturing distortion.

JPEG compression distortion is introduced in the saving process since most cameras use JPEG as their default storage format. We simulate this process with JPEG compression of the quality factor Q.

Network Architecture. After generating the simulated dataset, we utilize them to train the decoding network. We employ two convolutional blocks (Conv-BatchNorm-ReLU) with a 3×3 kernel as the basic network unit and skip-connection [29] is used between neighboring units. When we use 32×32 pixels to represent 1 bit message, given the input image I, we first use five residual blocks with stride 1 and output features $F_1 \in \mathbb{R}^{64 \times H \times W}$. Then we use several down-sampled convolutional blocks to generate $F_2 \in \mathbb{R}^{256 \times \frac{H}{32} \times \frac{W}{32}}$. The last layer employs a convolutional layer of 1×1 and Tanh to generate the final output watermark $M' \in \mathbb{R}^{1 \times \frac{H}{32} \times \frac{W}{32}}$. During network training, we set l_1 distance as the message reconstruction loss, which can be formulated by:

$$L = \left|\left| M - M' \right|\right|_1 \tag{8}$$

where $M \in \{0, 1\}^{1 \times \frac{H}{32} \times \frac{W}{32}}$ is the original message matrix.

Fig. 6. Experimental system. The left side shows the whiteboard and the test carrier used for the environment, and the projector is placed on the table on the right. The additional magnets (colourful dots for fixing the carrier) are only needed for the sake of the experiment.

Table 1. Based on the real-world environment, we set up the scopes of these parameters. During training, we uniformly sample these parameters and generate simulated dataset in each step.

t_+	γ_1	I_A	I_C	m
$(0, 0.2) \cup (0.8, 1)$	$(1, 2.5)$	$(0.05, 0.1)$	$(0.15, 0.3)$	$(0.9, 1.1)$
n	s	γ_2	σ	Q
$(-0.2, 0.2)$	$(-0.1, 0.1)$	$(0.4, 1)$	$(0, 0.1)$	$(50, 100)$

Training Details. The decoder network is executed on NVIDIA GeForce RTX 2080Ti. For gradient descent, Adam [30] is applied with a learning rate of 10^{-3}. During training,

Table 2. Configuration parameters of conducting real-world experiments.

Device	Mobile phone	iPhone8 Plus
	Projector	EPSON
Position	Shooting distance	60 cm
	Projecting distance	50 cm
	Projecting angle	up 10°
Watermark	Embedding intensity	$\alpha = 30/255$
	Capacity	8×8 bits
	Size	18.5 cm $\times$ 18.5 cm

we initialize the embedding intensity at $\alpha = 80/255$ and gradually decrease it to $30/255$. The decoder network is trained for 500 epochs with batch size 16. For training data, we randomly select 2595 images from ImageNet [31] and resize them to 256×256. For configuration parameters of the simulated dataset generation process, we uniformly sample them from scopes as shown in Table 1.

4   Real-World Experiments and Analysis

In this section, we first introduce the implementation details for our real-world experiments. Then comparative experiments of our method and baseline methods [10–12] are implemented. Finally, we implement additional experiments of the proposed method.

4.1   Implementation Details

The test dataset is USC-SIPI image dataset with 14 images [32]. All the test images are printed in A4 paper with 300dpi. The default projector and mobile phone we used are "EPSON EB-C301MN" with the refresh rate of 60 Hz and "iPhone8 Plus" with the camera resolution of 4032×3024. We use the embedding intensity $\alpha = 30/255$ for test. The details of the default experimental configuration are shown in Table 2, and our experimental system is shown in Fig. 6. To measure the visual quality of the watermarking image, we perform a mean opinion score (MOS) test. We ask 25 persons to assign a score from 1 (bad quality, the watermark clearly visible) to 5 (excellent quality, the watermark invisible) at the default shooting position. We use the mean value of every observer's score to represent the final MOS of the scheme. The robustness is evaluated by the average extraction accuracy of the captured images. We compare the messages and calculate the bit accuracy rate (Fig. 7).

Fig. 7. **Visual qualities.** We can see gray blocks in images with baseline methods.

Table 3. Mean opinion score (MOS) test compared with baseline methods.

Method	DCT [9]	DWT [10]	DCT-Cb [11]	Proposed
MOS	2.094	1.844	2.781	**4.144**

4.2 Visual Quality Comparison

The visual quality comparison results (MOS) are shown in Table 3. We can easily find that the proposed method achieves better MOS than other baseline methods. As shown in Fig. 3, the original images and captured images with different methods are displayed. In human eyes, the proposed projected pattern is just a pure white pattern with a certain intensity. But for the other schemes, obvious texture can be easily perceived. This is because the proposed method leverages the insensitivity of HVS with flicker, which greatly improves the visual quality of the watermarked image.

4.3 Robustness Tests

We conduct experiments on different conditions to compare the extraction performance of our method with baseline methods [10–12]. Explicitly speaking, the captured distances range from 30 cm to 90 cm and the captured angles range from left 75° to right 75°. As shown in Table 4, the proposed method maintains the best extraction bit accuracy in most distance cases, except for 30 cm and 90 cm. We can see that at 40 cm–80 cm, the proposed scheme can achieve the accuracy beyond 88%, and the closer shooting distance will result in better performance, which can be analyzed that closer shooting distance could get a clearer photograph, indicating higher bit accuracy. However, we can find that the proposed method doesn't perform best at 30 cm in all distance cases. We analyze the reason as: our method is based on color difference in different channels and shooting too closely can cause the captured image too bright, causing the color difference signal to disappear. And other methods are based on frequency modulation, so they are supposed to achieve the best performance with the clearest picture at the closest distance. Table 5 shows the performances at different angles. It can be easily seen that our method could achieve more than 90% of bit accuracy within angle $[-15°, 15°]$, and even at an angle of left 75°, the accuracy could still reach 71.63%. The performance on the front is not always best in all angle cases. That may be attributed to more intense specular reflection in the frontal.

Table 4. Bit accuracy (%) comparison of extracted message with different shooting distances.

Distance/cm	DCT [9]	DWT [10]	DCT-Cb [11]	Proposed
30 cm	91.74	92.35	**93.97**	90.85
40 cm	88.39	88.62	91.07	**96.88**
50 cm	90.40	92.13	92.63	**94.42**
60 cm	84.49	78.52	74.00	**90.07**
70 cm	80.58	82.31	85.38	**92.75**
80 cm	84.49	78.18	82.92	**88.84**
90 cm	86.38	87.05	**89.84**	83.37

Table 5. Bit accuracy (%) comparison of extracted message with different shooting angles.

Angle	DCT [9]	DWT [10]	DCT-Cb [11]	Proposed
Left 75°	60.94	63.39	61.61	**71.63**
Left 60°	80.47	81.58	**82.92**	77.79
Left 45°	78.01	77.46	82.59	**89.40**
Left 30°	83.15	82.03	82.37	**85.38**
Left 15°	77.57	76.45	80.92	**93.53**
Frontal	84.49	78.52	74.00	**90.07**
Right 15°	82.70	79.24	84.93	**92.97**
Right 30°	82.03	80.13	85.49	**95.54**
Right 45°	78.35	79.07	80.92	**87.72**
Right 60°	78.91	78.13	77.34	**89.17**
Right 75°	55.52	57.25	55.47	**86.38**

4.4   Additional Experiments

The Influence of the Noise-Aware Channel Simulation. Since the network is trained with the simulated data, the simulation performance greatly influences the network performance. In this section, we mainly explore the importance of different simulating operations with the following cases. The bit accuracy (%) results are shown in Tables 6 and 7, column (1): Without projecting color distortion (randomly selecting one from two patterns); column (2): Without synthesis distortion (regarding carrier images as whiteboards); column (3): Without capturing distortion; column (4): Iden (including all distortions). In all distortions, it's not hard to find that synthetic distortion is the most important among the three distortions. That's because the Retinex theory-based synthesis explains the basic process of the captured image generation.

Table 6. The influence of the noise-aware channel simulation with different distances.

Distance	W/o projecting color distortion	W/o synthesis distortion	W/o capturing distortion	Iden
30 cm	87.17	74.55	86.83	**90.85**
40 cm	95.76	83.48	95.42	**96.88**
50 cm	92.75	82.14	90.96	**94.42**
60 cm	86.61	75.56	85.16	**90.07**
70 cm	87.95	75.11	86.72	**92.75**
80 cm	82.81	73.77	83.26	**88.84**
90 cm	80.02	69.31	79.69	**83.37**

The Influence of Embedding Intensity. Embedding intensity α significantly influences the extraction accuracy in the real-world test. In this section, we mainly show and discuss the influence of embedding intensity. To determine appropriate α, we conduct a test on different intensities from 10/255 to 50/255 with the step of 10/255. For each intensity, we conduct the MOS test and the robustness test with the default setting. The corresponding results are shown in Table 8. It can be found that as the intensity increases, the visual quality gradually decreases while the robustness gradually increases. The reason is that although human eyes are not sensitive when flickering with 60 Hz, frequency is not the only restriction. When the intensity achieves a certain value, such artifacts can still be found even. Therefore, we should take a careful trade-off of visual quality and robustness and select the appropriate intensity $\alpha = 30/255$.

Adaptability to Different Devices. To reveals the versatility of the proposed method on different devices, we use five mobile phones ("iPhone8 Plus", "Mix2S", "Mi4", "Honor V20", "iPhone SE") and two projectors ("EPSON EB-C301MN", "NEC CR3117X") to test the extraction accuracy at the distance of 60 cm from the frontal. As shown in Table 9, the extraction accuracy is beyond 82% in all device pairs, which indicates the

Table 7. The influence of the noise-aware channel simulation with different angles.

Angle	W/o projecting color distortion	W/o synthesis distortion	W/o capturing distortion	Iden
L 75°	64.62	61.94	64.06	**71.63**
L 60°	73.32	64.51	72.21	**77.79**
L 45°	81.81	71.21	82.14	**89.40**
L 30°	79.80	67.30	79.80	**85.38**
L 15°	91.29	76.56	90.96	**93.53**
Frontal	86.61	75.56	85.16	**90.07**
R 15°	89.40	76.56	87.83	**92.97**
R 30°	94.31	77.12	92.08	**95.54**
R 45°	85.60	70.98	81.81	**87.72**
R 60°	86.05	72.32	84.49	**89.17**
R 75°	77.46	68.19	76.56	**86.38**

versatility of the proposed method. Besides, we found that the extraction accuracy with "NEC CR3117X" is higher than that with "EPSON EB-C301MN". We conclude that the "NEC CR3117X" has a higher projection resolution which influences the capture accuracy at the camera side.

Table 8. MOS-Accuracy. The performance across a range of intensity.

$\alpha(1/255)$	10	20	30	40	50
MOS	4.631	4.378	4.144	3.063	2.563
Accuracy (%)	70.65	77.57	90.07	94.08	94.75

Table 9. Bit accuracy (%) on different mobile phones and projectors.

Device	iPhone8 Plus	Mi 4	Mix2S	Honor V20	iPhone SE
EPSON	90.07	88.73	86.72	84.49	82.59
NEC	90.4	92.75	88.84	96.65	95.09

The Influence of Different 1-bit Block Sizes. In this section, we main explore the Influence of different block sizes that represent 1-bit message. To better clarify The Influence of different sizes, we utilize the size ranging from 8×8 to 64×64 pixels

Table 10. Bit accuracy (%) comparison with different 1-bit block sizes.

Block size	64 × 64	32 × 32	16 × 16	8 × 8
Accuracy	94.64	90.07	87.77	73.96

to represent 1-bit message (32 × 32 default) and adaptively change the stride for the network to re-train the network. Then we test these cases to generate the results shown in Table 10. We can easily find that the extraction accuracy increases when the block size is larger. We conclude that: when the block size is smaller, more possible distortions are introduced after capturing, so the extraction accuracy is poorer.

5   Conclusion

In this paper, we introduce a novel optical watermarking scheme based on noise simulation and deep neural network. To achieve better transparency, we utilize color-decomposition to embed watermark. As for robustness, we propose the noise-aware channel simulation model to generate the training dataset and employ the decoder network to extract the message. Extensive experiments demonstrate the superiority compared with baseline methods and reveal the broad applicability of our method.

Funding Statement. This work was supported in part by the Natural Science Foundation of China under Grant 62072421, 62002334, 62102386, 62121002 and U20B2047, Anhui Science Foundation of China under Grant 2008085QF296, Exploration Fund Project of University of Science and Technology of China under Grant YD3480002001, and by Fundamental Research Funds for the Central Universities WK5290000001.

References

1. Petitcolas, F.A., Anderson, R.J., Kuhn, M.G.: Information hiding-a survey. Proc. IEEE **87**(7), 1062–1078 (1999)
2. Katzenbeisser, S., Petitcolas, F.A.P.: Digital Watermarking, vol. 2. Springer, Artech House, London (2000)
3. Xiong, L., Han, X., Yang, C., Shi, Y.Q.: Robust reversible watermarking in encrypted image with secure multi-party based on lightweight cryptography. IEEE Trans. Circ. Syst. Video Technol. **32**, 75–91 (2021). https://doi.org/10.1109/TCSVT.2021.3055072
4. Bhaskar, A., Sharma, C., Mohiuddin, K., Singh, A., Nasr, O.A.: A robust video watermarking scheme with squirrel search algorithm. Comput. Mater. Continua **71**(2), 3069–3089 (2022)
5. Pereira, S., Pun, T.: Robust template matching for affine resistant image watermarks. IEEE Trans. Image Process. **9**(6), 1123–1129 (2000)
6. Cox, I.J., Kilian, J., Leighton, F.T., Shamoon, T.: Secure spread spectrum watermarking for multimedia. IEEE Trans. Image Process. **6**(12), 1673–1687 (1997)
7. Alhumyani, H., Alrube, I., Alsharif, S., Afifi, A., Amar, C.B.: Analytic beta-wavelet transform-based digital image watermarking for secure transmission. Comput. Mater. Continua **70**(3), 4657–4673 (2022)

8. Fang, H., Zhang, W., Zhou, H., Cui, H., Yu, N.: Screen-shooting resilient watermarking. IEEE Trans. Inf. Forensics Secur. **14**(6), 1403–1418 (2018)

9. Uehira, K., Suzuki, K., Ikeda, H.: Applications of optoelectronic watermarking technique to new business and industry systems utilizing flat-panel displays and smart devices. In: IEEE Industry Application Society Annual Meeting, pp. 1–9 (2014)

10. Uehira, K., Suzuki, M.: Digital watermarking technique using brightness-modulated light. In: IEEE International Conference on Multimedia and Expo, pp. 257–260 (2008)

11. Ishikawa, Y., Uehira, K., Yanaka, K.: Practical evaluation of illumination watermarking technique using orthogonal transforms. J. Display Technol. **6**(9), 351–358 (2010)

12. Uehira, K., Unno, H.: Effects of JPEG compression on reading optical watermarking embedded by using color-difference modulation. J. Comput. Commun. **6**(1), 56–64 (2017)

13. Oshita, K., Unno, H., Uehira, K.: Optically written watermarking technology using temporally and spatially luminance-modulated light. Electron. Imaging **2016**(8), 1–6 (2016)

14. Unno, H., Uehira, K.: Lighting technique for attaching invisible information onto real objects using temporally and spatially color-intensity modulated light. IEEE Trans. Ind. Appl. **56**(6), 7202–7207 (2020)

15. Unno, H., Yamkum, R., Bunporn, C., Uehira, K.: A new displaying technology for information hiding using temporally brightness modulated pattern. IEEE Trans. Ind. Appl. **53**(1), 596–601 (2016)

16. Unno, H., Uehira, K.: Display technique for embedding information in real object images using temporally and spatially luminance-modulated light. IEEE Trans. Ind. Appl. **53**(6), 5966–5971 (2017)

17. Cui, H., Bian, H., Zhang, W., Yu, N.: Unseencode: invisible on-screen barcode with image-based extraction. In: IEEE Conference on Computer Communications, pp. 1315–1323 (2019)

18. Zhang, L., et al.: Kaleido: you can watch it but cannot record it. In: Proceedings of the 21st Annual International Conference on Mobile Computing and Networking, pp. 372–385 (2015)

19. Song, K., Liu, N., Gao, Z., Zhang, J., Zhai, G., Zhang, X.P.: Deep restoration of invisible QR code from TPVM display. In: 2020 IEEE International Conference on Multimedia & Expo Workshops, pp. 1–6 (2020)

20. Nomura, Y., et al.: Evaluation of critical flicker-fusion frequency measurement methods using a touchscreen-based visual temporal discrimination task in the behaving mouse. Neurosci. Res. **148**, 28–33 (2019)

21. Menozzi, M., Lang, F., Naepflin, U., Zeller, C., Krueger, H.: CRT versus LCD: effects of refresh rate, display technology and background luminance in visual performance. Displays **22**(3), 79–85 (2001)

22. Liu, Y., Li, Y., You, S., Lu, F.: Unsupervised learning for intrinsic image decomposition from a single image. In: Proceedings of the IEEE/CVF Conference on Computer Vision and Pattern Recognition, pp. 3248–3257 (2020)

23. Land, E.H., Mccann, J.J.: Lightness and retinex theory. Josa **61**(1), 1–11 (1971)

24. Grosse, R., Johnson, M.K., Adelson, E.H., Freeman, W.T.: Ground truth dataset and baseline evaluations for intrinsic image algorithms. In: Proceedings of the IEEE Conference on Computer Vision, pp. 2335–2342 (2009)

25. Gugelmann, D., Sommer, D., Lenders, V., Happe, M., Vanbever, L.: Screen watermarking for data theft investigation and attribution. In: 10th International Conference on Cyber Conflict, pp. 391–408 (2018)

26. Fang, H., et al.: Deep template-based watermarking. IEEE Trans. Circ. Syst. Video Technol. **31**(4), 1436–1451 (2020)

27. Katayama, A., Nakamura, T., Yamamuro, M., Sonehara, N.: New high-speed frame detection method: Side trace algorithm (STA) for i-appli on cellular phones to detect watermarks. In: Proceedings of the 3rd International Conference on Mobile and Ubiquitous Multimedia, pp. 109–116 (2004)

28. Tancik, M., Mildenhall, B., Ng, R.: Stegastamp: invisible hyperlinks in physical photographs. In: Proceedings of the IEEE/CVF Conference on Computer Vision and Pattern Recognition, pp. 2117–2126 (2020)
29. He, K., Zhang, X., Ren, S., Sun, J.: Deep residual learning for image recognition. In: Proceedings of the IEEE Conference on Computer Vision and Pattern Recognition, pp. 770–778 (2016)
30. Kingma, D.P., Ba, J.: Adam: a method for stochastic optimization. In: International Conference on Learning Representations (2014)
31. Deng, J., Dong, W., Socher, R., Li, L.J., Li, K., Li, F.F.: ImageNet: a large-scale hierarchical image database. In: Proceedings of the IEEE Conference on Computer Vision and Pattern Recognition, pp. 248–255 (2009)
32. The USC-SIPI image database (2020). http://sipi.usc.edu/database/

Behavior Steganography in Social Network via Secret Sharing

Xuan Zhu[1] ⓘ, Qun Mo[1], Fengyong Li[2,3,4(✉)] ⓘ, Lei Zhang[1], and Chuan Qin[1] ⓘ

[1] School of Optical-Electrical and Computer Engineering, University of Shanghai for Science and Technology, Shanghai 200093, China
qin@usst.edu.cn
[2] College of Computer Science and Technology, Shanghai University of Electric Power, Shanghai 200090, China
fyli@shiep.edu.cn
[3] Guangxi Key Lab of Multi-source Information Mining and Security, Guangxi Normal University, Guilin 541004, China
[4] Computer Science Department, University of Victoria, Victoria, BC, Canada

Abstract. In this paper, we propose a new steganographic scheme based on social network behavior. Different from existing multimedia files based steganographic schemes, our scheme embeds the secret data within the behaviors of individuals in social network. To be specific, we firstly employ the (t, n) secret sharing strategy based on matrix multiplication to divide the secret data into multiple shares, and then transmits them by making "love" mark on the published news of each friend. For the receiver, since each share only contains a small part of valid secret data and a lot of redundant data, secret data can be correctly extracted from the published news of t friends, even if most of them are lost. Experimental results demonstrate the effectiveness of the proposed scheme. Compared with Zhang's scheme, proposed scheme can obtain higher robustness and larger embedding capacity.

Keywords: Behavior information · Social network · Steganography · Secret sharing

1 Introduction

Steganography, as an effective data hiding way, can embed secret data into cover data in an imperceptible way. In past decades, digital multimedia file-based steganography has attracted extensive research interests in the community of multimedia security [1, 2]. A majority of existing data hiding schemes utilized multimedia files as cover data, including text, image, audio and video, etc., and by slightly modifying cover data with well-designed mechanisms, secret data can be embedded into cover data to produce stego data. If stego data can be recovered to cover data losslessly after secret data extraction, this scheme is defined as reversible data hiding (RDH) method [3–6]. On the contrary, if stego data cannot be recovered to cover data, we call this scheme as steganographic method, because they mainly achieve the transfer of secret information. Since the performance of steganographic schemes is usually evaluated from two aspects, i.e., embedding rate (embedding capacity) and imperceptibility (distortion of cover or visual quality), the rate-distortion curve is thus commonly utilized in performance comparisons for different schemes.

Since most of the multimedia files on the Internet come from different image sources, it is difficult for them to maintain a unified format. In addition, due to the large amount of signal interference on the Internet, multimedia files containing secret information are easily affected so that the secret information cannot be extracted correctly. Therefore, steganographic methods based on multimedia files are not easily applied to Internet steganography. With the development of information technologies, such as Internet, big data and social network, etc., network information can be divided into three categories: 1) the information describing objective world; 2) the information recording human behavior; and 3) the information describing imaginary world (fictional world). The first category of information is the mainstream of network information, and conventional data hiding schemes with the requirements of perceptual and statistical lifelikeness are based on the first category of network information, such as multimedia data. While the second type of data reflects human behavior on the Internet. Behavioral information hiding is the use of human behavior to secretly transmit confidential information in the natural world. With the promotion and application of various technologies such as social networks and wearable devices, human behaviors are recorded and transmitted after being collected. More and more researches focus on the transmission of secret information by recording human behaviors in social network. If part of the secret data can be hidden in these behavioral information, it is more difficult to detect this form of data hiding than multimedia files. Considering the above problem, Zhang et al. firstly proposed a behavior steganography scheme based on social network behavior [7], in which secret data was embedded within the behaviors of the sender. Detailedly, on the sender side, the sender made "love" marks on the published news of his friends; while on the receiver side, the receiver can extract the secret data from the "love" marks. However, in this scheme, when the number of published news was small, secret data cannot be extracted correctly.

In this paper, we propose a new steganographic scheme based on social network behavior. We firstly employ the (t, n) secret sharing strategy based on matrix multiplication to divide the secret data into multiple shares, and then transmits them by making 'love' mark on the published news of each friend. For the receiver, since each share only contains a small part of valid secret data and a lot of redundant data, even if most of them are lost, secret data can be also correctly recovered from the published news of t friends. Extensive experiments demonstrate that our method outperforms Zhang's schemes with higher robustness and larger embedding capacity.

2 Framework Description

As a kind of modern communication platform, social network includes a lot of individuals (also called as users). In WeChat, an individual is able to see the news published by his friends, and also can mark "love" to approbate these comments on the published news. In this work, we propose a novel behavior steganography scheme in the WeChat based social network. In the scheme, the sender marks "love" on the news published by his friends to represent the secret data; on the receiver side, if the receiver is the friend of the sender, secret data can be correctly extracted from the sender's "love" marks.

The framework of proposed behavior steganography in social network is shown as Fig. 1. Suppose that, the sender has N friends, denoted as $F = \{F_1, F_2, ..., F(t, n)_N\}$, and the receiver is one of these N friends in F. We need to note two issues: (1) In some social networks, such as WeChat, the sender does not know whether one of his friends is also a friend of the receiver or not. That implies, the "love" mark behavior of the sender may not be seen by the receiver. In other words, secret data can only be extracted from the visible behavior information; (2) The sender should make "love" marks on the published news with a normal rate to avoid arousing any warden's suspicion. The reasonable "love" marking rate, denoted as r_x ($1 \leq x \leq N$), can be given according to the relationship between the sender and his friends.

In our scheme, suppose that, the sender has n friends for marking "love" on their published news, and the receiver has t friends and these friends are also the friends of the sender, thus, we utilize the (t, n) threshold secret sharing based on matrix operation to realize steganography on social network. Detailed procedures are described in the following section.

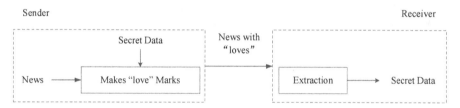

Fig. 1. The framework of behavior steganography based on social network.

3 Proposed Behavior Steganographic Scheme

Figure 2 shows the framework of proposed scheme, which mainly contains three phases: 1) secret data dividing, 2) data embedding based on social network behavior, and 3) data extraction. In the first phase, we present a secret sharing method based on matrix operation. In the second phase, the sender hides secret data with the behavior of "love" marking on the published news of each friend. In the third phase, the receiver extracts secret data by observing the "love" marking behavior of the sender.

3.1 Secret Sharing Based on Matrix Operation

Secret sharing can disperse the responsibility and enhance the security of the system and thus changes the traditional single mode of encryption, decryption and authentication. Shamir [8] first proposed the concept of (t, n) secret sharing and Thien and Lin [9] developed a (t, n) threshold secret image sharing scheme. Karnin et al. [10] employed matrix multiplication to further design an effective secret sharing scheme.

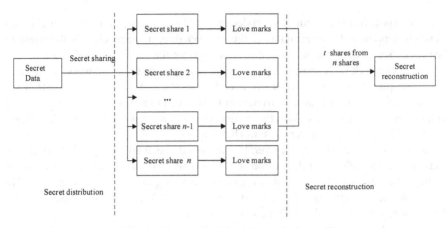

Fig. 2. The sketch of the proposed scheme.

Denote the secret data to be transmitted as a binary sequence consisting of L-bits, i.e., $\mathbf{m} = [m_1, m_2, \ldots, m_L]$. The (t, n) threshold secret sharing scheme can be constructed by matrix operation, where n is the number of total shares and t is the threshold that is the least number of shares to recover the secret data. Through a secret key, the n matrices $\mathbf{A}_1, \mathbf{A}_2, \ldots, \mathbf{A}_n$ with size of $L \times L/t$ are randomly generated, which should satisfy that the square matrix composed with any t of these n matrices is full rank. Thus, the n secret shares can be calculated as:

$$s_i = \mathbf{m} \cdot \mathbf{A}_i \tag{1}$$

When any t shares s_i sized $1 \times L/t$ are obtained, the L linear equations with L unknowns can be constructed. Thus, the L-bits secret data can be obtained by solving the linear equations.

An example of the $(2, 4)$ secret sharing for embedding 4-bits secret data, i.e., $t = 2$, $n = 4$ and $L = 4$, is given in the following. First, four matrices are randomly generated with a secret key:

$$\mathbf{A}_1 = \begin{bmatrix} 1 & 0 \\ 0 & 1 \\ 0 & 0 \\ 0 & 0 \end{bmatrix}, \ \mathbf{A}_2 = \begin{bmatrix} 0 & 0 \\ 0 & 0 \\ 1 & 0 \\ 0 & 1 \end{bmatrix}, \ \mathbf{A}_3 = \begin{bmatrix} 1 & 0 \\ 1 & 1 \\ 1 & 0 \\ 0 & 1 \end{bmatrix}, \ \mathbf{A}_4 = \begin{bmatrix} 0 & 1 \\ 1 & 0 \\ 1 & 0 \\ 0 & 1 \end{bmatrix} \tag{2}$$

Suppose that, the secret data $\mathbf{m} = [m_1, m_2, m_3, m_4] = [1, 0, 0, 1]$, and the corresponding four secret shares can be calculated as:

$$
\begin{aligned}
s_1 &= \mathbf{m} \cdot \mathbf{A}_1 = (m_1, m_2) = (1, 0), \\
s_2 &= \mathbf{m} \cdot \mathbf{A}_2 = (m_3, m_4) = (0, 1), \\
s_3 &= \mathbf{m} \cdot \mathbf{A}_3 = (m_1 \oplus m_2 \oplus m_3, m_2 \oplus m_4) = (1, 1), \\
s_4 &= \mathbf{m} \cdot \mathbf{A}_4 = (m_2 \oplus m_3, m_1 \oplus m_4) = (0, 0)
\end{aligned} \tag{3}
$$

Suppose that, the to-be-recovered secret data on the receiver side is $\mathbf{m'} = \left[m'_1, m'_2, m'_3, m'_4\right]$. When two shares ($t = 2$), such as $\mathbf{s}_1$ and $\mathbf{s}_3$, are received, with the assist of $\mathbf{A}_1$ and $\mathbf{A}_3$ generated by the secret key, four linear equations with four unknowns can be constructed:

$$\begin{cases} m'_1 = 1, \\ m'_2 = 0, \\ m'_2 \oplus m'_2 \oplus m'_3 = 1, \\ m'_2 \oplus m'_4 = 1. \end{cases} \tag{4}$$

Through solving the above linear equations, the secret data can be recovered, i.e., $\mathbf{m'} = [1, 0, 0, 1]$, which is the same as $\mathbf{m}$. Because the square matrix composed by any t matrices is full rank, the linear equations constructed with less than t shares has infinite solutions, which means secret data cannot be recovered in that scenario.

3.2   Behavior Steganography in Social Network

In our scheme, the sender has N friends $\mathbf{F} = \{F_1, F_2, ..., F_N\}$, and the secret data to be transmitted is a binary sequence consisting of L-bits, i.e., $\mathbf{m} = [m_1, m_2, ..., m_L]$. After N matrices $\mathbf{A}_x$ ($1 \leq x \leq N$) sized $L \times L/t$ are generated with secret key, we can calculate each share as

$$\mathbf{s}_x = \mathbf{m} \cdot \mathbf{A}_x = \left[s_{x,1}, s_{x,2}, ..., s_{x,L/t}\right]. \tag{5}$$

Notably, the parameters (t, n) of secret sharing will be discussed in the next subsection.

For each friend, an L/t bits-sequence $\mathbf{s}_x$ ($1 \leq x \leq N$) and a reasonable "love" rate r_x are generated. Here, both the probabilities of 0 and 1 in $\mathbf{s}_x$ are 1/2. Then, each bit in $\mathbf{s}_x$ is converted into another binary sequence $\mathbf{g}_x$ using inverse arithmetic coding with r_x, where the probabilities of 0 and 1 in $\mathbf{g}_x$ are $1 - r_x$ and r_x, respectively. Thus, the sender may begin the transmission of secret data. When observing a published news by his friend F_x, the sender takes a bit from $\mathbf{g}_x$, and marks "love" if the taken bit is "1" and does nothing if the taken bit is "0". For example, when a news is published by F_1, the "love" mark is made if the current bit taken from $\mathbf{g}_1$ is "1" and nothing is done if the bit is "0". In this way, secret data can be transformed into "love" behavior to all friends of the sender.

For the receiver side, if a sender's friend is also the friend of the receiver, the published news by this friend of the sender and the sender's love mark can be visible to the receiver. At the same time, the receiver collects the "0" and "1" information from these behavior information, and we can obtain Y ($1 \leq Y \leq N$) bit sequences:

$$\mathbf{h}_y = \left[h_{y,1}, h_{y,2}, ...\right], y = 1, 2, ..., Y. \tag{6}$$

where Y denotes the number of sender's friends who are the friend of the receiver, i.e., the number of common friends of the sender and the receiver, and the length of $\mathbf{h}_y$ depends on the length of news published by this common friend F_y. After using arithmetic coding on each $\mathbf{h}_y$, $\mathbf{p}_y$ can be obtained whose length is the same as that of $\mathbf{h}_y$. Then, from the Y bit sequences $\mathbf{p}_y$, the receiver randomly selects t bit sequences $\mathbf{p}_y$ corresponding to the t

common friends, whose lengths are longer than L/t, that is to say, the news published by these t common friends are all more than L/t. Using the same secret key, the t matrices $\mathbf{A}_x$ corresponding to these t common friends can be re-generated, and the L linear equations with full rank coefficient matrix can be established. Therefore, secret data $\mathbf{m} = [m_1, m_2,\ldots, m_L]$ can be recovered by the method described in Sect. 3.1.

3.3 Parameter and Security Analysis

In our scheme, our scheme involves several parameters, including the values (t, n) of secret sharing, the length L of secret data $\mathbf{m}$, and the number u_y of published news by each friend F_y $(1 < y < N)$, which are discussed in the following.

The Choice of Parameter n. Since the length of secret data $\mathbf{m}$ is L, the coefficient matrix size of the linear equations for secret data recovery is $L \times L$. Theoretically, the total number K of the $L \times L$ coefficient matrices with full rank is:

$$K = \left(1 - 2^{-L}\right)\left(1 - 2^{-L+1}\right) \cdots \left(1 - 2^{-1}\right) \times 2^{L^2} \tag{7}$$

For example, when $L = 2$, the number K of the matrices is 6, and they are:

$$\begin{bmatrix} 1 & 0 \\ 0 & 1 \end{bmatrix}, \begin{bmatrix} 1 & 1 \\ 0 & 1 \end{bmatrix}, \begin{bmatrix} 1 & 0 \\ 1 & 1 \end{bmatrix}, \begin{bmatrix} 1 & 1 \\ 1 & 0 \end{bmatrix}, \begin{bmatrix} 0 & 1 \\ 1 & 0 \end{bmatrix}, \begin{bmatrix} 0 & 1 \\ 1 & 1 \end{bmatrix}$$

For the sender, in order to conduct secret sharing, n matrices $\mathbf{A}_x$ sized $L \times L/t$ should be are generated by using the secret key, and the square matrix composed with any t matrices $\mathbf{A}_x$ should be full rank. Subsequently, we discuss the value of n. (1) For the condition $t = 1$, it means that the size of each generated matrix $\mathbf{A}_x$ is $L \times L$. Thus, the number n of generated matrices $\mathbf{A}_x$ is equal to K. (2) For the condition $1 < t < L$, since the square matrix must have the situation of full rank, the number n of generated matrices $\mathbf{A}_x$ is thus greater than t. (3) For the condition $t = L$, the size of each generated matrix $\mathbf{A}_x$ is $L \times 1$, and the number n of generated matrices $\mathbf{A}_x$ is increased with L. When $L = 2$, the three matrices can be generated (i.e., $n = 3$) as

$$\begin{bmatrix} 1 \\ 1 \end{bmatrix}, \begin{bmatrix} 1 \\ 0 \end{bmatrix}, \begin{bmatrix} 0 \\ 1 \end{bmatrix},$$

and the square matrix composed with any 2 matrices is full rank. When $L = 3$, the five matrices can be generated (i.e., $n = 5$) as

$$\begin{bmatrix} 1 \\ 1 \\ 1 \end{bmatrix}, \begin{bmatrix} 1 \\ 1 \\ 0 \end{bmatrix}, \begin{bmatrix} 1 \\ 0 \\ 1 \end{bmatrix}, \begin{bmatrix} 0 \\ 1 \\ 1 \end{bmatrix}, \begin{bmatrix} 0 \\ 0 \\ 1 \end{bmatrix},$$

and the square matrix composed with any 3 matrices is full rank. When $L = 4$, the nine matrices can be generated (i.e., $n = 9$) as

$$\begin{bmatrix} 1 \\ 1 \\ 1 \\ 1 \end{bmatrix}, \begin{bmatrix} 1 \\ 1 \\ 1 \\ 0 \end{bmatrix}, \begin{bmatrix} 1 \\ 1 \\ 0 \\ 1 \end{bmatrix}, \begin{bmatrix} 1 \\ 0 \\ 1 \\ 1 \end{bmatrix}, \begin{bmatrix} 0 \\ 1 \\ 1 \\ 1 \end{bmatrix}, \begin{bmatrix} 0 \\ 0 \\ 1 \\ 1 \end{bmatrix}, \begin{bmatrix} 1 \\ 0 \\ 0 \\ 1 \end{bmatrix}, \begin{bmatrix} 1 \\ 1 \\ 0 \\ 0 \end{bmatrix}, \begin{bmatrix} 0 \\ 1 \\ 1 \\ 0 \end{bmatrix}$$

and the square matrix composed with any 4 matrices is full rank. When $L = 5$, the thirteen matrices can be generated (i.e., $n = 13$) as

$$\begin{bmatrix} 1 \\ 1 \\ 1 \\ 1 \\ 1 \end{bmatrix}, \begin{bmatrix} 1 \\ 1 \\ 1 \\ 1 \\ 0 \end{bmatrix}, \begin{bmatrix} 1 \\ 1 \\ 1 \\ 0 \\ 1 \end{bmatrix}, \begin{bmatrix} 1 \\ 1 \\ 0 \\ 1 \\ 1 \end{bmatrix}, \begin{bmatrix} 1 \\ 0 \\ 1 \\ 1 \\ 1 \end{bmatrix}, \begin{bmatrix} 0 \\ 1 \\ 1 \\ 1 \\ 1 \end{bmatrix}, \begin{bmatrix} 0 \\ 0 \\ 1 \\ 1 \\ 1 \end{bmatrix}, \begin{bmatrix} 1 \\ 0 \\ 0 \\ 1 \\ 1 \end{bmatrix}, \begin{bmatrix} 1 \\ 1 \\ 0 \\ 0 \\ 1 \end{bmatrix}, \begin{bmatrix} 1 \\ 1 \\ 1 \\ 0 \\ 0 \end{bmatrix}, \begin{bmatrix} 0 \\ 1 \\ 1 \\ 1 \\ 0 \end{bmatrix}, \begin{bmatrix} 0 \\ 1 \\ 0 \\ 1 \\ 1 \end{bmatrix}, \begin{bmatrix} 1 \\ 0 \\ 1 \\ 0 \\ 1 \end{bmatrix}$$

and the square matrix composed with any 5 matrices is full rank. We can thus conclude that, with the increase of L and t, the value of n increases.

In our scheme, in order to ensure the effectiveness, the number n of the generated matrices $\mathbf{A}_x$ should be greater than the number Y of common friends of the sender and the receiver. Thereby, in real application, according to the length L of secret bits and the number Y of common friends, we can choose the appropriate value of t to make the number n of the generated matrices $\mathbf{A}_x$ greater than Y.

The Choice of Parameter t. 1) First, the published news by each friend should be considered according to the security. The numbers of published news are sorted according to the descending resulting in P_s, where $P_s > P_{s+1}$ where $1 < s < n - 1$, the number of friend n should satisfy:

$$n \times P_n \geq L \tag{8}$$

In this case, the secret data can be all embedded in the sender's making "love" behavior. The threshold t can be calculated by:

$$t = \lfloor L/P_n \rfloor$$
$$L \bmod t = 0 \tag{9}$$

where P_n represents the minimum number of published news by all friends. Then, we can adjust L and t to satisfy Eq. (9). From Eq. (8), we observe that $t \leq L$. When $p_x = 1$, that is to say, the number of news published by F_x is 1, i.e., $L = t$. When $L = t$, the size of matrix $\mathbf{A}_x$ is $L \times 1$. When $p_x > 1$, that is to say, $L > t$, the size of matrix $\mathbf{A}_x$ is $L \times L/t$.

2) When $n \times P_n < L$, that is to say, $n \times P_n$ bits of secret data can be embedded into the first P_n published news of n friends. Hence, the following Eq. (10) can be drawn. When the product value of the minimum number of published news posted by a friend and the number of friends is greater than the length of the secret data, all the secret data can be decrypted. When the product of the minimum number of published news posted by friends and the number of friends is less than the length of the secret data, $n \times P_n$ bits of secret data can be decrypted:

$$l = \begin{cases} L & n \times P_n \geq L \\ n \times P_n & n \times P_n < L \end{cases} \tag{10}$$

Analysis of System Security. When the receiver has the encryption key, i.e., the matrix assigned to each friend, secret data can be decrypted. In the practical example, the length of secret data is L, all possibility of decrypted matrix without full rank is:

$$P_1 = \frac{1}{2^{L^2}} \tag{11}$$

All possibility of decrypted matrix with full rank is:

$$P_2 = \left(1 - 2^{-L}\right)\left(1 - 2^{-L+1}\right)\cdots\left(1 - 2^{-1}\right) \tag{12}$$

With L increasing, the probability P approaches 0. It indicates that without encryption key, the decryption probability of secret data is related to the length of secret data L. With the increase of the secret data, the probability approaches 0 gradually.

4 Experimental Results and Discussions

In this section, we discuss decryption performance under different circumstances. Suppose that the length of secret data is 100, the number of friends of sender and receiver is 10, the minimum published news is 25, and the relationship between N, P and L satisfies Eq. (7).

Table 1 shows different matrix sizes under different parameters when all secret data can be extracted. In this table, the threshold is set as 4, 5, 10, and the corresponding public news are 25, 20 and 10, respectively. That is to say, the receiver can select 4 friends randomly from 10 friends to extract the secret data from their first 25 published news, select 5 friends from 10 friends randomly to extract the secret data from their first 20 published news, and select 10 friends to extract the secret data from their first 10 published news, respectively. Therefore, when the product value of the number of common friends and the minimum number of published news posted by friends is greater than the length of the secret data, different thresholds t can be set according to the actual situation, and all secret data can be embedded.

In Table 2, for the case $P \times n < L$, secret data are embedded in the first P published news of each friends. In the receiver side, secret data can be extracted from each friend. If the number of common friends is 10, it can be seen from Table 2 that the secret data is extracted from the first 8 published news of the 10 friends. At this time, the length of the secret data extracted is 80 bits. The secret data is extracted from the first 7 published news of 10 friends, and the length of the finally extracted secret data is 70 bits. The secret data is extracted from the first 6 published news of 10 friends, and the length of the finally extracted secret data is 60 bits. According to Sect. 3.3, the algorithm is feasible and effective.

Table 3 provides the comparison between the proposed scheme and Zhang's scheme. As can be seen from the table, for Zhang's scheme, only when N_D is greater than L, the probability of secret decryption approaches 1. Obviously, this mechanism may produce two problems. (1) If the number of published news is small, that is, N_D is much smaller than L, no secret data can be extracted. (2) In the steganography phase, if one published

Table 1. Matrix sizes under different parameters when all secret data can be extracted.

L	n	P_x(min)	P	t	$L \times L/t$
100	10	25	25	4	100×25
			20	5	100×20
			10	10	100×10

Table 2. Matrix sizes under different parameters when partial secret data can be extracted.

L	n	P_x(min)	P	t	$L \times L/t$
100	10	8	8	10	80×8
		7	7	10	70×7
		6	6	10	60×6

news is deleted or the published news is not visible to the receiver, the secret data cannot be decrypted correctly. Different from Zhang's method [7], the proposed scheme adopts secret sharing to design behavior steganography. In our scheme, when $n \times P_n \geq L$, secret data can be embedded with different thresholds, while $n \times P_n < L$, $n \times P_n$ bits can be embedded. Correspondingly, since the secret sharing mechanism is adopted, even if some published news are deleted or invisible to the receiver, secret data can also be decrypted by other L published news of other friends. Therefore, according to the above analysis, the proposed method has better performance than traditional social network behavior information hiding algorithm.

Table 3. Comparisons between Zhang's scheme [7] and our scheme.

Schemes	Zhang's scheme [7]	Proposed scheme
Embedding rate	1 bit per published news	1 bit per published news
Probability of decryption	$P = $ $\left(1 - 2^{-N_D}\right)\left(1 - 2^{-N_D+1}\right) \cdots$ $\left(1 - 2^{-N_D+L-1}\right)$	1
The number of published news	$N_D \gg L$	N_D

5 Conclusions

In this work, we propose an efficient method for behavior information hiding based on the social network. Secret sharing mechanism based on matrix operation is adopted in our steganographic scheme, and different threshold is set according to the published news. Proposed steganographic scheme can convert the secret data into "love" marks in social network, e.g., WeChat. Accordingly, the receiver makes "love" mark on the published news of his friends and the love "marking" rate assigned to each friend ensure the convert communication confidential. Since the secret sharing mechanism adds some data redundancy in original secret data, for the receiver, it can thus extract secret message correctly from the 'love' mark, even if part of "love" marks are lost. Compared with Zhang's method, our scheme has better performance. When the published news number is small, part of the secret data can be recovered, and the Zhang's method can recover the secret data only when the published news number is greater than the length of the secret data. Even if some published news are deleted or invisible to the receiver, secret data can also be extracted correctly. In future work, we will try to improve the embedding capacity in a given limited news.

Acknowledgement. This work was supported by the Natural Science Foundation of China (U20B2051), the Shanghai Science and Technology Committee Capability Construction Project for Shanghai Municipal Universities (20060502300), the Natural Science Foundation of Shanghai (21ZR1444600, 20ZR1421600) and the Research Fund of Guangxi Key Lab of Multi-source Information Mining & Security (MIMS21-M-02).

References

1. Fridrich, J.: Steganography in Digital Media: Principles, Algorithms and Applications. Cambridge University Press, Cambridge (2010)
2. Li, B., Wang, M., Li, X., Tan, S., Huang, J.: A strategy of clustering modification directions in spatial image steganography. IEEE Trans. Inf. Forensics Secur. **10**(9), 1905–1917 (2015)
3. Shi, Y.Q., Li, X.L., Zhang, X.P., Wu, H.T., Ma, B.: Reversible data hiding: advances in the past two decades. IEEE Access **4**, 3210–3237 (2016)
4. Li, X.L., Zhang, W.M., Gui, X.L., Yang, B.: Efficient reversible data hiding based on multiple histograms modification. IEEE Trans. Inf. Forensics Secur. **10**(9), 2016–2027 (2015)
5. Qin, C., Zhang, W., Cao, F., Zhang, X.P., Chang, C.C.: Separable reversible data hiding in encrypted images via adaptive embedding strategy with block selection. Sig. Process. **153**, 109–122 (2018)
6. Yi, S., Zhou, Y.C.: Separable and reversible data hiding in encrypted images using parametric binary tree labeling. IEEE Trans. Multimedia **21**(1), 51–64 (2019)
7. Zhang, X.: Behavior steganography in social network. In: Proceedings of the 12th International Conference on Intelligent Information Hiding and Multimedia Signal Processing (IIH-MSP), pp. 21–23 (2017)
8. Shamir, A.: How to share a secret. Commun. ACM **22**(11), 612–613 (1979)
9. Thien, C.C., Lin, J.C.: Secret image sharing. Comput. Graph. **26**(5), 765–770 (2002)
10. Karnin, E., Greene, J., Hellman, M.: On secret sharing systems. IEEE Trans. Inf. Theor. **29**(1), 35–41 (1983)
11. Jin, X., Su, L., Huang, J.: A reversible data hiding algorithm based on secret sharing. J. Inf. Hiding Priv. Prot. **3**(2), 69–82 (2021)
12. Liu, J., Zhang, R., Li, J., Guan, L., Jie, C.: A reversible data hiding algorithm based on image camouflage and bit-plane compression. Comput. Mater. Continua **68**(2), 2633–2649 (2021)

A Chaotic Image Encryption Algorithm Based on Sub-block Spiral Scans and Matrix Multiplication

Yongjin Xian[1], Xingyuan Wang[1(✉)], Xiaoyu Wang[1], Qi Li[1], and Bin Ma[2]

[1] Dalian Maritime University, Dalian 116026, China
xywang@dlmu.edu.cn
[2] Qilu University of Technology, Jinan 250353, China

Abstract. With the development of information technology, image secrecy technology has gradually received widespread attention. A chaotic image encryption scheme based on the mixture of sub-block spiral scans transform and matrix multiplication is proposed. Firstly, an increased sub-block segmentation spiral scanning method is presented, which enhances the effect of confusion during encryption. Secondly, a novel method of constructing the multiplying matrix of left and right has been utilized, which greatly reduces the encryption time while ensuring the encryption effect. Finally, the simulation and the analysis illustrate that the proposed algorithm has a greater cryptography effect and better key safety, while it can also effectively withstand exhaustive attacks, statistical attacks, and differential attacks.

Keywords: Chaos · Image encryption · Sub-block spiral scans transform · Matrix multiplication

1 Introduction

With the rapid development and popularization of information technology, human requirements for information security have gradually increased, and information security issues have also received widespread attention [1–4]. Due to the widespread use of images, it has become an urgent problem to be solved that how to make the image more secure [5–8]. Encryption is an effective technique to protect the image information [9]. Recently, many superior methods for image encryption have been proposed.

The method of transferring image pixels normally scrambles the pixel position by matrix transformation, thereby achieving the purpose of image encryption [10]. Since dynamic maps have an immediate sensitivity of value and have better properties unlike conventional cryptographic methods [11], numerous scholars have attempted to use chaotic maps for image encryption [12–15]. For instance, in [16], a new chaotic image encryption method with cyclic shift and sorting is proposed. And combined with chaos theory, many approaches have been presented for the encryption of images, such as analysis in frequency domains [17], substitution permutation network [18], combination chaotic system [19], randomly sampled noise signal [20], elementary cellular automata [21], DNA approach [22], and so on. For more security, the transform domain has been adopted in the encryption process [23–27]. After transforming the plaintext image into the transform domain, those elements are modified with designed rules then converted back to the spatial one. Under the guidance of this method, the permutation-substitution-diffusion network [24], theories of random fractional Fourier transforms [25], set partitioning in hierarchical trees [26], and nonlinear operations in cylindrical diffraction domain [27] are utilized in the chaotic image encryption algorithm to resist kinds of attacks.

With the study of the above literature, we find that most of the above methods based on chaotic maps may not be suitable for high-resolution images, as the chaotic window might appear when the chaotic sequence used for encryption is too long. At present, most scholars expand the chaotic interval that can be used for encryption by proposing or optimizing a new chaotic system. But for large resolution images, it is still not a good way to solve the problem. In this paper, a novel chaotic image encryption algorithm based on sub-block spiral scan transforms and matrix multiplication has been proposed to try to avoid the above problem. It is given that a sub-block spiral scan transformation to exchange all pixel positions, while the normal spiral scan would never achieve. In the process of scrambling and diffusion, it is designed that a method based on matrix left and right multiplication to further vary the pixels' positions and values for a better encryption effect.

The organization of this paper is as follows. In Sect. 2, the design of the proposed image encryption scheme is introduced in detail. The sub-block spiral scan transformation, and scrambling diffusion process via matrix left and right multiplication is provided. In Sect. 3, the simulation and security analysis of the proposed image cryptographic method are discussed. Eventually, the concluding remarks are set out.

2   Related Methods

2.1   Sub-block Spiral Scans Transformation

Spiral scans transformation is a scanning process that refers to scanning and rearranging elements from the center of the matrix. The spiral scans transformation is illustrated in Fig. 1, taking an 8 × 8 matrix as the example.

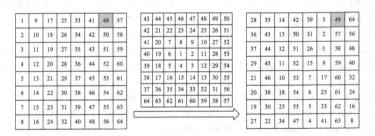

Fig. 1. 8 × 8 matrix Spiral scans transformation.

This paper presents a definition of advanced change based on spiral scans transformation in line with the idea of a transformation by spiral scans. Its order of scanning does not start from the center of the matrix but from the special position of the matrix, which can make every pixel of the image be changed by scan transformation. For comparison, an 8×8 matrix was taken as an example shown in Fig. 2. The pixel of position 49 in Fig. 1 had no change, while it was not expected in the processing of exchange, which was like the first and last pixels in the methods of Zigzag transformation. For better results, a block segmentation instrument was applied to make sure every pixel would be placed in a new location, as was illustrated in Fig. 2, the right matrix block of Fig. 1 was divided into 4×4 sub-block in which had 2×2 elements and rearranged by spiral scans transformation. The elements on the right side of Fig. 2 are completely changed from those on the left side of Fig. 1.

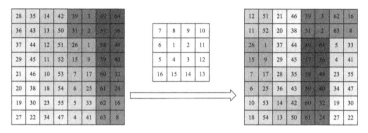

Fig. 2. 8×8 matrix block Spiral scans transformation process.

2.2 Chaotic System

This article took the logistic map of a chaotic one-dimensional structure and the following are the mathematical expressions:

$$x_{n+1} = \mu x_n (1 - x_n), \tag{1}$$

where, $x_n \in (0, 1)$, when the parameter $\mu \in (3.5699456, 4]$, the Logistic map reach the chaotic state. The resulting sequence x_n is disordered. The parameter within the scope $\mu \in (3.89, 4]$ is selected in this article, to avoid the periodic window.

2.3 Scrambling and Diffusion

Based on matrix multiplication, we obtained the new image matrix by using matrix left and right multiplication with two special random diagonal matrices to finish the processing encryption, respectively. The two special random diagonal matrices were determined by four chaotic random sequences, which were made up of Eq. (1) in this article. The left multiplying matrix was combined by the numerical values defined with one chaotic random sequence and the gradation with another, while the right one was combined by the other two. Elementary transformation of the matrix was applied in this method, to reduce huge calculations under the premise of ensuring that the rank of the image matrix is constant.

Furthermore, chaotic disturbance term diffusion was applied to obtain a better result of the ciphertext image as follows.

$$
\begin{cases}
T_i = \mathrm{mod}\left(\lfloor A^i \times 256 \rfloor,\ 256\right), \\
p'_1 = p_1 \oplus T_1, \\
p'_{i+1} = p_{i+1} \oplus p'_i \oplus T_{i+1}, \quad i = 2, 3, \cdots, N^*,
\end{cases}
\tag{2}
$$

where, A^i denotes the ith element of the chaotic sequence A, p_i denotes the grey value of the ith pixel in the image matrix p ordered by column preference, and p'_i denotes the grey value of the ith pixel of the diffused image p' obtained after chaotic diffusion. N^* denotes the number of pixel elements of the image matrix p.

2.4 Encryption Algorithm

The image in the proposed method is discussed with the rows of M and the columns of N. The encryption process of several main steps is established as follows:

Step 1. According to the sub-block spiral scans transformation, the plaintext image P was reorganized into P_1.

Step 2. With the initial value μ and x_1, an initial value was selected to produce 5 chaotic random sequences A_1, A_2, A_3, A_4 and A_5 in order after removing the first part sequence which had the length of T for randomness, where the length of A_1 and A_2 was M, the length of A_3 and A_4 was N and the length of A_5 was $M \times N$.

Step 3. L_{A_1} was defined as: $\lceil diag(A_1/mean(A_1)) \rceil$, where $diag(\cdot)$ is diagonal matrix transformation, $mean(\cdot)$ is mean function and $\lceil \cdot \rceil$ represents the rounding up function. Then the sequence A_2 was rearranged in ascending order and a transformation sequence S_{A_2} was obtained. L was obtained from L_{A_1} rearranging each row of L_{A_1} by S_{A_2}.

Step 4. Similarly to L_{A_1}, $R_{A_3} = \lceil diag(A_3/mean(A_3)) \rceil$. Then the sequence A_4 was rearranged in ascending order and a transformation sequence S_{A_2} was obtained. R was obtained from R_{A_3} rearranging each column of R_{A_3} by S_{A_2}.

Step 5. P_2 was owned after matrix formation as follows:

$$
P_2 \triangleq L \times P_1 \times R,
\tag{3}
$$

where L and R were obtained in Step 3 and Step 4, respectively.

Step 6. Let $P_3 = \lceil P_2 \rceil$, then $E = P_3 - P_2$, while E is taken as a decryption key.

Step 7. Ciphertext image matrix P_E was owned by the diffusion process with P_3 and A_5.

With the seven steps above, the ciphertext image was obtained, while the key sequence consists of μ, x_1, T and E. The inverse transformation can be used to complete its decryption project and the experimentally determined test.

When the algorithm proposed in this paper is applied to color images, three different channels of the grey-scale image are encrypted one by one, and the keys used in the encryption process for the three channels are independent of each other, from which they together form the key when encrypting the color image.

To better demonstrate the proposed encryption process, the flow chart of the proposed algorithm is shown in Fig. 3.

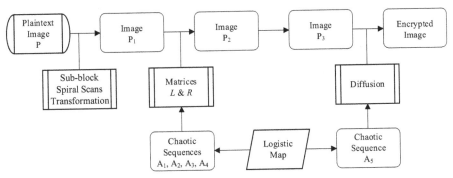

Fig. 3. Flow chart of the proposed encryption.

3 Results and Analysis

3.1 Simulation Result

Three grayscale images of Lena (256 × 256), Airplane (512 × 512), Baboon (1024 × 1024), and a color image of Peppers (512 × 512) were selected as the main plaintext images in this paper. The results of three grayscale image encryption were shown in Fig. 4. And the comparisons of encryption time with other algorithms are given in Table 1.

Table 1. Encryption time and comparisons (256 × 256 image).

Algorithm	Encryption time (s)
Proposed	0.5043
Ref. [28]	0.5554
Ref. [29]	1.6764
Ref. [30]	0.7124

3.2 Security Analysis

Key Analysis. The keyspace should be wide enough to effectively deal with numerous brute-force attacks. Although the number of keys in the keystream in our algorithm is short, the keyspace becomes extra huge due to the matrix row-column transformation and matrix multiplication, which highlights the superiority. In the proposed algorithm the key is $K = [\mu, x_1, T, E]$, where $\mu \in R$, $x_1 \in R$, $T \in R$ and $E \in R \times R$, so the keyspace is given as follows:

$$F(M, N) = 10^{14 \times (M \times N + 3)}, \tag{4}$$

where, the accuracy of the computer is 10^{-14}.

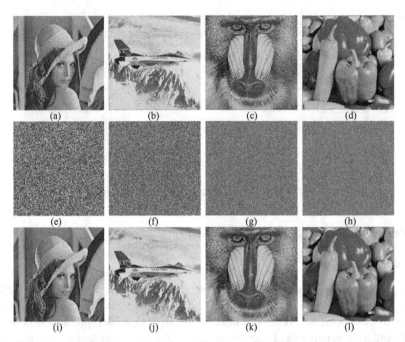

Fig. 4. Simulation results: (a) Lena (256 × 256), (b) Airplane (512 × 512), (c) Baboon (1024 × 1024), (d) Peppers (color, 512 × 512), (e) Ciphered Lena, (f) Ciphered Airplane, (g) Ciphered Baboon, (h) Ciphered Peppers, (i) Decrypted Lena, (j) Decrypted Airplane, (k) Decrypted Baboon, (l) Decrypted Peppers.

For the image with the pixel of 256 × 256, the keyspace is

$$F(256, 256) = 10^{14 \times (256 \times 256 + 3)} = 2^{\frac{14 \times 256 \times 256}{\log_{10} 2}} \times 10^{14 \times 3} > 2^{3,048,021}, \tag{5}$$

for the grayscale image with the pixel of 512 × 512, the keyspace is

$$F(512, 512) = 10^{3,670,058} > 2^{48,766,256}, \tag{6}$$

for the grayscale image with the pixel of 1024 × 1024, the keyspace is

$$F(1024, 1024) = 10^{14,680,106}, \tag{7}$$

for the color image with the pixel of 512 × 512, the keyspace is

$$(F(512, 512))^3 = 10^{3,670,058 \times 3} = 10^{11,010,174} > 2^{146,298,768}. \tag{8}$$

From Eq. (4), the size of the key is related to the size of the image, then the lower bound of the keyspace is a.

$$F(M, N) = 10^{14 \times (M \times N + 3)} \xrightarrow[M \to 0, N \to 0]{} 10^{14 \times 3}, \tag{9}$$

Obviously,

$$10^{14 \times 3} \approx 2^{139.5} > 2^{100}. \tag{10}$$

It can be seen that the lower bound on the keyspace of the proposed algorithm is greater than 2^{100}, which is large enough to ensure resistance to brute-force attacks.

Similarly, Table 2 offers a comparison of keyspaces. And we can get the conclusion that the keyspace is determined by the size of the image, which is almost close to the limits of computer representation while the required value is 2^{100} in the cryptosystem. So that brute-force attacks could be resisted by the proposed scheme.

Table 2. Keyspaces and comparison (512×512 image)

Algorithm	Keyspace
Proposed	$> 2^{48,766,256}$
Ref. [31]	$\approx 2^{300}$
Ref. [32]	$\approx 2^{446}$
Ref. [33]	$\approx 2^{520}$
Ref. [34]	$\approx 2^{256}$

Statistical Analysis. The results of histogram analysis, Chi-square test, adjacent pixel correlation, and information entropy are presented in this part. And there are outstanding statistical characteristics in the proposed algorithm.

Histogram Analysis. A significant metric used to evaluate the performance of a cipher system to resist attacks of statistical analysis is the histogram for the cryptographic image. Usually, some certain information of the image can be easily obtained, but the pixels are distributed evenly and statistical analysis attacks are extremely difficult to acquire intelligence when the histogram of the image is smooth. The flatter the histogram of a ciphertext image, the better the scheme. As presented in Fig. 5, the three pairs of histograms visually illustrate the security of this algorithm, and the histograms are more uniform after encryption. To make the results visible, we color the histograms of the RGB channels respectively shown as Fig. 5(g) and (h).

Chi-square Test. The chi-square test is used in this paper to obtain quantitative results, which can avoid visual spoofing.

The results of the chi-square test for the three encrypted images are given in Table 3, of which the histogram is given in Fig. 5. Both two experiment results confirm the truth that the proposed algorithm has a good ability to resist statistical attacks.

Adjacent Pixel Correlation. Correlation is a general criterion for evaluating the quantitative relationship between two adjacent pixels. A better encryption process method can counteract statistical analysis attacks, which occurred in an encrypted image with lower correlation.

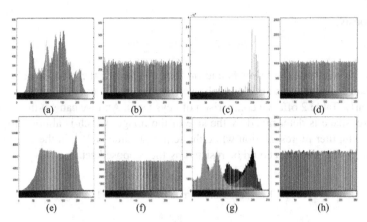

Fig. 5. Histogram: (a) Lena (256 × 256), (b) encrypted Lena, (c) Airplane (512 × 512), (d) encrypted Airplane, (e) Baboon (1024 × 1024), (f) encrypted Baboon, (g) Peppers (color, 512 × 512), (h) encrypted Peppers.

Table 3. Chi-square test.

Ciphertext image	P-value	H	Decision
Lena (256 × 256)	0.5043	0	Accept
Airplane (512 × 512)	0.6078	0	Accept
Baboon (1024 × 1024)	0.2802	0	Accept

In this paper, a plurality of pairs of adjacent pixels is arbitrarily chosen. And the correlation between the adjacent pixels of plaintext images and ciphertext images was calculated by Eqs. (11) and (12), while the results were shown in Fig. 6.

$$r_{xy} = \frac{\text{cov}(x, y)}{\sqrt{D(x)}\sqrt{D(y)}}, \qquad (11)$$

where

$$\begin{cases} \text{cov}(x, y) = \frac{1}{N^*} \sum_{i=1}^{N^*} (x_i - E(x))(y_i - E(y)) \\ D(x) = \frac{1}{N^*} \sum_{i+1}^{N^*} (x_i - E(x))^2 \\ E(x) = \frac{1}{N^*} \sum_{i=1}^{N^*} x_i \end{cases} \qquad (12)$$

x and y denote the set of pixels of two different images with the same number of elements in both sets, and N^* denotes the number of elements of set x.

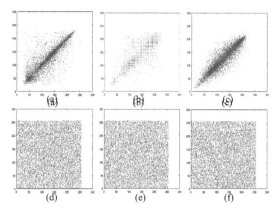

Fig. 6. Adjacent pixel correlation: (a) Lena (256 × 256), (b) Airplane (512 × 512), (c) Baboon (1024 × 1024), (d) encrypted Lena, (e) encrypted Airplane, (f) encrypted Baboon.

It could be seen that the plaintext image has a better correlation regardless of the direction. The proposed algorithm can be effective in Anti-statistical attacks, as the original image structure and features are traumatized, which greatly reduces the correlation after the action of the encryption scheme. The average correlation coefficients are listed in Table 4.

Table 4. Correlation between plain image and adjacent pixels of ciphertext image.

Direction	Lena		Airplane		Baboon		Peppers	
	Plaintext	Ciphertext	Plaintext	Ciphertext	Plaintext	Ciphertext	Plaintext	Ciphertext
Horizontal	0.9329	−0.0004	0.9668	0.0001	0.9677	−0.0011	0.9673	0.0001
Vertical	0.9650	0.0083	0.9600	0.0097	0.9401	0.0053	0.9684	0.0049
Diagonal	0.9066	0.0024	0.9392	0.0029	0.9168	0.0002	0.9623	0.00007

Information Entropy. Information entropy reflects the randomness of information. Its value can be calculated by Eq. (13):

$$H(s) = \sum_{i=0}^{2^L-1} p(s_i) \log_2 \frac{1}{p(s_i)}. \tag{13}$$

where $s = [s_i]_{2^L}$ and $p(s_i)$ represent the probability of s_i. In our experiment, $L = 8$, so $H(s, 8)=8$, which is the limit of the experiment results. In theory, the closer the information entropy is to 8, the less feasible it is to leak information.

The information entropies of the four test images before and after encryption are shown in Table 5. From the results in Table 5, after the encryption scheme proposed in this paper, the information entropies of the encrypted ciphertext images are limited to 8 on the left, which is very resistant to attacks.

Table 5. Information entropy.

Test image	Plaintext images	Ciphertext images
Lena (256 × 256)	7.4532	7.9973
Airplane (512 × 512)	5.1007	7.9993
Baboon (1024 × 1024)	7.4474	7.9998
Peppers (color, 512 × 512)	7.6698	7.9998

Resistance Differential Attack Analysis. A common aim is to define the ability of the image encryption device to withstand differential attacks through the number of changing pixel rate (NPCR) and unified averaged changed intensity (UACI). The NPCR and UACI are computed as follows:

$$D(i,j)=\begin{cases} 0, & \text{if } c_1(i,j) = c_2(i,j) \\ 1, & \text{if } c_1(i,j) \neq c_2(i,j) \end{cases}, \tag{14}$$

$$NPCR = \frac{\sum_{i,j} D(i,j)}{W \times H} \times 100, \tag{15}$$

$$UACI = \frac{1}{W \times H}\left[\sum_{i,j} \frac{|c_1(i,j) - c_2(i,j)|}{255}\right] \times 100, \tag{16}$$

where, $c_1(i,j)$ and $c_2(i,j)$ are the two values of the pixel (i,j) in the two images, respectively.

Table 6. NPCR and UACI values of ciphertext images with 100 random pixels.

Test image	NPCR (%)	UACI (%)
Lena (256 × 256)	99.6063	33.4395
Airplane (512 × 512)	99.5911	33.4523
Baboon (1024 × 1024)	99.6084	33.4448
Peppers (color, 512 × 512)	99.5949	33.4694

Table 6 displays the values of NPCR and UACI. The image cryptography system is tested to resist differential attacks.

Resistance to Cropping Attacks and Noise Attacks. To prevent the recipient from decrypting to achieve the goal, an attacker was used in the process of information transmission in the case of the fact that it could not decrypt encrypted text. The most popular two approaches were the cropping attack and noise attack.

After various levels of differential attack on the ciphertext image Lana was tested, it was the resistance effect illustrated in Figs. 7 and 8. In particular, it is shown that the results of the random cropping and regular cropping attacks and the decryption after the attacks are in Fig. 7. The findings indicate that the algorithm can counteract differential attacks.

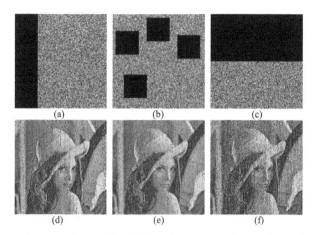

Fig. 7. Recovery after cropping attacks: (a) 1/4 degree vertical cropping of Fig. 4(b), (b) 1/4 degree vertical random cropping of Fig. 4(b), (c) 1/2 degree vertical cropping of Fig. 4(b), (d) Decrypted image of (a), (e) Decrypted image of (b), (f) Decrypted image of (c).

Fig. 8. Decryption results after salt and pepper noise: (a) strengths of 1%, (b) strengths of 5%, (c) strengths of 25%.

3.3 Comparison with Other Algorithms

The preceding section presents the test results of a set of indicators and essentially the average values are used to compare test indicators with other methods to compare the proposed algorithm. A comparison of the performance of the proposed encryption scheme with other image cryptosystems is described in Table 7. Compared to other algorithms, this comparison shows that our algorithm is successful in most respects. The new cryptosystem is therefore secure and effective.

Table 7. Comparisons with other methods.

Criteria		Ref. [35]	Ref. [36]	Ref. [37]	Ref. [38]	Proposed
Information entropy		7.9988	7.9976	7.9987	7.9967	7.9993
Correlation	Horizontal	−0.0016	0.0047	0.0018	−0.0020	−0.0003
	Vertical	0.0003	0.0118	0.0011	0.0010	0.0070
	Diagonal	0.0022	0.0021	0.0023	−0.0259	0.0014
NPCR		0.996093	0.9959	0.996083	0.9965	0.996002
UACI		0.334640	0.3349	0.334521	0.3332	0.334515

4 Conclusion

This paper proposes a kind of chaotic image encryption scheme based on the combination of sub-block spiral scans transform and matrix multiplication. Firstly, an improved sub-block segmentation spiral scanning method is presented, this method causes all pixel points to change their position. Secondly, a new method of constructing a multiplying matrix of left and right has been proposed, which greatly reduces the encryption time while ensuring the encryption effect. And based on this method, even in the large-resolution image encryption process, a very short chaotic sequence can satisfy the encryption requirements to greatly avoid the long sequence and the chaotic window, which makes the algorithm vulnerable to attack. Finally, the experimental analysis shows that the algorithm not only has a better encryption effect and higher sensitivity to keys; which effectively counteracts exhaustive attacks, statistical attacks, and differential attacks.

Acknowledgement. This work was supported by the National Natural Science Foundation of China under Grant 61672124 and 61701070, Liaoning Province Science and Technology Innovation Leading Talents Program Project under Grant XLYC1802013, Key R&D Projects of Liaoning Province under Grant 2019020105-JH2/103, Jinan City '20 universities' Funding Projects Introducing Innovation Team Program under Grant 2019GXRC031.

References

1. Wang, C.P., Wang, X.Y., Xia, Z.Q., Ma, B., Shi, Y.Q.: Image description with polar harmonic Fourier moments. IEEE Trans. Circ. Syst. Video Technol. **30**(12), 4440–4452 (2020)

2. Wang, C.P., Ma, B., Xia, Z.Q., Li, J., Li, Q., Shi, Y.Q.: Stereoscopic image description with Trinion Fractional-order continuous Orthogonal moments. IEEE Trans. Circ. Syst. Video Technol. (2021). https://doi.org/10.1109/TCSVT.2021.3094882

3. Li, X., Long, G., Li, S.: Encrypted medical records search with supporting of fuzzy multi-keyword and relevance ranking. In: Sun, X., Zhang, X., Xia, Z., Bertino, E. (eds.) ICAIS 2021. LNCS, vol. 12737, pp. 85–101. Springer, Cham (2021). https://doi.org/10.1007/978-3-030-78612-0_7

4. Duhayyim, M.A., Al-Wesabi, F.N., Marzouk, R., Hamza, M.A., Hilal, A.M., Eltahir, M.M.: Novel image encryption and compression scheme for IoT environment. Comput. Mater. Continua 71(1), 1443–1457 (2022)

5. Zheng, X., Cao, C., Deng, J.: DCDC-LSB: double cover dark channel least significant bit steganography. In: Sun, X., Zhang, X., Xia, Z., Bertino, E. (eds.) ICAIS 2021. LNCS, vol. 12737, pp. 360–375. Springer, Cham (2021). https://doi.org/10.1007/978-3-030-78612-0_29

6. Sanam, N., Ali, A., Shah, T., Farooq, G.: Non-associative algebra redesigning block cipher with color image encryption. Comput. Mater. Continua 67(1), 1–21 (2021)

7. Xia, Z.H., Wang, L., Tang, J., Xiong, N.N., Weng, J.: A privacy-preserving image retrieval scheme using secure local binary pattern in cloud computing. IEEE Trans. Netw. Sci. Eng. 8(1), 318–330 (2020)

8. Yuan, C.S., Xia, Z.H., Sun, X.M., Wu, Q.M.J.: Deep residual network with adaptive learning framework for fingerprint liveness detection. IEEE Trans. Cogn. Dev. Syst. 12(3), 461–473 (2019)

9. Zou, M.L., Liu, Z.X., Chen, X.Y.: A meaningful image encryption algorithm based on prediction error and wavelet transform. J. Big Data 1(3), 151–158 (2019)

10. Xian, Y.J., Wang, X.Y.: Fractal sorting matrix and its application on chaotic image encryption. Inf. Sci. 547, 1154–1169 (2021)

11. Wang, X.Y., Yang, J.J.: A privacy image encryption algorithm based on piecewise coupled map lattice with multi dynamic coupling coefficient. Inf. Sci. 569, 217–240 (2021)

12. Arab, A., Rostami, M.J., Ghavami, B.: An image encryption method based on chaos system and AES algorithm. J. Supercomput. 75(10), 6663–6682 (2019)

13. Wang, X., Gao, S.: Image encryption algorithm based on the matrix semi-tensor product with a compound secret key produced by a Boolean network. Inf. Sci. 539, 195–214 (2020)

14. Silva-García, V.M., Flores-Carapia, R., Rentería-Márquez, C., Luna-Benoso, B., Aldape-Pérez, M.: Substitution box generation using Chaos: an image encryption application. Appl. Math. Comput. 332, 123–135 (2018)

15. Wang, L.M., Dong, T.D., Ge, M.F.: Finite-time synchronization of memristor chaotic systems and its application in image encryption. Appl. Math. Comput. 347, 293–305 (2019)

16. Wang, X.Y., Feng, L., Zhao, H.Y.: Fast image encryption algorithm based on parallel computing system. Inf. Sci. 486, 340–358 (2019)

17. Abd Ellatif, A.A., Niu, X.M., Amin, M.: A new image cipher in time and frequency domains. Opt. Commun. 285(21–22), 4241–4251 (2012)

18. Belazi, A., Abd Ellatif, A.A., Belghith, S.: A novel image encryption scheme based on substitution-permutation network and chaos. Sig. Process. 128, 155–170 (2016)

19. Parvaz, R., Zarebnia, M.: A combination chaotic system and application in color image encryption. Opt. Laser Technol. 101, 30–41 (2018)

20. Liu, H.J., Kadir, A., Sun, X.B.: Chaos-based fast colour image encryption scheme with true random number keys from environmental noise. IET Image Proc. 11(5), 324–332 (2017)

21. Chai, X.L., Zheng, X.Y., Gan, Z.H., Han, D.J., Chen, Y.R.: An image encryption algorithm based on chaotic system and compressive sensing. Sig. Process. 148, 124–144 (2018)

22. Wu, J.H., Liao, X.F., Yang, B.: Image encryption using 2D Henon-Sine map and DNA approach. Sig. Process. 153, 11–23 (2018)

23. Singh, P., Yadav, A.K., Singh, K.: Phase image encryption in the fractional Hartley domain using Arnold transform and singular value decomposition. Opt. Lasers Eng. **91**, 187–195 (2017)

24. Belazi, A., Abd El-Latif, A.A., Diaconu, A.V., Rhouma, R., Belghith, S.: Chaos-based partial image encryption scheme based on linear fractional and lifting wavelet transforms. Opt. Lasers Eng. **88**, 37–50 (2017)

25. Annaby, M.H., Rushdi, M.A., Nehary, E.A.: Color image encryption using random transforms, phase retrieval, chaotic maps, and diffusion. Opt. Lasers Eng. **103**, 9–23 (2018)

26. Zhang, M., Tong, X.J.: Joint image encryption and compression scheme based on IWT and SPIHT. Opt. Lasers Eng. **90**, 254–274 (2017)

27. Wu, C., Wang, Y., Chen, Y., Wang, J., Wang, Q.H.: Asymmetric encryption of multiple-image based on compressed sensing and phase-truncation in cylindrical diffraction domain. Opt. Commun. **431**, 203–209 (2019)

28. Wang, X., et al.: S-box based image encryption application using a chaotic system without equilibrium. Appl. Sci. Basel **9**(4), 781 (2019)

29. Zhou, Y.C., Cao, W.J., Chen, C.L.P.: Image encryption using binary bitplane. Sig. Process. **100**, 197–207 (2014)

30. Wong, K.W., Kwok, S.H., Law, W.S.: A fast image encryption scheme based on chaotic standard map. Phys. Lett. A **372**(15), 2645–2652 (2008)

31. Xu, L., Gou, X., Li, Z., Li, J.: A novel chaotic image encryption algorithm using block scrambling and dynamic index based diffusion. Opt. Lasers Eng. **91**, 41–52 (2017)

32. Palacios-Luengas, L., Delgado-Gutiérrez, G., Díaz-Méndez, J.A., Vázquez-Medina, R.: Symmetric cryptosystem based on skew tent map. Multimedia Tools Appl. **77**(2), 2739–2770 (2017)

33. Souyah, A., Faraoun, K.M.: An image encryption scheme combining chaos-memory cellular automata and weighted histogram. Nonlinear Dyn. **86**(1), 639–653 (2016)

34. Hua, Z.Y., Jin, F., Xu, B.X., Huang, H.J.: 2D Logistic-Sine-coupling map for image encryption. Sig. Process. **149**, 148–161 (2018)

35. Shahna, K.U., Mohamed, A.: A novel image encryption scheme using both pixel level and bit level permutation with chaotic map. Appl. Soft Comput. **90**, 106162 (2020)

36. Diaconu, A.V.: Circular inter–intra pixels bit-level permutation and chaos-based image encryption. Inf. Sci. **355**, 314–327 (2016)

37. Cao, C., Sun, K.H., Liu, W.H.: A novel bit-level image encryption algorithm based on 2D-LICM hyperchaotic map. Sig. Process. **143**, 122–133 (2018)

38. Li, J.F., Xiang, S.Y., Wang, H.N., Gong, J.K., Wen, A.J.: A novel image encryption algorithm based on synchronized random bit generated in cascade-coupled chaotic semiconductor ring lasers. Opt. Lasers Eng. **102**, 170–180 (2018)

Robust Video Watermarking Using Normalized Zernike Moments

Shiyi Chen[1], Yi Chen[2], Yanli Chen[3], Limengnan Zhou[4], and Hanzhou Wu[1](✉)

[1] School of Communication and Information Engineering, Shanghai University,
Shanghai 200444, China
h.wu.phd@ieee.org
[2] School of Information Science and Technology, Southwest Jiaotong University,
Chengdu 610031, China
[3] School of Big Data and Computer Science, Guizhou Normal University,
Guiyang 550001, China
[4] School of Electronic and Information Engineering, University of Electronic Science
and Technology of China, Zhongshan Institute, Zhongshan 528402, China

Abstract. Digital video watermarking has become a hot research topic in recent years due to the increasing demand of protecting the intellectual property of video data. Even though many conventional video watermarking methods have been reported in past years, few of them are resistant to high-intensity geometric attacks, which motivates the authors in this paper to propose a video watermarking technique that is robust against high-intensity geometric distortion. To this purpose, the proposed method embeds the watermark information into the normalized Zernike moments of the target frames of the cover video sequence. The advantage is that the normalized Zernike moment preserves a strong invariance to geometric distortions such as rotation and scaling attacks. During data embedding, secret bits are embedded into adaptively selected moments with slight modifications to provide good robustness while maintaining the imperceptibility. The chrominance channel of the video data rather than the luminance one is used in our algorithm, as distortion in the former channel is less sensitive to the human visual system. Experimental results show that, compared with the existing scheme, the PSNR values of the proposed method gain about 7 dB averagely, meaning that the proposed method achieves high imperceptibility. Moreover, it is demonstrated that the proposed method is more robust against geometric distortions such as rotation and upscaling, which has verified the applicability and superiority of the proposed work.

Keywords: Video watermarking · Robust · Zernike moments · Information hiding · Copyright protection · Multimedia security

1 Introduction

Video watermarking is a technique for protecting digital video data from piracy. As illegal distribution of copyrighted digital video is ever-growing, video watermarking attracts an increasing amount of attention within the information security community. Over the last decade, various watermarking techniques have been introduced for copyright protection and data authentication. Based on the domain where the watermark information is embedded, this technique can be divided into three main classes: compressed, spatial and transform domain [1].

Among the above-mentioned three categories, transform domain algorithm is widely used due to its effectiveness in maintaining robustness against various attacks. The most commonly used transforms are singular value decomposition (SVD), discrete Fourier transform (DFT), discrete Cosine transform (DCT), discrete wavelet transform (DWT) and dual-tree complex wavelet transform (DT CWT) [1]. In [2], Huan et al.. Introduce an algorithm applying SVD on the DT CWT domain. In [3], Bhaskar et al.. Proposed a robust video watermarking scheme with squirrel search algorithm. For lack of a strong rotational invariance proved by mathematical principles, these methods are not robust to rotation attacks with a large angle, while this property is possessed by Zernike moment. In the image watermarking field, methods based on Zernike moment has been widely used, for example, in [4–6]. In [7], the author proposed a video watermarking algorithm based on Zernike moment. However, this algorithm only resists against rotation attacks rather than scaling attacks. Therefore, although contributions expended by predecessors have exceeded the development of robust watermarking techniques, problems like resistance to geometric attacks are still challenging in the video watermarking community and need further research.

In this paper, we propose a robust video watermarking algorithm based on normalized Zernike moments to resist against geometric distortions. Since different video compression algorithms are used on the Internet, the proposed algorithm is designed in the uncompressed domain for suiting any video compression standard. Because of the geometric-invariant property proved by mathematical principles, normalized Zernike moments are employed in our method as invariant features. For watermark embedding and extraction, Dither Modulation-Quantization Index Modulation (DM-QIM) is employed in the algorithm by using dither vectors and modulating the Zernike moments into different clusters to make an adequate trade-off between robustness and distortion [8]. To achieve high visual quality, we embed the watermark information into the U channel of the cover video sequence because distortion in luminance is more noticeable than that in chrominance as for human visual system [9]. The experimental results show that our approach maintains good visual quality and achieves great robustness to geometric attacks with high intensity comparing to the prior work.

The remainder of this paper is organized as follows. The preliminary knowledge related to the scheme is discussed in Sect. 2. In Sect. 3, we introduce the proposed video watermarking approach in detail. While in Sect. 4, experiments for imperceptibility and robustness evaluation of the proposed scheme is conducted. Finally, conclusions and future work are drawn in Sect. 5.

2   Preliminaries

In this section, we describe the preliminary knowledge of the proposed algorithm, which can be separated into four parts. In each part, we demonstrate the main contents and explain the reason why we use them.

2.1   Geometric Attacks

When watermarked videos are available online, some kinds of content-preserving attacks may be applied, which inevitably reduce the energy of the watermark inside the transmitted videos [6]. Among all these distortions, geometric attack is a relatively challenging one, since a slight geometric deformation often fails the watermark detection. In this paper, for practical applications, we mainly discuss the most common geometric attacks: rotation and scaling attacks.

Geometric attack is defined by a set of parameters that determines the operation performed over the target document, for example, scaling attack can be characterized by applying a scaling ratio to the sampling grid, and a similar conclusion can be given to rotation attacks. These common geometric attacks will cause two typical distortions in the document. One is the shifting of pixels in the spatial plane. The other is alteration of the pixel values due to interpolation [10]. Hence withstanding an arbitrary displacement of all or some of its pixels by a random amount is the main concern for resistance to geometric deformations.

2.2   Zernike Moments

In our method, we use normalized Zernike moments for data embedding due to its geometric invariance proved by mathematical principles, which is a modification of Zernike moments. Therefore, we first introduce Zernike moments in this part.

Zernike moments are orthogonal moments based on Zernike polynomial, which is a complete orthogonal set over the interior of the unit circle [11]. The set of these polynomials can be denoted in the following equation:

$$V_{nm}(x,y) = R_{nm}(\rho)e^{jm\theta} \tag{1}$$

where x, y denote the pixel position, $\rho = \sqrt{x^2 + y^2}$, and $\theta = tan^{-1}(y/x)$. n is a non-negative integer which represents the order and m is the repetition designed to satisfy the fact that $n - |m|$ is both non-negative and even. $R_{nm}(\rho)$ are radial Zernike polynomials, which are given by the equation below:

$$R_{nm}(\rho) = \sum_{s=0}^{n-|m|/2} \frac{(-1)^s \left[(n-s)!\right] \rho^{n-2s}}{s! \left(\frac{n+|m|}{2} - s\right)! \left(\frac{n-|m|}{2} - s\right)!} \tag{2}$$

After computing Zernike polynomials in Eq. (1), we can get the Zernike moments of order n with repetition m for a continuous image function:

$$A_{nm} = \frac{n+1}{\pi} \int \int_{x^2+y^2 \le 1} f(x,y)V_{nm}^*(\rho, \theta)dxdy \tag{3}$$

where V_{nm} represents the Zernike polynomial, and $*$ denotes complex conjugate.

For digital signal, the integrals are replaced by summations. Since the Zernike polynomial is a set over the interior of the unit circle, where each frame is reconstructed. By utilizing the properties of the Zernike polynomial set discussed above, frame image $f(x, y)$ can be reconstructed to $\hat{f}(x, y)$ in Eq. (4).

$$\hat{f}(x, y) = \sum_{n=0}^{N} \sum_{m} A_{nm} V_{nm}(\rho, \theta) \tag{4}$$

where A_{nm} represents the Zernike moments of order n with repetition m. A larger N results in a reconstruction result with more accuracy.

2.3   Invariant Properties of Normalized Zernike Moment

Based on the mathematical definition of Zernike moment, the amplitude of which can be used as a rotation-invariant feature. By utilizing the normalization technique, the normalized Zernike moments are invariant to both rotation and scaling attacks. The certification process is addressed in detail as follows.

Rotation Invariance. From Eq. (3), A_{nm} can be simplified as $A_{nm} = |A_{nm}| e^{jm\theta}$. After rotating each frame image clockwise by angle α, the relationship between the original and rotated frames in the same polar coordinate becomes

$$A'_{nm} = A_{nm} e^{-jm\alpha} \tag{5}$$

which means after rotation, the amplitude of the Zernike moment remains the same. As a result, it can be used as a rotation-invariant feature of each frame.

Scaling Invariance. After scaling the size of an image, the nonlinear interpolation will convert the content of the unit circle from the original one, which means that Zernike moments are not robust to scaling deformations.

$$m_{pq} = \sum_{x=0}^{M-1} \sum_{y=0}^{N-1} x^p y^q f(x, y) \tag{6}$$

To achieve scaling invariance, we can normalize each frame as shown in [12] before computing the Zernike moments. The normalization phase of which is concluded in a detailed way by the following four steps:

Step 1) Center the image by transforming $f(x, y)$ to $f_1(x, y) = f(x - \bar{x}, y - \bar{y})$. $(\bar{x}, \bar{y})$ is the centroid of $f(x, y)$, which can be calculated below.

$$\bar{x} = \frac{m_{10}}{m_{00}}, \bar{y} = \frac{m_{01}}{m_{00}} \tag{7}$$

where m_{10}, m_{01} and m_{00} are the moments of $f(x, y)$ as defined in Eq. (6).

Step 2) Apply a shearing transform from $f_1(x, y)$ to $f_2(x, y)$ in the x direction using Eq. (8) with $A_x = \begin{pmatrix} 1 & \beta \\ 0 & 1 \end{pmatrix}$ making sure that the μ_{30} of the resulting image is zero, which stands for central moments and is described in Eq. (9).

$$g(x, y) = A \cdot f(x, y) \tag{8}$$

Step 3) Apply a shearing transform from $f_2(x, y)$ to $f_3(x, y)$ in the y direction with $A_y = \begin{pmatrix} 1 & 0 \\ \gamma & 1 \end{pmatrix}$ so that the μ_{11} of the resulting frame reaches zero.

$$\mu_{pq} = \sum_{x=0}^{M-1} \sum_{y=0}^{N-1} (x - \bar{x})^p (y - \bar{y})^q f(x, y) \tag{9}$$

Step 4) Scale $f_3(x, y)$ in both x and y directions with $A_s = \begin{pmatrix} \alpha & 0 \\ 0 & \delta \end{pmatrix}$ to a prescribed standard size and achieve $\mu_{50} > 0$ and $\mu_{05} > 0$ from the outcome.

In [12], it is proved that image and its affine transforms have the same normalized image. Consequently, when it is employed in video algorithms, the same conclusion can be drawn. As a result, after normalization, the amplitude of the Zernike moments stays invariant to both rotation and scaling attacks.

2.4   Quantization Index Modulation

Quantization Index Modulation (QIM) [8] is an embedding operation used for information hiding, which preserves provably better rate distortion-robustness trade-offs than spread-spectrum and low-bit(s) modulation methods. In this paper, we use the modification of QIM: Dither Modulation (DM)-QIM algorithm. In this subsection, we introduce the basic theory of DM-QIM as follows:

Embedding Procedure. Suppose $f(n, m)$ is an image, where $n \in [1, N], m \in [1, M]$ and $W(k), k \in [1, N \times M]$, which is used as watermark. Let $d(k)$ be an array of uniformly distributed pseudo-random integers chosen within $[-\Delta/2, \Delta/2]$, which is generated according to a secret key. Dither vectors $d_0(k)$ and $d_1(k)$ are used for embedding the '0' and '1' bits of the watermark respectively. For simplicity, we combine the two vectors into $d_{W(k)}(k)$.

$$d_0(k) = d(k) \tag{10}$$

$$d_1(k) = d_0(k) - sign(d_0(k)) \times \frac{\Delta}{2} \tag{11}$$

where $f^w(n, m)$ denotes the watermarked image and Δ represents the quantization step, which is the most important parameter of QIM. The watermark embedding operation is performed below in Eq. (12).

$$f^w(n, m) = Q(f(n, m) + d_{W(k)}(k), \Delta) - d_{W(k)}(k) \tag{12}$$

where $Q(x, y)$ is defined below, and $round(x)$ returns the nearest integer of x.

$$Q(x, \Delta) = \Delta \times round(\frac{x}{\Delta}) \qquad (13)$$

Extraction Procedure. To extract the watermark data, we put the watermark bits '0' and '1' into (8) using the watermarked frame as an input instead of the original one, and then estimate the errors between the watermarked image and the results obtained above. By comparing the two errors, the one with the lower value represents the watermark bit. The extraction procedure is concluded below.

$$g^{W(k)}(n, m) = Q(\tilde{f}^w(n, m) + d_{W(k)}(k), \Delta) - d_{W(k)}(k) \qquad (14)$$

$$\tilde{W}(k) = argmin_{p \in [0,1]} \left| \tilde{f}^w(n, m) - g^p(n, m) \right| \qquad (15)$$

where $\tilde{f}^w(n, m)$ denotes the frame we received, and $g^{W(k)}(n, m)$ is used to calculate the watermark value in Eq. (15). $d_{W(k)}(k)$ is a dither vector used for embedding the watermark bit, Δ represents the quantization step, and both of them should be the same as the embedding procedure. $argmin(x)$ means the independent variable that minimizes the value of x.

3 Proposed Method

In this section, we introduce the proposed video watermarking algorithm in terms of embedding and extraction, which is demonstrated below separately.

3.1 Watermark Embedding

The watermark embedding procedure is demonstrated in Fig. 1, and some of the steps in the block diagram is explained in the following subsections.

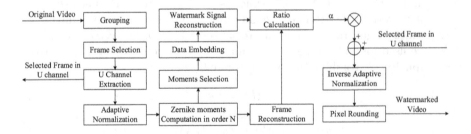

Fig. 1. Proposed robust watermarking framework

U Channel Extraction. In YUV format, Y represents the luminance channel and U, V are the two independent chrominance channels. As distortion in the chrominance channel is less sensitive to the human visual system than the luminance one [9], we extract the U channel in a YUV represented video for watermark embedding to enhance imperceptibility in the proposed method.

The following equation shows how to generate YUV signals from RGB sources:

$$\begin{bmatrix} Y \\ U \\ V \end{bmatrix} = \begin{bmatrix} 0 \\ 127 \\ 127 \end{bmatrix} + \begin{bmatrix} 0.2989 & 0.5866 & 0.1145 \\ -0.1688 & -0.3312 & 0.5000 \\ 0.5000 & -0.4184 & -0.0816 \end{bmatrix} \begin{bmatrix} R \\ G \\ B \end{bmatrix} \tag{16}$$

Adaptive Normalization. The adaptive normalization is almost identical as the procedure described in Sect. 2.3, except for step (4). After experiments, it is found that if videos in low resolution are normalized to a size much larger than the original one, more distortions will be produced.

To deal with this issue, the standard size $M \times M$ mentioned in Sect. 2.3, step (4) is set adaptively based on the video size. For example, if the U channel of the input video sequence is in a resolution of 176×144. Empirically, M can be set as 256 for higher accuracy. For different requests, M is open for adjusting.

Moments Selection. In [13], it is said that Zernike moments with repetition m = 4j, j integer, will deviate from orthogonality, meaning these moments cannot be computed accurately. In [14], $|A_{00}|$ and $|A_{11}|$ are independent of image, for that reason, they are not appropriate for watermark embedding. Given that conclusions can be drawn from Eq. (3) that $|A_{n,m}| = |A_{n,-m}|$, where $|x|$ denotes the amplitude, we can dismiss the latter ones so as to eliminate the embedding modifications. From what has been discussed above, we remove these moments to maximize the applicability and superiority of our algorithm.

Data Embedding. After selection, we embed watermark data into the amplitude of all these selected moments using DM-QIM, which has already been extensively discussed in Sect. 2.3. In this paper, watermark data for each target frame contains 1 bit, this embedding operation can be described below.

$$\left| A_{n,m}^w \right| = Q(|A_{n,m}| + d_w, \Delta) - d_w \tag{17}$$

where the superscript w indicates that it is the value after embedding. $Q(x,y)$ is a quantizer defined in Eq. (13), and $w = 0, 1$ represents the watermark bit. Δ is a quantization step, which is set based on the value of $|A_{n,m}|$, and $d_w \in [-\Delta/2, \Delta/2]$ is dither vector used for embedding watermark bit w.

Watermark Signal Reconstruction. The watermark signal $I_w(x, y)$ is reconstructed using Eq. (4) and multiplied with a coefficient based on the amplitude of both the original and the watermarked moment, which is demonstrated below.

$$I_w(x, y) = \sum_n^{N_{max}} \sum_m (\frac{|A_{nm}^w|}{|A_{nm}|} - 1) \times A_{nm} V_{nm}(\rho, \theta) \tag{18}$$

where x, y denote the pixel position, and A_{nm} represents the Zernike moment in order n and repetition m, while the one with a superscript w indicates that it is the value after embedding the watermark. $V_{nm}(\rho, \theta)$ denotes the Zernike polymonial, with $\rho = \sqrt{x^2 + y^2}$, and $\theta = tan^{-1}(y/x)$.

Finally, the watermark signal is added to the target frame with a coefficient α designed for controlling the embedding strength of the watermark and ensures the imperceptibility. We calculate the value of α with the following equation.

$$\alpha = \frac{\Theta I(x, y)}{\Theta I_r(x, y)} \tag{19}$$

where $x^2 + y^2 \leq 1$ and $\Theta(x)$ returns the mean value of x. $I(x, y)$ is the original frame image where all the data is in the unit circle. I_r is demonstrated in Eq. (20), which represents the reconstructed frame of the original one without selecting the appropriate moments for watermark embedding.

$$I_r(x, y) = \sum_{n}^{N_{max}} \sum_{m} A_{nm} V_{nm}(\rho, \theta) \tag{20}$$

In order to ensure visual quality, we choose to add the reconstruction to the original frame instead of replacement, since it is limited in the unit circle and the reconstruction effect is far from satisfactory even with a high order. This conclusion is verified in Fig. 2, which takes a 256 × 256 image of 'Lena' as an example to illustrate the reconstruction results with different orders. Furthermore, the reconstruction phase is rather time-consuming, for instance, when order is 30, it takes over 10 s to reconstruct only one image. So it is not a brilliant choice to replace the watermarked signal with the original one for data embedding.

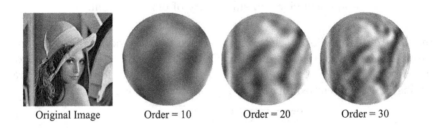

Original Image   Order = 10   Order = 20   Order = 30

Fig. 2. Reconstruction of 'Lena' with different orders

To sum up, the embedding procedure can be concluded as follows:

Step 1) Divide the input video into groups and select the target frames.

Step 2) Perform adaptive normalization for calculating Zernike moments.

Step 3) Calculate the Zernike moments from the normalized frame and select the appropriate ones as invariant features for watermark embedding.

Step 4) Compute the amplitude of the selected moments and embed the same watermark bit into all of them, using DM-QIM to embed watermark bit.

Step 5) Reconstruct the watermarked moments as the watermark signal and add it to the original frame with a coefficient α defined in Eq. (19).

3.2 Watermark Extraction

In Fig. 3, the process of watermark extraction is introduced, which is similar to the embedding procedure. After computing the Zernike moments and selecting the appropriate ones of each frame, we extract the watermark bit from each moment using the extraction step in DM-QIM by Eq. (14) and (15).

Majority Vote. From all the watermark bits extracted from the selected moments in one frame, to dismiss the mutations, we choose the one with the highest frequency as the extracted watermark bit of each frame for more accuracy.

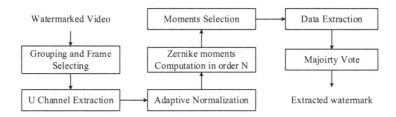

Fig. 3. Watermark extraction from Zernike Moments of the watermarked frame

The extraction procedure can be concluded in the following five steps:

Step 1) Divide the input video into groups and select the target frames.

Step 2) Perform adaptive normalization for calculating Zernike moments.

Step 3) Calculate the Zernike moments from the normalized frame and select the same moments used in watermark embedding procedure for extraction.

Step 4) Compute the amplitude of the selected moments and extract all the watermark bits using DM-QIM extraction method described in Sect. 2.4.

Step 5) Using Majority Vote to select the watermark bit with the highest frequency as the final extraction watermark bit for each target frame.

4 Experimental Results and Analysis

In this section, in order to evaluate the effectiveness of the proposed method, we conceive experiments to analyze the imperceptibility and robustness against geometric attacks by comparing our scheme with the existing approach [2].

4.1   Experimental Setup

All the experiments in this paper is implemented in the environment of Matlab R2016a on a PC with 8 GB RAM and 2.3 GHz Intel Core i5 CPU, running on 64-bit Windows 10. To evaluate our method fairly, we selected six standard video sequences in CIF format (352 × 288), i.e., *Akiyo, Foreman, Hall, Mother and Daughter, Paris* and *Silent* [15], and each testing video contains 300 frames.

For simulation, we normalize the frame image of each video in U channel to 256 × 256 and set the GOP (Group of Picture) length as 6, while the watermark length is 50, which is generated pseudo-randomly using a key, so that each GOP carries one watermark bit. After preliminary experiment in Sect. 4.2, we set the step length Δ to 30000, with $d_0 = 0$, $d_1 = 15000$. For simplicity, we embed each watermark bit into the first frame of one GOP, which represents the index frame. For fair comparison, the GOP in prior work [2] is also set to 6. The embedding strength T in [2] is set by 400 as the recommended value.

4.2   Parameter Setting

In this section, we conduct an experiment to find the optimal setting of Δ, which is the most important parameter in our scheme. To evaluate the accuracy of the extracted watermark, Normalized Cross Correlation (NCC) is exploited as a standard, which is demonstrated below by Eq. (21).

$$NCC(X,Y) = \frac{Cov(X,Y)}{\sqrt{Var(X) \cdot Var(Y)}} \tag{21}$$

where $Cov(X,Y)$ denotes the covariance between image X and Y, $Var(X)$ means the variance of X. The value range of NCC is $[-1,1]$ where '1' means complete match and '−1' indicates that the two images are exactly the opposite.

To evaluate the performance of different quantization step values, we use the six standard test video sequences mentioned above in Sect. 4.1, and the other parameters remain unchanged. In Fig. 4, it can be seen that the NCC value of our proposed method changes with the increase of quantization step and a maximum NCC value is reached by setting Δ to 30000 and 40000. Since the accuracy of the extracted watermark increases with the NCC value, so both can be chosen as the best quantization step. In the following discussions, we set $\Delta = 30000$ for experiment unless specific statement is presented.

4.3   Imperceptibility

For practical application, watermark imperceptibility is a very important requirement of a digital video watermarking algorithm. In this subsection, we adopt the peek signal-to-noise ratio (PSNR) as the standard to measure the visual quality of the final watermarked video, which is demonstrated below.

$$PSNR = 10 \cdot log_{10} \frac{max^2}{E}, E = \frac{1}{m \cdot n} \sum_{i=1}^{m} \sum_{j=1}^{n} |I(i,j) - K(i,j)|^2 \tag{22}$$

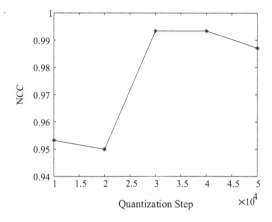

Fig. 4. NCC of the watermarked video for our scheme in different quantization steps

where $I(i,j)$ and $K(i,j)$ represent two different images, and $|x|$ represents the absolute value of x. m, n denotes the height and width of each frame, and max indicates the upper limit value of the pixel in each frame image.

The experimental results on the test video sequences are listed in Table 1. It can be concluded from the table that, the PSNR of watermarked videos in this paper are controlled around 37 dB, while the counterpart in [2] is 30 dB. Therefore, the PSNR values in our method gain about 7 dB averagely comparing to the prior work. Consequently, in terms of PSNR, our scheme outperforms the existing scheme [2] in imperceptibility, which results in better visual effects.

Table 1. PSNR of the proposed method and the existing work after watermarking

PSNR(dB)	Proposed method	Huan *et al.* [2]
Akiyo	38.9965	32.4720
Foreman	36.2325	30.1227
Hall	37.2345	29.4552
Mother and Daughter	37.1260	28.2724
Paris	36.5833	30.1578
Silent	36.9929	29.4093

4.4   Geometric Robustness

In this subsection, experiments are conducted to analyze the robustness of our method against geometric attacks. The experimental data in Table 2 is obtained by averaging the results of the aforementioned six standard test video sequences.

Table 2. NCC of the proposed method and the existing work after Scaling attack

NCC	Without attacks	Scaling 150%	Scaling 200%	Scaling 300%	Scaling 400%
Proposed	0.9934	0.9868	0.9934	0.9934	0.9870
Huan et al. [2]	0.9796	0.8560	0.9265	0.6935	0.6102

From Table 2, it can be observed that, before attacks, the accuracy in our method is 2% higher than that in approach [2]. After scaling attacks, the NCC value in our method relatively maintains the same value as the one without attacks. While in approach [2], the result decrease remarkably as the scaling factor increases from 200% to 300% and 300% to 400%. When the scaling factor reaches 400%, the NCC value in [2] is lower than our approach by 40%. As a result, the proposed method outperforms [2] notably in scaling attacks.

Table 3. NCC of the proposed method and the existing work after Rotation Attack

NCC	Rotate 30°	Rotate 60°	Rotate 90°	Rotate 120°
Proposed	0.9415	0.9356	0.9747	0.9287
Huan et al. [2]	0.6040	0.4746	0.4045	0.1540

In Table 3, the NCC of the proposed method and the existing work after rotation attack is given. It can be concluded that when the rotation angle increases, the NCC value in our method can be maintained, which is slightly lower than the one without any attack. While in [2], the NCC value drops significantly as the rotation angle rises, especially from 90° to 120°, which is lower than the value in our method from 60% to 80%. After the analysis above, our method performs remarkably better than [2] in robustness against rotation attacks.

From all the conclusions discussed above, our method outperforms [2] in both imperceptibility and geometric robustness against scaling and rotation. Therefore, we can jump to the conclusion that our method has a relatively good visual effect and a great robustness against geometric attacks.

5   Conclusion

In this paper, we propose a novel video watermarking scheme, which combines the benefits of both Zernike moments and normalization to resist against geometric distortions. Zernike moments are employed for its special invariant properties against rotation attacks. Normalization is used to normalize the target frame, so that the normalized Zernike moment is robust to both scaling and rotation attacks. After calculating the Zernike moments, we select some of the appropriate ones for watermark embedding according to certain principles to improve robustness and reduce modifications. With the heavy computation load and low accuracy for reconstructing Zernike moments, we use them to design watermark signal. The watermark embedded in each frame is obtained by taking the one with the highest frequency from all the candidate watermarks extracted from the amplitude of the selected Zernike moments to avoid errors. Based on the experimental results, our approach maintains good visual quality and achieves great robustness to rotation and scaling attacks comparing to the prior work.

In our method, it is shown that we apply a couple of forward and inverse normalizations, which produce inevitable distortions. To deal with this problem, it is necessary to design a new watermarking strategy to eliminate the loss. Meanwhile, as Zernike moment is computationally expensive, a watermark embedding algorithm with more efficiency needs to be explored. In future works, we will focus on the optimization for both preciseness and efficiency.

Acknowledgements. This work was partly supported by the National Natural Science Foundation of China (Grant Nos. 61901096, 62102112 and 61902235), and the Shanghai "Chen Guang" Program (Grant No. 19CG46).

References

1. Asikuzzaman, M., Pickering, M.: An overview of digital video watermarking. IEEE Trans. Circuits Syst. Video Technol. **28**(9), 2131–2153 (2018)
2. Huan, W., Li, S., Qian, Z., Zhang, X.: Exploring stable coefficients on joint sub-bands for robust video watermarking in DT CWT domain. IEEE Trans. Circ Syst. Video Technol. **32**(4), 1955–1965 (2021)
3. Bhaskar, A., Sharma, C., Mohiuddin, K., Singh, A., Nasr, O.A.: A robust video watermarking scheme with squirrel search algorithm. Comput. Mater. Continua **71**(2), 3069–3089 (2022)
4. Kim, H., Lee, H.: Invariant image watermark using Zernike moments. IEEE Trans. Circuits Syst. Video Technol. **13**(8), 766–775 (2003)
5. Xiong, L., Han, X., Yang, C., Shi, Y.: Robust reversible watermarking in encrypted image with secure multi-party based on lightweight cryptography. IEEE Trans. Circ. Syst. Video Technol. **32**(1), 75–91 (2021)
6. Hu, R., Xiang, S.: Cover-lossless robust image watermarking against geometric deformations. IEEE Trans. Image Process. **30**, 318–331 (2021)
7. Xu, G., Wang, R.: A blind video watermarking algorithm resisting to rotation attack. In: Proceeding of International Conference on Computer and Communications Security, pp. 111–114 (2009)
8. Chen, B., Wornell, G.W.: Quantization index modulation: a class of provably good methods for digital watermarking and information embedding. IEEE Trans. Inf. Theory **47**(4), 1423–1443 (2001)
9. Parraga, C.A., Brelstaff, G., Troscianko, T., Moorhead, I.R.: Color and luminance information in natural scenes. J. Opt. Soc. Am. A Opt. Image Sci. Vision. **15**(3), 563–569 (1998)
10. Xiang, S., Joong Kim, H., Huang, J.: Invariant image watermarking based on statistical features in the low-frequency domain. IEEE Trans. Circ. Syst. Video Technol. **18**(6), 777–790 (2008)
11. Khotanzad, A., Hong, Y.: Invariant image recognition by Zernike moments. IEEE Trans. Pattern Anal. Mach. Intell. **12**(5), 489–497 (1990)

12. Dong, P., Brankov, J., Galatsanos, N., Yang, Y., Davoine, F.: Digital watermarking robust to geometric distortions. IEEE Trans. Image Process. **14**(12), 2140–2150 (2005)
13. Xin, Y., Liao, S., Pawlak, M.: Geometrically robust image watermarking on a circular domain. Pattern Recogn. Lett. **40**(1), 3740–3752 (2007)
14. He, W., Sun, J., Yang, Z., Yang, D.: Video watermarking scheme based on normalization of pseudo-Zernike moment. In: Proceeding of International Conference on Measuring Technology and Mechatronics Automation, pp. 1080–1082 (2010)
15. Derf's Test Media Collection. https://media.xiph.org/video/derf/
16. Kamila, N., Mahapatra, S., Nanda, S.: RETRACTED: invariance image analysis using modified Zernike moments. Pattern Recogn. Lett. **26**(6), 747–753 (2005)
17. Asikuzzaman, M., Alam, M., Lambert, A., Pickering, M.: Imperceptible and robust blind video watermarking using chrominance embedding: a set of approaches in the DT CWT domain. IEEE Trans. Inf. Forensics Secur. **9**(9), 1502–1517 (2014)
18. Yuan, X., Pun, C.: Feature based video watermarking resistant to geometric distortions. In: Proceeding of IEEE International Conference on Trust, Security and Privacy in Computing and Communications, pp. 763–767 (2013)
19. Lin, C., Wu, M., Bloom, J., Cox, I., Miller, M., Lui, Y.: Rotation, scale, and translation resilient watermarking for images. IEEE Trans. Image Process. **10**(5), 767–782 (2001)
20. Zhao, Y., Wang, S., Zhang, X., Yao, H.: Robust hashing for image authentication using Zernike moments and local features. IEEE Trans. Inf. Forensics Secur. **8**(1), 55–63 (2013)
21. Zhou, X., Wang, L.: SoRS: an effective SVD-DWT watermarking algorithm with SVD on the revised singular value. In: Proceeding of IEEE International Conference on Software Engineering and Service Science, pp. 997–1002 (2014)
22. Keyvanpour, M.R., Khanbani, N., Boreiry, M.: A secure method in digital video watermarking with transform domain algorithms. Multimedia Tools Appli. **80**(13), 20449–20476 (2021). https://doi.org/10.1007/s11042-021-10730-5
23. Mareen, H., Praeter, J., Wallendael, G., Lambert, P.: A scalable architecture for uncompressed-domain watermarked videos. IEEE Trans. Inf. Forensics Secur. **14**(6), 1432–1444 (2018)
24. Chen, L., Zhao, J.: Informed histogram-based watermarking. Multimedia Tools Appli. **77**(6), 7187–7204 (2018)

An Improved Image Authentication Method Using QR Code Watermarking Approach

Xiaomei Liu[1], Bolin Zhang[1], Yuchen Wen[1], Xin Tang[1(✉)], and Haibo Su[2]

[1] School of Cyber Science and Engineering, University of International Relations, Beijing 100091, China
xtang@uir.edu.cn
[2] Personnel Division, University of International Relations, Beijing 100091, China

Abstract. Despite the progress in digital watermarking technology by optimizing the embedding method and enhancing the robustness of watermarking, the performance can still be improved using the Quick Response (QR) code technology. This paper proposes an improved QR code image watermarking approach by embedding texture-based QR code watermarking into the digital image. In contrast to the existing methods, an improved perceptual hash algorithm is used to extract image texture features, and therefore enhance the relevance of watermarking with image content, especially in light color images. In addition, the QR code method is combined with the reversible watermark algorithm in order to handle the problem that the original image is irreversibly modified. The experiments demonstrate that the proposed method can efficiently enhance the watermarking robustness, and resists common attacks.

Keywords: QR codes · Digital watermarking technology · Reversible data hiding · Image authentication

1 Introduction

Nowadays, the easy acquisition and tampering of digital images results in endless appearance of fake images, which greatly reduces the credibility of digital images [1–4]. Different from some information hiding techniques such as Linguistic steganography, etc., reversible digital watermarking technology is efficient in digital image protection [5–10]. However, with the continuous upgrade of the attack methods, higher requirements are put forward on the robustness of digital watermarks and the watermark relevance of image itself. Watermarks that are irrelated with digital image content can no longer cope with the different forms of attacks, such as copy attacks [11] that tackle the images by copying the watermarks.

As a mainstream coding technology, Quick Response (QR) codes are often used for watermark encoding in information hiding, due to its good error correction ability [12], referred to as QR code watermarking technology [13–18].

In this paper, the existing methods are classified into two types according to the content relevance between the watermark and the digital image. The first type consists of the methods that are irrelevant with the image content. Links, text information and icons are often converted into QR codes, in order to be embedded in the image. Although these methods can improve the watermark robustness. However, they are unable to resist copy attacks. The second type of methods consists of the content-based QR code watermarking technology, which can effectively resist copy attacks. However, transformation methods such as DCT and DWT are often used when the QR code is embedded, which causes irreversible changes to the original image, and therefore leads to unsatisfactory results in image authentication.

In this paper, an improved QR code watermarking algorithm is proposed. The image is first divided into smaller processing blocks in order to save more image texture features. The image features of each block are extracted and encoded into QR code as a watermark. The corresponding watermarked image is then obtained using the reversible watermark algorithm [19–22]. When image authentication occurs, the hamming distance is computed between the image features extracted from watermarks and those re-computed from the extracted original image. The main contributions of this paper are summarized as follows:

Firstly, the purpose of retaining more image texture features can be achieved using the improved perceptual hash algorithm to extract image features. When extracting image features, we not only consider the special features of the image, but also take the universal features into account. As a result, our proposal can effectively improve the protection of image with single color and simple pattern.

Secondly, the problem of irreversible changes caused by irreversible QR code watermarking is solved, by using an introduced reversible watermark algorithm. We use the Pixel-Value-Ordering (PVO) based reversible data hiding algorithm to embed the QR code, and realize the lossless operation of the carrier image. Therefore, when performing image authentication, unnecessary interference can be avoided, and a reliable authentication result can be obtained.

2   QR Code Watermarking Method

QR code has become a mainstream coding method due to its large data storage capacity and fast recognition speed. It is commonly used in website login, social platform, e-commerce payment, brand promotion, etc. [15,23]. The QR code technology provides a reliable solution for improving the robustness of watermarks. In [24], in order to transmit more information, the relevant URL is encoded as a QR code and more information can be viewed by scanning the QR code. This method is often used in advertisements applications, such as product promotion, for example. In [25,26], it is proved that icons can also be embedded in images or videos in the form of QR codes. In image copyright protection, if the authors want to embed some private invisible data, they can encode the private information as a QR code. This method not only ensures the vision effect of the original image, but also ensures that the extracted QR code can be correctly identified [27].

In recent years, researchers started to associate image content features with QR codes. The authors of [28] proposed a color document image authentication method, which stores the image color features in multiple QR codes, and then embeds them into image. The watermarked image is then converted to QR code, which is re-embedded in the blank area of the image. After these operations, the method not only performs image authentication, but also locates the tampered area. In [29], the authors proposed a transcript system in which the basic data of each student is encrypted and stored in a QR code, which is printed on the student's transcript. Even if the transcript is tampered, the real data can be obtained by decrypting the QR code.

In [16], the features of the image are extracted using a perceptual hash algorithm, and then converted into a QR code. However, the perceptual hash algorithm only considers the low-frequency features and totally ignores the high-frequency features, which results in authentication failure in a pure or light color image. In addition, QR codes embedded using the DCT and DWT transforms, bring irreversible changes to the original image. Consequently, an improved image authentication method using QR code watermarking is proposed.

3   The Proposed Model

The algorithm consists of QR code generation, watermark embedding and extraction, and image authentication. In this section, we first introduce the framework of the image authentication model, and then detail the whole process.

3.1   Framework

As shown in Fig. 1, the original image is divided into $m \times m$ sub-blocks in advance, here m equals to 2 for example. They are denoted by $Block_1$, $Block_2$, $Block_3$ and $Block_4$. The obtained blocks are processed using the DCT transform to obtain four frequency domain coefficient matrices denoted by FD_1, FD_2, FD_3 and FD_4. We then select the $n \times n$ $(n < m)$ low frequency matrix in the upper-left corner, and high frequency matrix in the bottom-right corner of each sub-block as image feature, which is the central idea of the improved perceptual hash algorithm.

The image feature are used to generate four QR codes denoted by QR_1, QR_2, QR_3 and QR_4 in Fig. 1. The generation processing is detailed in 3.2. We then embed the QR codes QR_1, QR_2, QR_3 and QR_4 in the Blocks $Block_1$, $Block_2$, $Block_3$ and $Block_4$ using a reversible watermarking method, respectively. At last, the watermarked image is obtained.

In the authentication stage, we extract the watermark and the original image from the watermarked image. By comparing the feature extracted from extracted QR codes and the feature recomputed from extracted original image, we can verify whether the image has been attacked, and locate the possible attack area.

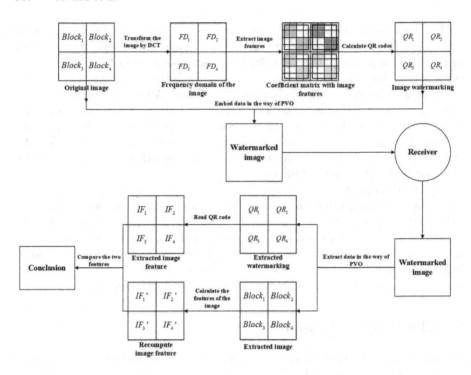

Fig. 1. Framework of the proposed authentication model.

3.2   Generating the QR Codes

In order to prevent copy attack, the watermark should relate to image feature. In our method, the image is transformed using DCT firstly. We preserve the special and universal characteristics of the image, which represent as the low frequency and high frequency coefficients in the DCT transform result. As shown in Fig. 2, we select the 8×8 low frequency matrix in the upper-left corner and the 8×8 high frequency matrix in the lower-right corner of a sub-block. The 8×8 DCT coefficients are marked as $(x_1, \ldots, x_{64})$ and $(y_1, \ldots, y_{64})$, and we calculate their average value and compare them one by one. For example, the mean value of $(x_1, \ldots, x_{64})$ is calculated and recorded as "d". We assume that the value of the corresponding position of x_i after transformation is x_i' ($1 \leq i \leq 64$). The (0,1) matrix can then be obtained according to formula (1).

$$\begin{cases} x_i' = 1, & if \quad x_i > d \\ x_i' = 0, & if \quad x_i \leq d \end{cases} \tag{1}$$

After comparison, the matrix elements are arranged into a sequence. and a 128 bit "01" string is obtained which is used to generate QR code as image feature.

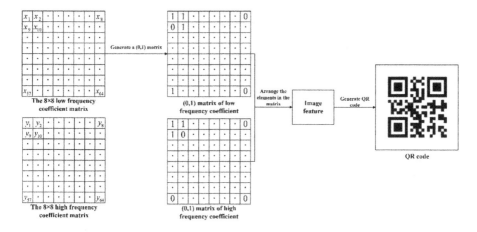

Fig. 2. Process of generating the QR codes.

3.3 Embedding the Watermark

In this section, the proposed PVO-based PEE embedding method is used to embed the watermark [21]. This method is a secure reversible watermarking algorithm. Firstly, the image is divided into non-overlapped blocks of equal size and then sorts the pixels in each block. Taking the ith block as example, the algorithm first sorts the n pixels $(x_1^i, x_2^i, \ldots, x_n - 1^i, x_n^i)$ in ascending order to obtain an ordered sequence $(x_{\sigma(1)}^i, x_{\sigma(2)}^i, \ldots, x_{\sigma(n-1)}^i, x_{\sigma(n)}^i)$, in which $\sigma : \{1, \ldots, n\} \to \{1, \ldots, n\}$ is the unique one-to-one mapping, such that $x_{\sigma(1)}^i \leq \ldots \leq x_{\sigma(n)}^i$, if $x_{\sigma(u)}^i = x_{\sigma(v)}^i$ and $u < v$ $(u, v \in \{1, n\})$, $\sigma(u) < \sigma(v)$. Afterwards, the error $x_{\sigma(n)}^i - x_{\sigma(n-1)}^i$ at the maximum end and the error $x_{\sigma(1)}^i - x_{\sigma(2)}^i$ at the minimum end, are calculated. According to the calculation results, the maximum and minimum of the ith block will be shifted or expanded to carry data as in Eqs. (2) and (3), respectively.

$$x_{\sigma(n)}^i = \begin{cases} x_{\sigma(n)}^i + b, & if \quad x_{\sigma(n)}^i - x_{\sigma(n-1)}^i = 1 \\ x_{\sigma(n)}^i + 1, & if \quad x_{\sigma(n)}^i - x_{\sigma(n-1)}^i > 1 \end{cases} \tag{2}$$

$$x_{\sigma(1)}^i = \begin{cases} x_{\sigma(1)}^i - b, & if \quad x_{\sigma(1)}^i - x_{\sigma(2)}^i = -1 \\ x_{\sigma(1)}^i - 1, & if \quad x_{\sigma(1)}^i - x_{\sigma(2)}^i < -1 \end{cases} \tag{3}$$

where b is a data to embed, and $b \in \{0, 1\}$.

Consequently, the watermark will be successfully embedded.

The specific process of data embedding is shown in Fig. 3. Note that we will take the embedding at the maximum side as an example. As shown in Fig. 3, there are four 2×2 blocks, where the second largest values are marked as green and the largest values are marked as red. After calculation, the obtained prediction errors of these blocks are $143 - 143 = 0$, $150 - 149 = 1$, $148 - 144 = 4$ and

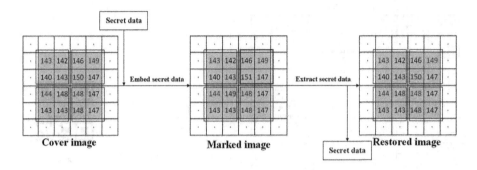

Fig. 3. Process of data embedding and data extraction.

$148 - 148 = 0$. Only one block can carry data, and a data bit $b = 1$ is embedded in it. The block is represented by a red rectangle, and the largest value becomes 151.

3.4 Extracting the Watermark

This section details the corresponding watermark extraction procedure. Taking the ith block as example, we can get an ascending order $(y^i_{\sigma(1)}, y^i_{\sigma(2)}, \dots, y^i_{\sigma(n-1)}, y^i_{\sigma(n)})$. For the maximum side, a secret bit b is extracted according to the rule shown in Eq. (4), and the largest pixel is recovered as in Eq. (5).

$$b = \begin{cases} 0, & if \ \ y^i_{\sigma(n)} - y^i_{\sigma(n-1)} = 1 \\ 1, & if \ \ y^i_{\sigma(n)} - y^i_{\sigma(n-1)} = 2 \end{cases} \tag{4}$$

$$y^i_{\sigma(n)} = \begin{cases} y^i_{\sigma(n)} - 1, & if \ \ y^i_{\sigma(n)} - y^i_{\sigma(n-1)} \geq 2 \\ y^i_{\sigma(n)}, & if \ \ y^i_{\sigma(n)} - y^i_{\sigma(n-1)} = 1 \end{cases} \tag{5}$$

For the minimum side, we exhibit the process of secret data extraction and original pixel recovery shown in Eqs. (6) and (7), respectively.

$$b = \begin{cases} 0, & if \ \ y^i_{\sigma(1)} - y^i_{\sigma(2)} = -1 \\ 1, & if \ \ y^i_{\sigma(1)} - y^i_{\sigma(2)} = -2 \end{cases} \tag{6}$$

$$y^i_{\sigma(1)} = \begin{cases} y^i_{\sigma(1)} + 1, & if \ \ y^i_{\sigma(1)} - y^i_{\sigma(2)} \leq -2 \\ y^i_{\sigma(1)}, & if \ \ y^i_{\sigma(1)} - y^i_{\sigma(2)} = -1 \end{cases} \tag{7}$$

A detailed illustration is shown in Fig. 3. The maximum prediction errors of these blocks are $143 - 143 = 0$, $151 - 149 = 2$, $149 - 144 = 5$ and $148 - 148 = 0$. It can be deduced that only the block with a maximum value of 151 is embedded a secret bit b=1, while the block with a maximum value of 149 is shifted.

At last, the original values of $y^i_{\sigma(n)}$ and $y^i_{\sigma(1)}$ are retained. Moreover, the original values of $(y^i_{\sigma(2)}, \dots, y^i_{\sigma(n-1)})$ are also retained, since they are not changed during the embedding process. Finally, the embedded watermark is extracted and the original image is recovered.

3.5 Image Authentication

Due to the reversibility of the PVO method, the image and the QR code can be lossless extracted from the watermarked image. In the verification stage, we analyze the comparison results of the image feature read from the extracted QR code and re-computed image feature of the extracted original image using the hamming distance, judging whether the image is attacked, or which part of the image is attacked. More precisely, if the Hamming distance is less than 5 and the QR code can be recognized, we then deduce that the image has not been attacked. On the contrary, if the hamming distance is larger than 5 or the QR code cannot be recognized, then this part of the image has been attacked.

4 Experiments and Analysis

In this section, we use grayscale image of 1024*1024 size from the USC-SIPI image database [30]. The performance of the proposed method is demonstrated, and its advantages are presented through experiments. The experiments were performed using MATLAB. A Java library was also used to encode and decode the QR codes which are size of 64*64 bits.

4.1 The Experimental Method

Firstly, the image is divided into several sub-blocks and the watermarking information should be generated from each image sub-block. The watermarking information is then encoded as QR code, which is the watermark image of the corresponding sub-block. Afterwards, a reversible data hiding method referred to as pixel-value-ordering (PVO) is used to embed the watermark image into matching chunk. As for the extraction step, the same separation pattern is used. The watermark image could be then extracted from the corresponding chunk. Finally, the watermarking information should be decoded from the watermark image. Note that the original image is lossless during the whole processing.

The experimental results are presented in Figs. 4, 5 and 6 when image is cut into 4, 6 or 9 sub-blocks. More precisely, Fig. 4(a) presents the original image and Fig. 4(b) represents several QR codes that are watermark images holding watermarking information generated from corresponding sub-blocks. The watermarking information can be identified using a QR decoder. Figure 4(c) shows the image that was embedded watermark images. Figure 4(d) includes four QR codes extracted form matching chunks. Figure 4(e) shows the recovered lossless image. When d is equal to 4, 6 or 9, PSNR between original image and image with watermark is 60.5368, 58.0432 or 56.2064.

(a) original image (b)watermark images(c) image with watermark(d) extracted watermark (e) recovered image

Fig. 4. Segmentation and processing results with d = 4.

(a) original image (b) watermark images (c) image with watermark (d) extracted watermark (e) recovered image

Fig. 5. Segmentation and processing results with d = 6.

(a) original image (b) watermark images (c) image with watermark (d) extracted watermark(e) recovered image

Fig. 6. Segmentation and processing results with d = 9.

4.2 Attack Detecting

To prove the possibility of tampering area location, a segmentation parameter is set. Even under the circumstances of cover attack or random line attack, the proposed method can locate the error in a smaller area. Afterwards, to testify the robustness under copy attack, the watermarking information of the original image is embedded into a new image. Table 1 presents the Hamming distance calculated between the recomputed image and extracted image features, as well as the QR code recognition results. Moreover, QR code itself has the ability to correct errors, after attacks, if QR code can still be identified, these attacks can be treated as non-malicious attacks. If not, these can be malicious attacks.

It can be seen from Figs. 7, 8 and Table 1 that, when cover attack occurs, the watermark image extracted from matching area might be damaged, or the Hamming distance is greater than 5. Thus, the watermark cannot be successfully identified. Owing to the separation, the tampering area can be located in few subblocks. This demonstrates that the more chunks, the more accurate tampering detecting would be. In Fig. 7 and 8, pixels of images are modified by attacks, when extracting watermarks form images by PVO, QR codes including quiet zone may be distorted.

To verify the robustness of the proposed method under copy attack, the watermark derived from Fig. 4(a) should be embedded into a different image. The new image and relevant results are presented in Fig. 9 and Table 1. It can be observed that the watermark can be extracted when the Hamming distance is far greater than 5, and therefore the copy attack can be recognized.

(a) cover attack   (b) extracted watermark

Fig. 7. The results under a cover attack.

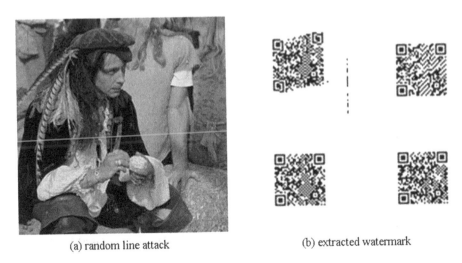

(a) random line attack   (b) extracted watermark

Fig. 8. The results under a random line attack.

(a) copy attack   (b) extracted watermark

Fig. 9. The results under a copy attack.

Table 1. Hamming distance and recognition results under different attacks.

Attack	Results (by sub-block)	1	2	3	4
Cover attack	Hamming distance	21	0	0	0
Cover attack	Recognition result	×	✓	✓	✓
Random line attack	Hamming distance	75	0	0	0
Random line attack	Recognition result	×	✓	✓	✓
Copy attack	Hamming distance	62	50	54	20
Copy attack	Recognition result	✓	✓	✓	✓

5   Conclusion

This paper proposed an improved image authentication method using QR code watermarking manner. The proposed method combines the improved perceptual hash algorithm and the reversible watermarking technique. Several experiments were conducted, and the obtained results were promising. The proposed method improves the image resistance and enhances the robustness of watermarking by applying the features of QR code and making the image lossless using PVO algorithm. It can defend against image attack using without changing the digital image. In future work, due to the simplicity of the proposed model, we expect to integrate deep learning method into image feature extracting and image segmentation to improve its performance.

Acknowledgements. This work was specially supported by Research Funds for NSD Construction, University of International Relations (2021GA08), National Natural Science Foundation of China (62172053, 62102113), Fundamental Research Funds for the Central Universities, University of International Relations (3262020T26, 3262021T13, 3262022T20).

References

1. Tang, X., Zhang, Y., Zhou, L.-N., Liu, D., Hu, B.-W.: Request merging based cross-user deduplication for cloud storage with resistance against appending chunks attack. Chin. J. Electron. **30**(2), 199–209 (2021)
2. Xin, Y., Li, Y.-Z., Lyu, S.-W.: Exposing Deep Fakes Using Inconsistent Head Poses. In: 2019 IEEE International Conference on Acoustics, Speech and Signal Processing, ICASSP, Brighton, pp. 8261–8265. IEEE (2019)
3. Tang, X., Zhou, L.-N., Hu, B.-W., Wu, H.-W.: Aggregation-based tag deduplication for cloud storage with resistance against side channel attack. Secur. Commun. Netw. **2021**(5), 1–15 (2021)
4. Tang, X., Huang, Y.-F., Chang, C.-C., Zhou, L.-N.: Efficient real-time integrity auditing with privacy-preserving arbitration for images in cloud storage system. IEEE Access **7**, 33009–33023 (2019)
5. Yang, Z.-L., Guo, X.-Q., Chen, Z.-M., Huang, Y.-F., Zhang, Y.-J.: RNN-Stega: linguistic steganography based on recurrent neural networks. IEEE Trans. Inf. Forensics Secur. **14**(5), 1280–1295 (2019)
6. Yang, Z.-L., Zhang, S.-Y., Hu, Y.-T., Hu, Z.-W., Huang, Y.-F.: VAE-Stega: linguistic steganography based on variational auto-encoder. IEEE Trans. Inf. Forensics Secur. **16**, 880–895 (2021)
7. Tang, X., Zhou, L.-N., Liu, D., Liu, B.-Y., Lü, X.-Y.: Reversible data hiding based on improved rhombus predictor and prediction error expansion. In: 2020 IEEE 19th International Conference on Trust, Security and Privacy in Computing and Communications, TrustCom, Guangzhou, pp. 13–21. IEEE (2020)
8. Liu, J., Zhang, R., Li, J., Guan, L., Jie, C.: A reversible data hiding algorithm based on image camouflage and bit-plane compression. Comput. Mater. Continua **68**(2), 2263–2649 (2021)
9. Qin, C., Zhang, W., Cao, F., Zhang, X.-P., Chang, C.-C.: Separable reversible data hiding in encrypted images via adaptive embedding strategy with block selection. Signal Process. **153**, 109–122 (2018)
10. Xiong, L., Han, X., Yang, C., Shi, Y.: Robust reversible watermarking in encrypted image with secure multi-party based on lightweight cryptography. IEEE Trans. Circuits Syst. Video Technol. **32**(1), 75–91 (2022)
11. Katzenbeisser, S., Veith, H.: Securing symmetric watermarking schemes against protocol attacks. Proc. SPIE **4675**(1), 260–268 (2002)
12. Goyal, S., Yadav, S., Mathuria, M.: Exploring concept of QR code and its benefits in digital education system. In: 2016 International Conference on Advances in Computing, Communications and Informatics, ICACCI, Jaipur, pp. 1141–1147. IEEE (2016)
13. Huang, H.-C., Chang, F.-C., Fang, W.-C.: Reversible data hiding with histogram-based difference expansion for QR code applications attacks. IEEE Trans. Consum. Electron. **57**(2), 779–787 (2011)
14. Bai, T.-T., Liu, Z., Peng, L.-U.: Geometrical attack resistant digital watermarking based on QR Code. Packaging Eng. **34**(11), 113–116 (2013)

15. Gao, Q., Chen, G.-X., Chen, Q.-F.: Double QR code watermarking algorithm based on DCT-SVD. Packaging Eng. **36**(17), 119–125 (2015)

16. Liu, X.-M., Tang, X.: Image authentication using QR code watermarking approach based on image segmentation. In: 2020 IEEE 19th International Conference on Trust, Security and Privacy in Computing and Communications, TrustCom, Guangzhou, pp. 1572–1577. IEEE (2020)

17. Zhou, Y., Luo, W.-W.: A QR data hiding method based on redundant region and BCH. J. Big Data **3**(3), 127–133 (2021)

18. Zhong, X.-W., Xiong, L.-Z., Xia, Z.-H.: A secure visual secret sharing scheme with authentication based on QR Code. J. Big Data **3**(2), 85–95 (2021)

19. Tang, X., Zhou, L.-N., Tang, G., Chen, Y.-X.: Reversible data hiding based on improved block selection strategy and pixel value ordering. In: 2021 IEEE 6th Cyber Science and Technology Congress, CyberSciTech, IEEE (2021)

20. Tang, X., Zhou, L.-N., Liu, D., Shan, W.-J., Zhang, Y.: Border following-based reversible watermarking algorithm for images with resistance to histogram overflowing. Int. J. Distrib. Sens. Netw. **16**(5), 1550147720917014 (2020)

21. Li, X.-L., Li, J., Li, B., Yang, B.: High-fidelity reversible data hiding scheme based on pixel-value-ordering and prediction-error expansion. Signal Process. **93**(1), 198–205 (2013)

22. Tang, X., Zhou, L., Tang, G., Wen, Y., Cheng, Y.: Improved fluctuation derived block selection strategy in pixel value ordering based reversible data hiding. In: Zhao, X., Piva, A., Comesaña-Alfaro, P. (eds.) IWDW 2021. LNCS, vol. 13180, pp. 163–177. Springer, Cham (2022). https://doi.org/10.1007/978-3-030-95398-0_12

23. Lin, Y., Lu, J.-H., Jun, Y.: Structure for two-dimensional barcode in test reports of anti-fake platform based on RSA digital signature. Qual. Tech. Supervision Res. **2015**(4), 55–57 (2015)

24. Chen, X.: An robust digital watermarking algorithm based on Arnold and DCT. J. Hu Zhou Univ. **40**(10), 29–34 (2008)

25. Liu, X., Gong, R.: Digital watermarking algorithm of QR Code based on DCT domain. Moder. Inf. Technol. **2**(12), 13–15 (2018)

26. Prabakaran, G., Bhavani, R., Ramesh, M.: A robust QR-code video watermarking scheme based on SVD and DWT composite domain. In: 2013 International Conference on Pattern Recognition, Informatics and Mobile Engineering, PRIME, Salem, pp. 251–257. IEEE (2013)

27. Yao, Y.-Z., Wang, F., Yan, W.-B., Yu, N.-H.: Image privacy preservation scheme based on QR code and reversible visible watermarking. J. Commun. **40**(11), 65–75 (2019)

28. Mohsin Arkah, Z., Alzubaidi, L., Ali, A.A., Abdulameer, A.T.: Digital color documents authentication using QR code based on digital watermarking. In: Abraham, A., Cherukuri, A.K., Melin, P., Gandhi, N. (eds.) ISDA 2018 2018. AISC, vol. 940, pp. 1093–1101. Springer, Cham (2020). https://doi.org/10.1007/978-3-030-16657-1_102

29. Dey, S., Agarwal, S., Nath, A.: Confidential encrypted data hiding and retrieval using QR authentication system. In: 2013 International Conference on Communication Systems and Network Technologies, Gwalior, pp. 512–517. IEEE (2013)

30. The USC-SIPI Image Database. http://sipi.usc.edu/database/, (accessed 9 January 2022)

A Cyberspace Security Knowledge System Based on Knowledge Graph

Bin Ma[1], Dongqi Li[1], Chunpeng Wang[1], Jian Li[1], Gang Li[1(✉)], and Xinan Cui[2]

[1] Shandong Provincial Key Laboratory of Computer Networks, Shandong Academy of Sciences, Qilu University of Technology, Jinan 250353, China
sdqluldq@126.com
[2] Zhongfu Information Inc., Jinan 250101, China

Abstract. Knowledge graph plays an important role in semantic search, data analysis and intelligent decision making, and has made remarkable achievements in many fields. However, it is rarely used in the field of network security, which hinders the systematic and structured development of network space security. In order to build a cyberspace security knowledge system to fill the gaps in this field, and to visualize cyberspace security knowledge, this paper proposes a construction method of network space security knowledge map, and uses bottom-up method to construct network security knowledge system. Firstly, Protégé is used to construct ontology of cyberspace security knowledge. Secondly, semantic relations between entities are extracted from cyberspace security data. Finally, the network security knowledge system is stored and displayed by Neo4j graphics database. The experimental results show that the method is effective and has important significance for the development of network space security.

Keywords: Ontology construction · Cyberspace security knowledge system · Knowledge graph

1 Introduction

With the rapid development of information technology, the Internet has gradually penetrated into all areas of society, while cyberspace security is also playing an increasingly important role in various fields. However, most of the massive information in cyberspace exists in the form of fragmentation, which makes network security protection face many problems. In order to solve this problem, knowledge graph based on cyberspace security came into being. It can integrate fragmented knowledge through information extraction [1, 2] in the form of formal knowledge organization.

Ontology can provide a unified way to describe the concept of pattern layer, and can completely and accurately represent the complex knowledge in the domain. Gruber [3] defines ontology as a conceptualized specification, which can be divided into general ontology and domain ontology. The latter is more difficult to construct than the former. Syed et al. [4] proposed a network security ontology, which aims to integrate network security information and combine different heterogeneous data and knowledge with

© The Author(s), under exclusive license to Springer Nature Switzerland AG 2022
X. Sun et al. (Eds.): ICAIS 2022, LNCS 13340, pp. 349–362, 2022.
https://doi.org/10.1007/978-3-031-06791-4_28

network security standards. Zhang et al. [5] proposed an ontology model for network security analysis, which reflects the security status of network nodes through three key sub-domains. After the definition of ontology is proposed, many ontologies established for network security problems appear. But there are few ontology constructions for analysis in the field of network space security in China, and there is a lack of certain relevance at the ontology level.

In order to further optimize the search engine, knowledge graph was proposed by Google on May 17, 2012. At present, knowledge mapping has been widely used in recommendation systems, information retrieval [6, 7] and other fields. The mature and commonly used large-scale knowledge mappings include Freebase [8] and Dbpedia [9]. In order to describe the important concepts in the field of network security and the concepts between them, researchers have adopted different construction methods to promote the development of knowledge mapping in this field. Manikandan et al. [10] uses convolutional neural networks to classify malware sentences and conditional random fields to predict labels. Sikos et al. [11] uses RDF to formalize the properties and relationships of network concepts, proposes a framework for network-aware knowledge, and automates inference for network applications. Li et al. [12] proposed an efficient knowledge graph recommendation system model. Yoo et al. [13] proposed EP-Bot (an Empathetic chatbot based on PolarisX), which can better understand a person's utterance by leveraging PolarisX, an auto-growing knowledge graph, which extracts new relational information and automatically expands the knowledge graph. Pingle et al. [14] proposed a feedforward neural network model, which uses network security-specific NER to vectorize network security entities and predict the relationship between network security entities. Ahh et al. [15] proposed Time-Aware PolarisX, an automatically extended knowledge graph containing temporal information. Yue et al. [16] proposed an end-to-end relation extraction method using Bidirectional Gated Recurrent Unit (BiGRU) neural network and dual attention mechanism for forestry knowledge graph construction. The above research on cyberspace security knowledge map at home and abroad is of great significance to the construction of cyberspace security knowledge map. But there is still room for improvement when extracting important concepts.

At present, there is no recognized and referential cyberspace security ontology and cyberspace security knowledge architecture based on knowledge map. In order to fully represent the category and semantic relationship of cyberspace security entities, this paper uses the structured and unstructured text data sets related to cyberspace security, and uses the combination of Development101 method [17] and statistical method to construct ontology, and then constructs the knowledge map by mining the concepts, entities and relationships of structured and unstructured text content.

This article is organized as follows. The second section introduces the principle and extraction results of TF-IDF, TextRank and LDA topic methods in ontology construction process. Section 3 introduces the important elements and construction process of cyberspace security map; Sect. 4 carries out knowledge storage and retrieval on the constructed knowledge map; finally, the fifth section summarizes the full text.

2 Ontology Construction

2.1 Generalizing the Concept of Cyberspace Security Domain

The core concept corresponds to the class in the ontology, and each core concept has many corresponding entities in the field of cyberspace security. TF-IDF algorithm, TextRank algorithm and LDA topic algorithm can extract the key words in the text. This paper uses these three algorithms to extract and filter the important word information in the field of cyberspace security, and finally determines the core concept of cyberspace security.

Term Frequency - Inverted Document Frequency (TF-IDF) is a weighted technology used in information retrieval and text mining, which is usually used to evaluate the importance of words to the corpus. The importance of a word increases proportionally with its frequency in the document and decreases inversely with its frequency in the corpus. Term Frequency (TF) represents the frequency of key entry in document D_i:

$$TF_{w,D_i} = \frac{count(w)}{D_i} \tag{1}$$

where $count(w)$ is the number of keywords w, and D_i is the number of all words in the document.

Inverse Document Frequency (IDF) represents the importance of a given entry. The main idea is that when a given entry appears at a high frequency in one text and at the same time appears at a low frequency in other texts, the higher the position of the word in the text is, the word should be given a high weight. IDF defines the following:

$$IDF_w = \log \frac{N}{\sum_{i=1}^{N} I(w, D_i)} \tag{2}$$

where N is the total number of all documents, indicating whether document D_i contains keywords. If it contains, it is 1, and if it does not contain, it is 0. If the word w does not appear in all documents, the denominator in the IDF formula is 0; therefore, it is necessary to smooth IDF:

$$IDF_w = \log \frac{N}{1 + \sum_{i=1}^{N} I(w, D_i)} \tag{3}$$

TF-IDF value of keyword w in document D_i:

$$TF - IDF_{w,D_i} = TF_{w,D_i} * IDF_w \tag{4}$$

TF-IDF algorithm is used to extract keywords, and the first 16 words with the largest weight are selected as the following examples:

Opinion	Security	Network	Cyberspace	Data	Information	Users	Technology
Web	Analysis	Encryption	Conduct	Storage	System	Attacker	Password

Fig. 1. TF-IDF algorithm to select the first 200 words word cloud results.

The word cloud can visually display keywords with high frequency in the text, and can filter a large number of low-frequency information. In this paper, the text after segmentation, using TF-IDF algorithm, using the word cloud to take the first 200 words for visual display, as shown in Fig. 1.

TextRank algorithm is an improved graph model for keyword extraction based on PageRank algorithm of Google search. TextRank was proposed by Mihalcea et al. [18] to construct a network through the adjacent relationship between words, and then the rank value of each node was iteratively calculated by TextRank. The keywords can be obtained by sorting the rank value.

Algorithm steps:

Step 1: Dividing text T to be processed by reference to sentence integrity, $T = [H_1, H_2, H_3, .., H_m]$.

Step 2: For each sentence H_i in text T, the word segmentation and part of speech tagging are performed respectively. Then perform the stop word operation, and only save the words of a specific part of speech, namely $H_i = [t_{i,1}, t_{i,2}, t_{i,3}, ..., t_{i,n}]$, is the keyword after the above operation is completed.

Step 3: The candidate keyword graph $G = (V, E)$ is constructed. V is the set of nodes generated by the previous step. E is the set of edges generated by the set of nodes V using the co-occurrence relationship, and this edge only exists when the size of the window is k. In other words, the maximum number of words that can be co-occurrence is k.

Step 4: According to the following formula, weights are calculated iteratively until convergence.

$$WS(V_i) = (1 - d) + d * \sum_{j \in In(V_i)} \frac{W_{ji}}{\sum_{V \in out(V_j)} W_{jk}} WS(V_j) \tag{5}$$

Among them, $WS(V_i)$ represents the rank value of node V_i, $In(V_i)$ represents the precursor node set of node V_i; $out(V_j)$ represents the set of subsequent nodes of node V_j; d (damping factor) damping coefficient is expressed as the probability of node transfer, and the value range is between 0 and 1, generally 0.85.

Step 5: The nodes after weight calculation are sorted from large to small, and then N words of importance in text H are obtained.

Using TextRank algorithm to extract keywords, under the condition of filtering part of speech as nouns, the extraction results of the first 16 words with the largest weight are as follows:

Security	Network	Data	Public	Opinion	Information	Technology	Cyberspace
User	System	Society	State	Website	Internet	Password	Aspect

The text uses TextRank algorithm to get keywords with weight from large to small, and uses the word cloud to take the first 200 words for visual display, as shown in Fig. 2.

Fig. 2. TextRank algorithm selects the top 200 words cloud results

Blei proposed the Latent Dirichlet Allocation (LDA) topic model in 2003, which is an unsupervised learning method to extract topic words from a document. It can generate multiple topics in the document and calculate the weight of each word in each topic [19].

$$P(term|doc) = \sum_{topic} P(term|topic) * P(topic|doc) \tag{6}$$

After the LDA topic model is applied to the network space security unstructured text, the top three topics are selected, and the top 6 keywords with the highest weight are selected for each topic. The results are shown in Table 1.

Table 1. Table captions should be placed above the tables.

The first theme		The second theme		The third theme	
Keywords	weight	Keywords	weight	Keywords	weight
Security	0.014	Cyberspace	0.021	Network	0.021
Cyberspace	0.010	Information	0.020	User	0.014
Server	0.008	Technology	0.015	Through	0.007
Mail	0.007	proceed	0.007	System	0.007
Service	0.007	Application	0.007	Data	0.007
Game	0.006	Internet	0.007	Standard	0.007

2.2 Establishing Class Hierarchy Structure

There are usually two ways to define classes and their levels:

(1) Top-down definitions: definitions of common concepts in the field and further refinement of definitions
(2) Bottom-down definitions: Start with leaf definitions for the most specific category, hierarchy, and then group these definitions.

In this paper, the bottom-up definition is used to divide cyberspace security knowledge into three categories: cyberspace security concepts, threats and protective measures. The top-level class is shown in Fig. 3.

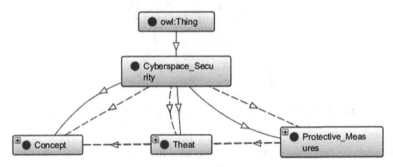

Fig. 3. Top-level class diagram of cyberspace security.

2.3 Definition Relations and Constraints

After defining the hierarchy of classes, it is necessary to establish the relationship between network space security knowledge. Based on the analysis of the content of cyberspace security, this paper establishes the inclusion, precursor, successor, brother and synonymous relationship. Entity relationships are shown in Table 2.

Table 2. Entity relationships.

Entity-relationship	Relationship description
Inclusion relation	A knowledge point contains the content of one or more other knowledge points
Precursor relationship	In two knowledge point entities, one knowledge point entity depends on the other, and there is a backward and forward order between the two knowledge points
The subsequent relationship	A knowledge point must be dependent on other knowledge entities, and the two must be sequential
The sibling relationship	Knowledge point entities are at the same level as each other and have the same parent node between knowledge points
The synonymy relationship	A knowledge point is named differently from another knowledge point, but expresses the same content

3 Construction of Network Space Security Knowledge Map

3.1 Element Definition

In the process of constructing cyberspace security knowledge graph, it is necessary to determine the elements required for construction. Among them, the most important is that the entity nodes, relationships and attributes are described as follows:

(1) Nodes: Nodes in the knowledge graph represent concepts and entities, where concepts are abstract things and entities are concrete abstract things. To simplify the description of a knowledge graph, entities and concepts can be collectively referred to as entities. And each entity has a unique entity name. According to the constructed ontology, it is divided into three categories: cyberspace security concept, threat and protective measures, and the corresponding entities of each category are determined.

(2) Entity relation: a relation is a particular relation that exists between two or more entities. This paper describes the internal relations among three types of entities, including physical security, network security and other specific relationships. The entity relations defined in this paper include inclusion, predecessor, successor, brother and synonymous relations. Inclusion relations generally exist between classes and knowledge entities. For example, network security protection measures include data encryption, identity recognition, identity authentication and other methods.

(3) entity attributes: entity attributes can also be understood as attribute relations, it belongs to a directed relationship. In this paper, the entity attributes of the cyberspace security direct-view ontology are defined as: importance (used to represent the importance of knowledge points in the entire knowledge system, which can be divided into: cognition, understanding, and mastery), difficulty (refers to the difficulty of knowledge points, which can be divided into: simple, medium, and difficult), chapter (represents the chapter to which the knowledge point belongs in

the cyberspace security textbook), node color (each node color represents different knowledge categories). Entity properties are shown in Table 3.

Table 3. Entity relationships.

Attribute	Type	Data format	Explanation
Importance	Data	String	The importance of knowledge point entities
Complexity	Data	String	Knowledge point entity understanding degree
Subordinate section	Data	String	Knowledge point entity location
The node color	System	String	Node color

3.2 Knowledge Graph Construction Process

Knowledge graph construction includes entity extraction and establishment of relationships between entities, and needs to effectively organize and store the relationships between entities.

High-quality data is an important underlying support when constructing knowledge graphs. Usually, knowledge sources can be structured data, semi-structured data and unstructured data. The process of constructing cyberspace security knowledge graph is: (1) According to relevant information on the Internet and unstructured text of cyberspace security, the field and scope of cyberspace security are determined. (2) Using statistical methods to analyze unstructured text, the concept class of cyberspace security is determined after screening. (3) According to the characteristics of physical security and data security in cyberspace security, the attributes of entities, entities and the relationship between entities are extracted, and a reasonable and accurate semantic network is obtained through knowledge fusion. (4) The extracted experimental results are represented by Neo4j graph database, and finally the knowledge map of cyberspace security can be obtained. The build process is shown in Fig. 4 below.

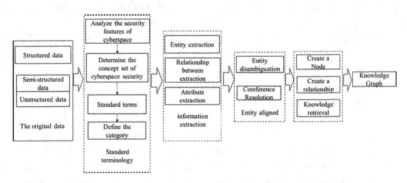

Fig. 4. Construction process of network space security knowledge map

4 Knowledge Storage and Retrieval

4.1 Knowledge Storing

Graph database is a non-relational database, the main purpose is to solve the limitations of the current relational database. It can clearly list the dependencies between data nodes. The storage based on graph structure uses nodes to represent entities, and edges to represent the relationship between entities, so that the data information provided can accurately express the relationship. Knowledge storage includes ontology layer and data layer. Data first enters ontology layer and then is stored in data layer. The concept of cyberspace security entity is determined in ontology layer, and the relationship between concepts is realized through constraint conditions. The storage method based on graph structure uses directed graph to model the data of knowledge graph, so the undirected relationship needs to be converted into two symmetrical directed relationships. For example, there is a "brother" relationship between "natural disaster impact" and "software and hardware impact". Because this relationship is a directed relationship, it is necessary to mark two symmetrical edges in the graph to represent the "brother" relationship between the two. This paper uses Neo4j graph database, which has high performance database with complete transaction characteristics, and has all the characteristics of mature database. Neo4j supports Cypher query language, Cypher is a descriptive graphic query language Table 4 shows the detailed information obtained after all the data are stored in Neo4j data.

Table 4. Statistics of knowledge base categories.

Category	Amount
Categories of entities	3
Categories of relationships	5
Categories of attributes	3
Node of concept	82
Node of threat	88
Node of action	192
All the nodes	362
All relationships	386

4.2 Knowledge Retrieval

In January 2008, SPARQL became the official standard for W3C. Like SQL, SPARQL is a descriptive structured query language. Users only need to refer to the syntax rules defined by SPARQL to describe their query information. For a SELECT statement, the SELECT clause specifies the content returned by the query; the FROM clause specifies the dataset to be used; MATCH is equivalent to SELECT in SQL, which is used to describe the data pattern of the production match; the WHERE clause is composed of a set of ternary patterns to specify the patterns that the returned data fragment needs to meet. This paper uses Neo4j Browser to retrieve and display data information in the network security part.

Creating Entity Nodes and Relationships in Network Security. The creation of network security entity nodes and relationships are shown in Table 5.

Table 5. Entity and relation creation statement.

Cypher statement
LOAD CSV WITH HEADERS FROM 'file:///course3.csv' AS line
create(:course3{cour_name:line.course,id:line.id,important:line.Degree of Importance ,
level: line. Complexity, belong: line. Subordinate Section})
LOAD CSV WITH HEADERS FROM "file:/// Contain.csv" AS line
match (from:course1{id:line.course_id1}),(to:course2 {id:line.course_id2})
merge (from)-[r:Contain]->(to)
LOAD CSV WITH HEADERS FROM "file:/// Sibling.csv" AS line
match (from:course4{id:line.course_id1}),(to:course4 {id:line.course_id2})
merge (from)-[r:Sibling]->(to)

Retrieval of Network Security Related Entities and Relationships

Search All Entities of Concept, Threat and Protection. Search network security entity node as shown in Table 6 below.

Table 6. Entity and relation creation statement.

Cypher statement
match (na:course1)-[re]->(nb:course2)
where na.cour_name ="Network Security"
WITH na,re,nb
match (nb:course2)-[re2]->(nc:course3)
return na,re,nb,re2,nc

We can clearly see the composition of network security from Fig. 5. Different colors represent different categories. Yellow represents network security, green represents the three subcategories of network security, and red represents entities under these three subcategories.

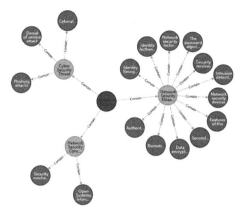

Fig. 5. Network security entity query results.

Retrieve All Entities and Relationships of Concepts, Threats and Protection Categories.
The relationships among all entity nodes and entities of network security are shown in
Table 7.

Table 7. Entity and relation creation statement.

Cypher statement
match (na:course2)-[re]->(nb:course3)
where na.cour_name ="Network Security Concept"or na.cour_name ="Cyber Security Threat"or na.cour_name ="Network Security Measure"
WITH na,re,nb
match (nb:course3)-[re2]->(nc:course4)
return na,re,nb,re2,nc

Figure 6 shows all entities and relationships contained in network security. The
relationship between entities in each entity category can be seen in more detail.

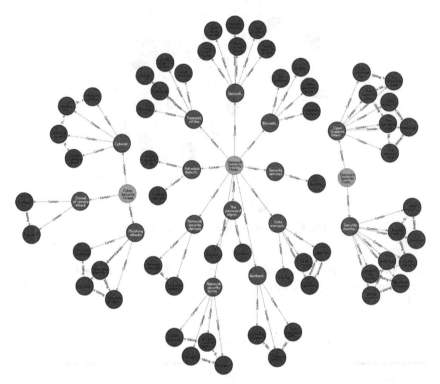

Fig. 6. Some entities and relation query results of network security.

5 Conclusion

This paper proposes a construction process of integrating multiple heterogeneous network space security unstructured data, and expounds the difficulties and challenges faced in the construction process. The purpose is to construct a semantically consistent and structurally reasonable network space security ontology and knowledge map.

This paper discusses the data sources and research contents of the construction of cyberspace security knowledge map, and puts forward the method of constructing cyberspace security knowledge map. Firstly, entities are extracted from unstructured texts, and then these entities are associated. The relationship information of text mining is stored in Neo4j graph database, and the attributes are set to achieve a variety of query and retrieval functions. Network space security knowledge map based on knowledge map can realize the association of network space security knowledge, which is beneficial to the integration of unstructured text information resources and improve query efficiency.

This article provides a reference for the research on the construction of cyberspace knowledge graphs, but there are still areas that can be studied. The amount of data used in cyberspace security corpus is relatively small, and the comprehensiveness of the cyberspace security knowledge graphs needs to be improved. The next step will be to crawl more cyberspace security texts from the web, increase the data volume of cybersecurity entities, and improve the comprehensiveness of the cyberspace security knowledge graph containing knowledge points.

Acknowledgement. This work was supported by the National Natural Science Foundation of China: (No: 61872203, No: 61802212), Shandong Provincial Natural Science Foundation: (No: ZR2019BF017, No: Z R2020MF054), the Jinan City '20 universities' Funding Projects (No: 2019GXRC031, No: 2020GXR C056), Provincial Educational Reform Project (NO: Z2020042), School-level teaching reform project (NO: 201804), and School-level key project (NO: 2020zd24).

References

1. Xu, Z.L., Sheng, Y.P., He, L.R., Wang, Y.F.: Review on knowledge graph techniques. J. Univ. Electron. Sci. Technol. Chin. **45**, 589–606 (2016)
2. Liu, Q., Li, Y., Hong, D., Yao, L.: Knowledge graph construction techniques. J. Comput. Res. Develop. **53**, 582–600 (2016)
3. Gruber, T.R.: Toward principles for the design of ontologies used for knowledge sharing? Int. J. Hum. Comput. Stud. **43**, 907–928 (1995)
4. Syed, Z., Padia, T., Finin, L., Mathews, A., Joshi: UCO: a unified cybersecurity ontology. In: Workshop on Artificial Intelligence for Cyber Security (2016)
5. Zhang, K., Liu, J.J.: Ontology construction for security analysis of network nodes. In: 2020 International Conference on Communications, Information System and Computer Engineering (CISCE), pp. 292–297 (2020)
6. Xiong, F., Gao, J.L.: Entity alignment for cross-lingual knowledge graph with graph convolutional networks. In: Proceedings of the 28th International Joint Conference on Artificial Intelligence, pp. 6480–6481 (2019)
7. Wang, X., Wang, D., Canran, X., He, X., Cao, Y., Chua, T.-S.: Explainable reasoning over knowledge graphs for recommendation. Proc. AAAI Conf. Artif. Intel. **33**, 5329–5336 (2019)
8. Bollacker, K., Evans, C., Paritosh, P.: Freebase: a collaboratively created graph database for structuring human knowledge. In: Proceedings of the 2008 ACM SIGMOD International Conference on Management of Data, pp. 1247–1250 (2008)
9. Lehmann, J., Isele, R., Jakob, M., et al.: Freebase: a collaboratively created graph database for structuring human knowledge. In: Proceedings of the 2008 ACM SIGMOD International Conference on Management of Data, pp. 1247–1250 (2008)
10. Manikandan, R., Madgula, K., Saha, S., et al.: Dbpedia-a large-scale, multilingual knowledge base extracted from Wikipedia. Seman. Web **6**, 167–195 (2015)
11. Sikos, L.F., Stumptner, M., Mayer, W., Howard, C., Voigt, S.: Automated reasoning over provenance-aware communication network knowledge in support of cyber-situational awareness. In: International Conference on Knowledge Science, Engineering and Management, pp. 132–143 (2018)
12. Li, T., Li, H., Zhong, S., et al.: Automated reasoning over provenance-aware communication network knowledge in support of cyber-situational awareness. In: International Conference on Knowledge Science, Engineering and Management, pp. 132–143 (2018)
13. Yoo, S., Jeong, O.: Bot: empathetic chatbot using auto-growing knowledge graph. Comput. Mater. Continua **67**(3), 2807–2817 (2021)
14. Pingle, A., Piplai, A., Mittal, S., Joshi, A., Holt, J., Zak, R.: RelExt: relation extraction using deep learning approaches for cybersecurity knowledge graph improvement. In: Proceedings of the 2019 IEEE/ACM International Conference on Advances in Social Networks Analysis and Mining, pp. 879–886 (2019)

15. Ahn, Y., Jeong, O.: Time-Aware PolarisX: auto-growing knowledge graph. Comput. Mater. Continua **67**(3), 2695–2708 (2021)
16. Yue, Q., Li, X., Li, D.: Chinese relation extraction on forestry knowledge graph construction. Comput. Syst. Sci. Eng. **37**(3), 423–442 (2021)
17. Noy, N.F., Mcguinness, D.L.: Ontology development 101: a guide to creating your first ontology (2001)
18. Mihalcea, R., Tarau, P.: TextRank: bringing order into text. In: Proceedings of the 2004 Conference on Empirical Methods in Natural Language Processing, pp. 404–411 (2004)
19. Blei, D.M., Ng, A.Y., Jordan, M.I.: Latent dirichlet allocation. J. Mach. Learn. Res. **3**, 993–1022 (2003)

Multi-carrier Steganography Algorithm Based on Executable Program

Zuwei Tian[1]([⊠]) and Zhichen Gao[2]

[1] College of Computer Science, Hunan First Normal University, Changsha 410205, China
35568625@qq.com
[2] Department of Applied Mathematics and Statistics, College of Engineering and Applied Sciences, Stony Brook University, Stony Brook, NY 11794-2300, USA

Abstract. Executable file steganography makes use of the redundancy of executable programs to hide secret information and realize the secure transmission of secret information, which is one of the research hotspots in the field of information security. Single carrier steganography has some problems, such as low security and insufficient steganography capacity. In order to further improve the concealment and solve the problem of too centralized hiding capacity, a technology of information decentralized hiding is introduced by using the working principle of threshold secret sharing. The encrypted secret information is divided into several blocks according to the agreed algorithm, and then is hidden into multiple executable files under the windows system folder. When users need secret information, the system will automatically extract and assemble this scattered and hidden information to form a complete secret information. In this way, even if a malicious attacker can get one or more executable files containing secret information, it cannot effectively extract the hidden information.

Keywords: Steganography · Executable program · Multi-carrier · Threshold secret sharing algorithm

1 Introduction

With the continuous expansion of computer application fields, people have higher and higher requirements for information security. Encryption technology only hides the information content itself without the existence of hidden information. The encrypted information data becomes a pile of random code, which is easy to expose the importance of the information itself. Encryption technology can not solve this problem well. Steganography is a kind of technique that tries to hide the existence of messages. PE file is a standard format for executable file and is applied extensively. A PE file is composed of DOS header, DOS stub, PE header, section table and section, which plays a very important role in the Windows operating system. PE files are widely used in Win32 executable programs, including EXE, DLL, OCX, SYS, SCR and so on. PE files are widely used in the Windows operating system. PE file has the characteristics of diversity, uncertainty of file size, and complexity of file structure and singleness of file format and so on, which

X. Sun et al. (Eds.): ICAIS 2022, LNCS 13340, pp. 363–372, 2022.
https://doi.org/10.1007/978-3-031-06791-4_29

makes it easy to be a carrier of information hiding, especially for that of large hiding capacity.

Steganography is based on cryptography, which hides the information in the original carrier after encryption without affecting its use. It not only hides the content of the information itself, but also hides the existence of the information. There are many public carriers such as images, text, audio, video and programs. Hiding information in these carriers can well realize the purpose of camouflage and hiding information. It is difficult for unauthorized users to judge whether there is hidden information from the public carrier, and it is more difficult to extract hidden information, so as to realize the safe storage and communication of secret information. It provides a new security technology for digital information [1–5]. At present, information hiding mainly takes multimedia digital resources such as image, video, audio and text as the carrier and research object, and has achieved many research results, which has attracted the attention of many research institutions and researchers. Different from executable files, images, video and audio itself have more redundant information. At the same time, due to the limited resolution of human visual and auditory organs, minor changes to images, video and audio will not cause human visual and auditory abnormalities, which is difficult to find. Therefore, steganography in these areas of images, video and audio has high concealment. Text information hiding mainly carries out steganography by modifying text syntax, text content and text format, and modifies the format and content of the text to a certain extent. There will be no abnormal text and will not affect the reading of the text. It has high concealment in vision. Software is an important part of computer system and a necessary condition for computer operation. People cannot live without software every day. Due to the complexity of software structure, the executability of program code, the uncertainty of file size and the diversity of executable files, software is very suitable as the carrier of information hiding. However, because the executable program has unique attributes such as behavior certainty, behavior self-evident and execution environment dependence, and the executable program is an organism composed of instruction code and related data, the modification of a byte of the executable program may lead to software exceptions, and even seriously affect the execution and function of the software. Hiding information in an executable program must ensure that it does not affect the enforceability and functionality of the software. After modifying the executable program carrier and hiding information, it will change some characteristics of the executable program itself, and may generate feature codes that are easy to be detected by the anti-virus software, which will be incorrectly identified as malware by the anti-virus software, which will cause the alarm of real-time protection software of the anti-virus engine and other systems, and the concealment will be affected. Due to these characteristics of executable programs, executable program steganography is more complex than image, video, audio and text steganography. It is necessary to analyze the data structure of executable programs, function recognition and assembly code analysis. The hidden information needs to be closely combined with software functions, that is, fine modification and accurate positioning are very important for executable program steganography (Fig. 1).

At present, executable program information hiding is mainly based on Java bytecode, PE file and other carriers. Elkhalil et al. proposed a scheme to encode the secret information by using the redundancy of the assembly instruction itself. The scheme uses

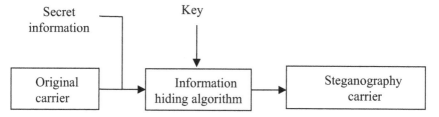

Fig. 1. Information hiding algorithm framework.

the secret key to randomly jump to a position in the code segment of the executable file to select the instruction, and then encodes and embeds the information according to the equivalent instruction set contained in the instruction block [6]. Based on the research of Hydran, Anckaert et al. Improved it from three aspects: instruction selection, instruction scheduling and code layout, and proposed Stilo steganography system for executable files [7]. Daemin et al. proposed a method of expanding the PE file code section for information hiding. The scheme hides the information in the code section by modifying the length of the PE file code section. In order to increase the secrecy, the information is stored in the operand of the selected instruction [8]. Li Qian et al. proposed an information hiding scheme to expand the code section of PE file and realize unlimited capacity. Firstly, the hidden information is preprocessed such as encryption, integrity verification, code camouflage and mixed original code. Then, the code section is expanded according to the preprocessed information length, and the position of each section table, import table and the value of each corresponding flag of PE header are corrected to ensure that the carrier PE file can be executed normally. The experimental results show that the scheme cannot only achieve information hiding without capacity limit, but also has certain concealment and robustness [9].

2   Analysis of PE File Structure

From the perspective of programmers, PE files are composed of many data structures, and each data structure is a series of orderly and meaningful data sets. The following introduces several data structures closely related to information hiding.

2.1   PE Header

PE header is IMAGE_NT_HEADERS structure. When loading PE files, the windows operating system will first read the PE header information and identify it. IMAGE_FILE_HEADER is located behind the PE header ID, with a size of 20 bytes. It stores the global attributes of the PE file, including the PE file running platform, PE file type, the number of sections in the PE file, PE file attributes, etc. Its definition is as follows:

```
typedef struct _IMAGE_FILE_HEADER
{
WORD   Machine;
WORD   NumberOfSections;
 DWORD   TimeDateStamp;
 DWORD   PointerToSymbolTable;
 DWORD   NumberOfSymbols;
 WORD   SizeOfOptionalHeader;
 WORD   Characteristics;
} IMAGE_FILE_HEADER;
```

The extended PE header is also called optional PE header. This structure stores more information than the standard PE header. The entry address when the file is executed, the default base address loaded by the PE file, the alignment unit of the section in disk and memory and other information are defined in this structure.

```
typedef struct _IMAGE_OPTIONAL_HEADER {
WORD   Magic;
BYTE   MajorLinkerVersion;
BYTE   MinorLinkerVersion;
DWORD   SizeOfCode;
DWORD   SizeOfInitializedData;
DWORD   SizeOfUninitializedData;
DWORD   AddressOfEntryPoint;
DWORD   BaseOfCode;
DWORD   BaseOfData;
DWORD   ImageBase;
DWORD   SectionAlignment;
DWORD   FileAlignment;
WORD   MajorOperatingSystemVersion;
WORD   MinorOperatingSystemVersion;
WORD   MajorImageVersion;
WORD   MinorImageVersion;
WORD   MajorSubsystemVersion;
WORD   MinorSubsystemVersion;
DWORD   Win32VersionValue;
DWORD   SizeOfImage;
DWORD   SizeOfHeaders;
DWORD   CheckSum;
WORD   Subsystem;
WORD   DllCharacteristics;
DWORD   SizeOfStackReserve;
DWORD   SizeOfStackCommit;
DWORD   SizeOfHeapReserve;
DWORD   SizeOfHeapCommit;
DWORD   LoaderFlags;
DWORD   NumberOfRvaAndSizes;
IMAGE_DATA_DIRECTORY DataDirectory[16];
} IMAGE_OPTIONAL_HEADER32;
```

2.2 Section Table

The section table immediately follows the IMAGE_NT_HEADERS, it is composed of multiple section table items. Each section table item describes the relevant information of a specific section in the PE file, such as section size, section attributes, location in file and memory, etc. The data structure definition of section table item is as follows:

```
typedef struct _IMAGE_SECTION_HEADER
{
    BYTE   Name[8];
    union {   DWORD  PhysicalAddress;
              DWORD  VirtualSize;
          } Misc;
    DWORD  VirtualAddress;
    DWORD  SizeOfRawData;
    DWORD  PointerToRawData;
    DWORD  PointerToRelocations;
    DWORD  PointerToLinenumbers;
    WORD   NumberOfRelocations;
    WORD   NumberOfLinenumbers;
    DWORD  Characteristics;
} IMAGE_SECTION_HEADER;
```

2.3 Relative Virtual Address and File Address

Because the alignment granularity is different, the image of the section in memory is different from that in the file. When reading and writing PE files by programming, it is often necessary to convert between RVA and file address.

Since the file header is the same in disk file and memory, the combination of all sections is all contents except the file header in PE file. In this way, all RVA fields in the file header data structure can locate the RVA to a specific section by comparison. Get the starting RAV0 of this section, and then you can find OFFSET (the offset address of the specified RVA from the section head). Because 0 is supplemented at the end of the section during alignment, this offset is the same in disk file and memory. That is, the offset between the starting address of the data in each section and the first address of the section is the same, which is the same in the file and memory. If D_{RVA} represents the relative virtual address of the data, D_{FOA} represents the file address of the data, SRVA represents the relative virtual address of the section, S_{FOA} represents the file address of the section, and D_H represents the relative offset of the data, then:

$$D_H = D_{RVA} - S_{RVA} \tag{1}$$

$$D_H = D_{FOA} - S_{FOA} \tag{2}$$

According to the above two formulas, the calculation formula of the address of the data in the file can be obtained as follows:

$$D_{FOA} = (D_{RVA} - S_{RVA}) + S_{FOA} \tag{3}$$

After obtaining the OFFSET address offset of an RVA from the section head in a section, the offset address of the RVA in the file can be calculated from the offset of the section in the file. The main steps are as follows:

Step 1: Judge which section the specified RVA is in.
Step 2: Calculate the starting RVA0 of this section.
Step 3: Calculate the offset OFFSET = RVA-RVA0.
Step 4: Find the offset address of the RVA relative to the disk file.

3   PE File Loading Process

The process of windows loader reading a PE file is as follows:

Step 1: First, read the DOS header, PE header and section table of the PE file. The loader reads the PE header offset in the DOS header and jumps to the PE header.
Step 2: The loader checks the validity of the PE head. If it is valid, jump to the end of the PE header, that is, the section table, otherwise "Illegal PE file" will be displayed.
Step 3: The loader reads the information of the section table, and according to whether the loading address defined by ImageBase in the PE header is available, if other modules have occupied it, the operating system allocates a new space, maps the section to the newly allocated memory space, and specifies the section attribute.
Step 4: Analyze the import table of the PE file, load the required DLL into the process space, and modify the address in the IAT table to the real memory address of the import function.
Step 5: The loader processes information such as the relocation table of the PE file and the TLS callback function.
Step 6: Generate the initialized heap and stack according to the data in the PE header.
Step 7: The loader jumps to the OEP (original entry point) of the PE file and starts execution.

4   Multi-carrier Steganography Algorithm Base on PE File

4.1   Multi-carrier Steganography Algorithm

Ker A. D. proposed the concept of multi-carrier image steganography for the first time in 2006. The research object has changed from single carrier to multi-carrier set. There is a certain correlation between carriers (Fig. 2).

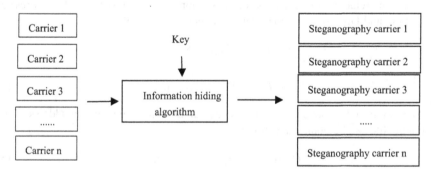

Fig. 2. Multi-carrier steganography model.

The embedding process of secret information is independent of each other in multi-carrier steganography. When extracting secret information, the extraction algorithm extracts the secret information from the steganography carrier and combines the extracted secret information. There are a large number of PE files in personal computers using Windows operating system. These PE files can be used for multi-carrier information hiding.

4.2 Threshold Secret Sharing Algorithm

Secret sharing is an effective mechanism to prevent the loss, destruction, tampering or illegal acquisition of secret information. It is an important means of information security and covert communication. In 1979, Shamir [10] and Blakley [11] independently proposed (k, n) threshold secret sharing algorithm. (k, n) threshold secret sharing algorithm is to divide a secret information into several sub secrets and distribute it to n participants. k or more participants can cooperate to reconstruct and recover the shared secret through Lagrange interpolation method. Any less than k participants cannot recover the shared secret, where k is called the threshold of the scheme.

Shamir's threshold secret sharing algorithm is based on Lagrange interpolation. Firstly, a polynomial of degree $k-1$ is constructed, and the secret information to be shared is taken as the constant term of the polynomial. Then, the secret information is divided into n sub secrets and distributed to n participants. Each sub secret is regarded as a coordinate point satisfying the polynomial, K or more participants cooperate and recover the shared secret through Lagrange interpolation algorithm, but less than k participants cannot obtain useful information. Blakley [11] proposed another threshold secret sharing algorithm using points in multidimensional space. In this algorithm, the shared secret is regarded as a point in k-dimensional space, and each sub secret is regarded as a $k-1$-dimensional hyper-plane equation containing this point. The shared secret can be determined by the intersection of any k $k-1$-dimensional hyper-planes. Similarly, Less than k, no useful information can be obtained.

The (k, n) threshold secret sharing scheme is simple and practical. The specific implementation is as follows:

(1) System Parameter

Suppose the number of participants is n, n is the threshold, and p is a large prime number, and it is required that $p > n$ and greater than the maximum value of secret s.

The secret distributor is D, $P = \{P_1, P_2, P_3, ...,P_n\}$ is a set of n participants; Both sub secret space and secret space are finite fields $GF(p)$.

(2) Distribute Secrets

The secret distributor D allocates the sub secret to n participants $P_i(0 \leq i \leq n)$ as follows:

Step 1: Randomly select a polynomial of degree $k-1$ on $GF(p)$: $f(x) = a_0 + a_1x + ... + a_{k-1}x^{k-1} \in Z_p[x]$, make $f(0) = a_0 = s$ a secret to be shared among n participants and D is a secret to $f(x)$.
Step 2: D select y non-zero elements different from each other $x_1, x_2, ..., x_n$ in Z_p, calculate $y_i = f(x_i)(1 \leq i \leq n)$.
Step 3: (x_i, y_i) is assigned to participant $P_i(1 \leq i \leq n)$, the value x_i is public, and y_i is the sub secret of P_i.

(3) Restore Secrets

Given any k point, you might as well set it as the previous k points are (x_1, y_1), (x_2, y_2), ... ,(x_k, y_k), Known from Lagrange interpolation formula:

$$f(x) = \sum_{i=1}^{k} y_i \prod_{j=1, j \neq 1}^{k} \frac{(x - x_j)}{(x_i - x_j)} \pmod{p} \tag{4}$$

$$\text{Namely} : s = f(0) = a_0$$

4.3   Multi-carrier Steganography Algorithm

In order to further improve the concealment and solve the problem of too centralized hiding capacity, an information decentralized hiding technology is proposed by using the working principle of threshold secret sharing algorithm, that is, the encrypted secret information is divided into several blocks according to the agreed algorithm, and then hidden into multiple PE files under the windows system folder. When users need secret information, the system will automatically extract and assemble this scattered and hidden information to form a complete secret information. In this way, even if a malicious attacker can get one or more PE files containing secret information, it cannot effectively extract the hidden information.

Randomly select n PE format files in the windows system folder, encrypt the information to be hidden and divide it into n sub blocks, then hide the information in sequence, and record the file name of the carrier PE file and the path information on the disk. The detailed implementation steps are as follows:

Step 1: Arbitrarily select n PE files from the system.
Step 2: Encrypt the information to be hidden and then divide it into n sub blocks.
Step 3: Use the function migration method to hide the N sub block information into n different PE files respectively.
Step 4: Record the file name of the carrier PE file and the path information on the disk.

4.4   Multi-carrier Extract Algorithm

According to the file name and path information of the carrier PE file, the above algorithm is used to extract secret information from n PE files respectively. According to the principle of threshold key, once the system is attacked, as long as the information embedded in more than k PE files is not damaged, the polynomial f(x) can be reconstructed by Lagrange interpolation formula to accurately extract all the hidden information. Even if the attacker obtains part of the sub secrets, as long as it is less than k, the original secrets cannot be obtained.

4.5 Multi-carrier Steganography Algorithm Automatic Destruction Technology

In order to improve security, when users correctly extract information, they can choose to automatically destroy the information hidden in multiple PE files and restore the PE files automatically. The specific implementation can restore the last section of the migrated function to the original function code location according to the hiding algorithm. The specific algorithm is as follows:

Step 1: Read the path and file name information where the recorded n carrier PE files are located.
Step 2: Reverse scan from the end of the last section. After finding a migrated function, copy the function code to the original function location.
Step 3: Repeat step 2 until all n PE files are processed.

5 Turn off Windows File Protection

The windows file protection function is used to protect specific types of files under Windows system folders, such as SYS, EXE, DLL, OCX, FON and TTF [12–16]. When an application attempts to replace a protected file, the protected file will only be temporarily replaced by a new file, but the protected file is backed up in the C:\windows\system32\dllcache folder. Soon, windows will copy the correct version of the file and replace it. In the process of decentralized hiding, because the information is scattered and hidden into multiple protected PE files under the windows system folder, in order to prevent the PE files with hidden information from being restored by the windows file protection function, by studying the implementation mechanism of the windows file protection function, turn off the windows file protection function before hiding to realize the effective hiding of information. An unpublished API function of windows SfcFileException() is used to turn off the windows file protection function. The SfcFileException() function is declared as follows:

DWORD WINAPI SfcFileException(DWORD dwUnknown0, PWCHAR pwszFile, DWORD dwUnknown1)

Parameter description: dwUnknown0 is unknown, set to 0. pwszFile is filename. dwUnknown1 is unknown, set to −1. Sfcfileexception can only prohibit windows file protection for a single file. The pwszFile parameter is UNICODE character, return value of 0 indicates success, return value of 1 indicates failure. In Windows XP, SfcFileException is located in SFC_OS.dll. There is no exported function name, but only the serial number 5. To hide information in PE files, it is often necessary to modify PE files. In order to prevent PE files with hidden information from being restored by windows file protection function, turn off windows file protection function by calling SfcFileException() function.

6 Conclusion

Based on the threshold secret sharing algorithm, this paper realizes the steganography of multi-carrier executable program, expands the steganography capacity and improves the security of secret information. Software steganography uses the redundancy of carrier program to hide secret information. It not only hides the content of secret information, but also hides the existence of information, which effectively improves the security of information. In order to further improve the concealment and solve the problem of too centralized hiding capacity, a technology of information decentralized hiding and automatic destruction is introduced by using the working principle of threshold secret sharing. The encrypted secret information is divided into several blocks according to the agreed algorithm, and then hidden into multiple PE files under the windows system folder. When users need secret information, the system will automatically extract and assemble these scattered and hidden information to form a complete secret information. In this way, even if the malicious attacker can get one or more PE files containing secret information, it cannot effectively extract the hidden information.

References

1. Malvar, H., Flomeio, D.: Improved spread spectrum: a new modulation technique for robust watermarking. IEEE Trans. Sig. Process. **51**(4), 898–905 (2003)
2. Jin, C.: Digital Watermarking Theory and Technology. Tsinghua University Press (2008)
3. Wang, Y.: Digital Watermarking Principle and Technology. Science Press (2007)
4. Cappellini, V., Bartolini, F., Barni, M.: Information theoretic aspects in digital watermarking. Sig. Process. **81**(6), 1117–1119 (2001)
5. Zeng, W., Yu, H., Lin, C.Y.: Multimedia Security Technologies for Digital Rights Management. Elsevier Academic Press, Salt Lake City (2006)
6. El-Khalil, R., Keromytis, A.D.: Hydan: hiding information in program binaries. In: Lopez, J., Qing, S., Okamoto, E. (eds.) ICICS 2004. LNCS, vol. 3269, pp. 187–199. Springer, Heidelberg (2004). https://doi.org/10.1007/978-3-540-30191-2_15
7. Anckaert, B., Sutter, B., Chanet, D., Bosschere, K.: Steganography for executables and code transformation signatures. In: Park, C.-S., Chee, S. (eds.) ICISC 2004. LNCS, vol. 3506, pp. 425–439. Springer, Heidelberg (2005). https://doi.org/10.1007/11496618_31
8. Daemin, S., Yeog, K., Keunduck, B., Sang, J.L.: Data hiding in windows executable files. Center for Information Security Technologies (CIST), Korea University, Seoul, Korea (2008)
9. Li, Q., Fang, Y., Tan, D.L., Zhang, C.S.: Research on information hiding technology based on PE file without capacity limit. Comput. Appl. Res. **28**(7), 2758–2760 (2011)
10. Shamir, A.: How to share a secret. Commun. ACM **22**(11), 612–613 (1979)
11. Blakley, G.R.: Safeguarding cryptographic keys. In: Proceedings of AFIPS 1979 National Computer Conference, pp. 313–317 (1979)
12. Beggar, B.: Disable WFP (windows file protection) (2011). http://blog.csdn.net/billbeggar/article/details/6403605
13. Microsoft. Windows file protection (2011). http://support.microsoft.com/?kbid=222193
14. Raff, E., Barker, J., Sylvester, J., Brandon, R., et al.: Malware detection by eating a whole EXE. arXiv arXiv:1710.09435 (2019)
15. Dai, Y., Li, H., Qian, Y.: A malware classification method based on memory dump grayscale image. Digit. Investig. **27**, 30–37 (2018)
16. Anderson, H. S., Kharkar, A., Filar, B., et al.: Learning to evade static PE machine learning malware models via reinforcement learning. arXiv arXiv:180108917 (2018)

Efficient Fragile Privacy-Preserving Audio Watermarking Using Homomorphic Encryption

Ruopan Lai[1], Xiongjie Fang[1], Peijia Zheng[1,2(✉)], Hongmei Liu[1(✉)], Wei Lu[1], and Weiqi Luo[1]

[1] School of Computer Science and Engineering, Guangdong Key Laboratory of Information Security Technology, Sun Yat-Sen University, Guangzhou 510006, China
{zhpj,luwei3}@mail.sysu.edu.cn
[2] State Key Laboratory of Information Security, Institute of Information Engineering, Chinese Academy of Sciences, Beijing 100093, China

Abstract. Audio has become increasingly important in modern social communication and mobile Internet. In cloud computing, practical cloud-based applications should achieve high computation efficiency and secure data protection simultaneously. In this paper, we study the application of an efficient encrypted audio fragile watermarking using homomorphic encryption and the batching technique SIMD in cloud computing. We firstly implement the algorithm of Haar wavelet transform in the encrypted domain (BS-HWT) using the batching technique SIMD with the fully homomorphic encryption scheme CKKS. By performing BS-HWT on the encrypted audio, we transform the encrypted audio signal into the encrypted frequency-domain coefficients. The encrypted fragile watermark is then embedded into the encrypted discrete wavelet transform domain. Our experimental results show that the proposed watermarking scheme is highly efficient and sensitive to common audio attacks. We also present the proposed scheme has a good ability of tamper localization.

Keywords: Audio watermarking · Secure watermarking · Discrete wavelet transform · Fully homomorphic encryption · Signal processing in the encrypted domain · Cloud computing

1 Introduction

With the advent of the mobile Internet era, users can easily generate pictures, audio, and videos through mobile phones, resulting in multimedia data bursting every day. As a significant part of multimedia data, audio plays an increasingly important role in people's daily lives and modern social communication. Most of the operating systems of smartphones and computers support voice interaction modules, such as Siri on iPhones, Bixby on Samsung phones, and Cortana on Windows. Meanwhile, voice messaging has become a mainstream communication method and an essential service in mobile social Apps, such as WhatsApp,

© The Author(s), under exclusive license to Springer Nature Switzerland AG 2022
X. Sun et al. (Eds.): ICAIS 2022, LNCS 13340, pp. 373–385, 2022.
https://doi.org/10.1007/978-3-031-06791-4_30

Facebook Messenger, Line, WeChat, etc. Motivated by the advances of cloud computing, people are willing to outsource their private multimedia data to the cloud to perform complex computing tasks for cost-saving and flexibility. Considering the privacy protection of personal audio, studying encrypted audio processing is meaningful and necessary.

Signal processing in the encrypted domain (SPED) has received considerable attention in recent years [2,9]. A general solution of SPED is homomorphic encryption (HE). HE allows us to operate the plaintexts via manipulating the ciphertexts without performing decryption. We can roughly classify existing HEs into partial homomorphic encryption (PHE) and fully homomorphic encryption (FHE). For example, Paillier encryption [16] is a famous PHE, which provides additive homomorphism. The first fully homomorphic encryption (FHE) was proposed by Gentry [11] which allows arbitrary homomorphic evaluation of circuits. Various FHE schemes [4,5,14] have been proposed since Gentry's construction. For example, Cheon et al. [7] proposed an approximate FHE scheme called CKKS, which supports the approximate arithmetic of encrypted real-number/complex-number messages.

With SPED techniques, the cloud server can perform processing and analysis directly on encrypted data without learning the private information. There are already many secure realizations of signal transformations in SPED, such as discrete Fourier transform (DFT) [3], discrete cosine transform (DCT) [1], and discrete wavelet transform (DWT) [22]. There are also many works on the development of privacy-preserving applications, such as privacy-preserving content-aware search [10], encrypted image reversible data hiding [20], privacy-preserving image feature extraction [19], secure verifiable diversity ranking search [13], privacy-preserving matrix QR factorization [21], privacy-preserving video anomaly detection and localization [12].

Considering that watermarking is a fundamental tool for achieving audio copyright protection and content authentication, it is necessary to seek efficient audio watermarking schemes in the encrypted domain. In this paper, we adopt CKKS as the cryptographic tool and design our privacy-preserving scheme. We focus on efficient fragile privacy-preserving audio watermarking in an audio authentication system in the cloud using CKKS and the batching technique single-instruction multi-data (SIMD). First, we propose an efficient batched implementation of secure Haar wavelet transform (BS-HWT) with the batching technique. By using BS-HWT, we first transform the audio signal into the encrypted frequency-domain coefficients. The fragile watermarks are then homomorphically embedded into all sub-bands. We can extract watermarks in the plaintext domain for audio content authentication and then detect whether the audio has been tampered with. We list the main contributions of this paper as follows.

1. We have proposed an efficient and secure fragile audio watermarking scheme in the encrypted domain based on the proposed batched discrete wavelet transform relying on the SIMD technique.
2. We have conducted several experiments on the proposed scheme to compare the running and performances under various attacks. The compassion results show our scheme has high computation efficiency and a good ability of tamper localization.

2. Fragile audio watermarking in the encrypted domain

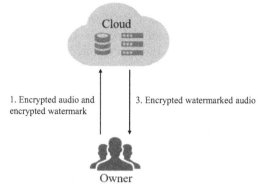

Fig. 1. System model

The rest of the paper is organized as follows. In Sect. 2, we introduce our security model, cryptographic tool, batching technique, and discrete wavelet transform. Section 3 presents the proposed efficient fragile privacy-preserving audio watermarking in the encrypted domain with batched secure (inverse) Haar wavelet transform. We give our experimental results in Sect. 4. Section 5 concludes the paper.

2 Problem Statement

2.1 System Model

We consider a cloud-based audio watermarking outsourcing system for content authentication involving two parties: the data owner $\mathcal{O}$ and the cloud server $\mathcal{S}$. In our application scenario, we assume that the data owner $\mathcal{O}$ has a huge quantity of sensitive data while is resource-constrained. $\mathcal{O}$ would like to outsource the task of watermarking to the clouds for authentication. To protect privacy, $\mathcal{O}$ will first encrypt audio data and watermark message and then distribute the ciphertexts to $\mathcal{S}$. After running the fragile audio watermarking algorithm in the encrypted domain, $\mathcal{S}$ will return the encrypted watermarked audio to the data owner $\mathcal{O}$, who can eventually recover the real watermarked audio from their encrypted versions. We sketch the system model in Fig. 1.

2.2 Threat Model

Throughout the paper, we adopt the semi-honest security setting. Specifically, the cloud server $\mathcal{S}$ is considered as an *honest-but-curious* party, which is honest to carry out the pre-defined protocols, but curious with the private data related to the data owner. More detailed discussions on semi-honest setting in privacy-preserving applications can be referred to [12,19].

2.3   Cryptographic Tool: CKKS

In our scheme, we use the FHE scheme CKKS proposed by Cheon et al. [7], which supports approximate arithmetic of encrypted real-number/complex-number messages. Let us use $[\![\cdot]\!]$ to denote the encryption operator. Then $[\![\xi]\!]$ means an encryption value of a complex-number message ξ. For ciphertexts $[\![\xi]\!]$, $[\![\eta]\!]$ and complex number z, we can use CKKS to homomorphically compute the sum, the difference, and the product of their plaintexts as

$$[\![\xi + \eta]\!] = [\![\xi]\!] \oplus [\![\eta]\!] \tag{1}$$

$$[\![\xi - \eta]\!] = [\![\xi]\!] \ominus [\![\eta]\!] \tag{2}$$

$$[\![\xi\eta]\!] = [\![\xi]\!] \otimes [\![\eta]\!] \tag{3}$$

$$[\![z\xi]\!] = [\![\xi]\!] \otimes z \tag{4}$$

where $\oplus$, $\ominus$, and $\otimes$ denote the homomorphic addition, subtraction, and multiplication, respectively. For convenience, we will use $[\![\xi]\!] + [\![\eta]\!]$, $[\![\xi]\!] - [\![\eta]\!]$, $[\![\xi]\!][\![\eta]\!]$ and $z[\![\eta]\!]$ to denote $[\![\xi]\!] \oplus [\![\eta]\!]$, $[\![\xi]\!] \ominus [\![\eta]\!]$, $[\![\xi]\!] \otimes [\![\eta]\!]$ and $[\![\xi]\!] \otimes z$, respectively.

2.4   Batching Technique: Single-Instruction Multiple-Data (SIMD)

For a power-of-two integer $k \leq N/2$ where N is the dimension of the cyclotomic polynomial ring, CKKS provides a technique to pack k complex numbers in a single polynomial using a variant of the complex canonical embedding map. The encoding/decoding techniques support the parallel computation over ciphertexts, yielding a better-amortized timing. Assuming that $\boldsymbol{v} = (v_0, v_1, \cdots, v_{n-1})$ is an n-dimensional vector. We use $[\![\boldsymbol{v}]\!]$ to denote a ciphertext of the polynomial into which the vector $\boldsymbol{v}$ is packed. Given two vectors $\boldsymbol{x} = (x_0, x_1, \cdots, x_{k-1})$, $\boldsymbol{y} = (y_0, y_1, \cdots, y_{k-1})$ and a complex number z, the SIMD-type homomorphic operations of CKKS can be expressed as

$$[\![\boldsymbol{x}]\!] + [\![\boldsymbol{y}]\!] = [\![(x_0 + y_0, x_1 + y_1, \cdots, x_{k-1} + y_{k-1})]\!] \tag{5}$$

$$[\![\boldsymbol{x}]\!] - [\![\boldsymbol{y}]\!] = [\![(x_0 - y_0, x_1 - y_1, \cdots, x_{k-1} - y_{k-1})]\!] \tag{6}$$

$$[\![\boldsymbol{x}]\!][\![\boldsymbol{y}]\!] = [\![(x_0 \times y_0, x_1 \times y_1, \cdots, x_{k-1} \times y_{k-1})]\!] \tag{7}$$

$$z[\![\boldsymbol{x}]\!] = [\![(x_0 \times z, x_1 \times z, \cdots, x_{k-1} \times z)]\!] \tag{8}$$

It shows that a single operation on the ciphertexts applies the homomorphic operation to every vector element. Here we $\{[\![\boldsymbol{x}_k]\!]\}_{k=0}^{N}$ to denote $\{[\![\boldsymbol{x}_0]\!], [\![\boldsymbol{x}_1]\!], \cdots, [\![\boldsymbol{x}_{N-1}]\!]\}$.

2.5   Discrete Wavelet Transform (DWT)

The discrete wavelet transform (DWT) is a tool used widely in the field of signal processing. With the different wavelet bases and decomposition levels, DWT

Algorithm 1. Batched secure Haar wavelet transform

1: **Input:** Encrypted signals $\{[\![x_k]\!]\}_{k=0}^{N}$ and the decomposition level L.
2: **Output:** Encrypted HWT coefficients $\{[\![c_k]\!]\}_{k=0}^{N}$.
3: Set $d = N/2$
4: **for** $j = 0$ to $L - 1$ **do**
5:     **for** $k = 0$ to $d - 1$ **do**
6:         $[\![c_k]\!] = \frac{1}{2}([\![x_{2k}]\!] + [\![x_{2k+1}]\!])$
7:         $[\![c_{k+d}]\!] = \frac{1}{2}([\![x_{2k}]\!] - [\![x_{2k+1}]\!])$
8:     **end for**
9:     **for** $k = 0$ to $N - 1$ **do**
10:         $[\![x_k]\!] = [\![c_k]\!]$
11:     **end for**
12:     $d = d/2$
13: **end for**
14: **return** $\{[\![c_k]\!]\}_{k=0}^{N}$

---

can extract different kinds of information from the media. According to Mallat's algorithm [15], DWT can be defined recursively as

$$a_j(k) = \frac{1}{\sqrt{2}} \sum_{l \in \mathbb{Z}} h_d(2k - l)a_{j-1}(l) \tag{9}$$

$$d_j(k) = \frac{1}{\sqrt{2}} \sum_{l \in \mathbb{Z}} g_d(2k - l)a_{j-1}(l) \tag{10}$$

where $h_d(k)$ and $g_d(k)$ are the low-pass decomposition filter coefficients and high-pass decomposition filter coefficients, respectively, and $j = 1, 2, 3, \cdots$ is the decomposition level of the input signal. $a_j(k)$ and $d_j(k)$, termed the approximation coefficients and detail coefficients respectively, can be computed from $a_{j-1}(k)$. $a_0(l)$ is defined as the input signal which is denoted by $x(l)$. In our paper, we will use the Haar wavelet transform (HWT) and the inverse Haar wavelet transform (IHWT) for watermarking.

3 Efficient Fragile Privacy-Preserving Audio Watermarking

3.1 Batched Secure Haar Wavelet Transform

We propose a batched implementation of secure Haar wavelet transform (BS-HWT) in Algorithm 1 to perform multi-level HWT in the encrypted domain. In BS-HWT, we perform L-level HWT-ED on encrypted signals $\{[\![x_k]\!]\}_{k=0}^{N}$ to obtain encrypted HWT coefficients $\{[\![c_k]\!]\}_{k=0}^{N}$ using SIMD in a batching manner. Assume the batch size is S, i.e., $[\![x_k]\!] = [\![(x_{k,0}, x_{k,1}, \cdots, x_{k,S-1})]\!]$, then $\{x_{k,i}\}_{k=0}^{N}$ is one signal block, $\{c_{k,i}\}_{k=0}^{N}$ are HWT coefficients of signal block $\{x_{k,i}\}_{k=0}^{N}$ and $\{c_{k,i}\}_{i=0}^{S}$ are HWT coefficients in position k of S signal blocks.

Algorithm 2. Batched secure inverse Haar wavelet transform

1: **Input:** Encrypted HWT coefficients $\{[\![c_k]\!]\}_{k=0}^{N}$ and the decomposition level L.
2: **Output:** Encrypted signals $\{[\![x_k]\!]\}_{k=0}^{N}$.
3: Set $d = N/2^L$
4: **for** $j = 0$ to $L - 1$ **do**
5:     **for** $k = 0$ to $d - 1$ **do**
6:         $[\![x_{2k}]\!] = [\![c_k]\!] + [\![c_{k+d}]\!]$
7:         $[\![x_{2k+1}]\!] = [\![c_k]\!] - [\![c_{k+d}]\!]$
8:     **end for**
9:     **for** $k = 0$ to $N - 1$ **do**
10:         $[\![c_k]\!] = [\![x_k]\!]$
11:     **end for**
12:     $d = 2d$
13: **end for**
14: **return** $\{[\![x_k]\!]\}_{k=0}^{N}$

3.2 Batched Secure Inverse Haar Wavelet Transform

We propose batched secure inverse Haar wavelet transform (BS-IHWT) in Algorithm 2 to perform multi-level IHWT in the encrypted domain to transform encrypted HWT coefficients to encrypted signals.

3.3 Efficient Fragile Privacy-Preserving Audio Watermarking

3.3.1 Encrypting Audio in a Batching Manner. We embed the fragile watermark on each audio frame. We frame the audio signals $x(k)$ into frames $x_i(k)$ with N points per frame. The fragile watermarks corresponding to the i-th frame are $w_i(k)(0 \le k < M)$ where M is the length of the watermarks. Given batch size S, we encrypt S frames $x_i(k)(0 \le i < S, 0 \le k < N)$ to N ciphertexts $\{[\![x_k]\!]\}_{k=0}^{N}$ to compute one group of encrypted HWT coefficients where $x_k = (x_0(k), x_1(k), \cdots, x_{S-1}(k))$. The corresponding fragile watermarks of S frames are encrypted to $\{[\![w_k]\!]\}_{k=0}^{M}$ the same as above where $w_k = (w_0(k), w_1(k), \cdots, w_{S-1}(k))$.

3.3.2 Watermark Embedding in the Encrypted Domain

Step 1 Encryption: $\mathcal{O}$ encrypts the audio frames and watermarks as in Sect. 3.3.1 and sends $\{[\![x_k]\!]\}_{k=0}^{N}, \{[\![w_k]\!]\}_{k=0}^{M}$ to $\mathcal{S}$ for watermarking.
Step 2 Pre-process: We pre-process the watermarks at the beginning. The data to be embedded can be expressed as $w_i'(j) = \gamma w_i(j)$, where γ is the embedding factor. Generally, γ is a very small value less than 1, e.g., 0.001. This pre-processing can be performed in the encrypted domain as $[\![w_k']\!] = \gamma[\![w_k]\!] = [\![\gamma w_k]\!], 0 \le k < M$.
Step 3 Transformation to Encrypted Frequency Domain: We perform multi-level BS-HWT (see Algorithm 1) on the encrypted audio frames $\{[\![x_k]\!]\}_{k=0}^{N}$ and obtain encrypted HWT coefficients $\{[\![c_k]\!]\}_{k=0}^{N}$.

Step 4 Encrypted HWT Coefficient Modification: With the watermarking key K_w, we determine the positions for watermark embedding and embed the fragile watermarks in all sub-bands of encrypted HWT coefficients as

$$\llbracket \boldsymbol{c}_{k'} \rrbracket = \llbracket \boldsymbol{c}_{k'} \rrbracket + \llbracket \boldsymbol{w}'_k \rrbracket$$
$$= \llbracket \boldsymbol{c}_{k'} + \gamma \boldsymbol{w}_k \rrbracket \tag{11}$$
$$k = 0, 1, \cdots, M - 1$$

or

$$\llbracket \boldsymbol{c}_{k'} \rrbracket = \llbracket \boldsymbol{c}_{k'} \rrbracket (\llbracket \boldsymbol{1} \rrbracket + \llbracket \boldsymbol{w}'_k \rrbracket)$$
$$= \llbracket \boldsymbol{c}_{k'} (\boldsymbol{1} + \gamma \boldsymbol{w}_k) \rrbracket \tag{12}$$
$$k = 0, 1, \cdots, M - 1$$

where k' is the position for k-th watermark embedding given by K_w, $\boldsymbol{1} = (1, 1, \cdots, 1)$ and $\llbracket \boldsymbol{c}'_{k'} \rrbracket$ is the encrypted modified HWT coefficient.

Step 5 Reconstruction of the Watermarked Audio: We combine the modified and the un-modified encrypted HWT coefficients together as $\{\llbracket \boldsymbol{c}'_k \rrbracket\}_{k=0}^N$, and perform the BS-IHWT (see Algorithm 2) to obtain the encrypted watermarked audio frames $\{\llbracket \boldsymbol{x}^w_k \rrbracket\}_{k=0}^N$.

3.3.3 Watermark Extraction and Detection in the Plaintext Domain

Step 1 Decryption: After receiving the encrypted watermarked audio frames $\{\llbracket \boldsymbol{x}^w_k \rrbracket\}_{k=0}^N$, $\mathcal{O}$ decrypt and obtain the watermarked audio frames $x^w_i(k)$ ($0 \leq i < S, 0 \leq k < N$).

Step 2 Watermark Extraction: We first perform HWT on the watermarked audio to convert the signal into the transform domain. With the watermarking key K_w, we can obtain the embedded watermark coefficients $c'_i(k')$. Suppose $c_i(k')$ is the corresponding coefficient of the original audio, the watermark extraction can then be given as

$$\hat{w}_i(k) = (c'_i(k') - c_i(k'))/\gamma$$
$$k = 0, 1, \cdots, M - 1 \tag{13}$$

or

$$\hat{w}_i(k) = (c'_i(k') - c_i(k'))/(\gamma c_i(k'))$$
$$k = 0, 1, \cdots, M - 1 \tag{14}$$

where $\hat{w}_i(k)$ denotes the extracted watermark.

Step 3 Watermark Detection: We compare the similarity of the extracted watermark sequence $\{\hat{w}_i(k)\}$ and the original watermark sequence $\{w_i(k)\}$ to perform watermark detection and tamper localization. If the similarity is high enough, we can say that the audio has not been tampered.

4 Experimental Results

In the experiment, all the test audios are 16-bit mono audios with a sample rate 16000 Hz. Due to the limitation of the paper, we only show the result of

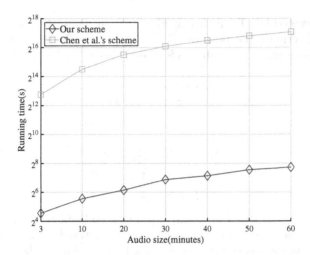

Fig. 2. Running time between Chen et al.'s scheme and our scheme.

two kinds of audio, each of which consists of 50 frames with 400 sample points per frame. The watermarks are the 12 MFCC coefficients [8] of each frame. Several metrics are employed in the experiments, including the sample Pearson correlation coefficient denoted as ρ, error rate (ER), and signal-to-noise ratio (SNR).

All the experiments were conducted on a 64-bit Ubuntu 18.04.5LTS PC with Intel Xeon Gold 6145 CPU @2.00 GHZ and 128 GB of RAM. We implemented our solution in PALISADE [18], an open-source lattice cryptography library. The parameter settings in our experiment are given as follows to ensure 128 bits of security. The bit-length of the scaling factor $= 50$, the level of BS-HWT $L = 3$, the dimension of the cyclotomic polynomial ring $= 2^{15}$, and the max batch size is 2^{14}.

4.1 Running Time

We compare the running time with Chen et al.'s scheme [6], which utilizes the Paillier cryptosystem [17] to do watermarking in the encrypted domain. The audio size increases from 3 min to 60 min. We show the average running time in Fig. 2. The running time of the two schemes grows linearly with the size of audio. Also, we can see Chen et al.'s scheme takes much more time than our scheme. When the audio size grows to 60 min, Chen et al.'s scheme will take 138767.8644 s while our scheme takes 211.5855 s.

4.2 Influence of Different Embedding Factors

We conduct an experiment to investigate the influence of the embedding factor γ on the watermarked audio. We choose different values of γ, perform watermark

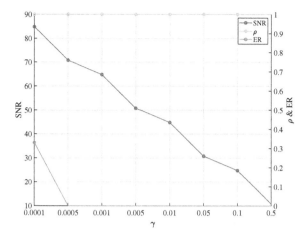

Fig. 3. Influence of different embedding factors.

embedding and extraction, and compute the values of ρ, ER, and SNR. Here, we assume the length of $\{w_{i,j}\}$ is L_w and define ER as $\frac{1}{L_w}\sum(|w_{i,j} - \hat{w}_{i,j}| > 0.001)$. The value of γ is chosen as 0.0001, 0.005, 0.001, 0.005, 0.01, 0.05, 0.1, and 0.5. The experimental result is shown in Fig. 3, from which we can see that when the value of γ changes, the curves of SNR change obviously, while the curve of ER and ρ changes slowly. In the following experiments, we adopt 0.0005 as the value of γ.

4.3 Various Attacks Applied to the Watermarked Audio and Temper Localization

The fragility of the watermarking scheme can be reflected by the degree that the watermark is destroyed after the audio is attacked. The severer the extracted watermark is destroyed, the higher fragility the watermarking scheme has. We consider three common attacks on the watermarked audio to test the fragility of the watermarking scheme.

(1) *Low-pass filtering:* Perform an nth-order low-pass Butterworth filtering with a cut-off frequency of 7 kHz.
(2) *Gaussian noising:* Addictive adding a Gaussian white noise to the water-marked audio with the intensity σ^2.
(3) *Compression:* Compress the watermarked audio using the MP3 Encod-ing/Decoding at 64 kb/s, 32 kb/s.

We apply three kinds of attacks with several different parameters to the watermarked audio and then perform watermark extraction and detection. We show the values of SNR, ER, and ρ in Table 1 for different audios. We can observe that the extracted watermark $\{\hat{w}_{i,j}\}$ is exactly the same with the original watermark $\{w_{i,j}\}$ without any errors when there is no attack applied to the

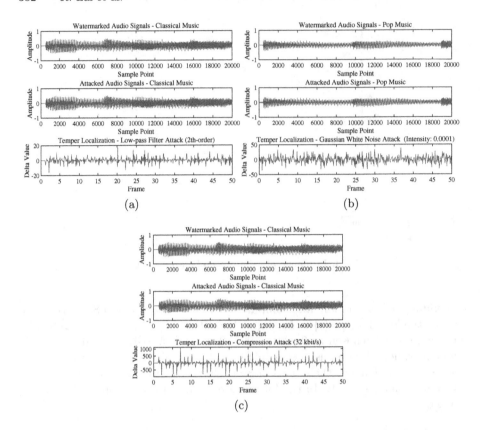

Fig. 4. Tamper localization in the watermarking scheme. Different kinds of watermarked audio before and after attacks and result of tamper localization.

watermarked audio. A lower SNR value means a stronger attack on the audio. When there is an attack performed on the watermarked audio, even it is a lightweight attack, it will cause apparent errors during the watermark extraction. For example, a Gaussian noise is added to produce an attacked audio with $\sigma^2 = 0.00005$, ρ is only 0.0408 and the ER is nearly 1.0, which means we can consider that the audio signal has already been tempered with.

We also conducted experiments to investigate the ability of tamper localization of the proposed watermarking scheme. The experimental results are shown in Fig. 4. With our detection mechanism, we are able to locate the juggled frames. We compute the difference between $\{\hat{w}_{i,j}\}$ and $\{w_{i,j}\}$. We consider $\hat{w}_{i,j} \approx w_{i,j}$ if $|\hat{w}_{i,j} - w_{i,j}| \leq 0.001$. The difference value of a normal frame is 0, while a juggled frame will have a non-zero difference. In Fig. 4, we can find that the proposed watermarking scheme can well locate the juggled frames against common attacks.

Table 1. Fragile watermark under various attacks. σ^2 denotes the intensity of Gaussian noise.

Attack	Classical music			Pop music		
	SNR	ρ	ER	SNR	ρ	ER
No attack	70.8079	1	0	66.5453	1	0
2nd Low-pass filtering	32.0425	0.0471	0.9850	24.9998	0.0497	0.9917
4th Low-pass filtering	26.7139	0.0200	0.9850	20.4203	0.0521	0.9917
Gaussian noising ($\sigma^2 = 0.00005$)	27.0774	0.0408	1.0000	22.6801	0.0379	1.0000
Gaussian noising ($\sigma^2 = 0.0001$)	24.1875	-0.0252	1.0000	19.6476	-0.0283	1.0000
Compression (64 kb/s)	-3.2859	-0.0320	0.9883	-3.0394	-0.0177	1.0000
Compression (32 kb/s)	-3.2858	-0.0296	0.9933	-3.0312	-0.0161	1.0000

5 Conclusions

In this paper, we proposed an efficient fragile privacy-preserving audio watermarking scheme in the cloud. We firstly propose the efficient algorithms BS-HWT and BS-IHWT using the batching SIMD technique. We then present an efficient fragile watermarking scheme in the encrypted domain using BS-HWT and BS-IHWT. The watermark extraction and detection are performed in the plaintext domain. We have also conducted experiments to investigate the system performances, including running time, the influence of different embedding factors, and temper localization under various attacks. The experimental results show that our scheme has a good ability of tamper localization and is more efficient than the previous scheme. In our future work, we will focus on developing more efficient watermarking schemes in the encrypted domain and bringing new privacy-preserving applications.

Acknowledgement. This work was supported in part by the Natural Science Foundation of Guangdong (2019A1515010746, 2022A1515011897), in part by the Science and Technology Projects in Guangzhou (202102080354), in part by the Open Foundation of Henan Key Laboratory of Cyberspace Situation Awareness (HNTS2022023).

References

1. Bianchi, T., Piva, A., Barni, M.: Encrypted domain DCT based on homomorphic cryptosystems. EURASIP J. Inf. Secur. **2009**, 1 (2009)
2. Bianchi, T., Piva, A.: Secure watermarking for multimedia content protection: a review of its benefits and open issues. IEEE Signal Process. Magaz. **30**(2), 87–96 (2013)
3. Bianchi, T., Piva, A., Barni, M.: On the implementation of the discrete fourier transform in the encrypted domain. IEEE Trans. Inf. Forens. Secur. **4**(1), 86–97 (2009)
4. Brakerski, Z.: Fully homomorphic encryption without modulus switching from classical GapSVP. In: Safavi-Naini, R., Canetti, R. (eds.) CRYPTO 2012. LNCS, vol. 7417, pp. 868–886. Springer, Heidelberg (2012). https://doi.org/10.1007/978-3-642-32009-5_50

5. Brakerski, Z., Vaikuntanathan, V.: Efficient fully homomorphic encryption from (standard) IWE. SIAM J. Comput. **43**(2), 831–871 (2014)
6. Chen, J., Zheng, P., Guo, J., Zhang, W., Huang, J.: A privacy-preserving multipurpose watermarking scheme for audio authentication and protection. In: 2018 17th IEEE International Conference on Trust, Security and Privacy in Computing and Communications/12th IEEE International Conference on Big Data Science and Engineering (TrustCom/BigDataSE), pp. 86–91. IEEE (2018)
7. Cheon, J.H., Kim, A., Kim, M., Song, Y.: Homomorphic encryption for arithmetic of approximate numbers. In: Takagi, T., Peyrin, T. (eds.) ASIACRYPT 2017. LNCS, vol. 10624, pp. 409–437. Springer, Cham (2017). https://doi.org/10.1007/978-3-319-70694-8_15
8. Davis, S., Mermelstein, P.: Comparison of parametric representations for monosyllabic word recognition in continuously spoken sentences. IEEE Trans. Acoust. Speech Signal Process. **28**(4), 357–366 (1980)
9. Erkin, Z., Franz, M., Guajardo, J., Katzenbeisser, S., Lagendijk, I., Toft, T.: Privacy-preserving face recognition. In: Goldberg, I., Atallah, M.J. (eds.) PETS 2009. LNCS, vol. 5672, pp. 235–253. Springer, Heidelberg (2009). https://doi.org/10.1007/978-3-642-03168-7_14
10. Fu, Z., Xia, L., Liu, Y., Tian, Z.: Privacy-preserving content-aware search based on two-level index. Comput. Mater. Continua **59**(2), 473–491 (2019)
11. Gentry, C.: Fully homomorphic encryption using ideal lattices. In: Proceedings of the Forty-First Annual ACM Symposium on Theory of Computing, pp. 169–178 (2009)
12. Guo, J., Zheng, P., Huang, J.: Efficient privacy-preserving anomaly detection and localization in bitstream video. In: IEEE Transactions on Circuits and Systems for Video Technology (2019)
13. Liu, Y., Peng, H., Wang, J.: Verifiable diversity ranking search over encrypted outsourced data. Comput. Mater. Continua **55**, 37–57 (2018)
14. López-Alt, A., Tromer, E., Vaikuntanathan, V.: On-the-fly multiparty computation on the cloud via multikey fully homomorphic encryption. In: Proceedings of the Forty-Fourth Annual ACM Symposium on Theory of Computing, pp. 1219–1234. ACM (2012)
15. Mallat, S.: A theory for multiresolution signal decomposition: the wavelet representation. IEEE Trans. Pattern Anal. Mach. Intell. **11**(7), 674–693 (1989). https://doi.org/10.1109/34.192463
16. Paillier, P.: Public-key cryptosystems based on composite degree residuosity classes. In: Stern, J. (ed.) EUROCRYPT 1999. LNCS, vol. 1592, pp. 223–238. Springer, Heidelberg (1999). https://doi.org/10.1007/3-540-48910-X_16
17. Paillier, P., Pointcheval, D.: Efficient public-key cryptosystems provably secure against active adversaries. In: Lam, K.-Y., Okamoto, E., Xing, C. (eds.) ASIACRYPT 1999. LNCS, vol. 1716, pp. 165–179. Springer, Heidelberg (1999). https://doi.org/10.1007/978-3-540-48000-6_14
18. PALISADE: PALISADE Lattice Cryptography Library (release 1.10.5) (2020). https://palisade-crypto.org/
19. Wang, Q., Hu, S., Wang, J., Ren, K.: Secure surfing: privacy-preserving speeded-up robust feature extractor. In: 2016 IEEE 36th International Conference on Distributed Computing Systems (ICDCS), pp. 700–710. IEEE (2016)
20. Xiong, L., Shi, Y.: On the privacy-preserving outsourcing scheme of reversible data hiding over encrypted image data in cloud computing. Comput. Mater. Continua **55**(3), 523–539 (2018)

21. Zhang, Y., Zheng, P., Luo, W.: Privacy-preserving outsourcing computation of QR decomposition in the encrypted domain. In: 2019 18th IEEE International Conference on Trust, Security and Privacy in Computing and Communications/13th IEEE International Conference on Big Data Science and Engineering (TrustCom/BigDataSE), pp. 389–396. IEEE (2019)
22. Zheng, P., Huang, J.: Discrete wavelet transform and data expansion reduction in homomorphic encrypted domain. IEEE Trans. Image Process. **22**(6), 2455–2468 (2013)

Robust Multi-watermarking Algorithm for Medical Images Using Patchwork-DCT

Yuan Li[1], Jingbing Li[1(✉)], Chunyan Shao[1], Uzair Aslam Bhatti[2], and Jixin Ma[3]

[1] Hainan University, Haikou 570100, China
Jingbingli2008@hotmail.com
[2] Nanjing Normal University, Nanjing 210000, China
[3] University of Greenwich, London 10 9LS, UK

Abstract. The fast development of digital information technology has made great improvement on medical imaging digital information technology. The medical images can not avoid the defect of suffering being attacked or tampered maliciously when they are transmitted, and medical image watermarking algorithms can solve the impact of these attacks or malicious tampering, watermarking algorithms techniques are required in the field of image processing. However, the effectiveness of most proposed watermarking algorithms under geometric attacks for medical images are not promise, such that have poor ability to ensure the safety of the medical images. This paper proposes a robust encrypted multiple watermarking algorithm for medical images based on Patchwork-DCT. First, the Patchwork shearing transform and Discrete Cosine Transform (DCT) are combined to extract robust feature vectors against geometric attacks on medical images. Second, considering with the relatively small capacity of medical images and comparatively high requirements for privacy, zero watermark technology is used to embed and extract the watermark. Finally, the Logistic Map encryption algorithm is implied to enhance the security of the watermark information. The experimental results show that the proposed algorithm can effectively embed and extract watermark information, producing relatively good effect on traditional attacks and geometric attacks. The proposed algorithm can be applied in many fields.

Keywords: Patchwork transform · Multiple watermarks · Zero watermarks · DCT · Logistic map

1 Introduction

Today, the widely used digitization plays a very important role in many fields such as science, engineering, medicine, et al. Especially, due to the increasing popularity of Internet technology, it is the era of big data nowadays, making the data transmitting requirements large [1–3]. However, these data can be attacked or tampered by others commonly during the transmission process. Consequently, the security of data transmission has received extensive attention [4]. As we known, a large number of digital medical products are required to be processed in the field of biomedicine, including but not limited to medical images such as ultrasound, X-ray photos, CT and MRI. In considering with the huge

© The Author(s), under exclusive license to Springer Nature Switzerland AG 2022
X. Sun et al. (Eds.): ICAIS 2022, LNCS 13340, pp. 386–399, 2022.
https://doi.org/10.1007/978-3-031-06791-4_31

included patient private information, it affects seriously once these medical images are tampered [5, 6]. However, the information can not avoid being stolen and tampered in the process of Internet based storage and transmission. Information protecting algorithms is urgently required for more safe medical image processing [7]. The current medical image protecting technologies include digital watermarking, image steganography and cryptography methods where the watermarking technology is used widely, which has very important applications in many aspects such as ensuring communication security and copyright protection [8, 9].

The most important measurements for verifying the performance of the digital water-marking are robustness, imperceptibility, and watermark capacity. Even for the most of the state of art algorithm, these performance cannot achieve best. Consequently, it is nec-essary to study digital watermarking algorithm that can achieve a balanced performance under these three characteristics [10, 11]. Especially, digital images in the biomedical field are quite different from traditional digital images, such that its quality specifica-tions are required extremely stableness and the relative visual quality on these images can not be changed. Take these into consideration, the watermarking algorithm must ensure the stableness of medical images and will not cause visual changes in the images. Under this premise, improving the robustness of watermarking algorithm for medical images against various attacks are significant [12, 13]. Accordingly, the embedding and extracting of watermarks using the watermarking algorithm should be fast. Inspired by this, a robust watermarking algorithm for medical images is proposed.

This paper presents the proposed robust watermarking algorithm to improve the security of medical images for Internet based storage and transmission. The algorithm is firstly based on Patchwork-DCT, combining the Logistic Map encryption algorithm and the perceptual hash algorithm (p-Hash). The Patchwork-DCT algorithm and the perceptual hash algorithm are then used to extract the feature vector of the medical image for the watermark is encrypted by the XOR operation to be embedded in the original medical image. Finally, cryptography and Logistic mapping are utilized together to solve the medical image anti-geometric attack problem, the watermark embedding and extraction problem, and the medical image visualization problem [14].

2 Basic Theories

2.1 Patchwork Transform

The proposed algorithm uses Patchwork transform to preprocess the medical images. "Patchwork" originally refers to the fabric that is made up of various shapes and colors rags. In the algorithm, a large amount of pattern redundancies are used to superimpose the signal into the spatial domain of the image, then the robustness of the watermarking algorithm will be improved. The algorithm is one of the most widely used algorithms [15]. When the Patchwork algorithm is used, selecting the point pairs in the carrier medical image, and dividing these point pairs into two types these are set as $A = \{ai\}$ and $B = \{bi\}$. Not only the point pairs can refer to pixels, but also some other characteristic value. Taking a set of point pairs (a, b) in the two sets, a is an element in A, b is an element in B. Calculating the difference between a and b as sub, a and b must be independent of each other and meet the principle of the uniform distribution. Calculating the sum of all subs as SUB, the variance of the SUB is as follows:

$$\sigma_{SUB}^2 = \sigma_a^2 + \sigma_b^2 \tag{1}$$

2.2 Discrete Cosine Transform

DCT can convert the original image information into a set of coefficients which represent different frequency components. It has two advantages: First, most of the signal's energy concentrates on a small range in the frequency domain. Second, the frequency domain decomposition maps the human visual system and allows the subsequent quantization process to meet its sensitivity requirements [16].

The two-dimensional discrete cosine transform (DCT) formula is as follows:

$$F(u, v) = c(u)c(v) \sum_{x=0}^{M-1} \sum_{y=0}^{N-1} f(x, y) \cos \frac{\pi(2x + 1)u}{2M} \cos \frac{\pi(2y + 1)v}{2N}$$
$$u = 0, 1, \ldots, M - 1; \quad v = 0, 1, \ldots, N - 1 \tag{2}$$

The parameters in the formula are:

$$c(u) = \begin{cases} \sqrt{1/M} & u = 0 \\ \sqrt{2/M} & u = 1, 2, \cdots, M - 1 \end{cases}$$

$$c(v) = \begin{cases} \sqrt{1/N} & v = 0 \\ \sqrt{2/N} & v = 1, 2, \cdots, N - 1 \end{cases}$$

The two-dimensional inverse discrete cosine transform (IDCT) formula is as follows:

$$f(x, y) = \sum_{u=0}^{M-1} \sum_{v=0}^{N-1} c(u)c(v)F(u, v) \cos \frac{\pi(2x + 1)u}{2M} \cos \frac{\pi(2y + 1)v}{2N}$$
$$x = 0, 1, \cdots, M - 1; \quad y = 0, 1, \cdots, N - 1 \tag{3}$$

Among them, x, y are sampling values in the spatial domain; u, v are sampling values in the frequency domain. In digital image processing, digital images are usually represented by a square pixel matrix, that is, $M = N$.

3 The Proposed Algorithm

In order to improve the algorithm's performance against geometric attacks, this paper proposes a medical image watermarking algorithm based on Patchwork transform, DCT, Logistic Map, et al. The algorithm consists five parts: Extracting the medical image feature vector, encrypting the digital watermark image, embedding the digital watermark into the medical image, extracting the digital watermark from the medical image, and decrypting and reconstructing the digital watermark.

3.1 Extracting Features

In the stage of extracting the medical image features, according to the human visual system and perceptual hash, the Patchwork-DCT algorithm is used to extract the feature sequences, they are the main basis when the watermark is embedded or extracted. Combining traditional watermarking technology with cryptography, Logistic Map, et al., the robustness and concealment of the algorithm will be improved and the security during remote transmission can also be enhanced.

To meet the requirements of the human visual system, selecting a human brain image (512×512 pixels) without any attack, and applying Patchwork transform in the original medical image. Then performing DCT on the new image to get the coefficient matrix. Finally, selecting the 4×8 features in the low frequency form a new matrix and generating the feature binary sequence of the 32-bit medical image. The flow chart of feature extraction is shown in Fig. 1.

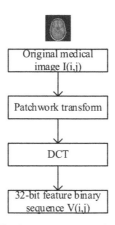

Original medical image I(i,j)

↓

Patchwork transform

↓

DCT

↓

32-bit feature binary sequence V(i,j)

Fig. 1. Feature extraction.

3.2 Encrypting Watermark Image

First, setting the initial value and the growth parameter (this time the initial value is set to 0.2, the growth parameter is set to 4), generating a chaotic sequence, and performing a total of 1023 iterations. Then, according to the Logistic chaotic sequence and the hash function, generating a binary sequence and setting greater than 0.5 to 1, and less than or equal to 0.5 to 0. Finally, the watermark is XORed with the sequences of the generated binary sequences, the chaotic scrambled watermark can be obtained, and the watermark can be encrypted. The flow chart of encrypting watermark image is shown in Fig. 2.

3.3 Embedding Watermark

When the watermark is embedded, the extracted feature vectors XOR with the encrypted watermark bit by bit, the watermark can be successfully embedded into the medical

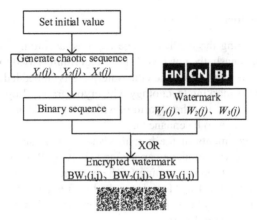

Fig. 2. Encrypting watermark image.

image. At the same time, the logical key will be obtained and stored in the third party. When the watermark is extracted, applying to obtain the logical key from the third party. By this way, the medical image can be protected better. The flow chart of embedding watermark is shown in Fig. 3.

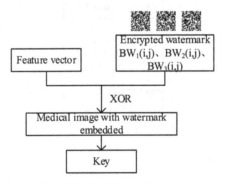

Fig. 3. Embedding watermark.

3.4 Extracting Watermark

When the watermark is extracted. First, performing Patchwork-DCT algorithm on the medical image to obtain the coefficient matrix, and then selecting the 4 × 8 matrix in the low-frequency coefficient. Through the hash function, the feature vectors of the medical image is obtained, and the feature vectors of the encrypted image XOR with the logical key to extract the encrypted watermark. The flow chart of extracting watermark is shown in Fig. 4.

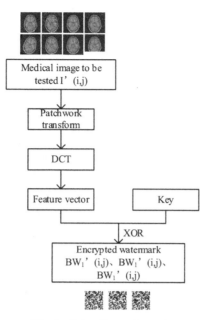

Fig. 4. Extracting watermark.

3.5 Decrypting and Reconstructing Watermark

When decrypting and reconstructing watermark, the same method is used to obtain the binary chaotic encryption sequence, and the values are sorted in the obtained binary chaotic encryption sequence. Then according to the position changes of the sorting of each value, the position space of the pixels is restored and the restored watermarks are obtained. Finally, calculating the normalized correlation coefficient (NC) between the original watermark and the restored watermark, and confirming the ownership of the

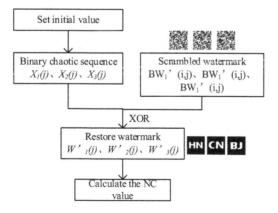

Fig. 5. Decrypting and reconstructing watermark.

medical image and the embedded watermark information. The flow chart of decrypting and reconstructing watermark is shown in Fig. 5.

4   The Proposed Algorithm

This article performs p-Hash on the 32-bit low-frequency data after Patchwork-DCT transform and lists the first 8 data in Table 1. According to the data in the table, after the medical image undergoes Patchwork-DCT transform, the symbols of the characteristic sequence remain unchanged, and obtaining a set of characteristic binary symbol sequence "11000010". Figure 6 shows the medical image after being attacked.

Table 1. Changes of Patchwork-DCT coefficients under different attacks for medical image.

Image Processing	PSNR (dB)	C(1,1)	C(1,2)	C(1,3)	C(1,4)	C(1,5)	C(1,6)	C(1,7)	C(1,8)	Sequence of coefficient symbols	NC
The original image	-	3.6	548.8	-1.6	-485.3	-163.5	-280.5	2.4	-152.0	11000010	1.00
Gaussian noise (5%)	14.8697	3.9	431.9	-1.4	-484.3	-116.2	-201.2	2.2	-107.1	11000010	1.00
JPEG compression (4%)	27.5819	3.5	626.1	-1.7	-517.5	-275.6	-338.6	2.5	-111.0	11000010	1.00
Median filter[5×5](10 times)	28.5551	3.7	542.1	-1.6	-523.0	-94.1	-232.3	2.4	-81.0	11000010	1.00
Rotation clockwise (15°)	14.8697	3.5	1.8	-1.7	-970.4	-1.7	-1.3	957.6	-401.6	11000010	0.86
Scaling (×0.5)	-	1.8	273.9	-8.0	-242.9	-81.5	-140.0	1.2	-75.9	11000010	1.00
Translation(5%, up)	18.2118	3.6	547.6	-1.6	-485.8	-163.7	-282.9	2.4	-153.3	11000010	0.96
Cropping(15%, Y direction)	-	3.4	551.0	-1.5	-439.8	-933.4	-325.5	2.3	-170.1	11000010	1.00

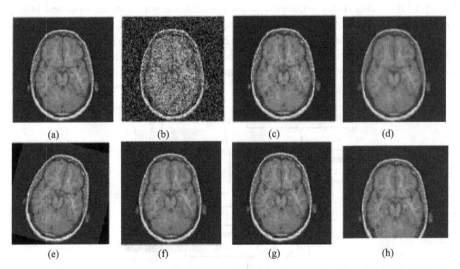

Fig. 6. Different attacks on the medical image. (a) Original image; (b) Gaussian noise (5%); (c) JPEG compression (4%); (d) Median filter [5 × 5] (10 times); (e) Rotation clockwise (15°); (f) Scaling (×0.5); (g) Translation (5%, up); (h) Cropping (15%, Y direction).

The recognition effect between different images also needs to be tested. Selecting multiple different medical images to do the same test, and extracting the 32-bit symbol feature sequence. Verifying the NC values between different medical images, and the results are shown in Table 2. The image used to detect the NC values between different medical images are shown in Fig. 7. According to Table 2, the NC values between different medical images are lower than 0.5, and the NC values of the same images are 1.00. It meets the requirements of the algorithm.

Table 2. Correlation coefficient value between different medical images.

Image	0	1	2	4	5	6
0	1.00	0.1825	-0.0556	0.0159	-0.0556	0.2857
1	0.1825	1.00	0.2549	0.3216	-0.1216	0.0784
2	-0.0556	0.2549	1.00	-0.1961	-0.0039	-0.3294
4	0.0159	0.3216	-0.1961	1.00	-0.0714	0.3492
5	-0.0556	-0.1216	-0.0039	-0.0714	1.00	-0.0833
6	0.2857	0.0784	-0.3294	0.3492	-0.0833	1.00

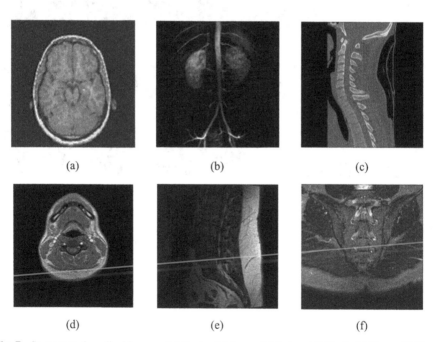

Fig. 7. Some tested medical images. (a) Brain; (b) Lung; (c) Spine; (d) Neck; (e) Knee; (f) Nose.

In the experiment, a gray-scale 512×512 pixels human brain image is selected as the original image, and three 32×32 pixels represents the original watermark image. In order to test the robustness of the proposed algorithm, the image are tested under different attack methods and intensity detection. In the process of embedding and extracting the watermark, the watermark's feature sequences in the medical image are extracted without modifying the original image. By this way, the medical image's visual quality is guaranteed well, where the watermark images are encrypted to improve the security of the watermark. When the medical image is not attacked, Fig. 8 shows the original medical image, watermark image, watermarked medical image and encrypted watermark, Fig. 9 shows the extracted watermark image. The two figures show, the medical image quality has hardly changed after the watermark is embedded, and the NC values of the extracted watermark are all 1, the requirements of the algorithm has been satisfied.

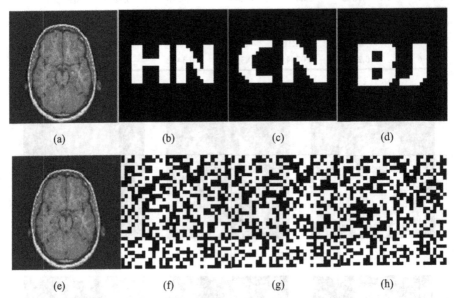

Fig. 8. Medical image and watermark: (a) Original medical image; (b) Original binary watermark 'HN'; (c) Original binary watermark 'CN'; (d) Original binary watermark 'BJ'; (e) Watermarked image; (f) Encrypted watermark 'HN'; (g) Encrypted watermark 'CN'; (h) Encrypted watermark 'BJ'.

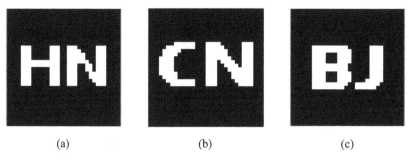

Fig. 9. Watermark extracted without attacks: (a) Extracted watermark 'HN'; (b) Extracted watermark 'CN'; (c) Extracted watermark 'BJ'.

4.1 Data Under Attack

Table 3 shows the PSNR and NC under different attacks, it shows that the proposed algorithm is effective in resisting attacks, and the algorithm embed multiple watermarks at the same time. When the image suffers a rotation attack, until the rotation is 20°, the NC of the extracted watermark is still 0.59, and the effect of extracting the watermark is great. When the image suffers a anti-scaling attack, until the scaling factor is 5.0, the NC of the extracted watermark is still 1.00, the watermarks are kept well. When the image suffers a translation attack, until it is moved up 20%, the NC of the extracted watermark is still 0.54, and when it is moved to the left by 40%, the NC of the extracted watermark is still 0.57, the effect of extracting the watermark is great. When the image suffers a cropping attack, until the y-axis is cut by 35%, the NC of the extracted watermark is still 0.60, and the effect of extracting the watermark is great.

4.2 Comparison

In this paper, in order to verify the effectiveness and robustness of the algorithm, and reduce the different test samples cause difference, choosing a 512×512 pixel "Lena" grayscale image as the original image, then comparing the algorithm with other watermarking algorithms. From an overall point of view, the algorithm has good robustness and provides a safe robust method for both medical images and ordinary images. Table 4 shows the comparison results, from the table, it is obvious that the ability of this algorithm is better when the image suffers traditional and geometric attacks. Only when it suffers rotation attacks, the NC is not as high as the NC value of the algorithm of Amit Kumar Singh.

Table 3. Data under attack.

Attacks	Intensity	PSNR(dB)	The watermark of 'HN' NC1	The watermark of 'CN' NC2	The watermark of 'BJ' NC3
Gaussian Noise	1	20.47	1.00	1.00	1.00
	5	14.31	1.00	1.00	1.00
	10	11.86	1.00	1.00	1.00
	20	9.80	0.94	0.94	0.90
	30	8.77	0.79	0.76	0.80
JPEG Compression	4	27.58	1.00	1.00	1.00
	10	31.29	1.00	1.00	1.00
	20	33.81	1.00	1.00	1.00
	30	34.83	1.00	1.00	1.00
	40	35.46	1.00	1.00	1.00
	50	35.97	1.00	1.00	1.00
Rotation Clockwise	2°	22.36	0.78	0.86	0.72
	5°	18.01	0.78	0.86	0.72
	10°	15.60	0.78	0.86	0.72
	15°	14.87	0.78	0.86	0.72
	18°	14.68	0.68	0.77	0.69
	20°	14.60	0.59	0.73	0.59
Scaling	0.5	-	1.00	1.00	1.00
	0.8	-	1.00	1.00	1.00
	2.0	-	1.00	1.00	1.00
	3.0	-	1.00	1.00	1.00
	5.0	-	1.00	1.00	1.00
Up Translation	2%	23.17	1.00	1.00	1.00
	5%	18.21	0.96	0.96	0.96
	8%	16.42	0.91	0.90	0.87
	10%	15.94	0.91	0.90	0.87
	15%	15.04	0.82	0.86	0.77
	20%	14.64	0.58	0.67	0.54
Left Translation	5%	17.32	0.95	0.92	0.90
	10%	15.57	0.95	0.92	0.90
	15%	14.74	0.95	0.92	0.90
	20%	14.48	0.95	0.92	0.90
	30%	14.26	0.77	0.74	0.67
	40%	13.82	0.68	0.70	0.57
Cropping (%) Y Direction	5%	-	0.96	0.96	0.96
	10%	-	1.00	1.00	1.00
	15%	-	1.00	1.00	1.00
	20%	-	0.90	0.88	0.84
	25%	-	0.74	0.76	0.74
	30%	-	0.65	0.70	0.65
	35%	-	0.60	0.64	0.60

Table 4. Comparison values of different algorithms.

Image Processing	Intensity of Attacks	A. Zear et al. [17] NC1	A. Kumar Singh et al.[18] NC2	The watermark of 'HN' NC3	The watermark of 'CN' NC4	The watermark of 'BJ' NC5
Gaussian Noise	1	0.88	0.74	1.00	1.00	1.00
	10	0.79	0.64	1.00	1.00	1.00
	25	0.63	0.52	1.00	1.00	1.00
JPEG Compression	4	0.11	0.32	1.00	1.00	1.00
	8	0.31	0.51	1.00	1.00	1.00
	25	0.91	0.72	1.00	1.00	1.00
Median Filter (10 times)	[3,3]	0.15	0.22	1.00	1.00	1.00
	[5,5]	0.04	0.17	1.00	1.00	1.00
	[9,9]	0.01	0.11	0.95	0.94	0.90
Rotation Clockwise	10°	0.21	0.85	0.76	0.84	0.72
	20°	0.17	0.81	0.58	0.71	0.66
Scaling	0.8	0.54	0.99	0.95	0.94	0.90
	2.0	0.92	0.99	1.00	1.00	1.00
Down Translation	8%	0.73	0.90	1.00	1.00	1.00
	15%	0.66	0.79	0.94	0.94	0.90
	20%	0.54	0.71	0.90	0.88	0.81
Left Translation	3%	0.77	0.91	0.95	0.94	0.90
	5%	0.74	0.81	0.95	0.94	0.90
	8%	0.70	0.77	0.82	0.76	0.83
Cropping	12%	0.76	0.88	0.90	0.88	0.84

5   Conclusion

This paper proposes a medical image multi-watermarking algorithm based on Patchwork-DCT and Logistic Map. Considering its ability on anti-shearing, Patchwork transform is combined with DCT to improve the algorithm's anti-geometric attack performance. In the process of watermark embedding and extracting, traditional watermarking technology is combined with cryptography technology, Logistic Map and third-party concepts to improve the robustness, concealment and security. Experimental results show that the algorithm has strong robustness and extract watermark information effectively even when suffering geometric attacks and conventional attacks. Take these into consideration, the proposed algorithm can be applied in many fields such as telemedicine and communication security, et al.

Acknowledgement. I would like to sincerely thank my tutor for guiding my thesis and my classmates for their enthusiastic help.

Funding Statement:. This work was supported in part by Key Research Project of Hainan Province under Grant ZDYF2021SHFZ093, the Natural Science Foundation of China under Grants 62063004 and 61762033, the Hainan Provincial Natural Science Foundation of China under Grants 2019RC018 and 619QN246, and the Major Scientific Project of Zhejiang Lab 2020ND8AD01.

References

1. Rajaragavi, R., Rajan, S.P.: Optimized U-Net segmentation and hybrid RES-net for brain tumor MRI images classification. Intell. Autom. Soft Comput. **32**(1), 1–14 (2022)
2. Das, T.K., Roy, P.K., Uddin, M., Srinivasan, K., Chang, C.: Early tumor diagnosis in brain MR images via deep convolutional neural network model. Comput. Mater. Continua **68**(2), 2413–2429 (2021)
3. Faragallah, O.S., Sallam, A.I., El-Sayed, H.S.: Visual protection using RC5 selective encryption in telemedicine. Intell. Autom. Soft Comput. **31**(1), 177–190 (2022)
4. Shoukat, M.U.: Improved multiple watermarking algorithm for Medical Images. In: Proceedings of 2020 3rd International Conference on Artificial Intelligence and Pattern Recognition, AIPR 2020, vol. 76, pp. 153–157 (2020)
5. Janani, T., Darak, Y., Brindha, M.: Secure similar image search and copyright protection over encrypted medical image databases. IRBM **42**(2), 83–93 (2021)
6. Basset, M., Mohamed, R., Chakrabortty, R.K., Ryan, M.J., Nam, Y.: Medical feature selection approach based on generalized normal distribution algorithm. Comput. Mater. Continua **69**(3), 2883–2901 (2021)
7. Mohammed, M.A., Abdulkareem, K.H., Garcia-Zapirain, B., Mostafa, S.A., Maashi, M.S.: A comprehensive investigation of machine learning feature extraction and classification methods for automated diagnosis of covid-19 based on x-ray images. Comput. Mater. Continua **66**(3), 3289–3310 (2021)
8. Abdulrahman, A.K., Ozturk, S.: A novel hybrid DCT and DWT based robust watermarking algorithm for color images. Multimedia Tools Appl. **78**(12), 17027–17049 (2019)
9. Li, S.K., Wang, A.L., Pang, J.P., Guo, L., Xin, K., Fan, S.X., Liu, F.P.: Research on robust algorithm of color holographic watermark based on DCT-DWT. IOP Conf. Ser. Mater. Sci. Eng. **563**(5), 052015 (2019)
10. Li, E., Fu, Z., Chen, S., Chen, J.: A two-stage highly robust text steganalysis model. J. Cyber Secur. **2**(4), 183–190 (2020)
11. Anasuodei, M., Eleonu, O.F.: An Enhanced satellite image compression using hybrid (DWT, DCT and SVD) algorithm. Am. J. Comput. Sci. Technol. **4**(1), 1–10 (2021)
12. Yan, Z.G., Lei, Y., Wang, H.R.: Research on digital image watermarking. Ind. Control **33**(11), 100–102 (2020)
13. Fu, C.J., Lan, S.K.: Digital watermarking algorithm based on DCT transform. Netw. Secur. Technol. Appl. **7**, 49–51 (2020)
14. Yuan, Z.H., Yang, B.L., Zhao, W.Q., Liu, Y.: A robust zero watermarking algorithm based on NSCT_DCT. In: Proceedings of the 2017 International Conference on Mechanical, Electronic, Control and Automation Engineering, MECAE 2017, pp. 128–132. Atlantis Press (2017)

15. Gan, L., Yang, Y.: Improved patchwork watermarking algorithm based on transform domain. J. Chengdu Univ. Inf. Technol. **32**(6), 623–627 (2017)
16. Li, W., Sun, Y.J.: Watermarking technology based on LWT-SVD-DCT algorithm. J. Luoyang Inst. Technol. (Nat. Sci. Edn.) **31**(1), 77–81 (2021)
17. Zear, A., Singh, A.K., Kumar, P.: A proposed secure multiple watermarking technique based on DWT, DCT and SVD for application in medicine. Multimedia Tools Appl. **77**(4), 4863–4882 (2016)
18. Singh, A.K., Kumar, B., Dave, M., Mohan, A.: Multiple watermarking on medical images using selective discrete wavelet transform coefficients. J. Med. Imaging Health Inf. **5**(3), 607–614 (2015)

Spatial Image Steganography Using a Correlational Model

Jiangqun Ni[1,2], Yichen Tong[1], Xianglei Hu[1(✉)], Wenkang Su[1], and Xiangui Kang[1]

[1] Sun Yat-sen University, Guangzhou 510006, China
huxlei3@mail.sysu.edu.cn
[2] Peng Cheng Laboratory, Cyberspace Security Research Center, Shenzhen, China

Abstract. Nowadays, the content-adaptive strategy is widely utilized in the image steganographic algorithms, among which the model-based methods, e.g., MiPOD, can be recognized as ones of the state-of-the-arts. However, the existing model-based designs merely adopt independent probability distribution, which could not make full use of the spatial information. In this paper, we propose a novel spatial image steganography based on a correlational model, i.e., Gaussian Markov random field, and utilize its conditional independence to decompose the graph into simple cliques and nodes, and then derive a practical form of KL divergence to minimize the statistical undetectability. Experiment results demonstrate that the proposed method can outperform or approximate the state-of-the-art algorithms when resisting detection of various steganalysis features.

Keywords: Steganography · Markov random field · Correlational model

1 Introduction

Information hiding has undergone a markable progress during this decade [3,14,18]. The current trend in image steganography is to embed the secret message while minimizing an embedding distortion between the cover and the stego. Such content-adaptive schemes are typically adopted by a covert communication system which includes the distortion designs and the steganographic codes. Since STCs (Syndrome Trellis Codes) approximates the rate-distortion bound for additive distortion [6], and therefore, designs of distortion attract more attention from researchers.

Currently, most of the steganographic distortion functions are heuristically designed. The state-of-the-art steganographic scheme, HILL (High-pass, Low-pass, and Low-pass) [13] utilized one High-pass filter and two Low-pass filters to the cover image and took the result as the map of embedding costs of all pixels. Similarly, S-UNIWARD (Spatial UNIversal WAvelet Relative Distortion) [10] and WOW (Wavelet Obtained Weights) [9] also introduce distortion functions

X. Sun et al. (Eds.): ICAIS 2022, LNCS 13340, pp. 400–411, 2022.
https://doi.org/10.1007/978-3-031-06791-4_32

using the residuals of various wavelet filters. However, all the above stegano-graphic distortions are merely designed in a heuristic manner due to the lack of formal connection between distortion and security as suggested in [2].

MG (Multivariate Gaussian) [8] measures statistical detectability rather than the empirically designed distortion function. By investigating the probability distribution of the cover image, it tries to minimize the KL divergence between cover and stego, and consequently achieves satisfactory security performance. It is worth noting that MG assumes that pixel variables are independent to each other, and therefore, the KL divergence for the whole image can be easily derived by summing up those of all pixels. Later, MG was generailzed to MVGG (Multivariate Generalized Gaussian) [16] and MiPOD (Minimizing the Power of Optimal Detector) [15], and the more accurate parameters have improved the security performance.

To better investigate the statistical characteristics of image model, this paper proposes an image steganographic scheme which take into account the correlation between pixel variables: First, we model the image as a Gaussian Markov random field (MRF), in which each pixel is correlated with its neighbors; then we utilize the conditional independence of MRF to simplify the KL divergence of between the joint probability distributions of cover and stego. At last, we can derive an optimal embedding through minimizing the proposed KL divergence with a certain payload constraint.

This paper is organized as follows. First, we introduce the correlational image model based on MRF in Sect. 2. Then, details of the proposed method are discussed in Sect. 3, including factorization of the MRF model and the proposed KL divergence. Section 4 shows the experimental results of our method in comparison to two state-of-the-arts, i.e., HILL and MiPOD, in terms of security performance. Finally, the paper is concluded in Sect. 5.

2   Correlational Model for Spatial Image Steganography

As mentioned above, model-based steganograhpic schemes, i.e., MiPOD, utilize an independent image model, which ignores the mutual influence of adjacent embedding modifications. In order to model the steganography more precisely, we take advantages of the correlational information among different pixels to approximate the non-additional steganography.

2.1   Cover Image Model

First, we must generalize the independent Gaussian model in MiPOD to the Gaussian Markov random field (Gaussian MRF), which is widely utilized in many areas of image processing and computer vision. Let $G = (V, E)$ denote the undirected graph of a Gaussian MRF (V is the set of nodes, and E includes all the edges), then the noise of each pixel is represented by a Gaussian node $x_i, i \in V$, and the joint probability density function of the Gaussian MRF is $\mathbf{x}_G \sim N(\mathbf{0}, \mathbf{\Sigma})$, where $\mathbf{\Sigma}$ is the covariance matrix of the MRF. Note that, due to the sparsity of the MRF, its precision matrix $\mathbf{Q}$, i.e., the inversion of covariance $\mathbf{\Sigma}$, must be a sparse matrix, where $Q_{i,j}$ is non-zero only when $i = j$ or $\{i, j\} \in E$.

An important property of MRF is the conditional independence: Any two subsets of variables are conditionally independent given a separating subset, $\mathbf{x}_A \perp \mathbf{x}_B | \mathbf{x}_S$, where every path from a node in a subgraph A to a node in B must pass through S. Conditional independence enables us to factorize the probability of the whole graph into the ones of clique units, and consequently reduces the computational complexity to a great extent.

2.2 Stego Image Model

Prevalent existing steganography methods adopt the Mutually Independent (MI) embedding strategy in which the modification of each pixel is independent of each other. Since the image noises are supposed to be correlational in the proposed cover model, the correlation of embedding modifications must be taken into consideration. Essentially, embedding can be recognized as adding some embedding noises $\mathbf{e}$ onto the cover image noises $\mathbf{x}$. In the case of ternary embedding, the distribution of e_i can be represented by:

$$
\begin{aligned}
\mathbb{P}(e_i = +1) &= \beta_i, \\
\mathbb{P}(e_i = -1) &= \beta_i, \\
\mathbb{P}(e_i = 0) &= 1 - 2\beta_i,
\end{aligned}
\tag{1}
$$

which conform to the payload constraint:

$$
R = \sum_i -2\beta_i \log_2(\beta_i) - (1 - 2\beta_i)\log_2(1 - 2\beta_i),
\tag{2}
$$

where R is the length of payload embedded on the cover.

As mentioned in Sect. 2, MiPOD incorporates the modification probability into KL divergence of the image model to measure the statistical undetectability of embedding, and the unit of the probability model is pixel. However, when adopting MRF instead of the independent model, the unit becomes the clique of the graph, i.e., $\mathbf{x}_{\{i,j\}}$ which denotes a pair of adjacent nodes $\{x_i, x_j\}$ in the graph, where i, j are the indice of pixel nodes. Therefore, we have to generalize the KL divergence from the uni-variable form to the bi-variable one. For the clique $\{i, j\} \in E$, the KL divergence between the marginal distributions of cover and stego variables can be calculated by:

$$
D_{\mathrm{KL}}(\mathbf{x}_{\{i,j\}} \| \mathbf{y}_{\{i,j\}}) = \boldsymbol{\beta}^T \cdot \mathbf{I}_{i,j}(\mathbf{0}) \cdot \boldsymbol{\beta}/2,
\tag{3}
$$

where $\boldsymbol{\beta} = [\beta_i, \beta_j]^T$ is the change probability vector and $\mathbf{I}_{i,j}(\mathbf{0}) = \begin{bmatrix} I_{ii} & I_{ij} \\ I_{ji} & I_{jj} \end{bmatrix}$ denotes the 2×2 Fisher information matrix for the clique $\{i, j\}$, and its mathematical derivation can be seen in Appendix.

To incorporate the change probabilities β_i into practical steganographic coding tools, it is necessary to transform β_i to the embedding cost: $c_i = \ln(1/\beta_i - 2)$ [5].

3 Spatial Steganography Based on Markov Random Field

Following the spirit of MiPOD, the proposed steganographic scheme designs embedding costs via minimizing the KL divergence between the cover and stego distribution, and notably, the proposed image model is supposed to be mutually correlational rather than independent, and therefore more spatial information has been brought in. However, it is difficult to deduce the closed form of KL divergence for a MRF, since the graph contains a large number of cycles, which would hinder the inference of marginal probability of each pixel node. Therefore, we must simplify the graph before optimizing the change probabilities β.

3.1 Factorization of a MRF for Steganography

As suggested in [17], a cyclic graph can be approximated by an acyclic graph through removing part of its edges. As for the proposed graph $G = (V, E)$ of the MRF, there are two categories of edges: horizontal and vertical, and acyclic subgraphs (G_v and G_h maintain the vertical and horizontal edges, respectively) can be obtained through removing one category of edges, seen as below:

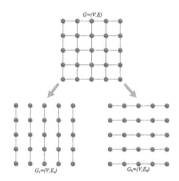

Fig. 1. Two acyclic graphs are derived from the orignal graph G.

Without loss of generalization, we take G_h as the example to calculate its probability distribution and deduce the KL divergence. As shown in Fig. 1, subgraph G_h is consisting of a series of Markov chains, which are supposed to be mutually independent since the vertical edges are removed. Therefore, the probability distribution of the subgraph G_h can be represented as:

$$P(\mathbf{x}_G) = \prod_m P(\mathbf{x}_m),\tag{4}$$

where $\mathbf{x}_m$ denotes the variable vector corresponding to the mth horizontal chain in the graph.

Next, the probability of the chain needs to be further factorized into cliques and nodes. Let $\mathbf{x}_m = \{x_{m,1}, x_{m,2}, ..., x_{m,N}\}$ be a chain containing N sequential pixel nodes, then its probability can be factorized according to the property of conditional independence (Given the value of node at coordinate $(m, 2)$, the conditional independence holds between node $(m, 1)$ and nodes $\{(m, 3)...(m, N)\}$, the row index m will be omitted here without confusion for ease of reading):

$$
\begin{aligned}
P(\mathbf{x}) &= P(x_1 x_3 ... x_N | x_2) P(x_2) \\
&= P(x_1 | x_2) P(x_3 ... x_N | x_2) P(x_2) \\
&= \frac{P(x_1 x_2)}{P(x_2)} \frac{P(x_2, x_3 ... x_N)}{P(x_2)} P(x_2) \\
&= \frac{P(x_1 x_2) P(x_2 ... x_N)}{P(x_2)},
\end{aligned}
\tag{5}
$$

where x_2 is acting as the separating node between x_1 and all other nodes in the chain.

The factorization can be iteratively proceeded on the remaining chain, and finally we have the completely factorized probability distribution of the mth chain:

$$
P(\mathbf{x}_m) = \frac{\prod\limits_{n=1}^{N-1} P(x_{m,n} x_{m,n+1})}{\prod\limits_{n=2}^{N-1} P(x_{m,n})},
\tag{6}
$$

which can be combined with (4) to derive the factorization of subgrah G_h:

$$
P(\mathbf{x}_{G_h}) = \prod_{m=1}^{M} \frac{\prod\limits_{n=1}^{N-1} P(x_{m,n} x_{m,n+1})}{\prod\limits_{n=2}^{N-1} P(x_{m,n})}.
\tag{7}
$$

Therefore, the KL divergence between cover and stego under the assumption of subgraph G_h can be decomposed into KL divergence of cliques and nodes:

$$
\begin{aligned}
D_{KL}(\mathbf{x}_{G_h} || \mathbf{y}_{G_h}) &= \sum_{m=1}^{M} D_{KL}(\mathbf{x}_m || \mathbf{y}_m) \\
&= \sum_{m=1}^{M} \sum_{n=1}^{N-1} D_{KL}(x_{m,n} x_{m,n+1} || y_{m,n} y_{m,n+1}) \\
&\quad - \sum_{m=1}^{M} \sum_{n=2}^{N-1} D_{KL}(x_{m,n} || y_{m,n}),
\end{aligned}
\tag{8}
$$

where $D_{KL}(x_{m,n} x_{m,n+1} || y_{m,n} y_{m,n+1})$ corresponds to (3) while (m, n) denotes the coordinate of ith 2-D node, and $D_{KL}(x_{m,n} || y_{m,n}) = \beta_{m,n}^2 / \sigma_{m,n}^4$ as mentioned in [15].

To simplify the optimization of (8), we replace the cross term in KL divergence of clique $\{i,j\}$ in an approximated manner (change probabilities $\boldsymbol{\beta}$ are spatially smooth [12]):

$$
\begin{aligned}
D_{\mathrm{KL}}(\mathbf{x}_{\{i,j\}}\|\mathbf{y}_{\{i,j\}}) &= \boldsymbol{\beta}^T \cdot \mathbf{I}(0) \cdot \boldsymbol{\beta}/2 \\
&= [\beta_i^2 I^{11} + \beta_i\beta_j I^{12} + \beta_i\beta_j I^{21} + \beta_j^2 I^{22}]/2 \\
&\approx [\beta_i^2 I^{11} + \beta_i^2 I^{12} + \beta_j^2 I^{21} + \beta_j^2 I^{22}]/2 \\
&= (\frac{\beta_i^2}{\sigma_i^4} + \frac{\beta_j^2}{\sigma_j^4})\frac{1+\rho_{i,j}^2}{(1-\rho_{i,j}^2)^2},
\end{aligned}
\tag{9}
$$

where σ_i, σ_j are the standard deviation of random variables x_i, x_j, and $\rho_{i,j}$ denotes the correlation coefficient between them. The closed form of Fisher information matrix $\mathbf{I}(0)$ is deduced in Appendix, and estimation of $\rho_{i,j}$ will be introduced in next subsection. Then, the KL divergence of chain term in (8) corresponding to chain $\mathbf{x}_m$ can be represented by the sum of individual terms:

$$
\begin{aligned}
D_{\mathrm{KL}}(\mathbf{x}_m\|\mathbf{y}_m) =& \frac{1+\rho_{1,2}^2}{(1-\rho_{1,2}^2)^2}\frac{\beta_1^2}{\sigma_1^4} + \frac{1+\rho_{N-1,N}^2}{(1-\rho_{N-1,N}^2)^2}\frac{\beta_N^2}{\sigma_N^4} \\
&+ \sum_{n=2}^{N-1}(2\frac{1+\rho_{n,n+1}^2}{(1-\rho_{n,n+1}^2)^2} - 1)\frac{\beta_n^2}{\sigma_n^4},
\end{aligned}
\tag{10}
$$

where the index m is omitted on the right side of equation, and it can be observed that the KL divergence would degrade into the independent model used in [8] when $\rho_{i,j} = 0$.

Then, after substituting (10) into (8), the optimal change probabilitites $\boldsymbol{\beta}_h$ can be solved for the subgraph G_h through a numerical method proposed in [8] while satisfying the payload constraint (2), and embedding costs $\mathbf{c}_h$ can be determined using equation $c_i = \ln(1/\beta_i - 2)$.

Similarly, embedding costs $\mathbf{c}_v$ can be also calculated for subgraph G_v which incorporates the correlation between pixels along the vertical direction. For content-adaptive steganography, the embedding cost actually indicates the priority of embedding, and the original MRF graph G should take into account simultaneously the horizontal and vertical information. Hereby, we use the average of $\mathbf{c}_h$ and $\mathbf{c}_v$ to approximate the $\mathbf{c}$ desired for G in an empirical manner: $\mathbf{c} = (\mathbf{c}_h + \mathbf{c}_v)/2$, which can be finally utilized in the steganographic coding tool or simulator.

3.2   Estimation of Parameters in MRF

Variance σ_i^2 can be estimated using the same method in [16], while it needs to revise for the estimation of the correlation coefficient $\rho_{i,j}$. Following the spirit of [16], variables x_i can be sampled by the residual of a high-pass filter, e.g. Wiener filter of size $(2,2)$, and are also assumed to be stationary signals as in [16], i.e., variance and correlation coefficients are approximately uniform within a small neighborhood. Consequently, the horizontal correlation coefficients can be estimated for G_h within a $(2k + 1) \times (2k + 1)$ neighborhood:

$$\hat{\rho}_{m_0,n_0} = \frac{(2k + 1) \sum\limits_{m=-k}^{k} \sum\limits_{n=-k}^{k-1} x_{m_0+m,n_0+n} \cdot x_{m_0+m,n_0+n+1}}{2k \sum\limits_{m=-k}^{k} \sum\limits_{n=-k}^{k} x^2_{m_0+m,n_0+n}}, \quad (11)$$

where $k = 3$ is chosen at default, (m_0, n_0) is the centering coordinate of the sliding window, and $\hat{\rho}_{m_0,n_0}$ is the estimator of correlation coefficient between x_{m_0,n_0} and x_{m_0,n_0+1}. Afterwards, we can apply smoothing filter, e.g., a 7×7 averaging filter, on $\hat{\rho}$ to stablize the estimation.

4   Experimental Results and Analysis

In this section, we will introduce the steps and parameters of our experiments. And we will also compare the the proposed method to the state-of-the-art distortion designs, i.e., HILL and MiPOD. The proposed method is called as Correlational Multivariate Gaussian (CMG), since it utilizes a correlation probability model.

4.1   Experiment Setup

Our experiments are carried on 10,000 8-bit grayscale images of size 512×512 compressed from BOSSbase 1.01 [1]. All the embedding schemes will be tested in 6 different embedding payload rates ($\{0.05, 0.1, 0.2, 0.3, 0.4, 0.5\}$ bits/pixel) using a embedding simulator.

To evaluate the security performance of steganography, we utilized a Fisher Linear Discriminant (FLD) ensemble [11] along with two popular steganalysis features: Spatial Rich Model (SRM) [7] and maxSRMd2 [4]. Nowadays, SRM is the standard feature and is consisting of 39 symmetrized sub-models with a total dimensions of 34,671. Whereas the maxSRMd2 is capable of taking advantage of extra information, the approximate embedding change probabilities extracted from stego images. The testing error P_E of classifier can be used to quantify the embedding security: the higher testing error P_E indicates the higher security performance of embedding. Training and testing of the ensemble is carried on the two disjoint sets of cover-stego pairs, which are randomly selected and derived from BOSSBase 1.01, and the whole process will be repeated ten times, and we use the average of testing error P_E, denoted by $\overline{P}_E$ to judge the security of the involved steganographic algorithms. Finally, we get curves of $\overline{P}_E$ w.r.t. the payload rate to demonstrate the security performance.

4.2   Comparison to Prior Arts

As shown in Table 1, the proposed CMG outperforms MiPOD in terms of security ($\overline{P}_E$) against steganalysis feature SRM about by $0.5-1.2\%$, and also comparable to HILL when the payload rate is above 0.2 bpp.

Table 1. Average testing error $\overline{P}_E$ (%) against steganalysis feature SRM.

Embedding scheme	Payload rate (bpp)					
	0.05	0.1	0.2	0.3	0.4	0.5
HILL	47.04	43.33	36.11	29.96	24.82	20.55
MiPOD	45.43	41.37	34.25	28.82	23.82	20.03
CMG	45.78	42.25	35.62	30.10	25.03	20.58

The maxSRMd2, a more powerful feature than SRM, should be given more attention and be included in a comprehensive measure of steganographic system's security. Table 2 demonstrates that the proposed CMG achieves the highest security among all three candidate embedding schemes when the security performance is practical (when $\overline{P}_E < 30\%$, the steganographic system might be assumed to be impractical.)

Table 2. Average testing error $\overline{P}_E$ (%) against steganalysis feature maxSRMd2.

Embedding scheme	Payload rate (bpp)					
	0.05	0.1	0.2	0.3	0.4	0.5
HILL	42.32	37.71	30.91	25.73	21.84	18.14
MiPOD	43.80	39.39	32.37	27.17	22.43	18.45
CMG	44.41	39.60	33.11	26.61	21.65	17.69

Figures 2 and 3 clearly demonstrate that each of HILL and MiPOD has its own advantage of security performance against either SRM or maxSRM, and the gap of $\overline{P}_E$ between them is more 1% on average. However, the proposed CMG can achieve or approximate the upper bound against **both** steganalysis features. Therefore, we can conclude that CMG can resist more comprehensive detections than HILL and MiPOD.

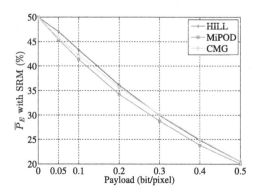

Fig. 2. Curves of $\overline{P}_E$ (%) against steganalysis feature SRM.

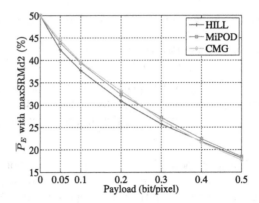

Fig. 3. Curves of $\overline{P}_E$ (%) against steganalysis feature maxSRMd2.

5 Conclusion

This paper proposes a spatial image steganography based on a Gaussian Markov random field, which incorporates the correlation between adjacent pixels. To make the optimization of MRF practical, the proposed method decomposes the cyclic MRF into two acyclic subgraphs respectively corresponding to horizontal and vertical edges. The optimum of each subgraph can be merged into an approximate optimum of the original MRF, and finally, optimal change probabilities will be converted to embedding costs utilized by steganographic codes.

Experimental results show that the proposed CMG outperforms or is comparable to the state-of-the-arts, i.e., HILL and MiPOD, against the prevalent steganalysis features. In the future, we might extend the CMD to more generalized graph models to achieve higher security.

Acknowledgements. This work was supported in part by the National Natural Science Foundation of China under Grants U1726315, 61772573 and U1936212 and U19B2022, in part by the Key-Area Research and Development Program of Guangdong Province under grant 2019B010139003, and in part by Shenzhen R&D Program under grant GJHZ20180928155814437.

A Appendix

We proposed an approximation to 2×2 steganographic Fisher Information matrix for clique $\{i, j\}$ as below:

$$\mathbf{I}_{i,j}(\mathbf{0}) = \begin{bmatrix} I_{ii} & I_{ij} \\ I_{ji} & I_{jj} \end{bmatrix}, \tag{12}$$

where $I_{ij} = I_{ji} = \sum_{k,l}\frac{1}{p_{k,l}}(\frac{\partial q_{k,l}(\beta_i,\beta_j)}{\partial \beta_i}|_{\beta_i,\beta_j=0}) \cdot (\frac{\partial q_{k,l}(\beta_i,\beta_j)}{\partial \beta_j}|_{\beta_i,\beta_j=0})$,

$$I_{ii} = \sum_{k,l}\frac{1}{p_{k,l}}(\frac{\partial q_{k,l}(\beta_i,\beta_j)}{\partial \beta_i}|_{\beta_i,\beta_j=0})^2, \quad I_{jj} = \sum_{k,l}\frac{1}{p_{k,l}}(\frac{\partial q_{k,l}(\beta_i,\beta_j)}{\partial \beta_j}|_{\beta_i,\beta_j=0})^2.$$

$q_{k,l}(\beta_i, \beta_j)$ denotes the joint probability of pixel i valued k with change probabilty β_i and pixel j valued l with change probabilty β_j in stego image. $q_{k,l}(\beta_i, \beta_j)$ holds (13) and its partial derivative become (14) and (15).

$$q_{k,l}(\beta_i, \beta_j) = (1 - 2\beta_i)\beta_j(p_{k,l-1} + p_{k,l+1}) + \beta_i(1 - 2\beta_j)(p_{k-1,l} + p_{k+1,l})$$
$$+\beta_i\beta_j(p_{k-1,l-1} + p_{k-1,l+1} + p_{k+1,l-1} + p_{k+1,l+1}) + (1 - 2\beta_i)(1 - 2\beta_j)p_{k,l} \quad (13)$$

$$\frac{\partial q_{k,l}}{\partial \beta_i}\Big|_{\beta_i=0, \beta_j=0} = -2p_{k,l} + p_{k-1,l} + p_{k+1,l}, \quad (14)$$

$$\frac{\partial q_{k,l}}{\partial \beta_j}\Big|_{\beta_i=0, \beta_j=0} = -2p_{k,l} + p_{k,l-1} + p_{k,l+1}. \quad (15)$$

Substitute (14) and (15) into (12), we can get:

$$I_{ij} = I_{ji} = \sum_{k,l} \frac{1}{p_{k,l}}(-2p_{k,l} + p_{k-1,l} + p_{k+1,l}) \cdot (-2p_{k,l} + p_{k,l-1} + p_{k,l+1}),$$

$$I_{ii} = \sum_{k,l} \frac{1}{p_{k,l}}(-2p_{k,l} + p_{k-1,l} + p_{k+1,l})^2,$$

$$I_{jj} = \sum_{k,l} \frac{1}{p_{k,l}}(-2p_{k,l} + p_{k,l-1} + p_{k,l+1})^2. \quad (16)$$

$p_{k,l}$ is the joint probability of pixel i valued k and pixel j valued l in cover image. In our work, pixels i and j obey two-dimensional Gaussian distribution $f(i, j)$ shown in (17). Though i, j are both discrete integer variables, we take them as continuous for differentiable:

$$f(i, j) = \frac{1}{2\pi\sigma_i^2\sigma_j^2\sqrt{1 - \rho^2}} \exp(-\frac{1}{2(1 - \rho^2)}(\frac{i^2}{\sigma_i^4} - \frac{2\rho ij}{\sigma_i^2\sigma_j^2} + \frac{j^2}{\sigma_j^4})). \quad (17)$$

Considering the Taylor approximation at points $(k \pm 1, l), (k, l \pm 1)$, we have:

$$f(k \pm 1, 1) \approx f(k, 1) \pm \frac{\partial f(x_i, x_j)}{\partial x_i}\Big|_{x_i=k, x_j=1} + \frac{1}{2} \cdot \frac{\partial^2 f(x_i, x_j)}{\partial x_i^2}\Big|_{x_i=k, x_j=1}, \quad (18)$$

$$f(k, 1 \pm 1) \approx f(k, 1) \pm \frac{\partial f(x_i, x_j)}{\partial x_j}\Big|_{x_i=k, x_j=1} + \frac{1}{2} \cdot \frac{\partial^2 f(x_i, x_j)}{\partial x_j^2}\Big|_{x_i=k, x_j=1}. \quad (19)$$

Given $p_{k,l} = f(k, l), p_{k\pm1,l} = f(k \pm 1, l), p_{k,l\pm1} = f(k, l \pm 1)$, taking advantage of (18) and (19), multiplication term in (16) can be approximated as:

$$-2p_{k,l} + p_{k-1,l} + p_{k+1,l} \approx \frac{\partial^2 f(x_i, x_j)}{\partial x_i^2}\Big|_{x_i=k, x_j=1}, \quad (20)$$

$$-2p_{k,l} + p_{k,l-1} + p_{k,l+1} \approx \frac{\partial^2 f(x_i, x_j)}{\partial x_j^2}\Big|_{x_i=k, x_j=1}. \quad (21)$$

By substituting (17)(20) and (21) into (16),and taking variables k, l continuous, (12) can be derived:

$$
\begin{aligned}
I_{ii} &= \sum_{k,l} \frac{1}{p_{k,l}} \left(-2p_{k,l} + p_{k-1,l} + p_{k+1,l}\right)^2 \\
&\approx \int_k \int_l \frac{1}{f(x_i, x_j)} \left(\frac{\partial^2 f(x_i, x_j)}{\partial x_i^2}\bigg|_{x_i=k, x_j=1}\right)^2 dk\, dl \qquad (22) \\
&= \frac{2}{\sigma_i^4 (1 - \rho^2)^2},
\end{aligned}
$$

$$
\begin{aligned}
I_{jj} &= \sum_{k,l} \frac{1}{p_{k,l}} \left(-2p_{k,l} + p_{k,l-1} + p_{k,l+1}\right)^2 \\
&\approx \int_k \int_l \frac{1}{f(x_i, x_j)} \left(\frac{\partial^2 f(x_i, x_j)}{\partial x_j^2}\bigg|_{x_i=k, x_j=1}\right)^2 dk\, dl \qquad (23) \\
&= \frac{2}{\sigma_j^4 (1 - \rho^2)^2},
\end{aligned}
$$

$$
\begin{aligned}
I_{ij} = I_{ji} &= \sum_{k,l} \frac{1}{p_{k,l}} \left(-2p_{k,l} + p_{k-1,l} + p_{k+1,l}\right) \cdot \left(-2p_{k,l} + p_{k,l-1} + p_{k,l+1}\right) \\
&\approx \int_k \int_l \frac{1}{f(x_i, x_j)} \left(\frac{\partial^2 f(x_i, x_j)}{\partial x_i^2}\bigg|_{x_i=k, x_j=1}\right) \cdot \left(\frac{\partial^2 f(x_i, x_j)}{\partial x_j^2}\bigg|_{x_i=k, x_j=1}\right) dk\, dl \qquad (24) \\
&= \frac{2\rho^2}{\sigma_i^2 \sigma_j^2 \cdot (1 - \rho^2)^2}.
\end{aligned}
$$

References

1. Bas, P., Filler, T., Pevný, T.: Break our steganographic system: the ins and outs of organizing BOSS. In: Proceedings of the 13th International Workshop on Information Hiding, pp. 59–70 (2011)
2. Bohme, R.: Advanced Statistical Steganalysis. Springer, Heidelberg (2010). https://doi.org/10.1007/978-3-642-14313-7
3. Chen, X., Zhang, Z., Qiu, A., Xia, Z., Xiong, N.N.: Novel coverless steganography method based on image selection and stargan. IEEE Trans. Netw. Sci. Eng. **9**(1), 219–230 (2022). https://doi.org/10.1109/TNSE.2020.3041529
4. Denemark, T., Sedighi, V., Holub, V., Cogranne, R., Fridrich, J.: Selection-channel-aware rich model for steganalysis of digital images. In: IEEE International Workshop on Information Forensics and Security (2014). https://doi.org/10.1109/WIFS.2014.7084302
5. Filler, T., Fridrich, J.: Gibbs construction in steganography. IEEE Trans. Inf. Forens. Secur. **5**(4), 705–720 (2010). https://doi.org/10.1109/tifs.2010.2077629

6. Filler, T., Judas, J., Fridrich, J.: Minimizing additive distortion in steganography using syndrome-trellis codes. IEEE Trans. Inf. Forens. Secur. **6**(3), 920–935 (2011). https://doi.org/10.1109/TIFS.2011.2134094
7. Fridrich, J., Kodovský, J.: Rich models for steganalysis of digital images. IEEE Trans. Inf. Forens. Secur. **7**(3), 868–882 (2012). https://doi.org/10.1109/TIFS. 2012.2190402
8. Fridrich, J., Kodovsky, J.: Multivariate gaussian model for designing additive distortion for steganography. In: IEEE ICASSP, pp. 2949–2953 (2013). https://doi. org/10.1109/ICASSP.2013.6638198
9. Holub, V., Fridrich, J.: Designing steganographic distortion using directional filters. In: International Workshop on Information Forensics and Security, pp. 234–239 (2012). https://doi.org/10.1109/WIFS.2012.6412655
10. Holub, V., Fridrich, J., Denemark, T.: Universal distortion function for steganography in an arbitrary domain. EURASIP J. Inf. Secur. **2014**(1), 1–13 (2014). https:// doi.org/10.1186/1687-417X-2014-1
11. Kodovský, J., Fridrich, J., Holub, V.: Ensemble classifiers for steganalysis of digital media. IEEE Trans. Inf. Forens. Secur. **7**(2), 432–444 (2012). https://doi.org/10. 1109/TIFS.2011.2175919
12. Li, B., Tan, S., Wang, M., Huang, J.: Investigation on cost assignment in spatial image steganography. IEEE Trans. Inf. Forens. Secur. **9**(8), 1264–1277 (2014). https://doi.org/10.1109/TIFS.2014.2326954
13. Li, B., Wang, M., Huang, J., Li, X.: A new cost function for spatial image steganography. In: International Conference on Image Processing, ICIP, pp. 4206–4210 (2014). https://doi.org/10.1109/ICIP.2014.7025854
14. Luo, Y., Qin, J., Xiang, X., Tan, Y.: Coverless image steganography based on multi-object recognition. IEEE Trans. Circuits Syst. Video Technol. **31**(7), 2779–2791 (2021). https://doi.org/10.1109/TCSVT.2020.3033945
15. Sedighi, V., Cogranne, R., Fridrich, J.: Content-adaptive steganography by minimizing statistical detectability. IEEE Trans. Inf. Forens. Secur. **11**(2), 221–234 (2016). https://doi.org/10.1109/TIFS.2015.2486744
16. Sedighi, V., Fridrich, J.J., Cogranne, R.: Content-adaptive pentary steganography using the multivariate generalized gaussian cover model. In: Proceedings of the SPIE, Electronic Imaging, Media Watermarking, Security, and Forensics, 2015, vol. 9409 (2015). https://doi.org/10.1117/12.2080272
17. Wainwright, M.J., Jordan, M.I.: Graphical Models, Exponential Families, and Variational Inference. Now Publishers (2008). https://doi.org/10.1561/2200000001
18. Yang, Z.L., Guo, X.Q., Chen, Z.M., Huang, Y.F., Zhang, Y.J.: Rnn-stega: linguistic steganography based on recurrent neural networks. IEEE Trans. Info. Forens. Secur. **14**(5), 1280–1295 (2019). https://doi.org/10.1109/TIFS.2018.2871746

Spatial Image Steganography Incorporating Adjacent Dependencies

Yichen Tong[1], Jiangqun Ni[1,2(✉)], Wenkang Su[1], and Xianglei Hu[1]

[1] Sun Yat-sen University, Guangzhou, China
tongych@mail2.sysu.edu.cn, {issjqni,huxlei3}@mail.sysu.edu.cn
[2] Peng Cheng Laboratory, Cyberspace Security Research Center, Shenzhen, China

Abstract. Most of the existing model-based image steganographic schemes in spatial domain assume the independence among adjacent pixels, thus ignores the embedding interactions among neighbouring pixels. In this paper, we propose a new image steganographic scheme by taking advantages of the correlations between each pixel and its eight-neighbourhood and determine the embedding cost of the pixel through the minimization of the KL-divergence between the cover and stego objects. Experimental results demonstrate that our scheme show superior or comparable performance to two state-of-the-art algorithms: HILL and MiPOD in resisting steganalysis detectors.

Keywords: Adaptive steganography · Model-driven · Neighbourhood correlation · KL divergence

1 Introduction

Spatial image steganography aims to hide messages into images by slightly modifying pixel values while minimizing detectability as much as possible. Currently, some scientists are trying to implement steganography using deep learning model [4,14,19], but some such as this paper will still further explore the traditional methods. In traditional methods, the steganography problem is often formulated as source coding with fidelity constraint since practical algorithms that embed near the theoretical payload-distortion bound are available for various distortion functions [9]. Under this scenery, the most crucial task in steganography becomes the design of distortion function.

Recently, refer to the design of distortion function, the vast majority have heavily relied on the heuristic principles, e.g. HILL, WOW, and UNIWARD [10]. For those heuristic attempts, designers should empirically quantify the impact of making an embedding change on the cover image using several kinds of filters. Intuitively, texture regions deserve lower cost while smooth regions have a higher cost.

HILL (High-pass, Low-pass and Low-pass) [13] sequentially adopts one high-pass filter and two low-pass filters on the cover image to obtain the cost map.

WOW (wavelet obtained weights) [9], which could be applied to both spatial and JPEG domain, also designs cost function with the help of a group of directional filters. These heuristics require sophisticated design and lack of strong theoretical support.

In order to design steganography mathematically, the model-based methods come into being. HUGO [16] is the first effort to consider the cover model when defining distortion function, which is finally to be a weighted sum of the difference between cover and stego images in SPAM (subtractive pixel adjacency matrix) [15] feature space. MG (Multivariate Gaussian) [8], the first attempt to measure statistical detectability, models the cover pixels as a sequence of independent but not necessarily identically distributed quantized Gaussians and employs KL divergence as the cost function. MVGG (Multivariate Generalized Gaussian) [18] is an extension to MG with an adequately adjusted variance estimator. Besides, MiPOD (Minimizing the Power of Optimal Detector) [17] minimizes the power of the most potent detector instead of the KL divergence.

In this paper, we propose a new steganographic scheme for spatial images by incorporating correlations between each pixel and its eight-neighbourhood. It integrates embedding impacts among neighbour pixels in the design of the overall distortion function, which we adopt the KL divergence between the cover and stego image. With the interactions between embedding changes adequately modelled, the proposed method performs superior or comparable to some of the state-of-the-art methods in resisting steganalysis detectors.

We first introduce notations in the next section and then describe the proposed model in Sect. 3. We test the proposed method and report the detection results under SRM [7] and maxSRMd2 [5] feature sets in Sect. 4, where we compare it with some existing state-of-the-art embedding schemes as well. The conclusion lies in Sect. 5.

2   Notations

In this paper, we use the symbol $i \in \{1, 2, ..., n\}$ to denote the i-th pixel in the image. σ_i and ρ_{ij} represent the variance of i and the correlation coefficient between i and j, respectively. The p.m.f. of pixel i with value m is denoted by p_m^i, and q_m^i is its stego version. Similarly, $p_{m,n,...}^{i,j,...}$ represents the p.m.f. of multi-pixel clique with pixels $(i, j, ...)$ valued $(m, n, ...)$, and $q_{m,n,...}^{i,j,...}$ denotes its stego version (The superscript i, j and subscript m, n may be omitted for simplicity). β_i denotes the change probability of the i-th pixel. In this paper, we set the change probability of modifying each pixel by +1 and -1 be the same.

3   The Method

The cover model built in this paper is shown as the left of Fig. 1, where each pixel interacts with its 8 neighbor pixels. The 9 pixels $\{0, 1, 2, 3, 4, 5, 6, 7, 8\}$, centered in pixel 0, are assumed to obey a 9-variate Gaussian distribution with zero means.

First, we decompose these 9 pixels as illustrated in Fig. 1 based on conditional independence. Then we propose a form of approximations to the KL divergence of 2-pixel clique and 4-pixel clique, with which the KL divergence of total 9 pixels can be easily obtained. The overall KL divergence is obtained by summing up the KL divergence of all such 9 pixels in the cover image (overlapped in practice). Finally, the optimal embedding change probabilities are derived through minimizing the overall KL divergence under a given payload constraint utilizing Lagrange multipliers and then converted to distortion cost for practical embedding.

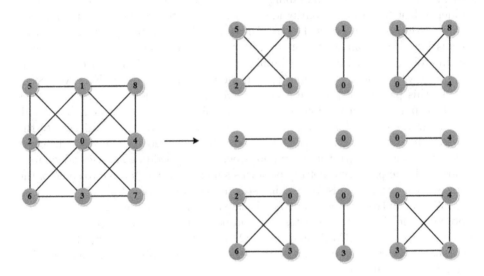

Fig. 1. Decomposition of a 9-pixel clique

3.1   Decomposition of a 9-Pixel Clique

Taking advantage of conditional independence, we first decompose the p.m.f. of 9-pixel clique $p(0 \sim 8)$ in terms of 1-variate Gaussian, 2-variate Gaussian and 4-variate Gaussian as Eq. (1) (for proof see Appendix A). Thus the corresponding KL divergence of pixels $\{0 \sim 8\}$ can be expressed as Eq. (2). Equation (1) indicates the interactions within 9-pixel clique, as shown in Fig. 1, it can be decomposed into one 1-pixel clique, four 2-pixel cliques and four 4-pixel cliques. Given the fact that the KL divergence of 1-pixel clique is already in MG, as long as we propose approximations to the KL divergences of 2-pixel clique and 4-pixel clique, the KL divergence of 9-pixel clique can be easily derived. The next subsection describes the details of the calculation for 2D and 4D divergence.

$$p(0 \sim 8) = \frac{p(1,0,2,5) \cdot p(3,0,2,6) \cdot p(3,0,4,7) \cdot p(1,0,4,8) \cdot p(0)}{p(0,1) \cdot p(0,2) \cdot p(0,3) \cdot p(0,4)}. \tag{1}$$

$$D_{KL}(p^{0\sim8}||q^{0\sim8}(\beta_0 \sim \beta_8)) = \sum_{(0,j,k,l)\in A} D_{KL}(p^{0,j,k,l}||q^{0,j,k,l}(\beta_0,\beta_j,\beta_k,\beta_l))$$

$$-\sum_{j=1}^{4} D_{KL}(p^{0,j}||q^{0,j}(\beta_i,\beta_j)) + D_{KL}(p^0||q^0(\beta_0)) \tag{2}$$

$$\approx (\sum_{(i,j,k,l)\in A} \frac{1}{2}\beta_{ijkl}^T \boldsymbol{I}_{ijkl}(0)\beta_{ijkl} - \sum_{(i,j)\in B} \frac{1}{2}\beta_{ij}^T \boldsymbol{I}_{ij}(0)\beta_{ij} + \frac{1}{2}\beta_i^2 I_i(0))|_{i=0},$$

where $A = \{(0,1,5,2),(0,3,2,6),(0,3,7,4),(0,1,8,4)\}$, $B = \{(0,1),(0,2),(0,3),(0,4)\}$, $\boldsymbol{\beta}_{ijkl} = [\beta_i,\beta_j,\beta_k,\beta_l]^T$, $\boldsymbol{\beta}_{ij} = [\beta_i,\beta_j]^T$, and $I_i(0), \boldsymbol{I}_{ij}(0), \boldsymbol{I}_{ijkl}(0)$ are respectively 1×1, 2×2 and 4×4 steganographic Fisher Information Matrix.

MG proposed an approxiamtion to $I_i(0)$ as (3), learned from which we construct 2D and 4D KL Divergence in Sect. 3.2.

$$I_i(0) = \sum_m \frac{1}{p_m^i}(\frac{\partial q_m^i(\beta_i)}{\partial \beta_i}|_{\beta_i=0})^2 \approx \frac{1}{\sigma_i^2}. \tag{3}$$

3.2 2D and 4D KL Divergence

For the 2-pixel clique (i,j) with values (m,n) , we assume its p.m.f. is $p_{m,n}$, and under the case of ternary embedding, then its stego pixel p.m.f. as well as the partial derivative of this p.m.f. are shown as:

$$q_{m,n}(\beta_i,\beta_j) = (1-2\beta_i)\beta_j(p_{m,n-1}+p_{m,n+1}) + \beta_i(1-2\beta_j)(p_{m-1,n}+p_{m+1,n})$$
$$+ \beta_i\beta_j(p_{m-1,n-1}+p_{m-1,n+1}+p_{m+1,n-1}+p_{m+1,n+1}) + (1-2\beta_i)(1-2\beta_j)p_{m,n}. \tag{4}$$

$$\frac{\partial q_{m,n}}{\partial \beta_i}|_{\beta_i=0,\beta_j=0} = -2p_{m,n} + p_{m-1,n} + p_{m+1,n},$$

$$\frac{\partial q_{m,n}}{\partial \beta_j}|_{\beta_i=0,\beta_j=0} = -2p_{m,n} + p_{m,n-1} + p_{m,n+1}. \tag{5}$$

We propose an approximation to two-dimensional KL divergence between the cover and stego as (6) in mimic of MG. The 2×2 steganographic Fisher Information matrix, which is the key component in (6), is approximated using (5) as below (for proof, see Appendix B). Note that $(\beta_i,\beta_j,\beta_k,\beta_l) = (\beta_1,\beta_2,\beta_3,\beta_4)$ in this subsection and Appendix B.

$$D_{KL}(p^{i,j}||q^{i,j}(\beta_i,\beta_j)) \approx \frac{1}{2}\beta_{ij}^T \boldsymbol{I}_{ij}(0)\beta_{ij} = \sum_{r,c=1}^{2} \frac{1}{2}\beta_r I_{ij}^{rc}(0)\beta_c \tag{6}$$

where $I_{ij}^{(11)}(0) \approx \frac{2}{\sigma_i^2(1-\rho_{ij}^2)^2}, I_{ij}^{(22)}(0) \approx \frac{2}{\sigma_j^2(1-\rho_{ij}^2)^2}, I_{ij}^{(12)}(0) = I_{ij}^{(21)}(0) \approx \frac{2\rho_{ij}^2}{\sigma_i\sigma_j(1-\rho_{ij}^2)^2}$,

Results in (6) are calculated employing Eq. (7), which is also a proposed approximation in mimic of (3).

$$I_{ij}^{rc}(0) = \sum_{m,n} \frac{1}{p_{m,n}} \cdot (\frac{\partial q_{m,n}}{\partial \beta_r}|_{\beta_i,\beta_j=0}) \cdot (\frac{\partial q_{m,n}}{\partial \beta_c}|_{\beta_i,\beta_j=0}) \tag{7}$$

Similarly, for 4-pixel clique (i, j, k, l) with values (m, n, s, t), the partial derivative of its p.m.f is given in (8), while the p.m.f. itself will not be given in this paper since it is too long and useless except for partial differential.

$$\frac{\partial q_{m,n,s,t}}{\partial \beta_i}\Big|_{\beta_i=0,\beta_j=0,\beta_k=0,\beta_l=0} = -2p_{m,n,s,t} + p_{m-1,n,s,t} + p_{m+1,n,s,t},$$

$$\frac{\partial q_{m,n,s,t}}{\partial \beta_j}\Big|_{\beta_i=0,\beta_j=0,\beta_k=0,\beta_l=0} = -2p_{m,n,s,t} + p_{m,n-1,s,t} + p_{m,n+1,s,t},$$

$$\frac{\partial q_{m,n,s,t}}{\partial \beta_k}\Big|_{\beta_i=0,\beta_j=0,\beta_k=0,\beta_l=0} = -2p_{m,n,s,t} + p_{m,n,s-1,t} + p_{m,n,s+1,t},$$

$$\frac{\partial q_{m,n,s,t}}{\partial \beta_l}\Big|_{\beta_i=0,\beta_j=0,\beta_k=0,\beta_l=0} = -2p_{m,n,s,t} + p_{m,n,s,t-1} + p_{m,n,s,t+1}.$$

$$(8)$$

Then, the KL divergence of 4-pixel clique is:

$$D_{KL}(p^{i,j,k,l}\|q^{i,j,k,l}(\beta_i, \beta_j, \beta_k, \beta_l)) \approx \frac{1}{2}\beta_{ijkl}^T \mathbf{I}_{ijkl}(0)\beta_{ijkl} = \sum_{r,c=1}^{4} \frac{1}{2}\beta_r I_{ijkl}^{rc}(0)\beta_c$$

$$(9)$$

where the element $I_{ijkl}^{rc}(0)$ located in the r-th row and c-th column of $\mathbf{I_{ijkl}}(\mathbf{0})$ can be calculated using (8) and (10):

$$I_{ijkl}^{rc}(0) = \sum_{m,n,s,t} \frac{1}{p_{m,n,s,t}} \cdot \left(\frac{\partial q_{m,n,s,t}}{\partial \beta_r}\Big|_{\beta_i,\beta_j,\beta_k,\beta_l=0}\right) \cdot \left(\frac{\partial q_{m,n,s,t}}{\partial \beta_c}\Big|_{\beta_i,\beta_j,\beta_k,\beta_l=0}\right)$$

$$(10)$$

For the sake of computationally efficient, we adapt the approximation equation below in the 4D KL divergence.

$$p(i, j, k, l) \approx \frac{(p(i, j)p(i, k)p(i, l)p(j, k)p(j, l)p(k, l))^z}{(p(i)p(j)p(k)p(l))^{3z-1}},$$

$$(11)$$

where z is a positive integer, and we set this hyper-parameter to be 1 in this work.

3.3   Optimization

Our steganographic task can be formulated as an optimization problem that minimizes the distortion under a given payload constraint. We take its optimal solution as the optimal change probabilities. The objective function is a weighted sum of the overall KL divergence and the total payload to be embedded, with Lagrange multiplier λ controls these two terms. The overall KL divergence equals the sum of the KL divergence of the 9-pixel cliques centered in pixel i, $i \in \{1, 2, ..., n\}$. The total payload embedded in the image is the sum of entropies:

$$\alpha n = \sum_{i=1}^{n} h(\beta_i),$$

$$(12)$$

where $h(x) = -2x\ln x - (1 - 2x)ln(1 - 2x)$. Differentiating the objective function w.r.t.β_i gives (13):

$$\frac{\partial}{\partial \beta_i}\left(\sum_{i=1}^{n} D_{KL}^{i} - \lambda\left(\sum_{i=1}^{n} h(\beta_i) - \alpha n\right)\right) = 0, \tag{13}$$

We solve (13) through several times of iterations, and thus obtain the optimal embedding change probabilities. The corresponding embedding distortion cost can be obtained using (14) [6], which will be used in STC for the practical embedding.

$$c_i = ln(\frac{1}{\beta_i} - 2). \tag{14}$$

4   Experimental Results and Analysis

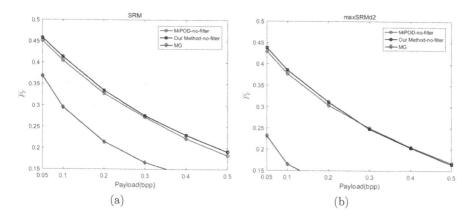

Fig. 2. The security performance in terms of average testing error $\overline{P_E}$ for MiPOD without filtered FI, MG and our method without filtered cost when detecting with the feature sets of SRM (a) and maxSRMd2 (b).

We conduct experiments on BOSSBase ver.1.01 [2], which contains 10,000 grey-scale images with a size of 512×512. The security performance is evaluated with two steganalysis feature sets: the 34,671-dimensional feature set SRM and its selection-channel-aware version called maxSRMd2 with ensemble classifiers [11]. The training set and test set, both of which contains 5000 images, are randomly selected by ten times. The average of the false-positive rate and false-negative rate across ten times are adopted as test error, denoted by symbol $\overline{P_E}$. The variance and covariance of pixels used in our method are estimated by a function named sklearn.empirical_covariance [1] in python. We also adjust the results for numerical stability by: $\rho = \min\{0.99, \rho\}, \sigma = max\{0.01, \sigma\}$

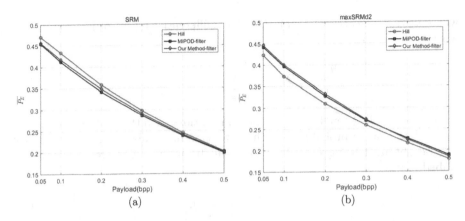

Fig. 3. The security performance in terms of average testing error $\overline{P_E}$ for Hill, MiPOD with filtered FI and our method with filtered cost when detecting with the feature sets of SRM (a) and maxSRMd2 (b).

Figures 2 and 3 show the average total probability of error $\overline{P_E}$ for payloads $R \in \{0.05, 0.1, 0.2, 0.3, 0.4, 0.5\}$ bpp(bits per pixel) for our method, MG and other prevailing embedding methods. Suggested by the spreading rule [12], we add a 9×9 average filter operation to our cost map before embedding and report the results in Fig. 3, while Fig. 2 remains cost map not be low-pass filtered. An average filter spreads the low costs of textural pixels to their neighbourhood, making the embedding more conservative. Comparison between Fig. 2 and Fig. 3 reflects that it indeed brings promotion on both two feature sets.

Figure 2 suggests that our method outperforms MiPOD and MG for both SRM and maxSRMd2 consistently without the low-pass filtering operation. If low-pass filter applied, Fig. 3 suggests that our method is superior to HILL and comparable to MiPOD in against the detection of maxSRMd2. As for the performance in resisting the detection of SRM, it is inferior to HILL while slightly superior to MiPOD. It may be due to our model can help the selection channel aware feature set maxSRMd2 to obtain more statistical information, which results in more accurate steganalysis on our method.

Table 1. Average testing error $\overline{P_E}$ versus payload in bits per pixel (bpp) for MiPOD with low-pass filtered Fisher Information and our method with low-pass filtered costs on 3000 relatively smooth images from BOSSbase ver1.01 using ensemble 1.0 classifier with two feature sets: SRM and maxSRMd2.

Feature	Algorithm	Payload (bpp)						
		0.05	0.1	0.2	0.3	0.4	0.5	0.6
SRM	MiPOD	0.4837	0.4600	0.4012	0.3343	0.2693	0.2090	0.1968
	Our method	0.4873	0.4688	0.4128	0.3506	0.2799	0.2206	0.2021
maxSRMd2	MiPOD	0.4742	0.4416	0.3755	0.3030	0.2434	0.1928	0.1766
	Our method	0.4599	0.4280	0.3662	0.3116	0.2573	0.2081	0.1734

In order to clearly show the efficiency of incorporating interactions within neighbourhood pixels in distortion design. We select 3000 relatively smooth images and conduct a series of experiments on it for payloads $R \in \{0.05, 0.1, 0.2, 0.3, 0.4, 0.5, 0.6\}$ bpp. These 3000 images are taken from the 5000th to the 8000th image in BOSSBase ver.1.01 after sorting them by noise level using algorithm provided in [3]. It is observed that our method outperforms MiPOD by 0.8–1.6% for $R \geq 0.3\,bpp$ against maxSRMd2, and is superior to MiPOD against SRM more obviously than experiments on 10000 images of BOSSBase ver.1.01. The reason is that embedding smoother regions with larger payload forces neighbourhood pixels simultaneously changed more, such that the assumption of independent pixels is no longer suitable in this case. Hence, our GMRF model performs better on relatively smooth images.

5   Conclusion

In this paper, we propose a new steganographic scheme for spatial images by incorporating correlations between pixels and their local eight-neighbourhood. The method obtains change probabilities by solving an optimization problem that aims to minimize the KL divergence under a payload constraint. To get the overall KL divergence, we decompose the 9-pixel clique into 1-pixel clique, 2-pixel clique and 4-pixel clique and propose an approximation of 2D and 4D KL divergence. With the interactions among embedding modifications taken into consideration, the proposed statistical model demonstrates superior or comparable security performance to some of the state-of-the-art methods, e.g. HILL and MiPOD. Moreover, it is more suitable for embedding relatively smooth images with a relatively large payload. Our future work plans to delineate the correlation between pixels more accurately.

Acknowledgements. This work was supported in part by the National Natural Science Foundation of China under Grants U1726315, 61772573 and U1936212 and U19B2022, in part by the Key-Area Research and Development Program of Guangdong Province under grant 2019B010139003, and in part by Shenzhen R&D Program under grant GJHZ20180928155814437.

Appendix

A   Decomposition of $p(0 \sim 8)$

Figure 1, illustrates 9 pixels of one block with index $\{0 \sim 8\}$, where every two pixels are adjacent if connected or independent if disconnected. Based on conditional independence, for two independent pixels, i, j, we can easily obtain:

$$p(i,j) = p(i|j) \cdot p(j) = p(i) \cdot p(j), \tag{15}$$

Let $i \leftrightarrow j$ represents adjacent pixels i, j, we proceed with a group of pixels according to conditional independence:

$$
\begin{aligned}
p(i, j_1, \ldots j_m) &= p(i|j_1, \ldots j_m) \cdot p(j_1, \ldots j_m) \\
&= p(i|j_k, i \leftrightarrow j_k) \cdot p(j_1, \ldots j_m).
\end{aligned}
\tag{16}
$$

Then, it's obvious to get (17) and subsequently we take the second term of former formula repeatedly and use (16) to simply them:

$$
p(0 \sim 8) = p(5|0 \sim 4, 6 \sim 8) \cdot p(0 \sim 4, 6 \sim 8) = p(5|0, 1, 2) \cdot p(0 \sim 4, 6 \sim 8),
\tag{17}
$$

$$
p(0 \sim 4, 6 \sim 8) = p(6|0 \sim 4, 7, 8) \cdot p(0 \sim 4, 7, 8) = p(6|0, 2, 3) \cdot p(0 \sim 4, 7, 8),
\tag{18}
$$

$$
p(0 \sim 4, 7, 8) = p(8|0 \sim 4, 7) \cdot p(0 \sim 4, 7) = p(8|0, 1, 4) \cdot p(0 \sim 4, 7),
\tag{19}
$$

$$
p(0 \sim 4, 7) = p(7|0 \sim 4) \cdot p(0 \sim 4) = p(7|0, 3, 4) \cdot p(0 \sim 4),
\tag{20}
$$

$$
\begin{aligned}
p(0 \sim 4) &= p(4|0, 1, 2, 3) \cdot p(0, 1, 2, 3) = p(4|0, 1, 3) \cdot p(0, 1, 2, 3) \\
&= \frac{p(0, 1, 3, 4)}{p(0, 1, 3)} \cdot p(0, 1, 2, 3),
\end{aligned}
\tag{21}
$$

$$
p(0, 1, 2, 3) = p(1|0, 2, 3) \cdot p(0, 2, 3) = p(1|0, 2) \cdot p(0, 2, 3) = \frac{p(0, 1, 2)}{p(0, 2)} \cdot p(0, 2, 3),
\tag{22}
$$

For the numerator and denominator in first term in (21):

$$
p(0, 1, 3, 4) = p(3|0, 1, 4) \cdot p(0, 1, 4) = p(3|0, 4) \cdot p(0, 1, 4) = \frac{p(0, 3, 4)}{p(0, 4)} \cdot p(0, 1, 4),
\tag{23}
$$

$$
p(0, 1, 3) = p(1|0, 3) \cdot p(0, 3) = p(1|0) \cdot p(0, 3) = \frac{p(0, 1)}{p(0)} \cdot p(0, 3),
\tag{24}
$$

Substitute (22), (23) and (24) into (21), (21) into (20), (20) into (19), (19) into (18) and (18) into (17) in turn, (17) can be expressed as:

$$
p(0 \sim 8) = \frac{p(1, 0, 2, 5) \cdot p(3, 0, 2, 6) \cdot p(3, 0, 4, 7) \cdot p(1, 0, 4, 8) \cdot p(0)}{p(0, 1) \cdot p(0, 2) \cdot p(0, 3) \cdot p(0, 4)}.
\tag{25}
$$

B   2D and 4D Steganographic Fisher Information matrix

We mimic Eq. (3), where one-dimensional steganographic Fisher Information proposed, to construct 2D and 4D steganographic Fisher Information matrix in this proof. First, elements in 2D steganographic Fisher Information matrix are approximated as:

$$
\begin{aligned}
I_{ij}^{(12)}(0) = I_{ij}^{(21)}(0) &= \sum_{m,n} \frac{1}{p_{m,n}} \left(\frac{\partial q_{m,n}(\beta_i, \beta_j)}{\partial \beta_i} \Big|_{\beta_i, \beta_j = 0} \right) \cdot \left(\frac{\partial q_{k,l}(\beta_i, \beta_j)}{\partial \beta_j} \Big|_{\beta_i, \beta_j = 0} \right), \\
I_{ij}^{(11)}(0) &= \sum_{m,n} \frac{1}{p_{m,n}} \left(\frac{\partial q_{m,n}(\beta_i, \beta_j)}{\partial \beta_i} \Big|_{\beta_i, \beta_j = 0} \right)^2, \\
I_{ij}^{(22)}(0) &= \sum_{m,n} \frac{1}{p_{m,n}} \left(\frac{\partial q_{m,n}(\beta_i, \beta_j)}{\partial \beta_j} \Big|_{\beta_i, \beta_j = 0} \right)^2.
\end{aligned}
\tag{26}
$$

$p_{m,n}$, the abbreviation of $p_{m,n}^{i,j}$, is the probability $P\{i = m, j = n\}$, which can viewed as a point $f(x_i = m, x_j = n)$ in the two-dimensional Gaussian distribution. Although x_i, x_j are both discrete integer variables, we suppose $f(x_i, x_j)$ is continuous for differentiate:

$$f(x_i, x_j) = \frac{1}{2\pi\sigma_i\sigma_j\sqrt{1 - \rho_{ij}^2}} \exp\left(-\frac{1}{2(1 - \rho_{ij}^2)}\left(\frac{x_i^2}{\sigma_i^2} - \frac{2\rho_{ij}x_ix_j}{\sigma_i\sigma_j} + \frac{x_j^2}{\sigma_j^2}\right)\right). \quad (27)$$

Given $p_{m,n} = f(m, n), p_{m\pm 1,n} = f(m \pm 1, n), p_{m,n\pm 1} = f(m, n \pm 1)$, considering the Taylor approximation at points $(m \pm 1, n), (m, n \pm 1)$, we have:

$$f(m\pm 1, n) \approx f(m, n) \pm \frac{\partial f(x_i, x_j)}{\partial x_i}\Big|_{x_i=m,x_j=n} + \frac{1}{2} \cdot \frac{\partial^2 f(x_i, x_j)}{\partial x_i^2}\Big|_{x_i=m,x_j=n}, \quad (28)$$

$$f(m, n\pm 1) \approx f(m, n) \pm \frac{\partial f(x_i, x_j)}{\partial x_j}\Big|_{x_i=m,x_j=n} + \frac{1}{2} \cdot \frac{\partial^2 f(x_i, x_j)}{\partial x_j^2}\Big|_{x_i=m,x_j=n}. \quad (29)$$

$$- 2p_{m,n} + p_{m-1,n} + p_{m+1,n} \approx \frac{\partial^2 f(x_i, x_j)}{\partial x_i^2}\Big|_{x_i=m,x_j=n}, \quad (30)$$

$$- 2p_{m,n} + p_{m,n-1} + p_{m,n+1} \approx \frac{\partial^2 f(x_i, x_j)}{\partial x_j^2}\Big|_{x_i=m,x_j=n}. \quad (31)$$

After substituting (5), (27), (30) and (31) into (26), and taking variables m, n, s, t continuous, we can finally derive (32)–(34). We give an example formula for element ij in 4×4 Fisher Information matrix as (35), which can be easily generalized to other elements, their calculation results do not list because of the length limit.

$$I_{ij}^{(11)}(0) = \sum_{m,n} \frac{1}{p_{m,n}}(-2p_{m,n} + p_{m-1,n} + p_{m+1,n})^2$$
$$\approx \int_m \int_n \frac{1}{f(x_i, x_j)}\left(\frac{\partial^2 f(x_i, x_j)}{\partial x_i^2}\Big|_{x_i=m,x_j=n}\right)^2 dm dn = \frac{2}{\sigma_i^2(1 - \rho_{ij}^2)^2}. \quad (32)$$

$$I_{ij}^{(22)}(0) = \sum_{m,n} \frac{1}{p_{m,n}}(-2p_{m,n} + p_{m,n-1} + p_{m,n+1})^2$$
$$\approx \int_m \int_n \frac{1}{f(x_i, x_j)}\left(\frac{\partial^2 f(x_i, x_j)}{\partial x_j^2}\Big|_{x_i=m,x_j=n}\right)^2 dm dn = \frac{2}{\sigma_j^2(1 - \rho_{ij}^2)^2}. \quad (33)$$

$$I_{ij}^{(12)}(0) = I_{ij}^{(21)}(0)$$

$$= \sum_{m,n} \frac{1}{p_{m,n}} (-2p_{m,n} + p_{m-1,n} + p_{m+1,n}) \cdot (-2p_{m,n} + p_{m,n-1} + p_{m,n+1})$$

$$\approx \int_m \int_n \frac{1}{f(x_i,x_j)} \left(\frac{\partial^2 f(x_i,x_j)}{\partial x_i^2}\Big|_{x_i=m,x_j=n}\right) \cdot \left(\frac{\partial^2 f(x_i,x_j)}{\partial x_j^2}\Big|_{x_i=m,x_j=n}\right) dm\, dn \qquad (34)$$

$$= \frac{2\rho_{ij}^2}{\sigma_i \sigma_j \cdot (1-\rho_{ij}^2)^2}.$$

$$I_{ijkl}^{ij}(0) = \sum_{m,n,s,t} \frac{1}{p_{m,n,s,t}} \cdot \left(\frac{\partial q_{m,n,s,t}}{\partial \beta_i}\Big|_{\beta_i,\beta_j,\beta_k,\beta_l=0}\right) \cdot \left(\frac{\partial q_{m,n,s,t}}{\partial \beta_j}\Big|_{\beta_i,\beta_j,\beta_k,\beta_l=0}\right)$$

$$= \sum_{m,n,s,t} \frac{1}{p_{m,n,s,t}} \cdot (-2p_{m,n,s,t} + p_{m-1,n,s,t} + p_{m+1,n,s,t})$$

$$\cdot (-2p_{m,n,s,t} + p_{m,n-1,s,t} + p_{m,n+1,s,t}) \qquad (35)$$

$$\approx \int_m \int_n \int_s \int_t \frac{1}{f(x_i,x_j,x_k,x_l)} \left(\frac{\partial^2 f(x_i,x_j,x_k,x_l)}{\partial x_i^2}\Big|_{x_i=m,x_j=n,x_k=s,x_l=t}\right)$$

$$\cdot \left(\frac{\partial^2 f(x_i,x_j,x_k,x_l)}{\partial x_j^2}\Big|_{x_i=m,x_j=n,x_k=s,x_l=t}\right) ds\,dt\,dm\,dn.$$

References

1. Scikit-learn 0.19.1 documentation. https://scikit-learn.org/stable/modules/covariance.html. Accessed 7 Nov 2019
2. Bas, P., Filler, T., Pevný, T.: Break our steganographic system: the ins and outs of organizing BOSS. In: Proceedings of the 13th International Workshop on Information Hiding, pp. 59–70 (2011)
3. Chen, G., Zhu, F., Heng, P.A.: An efficient statistical method for image noise level estimation. In: 2015 IEEE International Conference on Computer Vision (ICCV), pp. 477–485 (2015). https://doi.org/10.1109/ICCV.2015.62
4. Chen, X., Zhang, Z., Qiu, A., Xia, Z., Xiong, N.N.: Novel coverless steganography method based on image selection and stargan. IEEE Trans. Netw. Sci. Eng. **9**(1), 219–230 (2022). https://doi.org/10.1109/TNSE.2020.3041529
5. Denemark, T., Sedighi, V., Holub, V., Cogranne, R., Fridrich, J.: Selection-channel-aware rich model for steganalysis of digital images. In: IEEE International Workshop on Information Forensics and Security (2014). https://doi.org/10.1109/WIFS.2014.7084302
6. Filler, T., Judas, J., Fridrich, J.: Minimizing additive distortion in steganography using syndrome-trellis codes. IEEE Trans. Inf. Forens. Secur. **6**(3), 920–935 (2011). https://doi.org/10.1109/TIFS.2011.2134094
7. Fridrich, J., Kodovský, J.: Rich models for steganalysis of digital images. IEEE Trans. Inf. Forens. Secur. **7**(3), 868–882 (2012). https://doi.org/10.1109/TIFS.2012.2190402
8. Fridrich, J., Kodovsky, J.: Multivariate gaussian model for designing additive distortion for steganography. In: IEEE ICASSP, pp. 2949–2953 (2013). https://doi.org/10.1109/ICASSP.2013.6638198

9. Holub, V., Fridrich, J.: Designing steganographic distortion using directional filters. In: International Workshop on Information Forensics and Security, pp. 234–239 (2012). https://doi.org/10.1109/WIFS.2012.6412655

10. Holub, V., Fridrich, J., Denemark, T.: Universal distortion function for steganography in an arbitrary domain. EURASIP J. Inf. Secur. **2014**(1), 1–13 (2014). https://doi.org/10.1186/1687-417X-2014-1

11. Kodovský, J., Fridrich, J., Holub, V.: Ensemble classifiers for steganalysis of digital media. IEEE Trans. Inf. Forens. Secur. **7**(2), 432–444 (2012). https://doi.org/10.1109/TIFS.2011.2175919

12. Li, B., Tan, S., Wang, M., Huang, J.: Investigation on cost assignment in spatial image steganography. IEEE Trans. Inf. Forens. Secur. **9**(8), 1264–1277 (2014). https://doi.org/10.1109/TIFS.2014.2326954

13. Li, B., Wang, M., Huang, J., Li, X.: A new cost function for spatial image steganography. In: International Conference on Image Processing, ICIP, pp. 4206–4210 (2014). https://doi.org/10.1109/ICIP.2014.7025854

14. Luo, Y., Qin, J., Xiang, X., Tan, Y.: Coverless image steganography based on multi-object recognition. IEEE Trans. Circuits Syst. Video Technol. **31**(7), 2779–2791 (2021). https://doi.org/10.1109/TCSVT.2020.3033945

15. Pevný, T., Bas, P., Fridrich, J.: Steganalysis by subtractive pixel adjacency matrix. IEEE Trans. Inf. Forens. Secur. **5**(2), 215–224 (2010). https://doi.org/10.1145/1597817.1597831

16. Pevný, T., Filler, T., Bas, P.: Using high-dimensional image models to perform highly undetectable steganography. In: Information Hiding, 12th International Conference, vol. 6387, pp. 161–177 (2010). https://doi.org/10.1007/978-3-642-16435-4_13

17. Sedighi, V., Cogranne, R., Fridrich, J.: Content-adaptive steganography by minimizing statistical detectability. IEEE Trans. Inf. Forens. Secur. **11**(2), 221–234 (2016). https://doi.org/10.1109/TIFS.2015.2486744

18. Sedighi, V., Fridrich, J.J., Cogranne, R.: Content-adaptive pentary steganography using the multivariate generalized gaussian cover model. In: Proceedings of the SPIE, Electronic Imaging, Media Watermarking, Security, and Forensics 2015, vol. 9409 (2015). https://doi.org/10.1117/12.2080272

19. Yang, Z.L., Guo, X.Q., Chen, Z.M., Huang, Y.F., Zhang, Y.J.: RNN-stega: linguistic steganography based on recurrent neural networks. IEEE Trans. Inf. Forens. Secur. **14**(5), 1280–1295 (2019). https://doi.org/10.1109/TIFS.2018.2871746

IoT Security

A Trust-Based Malicious Detection Scheme for Underwater Acoustic Sensor Networks

Kun Liang[1], Shijie Sun[2], Xiangdang Huang[2], Qiuling Yang[2(✉)], and N. Xiong Neal[3]

[1] School of Cyberspace Security (School of Cryptology), Hainan University, Haikou, China
[2] School of Computer Science and Technology, Hainan University, Haikou, China
990709@hainanu.edu.cn
[3] Department of Mathematics and Computer Science, Northeastern State University, Tahlequah, OK 74464, USA

Abstract. Underwater acoustic sensor networks (UASNs) have been widely applied in the fields of maritime and underwater industries and national defense. However, due to the unattended deployment environment of UASNs, the sensor nodes are vulnerable to malicious attacks and are easily compromised to be malicious nodes. In recent years, trust models are proved as an effective and efficient tools for identifying malicious nodes possessing valid identity information. We propose a trust-based malicious identification scheme (TMIS) for UASNs. First of all, the impact of underwater environment on communication trust is quantified, which makes communication trust effectively reflect the behavior of the attacks that cause communication failure such as selective forwarding attacks. Second, communication traffic is exploited to effectively reflect the behavior of the attacks that transmit or receive an abnormal number of packets, such as DOS attack. Third, we train the prediction model with SVM and K-means++ algorithms. Finally, two trust update mechanisms are proposed to cope with the dynamic environment of UASNs and On-Off attacks. The simulation results show that TMIS can effectively identify malicious nodes in complex underwater environment compared to the other three kinds of identification schemes. In particular, the larger the rate of malicious nodes is, the better TMIS performs relatively.

Keywords: UASNs · Malicious node detection · Trust mode

1 Introduction

In recent years, underwater acoustic sensor networks (UASNs) have attracted a lot of attention from some research communities, because UASNs can be used in a wide range of maritime and underwater industries and national defense, such as ocean sampling, environmental monitoring, oceanographic data collection, disaster prevention, distributed tactical surveillance, mine reconnaissance, and assisted navigation by providing exploration and monitoring services below water surface [1–3]. However, due to the inaccessible and even hostile underwater deployment environment of UASNs, sensor nodes likely encounter diverse malicious attacks and have no enough capability to cope with them due to limited software and hardware resources.

© The Author(s), under exclusive license to Springer Nature Switzerland AG 2022
X. Sun et al. (Eds.): ICAIS 2022, LNCS 13340, pp. 427–440, 2022.
https://doi.org/10.1007/978-3-031-06791-4_34

To solve the above problem, some traditional security technologies such as cryptography technology, key management, and authentication mechanism have been extensively studied and applied in UASNs [4]. However, these technologies cannot effectively cope with the internal attackers that generally have a copy of valid identity information. Trust management is an effective technology in coping with the internal attacks and increasing the tolerance of the networks to the internal attacks. However, due to the complex, dynamic, and harsh deployment environment of UASNs, the application of trust management is facing many challenges. First, due to the high bit error rate and packet collision of underwater channel, the probability of communication failure is high. So, non-cooperative behavior of malicious nodes can be concealed, which largely lessen the performance of trust management [17]. Second, the selection of a kind of trust evidence generally should consider three factors. The first one is the effectiveness of the evidence on reflecting the performance of attacks. The second one is the cost for obtaining the trust evidence. The lower the cost is, the longer the lifetime of UASNs is. The last one is the reliability of the evidence, but there are few works taking this factor into account. Moreover, the evidence should be obtained by observing the behavior of a trustee but offered by the trustee. This is because the authenticity of the evidence offered by the trustee cannot be ensured. That is, the evidence can be forged by the trustee. In existing some of state of the art trust models [5, 17], energy evidence is adopted to reflect the performance of DoS attack, Selective forwarding, Sybil attack, Wormhole attack, Hello flood attack, and Fake routing attack. Indeed, the rate of energy consumption is an important evidence for reflect the effect of many attacks. However, these studies didn't take the third factor into account. Third, how to cope with the attacks that aim at trust management is also challenge. For example, in an on-off attack, the malicious node is able to perform bad or good behavior alternately. After launching malicious attacks for a period of time, the adversary can choose to behave normally to increase its trust level. Repeating this process, it is difficult to identify the adversary based on the level of trust value [5].

To solve the above-mentioned problems, we propose TMIS to cope with them. First, in order to quantify the impact of underwater channel on communication trust, we model the success probability that two neighbor nodes interact once. Then, in the phase of generation of trust evidences, we combine communication evidence with the success probability of two neighbor nodes' interactions in normal situations, which can extremely reduce the impact of high packet-bit-error rate and packet collision on the authenticity of communication trust. Secondly, we select communication traffic as a kind of trust attribute, which is collected by observation and able to effectively and reliably reflect the performance of the attacks that cause an abnormal number of packets between neighbor nodes. Considering on-off attacks that aim at undermining the functions of trust management, we adopt two kinds of trust update methods, namely, event-based and time-based trust update, which can achieve the effect of rising slowly and falling quickly.

2 Related Work

Up to now, there have existed many trust models researched for detecting malicious nodes [6, 22], intrusion detection [7, 21], secure data collection [8], and access control

[9]. In order to understand the research status, a review of existing trust management schemes, as follows, is presented and classified by mathematical methods.

S. Ganeriwal et al. [10] proposed a reputation system named RFSN (Reputation-based Framework for High Integrity Sensor Networks) based on beta distribution. In this scheme, many concepts such as reputation and trust were defined, and this system employed the Bayesian formulation. In particular, the beta distribution was used in reputation representation, updating, and integration. Moreover, the reputation updating adopted the idea of aging of observations with time. However, only taking into account successful and unsuccessful interactions between any two neighbor nodes as trust attributes is not enough for accurate malicious node identification. To the best of our knowledge, Josang et al. [11] first proposed a trust model based on subjective logic. In addition, the subjective logic and beta distribution in this scheme can be used in solving the uncertainty and fuzziness of observations. However, it didn't refer to trust updating for fusing history observations. Ren et al. [12] proposed a subjective logic-based trust management for unattended wireless sensor networks to deal with subjectivity and uncertainty of trust evaluation. The main research interest is to guarantee the security of the storage of observations. In [13], Feng et al. proposed a trust calculation algorithm for wireless sensor nodes based on node behavior and D-S evidence theory. This scheme can solve the imprecision and uncertainty of observations. However, it didn't fuse history trust evidences, which reduce the robustness of this scheme. In [20], a trust model named ARTMM was proposed, which is known as the first trust model for UASNs. In ARTMM, the trustworthiness of sensor nodes is described by link trust, data trust, and node trust. The ARTMM takes the unreliability of the acoustic channel and the fluidity of seawater into account while evaluating the integrated trust value. However, the effect on network layers caused by attacking is ignored in ARTMM, and only using fuzzy logic is hard to acquire an accurate description of the trust relationship. To the best of our knowledge, Bin et al. [14] first employed cloud model into trust models for node selection in wireless sensor networks. In theory, cloud model can better demonstrate the randomness, fuzziness, and uncertainty of subjective trust. In [15], Jiang et al. proposed a cloud model-based trust management for detecting malicious nodes in UASNs. Taking into account characteristics of underwater channel, packet loss, used as a kind of trust evidence, in the model was analyzed layer by layer from the physical layer to the transport layer. However, the trust evidence of energy consumption is difficult to verify its authenticity, because only a sensor node itself knows its real residual energy. Both of the two schemes didn't refer to how to fuse history observations. In [16], U. Jayasinghe et al. proposed a SVM-based trust computational model for IoT services. This model includes three kinds of metrics, namely, knowledge, experience, and reputation. However, it didn't give an algorithm for trust updating. In [5], Guangjie Han et al. proposed a SVM-based trust model for identifying malicious attacks in UASNs. This model adopted three kinds of trust evidences, namely, communication trust, packet trust, and energy trust. However, this scheme didn't take into account the impact of underwater environment on communication trust, which makes the communication trust not accurate. In [17], Jinfang Jiang et al. proposed a dynamic trust evaluation and update mechanism based on C4.5 decision tree in UASNs. In addition, they designed two kinds of trust update, which make this model more flexible to cope with dynamic behavior of

UASNs. However, this model didn't take into account the impact of underwater environment on trust evaluation. In [18], Yu He et al. proposed a trust update mechanism based on reinforcement learning in UASNs. The authors took into account the impact of underwater environment on trust update.

3 Network and Attack Model

As illustrated in Fig. 1, we assume that, in this network model, all sensor nodes are homogeneous, that is, these nodes are armed with uniform software and hardware resources, and randomly and 3D-dimensionally deployed under a piece of specific ocean surface, and the cluster heads are selected from the sensor nodes by clustering protocols, and autonomous underwater vehicles(AUVs) can dynamically change their position in order to execute special tasks, which possess more software and hardware resources compared to the sensor nodes.

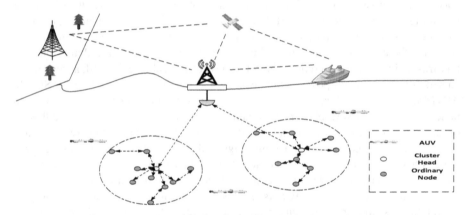

Fig. 1. Network model of underwater acoustic sensor networks.

Moreover, some assumptions are given as follows. Firstly, every node previously holds a unique ID so that each node stores the information about its neighbor nodes. Secondly, the communication between sensor nodes and AUVs is secure by default in order to ensure the integrity and confidentiality of trust evidences sent to AUVs. Thirdly, each node maintains a historical time window and a current time window for storing observations collected from behavior of neighbor nodes.

We assume that an attacker aiming at this network can capture or compromise some sensor nodes by acoustic signal detectors. Then, the attacker can obtain secret identity information of the sensor nodes so that it can inject malicious nodes, possessing valid identities, into this network. Furthermore, the attacker can launch more malicious attacks including DoS, Selective forwarding, Packet tampering, Sybil attack, Wormhole attack and On-Off attack.

4 Overview of TMIS

In this section, we will introduce the TMIS scheme. we firstly make an overview of it. This scheme mainly includes channel model, trust evidence generation, trust evaluation, and trust update.

4.1 Channel Model

In this paper, we adopt the underwater acoustic channel model investigated in [19] that can reflect the effects of path-loss, multiple propagation paths and ambient noise of underwater acoustic channel. In this study, it is assumed that Slotted-Aloha is adopted as the MAC protocol of UASNs, each sensor j is modeled as an M/G/1 queue with a generally distributed service time with μ_j and generates data frames of fixed size while following a Poisson process at rate λ_j. The probability of a successful communication (both packet transmission error and packet collision will not occur) between two neighbor nodes can be modeled as follows:

$$P_{w,p}(\beta_n) = (1 - P_e(\beta_n))\rho \prod_{j=1}^{\overline{U}-1} \left(1 - \frac{\lambda_j}{\mu_j}\rho\right) \tag{1}$$

where β_n represents the density of cluster headers, $\frac{\lambda_j}{\mu_j}$ is the utilization factor of neighbor sensor j, which indicates the probability that queue j is empty, ρ is the probability that a queued packet is indeed transmitted, $\overline{U}$ is the average number of associated sensors per cluster header. Besides, $P_e(\beta_n)$ is the packet error probability and obtained by Eq. 2.

$$P_e = 1 - (1 - P_b)^{L_p}$$

$$P_b = Q(\sqrt{\gamma})$$

$$\gamma = \frac{|H(f)|^2 P_{tx}}{I + N(f)} \tag{2}$$

where P_b is the bit error probability, L_p is the number of a packet in bits, γ is the signal-to-interference-and-noise ratio (SINR), I is the interference from the other clusters, and $Q(\cdot)$ is the Q-Function.

In order to make Eq. 1. able to be used for each node, we adjust it as follows:

$$P_l = (1 - P_e(l))\rho \prod_{j=1}^{n-1} \left(1 - \frac{\lambda_j}{\mu_j}\rho\right) \tag{3}$$

where l represents the length of packets, n represents the number of target node's neighbor nodes.

Using the above channel model, we can calculate the probability that one interaction succeeds between neighbor nodes without packet error and packet collision. It is assumed that, after transmitting a data packet to its target node, a sensor node waits ACK packet in order to know if the data packet is received successfully, and the longest waiting time is N time slots. That is, the data packet is not received successfully by the target node if its waiting time is longer than the longest waiting time. The successful one-interaction probability P_{inter} between two neighbor nodes can be formulated as follows.

$$P_{inter} = P_{l_d} * P_{ack}$$

$$P_{l_d} = (1 - P_e(l_d)) \prod_{j=1}^{n-1} \left(1 - \frac{\lambda_j}{\mu_j} \rho\right)$$

$$P_{ack} = P_{l_a} + (1 - P_{l_a})P_{l_a} + \ldots + (1 - P_{l_a})^{N-1} P_{l_a} \tag{4}$$

where P_{l_d} represents the probability of a data packet successfully received by target node, l_d represents the length of the data packet, P_{ack} represents the probability that the transmitting node successfully receives an ACK from the target node within N time slots, and l_a represents the length of the ACK packet.

4.2 Generation of Trust Evidences

Due to the unattended underwater environment, sensor nodes are very likely to suffer a variety of malicious attacks, and the behavior characteristics of these attacks are not exactly the same, as exhibited in Table 1.

Table 1. The performance of different attacks.

Attack type	Performance of corresponding attack
DoS	More traffic
Selective forwarding	Less traffic and communication failure
Packet tampering	Data abnormality
Sybil	More traffic
Wormhole	More traffic

Each sensor records the behaviors of its neighbor nodes as it interacts with them. These records are raw and therefore cannot be directly used in trust evaluation. In order to solve it, we will normalize the records and generate trust evidences. Moreover, we employ three kinds of trust attributes to reflect the performance of these attacks, namely, communication trust, packet trust, and traffic trust.

Communication Trust. Communication trust depends on the number of successful and unsuccessful interactions between two neighbor nodes during a given time interval. Due to the packet bit error and packet collision in UASNs, it is possible that normal sensor nodes have low trust value, so it is hard to identify malicious nodes from normal nodes.

In order to solve it, we need to make channel estimation. By Eq. 4, we can quantify the probability of one-interaction success between two neighbor nodes. Moreover, we propose an advanced generation method based on Subjective Logic theory. Assume that s represents the number of successful interactions, u represents the number of unsuccessful interactions, we can obtain communication trust by Eq. 5:

$$T_c^t = \begin{cases} T_c^{t-1}, ceil\left(\frac{1}{1-P_{inter}}\right) < s+u \\ \frac{2(s+(s+u)(1-P_{inter}))+1}{2(normalization+1)}, else \end{cases}$$ (5)

where T_c^{t-1} represents the communication trust of the previous time slot. $ceil(\cdot)$ represents a function of rounding up.

Packet Trust. Some attacks, such as packet tampering, aim at data corruption, so packet evidence play an important role in trust evaluation. Due to the spatial and time correlation of underwater environment information, environment data follows normal distribution [5] and varies slowly. If the data value in a packet is in a given range, it is not accepted and considered as a normal packet. Assuming that, in a period of time, the number of normal data is n, and the number of abnormal data is a, the packet trust can be expressed as follows:

$$T_d = \frac{2n+1}{2(n+a+1)}$$ (6)

Packet Trust. In general, most of malicious attacks would consume more or less energy than normal node. For example, DoS attacks can cause network congestion by transmitting a mass of request packets or sync packets to target nodes, so the target nodes cannot provide normal network service. Therefore, the attackers will consume a lot of energy for transmitting the packets. So the rate of energy consumption or the amount of remaining energy is a kind of effective evidence for reflecting the performance of the attacks that consume more or less energy than normal sensor nodes. However, it is not practical that energy evidence is collected by observing the energy consumption rate or remaining energy of a neighbor node, and energy evidence can be forged in order to obtain more high trust level. Therefore, we adopt the traffic evidence to reflect the energy consumption rate, which is easy to be collected by observing and almost impossible to be forged. So traffic evidence is reliable. And it can effectively reflect the performance of DoS attacks, Selective attacks, Wormhole attacks by observing the traffic changes of neighbor nodes. Assuming that every sensor records the amount of generated traffic from or transmitted traffic to their neighbor nodes, we can obtain the traffic trust by calculating the following equation.

$$T_f = 1 - \left|\frac{r_t - r_a}{r_a}\right|$$ (7)

where r_r and r_a are the rate of traffic and average traffic from a neighbor node in a period of time slot, respectively.

4.3 Prediction Model Training

Each sensor is responsible for generating the three kind of trust evidences and saving them in its storage devices. After generating the three kinds of trust evidences, many existing trust models calculate the final trust value of the trustee by combining each weighted trust attribute. However, there are many drawbacks in this kind of approach [16]. First of all, due to lack of prior knowledge and the infinite number of possibilities, it is difficult to estimate weighting factors for every trust attribute. Second, it is unreasonable to evaluate if the trustee is malicious or not by employing a threshold-based classification system.

Machine learning can overcome the weaknesses. it is a powerful artificial intelligence method to find laws from a large number of data and can improve own classification performance by continuously training. Due to the characteristic that the number of samples is small in UASNs, support vector machine (SVM) algorithm is a good choice. In addition, this algorithm can save storage space, because only on support vector the samples are useful and worthy of being stored. And the computation complexity of this algorithm is low relatively. In our scheme, when the current time window of a sensor node is filled, it sends the trust evidences in history window to the AUV nearest to itself and replaces the history time window with the current time window. It is assumed that the data of each AUV is synchronous, and the AUVs have enough capability to provide the training and storage services for all the sensors. Then, the AUV trains a prediction model on the history trust evidences collected from the same cluster, which can cope with the situation where there are short of trust evidences for training a prediction model in UASNs. Finally, the prediction model is sent back to every sensor.

In order to achieve this, we use K-means++ to identify two different labels, namely 1 or −1, because it is simple and quick compared to other unsupervised learning algorithm. Then, the labeled training set is provided for SVM algorithm to train a classification model. Currently, many toolboxes of SVM have been developed, such as BSVM, HeroSVM, LIBSVM, etc. Here, we employ the LIBSVM toolbox to train a predict model. LIBSVM is a simple, easy-to-use, fast and effective SVM pattern recognition and regression software package developed and designed by Professor Lin Chih-Jen of National Taiwan University. The software has relatively few adjustments to the parameters involved in the SVM, and provides a lot of default parameters, which can solve many problems by using these default parameters. Moreover, we set the Kernel function of the training algorithm as Radial Basis Function Kernel (RBFK) due to the smaller number of the sample attributes compared to the number of the training samples.

4.4 Trust Update

To the best of our knowledge, most of existing trust models only employ a kind of update mode, which is not flexible enough to cope with the dynamic behavior of UASNs. In addition, On-Off attackers can perform good or bad behavior periodically, which looks like normal phenomenon due to the dynamic underwater environment. Moreover, after launching malicious attacks a period of time, the adversary can increase own trust value by behaving normally. Therefore, trustors cannot correctly evaluate if the trustees are malicious or not. In this paper, we will adopt two kinds of update methods, namely, event-based trust update and time-based trust update.

First, we focus on the events-based trust update. The main idea is to observe the significant change of the trust evidences. In other words, at the time slot i, if the value of a trust attribute in next n time slots is always less than that of time slot i, and the differences are all more than a preset threshold, the events-based trust update is triggered. This behavior will be penalized by the following equation.

$$T_x^{new} = \prod_{j=i+1}^{i+n} T_x^j,$$

$$\forall j \in [i+1, j+n], T_x^i - T_x^j > \alpha, n > \beta \tag{8}$$

where α, β are thresholds.

Second, we focus on the time-based trust update. The history trust evidences can be used as reference for node evaluation at present. In this paper, we adopt the time forgetting method to fuse the history trust evidences. The main idea is that the fresher a trust evidence is, the larger the weight for it is. At the end of a time window, the time-based trust update is triggered. It is updated by the following equation.

$$T_x^{new} = \sum_{j=i}^{i+m} T_x^j \left(1 - \frac{m+i-j}{m+1}\right) \tag{9}$$

where m is the number of time slots in a time window.

5   Simulation Analysis

In this section, to verify the performance of TMIS in the identification accuracy of malicious nodes, we will do comparative experiments. The selected reference objects are STMS [5], TMC [15], ARTMM [20]. The three trust models are all the state of the art schemes and representative for UASNs. In this simulation, experiment parameters are set as Table 2.

As demonstrated in Fig. 2, the four trust models are compared in detection accuracy with simulation time on condition that the rate of malicious nodes is 25%. It is obvious that our scheme, called TMIS, performs better compared to the other three trust models from 600 s. the detection accuracy is calculated once an interval of 200 s. It is observed in Fig. 2 that, before 600 s, the performance of TMIS and STMS is more poor than TMC, but it gradually increases over time. This is because the classification accuracy of machine learning extremely depends on the amount of training set. Due to the lack of trust evidences at the beginning of simulation, the detection accuracy of TMIS is not high enough. However, as time goes on, the number of trust evidences collected by sensor nodes increases, and the advantage of TMIS and STMS both based on SVM in identifying malicious nodes is emerged gradually. It is also shown that the detection accuracy of TMIS is higher than STMS. This is because TMIS takes into account the impact of packet collision and underwater environment, including ambient noise, multipath effect, and path attenuation, on the generation of trust evidences, which makes the trust evidences more effectively reflect the performance of malicious nodes. In addition, the detection accuracy of TMC and ARTMM is relatively lower than them. This is because these

Table 2. Experiment parameters.

Parameters	Value
The size of the UASN	1000 m * 1000 m * 1000 m
The number of sensor nodes	30–70
Node placement	Randomly deployed
Frequency	20 kHz
Shipping activity	0–1
Wind speed	0–3 m/s
Spreading factor	1.5
Acoustic speed	1500 m/s
The length of time slots	200 s

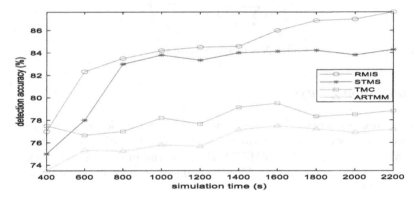

Fig. 2. Detection accuracy comparison with simulation time.

two schemes both refer to assign weight to every trust attribute. Due to lack of prior knowledge and the infinite number of possibilities, it is difficult to estimate weighting factors for every trust attribute.

As illustrated in Fig. 3, we compare the detection accuracy with the proportion of malicious nodes ranging from 10% to 30% and calculate once an interval of 5%. From the whole simulation, TMIS performs best among the four detection schemes. Especially, the larger the proportion of malicious nodes is, the better TMIS performs compared to the other three detection schemes. In addition, the detection accuracy of the four identification schemes gradually decreases as the rate of malicious nodes increases. However, our scheme is relatively stable. It is also seen in Fig. 3 that TMIS and STMS both based on SVM outperform TMC and ARTMM from 10%. This is because Machine Learning is easier to learn laws from more malicious nodes whose attack features are different. However, TMC and ARTMM are difficult to learn the laws from the malicious nodes. Moreover, the performance of TMIS outperforms STMS, because TMIS can quantify the impact of underwater environment and packet collision on communication trust, which extremely improves the identification accuracy of TMIS.

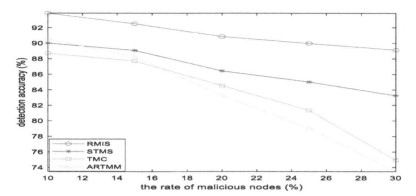

Fig. 3. Detection accuracy with the rate of malicious nodes.

As illustrated in Fig. 4, we compared the identification accuracy of the four schemes under different interaction frequencies. The proportion of malicious nodes and the size of time slots are set as 25% and 200 s, respectively. It is observed that the performance of the four schemes has no big difference as the frequency of node interaction is less than 0.03. This is because the performance of Machine Learning extremely the quality of training set. When the frequency of interactions between nodes is low, the trust evidences have no enough capacity to reflect the features of malicious nodes. With the frequency of node interactions increasing, TMIS and STMS show a clearer advantage compared to the other two schemes. That is, the more frequently two nodes interact, the better TMIS performs. However, the size of time slots affects the timeliness of TMIS. Therefore, the length of time slots is set according to actual needs of applications.

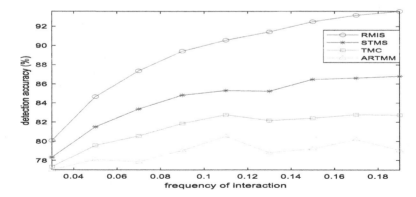

Fig. 4. Detection accuracy with the frequency of interaction between nodes.

As illustrated in Fig. 5, the detection accuracy of SMIS are compared under three rates of malicious nodes, 0.1, 0.2, and 0.3, as the frequency of node interaction increases from 0.01 to 0.3. This figure has the insight that the smaller the proportion of malicious nodes is, the more TMIS depends on the frequency of node interaction in order to improve own identification accuracy of malicious nodes. This is because the smaller the proportion of malicious nodes is, the less the samples about malicious nodes are. In addition, with the frequency of node interaction decreasing, the effectiveness of trust evidences weakens. Therefore, TMIS is harder to extract the features of malicious nodes.

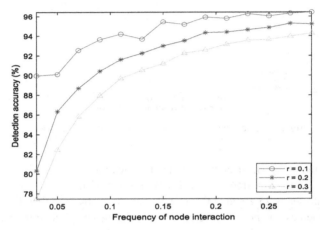

Fig. 5. Detection accuracy with the frequency of node interaction under the rate of malicious nodes.

6   Conclusion

Due to the dynamic and complex underwater environment, most of existing trust models cannot perform well enough in identification accuracy. In order to solve it, we propose a trust-based malicious identification scheme for UASNs. Firstly, we quantify the impact of underwater environment and packet collusion on communication trust. Then, we choose a kind of objective trust attribute called traffic trust, which can be collected by observation. In addition, we employ SVM and K-means algorithms to extract features from the trust evidences, which are more suitable to the dynamic underwater environment and complex attack patterns. Finally, we adopt two kinds of trust update in order to further improve the identification accuracy of TMIS. By the two kinds of trust update the trust value of trust attributes can achieve the effect of rising slowly and falling quickly, which can effectively cope with ON-OFF attacks. Moreover, the simulation results show that TMIS performs better than the other three identification schemes in terms of the detection accuracy of malicious nodes.

Acknowledgement. This work was supported by Key Research and Development Program of Hainan Province (ZDYF2020199), National Natural Science Foundation of China (61862020), the

Hainan Provincial Natural Science Foundation of China (2019RC096, 620RC560), the Scientific Research Setup Fund of Hainan University (KYQD(ZR)1877).

References

1. Darehshoorzadeh, A., Boukerche, A.: Underwater sensor networks: a new challenge for opportunistic routing protocols. IEEE Commun. Mag. **53**(11), 98–107 (2015)
2. Pompili, D., Melodia, T.: Three-dimensional routing in underwater acoustic sensor networks. In: Proceedings of the 2nd ACM International Workshop on Performance Evaluation of Wireless Ad Hoc, Sensor, and Ubiquitous Networks, pp. 214–221 (2005)
3. Koo, S., Song, Y., Lim, S.H., Oh, M.H., Seo, S.N., Baek, S.: Development of a remote supervisory control and data acquisition system for offshore waste final disposal facility. J. Coast. Res. **90**(SI), 205–213 (2019). https://doi.org/10.2112/SI90-025.1
4. Han, G., Long, X., Zhu, C., Guizani, M., Zhang, W.: A high-availability data collection scheme based on multi-AUVs for underwater sensor networks. IEEE Trans. Mob. Comput. **19**(5), 1010–1022 (2019)
5. Han, G., He, Y., Jiang, J., Wang, N., Guizani, M., Ansere, J.A.: A synergetic trust model based on SVM in underwater acoustic sensor networks. IEEE Trans. Veh. Technol. **68**(11), 11239–11247 (2019)
6. Su, S., Tian, Z., Liang, S., Li, S., Du, S., Guizani, N.: A reputation management scheme for efficient malicious vehicle identification over 5G networks. IEEE Wirel. Commun. **27**(3), 46–52 (2020)
7. Ponnusamy, V., Yichiet, A., Jhanjhi, N.Z., Humayun, M., Almufareh, M.F.: IoT wireless intrusion detection and network traffic analysis. Comput. Syst. Sci. Eng. **40**(3), 865–879 (2020)
8. Lin, K., Ge, X., Wang, X., Zhu, C., Ryu, H.G.: Research on secure data collection in wireless multimedia sensor networks. Comput. Commun. **35**(15), 1902–1909 (2012)
9. Paul, N.R., Raj, D.P.: Enhanced trust based access control for multi-cloud environment. Comput. Mater. Continua **69**(3), 3079–3093 (2021)
10. Ganeriwal, S., Balzan, L.K., Srivastava, M.B.: Reputation-based framework for high integrity sensor networks. In: Proceedings of the 2nd ACM Workshop on Security of Ad Hoc and Sensor Networks (SASN), pp. 66–77. ACM Press, New York (2004)
11. Josang, A., Hayward, R., Pope, S.: Optimal trust network analysis with subjective logic. In: Proceedings of the 2008 Second International Conference on Emerging Security Information, Systems and Technologies, IEEE Computer Society, pp.179–184 (2008)
12. Ren, Y., Zadorozhny, V.I., Oleshchuk, V.A., Li, F.Y.: A novel approach to trust management in unattended wireless sensor networks. IEEE Trans. Mob. Comput. **13**(7), 1409–1423 (2013)
13. Feng, R., Xu, X., Zhou, X., Wan, J.: A trust evaluation algorithm for wireless sensor networks based on node behaviors and ds evidence theory. Sensors **11**(2), 1345–1360 (2011)
14. Ma, B.: Cross-layer trust model and algorithm of node selection in wireless sensor networks. In: Proceedings of the Communication Software and Networks (ICCSN'09), pp. 812–815 (2009)
15. Jiang, J., Han, G., Shu, L., Chan, S., Wang, K.: A trust model based on cloud theory in underwater acoustic sensor networks. IEEE Trans. Industr. Inf. **13**(1), 342–350 (2015)
16. Jayasinghe, U., Lee, G.M., Um, T.W., Shi, Q.: Machine learning based trust computational model for IoT services. IEEE Trans. Sustain. Comput. **4**(1), 39–352 (2018)
17. Jiang, J., Zhu, X., Han, G., Guizani, M., Shu, L.: A dynamic trust evaluation and update mechanism based on C4. 5 decision tree in underwater wireless sensor networks. IEEE Trans. Vehicul. Technol. **69**(8), 9031–9040 (2020)

18. He, Y., Han, G., Jiang, J., Wang, H., Martinez-Garcia, M.: A trust update mechanism based on reinforcement learning in underwater acoustic sensor networks. IEEE Trans. Mob. Comput. **21**(3), 811–821 (2020)

19. Song, Y.: Underwater acoustic sensor networks with cost efficiency for internet of underwater things. IEEE Trans. Indust. Electron. **68**(2), 1707–1716 (2021)

20. Han, G., Jiang, J., Shu, L., Guizani, M.: An attack-resistant trust model based on multidimensional trust metrics in underwater acoustic sensor network. IEEE Trans. Mob. Comput. **14**(12), 2447–2459 (2015)

21. Yang, E., Joshi, G.P., Seo, C.: Improving the detection rate of rarely appearing intrusions in network-based intrusion detection systems. Comput. Mater. Continua **66**(2), 1647–1663 (2021)

22. Nayak, R.P., Sethi, S., Bhoi, S.K., Sahoo, K.S., Jhanjhi, N., et al.: Tbddosa-md: trust-based ddos misbehave detection approach in software-defined vehicular network (sdvn). Comput. Mater. Continua **69**(3), 3513–3529 (2021)

Multi-level Federated Learning Mechanism with Reinforcement Learning Optimizing in Smart City

Shaoyong Guo[1], Baoyu Xiang[1]([✉]), Liandong Chen[2], Huifeng Yang[2], and Dongxiao Yu[3]

[1] State Key Laboratory of Networking and Switching Technology, Beijing University of Posts and Telecommunications, Beijing 100876, People's Republic of China
syguo@bupt.edu.cn, 473429384@qq.com

[2] Information and Telecommunication Branch, Stat Grid HeBei Electric Power Company Co., Ltd., Shijiazhuang, People's Republic of China
power3667@sina.com

[3] School Computer Science and Technology, Shandong University, Qingdao, People's Republic of China
dxyu@sdu.edu.cn

Abstract. While taking account into data privacy protection, federated learning can mine local data knowledge and gather data value, which has been widely concerned by the Smart city and Internet of Things. At present, a large amount of data is generated by the massive edge network in the smart city, but the resources of the edge side are limited. How to reduce the communication overhead between the edge and the centralized cloud server, improve the convergence speed of data model, and avoid resource waste caused by synchronized blocking of federated learning has become the core issue for the integration of federated learning and the Internet of Things in the smart city. For this reason, this paper designs a multi-level federated learning mechanism in the smart city, and uses reinforcement learning agents to select nodes to offset the influence of the non-IID data that is not independent and identically distributed. At the same time, asynchronous non-blocking updating method is used to perform model aggregation and updating of federated learning to release the resources of faster devices and improving the efficiency and stability of federated learning. Finally, simulation results show that the proposed method can improve the efficiency of federated learning tasks in edge network scenarios with a lot of devices in the smart city.

Keywords: Smart city · Federated learning · Reinforcement learning · Edge network

1 Introduction

Under the edge network in the smart city, devices with excellent performance can well collect user information and deploy some crowd-aware tasks [1]. Therefore, it is of great value to study and explore the distributed data in the mobile edge network. At present, the application of federated learning technology in the field of data distributed learning solves the problem of data privacy protection, and gradually becomes a trend. However, there are still some problems if applying federated learning in the edge network with a lot of devices, so we designed a multi-level federated learning mechanism to be suitable for this scenario in the smart city.

The previous data collection usage pattern was that each device collected user data and then uploaded it centrally to the background central server. The cloud central server aggregated user data and processed it, then trained the data, got an optimized model, and then provided better services to each user. However, there are great privacy security problems in this way. Each device uploads its local data to the central server, which is equivalent to exposing its own privacy. Once a malicious attacker attacks the system, there will be a great risk of user privacy data leakage. Especially at present, data owners pay more and more attention to data privacy protection, and various countries have also implemented relevant legislation on data privacy protection, such as the European Commission's General Data Protection Regulation (GDPR) [2] and the U.S.'s Bill of Rights on Consumer Privacy [3]. Therefore, this traditional data usage pattern is unsustainable, and a new data sharing joint training technology to protect data privacy and security is needed to replace it.

In order to solve the privacy security problems brought by the traditional data usage mode, Google proposed the concept of federated learning and applied it to the virtual keyboard function of smart phones [4]. Federated study refers to each device retain their data is not shared, initial global model released by the central server, the devices download global model and use their local data training local model, then upload the local model. Finally, a central server aggregates the local models into a global model. Federated learning task refers to repeating this process, until the global model fulfills the requirements of the iterative convergence [5].

In the edge network of the smart city, there are still many problems. Due to the different usage habits of users, the data on each device does not meet the assumption of independent identical distribution of model training, which will lead to slow convergence of the model and reduce the final model effect. On the other hand, due to the large number of mobile devices in the edge network, even if the original data is not transferred, it will cause a huge burden on the central server. Finally, because federated learning uses synchronous blocking model aggregation updates, high performance devices will waste resources while waiting for model updates.

Based on the above problems, we propose a multi-level federated learning mechanism under the edge networks in the smart city to realize efficient federated learning under the premise of protecting data privacy. Our main contributions are as follows:

(1) On the background of the edge network in the smart city, design a multi-level federated learning mechanism, in order to solve the huge amount of Iot device burden to the central server.

(2) By means of reinforcement learning, the nodes used for model updating are selected to eliminate the problem of slow convergence and reduced effect caused by non-independent iden-distributed data on each device.

(3) Asynchronous non-blocking update with parameter weight correction is used to update the global model, which frees up resources of the devices with high performance, speeds up federated learning tasks and improves the stability of federated learning.

2   Related Work

Federated learning has been proposed to solve the user privacy leakage problem in machine learning tasks, which has received much attention in academia and industry. In [6], the author proposed an architecture based on blockchain network in the computational scenario, called "FLchain", to enhance the security of joint learning. In [7], the author proposed an incentive mechanism combining contract theory to encourage work nodes to work actively to ensure reliable federated learning. In [8], the author mainly analyzes and optimizes the uncertainties of federated learning tasks in wireless channels and the heterogeneous power constraints and local data size differences of local mobile devices. In [9, 10], the author focuses on privacy protection in the federated learning process.

In [11], in order to solve the problem of non-IID data in federated learning, the authors propose a method of deep network joint learning based on iterative model averaging. In [12], the author, aiming at the analysis and improvement of [11]. In [13], the author proposes a Favor, an empirically driven control framework that can intelligently select client devices to participate in each round of federated learning through reinforcement learning to balance biases introduced by non-IID data and accelerate convergence.

In other aspects, in order to solve the trust problem of multi-party participation and ensure data sharing collaboration, the author in [14] combines blockchain technology with federated learning, and specifically analyzes its role in the industrial Internet of Things. In [15], the author uses multi-objective evolutionary algorithm to optimize the structure of neural network model in federated learning to minimize communication cost and global model testing errors at the same time. In [16], the author proposed a blockchain federated learning architecture, analyzed and solved its end-to-end delay, optimized the training speed of each iteration model, and analyzed and optimized the block generation rate from three aspects of information exchange, calculation and consensus. In [17], the author proposes a hierarchical incentive mechanism design for federated learning, which takes into account the formation of multiple model owners and multiple alliances.

3   Architecture of System Model

Under the edge networks in the smart city, there are a lot of Iot devices. The rapid development of technology enables these devices to collect user behavior data easily and accurately. In recent years, with the rapid development of mobile communication technology, edge computing theory and technology have attracted more and more attention from researchers and engineers around the world. They can significantly combine cloud capacity and devices demand through network edge, thus accelerating content delivery and improving user service quality [18]. Traditionally, the data on the edge device is aggregated by the edge server and then modeled as a whole to explore its hidden great value. However, this method does not take into account the privacy security of users, and the transmission of the original user behavior data has a considerable risk of privacy leakage. With more and more attention paid to privacy security, the traditional way of data migration under the edge network is obviously not sustainable. Therefore, we propose a multi-level federated learning mechanism under mobile edge network in the smart city combined with reinforcement learning technology to optimize edge computing and make safe and effective use of privacy data on massive mobile devices with the premise of protecting data privacy and security, see Fig. 1 below.

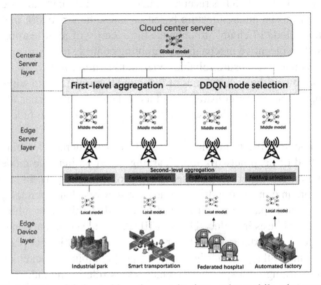

Fig. 1. Multi-level federated learning mechanism under mobile edge network.

The bottom layer is the edge device layer in the smart city with the raw user data. There are industrial park, smart transportation, federated hospital and automated factory. They generate a large amount of data every day, which is closely related to city information and user behavior, and is crucial to the construction of smart city.

The middle layer is the edge servers for each region, and the top layer is the cloud center server. Each edge server is connected to mobile smart device in a region, and the cloud center server is connected to edge servers in all regions. The edge server is the client of the first level federated learning, and the central server of the second level federated learning. The intelligent devices in each area are the clients of the second level federated learning. Therefore, in the edge network of the smart city, the principle of multi-level federated learning mechanism design is the first-level federated learning led by a cloud center server and the second-level federated learning led by multiple edge servers, in order to build a better smart city. The advantage of this design is to free the cloud center server from the massive mobile smart devices in the edge network, reduce its computing and communication burden, and at the same time can sense all the device data in the network.

In the edge network of the smart city, the specific workflow of the multi-level federated learning mechanism we designed is as follows:

(1) When a new federated learning task arrives, the cloud center first detects whether the task has been processed before, and if so, it finds a matching model from the stored records of the cloud service center and returns the model results. Otherwise, an initial global model is initiated through the cloud service center or the initial model is uploaded by the requestor.

(2) Each edge server downloads the global model from the cloud service center and broadcasts it to each edge device connected to it.

(3) Each edge device receives the global model from the edge server, and then performs iterative training with its own local data based on this model to obtain the updated local model.

(4) The edge server selects some edge devices to upload their local models through relevant policies, and aggregates the local models to obtain a second-level global model.

(5) Cloud central server through the edge of the reinforcement learning node selection algorithm to choose the optimal server subset, the selected edge servers upload their aggregation good secondary global model, a central server then aggregates their secondary global model into a global model, and test the accuracy of the model in the test data.

(6) Repeat the above steps until the global model meets the target requirements.

4   Nodes Selection Strategy

4.1   First-Level Edge Severs Selection

Reinforcement learning is an agent's learning in a way of "trial and error", and the agent's behavior is guided by the return obtained through interaction with the environment. The goal is to make the agent get the maximum return. In this way, reinforcement learning can acquire knowledge in the action-evaluation environment and improve the action plan to adapt to the environment [19, 20].

Reinforcement learning is a time-related sequential decision making problem, which follows the Markov Decision Process and consists of <S, A, R, P> quaternions, where S stands for state, A stands for action, R stands for reward, and P stands for state transition probability matrix [21, 22]. The state transition diagram is as Fig. 2 below:

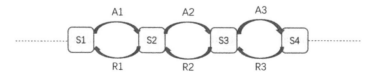

Fig. 2. State transition diagram.

The goal of reinforcement learning is to obtain the maximum cumulative reward value $R = \sum_{t=1}^{T} \gamma^{t-1} r_t$ through the state action sequence, where $\gamma \in (0, 1]$ is a factor discounting of future rewards. To achieve this goal, reinforcement learning algorithm uses a value function $Q(S_t, a)$ to estimate the future cumulative reward value after performing action a in state S_t.

$$Q_\pi(s_t, a) = E_\pi\left[\sum_{k=1}^{\infty} \gamma^{k-1} r_{t+k-1}|s_t, a\right] = E_{s_{t+1},a}\left[r_t + \gamma Q_\pi(s_{t+1}, a)|s_t, a_t\right] \quad (1)$$

where π is the probability or strategy from the state to the choice of possible measures. The optimal value function is $Q^*(s_t, a)$, which represents the maximum cumulative future reward after performing an action a in the state s_t.

$$Q^*(s_t, a) = E_{s_{t+1}}\left[r_t + \gamma \max_a Q_*(s_{t+1}, a)|s_t, a\right] \quad (2)$$

The goal of reinforcement learning agent learning is to make its value function approximate to $Q^*(s_t, a)$. Deep reinforcement learning uses deep neural network to represent Q and updates Q through the gap between them. The loss function can be expressed as the following formula [13]:

$$l_t(\theta_t) = \left(r_t + \gamma \max_a Q^*(s_{t+1}, a|\theta_t) - Q(s_t, a|\theta_t)\right)^2 \quad (3)$$

We adopt DDQN model, replacing $r_t + \gamma \max_a Q(s_{t+1}, a|\theta_t)$ with $Q_{t\,arg\,et}(s_t, a|\theta_t)$, and periodically update $Q_{t\,arg\,et}$ with Q.

In the first-level federated learning, we treat the selection of edge servers as a deep reinforcement learning problem and use the Double Deep Q-Learning Network (DDQN) to train this problem [3].

The selection of edge servers is described as a problem of deep reinforcement learning, which requires the clarification of state S, action A, and reward R. Meanwhile, we use DQN network as reinforcement learning agent to interact with the environment. Instead of collecting or examining any data samples from a device, the agent simply passes in the convolutional layer weights of the global model, thus preserving the higher level of privacy than traditional federated learning. It only depends on the weights of model to determine which information on the edge server aggregation model can improve the global model to the greatest extent, Because, there is an implicit relationship between the data distribution on the device and the local model weights acquired through training on these data, this effect is captured by the secondary aggregation model of the edge server and is perceived by the central server. Therefore, through this choice of reinforcement learning, the problems of slow convergence and declining effect of models caused by non-independent identically distributed data on each device can be eliminated.

In the optimization module of reinforcement learning node selection, we can dynamically adjust the environment state according to different tasks, and then train the reinforcement learning agent to adapt to different task types.

During the selection process of edge servers in our example, it is assumed that the state of federated learning in round t is S_t, which means the convolutional layer parameter of the global model. The purpose of using convolutional layer parameters is that the convolutional layer can better extract data features, and the training of reinforcement learning can be accelerated with a small data dimension. In other categories of tasks, the definition of state can be considered in context. The action of federated learning in round t is A_t. In the training process, it means to select the server with the highest Q value from N edge servers, and then compare the maximum Q value of this step action with the optimal Q value function. However, when the federated learning nodes are selected for use, the K choices with the highest Q value are selected to participate in the next round of federated learning. The reward of round t is R_t, which is expressed as follows:

$$R_t = \beta^{\Omega_t - \Omega} - 1 \tag{4}$$

where Ω_t is the accuracy of the global model in round t on the validation set. Ω is target accuracy. $\beta^{\Omega_t - \Omega}$ adopts the form of index in order to magnify the reward brought by the improvement of training accuracy, and -1 is in order to use fewer rounds [13].

Therefore, the cumulative future rewards for DDQN reinforcement learning agent learning can be expressed as follows:

$$R_{total} = \sum_{t=1}^{T} \gamma^{t-1} R_t = \sum_{t=1}^{T} \gamma^{t-1} (\beta^{\Omega_t - \Omega} - 1) \tag{5}$$

4.2 Second-Level Mobile Equipment Selection

In the second-level federated learning, the edge server selects a subset of the devices that is connected to itself for the second aggregation of the local model, so as to obtain a second-level global model of the edge server. FedAvg method is adopted for this part of choosing devices, as shown in Fig. 3 below.

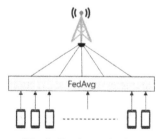

Fig. 3. Devices selection

FedAvg means that each device first iteratively trains the local model, then the edge server randomly selects part of the mobile devices, collects their local model, and performs weighted aggregation according to the proportion of its data [11], as shown below:

$$W_g^t = \sum_{i=1}^{k} \frac{D_i}{D} W_i^t \tag{6}$$

where W_g^t is the global model parameter of round t, k is the number of the devices selected to participate in second-level federated learning, D_i is the data size on device i, D is the data sum of k devices, and g is the local model of round t training on device i.

The adoption of FedAvg in the second federated learning phase is a good way to reduce the huge communication overhead burden caused by the massive devices. The update aggregation mode of FedAvg is still affected by the non-IID data of each device to a certain extent, but the edge server selection through DQN reinforcement learning method in the first-level federated learning we designed can make up for this loss.

5   Asynchronous Non-blocking Update with Parameter Weight Correction

The federated learning tasks' training speed conforms to the traditional barrel principle and is determined by the weakest and slowest learning speed of the device participating in the task. The traditional federated learning mechanism uses synchronous blocking model updating, that is, the global model will be updated and the next round of federated learning will be carried out only after all the devices has been trained and the local model uploaded. However, in smart cities, a lot of devices participating in federated learning are highly free and flexible. Asynchronous update training is more suitable for federated learning tasks in smart cities due to different time of equipment joining, differences in node resources and computing power, learning interruptions and network blocking caused by various external factors.

If we continue to use the synchronous approach, computing and storage resources of some devices with high performance will be idle for waiting to be blocked after their fast training, resulting in wasting of resources and inefficiency. Meanwhile, the whole federated learning task will be weighed down by a few devices with poor performance. This disadvantage is magnified when individual devices fail.

In [19], it is recommended to improve the energy efficiency of federated learning by reducing the CPU cycle frequency of faster mobile devices in the training group. Since all devices are iterative synchronous, as long as they complete the training before the slowest device in each iteration, they can maintain the federated learning's speed. But instead of speeding up federated learning, having faster devices slow down their CPU frequency to wait for slower ones, we think this is another way to waste faster resources.

Therefore, we design a parameter weight correction method based on time and accuracy to realize asynchronous federated learning, which frees up resources of faster devices and speeds up training of federated learning tasks. As shown in Fig. 4 below.

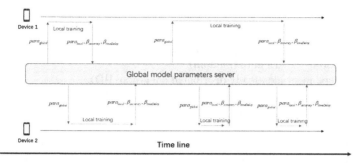

Fig. 4. Asynchronous federated learning with parameter weight correction.

In the learning process, each device communicates with the global model parameter server independently and asynchronously. Each device downloads the global model according to its own time line, carries out local training and uploads local training results, as well as the accuracy $\beta_{accuracy}$ and delay $\beta_{timeDelay}$ of the local model. These two parameters are used to correct the update of global model parameters. $\beta_{timeDelay}$ is defined as follows:

$$\beta_{timeDelay} = t_{upload} - t_{download} \tag{7}$$

We hope that when the local model updates the global model, its parameter weight will be positively correlated with the accuracy of the local model and negatively correlated with the time delay of the model, and the weight coefficient will decline gently when the time delay is large. So we define the weight correction coefficient α as follows:

$$\alpha = \beta_{accuracy} * z^{\beta_{timeDelay}} \tag{8}$$

where $z \in (0, 1)$.

In the process of asynchronous federation learning, the local model parameters trained by each node need to be multiplied by the weight coefficient α before participating in the update of the global model. During this process, optimization algorithms of other strategies may be added. After the global model is updated, it will be sent to each node for a new round of learning tasks.

6   Simulation Results

We implemented the simulation experiment of multi-level federated learning mechanism under the edge network proposed in this paper. We coded with Python3.7 and tensorflow2.0. For simulating the the edge network, we simulated 100 mobile devices, 10 edge servers and a central server. And assign the open data set MNIST to 100 mobile devices according to different policies. The task model is a three-layer convolutional neural network. The first layer consists of 32 convolutional layers with THE size of 3 × 3, the second layer consists of a full connection layer with 128 neurons, and the last layer is the output layer.

There are four data allocation strategies:

(1) Data is completely distributed according to independent identical distribution (IID).
(2) Data randomly distribution(random).
(3) Non-independent identically distributed data (non_IID).
(4) Part of devices is not independently and identically distributed, and part of devices is randomly distributed (real_random_non_IID).

We think that the fourth scenario is more close to real life. Among them, the non-independent identically distributed data of data can be divided into 1.0, 0.8, 0.6, 0.2 according to the proportion. This parameter is the ratio of the same label data in a device.

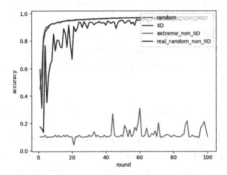

Fig. 5. Different data distribution in mobile edge networks.

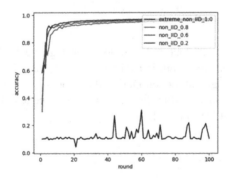

Fig. 6. Non-IID data and different proportions.

Figure 5 shows the relationship between the communication rounds of multi-level federated learning with different data distributions and model accuracy under mobile edge networks. Figure 6 shows the relationship between the communication rounds of multilevel federated learning and model accuracy under not independent identically distribution with different proportions. It can be seen from Fig. 5 that random distribution and independent identical distribution are better than real_random_non_IID, with faster convergence and higher model accuracy. In Fig. 5, extreme_non_IID_1.0 is in the same condition as extreme_non_IID_1.0 in Fig. 6, that is, extreme non-independent identically distributed data, and the data on each mobile device are of the same label. In this case, the federated learning method cannot be used to train the model. Figure 6 shows that the smaller the proportion of the same label data is, the larger the proportion of random data is, and the model has faster convergence and higher model accuracy, indicating that the non-independent identically distributed data will have a bad impact on federated learning tasks.

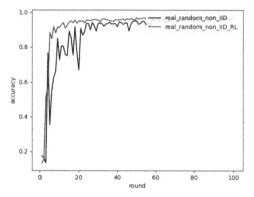

Fig. 7. Contrast graph of reinforcement learning agent node selection.

Figure 7 shows the relationship between the communication rounds of the federated learning mechanism designed by us and the model accuracy when the reinforcement learning agent is used to select nodes and that is not used. The experimental environment is a real non_IID scenario. It can be seen that the selection of reinforcement learning agent speeds up the convergence of federated learning tasks, improves the accuracy of the model, and effectively improves the efficiency of the multi_level federated learning mechanism designed by us over mobile edge network.

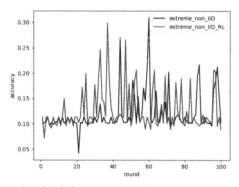

Fig. 8. The contrast graph of reinforcement learning node selection under extreme Non-independent identically distributed data.

Unlike Fig. 7, Fig. 8 shows an extreme non_IID data distribution, in which reinforcement learning agent node selection optimization is useless because it does not pick good data nodes at all, i.e. they are all bad. On the other hand, it can be explained that after iterative training, the reinforcement learning agent obtains the ability to select the current optimal nodes according to the training state of the current federated learning task, so as to accelerate the convergence of the model and improve the performance of the model.

In Sect. 5, we propose an asynchronous federated learning method based on local model accuracy and time delay for parameter weight correction. In this way, avoid the resource waste caused by faster devices waiting for federated learning tasks and accelerate federated learning tasks.

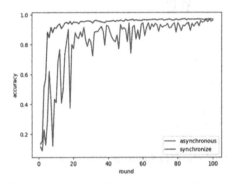

Fig. 9. The contrast graph of Asynchronous and Synchronize.

Figure 9 shows that compared with synchronous training, asynchronous training has a slower convergence, but it can still achieve the same model effect as synchronous training within a limited training time.

7 Conclusion

In the future, we will further improve the proposed solution and try to apply it to the real edge network environment for building a smart city. At the same time, we will continue to explore federated learning technology and its application, and actively solve its problems.

Acknowledgement. This work is supported by National Key R&D Program of China (2019YFB2102301), the National Natural Science Foundation of China (62072049), Key R&D Program of Hebei Province (20310103D), and Key Project Plan of Blockchain in Ministry of Education of the People's Republic of China (2020KJ010802).

References

1. Lim, W.Y.B.: Federated learning in mobile edge networks: a comprehensive survey. IEEE Commun. Surv. Tutor. **22**(3), 2031–2063 (2020)
2. Custers, B., Sears, A., Dechesne, F., Georgieva, I., Tani, T., Hof, S.V.D.: EU Personal Data Protection in Policy and Practice. TMC Asser Press, Hague (2019)
3. Gaff, B.M., Sussman, H.E., Geetter, J.: Privacy and big data. Computer **47**(6), 7–9 (2014)
4. Hard, A., Rao, K.: Federated learning for mobile keyboard prediction. arXiv preprint arXiv: 1811.03604 (2018)
5. Yang, Q., Liu, Y.: Federated machine learning: concept and applications. ACM Trans. Intell. Syst. Technol. **10**(2), 12–112 (2019)
6. Majeed, U., Hong, C.S.: FLchain: federated learning via MEC-enabled blockchain network. In: Asia-Pacific Network Operations and Management Symposium (APNOMS), pp. 1–4 (2019)
7. Kang, J., Xiong, Z., Niyato, D., Xie, S., Zhang, J.: Incentive mechanism for reliable federated learning: a joint optimization approach to combining reputation and contract theory. IEEE Internet Things J. **6**(6), 10700–10714 (2019)
8. Tran, N.H., Bao, W., Zomaya, A., Nguyen, M.N.H., Hong, C.S.: Federated learning over wireless networks: optimization model design and analysis. In: IEEE INFOCOM 2019-IEEE Conference on Computer Communications, pp. 1387–1395 (2019)
9. Lu, Y., Huang, X., Dai, Y., Maharjan, S., Zhang, Y.: Differentially private asynchronous federated learning for mobile edge computing in urban informatics. IEEE Trans. Indust. Inf. **16**(3), 2134–2143 (2020)
10. Lu, X., Liao, Y., Lio, P., Hui, P.: Privacy-preserving asynchronous federated learning mechanism for edge network computing. IEEE Access **8**, 48970–48981 (2020)
11. Mcmahan, H.B., Moore, E., Ramage, D., Hampson, S., Arcas, B.A.: Federated Learning with Non-IID Data (2018)
12. Zhao, Y., Li, M., Lai, L.: Communication-efficient learning of deep networks from decentralized data. In: International Conference on Artificial Intelligence and Statistics (2017)
13. Wang, H., Kaplan, Z., Niu, D., Li, B.: Optimizing federated learning on non-iid data with reinforcement learning. In: IEEE INFOCOM 2020 - IEEE Conference on Computer Communications, pp. 1698–1707 (2020)
14. Lu, Y., Huang, X., Dai, Y., Maharjan, S., Zhang, Y.: Blockchain and federated learning for privacy-preserved data sharing in industrial IoT. IEEE Trans. Indust. Inf. **16**(6), 4177–4186 (2020)
15. Zhu, H., Jin, Y.: Multi-objective evolutionary federated learning. IEEE Trans. Neural Netw. Learn. Syst. **31**(4), 1310–1322 (2019)
16. Kim, H., Park, J., Bennis, M., Kim, S.: Blockchained on-device federated learning. IEEE Commun. Lett. **24**(6), 1279–1283 (2019)
17. Lim, W.Y.B.: Hierarchical incentive mechanism design for federated machine learning in mobile networks. IEEE Internet Things J. **7**(10), 9575–9588 (2020)
18. Wang, X., Han, Y., Wang, C., Zhao, Q., Chen, X., Chen, M.: In-edge AI: intelligentizing mobile edge computing, caching and communication by federated learning. IEEE Network **33**(5), 156–165 (2019)
19. Wang, X., Wang, C., Li, X., Leung, V.C.M., Taleb, T.: Federated deep reinforcement learning for internet of things with decentralized cooperative edge caching. IEEE Internet Things J. **7**(10), 9441–9455 (2020)
20. Zhan, Y., Li, P., Guo, S.: Experience-driven computational resource allocation of federated learning by deep reinforcement learning. In: 2020 IEEE International Parallel and Distributed Processing Symposium (IPDPS), pp. 234–243 (2020)

21. Ali, M., Mujeeb, A., Ullah, H., Zeb, S.: Reactive power optimization using feed forward neural deep reinforcement learning method: (deep reinforcement learning dqn algorithm). In: Asia Energy and Electrical Engineering Symposium (AEEES), pp. 497–501 (2020)
22. Zuo, G., Du, T., Lu, J.: Double DQN method for object detection. In: 2017 Chinese Automation Congress (CAC), pp. 6727–6732 (2017)
23. Hasselt, H.V., Guez, A., Silver, D.: Deep reinforcement learning with double q-learning. In: Proceedings of the Thirtieth AAAI Conference on Artificial Intelligence (AAAI) (2016)

A Scheme to Improve the Security of IoT Communication

Junjie Fu[1,2], Xiaoliang Wang[1,2(✉)], Yuzhen Liu[1,2], Qing Yang[3], and Frank Jiang[4]

[1] School of Computer Science and Engineering, Hunan University of Science and Technology, Xiangtan 411201, China
fengwxl@hnust.edu.cn
[2] Hunan Key Laboratory for Service Computing and Novel Software Technology, Xiangtan 411201, China
[3] School of Computer Science and Information Engineering, Guangzhou Maritime University, Guangzhou 510725, China
[4] Centre for Cyber Security Research and Innovation (CSRI), Deakin University, Geelong 3220, Australia

Abstract. In the Internet of Vehicles scenario of the Internet of Things, the security of transmission has become a big challenge. In order to deal with such security risks, we add AES encryption mechanism to the classic Ad hoc On-Demand Distance Vector Routing (AODV) routing protocol in mobile sensor networks and design an AODV-AES encrypted communication protocol, which can be applied to wireless sensor networks of Internet of Vehicles. The protocol has the following advantages: low delay, low energy consumption, and high security. The above advantages show that the AODV-AES encryption communication protocol meets the characteristics of low delay, limited memory, and energy storage of mobile sensor nodes. We also compare several protocols through NS2 simulation software, add blackhole attacked in malicious node attacks, and analyze the average end-to-end delay when attacked by different numbers of nodes. In addition, we also analyze the changing trend of source node energy consumption when attacked in different scenarios. The experimental results show that the AODV-AES encryption communication protocol can not only meet the function of encrypting and decrypting privacy information, but also effectively reduce the average end-to-end delay and reduce the energy consumption of the source node when attacked. It shows that the AODV-AES encryption communication protocol can be applied to the wireless mobile sensor network of the Internet of Vehicles, and improve communication security.

Keywords: Internet of Things · AODV-AES · Encrypted communication

1 Introduction

On the Internet of Vehicles scenario of the Internet of Things, the mobile wireless sensor network is a very important module [13], in which the wireless sensor can

X. Sun et al. (Eds.): ICAIS 2022, LNCS 13340, pp. 455–468, 2022.
https://doi.org/10.1007/978-3-031-06791-4_36

receive the information sent by the source center or other sensor nodes in the sensor network, and can also transmit or actively send messages as a relay node [19]. With the development of science and technology, illegal third-party eavesdroppers and attackers may secretly send false data packets [20], or intercept the data packet information sent by sensor networks, which greatly threatens the privacy information and information transmission efficiency in the transmission process [15]. For such problems, the reason why third-party attackers can easily steal privacy information is that they intercept communication packets by amplifying the vulnerabilities of communication protocols. If we want to weaken or prevent third-party attackers from obtaining privacy information in communication information, we can start with the improvement and optimization of communication protocols of wireless sensor networks, this is also the focus of most encrypted communication protocols [18]. Secondly, the algorithm of asymmetric encryption mechanism may spend more time and cost in the process of generating ciphertext and decryption, such as elliptic curve encryption mechanism and RSA encryption mechanism. The encryption speed gap between symmetric and asymmetric encryption mechanisms may reach a thousand times [23]. Considering that we want to solve the security problem on the Internet of Vehicles communication, the primary requirement of vehicle communication is real-time. The lower the delay of the encryption algorithm, the better. Low delay is the first consideration. The second point is low energy consumption [17]. We consider not only the sensors configured on the vehicle, which can be powered by the vehicle. Generally, its capacitance is large [16]. We mainly consider the temporary wireless sensor with limited energy consumption, that is, an external sensor is randomly placed on the vehicle. The external sensor is characterized by limited energy content [3]. Broadcast transmission of data packets containing privacy information by the source vehicle through the random movement of the vehicle. Vehicles with sensors including relay nodes are selected within the preset range to form a completely mobile wireless sensor network. The Internet of Vehicles is used as the carrier for the movement of sensor nodes. This setting also improves the randomness of point selection and improves the security of the protocol in terms of the physical structure. At the same time, the main purpose of third-party attack nodes is to intercept and analyze privacy information, and will not focus a lot of energy on the search of relay wireless sensor nodes, that is, relay node vehicles that may change; Secondly, the relay node may go out of the transmission range of the source node, which may change the vehicle for each round of privacy information transmission. The vehicles attacking nodes will not record and update these relay node vehicles that will change at any time. In order to solve the security and performance problems of such protocols, we designed an AODV-AES encrypted communication protocol based on the wireless sensors that can send and receive information on the Internet of Vehicles [14], which is based on the classic AODV routing protocol and added the AES encryption mechanism. At the same time, it is a communication protocol with symmetric encryption mechanism, which has the advantages of small keyspace and low encryption and decryption delay. These two advantages meet the characteristics of limited storage space and low delay of mobile wireless sensor nodes on the Internet of Vehicles.

2   Related Work

We found that when solving the problem of communication security, most of the solutions are to improve and optimize the communication protocol to enhance security. Geetha et al. [7] discussed the application of the DES algorithm in wireless networks, which also enhances the protection of privacy information. He mentioned a variety of security requirements, the self-organization requirements of sensor nodes, authentication requirements, positioning security requirements, and time synchronization requirements between sensors. The purpose of this last point is to enable some sensor nodes that do not need to work temporarily in wireless sensor networks to be idle intermittently, which can reduce the corresponding energy consumption and meet the main characteristics of limited mobile sensor resources. Hammi et al. [9] also did research in the sensor network in the Internet of Things, introduced a lightweight communication protocol with encryption and authentication, and also controlled the energy consumption lower. They thought that a new Internet of Things device must be authenticated before joining the sensor network, and proposed a two-way authentication protocol; In the key generation stage, a strong key is designed to form secondary protection for the original encryption key, which has been improved in security strength, because the strong key adopts the once generated algorithm, which makes it nonreversible, increases the difficulty of decoding by third-party attackers, and indirectly improves the security of encrypted communication protocol. In the research direction of multiple authentications in the Internet of Things communication, Lee et al. [12] proposed a multiple authentication protocol, which is based on biological characteristics and aims to protect intelligent devices from malicious attacks by third-party attackers. The protocol they designed is characterized by applying the Honey List mechanism to sensor networks. Chu et al. [6] considering the limited energy storage of wireless sensors, a lightweight and low-cost communication protocol for generating keys from keygen function containing only XOR operation is designed. The principle is to add new codes to plaintext many times to improve the security of generating ciphertext. Boakye-Boateng et al. [4] found that when fog computing is directly applied to wireless sensor networks, the delay and computational overhead will be much greater than the design requirements. Therefore, a no packet loss encryption protocol is designed. This protocol is designed based on One-Time Pads, which has the advantage of distributed characteristics and greatly improves the security of ciphertext. Ajaykumar et al. [2] analyzed and compared a variety of communication protocols and encryption mechanisms in wireless sensor networks in recent years, and understood the advantages and disadvantages of various algorithms. They believe that the security and efficiency of the communication protocol should be considered in the communication of wireless sensor networks. They also summarize that the commonly used encryption mechanisms include

AES, DES, RSA, and ECC. They believe that when evaluating whether the encryption mechanism is suitable for an application scenario, the timeliness, energy consumption, and computing overhead of the confidentiality mechanism should be considered. In addition to directly applying the encryption mechanism to mobile wireless sensor networks, another method is data aggregation, and the advantage of data aggregation is that it can effectively reduce energy consumption. Agarwal et al. [1] designed the OLWS clustering protocol. When selecting the cluster head, they designed new calculation formulas for weight and node centrality and set the standard of signal strength during aggregation analysis, which can assist in the connection of the best route. Jasim et al. [10] proposed SEEDA aggregation protocol, which is characterized by adding verification of aggregated data to judge whether the data is real information. At the same time, before transmitting encrypted data, the data set will be divided into blocks to reduce the probability of intercepted privacy information disclosure. Zhou et al. [24] considering that it is still difficult to aggregate a large number of wireless sensor data into one, used homomorphic encryption mechanism and CRT theorem to design PIMA aggregation algorithm, which provides a solution to the problem of wireless sensor data aggregation and enhances the security of wireless sensor network communication. Yang et al. [22] designed a security clustering protocol using game theory to optimize the trust mechanism of wireless sensor networks. Because the trust value of the third-party attacking node will be low, the dynamic game judgment of the trust value can be made before the sensor transmits information. If an attacking node is detected, the trust mechanism will not continue to transmit information from this node. This protocol can also increase the transmission efficiency of relay sensor nodes.

3   Network Architecture

The network architecture of encrypted communication protocol on the Internet of Vehicles contains three main structures: source vehicle, privacy information receiving node vehicle, and malicious node vehicle that will carry out blackhole attack.

Figure 1 is a description of the network architecture. In the figure, we assume that the white vehicle is used as the source node to transmit privacy information to the target receiving node vehicle; Taking the mobile yellow vehicle as the relay and forwarding node for transmitting information; There is also a malicious node that will use three third-party illegal red vehicles as a blackhole attack. This setting meets the mobility of wireless sensor networks on the Internet of Vehicles, meanwhile including the mobility of malicious attack nodes.

4   Proposed Scheme

4.1   Basic Model

In this scheme, we used the very classical AODV routing protocol in our mobile sensor network as the basic routing protocol. The AODV protocol is divided

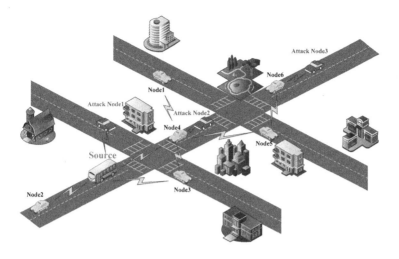

Fig. 1. Network architecture (Color figure online)

into several stages: first, when a source node needs to send a packet to the receiving node, but there is no direct path, the source node will make a broadcast request (RREQ), and when the surrounding nodes receive the broadcast, they will find out whether they have the routing information to the receiving node. If there is routing information, RREQ will be forwarded along the route to the receiving node. After receiving RREQ, the receiving node needs to send a response (RREP) and send it back along the original route. When the source node receives RREP, a complete propagation link is successfully connected [5].

The relay nodes in the AODV protocol broadcast the Hello information periodically [21], to make the surrounding nodes aware of their position, and also for the subsequent construction and update of their routing tables. This feature is very consistent with the Internet of Vehicles, facilitating the search for vehicles that can network.

Figure 2 is a description of the AODV routing protocol, and the dashed circle is the range broadcast by each mobile wireless sensor. The green lines represent the process of normal node broadcast within the wireless sensor network. The red line is the spurious RREP feedback immediately after the attack node received the RREQ. The two blackhole attack nodes in Fig. 2 are attacking.

4.2 AODV-AES Implementation Details

The following are the four steps of communication encryption by AODV-AES in mobile wireless sensor networks on the Internet of Vehicles.

Replace Original Bytes. When replacing original bytes, which need to be treated individually for each, an S-Box 16 * 16 bytes matrix is will be used.

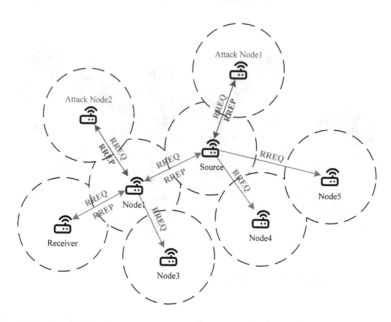

Fig. 2. AODV broadcast with attack nodes (Color figure online)

The methods of substitution are: the first four bytes were used to map the row and column value of the index value of a new output element, using this new element value as the value after replacement. A brief description of the algorithm that replaces original bytes follows.

Algorithm 1. Replace Original Byte

Input: Original Byte $OB[i][4]$
Output: Replaced Value $Result_{ROB}[m][n]$
1: **while** $Ob[i][4] \neq 0$ **do**
2:     **for** $m = 0; m < 4; m + +$ **do**
3:         **for** $n = 0; n < 4; n + +$ **do**
4:             $Result_{ROB}[m][n] = SBox[OB[m][n]]; //$From SBox
5:         **end for**
6:     **end for**
7:     **return** $Result_{ROB}[m][n]$;
8: **end while**

Row Shift. The operation of this step of a row shift is relatively easy because of the defined matrix of 4 * 4, shifted row requires only the latter three rows to be shifted, the line i shift i bytes to the left, and below is a brief description of the algorithm for the row shift.

Algorithm 2. Row Shift

Input: Privacy Information $OB[i][4]$
Output: Row Shift Value $Result_{RS}[m][n]$
1: **while** $Ob[i][4] \neq 0$ **do**
2:     $X_k = Rand()$ mod $EndNum$;
3:     **for** $m = 1; m < 4; m + +$ **do** //Line 0 is not processed
4:       **for** $n = 0; n < 4; n + +$ **do**
5:         $temp[n] = OB[m][(m + n)mod\ 4]$;
6:       **end for**
7:       **for** $n = 0; n < 4; n + +$ **do**
8:         $Result_{RS}[m][n] = temp[n]$;
9:       **end for**
10:    **end for**
11:    **return** $Result_{RS}[m][n]$;
12: **end while**

Confusion Column. The basic principle of a confusion column is a matrix multiplication operation, whereby each column is confused in turn by matrix multiplication. The key point is the coefficient setting for the confounder column, with the criteria set as in (1) (2) (3). M(a), N(a) and C(a) are matrix calculation formulas for the confusion column.

$$M(a) = M(a)\,mod\,(a^4 + 1) \tag{1}$$

$$N(a) = 03 * a^3 + 01 * a^2 + 01 * a + 02 \tag{2}$$

$$C(a) = M(a) * N(a) \tag{3}$$

Round Key Addition. The final step is the round key addition, and this step can be understood as adding bytes in turn, with the common approach being XOR operation, described below by its algorithm.

Algorithm 3. Round Key Addition

Input: Original Byte $OB[i][4]$, Number of rounds $R[j][4]$
Output: Round Key Addition Value $Result_{RKA}[m][n]$
1: **while** $Ob[i][4] \neq 0$ **do**
2:     **for** $m = 0; m < 4; m + +$ **do**
3:       **for** $n = 0; n < 4; n + +$ **do**
4:         $Result_{RKA}[m][n] \oplus = R[m][n]$;//XOR
5:       **end for**
6:     **end for**
7:     **return** $Result_{RKA}[m][n]$;
8: **end while**

Decrypt Information. The above four steps are the encryption key step of the AES encryption mechanism, and when the mobile wireless sensor node of the receiving vehicle receives ciphertext, it only will proceed three steps, which is the inverse operation of three of the above four encryption key steps, the confusion column of the third step does not do. After the operation of the inverse operation, the corresponding plaintext information is will be obtained. Finally, after the ciphertext is obtained, the hash value of the ciphertext will be calculated for simple authentication to ensure that the privacy information is not tampered with by the attacker.

5   Blackhole Attack

To verify the security of the AODV-AES encrypted communication protocol and the performance of energy consumption and delay after being attacked, we added some blackhole attack nodes to simulate the attack. When the blackhole attack node receives the RREQ forwarded to itself, the received information is not carefully analyzed, but instead immediately sends an RREP back along the original path, which can cause a misleading effect on the transmission of the source node, because the attack node would indicate that it has a route to the receiving node, trying to wipe its own illegal identity by sending a malicious RREP [11]. This creates a path for the source node to send the packet to the wrong nodes, increasing the danger that the information is intercepted.

But the AODV-AES protocol designs an encrypted authentication mechanism and if the blackhole attack node deceives the source node, in the next stage of information transmission authentication, it will be identified as the attacking node and make its attack invalid. Even if the attack node gets ciphertext, the attacker also has no key, the encryption mechanism of AODV-AES will make it difficult to obtain plaintext. The encryption and authentication mechanisms together protect the transmission of privacy information.

6   Simulation and Performance Analyses

6.1   Simulation Environment and Parameters

We used NS-2.30 simulation software in the system of ubuntu10.04 to conduct the experiments, and Fig. 3 is the dynamic visualization of the simulation environment by Nam tool in NS-2.30. As can be seen, this is a scene with 60 mobile wireless sensor network nodes. The green node represents an ordinary relay node with sufficient energy. The red node is an aggressive and destructive malicious node, which is used to verify the security of AODV-AES protocol. The blue is the privacy information receiving node and the brown is the source node. The black circle in the figure is the dynamic visualization form of node broadcasting. The speed of viewing the visualization process can be adjusted in the upper right corner. Through this visual simulation, we can more clearly see the movement

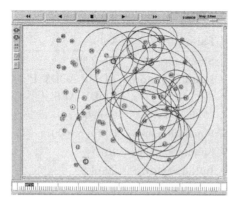

Fig. 3. Simulation environment (Color figure online)

trend, energy consumption status, and transmission information link trajectory of each wireless sensor node.

Table 1 is a description of the parameter case of our designed simulation experiment. We first set up the moving speed, the scene range, simulation time, and energy consumption of mobile sensor nodes for various situations through the Setdest tool in simulation software, then we can generate the simulation scenarios.

It should be noted that the Idle Power in Table 1 is the energy consumption of the sensor when it is idle. RX Power is the energy consumption of the sensor receive packet. TX Power is the energy consumption of the sent packet. Sleep Power is the energy consumption of the sensor when it is dormant. Transition Power is the energy required to switch between dormant and idle states. Transition Time is the time required to switch between dormant and idle states.

6.2   Performance Analysis

In contrast experiments, we contrast two major performance parameters applied to wireless sensor networks on the Internet of Vehicles: source node energy consumption and average end-to-end delay.

Energy Consumption. In the experiment of contrast energy consumption, we introduce AODV-P encryption communication protocol for comparison, AODV-P is also a kind of encryption communication protocol. We apply the Caesar encryption mechanism [8] to the AODV protocol after a slight improvement, then generated an AODV-P protocol. The classical Caesar encryption mechanism only has the shifting encryption stage: by setting the private key K as the number of bits that the encryption needs to move, the ciphertext is output after shifting the plaintext bit.

Table 1. Simulation Parameters.

Parameter	Values
Simulator	NS-2.30
Routing protocol	AODV AODV-P
	AODV-AES
Node speed	20 m/s
Simulation area	600 m × 600 m
Simulation time	10 s
Initial energy	200 J
Idle power	1.15 J
Rx power	1.2 J
Tx power	1.6 J
Sleep power	0.001 J
Transition power	0.2 J
Transition time	0.005 s

We incorporated a simple authentication protection mechanism on this basis. Hashes of plain and ciphertext were calculated as the two identifiers protected by authentication. After the receiving node receives the ciphertext, it is important to check that the received and computed identifiers are consistent to determine whether the plaintext is decrypted correctly and whether it has been tampered with maliciously by the attacker.

We divided the energy consumption contrast experiments into three groups, which were performed in scenarios with 40, 50, and 60 sensor points. Contrasting the AODV, AODV-P, and AODV-AES protocols energy consumption changing trend of source nodes when attacked by different numbers of blackhole attacking nodes.

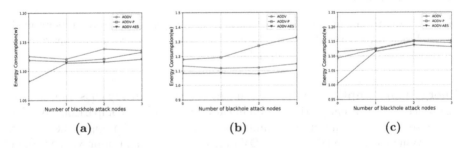

(a)   (b)   (c)

Fig. 4. Source node energy consumption under different number of blackhole attack nodes. (a) 40 nodes; (b) 50 nodes; (c) 60 nodes.

Figure 4a describes the first set of experiments aimed at contrasting the trend of source node energy consumption change when source nodes are attacked by different numbers of blackhole attack nodes under 40 nodes number scenarios after simulation using a variety of protocols. From the figure, the source node energy consumption of the AODV-AES protocol is lower than that of the AODV and AODV-P protocol in the four attacked scenarios with 0 to 3 attacked nodes, especially when they are not attacked, and the effect of low energy consumption is the most obvious.

Figure 4b describes the second set of experiments aimed at contrasting the trend of source node energy consumption change when source nodes are attacked by different numbers of blackhole attack nodes under 50 nodes number scenarios after simulation using a variety of protocols. When the AODV-P protocol is attacked in the 50 nodes scenario, the source node energy consumption all exceeds that of the AODV and AODV-AES protocol. Meanwhile, the AODV-AES protocol still maintains the lowest source node energy consumption among these several protocols after the AODV-AES protocol is attacked in the scenario of 50 nodes.

Figure 4c describes the third set of experiments aimed at contrasting the trend of source node energy consumption change when source nodes are attacked by different numbers of blackhole attack nodes under 60 nodes number scenarios after simulation using a variety of protocols. AODV-AES still maintains the lowest energy consumption of the source node in four cases, especially when it is not attacked.

After comprehensively comparing Fig. 4a, Fig. 4b and Fig. 4c, we find that the AODV-AES encryption communication protocol can maintain a low energy consumption with the increase of the total number of nodes and the number of attacked nodes. It shows that the AODV-AES encryption communication protocol is suitable for mobile wireless sensor networks characterized by low energy consumption on the Internet of Vehicles, and increases communication security.

Delay. We design experiments to compare the average end-to-end delay of AODV and AODV-AES protocol in different numbers of blackhole attack nodes.

As can be seen from Fig. 5, when attacked by different numbers of blackhole attack nodes, the average end-to-end delay of AODV-AES is all lower than that of the AODV. This indicates that AODV-AES will also have a low end-to-end delay under the premise of ensuring encrypted communication. It also shows once again that the AODV-AES encryption communication protocol is suitable for the mobile wireless sensor network of the Internet of Vehicles characterized by low delay, and can increase communication security.

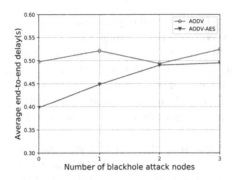

Fig. 5. Average end-to-end delay under different number of blackhole attack nodes

7   Conclusion

In order to deal with the transmission of security hidden danger in the mobile sensor network of the Internet of Vehicles, we add AES encryption mechanism to the classic AODV routing protocol in the mobile sensor network and design the AODV-AES encrypted communication protocol, which has three advantages. Low delay, low energy consumption, and high security. Moreover, the encryption mechanism of AODV-AES is a symmetric encryption mechanism, and the key occupies a small space. The above advantages show that AODV-AES encryption communication protocol meets the requirements of mobile sensor nodes on the Internet of Vehicles, low delay, limited memory and energy storage. We design comparative experiments to simulate the energy consumption and delay performance of AODV, AODV-P, and AODV-AES under the blackhole attack environment. The results show that when AODV-AES is attacked by different numbers of blackhole attack nodes under different scenarios nodes, and on the premise of ensuring encrypted transmission, it can control the average end-to-end delay and source node energy consumption well, which are better than AODV protocol and AODV-P encrypted communication protocol. It is again indicated that the AODV-AES encrypted communication protocol can be applied in mobile wireless sensor networks with the Internet of Vehicles as required by low energy consumption, low delay, and high-security standards.

Acknowledgements. This work is supported by the Key Project of Hunan Provincial Department of Education (20A191) and Hunan Teaching Research and Reform Project (2019).

References

1. Agarwal, H.K., Tripathi, M.: OLWS: optimized light weight secure clustering protocol for wireless sensor networks. In: 2019 4th International Conference on Information Systems and Computer Networks (ISCON), pp. 799–804 (2019)

2. Ajaykumar, N., Sarvagya, M.: Secure and energy efficient routing protocol in wireless sensor network: a survey. In: 2017 International Conference on Advances in Computing, Communications and Informatics (ICACCI), pp. 2313–2322 (2017)
3. Baroudi, U.: Robot-assisted maintenance of wireless sensor networks using wireless energy transfer. IEEE Sens. J. **17**(14), 4661–4671 (2017)
4. Boakye-Boateng, K., Kuada, E., Antwi-Boasiako, E., Djaba, E.: Encryption protocol for resource-constrained devices in fog-based IOT using one-time pads. IEEE Internet Things J. **6**(2), 3925–3933 (2019)
5. Chakeres, I., Belding-Royer, E.: AODV routing protocol implementation design. In: Proceedings of the 24th International Conference on Distributed Computing Systems Workshops, 2004, pp. 698–703 (2004)
6. Chu, S.I., Huang, Y.J., Lin, W.C.: Authentication protocol design and low-cost key encryption function implementation for wireless sensor networks. IEEE Syst. J. **11**(4), 2718–2725 (2017)
7. Geetha, B., Monika, R., Thejasvi, R., Vibaasundari, N.: A study of different routing protocols and encryption algorithms in wireless networks. In: 2017 IEEE International Conference on Power, Control, Signals and Instrumentation Engineering (ICPCSI), pp. 1213–1217 (2017)
8. Gowda, S.N.: Innovative enhancement of the Caesar Cipher algorithm for cryptography. In: International Conference on Advances in Computing, pp. 1–4 (2016)
9. Hammi, M.T., Livolant, E., Bellot, P., Serrhrouchni, A., Minet, P.: A lightweight IOT security protocol. In: 2017 1st Cyber Security in Networking Conference (CSNet), pp. 1–8 (2017)
10. Jasim, A.A., Idris, M.Y.I.B., Azzuhri, S.R.B., Issa, N.R., Mohamed Noor, N.B.E.A.: Secure and energy-efficient data aggregation method based on an access control model. IEEE Access **7**, 164327–164343 (2019)
11. Kumari, A., Krishnan, S.: Analysis of malicious behavior of blackhole and rushing attack in manet. In: 2019 International Conference on Nascent Technologies in Engineering (ICNTE), pp. 1–6 (2019)
12. Lee, J., Yu, S., Kim, M., Park, Y., Das, A.K.: On the design of secure and efficient three-factor authentication protocol using honey list for wireless sensor networks. IEEE Access **8**, 107046–107062 (2020)
13. Liang, Y., Wu, X., Meng, X., Zhang, K.: Design and implementation of a 780 mhz wireless sensor network for electric vehicle management system. In: 2019 IEEE 19th International Conference on Communication Technology (ICCT), pp. 967–971 (2019)
14. Nanda, A., Puthal, D., Rodrigues, J.J.P.C., Kozlov, S.A.: Internet of autonomous vehicles communications security: overview, issues, and directions. IEEE Wirel. Commun. **26**(4), 60–65 (2019)
15. Nazeer, M.I., Mallah, G.A., Memon, R.A.: A hybrid scheme for secure wireless communications in IoT. Intell. Autom. Soft Comput. **29**(2), 633–648 (2021)
16. Piran, M.J., Verma, V.G.M.S., Suh, D.Y.: Energy-efficient transmission range optimization model for WSN-based internet of things. Comput. Mater. Continua **67**(3), 2989–3007 (2021)
17. Singh, A.K., Alshehri, M., Bhushan, S., Kumar, M., et al.: Secure and energy efficient data transmission model for WSN. Intell. Autom. Soft Comput. **27**(3), 761–769 (2021)
18. Butt, T.M., Riaz, R., Paul, A.C.C.S.S.R.: Cogent and energy efficient authentication protocol for WSN in IOT. Comput. Mater. Continua **68**(2), 1877–1898 (2021)
19. Tang, C.: Research and analysis of WSN node location in highway traffic based on priority. J. Quant. Comput. **2**(1), 1–9 (2020)

20. Wang, D., Ren, P., Du, Q., Sun, L., Wang, Y.: Security provisioning for miso vehicular relay networks via cooperative jamming and signal superposition. IEEE Trans. Vehicul. Technol. **66**(12), 10732–10747 (2017)

21. Wu, S.L., Ni, S.Y., Tseng, Y.C., Sheu, J.P.: Route maintenance in a wireless mobile ad hoc network. In: Proceedings of the 33rd Annual Hawaii International Conference on System Sciences, p. 10, vol. 2 (2000)

22. Yang, L., Lu, Y., Liu, S., Guo, T., Liang, Z.: A dynamic behavior monitoring game-based trust evaluation scheme for clustering in wireless sensor networks. IEEE Access **6**, 71404–71412 (2018)

23. Yassein, M.B., Aljawarneh, S., Qawasmeh, E., Mardini, W., Khamayseh, Y.: Comprehensive study of symmetric key and asymmetric key encryption algorithms. In: 2017 International Conference on Engineering and Technology (ICET), pp. 1–7 (2017)

24. Zhou, Q., Qin, X., Liu, G., Cheng, H., Zhao, H.: An efficient privacy and integrity preserving data aggregation scheme for multiple applications in wireless sensor networks. In: 2019 IEEE International Conference on Smart Internet of Things (SmartIoT), pp. 291–297 (2019)

Energy Efficiency Maximization for UAV and Electric Vehicle Assisted Mobile Edge Computing on the Edge Side

Qiang Tang[1], LinJiang Li[1], Jin Wang[1(✉)], Gwang-jun Kim[2], and Bin Tang[1]

[1] Hunan Provincial Key Laboratory of Intelligent Processing of Big Data on Transportation, School of Computer and Communication Engineering, Changsha University of Science and Technology, Changsha 410114, Hunan, China
jinwang@csust.edu.cn

[2] Department of Computer Engineering, Chonnam National University, Gwangju 61186, Korea

Abstract. The research on the Internet of Things (IoT) and edge computing, especially Unmanned Aerial Vehicles assisted Mobile Edge Computing (UAV assisted MEC) attracted more and more interests of researchers. Nowadays, Electric Vehicles (EV) was introduced into the UAV assisted MEC system to improve system suitability and robustness. In this paper, an UAV and EV assisted MEC system was proposed and a paralled processing was involved with the goal of the edge side energy efficiency maximization, by jointly optimizing the communication scheduling, computing frequency and the trajectory of the UAV. The problem was formulated as a Mixed Integer Non-Liner Programming (MINLP), which was hard to solve. Therefore, the MINLP was divided into three sub-problems by applying the Block Coordinate Descent (BCD) method and solved by using Exhaustive Method (EM) and Successive Convex Optimization (SCO). In addition, a heuristic algorithm was put forward to get the optimization solution. The simulation results showed that our strategy has better performance compared with other benchmarks.

Keywords: Mobile edge computing · Electric vehicles · UAV trajectory

1 Introduction

The UAV assisted MEC systems attracted more and more attention due to their advantages such as easy deployment, controllable mobility, and superior communication links, that could solve many problems [1–3]. By adding UAVs with computing capability to the MEC system, the issue of insufficient computing resources could be relieved [4]. Thanks for the easy deployment of UAV and the air-to-ground communication systems with Line-of-Sight (LoS) links, the impact of ground noise could be mitigated [5]. Considering the mobility of UAVs, the shortened communication distance between users and the edge computing server benefited the establish of strong communications links and the communication efficiency [6].

However, there were still some issues in the above UAV assisted MEC systems [7], such as the insufficient energy capacity and weak computing stability. Some researchers

© The Author(s), under exclusive license to Springer Nature Switzerland AG 2022
X. Sun et al. (Eds.): ICAIS 2022, LNCS 13340, pp. 469–481, 2022.
https://doi.org/10.1007/978-3-031-06791-4_37

had proposed a UAV assisted MEC with Base Station (BS) system to deal with these problems [8]. However, the BS had many limitations, such as immovability and expensiveness. Combining with the design idea of the EV in IoV [9–11], we used EV replacing the BS in our system to solve those shortcomings.

In this paper, we considered an UAV and EV assisted MEC system to enhance the energy efficiency of the edge side. The UAV was responsible for collecting data from the terminals and forwarding data to the EV. Meanwhile, the EV handled those data. An energy efficiency maximization problem was formulated and solved approximately. Finally, an optimized computing offloading strategy named PABCD (Paramenter Assisted Block Coordinate Descent) was proposed.

2 System Model and Problem Formulation

As shown in Fig. 1, an offloading process was considered in our UAV and EV assisted MEC system. To handle this process, we defined that UEs on the ground firstly offloaded data to the UAV, then the UAV forwarded data to the EV, the EV was responsible for computing and processing tasks finally.

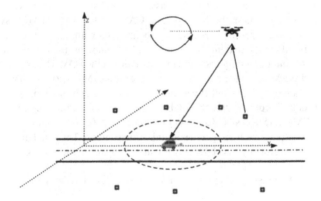

Fig. 1. Schematic diagram of physical model.

Without loss of generality, a 3-D Cartesian coordinate system was employed. There were K user equipment (UE) located at $[w_k, 0]^T$ (the $()^T$ denoted the transpose operator), where $w_k = [x_k, y_k]^T$ and $k \in K = \{1, 2, 3, ..., K\}$. The EV stayed at position $[q_{EV}, 0]^T$, where $q_{EV} = [x_{EV}, y_{EV}]^T$. In order to dynamically design the trajectory of the UAV, we discretized the work cycle T into $N + 2$ time slot with the equal interval as $\delta = (T/(N+2))$. Due to the small time slot, the UAV was considered static and its coordinates were defined as $[q[n], H]^T$, where H was the flight height, $q[n] = [x[n], y[n]]^T$ and $n \in N = \{1, 2, 3, ..., N\}$.

2.1 Communication and Computing Model

Communication Model. As shown in Fig. 2, we considered a three-stage parallel approach to improve the communication efficiency of the system. Firstly, the UE offloaded

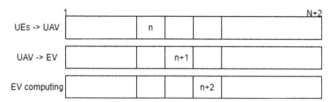

Fig. 2. The process of communication.

data to the UAV at the n-th time slot. Then, the UAV forwarded the data to the EV at the $(n + 1)$-th time slot. Finally, the EV processeed these data at the $(n + 2)$-th time slot. We applied the one-to-one communication in all time slots [12], in which the noise could be ignored.

The channels between the UEs and the UAV, and between the UAV and the EV were assumed to be dominated by the LoS, with no small scale fading. Thus, we used the free-space path loss model [13] to establish the channel power gain from the k-th UE to the UAV in the uplink at the n-th time slot, show as:

$$h_k[n] = \frac{\beta_0}{\|q[n] - w_k\|^2 + H^2}, \forall k \in K, \forall n \in N \tag{1}$$

Analogously, the channel power gain between the UAV and the EV could be expressed as:

$$h_U[n+1] = \frac{\beta_0}{\|q[n+1] - q_{EV}\|^2 + H^2}, \forall n \in N \tag{2}$$

where β_0 represented the reference channel gain at $d = 1m$.

We denoted $\alpha_k[n]$ as the communication status of the k-the UE with the UAV at the n-th time slot. According to Fig. 2, we knew that $\alpha_k[n]$ could also express the communication status of the UAV with the EV at the n-th time slot and it should satisfy:

$$\alpha_k[n] = \{0, 1\}, \sum_{k=1}^{K} \alpha_k[n] = 1, \forall k \in K, \forall n \in N \tag{3}$$

The bandwidth between the UEs and the UAV was denoted as B_{U2U}, the bandwidth between the UAV and the EV was treated as B_{U2E}, and the noise power was σ^2. The UE transmitted power and the UAV forwarded power was regarded as P_{UE} and P_{UAV}, respectively. Then the transmission rate between the k-th UEs and the UAV [14] was formulated as:

$$r_k[n] = B_{U2U} \cdot \alpha_k[n] \cdot log_2\left(1 + \frac{P_{UE}h_k[n]}{\sigma^2}\right), \forall k \in K, \forall n \in N \tag{4}$$

Similarly, the transmission rate between the UAV and the EV was formulated as:

$$r_k^U[n] = B_{U2E} \cdot \alpha_k[n] \cdot log_2\left(1 + \frac{P_{UAV}h_U[n+1]}{\sigma^2}\right), \forall k \in K, \forall n \in N \tag{5}$$

We defined $l_k[n]$ as the tasks offloaded by k-th UE to the UAV at the n-th time slot and $l_k^U[n+1]$ as the tasks forwarded by the UAV to the EV at the $(n+1)$-th time slot. In this case, the amount of offloaded data and forwarded data should satisfy:

$$\alpha_k[n] \cdot log_2\left(1 + \frac{P_{UAV}h_k[n]}{\sigma^2}\right) \geq \frac{l_k[n]}{B_{U2U}\delta}, \forall k \in K, \forall n \in N \tag{6}$$

$$\alpha_k[n] \cdot log_2\left(1 + \frac{P_{UAV}h_U[n+1]}{\sigma^2}\right) \geq \frac{l_k^U[n+1]}{B_{U2E}\delta}, \forall k \in K, \forall n \in N \tag{7}$$

Computing Model. To reduce the complexity of the model, we assumed $l_k[n]$ as the amount of data processed by EV at the $(n+2)$-th time slot. $\frac{f[n+2]}{C} \cdot \delta$ was regarded as the amount of data processed [15] by the EV at the $(n+2)$-th time slot, and it met the following conditions:

$$\sum_{k=1}^{K} l_k[n] = \frac{f[n+2]}{C} \cdot \delta, \forall n \in N \tag{8}$$

where C was the required CPU cycles per input-bit at EV like the computation of the UAV.

The computing energy consumption at the $(n+2)$-th time slot was:

$$E_{comp}[n+2] = \lambda_c \cdot f[n+2]^3 \cdot \delta, \forall n \in N \tag{9}$$

where λ_c denoted the effective CPU switch capacitance, and we set $f[n+2]$ as the CPU frequency of the EV at the n-th time slot with a unit of cycles per second.

2.2 Energy Consumption Model and Energy Efficiency

There were two parts for the total energy consumption, including the flying and forwarding energy of the UAV, along with the computing and standby energy of the EV. For the first part, the energy consumption of the UAV during one flight period was E_{fly}, and we defined E_{comm} as the forwarding energy consumption of the UAV for data transmission to EV. For the second part, the energy consumption of computing on the EV was denoted as Ecomp. Meanwhile, the standby energy consumption of the EV immovably was E_{EV}.

A complete flight energy consumption model [16] could be represented by:

$$E_{fly} = \sum_{n=1}^{N}\left(C_1\|v[n]\|^3 + \frac{C_2}{\|v[n]\|}\left(1 + \frac{\|a[n]\|^2}{g^2}\right)\right) \cdot \delta \tag{10}$$

where $\|\cdot\|$ meant the norm 2 function. $v[n]$, $a[n]$ and g denoted speed, acceleration and acceleration of gravity respectively. $C_1 > 0$ and $C_2 > 0$ were constants which were related to the UAV's wing area, load factor and wing span efficiency etc.

For the forwarding energy consumption, we formulated it as:

$$E_{comm} = \sum_{n=1}^{N}\sum_{k=1}^{K} \alpha_k[n] \cdot P_{UE} \cdot \delta \tag{11}$$

Combining formula (9), we knew that:

$$E_{comp} = \sum_{n=1}^{N} \lambda_c \cdot f[n+2]^3 \cdot \delta \tag{12}$$

We defined P_{EV} as the standby power of the EV, so the standby energy consumption of EV was:

$$E_{EV} = \sum_{n=1}^{N} \sum_{k=1}^{K} \alpha_k[n] \cdot P_{EV} \cdot \delta \tag{13}$$

Above all, the total energy consumption of the system was: $E_{total} = E_{fly} + E_{comm} + E_{comp} + E_{EV}$. In addition, we defined θ as the energy efficiency and it was formulated as:

$$\theta = \frac{\sum_{n=1}^{N} \sum_{k=1}^{K} l_k[n]}{E_{total}} \tag{14}$$

2.3 Problem Formulation

We optimized the energy efficiency maximization of the edge side by jointly formulating a optimization problem with the communication scheduling, the computing frequency of the EV and trajectory of the UAV. A collection of trajectory, acceleration and speed of the UAV was defined as $Q = \{q[n], a[n], v[n]\}$. The communication scheduling was denoted as $A = \{\alpha_k[n]\}$. The computing frequency of the UAV was denoted as $F = \{f[n+2]\}$. The formulated problem was represented as:

$$P1:$$

$$\max_{\{Q,A,F\}} \theta$$

$$s.t.$$

$$C1: \alpha_k[n] \cdot log_2\left(1 + \frac{P_{UE}h_k[n]}{\sigma^2}\right) \geq \frac{l_k[n]}{B_{U2U}\delta}, \forall k \in K, \forall n \in N$$

$$C2: \alpha_k[n] = \{0, 1\}, \sum_{k=1}^{K} \alpha_k[n] = 1, \forall k \in K, \forall n \in N$$

$$C3: \alpha_k[n] \cdot log_2\left(1 + \frac{P_{UAV}h_U[n+1]}{\sigma^2}\right) \geq \frac{l_k^U[n+1]}{B_{U2E}\delta}, \forall k \in K, \forall n \in N$$

$$C4: \sum_{k=1}^{K} l_k[n] = \frac{f[n+2]}{C} \cdot \delta, \forall n \in N$$

$$C5: f[n+2] \geq 0, \forall n \in N$$

$$C6 : q[n+1] = q[n] + v[n] \cdot \delta + \frac{1}{2}a[n] \cdot \delta, \forall n \in N$$

$$C7 : v[n+1] = v[n] + a[n] \cdot \delta, \forall n \in N$$

$$C8 : q[1] = q[N+1], v[1] = v[N+1]$$

$$C9 : \|a[n]\| \leq A_{max}, \forall n \in N$$

$$C10 : \|v[n]\| \leq V_{max}, \forall n \in N$$

Due to the non-convexity of the objective function and the constraints C1, C2 and C3, the problem P1 was a MINLP problem. Hence, we found it was hard to solve by standard convex optimization techniques. Taking into account the above factors, we used BCD technology to divide the problem P1 into three sub-problems. The first one, named communication scheduling problem, could be addressed by exhaustive method with given the UAV trajectory and the computing frequency. The second sub-problem could be solved with given the UAV trajectory and the communication scheduling, and we called it computing resource allocation problem. Finally, we used SCO techniques as well as the standard convex optimization solver to optimize this trajectory problem with the optimal solutions of the other sub-problems.

3   Optimization Method and Process

3.1   Communication Scheduling and Computing Resource Allocation Problems

Communication Scheduling Problem.   With the given Q and F, we could get a new P2 problem as follows:

$$P2 :$$

$$max\,\theta = \frac{\sum_{n=1}^{N}\sum_{k=1}^{K}l_k[n]}{\partial}$$
$$\{A\}$$

$$s.t.\,C1, C2, C3$$

Through the analysis of the objective function θ, combining with C2, we decomposed the P2 problem into N sub-problems, where we defined $\theta = \sum_{n=1}^{n=N}\theta_1$. Then, we solved the sub-problems using the EM. As described in constraint C1 and C3, we could see that θ_1 would change with the value of $l_k[n]$, meanwhile, $\sum_{k=1}^{K}l_k[n]$ would change with $\alpha_k[n]$. Thus, by comparing different θ_1 under the different value of k, we set $\alpha_k[n] = 1$ when the θ_1 was the largest. By solving N sub-problems, we could get the solution set of A.

$$\partial = \sum_{n=1}^{N} \left(C_1 \|v[n]\|^3 + \frac{C_2}{\|v[n]\|} \left(1 + \frac{\|a[n]^2\|}{g^2} \right) \right) \cdot \delta + \sum_{n=1}^{N} \gamma_c \cdot f[n+2]^3 \cdot \delta$$

$$+ \sum_{n=1}^{N} \sum_{k=1}^{K} \alpha_k[n] \cdot (P_{UE} + P_{EV}) \cdot \delta$$

Computing Resource Allocation Problem. Combining θ, C2 and C4, with Given Q and a, We Could Get P3:

$$P3:$$

$$\max_{\{F\}} \theta_2 = \sum_{n=1}^{N} \frac{f[n+2]}{\left(C_1 \|v[n]\|^3 + \frac{C_2}{\|v[n]\|} \left(1 + \frac{\|a[n]\|^2}{g^2} \right) \right) + \gamma_c \cdot f[n+2]^3 + P_{UE} + P_{EV}} \cdot \frac{1}{C}$$

$$s.t.\, C5$$

Similar as problem P2, we decomposed the P3 problem into N sub-problems, where we defined $\theta_2 = \sum_{n=1}^{N} \theta_{2,n}$. By deriving $f[n+2]$ in $\theta_{2,n}$, we knew that $\theta_{2,n}$ and θ_2 could get the maximum when $f[n+2]$ satisfied the following conditions:

$$f[n+2] = \sqrt[3]{\frac{C \cdot \left(C_1 \|v[n]\|^3 + \frac{C_2}{\|v[n]\|} \left(1 + \frac{\|a[n]\|^2}{g^2} \right) \right) + P_{UE} + P_{EV}}{2\gamma_c}} \tag{15}$$

Above all, we could get the solution set of F.

3.2 Trajectory Problems

In this section, the final sub-problem of P1 for optimizing the UAV trajectory was solved with the optimal solution of P2 and P3. $\sum_{n=1}^{N} \sum_{k=1}^{K} l_k[n]$ would be a fixed value with the given A and F, and E_{comm}, E_{comp} and E_{EV} were fixed, too. Therefore, we needed to minimize the E_{fly}. Accordingly, this problem could be reformulated as:

$$P4:$$

$$\min_{\{Q\}} E_{fly}$$

$$s.t.\, C1, C3, C6 - C9$$

By analyzing constraints C1 and C3, we saw that the problem P4 was a non-convex optimization problem. Thus, an approximate solution was obtained by introducing SCO techniques with a slack variable:

$$\tau[n] \geq 0 \tag{16}$$

And it should follow:

$$\|v[n]\|^2 \geq \tau[n]^2 \tag{17}$$

Therefore, E_{fly} could be relaxed to be:

$$E_{fly}^* = \sum_{n=1}^{N} \left(C_1 \|v[n]\|^3 + \frac{C_2}{\tau[n]} \left(1 + \frac{\|a[n]\|^2}{g^2} \right) \right) \cdot \delta \tag{18}$$

According to (17) and (18), it could be inferred that $E_{fly}^* \geq E_{fly}$. So, replacing E_{fly} by E_{fly}^*, the objective function of problem P4 could be released into a convex problem for $v[n]$ and $\tau[n]$ jointly. For the non-convex constraint (17), the first-order Taylor expansion was applied to deal with it. Thus, for any given feasible point $\tau_r[n]$, it followed:

$$\|v[n]\|^2 \geq \|\tau_r[n]\|^2 + 2v_r^T[n](v[n] - v_r[n]) \triangleq \psi_{lb}(v[n]) \tag{19}$$

where equality held at the point $v[n] = v_r[n]$. Then, constraint (17) could be transformed to:

$$\psi_{lb}(v[n]) \geq \tau[n]^2 \tag{20}$$

Further, constraints of C1 and C3 were handled by using SCO techniques, which could obtain an approximate solution of problem P4. Specifically, constraint C1 was nonconvex with respect to $q[n]$, considering the expression of $log_2\left(1 + \frac{P_T \lambda_0}{\|q[n] - w_k\|^2 + H^2} \right)$ in Left Hand Side (LHS), but it was convex with respect to $\|q[n] - w_k\|$, where $\lambda_0 = \frac{B_0}{\sigma^2}$.

The lower bound function of the LHS in C1 could be transformed to $g_1[n]$ by using the first-order Taylor expansion. Similarly, the LHS of the formula in C3 could also be lower-bounded. These functions were expressed in (21) and (22)

$$g_1[n] = log_2\left(1 + \frac{P_{UE} \lambda_0}{\|q_j[n] - w_k\|^2 + H^2} \right)$$
$$- \frac{log_2(e) P_{UE} \lambda_0 \left(\|q[n] - w_k\|^2 - \|q_j[n] - w_k\|^2 \right)}{\left(\|q_j[n] - w_k\|^2 + H^2 \right)\left(\|q_j[n] - w_k\|^2 + H^2 + P_T \lambda_0 \right)} \tag{21}$$

$$g_2[n+1] = log_2\left(1 + \frac{P_{UAV} \lambda_0}{\|q_j[n+1] - q_{EV}\|^2 + H^2} \right)$$
$$- \frac{log_2(e) P_{UAV} \lambda_0 \left(\|q[n+1] - q_{EV}\|^2 - \|q_j[n+1] - q_{EV}\|^2 \right)}{\left(\|q_j[n+1] - q_{EV}\|^2 + H^2 \right)\left(\|q_j[n+1] - q_{EV}\|^2 + H^2 + P_U \lambda_0 \right)} \tag{22}$$

Considering the lower bound functions and the approximately convex expression, we could get the following new problem P4.1:

$$P4.1:$$

$$\min_{\{Q\}} E^*_{fly}$$

$$s.t.$$

$$C1^* : \alpha_k[n] \cdot g_1[n] \geq \frac{l_k[n]}{B_{U2U}\delta}, \forall k \in K, \forall n \in N$$

$$C3^* : \alpha_k[n] \cdot g_2[n+1] \geq \frac{l_k^U[n+1]}{B_{U2E}\delta}, \forall k \in K, \forall n \in N$$

$$C6 - C9$$

$$C10 : \|v[n]\|^2 \geq \|\tau_r[n]\|^2 + 2v_r^T[n](v[n] - v_r[n]) \triangleq \psi_{lb}(v[n]), \forall n \in N$$

$$C11 : \psi_{lb}(v[n]) \geq \tau[n]^2, \forall n \in N$$

Obviously, problem P4.1 was convex, where standard convex optimization tools were proposed to get the solution, such as CVX [17].

As shown in Table 1, where $P = \{P_{UE}, P_{UAV}, P_{EV}\}$, $B = \{B_{U2U}, B_{U2E}\}$, the steps 3–5 were the process for solving three sub-problems, alternately. After getting the EE (energy efficiency), we made h_k and h_U change within the feasible region so that our optimal solution would not fall into the local optimal.

Table 1. Problem P1 optimization algorithm.

Input: Q, W, q_{EV}, σ^2, P, B, pa
1 set iteration tolerance $\varepsilon > 0$, E_{comm}, E_{EV}, **A, F**, l_k, l_k^U, h_k, h_U
2 **while** the fractional decrease of the objective value of problem **P1** was more than tolerance ε **do**
3   updated **A**, l_k, l_k^U with **Q** and **F** by EM.
4   updated **F** and E_{comm} with given **Q** and **A** by (15).
5   updated **Q**, E_{fly}, l_k and l_k^U with given **A** and **F** by CVX.
6   got EE with l_k, l_k^U, E_{fly}, E_{comm}, E_{comm}, E_{EV}
7   let h_k/pa and $h_U * pa$ replace h_k and h_U, respectively
8 **end**
Output: EE

4 Numerical Results

In this section, numerical simulation results were provided to evaluate the performance of our proposed algorithm and the detail parameters values were shown in Table 1 [10, 14]. We measured the superiority of our algorithm by analyzing the energy efficiency in the simulation results and proposed two comparison schemes:

Without PA (WPA): By solving the three sub-problems alternately, an optimized energy efficiency was obtained and its solution schemes of the three sub-problems were the same as the PABCD without parameter;

Fixed Trajectory Over UEs (FTOU): In this scheme, the UAV choosed the straight line between two adjacent UEs as the fixed trajectory. The UAV could establish a better communication channel with Terminals.

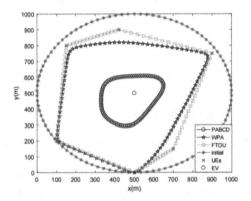

Fig. 3. The trajectory of UAV in all schemes.

The PABCD and WPA shared an initial trajectory, while the FTOU was a fixed trajectory as shown in Fig. 3. It could be found that the UAV trajectory of the PCBCD was smaller than the WPA schemes. There were many factors responsible for this phenomenon. Firstly, the parameter in the PABCD would cause the trajectory in the next iteration to have a larger solution space, so its trajectory could be smaller. Then, energy efficiency would change (it would enlarge first, and then reduce) with reducing of the flying energy consumption of the UAV.

In Fig. 4, we observed that the optimization of the PACBD was optimal. Compared with the WPA, we could obviously see that the optimization result of the PABCD was better, which also proved that our design of the PABCD algorithm was meaningful. On the other hand, with the performance of the WPA, its trajectory fell into the local optimal solution. For the FTOU, since the UAV trajectory of the FTOU was unchanged, the rest of the variables would be fixed during the iterative solution process, resulting in its energy efficiency stayed at a specific value.

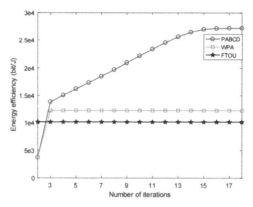

Fig. 4. Convergence of energy efficiency.

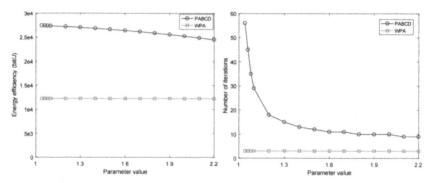

Fig. 5. Performance of the PABCD and WPA under different parameters.

Figure 5 plotted that the optimal value and the number of iterations obtained by the PABCD would be larger as the parameter decreases. In particular, when the parameter was close to 1, the optimization result would converge to the optimal value but it would spend more iterations. This was because that the search for the solution space would be more 'detailed' and the number of iterations would increase when the parameter was close to 1. Then, we set the parameters as 1.04, 1.06 and 1.08, as shown in Fig. 5, where these optimal values were closer to 274.5 * 100(bit/J). Combining with Fig. 4, we had reason to believe that this value was the optimal value approximately in this case. For the WPA, we could see that its snergy efficiency would unchanged as parameter changes, because the parameter was not involved in the optimization process of it.

We could see that the result of the PABCD was the best in these schemes, as shown in Fig. 6, where the number of UEs change would influence the optimality of this system. By comparing the FTOU, WPA and PABCD, it was not hard to find that the optimized trajectory had greater energy efficiency than the fixed trajectory.

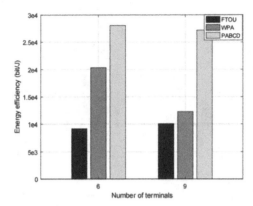

Fig. 6. Performance of all schemes under different terminals.

5 Conclusions

In this paper, an UAV and EV assisted MEC system was proposed, where UEs on the ground offloaded data to the UAV, and the UAV forwarded data to the EV. Meanwhile, the EV was responsible for computing and processing tasks. We maximized the energy efficiency of the edge side in this system by jointly optimizing the communication scheduling, computing frequency and the trajectory of the UAV. The problem was formulated as a MINLP, and we divided it into three sub-problems by applying the BCD method, and solved it by using the EM method as well as SCO. Finally, an optimal strategy PABCD was put forward. In order to illustrate the performance of PABCD, we proposed two schemes WPA and FTOU, and the simulation results showed that the PABCD had the best performance.

Acknowledgement. This work was jointly supported by Natural Science Foundation of Hunan Province, China (Grant No. 2021JJ30736), Changsha Municipal Natural Science Foundation (Grant No. kq2014112), and the Outstanding Youth Project of Hunan Province Education Department (Grant No. 18B162).

References

1. Zhang, J.: Computation-efficient offloading and trajectory scheduling for multi-UAV assisted mobile edge computing. IEEE Trans. Veh. Technol. **69**(2), 2114–2125 (2020)
2. Zhang, K., Gui, X., Ren, D., Li, D.: Energy-latency tradeoff for computation offloading in UAV-assisted multiaccess edge computing system. IEEE Internet Things J. **8**(8), 6709–6719 (2021)
3. Noorwali, A., Javed, M.A., Khan, M.Z.: Efficient UAV communications: recent trends and challenges. Comput. Mater. Continua **67**(1), 463–476 (2021)
4. Sheng, Z., Mahapatra, C., Leung, V.C.M., Chen, M., Sahu, P.K.: Energy efficient cooperative computing in mobile wireless sensor networks. IEEE Trans. Cloud Comput. **6**(1), 114–126 (2018)

5. Zhou, F., Wu, Y., Hu, R.Q., Qian, Y.: Computation rate maximization in UAV-enabled wireless-powered mobile-edge computing systems. IEEE J. Sel. Areas Commun. **36**(9), 1927–1941 (2018)
6. Li, S., Duo, B., Yuan, X., Liang, Y., Renzo, M.D.: Reconfigurable intelligent surface assisted UAV communication: joint trajectory design and passive beamforming. IEEE Wire. Commun. Lett. **9**(5), 716–720 (2020)
7. Almutairi, J., Aldossary, M.: Investigating and modelling of task offloading latency in edge-cloud environment. Comput. Mater. Continua **68**(3), 4143–4160 (2021)
8. Zhang, T., Xu, Y., Loo, J., Yang, D., Xiao, L.: Joint computation and communication design for UAV-assisted mobile edge computing in IoT. IEEE Trans. Ind. Inf. **16**(8), 5505–5516 (2020)
9. Jiang, F., Wang, K., Dong, L., Pan, C., Xu, W., Yang, K.: Deep-learning-based joint resource scheduling algorithms for hybrid MEC networks. IEEE Internet Things J. **7**(7), 6252–6265 (2020)
10. Liu, Y.: Joint communication and computation resource scheduling of a UAV-assisted mobile edge computing system for platooning vehicles. IEEE Trans. Intell. Transp. Syst. (2021). https://doi.org/10.1109/TITS.2021.3082539
11. Li, M., Cheng, N., Gao, J., Wang, Y., Zhao, L., Shen, X.: Energy-efficient UAV-assisted mobile edge computing: resource allocation and trajectory optimization. IEEE Trans. Veh. Technol. **69**(3), 3424–3438 (2020)
12. Hua, M., Wang, Y., Li, C., Huang, Y., Yang, L.: UAV-aided mobile edge computing systems with one by one access scheme. IEEE Trans. Green Commun. Netw. **3**(3), 664–678 (2019)
13. Zhang, S., Zeng, Y., Zhang, R.: Cellular-enabled UAV communication: a connectivity-constrained trajectory optimization perspective. IEEE Trans. Commun. **67**(3), 2580–2604 (2019)
14. Tse, N., David, V., Hanly, S.: Multiaccess fading channels-part i: polymatroid structure, optimal resource allocation and throughput capacities. IEEE Trans. Inf. Theory **44**(7), 2796 (1998)
15. You, C., Huang, K., Chae, H.: Energy efficient mobile cloud computing powered by wireless energy transfer. IEEE J. Sel. Areas Commun. **34**(5), 1757–1771 (2016)
16. Liu, Y., Xiong, K., Ni, Q., Fan, P., Letaief, K.B.: UAV-assisted wireless powered cooperative mobile edge computing: joint offloading, CPU control, and trajectory optimization. IEEE Internet Things J. **7**(4), 2777–2790 (2020)
17. Grant, M., Boyd, S.: CVX: MATLAB software for Disciplined Convex Programming, Version 2.0 Beta. http://cvxr.com/cvx (2012)

Risk Assessment of Electric Energy Metering Automation System Based on Bayesian Network

Weihua Li[1], Shaocheng Wu[1], Yue Ma[1], Tao Liu[1], Yali Bai[2], and Jinxin Zuo[3(✉)]

[1] Shenzhen Power Supply Co. Ltd., Shenzhen 518001, China
[2] Department of Communication Engineering, University of Science and Technology Beijing, Beijing 100083, China
[3] School of Cyberspace Security, Beijing University of Posts and Telecommunications, Beijing 100876, China
zuojx@bupt.edu.cn

Abstract. In the ubiquitous network environment, the security threats facing the metering automation system are also increasing. The risk assessment of electric energy measurement automation system is an important goal of power grid security, but it faces difficulties such as single hidden danger identification means and lack of dynamic assessment models. To improve the accuracy and rationality of the system risk assessment, this paper realizes the dynamic risk assessment of the electric energy metering automation system. First, a risk assessment index system is established from the three aspects of technology, management, and regulations. Secondly, based on analytic hierarchy process, we analyzed the weight of the risk assessment indicator to obtain the subjective weight of the risk assessment indicator. Then, the Bayes grid method is improved by the method of probability distribution, which quantitatively describe the relationship between parent nodes and child nodes. Through the improved Bayesian grid method, the objective weight of the risk assessment indicator is obtained, and the comprehensive weight of the assessment indicator is calculated through combination weighting, which realizes the comprehensive risk assessment of the measurement automation system. Finally, the simulation experiment analysis and the sensitivity analysis of the proposed model are carried out. The result shows that the safety guarantee goal of the electric energy metering automation system depends to a large extent on the technical reliability.

Keywords: Electric energy measurement automation · Risk assessment · Bayes · Analytic hierarchy process · Probability distribution

1 Introduction

Due to the increasing demand for electricity in our country, the inspection and maintenance of electric energy metering devices will be very difficult. The application of measurement automation system can reasonably allocate effective resources, and greatly improves work efficiency and quality efficiency [1].

However, under the ubiquitous network environment, the data of the metering terminal user terminal is increasing, and the security threats facing the metering automation system are also increasing. One of the important goals of the smart grid is to ensure the safety of the metering automation system, and to be able to predict the security risk level of the system in time [2]. How to make a reasonable and accurate risk assessment of the safety status of the electric energy metering automation system is the focus and difficulty of safety protection for electric metering automation system.

Identifying and analyzing the risk factors and risk levels of the system, and mining the causal links and regularities between indicators are the basis for establishing an effective measurement security risk assessment model [3]. However, due to factors such as the network structure and the diversity of load characteristics and distribution characteristics in the system, it is difficult to form a universal evaluation system for the safety assessment of electric energy measurement. In view of this, this article integrates the literature [4–7], which proposed risk indicators such as illegal network intrusion and metered user management, and adds consideration of system operation management and regulatory indicators to build a complete system risk assessment index system. By calculating system security risks quickly and accurately, the management personnel could conduct system control in advance to enhance the initiative of the safe operation of the power grid.

The main contributions of this article are as follows:

1. The measurement automation system safety risk assessment index system has been established from the three dimensions of technology, management, and regulations.
2. Construct a safety risk assessment model for the measurement automation system. The proposed model can effectively identify the key influencing factors that lead to system security risks, and conduct a dynamic and intelligent comprehensive assessment of the security risks of the metering automation system.
3. Based on Netica Bayes and Yaahp, the simulation experiment analysis and the sensitivity analysis of the model are carried out.

2   Related Works

The demand for global monitoring of power grid operation, prevention and control of the entire network, and centralized decision-making is increasingly prominent [8]. Research on power grid risk protection and active dispatch control strategies is an important means to improve the level of regulation and promote the transformation of empirical regulation to analysis and intelligence [9]. However, in the face of the uncertainty of the risk indicators of the electric energy metering automation system, the existing risk protection measures are still mainly in the passive control stage [10, 11], which demanding to wait for scenarios or failures that need to be adjusted before formulating and implementing strategies. However, this kind of risk prevention and control method cannot make full use of resources with a large risk prevention and control time constant, making the grid security in a passive position [11]. Due to the lack of initiative in the existing grid risk safety prevention and control methods, it is impossible to accurately analyze and predict risks before they arrive.

At present, research on risk assessment in the power field mainly focuses on concept establishment and necessity analysis [12, 13], risk indicator improvement [14–18], and risk-based dispatch decision-making [19]. Among them, the literature [15] earlier proposed the related concepts of risk assessment, and established risk assessment indicators; literature [16, 17] further added equipment overload, loss of load and other indicators to enrich Evaluation system. Literature [20] proposed using deep learning algorithm to evaluate the security elasticity of power system. Literature [21] based on statistical analysis methods, the annual failure rate distribution of transmission lines is obtained, and the ice damage faults of transmission lines are comprehensively analyzed.

Although the above studies have modeled the severity, this type of risk assessment method based on certainty assumptions and model-driven has been difficult to accurately estimate the real risk of system. As a result, data-driven risk assessment methods have received widespread attention in recent years [22–27], but most of them are still mainly aimed at indicator improvement under data-driven methods [23] and assumptions based on deterministic failures [24]. There are only a few studies that combine scenario probability with risk assessment [25, 26].

Although the above-mentioned results have been achieved, it does not measure the risks in future scenarios, and does not use the results of the security risk assessment to guide regulation. Therefore, this article proposes risk indicators such as illegal network intrusion and metered user management, and adds consideration of system operation management and regulatory indicators to build a complete system risk assessment index system.

3 Safety Risk Assessment Indicators for Electric Energy Metering Automation Systems

3.1 Index System

Referring to the relevant research on the risk of metering automation system, a safety risk assessment system for electric energy metering automation systems is established from technology, management, laws and regulations, as shown in Fig. 1.

1. Technical risk. The technical guidelines are defined as A, which can be divided into four categories: illegal network intrusion [10], data storage and processing, identity authentication and access control, and system operation security [26]. $A_1 = \{A_{11}, A_{12}, A_{13}, A_{14}\}$, indicates the impact sub-criteria A_1. The impact indicators of illegal network intrusion include: DDoS attack A_{11}, man-in-the-middle attack A_{12}, unknown source risk A_{13}, and malicious access point A_{14}. $A_2 = \{A_{21}, A_{22}, A_{23}, A_{24}\}$, indicates the impact sub-criteria level A_2, the impact indicators of data storage and processing include: data sharing risk A_{21}, data theft or loss A_{22}, data isolation risk A_{23}, and data backup and recovery risk A_{24}. $A_3 = \{A_{31}, A_{32}, A_{33}\}$, indicates the impact of sub-criteria level A_3. The impact indicators of identity authentication and access control include: identity information validity A_{31}, cross-domain access risk $A32$, and access authority management A_{33}. $A_4 = \{A_{41}, A_{42}, A_{43}\}$, represents the impact sub-criteria level A_4. The impact indicators of system operation risk include:

system monitoring real-time performance A_{41}, system interface risk A_{42}, and system patch management A_{43}.

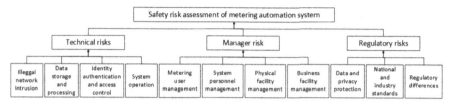

Fig. 1. Risk assessment index system.

2. Manage risks. Management criteria is defined as B, which can be divided into four dimensions: metering user management B_1, system internal personnel management B_2, physical facility management B_3, and business operation management B_4 [27]. $B_1 = \{B_{11}, B_{12}\}$, indicates the impact sub-criteria B_1, the impact indicators for measuring user management include: user illegal behavior response B_{11}, user authentication and access authorization B_{12}. $B_2 = \{B_{21}, B_{22}, B_{23}\}$, indicates the impact sub-criteria level B_2, the impact indicators of the internal personnel management of the system include: measurement key management B_{21}, access authority distribution and monitoring B_{22}, and illegal and malicious operations B_{23}. $B_3 = \{B_{31}, B_{32}, B_{33}\}$, indicates the impact of sub-criteria level B_3. The impact indicators of physical facility management include: natural disaster response B_{31}, man-made accident response B_{32}, and physical host security B_{33}. $B_4 = \{B_{41}, B_{42}, B_{43}\}$, represents the impact sub-criteria level B_4. The impact indicators of business operation management include: system asset management and identification B_{41}, critical business chain review B_{42}, and resource integration, allocation and supply B_{43}.

3. Regulatory risks. Regulatory standards are defined as C, which can be divided into three dimensions: data, privacy protection C_1, national and industry standards C_2, and differences in standards and regulations C_3 [28]. $C_1 = \{C_{11}, C_{12}\}$, indicates the impact sub-criteria C_1, the impact indicators of data and privacy protection include: illegal misuse of user information C_{11}, privacy leakage risk C_{12}. $C_2 = \{C_{21}, C_{22}\}$, indicates the impact of the sub-criteria level C_2. The impact indicators of national and industry standards include: consistency with national and industry regulations C_{21}, and completeness of industry standards C_{22}. $C_3 = \{C_{31}, C_{32}\}$, indicates the impact of sub-standard level C_3. The impact indicators of differences in standards and regulations include: cross-regional regulatory differences C_{31}, and industry regulations have no unified standard C_{32}.

3.2 Evaluation Level

According to GB/T 22240-2020 and other standards [29], this article divides the security risk level of the measurement automation system into 5 levels: very safe (I), safe (II), relatively safe (III), relatively dangerous (IV), and very dangerous (V), the corresponding safety risk comprehensive score is 80 points or more, 70–80 points, 60–70 points, 50–60 points, 0–50.

4 Construction of a Safety Risk Assessment Model for Measurement Automation System

To avoid the subjective experience brought by the traditional methods, this paper uses the analytic hierarchy process to calculate the subjective weight of the assessment indicators. We improved the Bayesian network method through the probability distribution method, which clarifies the causal relationship between root node and the child node. Also, prior knowledge and objective evidence are effectively integrated. In addition, the system risk impact factors are combined and weighted, and the security risk is evaluated dynamically and comprehensively.

4.1 Determination of the Subjective Weight

The Analytic Hierarchy Process (AHP) method [30] is an analysis method for systematic qualitative calculation of the weights of evaluation indicators, which basic principle is dividing the complex evaluation system according to the target level, criterion level, sub-criteria level, indicator level and other levels, and then analyze the influencing factors of the interaction between the influencing factors in the system.

1. Construct a judgment matrix. After the evaluation content is divided and processed, experts in the field of electric energy measurement automation are invited to use the "1–9" scaling method [31] to analyze the impact factors in the two-level evaluation index system. Evaluate the scores to determine the value, and compare them in pairs to obtain the ranking results of the evaluation indicator weights layer by layer, thereby constructing the n-th order judgment matrix P.

$$P = \begin{bmatrix} P_{11} & P_{12} & \cdots & P_{1n} \\ P_{21} & P_{22} & \cdots & P_{2n} \\ \cdots & \cdots & \vdots & \cdots \\ P_{n1} & P_{n2} & \cdots & P_{mn} \end{bmatrix} \tag{1}$$

See Eq. (1), where $p_i (i = 1, 2, \ldots, n)$ represents the impact factor; p_{ij} represents the relative importance indicator of p_i to p_j; n is the order of the judgment matrix.

2. Calculation of the relative weight of evaluation indicators. For the judgment matrix P constructed above, the product R_i of each row element is calculated first, then normalize r_i, and use the square root method to solve the eigenvector α_i' $(i = 1, 2, \ldots n)$, and then the eigenvector set of the judgment matrix P can be obtained $\alpha' = \left(\alpha_1', \alpha_2', \cdots, \alpha_n'\right)$, which can been seen in Eq. (2), (3), (4).

$$R_i = \prod_{j=1}^{n} P_{ij} \tag{2}$$

$$r_i = \sqrt[n]{R_i} \tag{3}$$

$$\alpha'_i = \frac{r_i}{\sum_i^n r_i} \tag{4}$$

3. Consistency test. In order to ensure the accuracy of the judgment matrix P, the value of the random consensus ratio (CR) needs to be determined. The smaller the CR value, the higher the consistency, the higher the accuracy, and the more consistent with reality. When CR < 0.1, it means that it meets the consistency inspection requirements and falls into the acceptable range; otherwise, it does not meet the consistency inspection requirements and no results can be obtained. The specific calculation formula is as follows.

$$CI = \frac{\lambda_{max} - n}{n - 1} \tag{5}$$

$$CR = \frac{CI}{RI} \tag{6}$$

where n represents the order of the judgment matrix; λ_{max} is the maximum eigenvector of the judgment matrix; CI is the general consistency indicator of the judgment matrix; RI is the average random consistency indicator of the judgment matrix, and CR is the judgment consensus ratio of the matrix.

4.2 Determination of Objective Weights

This paper evaluates the probability of one-off events based on the Bayesian grid method, thereby describing the interrelationship between the first probability and the later probability. It has the advantages of dynamic calculation, meets the needs of establishing the risk assessment model of the dynamic intelligent measurement automation system.

Bayes grid method [32] is a belief network. The grid structure is a directed acyclic graph describing the relationship between nodes. The conditions in the network parameters Probability expresses the intensity of influence between nodes, from the parent node (cause) to the child node (outcome), that is, the cause points to the result, that is, BN equals (network structure, network parameter), network structure equals (child node set, directed edge set). Among them, the directed edge set reflects the causal dependence between node variables.

1. Determine the network structure. According to the risk assessment system, the impact factors are divided from static and dynamic aspects to construct a Bayes network diagram of dynamic risk assessment. There are a total of 31 influencing factors for assessing the vulnerability of parent nodes. These factors mainly include static factors and dynamic factors. The static factors are input by investigators on-site inspection and mainly include B and C indicators. The factors are monitored by the measurement automation system, and mainly include A-type indicators.

2. Determine the network parameters. The network parameters represent the basic char-
    acteristics of the evaluation object and the degree of dependency between the parent
    and child nodes, including two parts: node variable parameters and conditional prob-
    ability tables. The node variable parameters are the determination of constitutional
    probability and subsequent probability; the conditional probability table is used to
    quantify the parent the degree of influence of the node on the sub-nodes, that is, the
    level of security risk occurrence of the metering automation system.

The Bayes grid method is used to calculate the objective weight of the evaluation
indicator, and to evaluate the security status of the measurement automation system.
When calculating the score of each layer of the Bayes network (BN) node [32], first set
the full score of each evaluation indicator to 100 points, and multiply the first probability
when all the nodes are in a state that is beneficial to the safety of the measurement
automation system by 100. The calculation formula for the probability P, the weight of
each evaluation indicator in the Bayes network is as follows:

$$P(Y \mid X) = \frac{P(Y \cap X)}{P(Y)} = \frac{P(X)P(Y \mid X)}{P(Y)} \tag{7}$$

$$\alpha''(A_{1n}) = \frac{P(A_{1n} \mid A_1)}{P(A_{11} \mid A_1) + P(A_{12} \mid A_1) + \cdots + P(A_{1n} \mid A_1)} \tag{8}$$

where n is the number of nodes; X and Y are random variables, $Y = y$ is a set of event
hypotheses, $X = x$ is a set of conditions, the probability of impact on event $Y = y$ before
the condition $X = x$ occurs $P(Y)$ is called the first probability. After the condition $X = x$ occurs, the impact $P(Y|X)$ on the event $Y = y$ is called the later probability.

4.3 Improvement of Bayes Grid Method

In order to make the measurement security risk assessment results more accurate, the
weights of nodes listen to the opinions of multiple experts and appropriately integrate
them. In order to reduce the impact of individual experts' subjectivity, this paper adopts
probability allocation [33] and triangular fuzzy method [34] to determine the node
conditional probability table and the root node prior probability table.
    Determine the influence weight of each parent node on the child node and perform
normalization processing, where is the influence weight of the parent node on the child
node.

$$\sum_{i=1}^{m} w_i = 1, w_i \in [0, 1] \tag{9}$$

Calculate the weighted average state distance from the child node to the parent node
according to the following formula:

$$E_s = \sum_i |U_s - C_s|_i \times w_i \tag{10}$$

where U_s represents the state of the parent node; C_s represents the state of the child
node; s represents the state of the node.

Formula (7) is a conventional formula for calculating conditional probability. The improved conditional probability by the method of probability distribution is shown in formula (3–11), where R is the result distribution indicator given by the expert.

$$U_s = \frac{e^{-RE_s}}{\sum_{s_1}^{s_m} e^{-RE_s}} \tag{11}$$

4.4 Determining the Weight of Indicator Combination

The subjective and objective weights calculated by the AHP method and the Bayes network method are combined to assign weights [35] to obtain the comprehensive weights of the evaluation indicators. The calculation formula is:

$$W_i = \frac{\alpha_i' \alpha_i''}{\sum_{i=1}^{n} \alpha_i' \alpha_i''} (i = 1, 2 \ldots, n) \tag{12}$$

5 Experiment and Analysis

Based on the corresponding energy metering index system in Fig. 1, this paper establishes an electrical energy metering automation dynamic risk assessment model. The evaluation process of the model is as follows.

5.1 Calculate Subjective Weight

Comprehensive analysis is carried out from levels to the system risk influence factors, that is, the evaluation index system is divided into target level, criterion level and sub-criteria level. Among them, the target layer is analyzed from both static and dynamic perspectives; the first-level indicator criterion layer mainly includes three aspects: technical risk A, management risk B, and regulatory risk C. The second-level indicator has 11 sub-criteria layers. Among them, the decision goal is the security assurance of the measurement automation system. The three criterion-level elements are technical risk A, management risk B, and regulatory risk C.

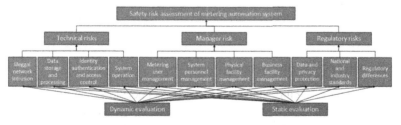

Fig. 2. Hierarchical structure model based on Yaahp.

1. Build a hierarchical structure model. According to the evaluation index system and layering method listed in Fig. 1, this paper generates an analytic hierarchy process model based on Yaahp decision analysis software. This model includes 1 decision objective, 3 criterion-level intermediate elements, and 11 sub-criteria-level intermediate elements, as shown in Fig. 2.

2. Calculate the sorting weight. In this paper, the subjective weight of each evaluation indicator is calculated by formulas (1)–(6). According to the judgment matrix scaling method listed in Session 4, the judgment matrix is established as Table 1. The calculation results of the ranking weight of each criterion-level element to the decision objective are shown in Fig. 3. As shown in Fig. 3, technical risks accounted for 41.47%, management risks accounted for 33.33%, and regulatory risks accounted for 25.55%. Taking the criterion-level evaluation indicator as an example, it is calculated that the maximum eigenvector of the judgment matrix is 3.0324, and the consistency test result CR is 0.0311, which is less than 0.1, which meets the consistency test requirements.

Table 1. Judgment matrix at criterion level.

Criterion layer	A	B	C
A	1.0000	1.5000	1.4000
B	0.6667	1.0000	1.6000
C	0.7143	0.6250	1.0000

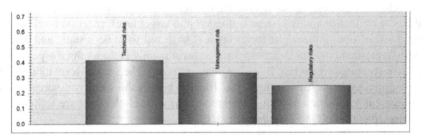

Fig. 3. The ranking weights of decision-making targets by each criterion layer.

5.2 Calculating Objective Weights

In order to test the feasibility of the safety risk assessment model of the electric energy metering automation system proposed in this article, this article adopts the assessment index system proposed in Part 3, using the 31 kinds of assessment indicators listed in Session 3, and using the improved Bayesian grid method to obtain the objective weight of the system risk assessment indicator.

1. Constructing the Bayes network structure. This paper uses Netica Bayes [16] network software and the evaluation index system proposed in Part 3 to generate a system security evaluation risk structure, as shown in Fig. 4.
2. Determine network parameters. As shown in Fig. 4, the quantity to be decided by the model is defined as "Evaluation", which represents whether the measurement system is prone to security risks; the criterion layers of the model are A, B, C and its sub-layers A = $\{A_i, i = 1, 2, 3, 4\}$, B = $\{B_i, i = 1, 2, 3, 4\}$, C = $\{C_i, i = 1, 2\}$.
3. Calculate the score of each level node. Using the node score as the input, calculate the final score of each BN node of level one according to formulas (7)–(11) and the Bayes grid method, and then quantify the weight of each evaluation indicator of level one, and so on, The weight of each evaluation indicator of the measurement automation system and the comprehensive score of safety risk can be obtained. Through calculation, BN node scores and security risk scores at each level of the measurement automation system can be obtained, as shown in Table 2.

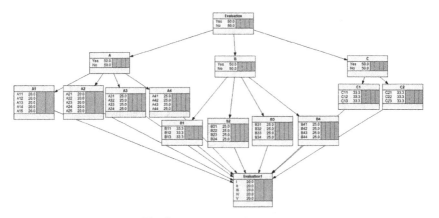

Fig. 4. Bayes network structure.

5.3 Determining the Overall Weight

Taking technical risks A, management risk B, and regulatory risk C in the standard level as the final evaluation indicators, the AHP method and the improved Bayes method are used to calculate the subjective and objective weights of each evaluation indicator, and the evaluation indicators are The subjective and objective weights are combined for weighting, and the comprehensive weight of each evaluation indicator is calculated by formula (12). The calculation results are shown in Table 3.

It can be seen from Table 3 that, among the first-level assessment indicators, the comprehensive weight of the technical risk assessment indicator A is 0.4729, followed by the management indicator B, which has a weight of 0.3242. The weight of class indicator C is 0.2029. Then it is inferred that the safety guarantee goal of the electric energy metering automation system depends to a large extent on the technical reliability, which is consistent with the actual situation.

Table 2. Comprehensive assessment results of safety risks of measurement automation systems.

Criterion layer	Sub-criteria layer	Score of Sub-criteria layer BN node	Indicator weight of sub-criteria layer	Evaluation score of criterion layer	Evaluation indicator weight of criterion layer
A	A$_1$	68.00	0.2306	70.00	0.3888
	A2	70.33	0.2385		
	A3	80.00	0.2713		
	A4	76.50	0.2596		
B	B1	83.00	0.2331	60.00	0.3333
	B2	87.00	0.2444		
	B3	96.00	0.2697		
	B4	90.00	0.2528		
C	C1	62.50	0.5000	50.00	0.2779
	C2	62.50	0.5000		

Table 3. Comprehensive weighting table of evaluation indicators.

Criterion layer	Subjective weight	Objective weight	Comprehensive weight
A	0.4167	0.3888	0.4729
B	0.3333	0.3333	0.3242
C	0.2500	0.2779	0.2029

5.4 Sensitivity Analysis

This paper uses sensitivity analysis to determine the degree of influence of the indicator weight change of the criterion level on the decision evaluation value, so as to guide the management personnel of the electric energy measurement automation system to make decisions at a higher level.

First, as shown in Fig. 5, 6 and 7, the sensitivity analysis curves of A, B, and C indicators respectively. Taking Fig. 5 as an example, the abscissa is the weight change of technical indicators, and the ordinate is the weight change of static evaluation and dynamic evaluation. For indicator A, the more attention is paid to dynamic evaluation methods, the more obvious the advantages of category A indicators are, On the contrary, as shown in Fig. 6 and Fig. 7, for the B and C indicators, compared to dynamic evaluation, the more important the static evaluation method is.

Secondly, by observing Fig. 5, 6 and 7, we can find that there is a change point in all three sensitivity analysis curves. The values of the three change points are (0.4700, 0.5200), (0.2500, 0.5022), (0.1700, 0.5022), and these points marked where the weight

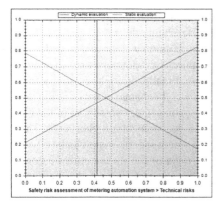

Fig. 5. Sensitivity analysis of A.

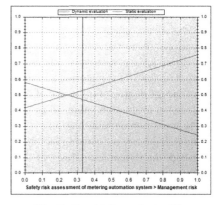

Fig. 6. Sensitivity analysis of B.

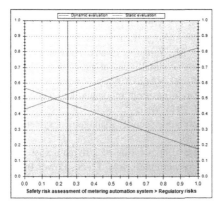

Fig. 7. Sensitivity analysis of C.

ranking changes. Taking the change points (0.4700, 0.5200) in the sensitivity curve of A-type indicators as an example, it shows that when the weight of technical indicators is less than 0.4700, compared with dynamic evaluation, the weight of static evaluation is higher; and when the weight of technical indicators is When it is greater than 0.4700, the dynamic evaluation method accounts for a higher proportion.

6 Conclusion

This paper constructs a safety risk assessment model of electric energy metering automation system based on fuzzy analytic hierarchy process and improved Bayesian network, which includes the construction of a Bayesian network-based metering automation system risk assessment reasoning network structure and a metering automation system security risk assessment system. Corresponding risk assessment calculation model.

The model combines the traditional AHP method with the improved Bayes network method to combine the weights of the evaluation indicators and calculates the comprehensive weights of the evaluation indicators, which improves the rationality of the evaluation indicator, and realizes the comprehensive assessment of subjective and objective risks measurement for automation system. Determine the safety risk level of each evaluation indicator according to the principle of maximum weight, and consider that the system risk level is relatively safe and below requires relevant personnel to conduct an in-depth review of the metering automation system. Finally, through sensitivity analysis, determine the degree of influence of the indicator weight change of the criterion level on the decision evaluation value, so as to guide the management personnel of the electric energy measurement automation system to make decisions at a higher level. Through this model, the key influencing factors leading to system security risks can be effectively identified, the dynamic analysis of the security risks of the measurement automation system is realized, and the basis for reducing the security risks of the measurement automation system can be provided.

References

1. Jin, L., Mesiar, R., Qian, G.: Weighting models to generate weights and capacities in multicriteria group decision making. IEEE Trans. Fuzzy Syst. **26**(4), 2225–2236 (2018)
2. Wang, L., Chen, Y., Yang, M., Yang, S., Zhang, H.: Research on deepening application of measurement operation data and intelligent fault recognition based on cloud platform. Electr. Measure. Instrument. **57**(7), 87–92 (2020)
3. Dong, X., Qiao, K.: Research for orient mode and key technology of China's smart gird. J. Electric Power **25**(4), 287–291 (2010)
4. Zhang, F.: Risk-based information security management system. Netw. Secur. Technol. Appl. **3**, 5–6 (2019)
5. Ma, H.: The construction and application of a dynamic assessment model of information security risks for electric power enterprises. Electr. Power Inform. Commun. Technol. **15**, 22–25 (2017)
6. Santos, R., Marinho, R., Schmitt, G.R.: A framework and risk assessment approaches for risk-based access control in the cloud. J. Netw. Comput. Appl. **74**, 86–97 (2016)
7. Ding, G., Fan, B., Lan, H., Long, T., Wang, J.: Research on smart grid information security threats and defense strategies. Electr. Power Inform. Commun. Technol. **12**(5), 58–63 (2014)
8. Cao, J., Yang, M., Zhang, D., Ming, Y.: Energy internet-information and energy infrastructure integration. South. Power Grid Technol. **8**(4), 1–10 (2014)
9. Yang, S., Tang, B., Yao, J., Li, F.: Automatic intelligent dispatching architecture and key technologies of power grid based on situation awareness. Power Syst. Technol. **38**(1), 33–39 (2014)
10. Sun, Y., Wu, J., Li, G.: Dynamic economic dispatch of power system containing wind farm based on wind speed forecast and stochastic programming. Proc. Chin. Soc. Electr. Eng. **29**(4), 41–47 (2009)
11. Cheng, Z.: Key technologies for optimal dispatching of intelligent distribution networks. Electron Technol. **49**, 186–188 (2020)
12. Mccalley, J.D., Vittal, V., Abi-Samra, N.: An overview of risk based security assessment. Power Engineering Society (1999)
13. Kirschen, S., Jayaweera, D.: Comparison of risk-based and deterministic security assessments. Gener. Trans. Distrib. **1**, 527–533 (2007)
14. Mccalley, D., Fouad, A.: A risk-based security indicator for determining operating limits in stability-limited electric power systems. IEEE Trans. Power Syst. **12**(3), 1210–1219 (1997)
15. Ni, M., James, D.: Online risk-based security assessment. IEEE Trans. Power Syst. **18**(1), 258–265 (2003)

16. Hu, S., Chao, Z., Zhong, H., Xie, M., Luo, W., Liu, M.: Modeling and application of risk consequence value of power grid dispatching operation. Autom. Electr. Power Syst. **40**(7), 54–60 (2016)
17. Chen, W., Jiang, Q., Cao, Y., Han, Z.: Risk assessment of power system voltage collapse. Power Syst. Technol. **19**, 36–41 (2005)
18. Shi, H., et al.: On-line assessment of transmission network operation risk. Power Syst. Technol. **6**, 43–48 (2005)
19. Yong, J., Mccalley, D., Voorhis, V.: Risk-based resource optimization for transmission system maintenance. IEEE Trans. Power Syst. **21**(3), 1191–1200 (2006)
20. Jeyaraj, P.R., Kathiresan, A.C., Asokan, S.P., Rajan, E., Rezk, H.: Power system resiliency and wide area control employing deep learning algorithm. Comput. Mater. Continua **68**(1), 553–567 (2021)
21. Tang, B., Zhang, S., Tang, F., Jun, H.L., Zou, X.Z.: Research and analysis on the annual failure rate of transmission line ice damage. Electr. Measur. Instrument. **57**(17), 29–33 (2020)
22. Li, Q., Yang, X., Liu, Z., Li, Z., Zhao, S., He, X.: Gray cluster analysis-based transmission line galloping classification early warning scheme. Electr. Measure. Instrument. **57**(17), 45–51 (2020)
23. Huang, J., Hua-Qiang, Z.Y.: Power grid security risk assessment based on comprehensive element influence indicator. Sci. Technol. Eng. **17**(23), 201–208 (2017)
24. Dong, M., Nassif, A., Li, B.: A data-driven residential transformer overloading risk assessment method. IEEE Trans. Power Delivery **34**, 387–396 (2019)
25. Shi, X., Qiu, R., Mi, T., He, X., Zhu, Y.: Adversarial feature learning of online monitoring data for operational risk assessment in distribution networks. IEEE Trans. Power Syst. **35**(2), 975–985 (2019)
26. Chen, H., Liu, P., Wu, G., Kuang, B.: Analysis of the impact of low-frequency power grid faults on the operational safety of nuclear power plants. In: Thermal Power Generation, pp. 1–8 (2015)
27. Jiang, Y., Wu, Y., Luan, Y., Zhou, B., Zhao, Z., Zhou, H.: The upgraded functions and applications of the comprehensive load forecasting platform of Yunnan power grid. Yunnan Electr. Power Technol. **46**(6), 44–47 (2018)
28. Ma, X., Zhang, L.: Interpretation of gao's 'protection of critical infrastructure: taking measures to respond to major network security risks facing power grids. Inform. Secur. Commun. Confident. **12**, 73–78 (2019)
29. He, Z., Wang, Y., Liu, J.: The status quo of China's network security grade protection and the study of 2.0 standard system. Inform. Technol. Netw. Secur. **38**(3), 9–14 (2019)
30. Li, X., Liu, X., Gu, Q., Chen, B., Ge, L., Chen, G.: PCA and AHP hybrid risk assessment method for electronic transformer electric energy measurement and trade settlement". Electr. Measur. Instrument. **55**(14), 1–7 (2018)
31. Wang, B., Yin, J., Hu, S., Luo, Y., Pan, Y., Xiao, X.: Research on reliability allocation technology of smart energy meter based on AHP and group decision. Electr. Measur. Instrument. **58**(12), 1–7 (2021)
32. Fu, G.: Analysis and research on probabilistic prediction of wind power based on bayesian method. North China Electric Power University (Beijing) (2019)
33. Wang, J.: Reliability analysis of power lines and their secondary equipment under multiple uncertain factors. University of Electronic Science and Technology of China (2020)
34. Zhang, J.: Research on decision optimization of renewable energy power project investment portfolio. Ph.D. Dissertation, North China Electric Power University (Beijing) (2020)
35. Liu, et al.: Evaluation model of network security situation based on support vector machine and self-adaptive weight. Computer Systems Applications (2018)

Dynamic Encryption of Power Internet of Things Data Based on National Secret Algorithm

Jing Zhou[1], Qian Wu[1], Jin Li[2(✉)], and Jiaxin Li[3]

[1] Shenzhen Power Supply Co. Ltd., Shenzhen 518001, China
[2] School of Cyberspace Security, Beijing University of Posts and Telecommunications,
Beijing 100876, China
li_jin@bupt.edu.cn
[3] Department of Communication Engineering, University of Science and Technology Beijing,
Beijing 100083, China

Abstract. The power Internet of Things is the evolution direction of the power industry. While improving the convenience of power grid operations, it also brings emerging network security risks to traditional industries. The national secret algorithm can integrate the characteristics of the power Internet of things for deployment and application, and improve the industry security of the power Internet of things. Based on the characteristics of the power Internet of Things architecture, the security analysis of the interconnection of power grids is carried out, combined with the calculation points of the national secret algorithm, the business application scenarios of the national secret algorithm in the power industry are discussed, and a kind of electricity information encryption is proposed for the communication requirements of the power terminal and the grid platform. In the transmission scheme, SM2 is applied to the encrypted communication between the power terminal and the power grid platform server to solve the security issues such as identity authentication and encrypted transmission, and to improve the security efficiency of the power Internet of Things.

Keywords: Power internet of things · National secret algorithm · Network security · Encrypted transmission

1 Introduction

Electric energy is an important support for social life and production, and the electric power system is a basic industry that guarantees people's livelihood and promotes social and economic development. The power system has a complex structure. From the perspective of equipment composition, the power system mainly includes power generation equipment, power conversion equipment, power transmission equipment, and distribution and consumption equipment; from the perspective of network composition, the power grid is mainly divided into power transmission grids and power distribution networks [1, 2]. In view of the particularity of the power industry, a complete security monitoring system needs to be established, and massive connections need to be built based on new technologies such as 5G industrial network, narrowband Internet of Things, low-power wide area network LPWAN [3], so as to realize the deployment of data collection and monitoring and control systems. And communications, but also provide support for intelligent power services. The power Internet of Things connects the originally isolated power equipment in series and opens up the information channel of the closed network. While improving the convenience of power system operation, it also brings emerging network security risks to the traditional industry of power. As the encryption algorithm of my country's independent intellectual property rights, the national secret algorithm can be deployed and applied by integrating the characteristics of the power Internet of things to improve the industry security of the power Internet of things [4, 5].

This paper combines the development characteristics of the power Internet of Things, carries out the security analysis of the power Internet of Things [6], combines the calculation points of the national secret algorithm, discusses its application in the power Internet of Things industry, designs a typical application scenario, and proposes a kind of electricity based on SM3 and SM9. The information collection and transmission scheme can effectively support the safe development of power information transmission business and provide reference ideas for industry research and industrial production.

2 Power Internet of Things Architecture and Security Analysis

2.1 Network Architecture

According to the current operating status of power grid transmission, transformation, distribution and power consumption business, the overall framework design of the power Internet of Things is shown in Fig. 1 which according to [7], including 4 layers, of which the perception layer realizes the perception of power terminal equipment information, relying on RFID and other technologies realize the aggregation of terminal status information, realize line monitoring and video monitoring in the transmission link, equipment inspection and video monitoring in the substation link, distribution automation in the power distribution link, equipment monitoring and remote copying in the power utilization link Information collection in various links such as tables and customer relationships; at the network layer, a comprehensive use of wired communications, wireless communications, satellite communications, operator dedicated lines, 5G and other technologies to build a dedicated power communication system has formed a wide-area connection of the power Internet of Things; At the platform layer, the information and data of all links are transmitted to the management platform through the power communication system to realize the integration, analysis and processing of information; at the application layer, through differentiated decision-making on power services in different industries, providing intelligent professional use for different industries Electricity service realizes the high efficiency and intelligence of electric power distribution and power dispatching. Through the power Internet of Things, the existing power system infrastructure resources can be reasonably and effectively integrated, and the efficiency of power utilization can be improved. At the same time, it can promote the rapid access to the grid of new energy industries such as green power, and improve the automation and intelligence of the power system [8].

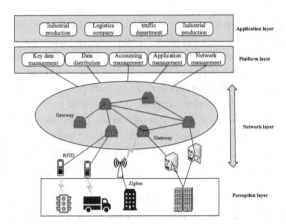

Fig. 1. Power IoT system architecture.

2.2 Safety Analysis

An important feature of the power Internet of Things is the ubiquity of the power communication network. A large number of public network protocols are deployed in the power communication network to improve the level of power grid supervision and at the same time provide a suitable platform for most Internet attack methods. Combined with the power Internet of Things architecture, this article believes that its security risks are mainly reflected in the following aspects.

One is identity authentication. With the evolution of the open interconnection of the power Internet of Things, there are massive network connections in the power Internet of Things [9], especially in the mobile, ubiquitous, hybrid, and wide-area interconnection environment. The power Internet of Things has deployed sensor devices, mobile terminals, how to identify a large number of internal and external network data collection, control and management equipment such as video surveillance, smart meters, charging piles, office computers, etc., to realize the accurate positioning of the business system on the massive power equipment, is to prevent the identification of wrong identification and malicious counterfeiting A problem that must be faced when entering.

The second is the network boundary. In the past, the power grid was an isolated network, which used a proprietary protocol to achieve industrial control, and had a clearer boundary with other networks. The Internet of Power Things is an important content of the Industrial Internet, especially the use of cloud platforms, which further dilutes the boundary between the power grid and the public network. At the same time, with the development of the Internet of Power Things, it is bound to use public network resources such as telecom operators 5G slicing or The MPLS VPN network realizes communication networking, which leads to an increase in the scale of the interface between the power grid and the Internet, weakens the network boundary of the industrial network, and increases the source of risk.

The third aspect is encrypted transmission. There is a large amount of communication data in the power Internet of Things. Whether it is the communication between the perception layer RFID terminal perception network, or the communication between the network layer power terminal and the platform layer system, it must face the encryption problem of transmission data to prevent man-in-the-middle hijacking attacks. To realize the tampering of information such as power data, so the demand for data transmission encryption is huge [10].

3 National Secret Algorithm Application Analysis

The cryptographic algorithm has the function of data encryption and identity authentication, and the deployment of cryptographic equipment at the network boundary can also play a role in network isolation. The deployment of cryptographic algorithms in the power Internet of Things can achieve network and information security protection.

3.1 Overview of National Secret Algorithm

The national secret algorithm is a series of algorithms formulated by the National Cryptography Bureau. The national secret algorithm includes a series of technologies such as cryptographic algorithm programming, algorithm chip, and encryption card implementation. Specific classifications include SM1 symmetric encryption, SM2 cipher hash algorithm, SM3 symmetric encryption algorithm [11], SM4 symmetric encryption algorithm, SM7 block cipher algorithm, SM9 [12] identification cipher algorithm, and ZUC algorithm. The national secret algorithm has a wide range of applications, and is used to encrypt and protect sensitive internal information, administrative information, economic information, etc.: SM1 can be used for enterprise access control management, transmission encryption and storage encryption of various sensitive information within the enterprise to prevent Illegal third parties obtain information content; it can also be used for various security certifications, online banking, digital signatures.

3.2 Power Industry Applications

At present, the communication protocol of some business data of the electric power adopts certain security authentication and encryption methods, but the application scenarios are not common. In most business scenarios, there are still security risks such as theft or forgery of protocol data packets, data tampering, and identity forgery by third parties. The use of domestic cryptographic algorithms is conducive to improving security strength and ensuring the safe operation of the power system. Among them, SM1 and SM7 algorithms are widely used in smart meter card communication; SM3 can be used to verify the integrity of sensitive data, for example, SM3 is used to sign during the transmission of meter data to verify that the power data has not been modified; SM2, SM4, SM9, and ZUC algorithms have good application prospects in the secure transmission of power messages. The following describes the SM2 digital signature generation and verification process, SM2 encryption and decryption process [13, 14].

Generally, users use digital signatures to ensure the non-repudiation of messages. The reliability of messages digitally signed by the signee is determined by the verifier by verifying the signature attached to the message. When the message M needs to be digitally signed, the signer user A first needs to have the public key P_A and the corresponding private key d_A, and the signer user B who receives the signed message needs to have the public key P_A of the user A. User A uses d_A to generate a signature, and user B uses P_A for verification. According to the SM2 standard published by the National Cryptographic Administration [15], the hash value Z_A must be calculated for signature verification in the SM2 digital signature algorithm, $Z_A = H_{256}(ENTL_A \parallel ID_A \parallel a \parallel b \parallel x_G \parallel y_G \parallel x_A \parallel y_A)$. Among them, H_{256} () is the password hash function, which calculates a series of parameters of user A, ENTLA is two bytes converted from the length of user IDA, the parameters of a and b elliptic curve equation, the elliptic curve base point H_{256}, x_A and y_A are the coordinates of P_A. Then user A performs the following operations to realize the digital signature [16]:

(1) Let $M = Z \parallel M$;
(2) Calculate $e = H_v(\overline{M})$ and convert e to an integer;
(3) Generate a random number k in the interval $[1, n - 1]$, where n is the order of the base point G;
(4) Calculate $(x_1, y_1) = [k]G$, and convert x1 to an integer;
(5) Calculate $r = (e + x_1) \bmod n$, if $r = 0$ or $r + k = n$, then return to step 3;
(6) Calculate $s = ((1 + d_A)^{-1} * (k - r*d) \bmod n$, if $s = 0$, return to step 3;
(7) Convert r and s to byte string, then the signature of message M is (r, s).

In order to verify the received message M' and (r', s'), the sign verifier user B also needs system parameters, Z_A and P_A, then implement the following operations:

(1) Does r' belong to $[1, n - 1]$. If yes, proceed to the next step; otherwise, the verification fails;
(2) Does s' belong to $[1, n - 1]$. If yes, proceed to the next step; otherwise, the verification fails;
(3) Set $M' = Z \parallel M'$;
(4) Calculate $e' = H_v(\overline{M})$, and convert e' to an integer;
(5) Convert r' and s' to integers, calculate $t = (r' + s') \bmod n$, if $t = 0$, the verification fails;
(6) Calculate $(x_1', y_1') = [s'] G + [t] P_A$, and convert x_1' to an integer;
(7) Calculate $R = (e + x_1') \bmod n$, check whether R and r' are the same, if they are the same, the digital signature verification passes; otherwise, the verification fails.

The public key encryption algorithm means that the key used by the sender to encrypt data is the public key of the receiver, and the receiver needs to use its own private key to decrypt and restore the plaintext. When the message M needs to be encrypted, the encrypting user A first needs to obtain the elliptic curve system parameters and the public key P_B of the recipient user B, and perform the following operations [17]:

(1) Generate a random number k in the interval $[1, N - 1]$, where N is the order of the elliptic curve point group;
(2) Calculate $C_1 = [k]G = (x_1, y_1)$, and convert the elliptic curve point C_1 into a bit string;

(3) Calculate S = [h]PB, where h is the cofactor of the order, judge whether S is the infinity point, and if so, exit with an error;
(4) Calculate the elliptic curve point $[k]P_B = (x_2, y_2)$, and convert the data types of x_2 and x_2 into bit strings;
(5) Calculate t = KDF $(x_2 \parallel y_2, klen)$, judge whether t is a string of all 0 bits, if so, return Step 1;
(6) Calculate $C_2 = M \oplus t$;
(7) Calculate C_3 = Hash $(x2 \parallel M \parallel y2)$, and finally get the ciphertext $C = C_1 \parallel C_2 \parallel C_3$.

After user B as the decryptor receives the ciphertext C, in order to decrypt the plaintext, the parameters of the elliptic curve system and B's own private key dB are required, and perform the following calculations [18]:

(1) Take out the C_1 part of the ciphertext, convert it to a point on the elliptic curve, and verify whether it satisfies Elliptic curve equation, if satisfied, proceed to the next step, otherwise exit with an error;
(2) Calculate the elliptic curve point S = $[h]C_1$, where h is the cofactor of the order, and judge whether S is infinite
    Stay far away, if yes, exit with an error;
(3) Calculate the elliptic curve point $[d_B]C1 = (x_2, y_2)$, and convert the data types of x_2 and y_2 into bit strings;
(4) Calculate t = KDF d$(x_2 \parallel y_2, klen)$, if t is a string of all 0 bits, exit with an error;
(5) Take out the bit string C_2 from C and calculate $M' = C_2 \oplus t$;
(6) Calculate u = Hash $(x2 \parallel M' \parallel y2)$, judge whether u is equal to C_3, if it is equal to C_3, get the plaintext M', otherwise exit with an error.

4   Typical Applications

Combining with the main scenarios described in the "5G Network Slicing Enable Smart Grid" [19] issued by China Telecom, Huawei and State Grid, this article discusses the encryption problem of power Internet of Things under the scenario of low-voltage power consumption information collection, and gives a solution based on SM2 Plan and analyze its benefits.

4.1   Electricity Acquisition System

As shown in Fig. 2, It's a schematic diagram of the power acquisition system architecture. The access architecture. The power collection system is composed of three parts: power grid platform, data channel, and power terminal. It realizes real-time data collection of power grid and power meter, and completes time-of-use power billing statistics and energy balance. There are many communication methods to realize the transmission of power information, and narrowband communication technology is more commonly used. Through periodic collection, the continuous tracking of the power of important users is realized, and the power service capability is improved.

In the system architecture shown in Fig. 2, there are two practical requirements for security:

One is the problem of encrypted transmission, which requires encrypted transmission protection for the communication between the power grid platform and the power terminal to prevent information from being hijacked and maliciously modified during transmission.

The second is the identity authentication problem of a large number of terminals. Each terminal has a unique code to realize identity identification. However, the power terminal involves a large number of households, and the power grid platform needs to realize the identity authentication of the power terminal.

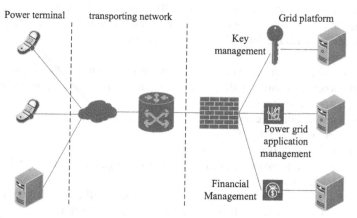

Fig. 2. Schematic diagram of power collection and transmission system architecture.

4.2 SM2-Based Encrypted Communication

Aiming at the identity authentication problem and encrypted transmission problem raised in the previous section, a SM2-based encrypted transmission scheme is proposed, which can simplify the exchange of digital certificates in the encryption process and make the encryption algorithm easier to deploy and apply.

Electricity data collection is mainly the communication between the electric meter terminal and the grid platform, which has the characteristics of many-to-one communication, that is, a large number of electric meter terminals communicate with the grid platform server. It is divided into two business modes. The first is initiated by the meter terminal and reports power data to the grid platform, which is mainly used for periodic power data reporting; the second is initiated by the power grid platform server and is mainly based on power data query Demand. The collection and transmission of power information is a two-way business, which can be encrypted using symmetric or asymmetric cryptographic algorithm methods. No matter which method is used, key management is a considerable problem. The two methods are analyzed separately as follows.

If the symmetric cipher algorithm uses a pre-shared key, the security of the meter terminal will have an excessive impact on the entire power grid because the keys of the two communicating parties are stored on the side of the meter. At the same time, each time the grid platform server needs to query the corresponding key according to the user's identity, it will bring an additional burden of identity authentication, and it is easy to form a denial of service attack of the grid platform server when a large number of power terminals communicate at the same time.

If an asymmetric cryptographic algorithm is used, the meter terminal needs to store the public key of the power supply station and its own private key, and the power grid platform stores its own private key and the public key of the user's meter. The meter terminal uses the public key of the power grid platform when reporting power data. With key encryption, the power grid platform uses its own private key to decrypt data; when the power grid platform sends data to the meter terminal, it uses the public keys of different meter terminals for encryption, and then the meter terminal uses its own private key to decrypt. Due to the asymmetry of the two-way channel between the electricity meter terminal and the grid platform server in the power communication, the amount of information transmitted by the electricity meter terminal to the server is significantly higher than the amount of data transmitted by the server to the power terminal. Therefore, the server does not decrypt the data. The need for key query can reduce the possibility of service being attacked by denial of service.

The above method solves the problem of information encrypted transmission, but there is still the problem of identity authentication. A large number of electric meter terminal meters use the public key of the power grid platform for transmission, and how to perform information identification is a problem that must be considered. To this end, a digital signature mechanism based on SM2 is further proposed. The main idea is that the meter terminal uses a hash algorithm to generate a message digest from the message during message transmission, and then uses its own private key to encrypt the digest. The summary sends the digital signature of the message and the message to the power grid platform server. The server uses the same hash algorithm to calculate the message summary from the received original message, and then uses the public key of the power terminal to match the message. The attached digital signature is decrypted. If the two digests are the same, the receiver can confirm that the message is from the sender [20].

The SM2-based information transmission mechanism is specifically as follows. Take power information reporting as an example, where the meter terminal is referred to as ET and the grid platform server is referred to as ES:

A1. KGC publishes system parameters, and generates ET public key private key and ES public key private key according to the user's power code;

A2. ET stores the personal private key and the public key of the power platform; ES stores the public key of the meter terminal and its own private key.

A3. ET establishes communication with ES. If it is the first data packet initialized, sign it, see the next step for details; otherwise, use ES public key encryption to obtain encrypted data packet EP, and send EP.

A4. ET uses SM3 to compress the message date. The message data only takes the user information code, and the message digest $H = \text{hash(date)}$ is obtained after compression.

A5. ET uses its own private key to use SM2 signature algorithm to sign digest H to obtain signature information SP.

A5. ET attaches the signature information SP to the original information to form a combined data packet, encrypts it to obtain EP, and sends it.

A6. After ES receives the data EP, it uses its own private key to decrypt it, obtains the decrypted data packet DP, and starts the data packet counter to label the received data packet.

A7. If the DP is the first data packet, the combined data packet is obtained, the SP is extracted, the public key corresponding to the ET is calculated, the information to be signed and the signature are input, and SM2 is used to verify whether the signatures are consistent. If they are consistent, the identity is verified the identity of the card.

A8. After the communication ends, the counter of ES is cleared.

5 Experiment Analysis

In the hardware environment, as shown in Fig. 3, this article uses two hosts in the LAN to simulate ET and ES. The communication process between ET and ES is implemented using python socket. The transmission layer protocol uses TCP, and Socket is used to simulate the power information transmission between ET and ES. The transmission content is mainly user power code, power information, current time and other information. The encryption code of SM2 uses the GMSSL open-source package [21–26]. GMSSL is a python implementation of an open-source encryption package that supports SM2/SM3/SM4/SM9 and other national encryption algorithms.

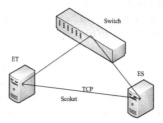

Fig. 3. Hardware environment diagram.

Through analysis, unencrypted information can easily cause information leakage and man-in-the-middle attacks in an open network environment. In the local area network environment, the man-in-the-middle attack test frameworks MITMF and Ettercap can be deployed on the third terminal to implement address spoofing technology to achieve session hijacking, which can easily achieve information tampering. However, after encrypting the transmitted information, the ET sends the encrypted data to the ES, which can realize the protection of the data information. In terms of fighting against middleman hijacking, the data is encrypted using the public key of ES, but it can only be decrypted at the ES platform server, and the middleman cannot perform correct decryption. This transmission can effectively ensure the security of information transmission.

In addition, the first data packet of each power user is the signature data, which plays the role of identity authentication. In this process, ET uses its own private key to encrypt the digest information to realize the signature. The ES end receives the signature and needs to use its own private key to decrypt the information. Encoding of ET, and then calculating the public key of ET, there is a problem of ES end response when a large number of users access, but because ES end only verifies the first data packet of each ET, subsequent communication is no longer verified, so ES is also reduced. The response pressure forms the protection of ES.

6 Conclusion

The power Internet of Things is the focus of the construction of the power industry. It opens up the originally isolated power equipment network, realizes the communication series of a large number of equipment, builds the information channel of the traditional industry, and improves the operation efficiency of the power system. This article combines the development characteristics of the power Internet of Things, carries out a security analysis of the interconnection and intercommunication of power, combines the calculation points of the national secret algorithm, discusses its application in the power Internet of things industry, and presents the encryption between the SM2-based power terminal and the grid platform server. The communication mode solves security issues such as identity authentication and encrypted transmission, and provides reference ideas for industry research and industrial production. The future work has two aspects. One is to expand the application of encrypted communication in other power business scenarios to further improve the security of the power grid; on the other hand, the current mechanism is only based on the business characteristics of power transmission, and the first data packet is used for identity authentication. In other businesses, the optimization of the number of identity authentication can be studied, and the next step is to seek effective methods to enhance identity authentication under the premise of controlling ES pressure.

References

1. Fang, X., Misra, S., Xue, G., Yang, D.: Smart grid-the new and improved power grid: a survey. IEEE Commun. Surv. Tutor. **14**(4), 944–980 (2012)
2. Aoufi, S., Derhab, A., Guerroumi, M.: Survey of false data injection in smart power grid: attacks, countermeasures and challenges. J. Inf. Secur. Appl. **54**, 2214–2226 (2020)
3. Yang, W., Mao, W., Zhang, J., Zou, J.: Narrowband wireless access for low-power massive internet of things: a bandwidth perspective. IEEE Wirel. Commun. **24**(3), 138–145 (2017)
4. Kimani, K., Oduol, V., Langat, K.: Cyber security challenges for IoT-based smart grid networks. Int. J. Crit. Infrastruct. Prot. **25**, 36–49 (2019)
5. Shrestha, M., Johansen, C., Noll, J., Roverso, D.: A methodology for security classification applied to smart grid infrastructures. Int. J. Crit. Infrastruct. Prot. **28**, 100342 (2020)
6. Wang, Y., Wu, L., Yun, Y.: Security authentication method of terminal trusted access in smartgrid. Int. J. Secur. Appl. **9**(7), 337–346 (2015)
7. Sun, H., Guo, Q., Zhang, B., Wu, W.: Integrated energy management system: concept, design, and demonstration in China. IEEE Electrific. Mag. **6**(2), 42–50 (2018)
8. Lu, Q., Cui, W.: Research on security monitoring and analysis technology of ubiquitous power internet of things germinal layer. Inf. Technol. **44**(2), 121–125 (2020)
9. Li, P.Z., Xiao, Z.F., Chen, Z.W.: The research on communication technology matching of power terminal communication access network. Procedia Comput. Sci. **155**, 785–790 (2019)
10. Luo, Z., Xie, J.H., Gu, W.: Development of power grid information security support platformbased on SM2 cryptosystem. Autom. Electr. Power Syst. **38**(6), 68–74 (2014)

11. Tong, W.: The research of the SM2, SM3 and SM4 algorithms in WLAN of transformer substation. In: 3rd International Conference on Electronic Information Technology and Computer Engineering (EITCE), pp. 276–283 (2019)
12. Tian, C., Wang, L., Li, M.: Design and implementation of SM9 Identity based Cryptograph algorithm. In: 2020 International Conference on Computer Network, Electronic and Automation (ICCNEA), pp. 96–100 (2020)
13. Ding, F., Long, Y., Wu, P.: Study on secret sharing for SM2 digital signature and its application. In: 14th International Conference on Computational Intelligence and Security (CIS), pp. 205–209 (2018)
14. Yang, A.: Provably-secure (Chinese government) SM2 and simplified SM2 key exchange protocols. Sci. World J. (2014)
15. National cryptography authority, SM2 elliptic curve public key cryptography algorithm, pp. 65–68 (2010). https://www.occa.gov.cn/sca/xwdt/2020-12/08/content_1060792.shtml
16. Wang, Z., Zhang, Z.: Overview on public key cryptographic algorithm SM2 based on elliptic curves. J. Inf. Secur. Res. 16(5), 12–17 (2016)
17. Wang, Z.H., Zhang, Z.F.: Overview of SM2 elliptic curve public key cryptography algorithm. Inf. Secur. Res. 2(11), 972–982 (2016)
18. Bai, L., Zhang, Y., Yang, G.: SM2 cryptographic algorithm based on discrete logarithm problem and prospect. In: 2012 2nd International Conference on Consumer Electronics, Communications and Networks (CECNet), pp. 1294–1297 (2012)
19. Xia, X.: A survey on 5G network slicing enabling the smart grid. In: 2019 IEEE 25th International Conference on Parallel and Distributed Systems (ICPADS), pp. 911–916 (2019)
20. Hong, N., Zheng, X.: A security framework for internet of things based on sm2 cipher algorithm. In: 2013 International Conference on Computational and Information Sciences, pp. 13–16 (2013)
21. Guo, Q., Ke, Z., Wang, S., Zheng, S.: Persistent fault analysis against SM4 implementations in libraries crypto++ and GMSSL. IEEE Access 9, 63636–63645 (2021)
22. Jia, R., Xin, Y., Liu, B., Qin, Q.: Dynamic encryption and secure transmission of terminal data files. Comput. Mater. Continua 71(1), 1221–1232 (2022)
23. Li, L., Xu, C., Yu, X., Dou, B., Zuo, C.: Searchable encryption with access control on keywords in multi-user setting. J. Cyber Secur. 2(1), 9–23 (2020)
24. Ali, M., Xu, C., Hussain, A.: Authorized attribute-based encryption multi-keywords search with policy updating. J. New Media 2(1), 31–43 (2020)
25. Feng, T., Pei, H., Ma, R., Tian, Y., Feng, X.: Blockchain data privacy access control based on searchable attribute encryption. Comput. Mater. Continua 66(1), 871–890 (2021)
26. Doss, S., Paranthaman, J., Gopalakrishnan, S., Duraisamy, A.: Memetic optimization with cryptographic encryption for secure medical data transmission in IoT-based distributed systems. Comput. Mater. Continua 66(2), 1577–1594 (2021)

Research on Power Mobile Internet Security Situation Awareness Model Based on Zero Trust

Zaojian Dai[1,2(✉)], Nige Li[1,2], Yong Li[1,2], Guoquan Yuan[3], Xinjian Zhao[3], Ran Zhao[3], and Fan Wu[4]

[1] Institute of Information and Communication, Global Energy Interconnection Research Institute, Nanjing 210003, China
daizaojian@geiri.sgcc.com.cn
[2] State Grid Key Laboratory of Information and Network Security, Nanjing 210003, China
[3] State Grid Jiangsu Electric Power Company, Nanjing 210003, China
[4] Computer Science Department, Tuskegee University, Tuskegee, AL 36088, USA

Abstract. With the rapid development of modern mobile Internet services, the business architecture and network environment of power mobile Internet are also undergoing significant changes. In view of the current network security protection method of tradition is very difficult to adapt to the safety of power for mobile business diversification demand, unable to effectively defense complex network attacks and threats, internal network security accidents frequent this present situation, proposed a based on the difference of privacy and UEBA (User Entity behaviors Analytics) of the power of mobile Internet network security situational awareness model. UEBA is used to realize network situation awareness of power mobile interconnection business terminals, and the privacy of user data is effectively protected by introducing differential privacy mechanisms. At the same time, aiming at the shortcoming of a high false-positive rate of first access warning in UEBA, the optimization of the first access evaluation mechanism is introduced, and the recommendation score between users and visiting entities is predicted by the method based on the recommendation system. Experimental analysis shows that the proposed method can effectively reduce the false alarm rate of first access warnings. And compare our method with the general situation awareness scheme, it has obvious advantages.

Keywords: Zero trust · Differential privacy · UEBA · Situational awareness

1 Introduction

With the rapid development of mobile offices and other services, the business architecture and network environment of power mobile interconnection have undergone significant changes. However, the traditional network security architecture based on boundary protection is difficult to adapt to the safety of power for mobile business diversification demand, for some advanced persistent threat attacks cannot be an effective defense, such as new DDoS attacks [1], network safety accidents happen frequently, for enterprises have been aware of the urgency of the problem, using the traditional security defense technology can only separate one or a few indicators reflect the status of the network, already cannot satisfy the administrator timely grasp the demand, the security situation in the network as a whole is not able to help them solve from internal security problems.

In the era of big data, internal threats often bring hazards such as data leakage [2] and are difficult to detect due to their concealment and transparency. The main reason is that internal attackers have relevant knowledge of the organization and can access the core assets and sensitive data of the organization to attack the assets, business, and reputation of the organization. Therefore, the weakest link of security is human, and the essence of zero-trust security is to change from the traditional network boundary as the center to the user identity as the center, identity and access control as the cornerstone of trust reconstruction. Only by establishing a user-centered network security situation analysis system can we discover and terminate internal threats in a more timely manner and prevent information leakage in the bud.

Network security situational awareness technology also gradually become a hot research topic in the field of network security in recent years. The connection of situational awareness that focuses on global early warning of external attacks and User and Entity Behavior Analytics (UEBA) that focuses on internal threat detection can efficiently solve account security and data security issues in the dimensions of people, assets, and applications. UEBA is a new method to detect user activities and internal attacks within an organization. It emphasizes the depiction of normal behaviors of users and entities through machine learning and the use of data models and rules, to detect abnormal behaviors. Compared with traditional misuse detection, UEBA performs anomaly detection by characterizing normal behavior and establishing a baseline, so it can detect abnormal behavior and unknown threats.

In recent years, the issue of user data privacy has also received great attention. During data transmission in organizations, there is little or no privacy protection for users, which leads to many problems such as user data theft and sensitive information disclosure. Therefore, because of insider threats, before using advanced machine learning and artificial intelligence technology to analyze data, privacy protection is still required before data delivery.

This paper proposes a power mobile interconnection network security situation awareness model based on differential privacy and UEBA. UEBA is used to conduct network situation awareness on power mobile interconnection service terminals. At the same time, the privacy of user data is effectively protected by introducing a differential privacy mechanism. At the same time, because of the shortcomings of the widespread deployment of the first access warning in the UEBA service, the optimization of the first access evaluation mechanism is introduced, and the recommendation score between the user and the visiting entity is predicted through the method based on the recommendation system, thereby reducing the false alarm rate of the first access warning. The paper is organized as follows. Section 2 is the research introduction and existing problems in related fields. Section 3 puts forward the concrete model of this paper and elaborates its details. In Sect. 4, experiments are carried out to prove the proposed scheme. Section 5 is the summary of the thesis and the prospect of future work.

2 Related Work

Bass first introduced the concept of cyberspace situational awareness in 1999 [3, 4]. He believes that network situational awareness based on convergence is the development direction of network management. Since Bass, relevant researches have been focused on the network security situation, and gradually studied the concept of network security situation awareness. Although current researches mostly divide network security situation awareness into three functional modules of situation extraction, situation assessment, and situation prediction, there are still different researchers who divide network security situation awareness into different stages. Therefore, scientific and comprehensive definitions of network security situational awareness and reasonable division of different stages are still problems to be discussed and solved.

At present, the domestic mainstream situational awareness solutions can be roughly divided into three types from the technical implementation: situational awareness based on traffic, situational awareness based on SIEM (Security Information Event Management), and situational awareness based on product integration. Literature [5] on the analysis of the three traditional solutions, the thought and the traditional compared to situational awareness based on flow, SIEM UEBA (User Entity behaviors Analytics, User Entity Behavior analysis) don't care about all kinds of mass alarm, don't focus on one of the top events, but the "abnormal users" and "User exception" Behavior has the high hit rate, make the abnormal events of the alarm is more in line with the business scenario. UEBA emphasizes the use of machine learning and data models and rules to describe the normal behaviors of users and entities and detect abnormal behaviors. Compared with traditional misuse detection, UEBA performs anomaly detection by characterizing normal behavior and establishing a baseline, so it can detect abnormal behavior and unknown threats. At the same time, with the development of deep learning, due to its many advantages, it is more and more introduced into the field of network security.

The combination of security information Event Management (SIEM) and UEBA is used in most enterprise management. Many enterprises at home and abroad have independently developed products based on UEBA. Exabeam predicts the event schedule through a series of expert rules and service logs [6]. GURUKUL focuses on detecting threats that exceed signature, rule, and pattern capabilities, predicting risk scores, and finding and stopping threats immediately; LogRhythm quickly displays events and their priorities through multidimensional behavior analysis [7]. What all of these products have in common is that they are designed to detect insider threats, data breaches, identity theft, and other aberrant behavior by normal users. In China, Qiming Stars is used to detect abnormal behaviors such as data leakage and account number leakage by employees. Guan'an [8] is also used for data breach analysis. In the application Security Report released by Gartner in 2018, there are fewer and fewer single UEBA products, and their development trend is to be merged into other products as a core engine to play a role [9].

Situational awareness requires the acquisition of large amounts of data for storage and analysis, but in the process, there is little privacy protection for users, which can lead to the disclosure of private data. The need to protect stored data increases. S. Nithyanatham and g. singaravel [10] proposed a hybrid deep learning framework for privacy protection in geographically distributed data centers. Differential privacy, first formally introduced in a seminal work by Dwork [11], is considered a powerful tool for providing this protection. Differential Privacy is a Privacy protection method based on data distortion. Based on a solid mathematical foundation, differential Privacy is defined strictly and a quantitative evaluation method is provided, which makes the Privacy protection level provided by data sets with different parameter processing comparable. Differential privacy makes the difference in the output result due to the presence or absence of a single piece of information trivial, thus providing privacy for a given piece of information so that an attacker cannot determine its existence or absence. In this paper, we combine differential privacy and UEBA for anomaly detection [12].

3   Network Security Situational Awareness Model

This paper proposes a power mobile Internet security situation awareness model based on differential privacy and User Entity Behavior Analytics (UEBA). We assume that data collection and privacy protection are set in the client, and situation awareness is deployed in the organization's mobile security monitoring platform. The application scenario of this model is shown in Fig. 1.

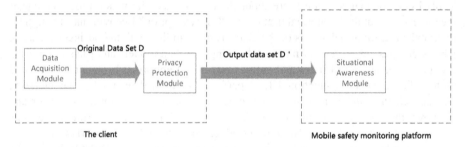

Fig. 1. Model application scenario.

In this model, we set up a privacy protection agent, using a differential privacy basis to protect data. At the same time, to prevent internal threats, real-time analysis of user behavior based on UEBA, an abnormal warning is issued. The network security situational awareness model based on differential privacy and UEBA is shown in Fig. 2.

The model is divided into five levels: situation data acquisition, situation data preprocessing, privacy protection processing, situation analysis, and situation prediction.

Data collection is to collect the perceived user terminal environment data based on predefined network security situation indicators. It mainly receives the situation information from massive multi-source heterogeneous data and converts it into an understandable format to provide original data for data preprocessing. Data preprocessing is to standardize and classify the original data through a data processing algorithm, generate standardized data, extract characteristic data or situation factors from it, ensure the comprehensiveness and accuracy of data, and lay a foundation for situation analysis.

Considering internal threats, a privacy protection processing module is added to the model, which protects user data at the client end and then sends it to the situational awareness module for analysis to prevent sensitive data leakage and internal attacks.

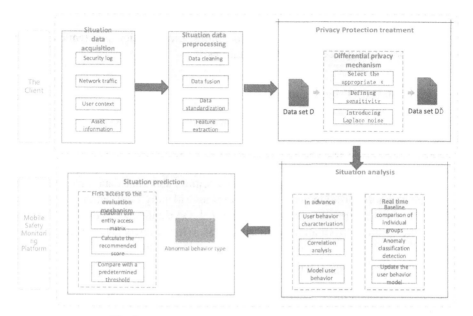

Fig. 2. Network security situational awareness model.

Situation analysis is the core of the network security situation awareness model. It is a dynamic process of understanding the current security situation. It identifies whether the user behavior deviates from the normal range to obtain the security status of the network.

Based on security situation information, current network security situation, and network situation history, situation prediction predicts the changing trend of future network situations, gives feedback results, and determines whether to issue an alarm.

3.1 Situation Data Collection

This link is mainly used to collect network status-related data, including logs and log agents, security products, external intelligence, internal scanning, and manual information entry. These data can be roughly divided into three categories of mobile terminal user data, including user identity data, device entity identity data, and user behavior data [13].

User identity data includes registration information, user asset information, VPN logs, OA logs, access control face brush logs, work order logs, security logs, etc. Device entity identity data includes IP address, MAC address, network traffic, threat intelligence, application system logs, etc. User behavior data is divided into network behavior information and terminal behavior information. Through Deep Packet Inspection (Deep Packet Inspection, DPI) system including log the source address, the destination address, source port, destination port, and protocol type, audit information, application session identification information, application session flow statistics, network transport layer flow statistics, application-layer traffic statistical information such as network behavior.

The Endpoint Detection and Response (EDR) system collect terminal behavior information such as memory operations, disk operations, file operations, system calls, port calls, network operations, and registry operations.

3.2 Situation Data Preprocessing

The data collected in the network environment is complex and diverse. To comprehensively extract characteristic data or situation factors, it is necessary to process the data to obtain standardized data and save the perceived network data in real-time, to improve the speed and efficiency of perception.

Data cleaning according to preset the rules to remove abnormal data values, to fill the gap value, the normalization processing various user identity information (registration information, user information assets, VPN, journal, OA), entity status data (IP address, MAC address, threat information, application system logs), safety data sources (such as packets, flow, log files, alarm, threat source), etc., according to the needs of the database storage and indexing, and complete the standardization of data.

Data fusion refers to the comprehensive processing of multi-sensor or multi-source information to obtain more accurate and reliable conclusions. In data fusion, raw data is related to making it more meaningful (for example, the IP address associated with the user), and provide a rich context for refining the historical record (for example, authentication and equipment use, port protocol), to be prepared for the next trend of feature extraction is the typical algorithm of data fusion with bayesian networks and D - S evidence reasoning.

The situation feature extraction is carried out by a machine learning algorithm, which provides input for the subsequent modeling analysis of user behavior anomaly and entity behavior anomaly. Currently, commonly used algorithms include convolutional neural networks and particle swarm optimization algorithm [14].

After obtaining the situation characteristics, the clustering algorithm is used for classification. Due to the richness of clustering methods, it is very important to compare various methods and determine which method is suitable for a given data set [15].

3.3 Privacy Protection

The privacy protection module carries out differential privacy protection for the collected data and sends the processed data set to the mobile monitoring platform.

If the difference between adjacent data sets D_1 and D_2 is at most one data record, given that the random algorithm K provides differential privacy, Range (K) represents the value Range of the random algorithm K, $Pr[*]$ represents the probability that the query result is S after the data set is added with the same random noise. For the two data sets D_1 and D_2 with only one record difference, The probability of obtaining the same value should be so close that even if an attacker has sufficient background knowledge, it is impossible to find individual user privacy data in the final result. Algorithm K satisfies the output result $S \in Range(K)$ on D1 and D2 by Eq. (1):

$$Pr[K(D_1) = S] \le e^{\varepsilon} \times Pr[K(D_2) = S] \tag{1}$$

where, ε is the privacy protection budget factor, which is used to measure the intensity of privacy protection. The value of ε is directly proportional to the protection effect and inversely proportional to the degree of data distortion.

We use the Laplace mechanism to add noise to realize differential privacy. Firstly, we select an appropriate privacy protection budget factor ε, ranging from 0 to 1, according to the requirements of privacy protection. Then we define sensitivity Δf, which stands for a mapping function $f : D \rightarrow R^d$, which represents a mapping of data set D to a D-dimensional space, and its maximum range of variation, such as the number of queries, sensitivity is 1.

$$\Delta f = \max_{D1,D2} ||f(D1) - f(D2)|| \tag{2}$$

Add random variable x satisfying Laplace distribution to $f(D)$, where, the probability density function of random variable x is

$$p(x|\mu, \lambda) = \frac{1}{2\lambda} e^{-\frac{|x-\mu|}{\lambda}} \tag{3}$$

μ is the location parameter, which defaults to 0. $\lambda > 0$ is a scale parameter, which satisfies:

$$Lap(\lambda) = \frac{\Delta f}{\varepsilon} \tag{4}$$

The final return result A(D) satisfies:

$$A(D) = f(D) + (Lap_1\left(\frac{\Delta f}{\varepsilon}\right) \cdots Lap_d\left(\frac{\Delta f}{\varepsilon}\right))^T \tag{5}$$

Finally, the privacy protection module sends the data set D 'obtained after processing by the differential privacy mechanism to the mobile security monitoring platform.

3.4 Situation Analysis

Situation analysis is the core of network security situation awareness. By analyzing characteristic data, we can get the relevant factors that affect network security situations. Based on these factors, we can identify network attacks and detect network threats. UEBA through the analysis of the behavior of internal users and assets, these objects are portrait building, continuous learning, and behavior to form a picture of the baseline testing different from baseline behavior as the entry point, combined with dimension reduction, clustering, and decision tree-based computing model of abnormal behavior, the comprehensive score of users and assets, to identify behavior, the ghost has the latent threat of invasion and external invasion behavior, thus warning ahead of time.

Based on the idea of UEBA, the situational awareness module analyzes the behavioral characteristic data in advance, characterizes the user behavior, makes the association analysis, establishes the continuous user behavior baseline, and forms the user behavior model.

Behavior characterization refers to the continuous tracking and portrait of the behaviors of all users and entities based on time series [16]. For example, attributes of the user include the accounts, applications, files, devices, online time, and location. The mapping process is the process of establishing a baseline through which all network activities of users and entities are completely visualized.

Association analysis can be divided into three types: situational association, rule association, and behavior association. We mainly use behavior association, which analyzes User and Entity Behavior Analytics (UEBA) security events in multiple dimensions based on typical security scenarios. Specifically, real-time correlation analysis is conducted from four dimensions of user, device, application, and data to form an automatic and continuous analysis process.

In the stage of behavior modeling, individual behavior is analyzed from multidimensional time series, location, and region. Not only individual behavior is analyzed, but also group behavior is analyzed. Based on the data of behavior characterization and association analysis, group baseline and individual baseline are established.

First, define the individual baseline for us to evaluate the user's behavior in the past time; The group baseline allows us to assess the behavior of users based on the behavior of the group to which they belong. Second, the meaning of user behavior must be defined. This involves determining the temporal granularity of the analysis (hourly, daily, weekly, and so on) and identifying a set of characteristics that describe the access patterns of each user over each period. Finally, the user behavior model is constructed by learning user behavior characteristics, association analysis, and baseline establishment.

Through the user behavior model trained by previous data, real-time situation analysis of user behavior is carried out. This is to identify deviations from the normal baseline by comparing real-time user behavior data with individual and group behavior. There are various algorithms for calculating the deviation from the baseline of behavior, using density, mean, variance, similarity, and so on. If it is determined that the behavior deviates from the normal baseline, machine learning algorithms such as isolated forest, SVM, k-means clustering are used for abnormal behavior classification detection. Because different algorithms have their limitations, it is difficult to have one algorithm suitable for all scenarios, and the results of abnormal detection need to be verified and fed back. Otherwise, the data is added to the dataset to update and train the user behavior model.

3.5 Situation Prediction

Situation prediction is the purpose of network security situation awareness. For example, A.A. Almazroi and R. Sher use the tree based ensemble model to predict the case of COVID-19 -19 in Saudi Arabia [17]. Given the high false positive rate of the first visit alarm [18], we can introduce the first visit evaluation mechanism when the result of a situation analysis is the first visit alarm. L. Palaniappan and K. Selvaraj [19] overview and rating similarity analysis of recommendation system using deep learning. The specific flow of this process is shown in Fig. 3.

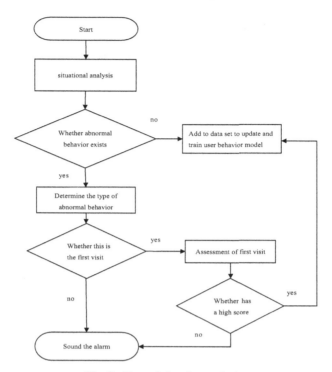

Fig. 3. Flow of situation analysis.

The specific steps of the first visit assessment are:

(1) Suppose an access recommendation system contains M users and N entities, first
establish the user entity access matrix:

$$R = \{r_{ij}\}_{m \times n} \tag{6}$$

r_{ij} indicates the number of times the user accesses the network entity. If the user
has not accessed the network entity, r_{ij} is 0.

(2) The access recommendation score is calculated based on the user's entity access
preference and the user group portrait of the entity. Entities from the user access
preference Angle calculation recommended scores method includes: use of collaborative filtering recommendation algorithm based on project ideas, by studying
the user access to the entity's history data, calculate the history access entities and
the similarity to access the target entity, and using the similarity as the weight,
weighted for each user's access to the entity's visits, to get access to target entity
recommendation scores $S(u_i)$.

$$S(u_i) = \sum_{j=1}^{n} Q_1 \times r_{ij} \tag{7}$$

where, u_i represents the user, Q_1 represents the similarity between entities. And we can
use the cosine similarity algorithm and Pearso similarity algorithm to calculate.

From the view of the access user group portrait of entity recommendation scores method includes: by studying the past visited the users of the entity data, calculate the user and the current user's similarity, and using the similarity as the weight, the weighted number of visits to the target entities, each user to get access to target entity recommendation scores $S(e_j)$.

$$S(e_j) = \sum_{i=1}^{m} Q_2 \times r_{ij} \qquad (8)$$

where, e_i represents the entity and Q_2 represents the similarity between users. The final access recommendation score is $S(u_i, e_j)$.

$$S(u_i, e_j) = S(u_i) + S(e_j) \qquad (9)$$

(3) Compare the access recommendation score $S(u_i, e_j)$ with the predetermined threshold, if it is greater than the predetermined threshold, the first access alert is suppressed, and the data is added to the dataset to update and train the user behavior model. If it falls below a predetermined threshold, an alarm is still emitted. The ideal predetermined threshold is trained by selecting several different recommendation scores in the early stage in this mechanism, and the results are verified and fed back. Finally, the recommendation score with the highest accuracy is selected as the predetermined threshold.

4   Experimental Proof

The experiment in this paper was conducted in the Python environment. We collected the visits (days) of 100 users to some network entities in a month as the experimental data set, 70% as the training set, and 30% as the test to verify the effectiveness of the first access evaluation algorithm.

Firstly, the user entity access matrix is established, including 70 users (u_1–u_{70}) and 10 network entities (e_1–e_{10}). We take 30 users in the test set as first-time users accessing the network entity e_{10}, and use the algorithm designed in this paper to test the recommended score of first-time users accessing the network entity. When calculating the recommended score $S(e_j)$ of the target entity e_{10}, the result score is multiplied by the reduction coefficient 0.1.

The calculated access score compares the access times of these 30 users in the source data, as shown in Fig. 4 (Table 1):

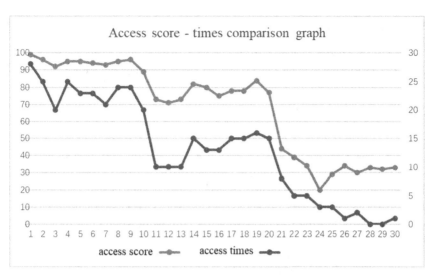

Fig. 4. Access score-times comparison diagram

Table 1. Comparison with the general scheme

	General situational awareness schemes	Network security situational awareness model based on zero trust
Access control	Take the network boundary as the center and use traditional security protection policies	Based on the concept of zero trust, user identity as the center, continuous monitoring
Privacy protection	There is no	Differential privacy is used to protect sensitive user data from being leaked
The first visit	Issue first access alert	Starting the first access evaluation mechanism greatly reduces the false alarm rate of the first access alarm
Safety protection	It is difficult to effectively protect against external advanced persistent threats and endogenous threats	UEBA technology can not only guard against external attacks but also detect abnormal behaviors of normal internal users, ensuring endogenous security

As can be seen from the diagram, in the source data access times more users on the network entities also have higher recommendation scores, we will be the ideal threshold is set to 70 points, in the heart of the test users to have 66.7% of the first visit to the alarm can be suppressed, compared with other schemes in general on the first visit to alert Settings, first visit to alert our scheme can effectively reduce the rate of false positives.

Compared with the general situation awareness scheme, our scheme has more advantages. The following is a comprehensive analysis and comparison.

5   Future Research Directions

This paper introduces a security situation awareness model of power mobile Internet based on zero trust. This model can be used on the client and mobile security monitoring platform. Compared with other schemes, this scheme can effectively prevent external attacks and internal threats, and protect users' private data to prevent sensitive data leakage. We propose an access recommendation method based on collaborative filtering to reduce the false positives from these alerts. The work to be done in the future is to further study the user behavior analysis of this scheme to improve the accuracy of abnormal behavior classification. It is also possible to implement our proposed solution in a federated learning environment, where the data comes from different nodes, and then execute our proposed model on the provider side to protect the user's private data.

Funding Statement.   This work is supported by the science and technology project of State Grid Corporation of China Funding Item: "Research on Dynamic Access Authentication and Trust Evaluation Technology of Power Mobile Internet Services Based on Zero Trust" (Grand No. 5700-202158183A-0-0-00).

Conflicts of Interest.   The authors declare that they have no conflicts of interest to report regarding the present study.

References

1. Sood, I., Sharma, V.: Computational intelligent techniques to detect ddos attacks: a survey. J. Cyber Secur. **3**(2), 89–106 (2021)
2. Si, D., Hua, C., Yang, H.: A security threat analysis system based on machine learning. Inf. Technol. Netw. Secur. **4** (2019)
3. Bass, T.: Multisensor data fusion for next generation distributed intrusion detection systems. In: Proceedings of the IRIS National Symposium on Sensor and Data Fusion, vol. 24, no. 28, pp. 24–27. COAST Laboratory, Purdue University, 1 (1999)
4. Bass, T.: Intrusion systems and multisensory data fusion. Commun. ACM **43**(4), 99–105 (2000)
5. Xu, F.: Status and development analysis of network security situation awareness technology based on UEBA. Netw. Secur. Technol. Appl. **10**, 10–13 (2020)
6. Exabeam: User and Entity Behavior Analytics (2020). https://www.exabeam.com/siem-guide/ueba
7. Logrhythm: User and Entity Behavior Analytics (UEBA) (2020). http://logrhythm.com/-sol utions/security/user-and-entity-behavior-analytics
8. Hu, S.Y.: Analysis of data leakage based on UEBA. Inf. Secur. Commun. Secur. **000**(008), 26–28 (2018). (in Chinese)
9. Litan, A., Sadowski, G., Bussa, T.: Market guide for user and entity behavior analytics(G00349450) (2018). https://www.gartner.com/en/documents/-3872885

10. Nithyanantham, S., Singaravel, G.: Hybrid deep learning framework for privacy preservation in geo-distributed data centre. Intell. Autom. Soft Comput. **32**(3), 1905–1919 (2022)
11. Dwork, C., Pottenger, R.: Toward trolling privacy. J. Am. Med. Inform. Assoc. **20**(1), 102–108 (2013)
12. Rashid, F., Ali, M.: User and event behavior analytics on differentially private data for anomaly detection. In: 2021 7th IEEE International Conference on Big Data Security on Cloud (BigDataSecurity), IEEE International Conference on High Performance and Smart Computing, (HPSC) and IEEE International Conference on Intelligent Data and Security (IDS), pp. 81–86. IEEE (2021)
13. Mo, F., Shuai, Jia, S.: Application of user entity behavior analysis technique based on machine learning in account anomaly detection. Commun. Technol. **53**(05), 1262–1267 (2020)
14. Lei, J.: User behavior feature extraction and safety warning modeling technology. J. China Acad. Electron. Sci. **14**(04), 368–372 (2019)
15. Mostafa, S.M.: Clustering algorithms: taxonomy, comparison, and empirical analysis in 2d datasets. J. Artif. Intell. **2**(4), 189–215 (2020)
16. Xie, K., Wu, J.: User portrait and user behavior analysis based on big data platform. China Inf. **000**(003), 100–104 (2018)
17. Almazroi, A.A., Sher, R.: COVID-19 cases prediction in saudi arabia using tree-based ensemble models. Intell. Autom. Soft Comput. **32**(1), 389–400 (2022)
18. Tang, B., Hu, Q., Lin, D.: Reducing false positives of user-to-entity first-access alerts for user behavior analytics. In: 2017 IEEE International Conference on Data Mining Workshops (ICDMW), pp. 804–811. IEEE (2017)
19. Palaniappan, L., Selvaraj, K.: Profile and rating similarity analysis for recommendation systems using deep learning. Comput. Syst. Sci. Eng. **41**(3), 903–917 (2022)

A New Transparent File Encryption Method Based on SM4 for Android Platform

Yuheng Li[1], Yongzhong Li[2(✉)], and Shipeng Zhang[3]

[1] Suzhou Institute of Technology, Jiangsu University of Science and Technology,
Suzhou 215600, China
[2] School of Computer Science and Engineering, Taizhou Institute of Science and Technology
NJUST, Taizhou 225300, China
liyongzhong61@163.com
[3] School of Computer Science, Jiangsu University of Science and Technology, Zhenjiang
212003, China

Abstract. With the rapid development and wide using smart phones, the protection of privacy data in mobile phones is becoming more and more important. For the data security problem of Android platform, a new transparent encryption method based on SM4 with file filter driver is designed and implemented, according to the technology of file transparent encryption and decryption system based on hook transparent encryption technology and file filtering driven transparent encryption technology used on windows platform. The transparent encryption system is different from the traditional APP development method of Android system. By intercepting the system call function and using the secret-key converted from the host MAC address, the encryption and decryption SM4 algorithm is written into the kernel, which fundamentally guarantees the security of user information. At the same time, the user's security experience is improved by putting authentication on the screen unlocking. The system design and implementation are described in this paper from system requirement analysis to overall design and detailed design of each module. Android application development technology and cross-compiling principle are used in the coding process. The system test results show that the system can effectively transparently encrypt files and protect the privacy of mobile files.

Keywords: Transparent encryption · Privacy protection · Android · SM4

1 Introduction

With the rapid development of the mobile communication technology and mobile Internet, the smart phone has been widely used. However, the security of the smart phone and the protection of the user's privacy have arisen extensive attention [1, 2], especially the smart phone's data security.

At present, file transparent encryption technology has become increasingly mature [1–3]. However, it is mostly used in Windows platform, and the application market for Android mobile phone file encryption software is uneven, and users are required to enter

X. Sun et al. (Eds.): ICAIS 2022, LNCS 13340, pp. 520–531, 2022.
https://doi.org/10.1007/978-3-031-06791-4_41

passwords to verify every time they encrypt and decrypt files, which greatly reduce the encryption efficiency and user experience [3]. The transparent file encryption technology is divided into two kinds, the hook transparent encryption technology and the file filter driven transparent encryption technology [1–4]. The file filter driven transparent encryption technology and SM4 algorithm have been adopted in this system, the algorithm is written to the kernel by intercepting and modifying the system calls. The key of the algorithm converted from the terminal mac address, the function of transparent file encryption is achieved by the file filter driven and the terminal mac address, so that user's data can be protected very well.

A transparent encryption system based on Android file filter driver is designed in this paper. In the kernel layer, the encryption and decryption algorithm is written into the kernel by intercepting system calls, so as to improve user experience and encryption efficiency. The system's authentication is placed in the screen lock.

2 Android System Architecture and SM4 Algorithm

2.1 Android Architecture

Android system architecture is based on the Linux kernel and is bottom-up structure. It is mainly divided into four layers, as shown in Fig. 1, the Linux Kernel layer, the Library layer, the Application Framework layer and the Application layer. The Linux kernel layer provides the underlying drivers for various hardware of Android devices, such as display driver, audio driver, etc.

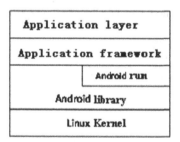

Fig. 1. Android system architecture.

The system runtime layer mainly provides the main features support for Android system through some C/C++ libraries, such as SQLite library, etc. The application framework layer mainly provides various APIs that may be used to build applications. Application Programming Interface (API); the application layer includes all applications installed on mobile phones [5].

2.2 SM4 and AES Algorithm

SM4 Algorithm. SM4 algorithm [6] is a block cipher algorithm. SM4 is similar to the DES and AES algorithms, but SM4 algorithm adopts four branch generalized unbalanced

Feisal structure. The packet length and key length are 128 bits. The encryption and decryption algorithm and key expansion algorithm adopt 32 rounds of nonlinear iterative structure, and each round of iteration completes 32-bit Encryption/ Decryption operation. In SM4, the structure of the encryption algorithm and the decryption algorithm are the same, except that the round key used is opposite, where the decryption round key is the reverse order of the encryption round key. The algorithm structure is shown in Fig. 2, the round operation of each round of SM4 algorithm includes round key addition, S-box replacement and linear operation. The input of each round is four 32-bit words. After XOR with the key, one round of encryption is completed through four s boxes and a linear layer.

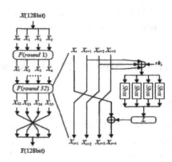

Fig. 2. Encryption and decryption structure of SM4.

AES Algorithm.   AES is known as the advanced encryption standard. The AES algorithm requires a 128-bit or 16-byte length of plaintext, and the length of the secret key can be divided into 128-bit, 192-bit, or 256-bit (16, 24, or 32 bytes) [6, 7]. The AES encryption process involves four operations: AddRoundKey, SubBytes, ShiftRows, and MixColumns. The decryption process is the corresponding inverse operation of the encryption [8].

3   Principle of Transparent Encryption Technology

Transparent encryption refers to the process of encrypting and decrypting files without changing the user's operating habits. It is a passive compulsory encryption technology [1–8], which is insensitive to users. When the user opens or edits the specified file, the system will automatically encrypt the unencrypted file and decrypt the encrypted file. Encrypted files leave the current usage environment, which can not automatically decrypt and protect the contents of files.

Transparent encryption technology can be divided into user-mode implementation and kernel-mode implementation according to the location of implementation. They correspond to the two main transparent encryption technologies, namely hook transparent encryption and file filter-driven transparent encryption. According to encryption efficiency, hook encryption technology encrypts the whole file in the application layer, and encrypts and decrypts the file relatively slowly. Driving transparency technology encrypts and decrypts the file dynamically in the driver layer, which has high efficiency. So file filter-driven transparent encryption is used in this paper.

File Driver Encryption (IFS) technology is based on Windows File System Filter Driver (IFS) technology [1–3, 9, 10], which works in the kernel layer of Windows. Without affecting the upper and lower interfaces, it can intercept all file system requests, so that new functions can be added without modifying the upper software or the lower driver [1–3, 8–12], as shown in Fig. 3.

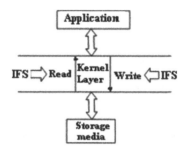

Fig. 3. Drives transparent encryption.

It is characterized by high encryption efficiency and security, but the technical threshold is high. It is necessary to understand the Windows system kernel in depth and difficult to develop. All tables and figures with text only should be boxed in; i.e., a box should be drawn around the table or figure either by hand with a ruler or with a draw facility on.

4 Design and Implementation of Transparent File Encryption System

4.1 Overall Designs

This system is a transparent file encryption system based on Android platform. It mainly completes the encryption and decryption of specified files, and takes into account the user's good experience, so as to ensure the personal information security of Android users. The frame design of the whole system is shown in Fig. 4.

The system uses MVP (Model, View, Presenter) framework. Model (model) receives the control information from the controller, completes the operation of reading and writing files and encryption and decryption. View (user interface) mainly realizes the interaction with users and updates the user's encryption policy customization to relevant database items. Presenter is responsible for logical processing, customizing and updating the monitoring list according to the user's encryption strategy, monitoring and accepting the data read and write operations applied in the list, and passing the information to Model. MVP is evolved from MVC framework [14]. It cuts off the connection between View and Model, makes View interact only with Presenter, increases readability and reusability, and reduces the cost of later testing and maintenance [15].

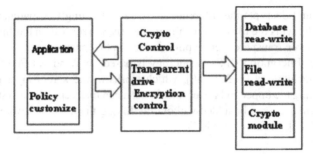

Fig. 4. System overall design framework.

In the choice of encryption algorithm, we chose the SM4 encryption algorithm that independently developed by China and currently popular encryption algorithm AES. The reason for making these two choices is mainly considering the following reasons:

(1) The reason why chose SM4 as the encryption algorithm for this design, we mainly consider that SM4 is an encryption algorithm independently developed by China. The emergence of encryption algorithms such as SM4 independently developed by China is an essential measure to ensure the security of encryption algorithms and an inevitable measure to get rid of foreign technical control. We can only do our own encryption standards and continue to promote the standardization process of encryption algorithms in China. Only then can China's algorithm standard become an international standard.

(2) The reason why AES is selected as the encryption algorithm is because AES encryption algorithm is one of the most popular algorithms in symmetric encryption, and it replaced the original DES encryption algorithm. For now, AES is still a primary consideration in some encryption scenarios. At least for now, the AES encryption algorithm does not show a decline, nor does it show obvious problems in security;

The system authenticates the user through screen lock when the mobile phone starts. When the system intercepts the user to read the file, it calls the function module of the kernel to decrypt the cipher-text, and then transmits the decrypted plaintext to the application layer for the user to read. When the system intercepts the user to write the file, it stores the plaintext encryption on the storage device to improve the user experience and security performance.

4.2 Design and Implementation of Encryption and Decryption Module

The performance of the encryption module affects the security of the transparent encrypted file system [10–19]. For the encryption algorithm, we have made the following two choices: SM4 algorithm is a block cipher algorithm. The packet length is 128 bits, and the key length is also 128 bits. AES algorithm requires a 128-bit or 16-byte length of plaintext, and the length of the secret key use 128-bit. Figure 5 shows the working flow chart of the encryption module.

Regardless of whether SM4 encryption algorithm or AES encryption algorithm is used, the functions we want to achieve are consistent. Figure 5 shows the workflow diagram of the encryption module.

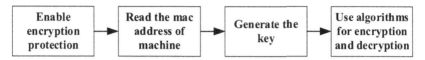

Fig. 5. Workflow of encryption module.

By reading the MAC address of the Android terminal, after a series of replacement transformations and other operations, it is transmitted to the encryption algorithm of the kernel module as the encryption key of the current device. Among them, accessing the MAC address of the Android terminal requires reading the address under/sys/class/net/wlan0. Therefore, each terminal has its own unique key. If the terminal is changed, the files of the local terminal will not be able to view. The function plays a vital role in protecting the privacy of mobile files.

The decryption process is the same as the encryption process, only using the corresponding decryption algorithm. Workflow diagram decryption module is similar to Fig. 5.

4.3 Design and Implementation of the Whole System

The whole design module of the system is divided into application layer module and kernel module. The application layer module mainly completes the function of customizing encryption strategy and interacting with users; the kernel module completes the functions of monitoring, encryption and decryption, data reading and writing according to the setting of application module.

The overall design flow chart of the system is shown in Fig. 6. After the system starts to run, the user carries out the "policy customization" operation at the user level, enters the kernel layer after the policy formulation, and monitors the reading and writing operations of the files. In order to read a file, the first step is to determine whether the file is an open encrypted protected file. If it is, it decrypts and passes the data to the user; if it is to write a file, it is still necessary to determine whether the file is an open encrypted file, and if it is, it is encrypted and writes the data to the database or SD card. If the read-write operation file is not the file protected by the policy, then the normal read-write operation can be carried out.

In the architecture of Android system, most core services need the support of Linux kernel layer. Because the filter driver file transparent encryption technology is adopted, the most fundamental implementation of the read-write monitoring module is the implementation of file read-write monitoring by Linux kernel.

The index node in Linux file system is including files, directories and hardware devices. The index node corresponds to each file one by one, so the Linux kernel can control all files, directories, hardware devices, etc. of the entire file system by managing the index node. As shown in Fig. 7, it is the read-write hierarchy of Linux kernel files.

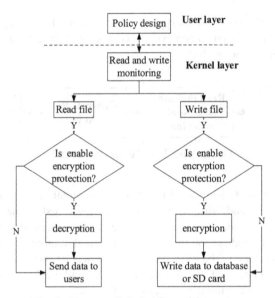

Fig. 6. The overall design flow of the system.

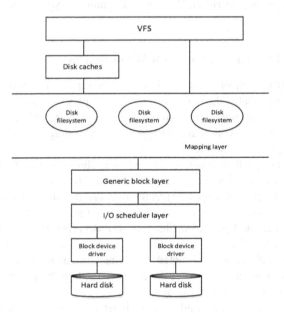

Fig. 7. File read/write flow of Linux.

4.4 Design and Implementation of Kernel Module

System calls under Linux are implemented with soft interrupts. The interrupt program handles different system calls according to the system call number. Through the soft interrupt program, the program will be trapped in the kernel space for system call processing.

In addition, Linux provides a program that can load kernel modules, namely LKM (Loadable Kernel Module), which is mainly used to dynamically extend the functions of the Linux kernel [9]. Figure 8 shows the workflow diagram of the kernel module.

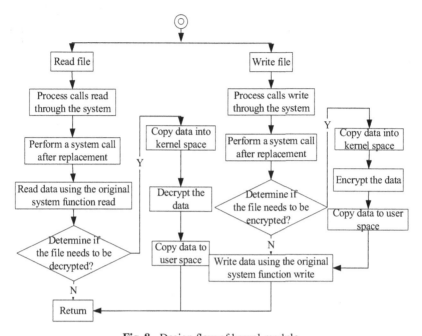

Fig. 8. Design flow of kernel module.

When run the process of writing files, the encryption process, is executed, the interception system calls write. At this run point, the kernel module gets the file name and structure. Comparing with the file name and file structure in the encryption strategy formulated by the application layer, if the file name and file structure match, the data will be copied to the kernel space, and SM4 or AES symmetric encryption operation is performed on the data through the pre-written encryption function. The key is obtained from the application layer and encrypted. Then the file is copied to the user space, and the data is written into the storage medium by calling the original system function write. If the current operation of the file is not specified in the encryption policy, the normal file write operation is run.

When the read file operation is performed, the interception system calls read. Get the file name and structure of the file currently operating in the kernel module. Comparing with the file name and file structure in the encryption strategy formulated by the application layer, if the file name and file structure match, the file will be copied to the kernel space and decrypted. After the plaintext data is transferred to the kernel space, if the current operation file is not specified in the encryption policy, the file reading operation will be performed normally.

5   System Testing

The system is installed on API18 simulator and successfully implements the transparent encryption function of txt and doc file format on SD card. After the encryption is successful, the files can be viewed normally at the local terminal. Replacing the terminal and viewing it on the PC and another mobile phone is random code, thus completing the privacy protection of Android mobile phone files, as shown in Fig. 9, 10 and Fig. 11 that are DOC file protected test result.

Fig. 9. Views encrypted DOC File on local Phone.

Fig. 10. Views encrypted DOC File on PC.

Figure 12, 13 and Fig. 14 that is TXT file protected test result are given.

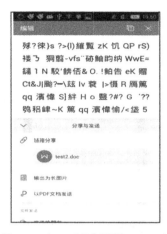

Fig. 11. Views encrypted DOC File on another Phone.

Fig. 12. Views encrypted TXT File on local Phone.

Fig. 13. Views encrypted TXT File on the PC.

Fig. 14. Views encrypted TXT File on another Phone.

6 Conclusion

According to the test results, when the encryption is completed, the files can be viewed normally on the local mobile phone after the authentication of screen lock, but not in other environments. The transparent encryption function of files under Android platform has been successfully implemented. The system uses file filtering to drive transparent encryption technology. By intercepting system calls and using keys converted from MAC address of host computer, the encryption and decryption algorithm is written into the kernel. In the process of encryption, the plaintext of files only appears in the kernel layer, which has the characteristics of security, stability and efficiency. However, the software user interface for this system can also be beautified, and the type of file data for encryption protection can also be increased, which will become the next research content.

Acknowledgement. For successful completion of this paper, first of all, I would like to thank Professor Li Yongzhong, the instructor, and graduate students Zhang Shipeng and Shen Cheng for their patient guidance and help.

Funding Statement. Project supported by National Nature Science Foundation of China (Grant No. 61471182); Postgraduate Research & Practice Innovation Program of Jiangsu Province (Grant No. KYCX20_2993); Jiangsu postgraduate research innovation project (SJCX18_0784).

References

1. Wang, G., et al.: SpaCCS 2020. LNCS, vol. 12383, pp. 137–145 (2021)
2. Cheng, S.: Research and Design of file Transparent Encryption Technology Based On Android Platform. China (2018)

3. Wang, Y., Li, Y., Lu, S.: Research and implementation of file transparent encryption technology based on android. Comput. Technol. Dev. **2014**(09), 137–140 (2014)
4. Mei, K., Li, Y.: Transparent file safety encryption method of enterprise lan based on filter driver. Comput. Technol. Dev. **2012**(04), 238–241 (2012)
5. Guo, L.: The First Line of Code-Android. 2nd edn. The People's Posts and Telecommunications Press, Beijing (2016)
6. Office of state commercial cipher administration. Block Cipher for WLAN Products-SMS4. http://www.oscca.gov.cn/UpFile/200602101642319790.pdf
7. Zhu, S.: Design and implementation of AES algorithm based on FPGA. M.S. Dissertation, West Normal University, China (2016)
8. Luo, Z.: Improvement and application of the AES algorithm based on multi-core android platform. M.S. Dissertation, Shanghai Normal University, China (2016)
9. Yang, D., Ye, P., Zhen, L.: The application of transparent decryption in trusted storage of electronic documents. Electron. Sci. Technol. **04**(04), 147–150 (2017)
10. Qian, J.: Design and implementation of phone privacy protection system based on android. M.S. dissertation, University of Electronic Science and Technology, China (2014)
11. Wang, Q., Zhou, Q., Liu, Y., et al.: Research on file system transparent encryption techniques. Comput. Technol. Dev. **2010**(03), 147–150 (2010)
12. Zhou, S.: The Reveal and Prevention in Android Security Technology. The People's Posts and Telecommunications Press, Beijing (2015)
13. Sun, X., Yang, T., Hu, X.: A file system protection scheme based on file filter driver and truecryp. Modern Comput. (professional) **2016**(03), 77–80 (2016)
14. Lin, Y.: Application of MVVM design pattern and MVP design pattern based on ZK. J. Chongqing Univ. Arts Sci. (Nat. Sci. Edit.) **2012**(06), 72–78 (2012)
15. Zeng, L.: Application research of MVP for android. Comput. Eng. Softw. **2016**(06), 75–78 (2016)
16. Fu, C.: Design of transparent encryption system for documents based on windows kernel. J. Chongqing Univ. Educat. **28**(03), 171–173 (2015)
17. Alshambri, H.A., Alassery, F.: Securing fog computing for e-learning system using integration of two encryption algorithms. J. Cyber Secur. **3**(3), 149–166 (2021)
18. Kumar, T.M., Karthigaikumar, P.: Implementation of a high-speed and high-throughput advanced encryption standard. Intell. Automat. Soft Comput. **31**(2), 1025–1036 (2022)
19. Xu, C., Mei, L., Cheng, J., Zhao, Y., Zuo, C.: IoT services: realizing private real-time detection via authenticated conjunctive searchable encryption. J. Cyber Security **3**(1), 55–67 (2021)

Calibration of Multi-dimensional Air Pressure Sensor Based on LSTM

Tao Wang[1,2,3], Pengyu Liu[1,2,3(✉)], Wenjing Zhang[4], Xiaowei Jia[5], Yanming Wang[6], and Jiachun Yang[7]

[1] Beijing University of Technology, Beijing 100124, China
liupengyu@bjut.edu.cn
[2] Beijing Laboratory of Advanced Information Networks, Beijing 100124, China
[3] Beijing Key Laboratory of Computational Intelligence and Intelligent System, Beijing 100124, China
[4] Gohigh Data Networks Technology Co., Ltd., Beijing 100124, China
[5] Department of Computer Science, University of Pittsburgh, Pittsburgh 15260, USA
[6] Shijiazhuang Posts and Telecommunications Technical College, Shijiazhuang 050021, China
[7] Tianjin Huayuntianyi Special Meteorological Detection Technology Co., Ltd., Tianjin 300392, China

Abstract. The calibration of the air pressure sensor is of great significance for improving the measurement accuracy of the sensor and the accuracy of atmospheric prediction. In view of the problem that there are few deep learning methods that can be applied to sensor calibration, and the accuracy cannot meet the requirements of practical applications, this paper considers the temporal characteristics of the measurement data of the air pressure sensor, and proposes a multi-dimensional air pressure sensor calibration based on LSTM. The test results on the pressure sensor data set in the interval of [0 kPa, 1100 kPa] and [−30 °C, 30 °C] show that the error of the pressure sensor is reduced from 1.4 kPa to about 0.55 kPa compared with other sensor calibration methods proposed in this paper. In addition to better calibration results, it has good generalization ability, which can be applied to similar sensor calibration.

Keywords: LSTM · Sensor calibration · Sequentially · Error correction

1 Introduction

High altitude weather detection is of great significance for natural disaster warning, weather forecast and daily production guidance, so various meteorological weather detection technologies have emerged. Among them, radiosonde has been favored by its excellent cost performance, convenient delivery and good measurement accuracy, so it has become the main method of high-altitude weather detection at present. The various sensors carried in the radiosonde are the main method of measuring data. Taking the air pressure sensor as an example, it is affected by the complex and changeable high-altitude environment and its own production process. The measurement results of the pressure sensor will have some errors with the actual results, which will directly affect the accuracy of weather prediction. There is still a certain gap between the measurement accuracy of the domestic air pressure sensor and that of the Finland Visala, so how to reduce the measurement error of the air pressure sensor through calibration has become an urgent problem to be solved [1].

At present, there are few calibration methods for air pressure sensors at home and abroad, and the effect is not ideal and the generalization ability is not strong. With the development of computer technology, the appearance of neural network provides a new direction to solve the above problems [2]. BP neural network has been widely used due to its good approximation ability and mature training methods, but the calibration results depend on a large amount of data for training. The network itself has many shortcomings such as slow convergence speed, long training time, unsatisfactory accuracy and weak generalization ability, so LM algorithm is proposed to enhance BP neural network, but the final effect is only to improve some calibration accuracy [3]. Another commonly used calibration method is the RBF neural network. Compared with the BP neural network, the RBF neural network has the only best approximation characteristic, there is no local minimum problem, and the learning convergence process is much better than the BP neural network. Compared with BP neural network, the calibration speed and generalization ability of pressure sensor are greatly improved by this method, but there is still a certain gap in the requirement of high precision and strong generalization ability of air pressure sensor [4].

In view of the characteristics of high frequency acquisition, large amount of data acquisition and wide distribution range of pressure sensor in high altitude environment, there should be a close connection between time sequence characteristics in the whole acquisition process, which can more generally show the change of pressure sensor. In this paper, a calibration model of multi-dimensional pressure sensor is proposed based on LSTM network [5]. The calibration accuracy and generalization ability of the model are improved by using time sequence characteristics and multi-dimensional input. In the measurement range of the air pressure sensor [0 kPa, 1100 kPa] and [-30 °C, 30 °C] used in this paper, it not only effectively reduces the calibration error, but also has better generalization ability in the whole range than the above two networks.

2 Materials and Methods

2.1 Analysis of Data Characteristics of Air Pressure Sensor

Timing Characteristics. The frequency of the sensor is an important indicator of the working state of the pressure sensor. Its distribution directly reflects whether the sensor is in normal working state. The pressure distribution interval of the experimental data used in this paper is [0 kPa, 1100 kPa]. In order to analyze the timing characteristics of the pressure sensor distribution, we take rough sampling of the working frequency in the pressure interval and draw the scatter diagram of the working frequency distribution of the pressure sensor, as shown in Fig. 1:

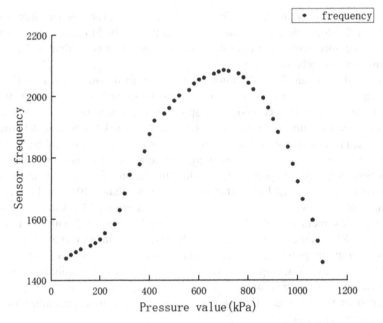

Fig. 1. Scatterplot of pressure sensor frequency distribution.

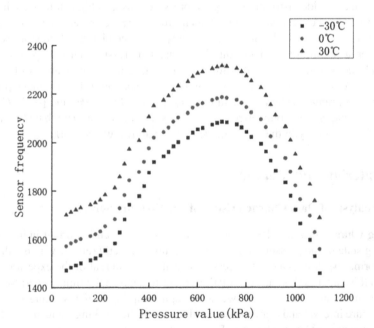

Fig. 2. Pressure sensor frequency temperature contrast diagram.

In the figure, we can find that the working frequency of the air pressure sensor presents a corresponding non-linear continuous relationship with the increase of air pressure. If the sampling frequency is large enough, the overall curve should be a continuous trend [6]. Therefore, it can be shown that with the change of time, the working state of the air pressure sensor has a certain time sequence correlation. The temperature range measured by the air pressure sensor is [−30 °C, 30 °C]. In order to analyze the working frequency variation trend of the air pressure sensor at different temperature points, a comparative analysis diagram of the air pressure sensor frequency and temperature is made as shown in Fig. 2. From the figure, we can find that the overall trend of the working frequency of the air pressure sensor at different temperature points is continuous, so it can be inferred that the data collected by the air pressure sensor at different temperature points still has time-series correlation.

Multi-dimensional Input of Pressure Sensor. Based on the comparison diagram of frequency and temperature of the air pressure sensor shown in Fig. 2, we find that as the working indicator of the air pressure sensor, the frequency of the sensor is closely related to the state and measurement data of the sensor, so the frequency of the sensor has become one of the input dimensions considered in this paper. In addition to the sensor frequency, the returned data of the air pressure sensor includes sensor number, air pressure measurement value, temperature value, air pressure original value and temperature original value, etc. [7]. Temperature is one of the important measurement data of the air pressure sensor, and the change trend in the high-altitude complex and changeable environment is directly related to the stable state of the sensor. In order to further confirm the influence of temperature change and pressure error, we constructed a three-dimensional scatter diagram between the original pressure value, the original temperature value and the pressure measurement point according to the data returned by the sensor, as shown in Fig. 3.

The original values of air pressure and temperature are the initial data of air pressure and temperature returned by the air pressure sensor. We select some characteristic significant air pressure points in the range of 0–1100 kPa to reflect the overall change trend of air pressure sensor data in the range [8]. It can be seen from the figure that with the increase of the pressure measurement point, the original value of pressure and the original value of temperature on the whole show a linear change and the transformation trend is consistent. Ideally, the three should form a smooth plane. However, the local area in the figure is not smooth enough, which indicates that the air pressure and temperature are fluctuating during the collection process. Therefore, we judge that temperature fluctuation is an important influencing factor in the process of pressure sensor data collection. When designing the input content of the model, we take temperature factor as one of the input dimensions to reduce the error caused by temperature change.

Based on the pressure data needed to be measured by the pressure sensor itself, combined with temperature fluctuation factors and frequency distribution, the input of this paper is finally confirmed including pressure measurement value, temperature measurement value, original pressure value, original temperature value, real pressure value and frequency.

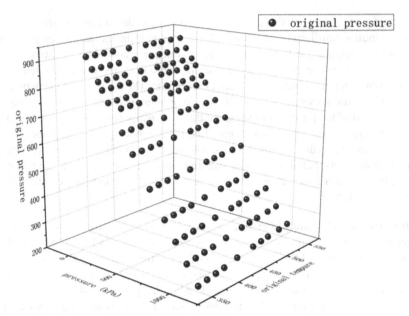

Fig. 3. Scatter plot of the relationship between pressure and temperature.

2.2 Calibration Model of Air Pressure Sensor Based on LSTM

Principle of LSTM Model. Long-short-term memory network (LSTM) was originally developed from recurrent neural network (RNN). RNN is generally used to deal with short-term dependence. When the time series is too long, its processing effect on long-term dependence is unsatisfactory.

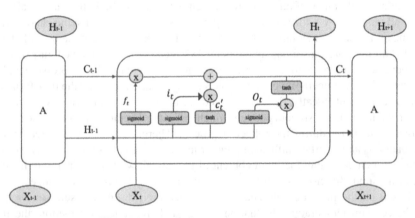

Fig. 4. Long and short-term memory module.

The LSTM network can maintain the learning information during the long-term sequence learning process, so it can solve the problems of gradient disappearance and gradient explosion [9]. The difference from RNN is that its memory block is mainly composed of a cell structure and three different gate structures. The storage unit of LSTM can store the unit state of the latest data processing [10]. When the information arrives at the storage unit, the result is controlled through the combination of unit states, and then the unit states are refreshed to realize long time sequence feature memory. Its three gate structures are forget gate, input gate and output gate. Its overall structure is roughly shown in Fig. 4.

The forget gate determines which information the cell state should retain and which information should be discarded. According to Formula (1), the two vectors H_{t-1} and X_t are spliced and passed through the sigmoid function, and the value range of the output result is [0, 1]. By multiplying with the previous cell state C_{t-1}, when the output result is 0, the corresponding characteristic information will be forgotten, and the corresponding characteristic information will be completely retained only when the result is 1. In this way, long-term memory of sequence features can be realized, so that effective information can be retained for a longer period of time [11].

$$f_t = \sigma(W_f[H_{t-1}, X_t + b_f]) \tag{1}$$

$$i_t = \sigma(W_i[H_{t-1}, X_t] + b_i) \tag{2}$$

$$C'_t = \tanh(W_c[H_{t-1}, X_t] + b_c) \tag{3}$$

$$C_t = f_t * C_{t-1} + i_t * C'_t \tag{4}$$

$$O_t = \sigma(W_o[H_{t-1}, X_t] + b_o) \tag{5}$$

$$H_t = O_t * \tanh(C_t) \tag{6}$$

The input gate determines which new information is stored in the cell state. As shown in Formula (2) and Formula (3), i_t is obtained through sigmoid function after splicing vector H_{t-1} and X_t to determine which information in the new input should be retained or discarded. Then, the splicing results are obtained through tanh function to obtain the candidate cell state C'_t. Finally, the candidate cell state C'_t and the pre-cell state C_{t-1} are multiplied by the corresponding sigmoid function results as the updated cell state [12]. The realization principle is shown in Formula (4). The output gate determines which information of this unit should be used as the output. According to Formula (5) and Formula (6), we can find that the output information of this unit can be obtained by multiplying vector H_{t-1} and X_t through sigmoid function and then C_t scaled by tanh function [13].

The LSTM structure proposed in this paper is shown in Fig. 5, and its input layer includes six dimensions of data including pressure measurement value, temperature measurement value, original pressure value, original temperature value, real pressure value and frequency. The input data was passed through two LSTM layers and two Dropout layers, and finally the dimensions of the output were adjusted through the

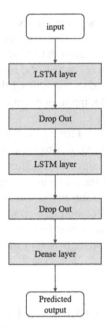

Fig. 5. The structure of our framework.

Dense layer to obtain the final predicted barometric calibration [14]. Adam was used as the optimizer, and mean absolute error and root mean square error were used as evaluation indicators [15].

Data Set. The data used in this paper is based on the data information of the new M-pressure sensor. According to the measurement range of [0 hPa, 1100 hPa] and [−30 °C, 30 °C], a batch of data is collected every 10hPa in the pressure range, and a temperature collection point is set every 5 °C in the temperature range, thus forming the data set required by the experiment in this paper. First, the experimental data is scaled and preprocessed, and the data set was divided into training set and test set after feature selection. Among them, 70% were used as training set for model training, and 30% were used as test set to verify model performance.

3   Experimental Results and Comparative Analysis

3.1   Experimental Results

In view of the fact that the air pressure sensor is a precision measuring instrument, by comparing the error between the predicted air pressure value and the actual air pressure value, it is found that the numerical gap between the two is relatively small. In order to display the error distribution more intuitively, the sensor calibration as shown in Fig. 6 is drawn. The error scatter point line chart of, the abscissa is the air pressure calibration point, and the ordinate is the error of the air pressure measurement value. From Fig. 6 we find that the error fluctuation range of the air pressure sensor after the model calibration proposed in this paper is reduced to 0.45 kPa–0.65 kPa. The overall deviation of the error along with the change of air pressure is not large, which can meet the theoretical error range requirements. Prove the effectiveness of the model.

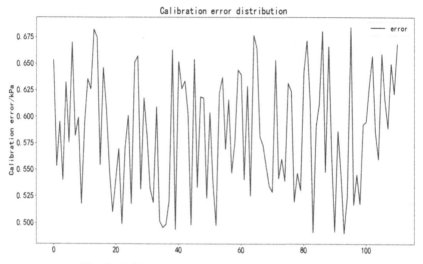

Fig. 6. Calibration error distribution of pressure sensor.

3.2 Comparative Experiment

In order to prove the advantages of the method proposed in this paper, BP neural network and RBF network which have been used in sensor data calibration are selected as comparisons, and the specific point comparison method, average absolute error (MAE) and root mean square error (RMSE) are used as evaluation methods [16]. In the interval of [0 kPa, 1100 kPa], 12 pressure points were selected as specific points. BP neural network and RBF network were used as comparison to obtain binomial parameters through the training of a large number of data collected at specific points. The input was the measured pressure value, the original pressure value and the original temperature value, and the output was the calibrated air pressure value. The comparative effect of this method is shown in Table 1.

It can be seen from Table 1 that the error range of BP neural network is 0.9–1.1 kPa, while that of RBF neural network is 0.7–0.8 kPa. By contrast, the error range of the model proposed in this paper is 0.5–0.7 kPa. Compared with the better RBF model, the performance is improved by about 21% and the calibration results of all selected collection points are improved to some extent. At the same time, the fluctuation range of error is more average, so it has higher stability The overall error curve distribution is shown in Fig. 7.

Table 1. Error comparison table for specific collection points.

Standard pressure /hPa	Error of BP neural network/hPa	Error of RBF neural network/hPa	Error of LSTM neural network/hPa
1100	0.967	0.783	0.586
1000	1.206	0.826	0.654
900	0.905	0.794	0.621
800	0.833	0.711	0.542
700	0.861	0.795	0.589
600	0.914	0.801	0.613
500	0.969	0.733	0.566
400	0.981	0.758	0.627
300	1.042	0.661	0.645
200	0.884	0.738	0.611
100	0.909	0.752	0.517
5	0.917	0.763	0.524

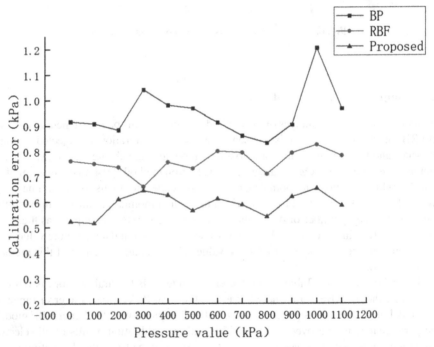

Fig. 7. Comparison of specific points of calibration error.

The mean absolute error is the average value measuring the difference between the actual value and the predicted value. The smaller the value is, the higher the prediction accuracy is. The calculation method is shown in Formula (7). The root mean square error is the average root of the mean square of all errors. The smaller the value is, the better the prediction accuracy is. The calculation method is shown in Formula (8):

$$MAE = \frac{1}{N} \sum_{t=1}^{N} |y_t - \hat{y}| \tag{7}$$

$$RMSE = \frac{1}{N} \sum_{t=1}^{N} (y_t - \hat{y})^2 \tag{8}$$

Table 2 shows the performance results of the three models after MAE and RMSE are used as evaluation indexes. The calibration effect of the proposed method in this paper is also better than that of BP neural network and RBF network. It can be seen that the calibration performance is significantly improved after considering the timing characteristics and the input dimensions that affect the pressure sensor data, which proves the superiority of this method.

Table 2. Network performance evaluation comparison table.

Neural network	MAE	RMSE
BP	0.954	0.9537
RBF	0.738	0.7608
LSTM	0.539	0.5928

4 Conclusions

According to the working frequency of the air pressure sensor, the time series correlation of the air pressure sensor data is analyzed, and the multiple factors affecting the calibration error are analyzed to confirm the dimension of the model input. Based on LSTM network, a multidimensional barometric calibration model is proposed. By comparing the results, it is found that LSTM can better learn sensor data characteristics by adjusting parameters than calibration models that use polynomial fitting such as BP neural network and RBF network, and the overall pressure measurement error is reduced from 1.4 hPa to 0.55 hPa after considering timing characteristics. The calibration accuracy and generalization ability of the model are both better, which proves the feasibility of the proposed method in the calibration of pressure sensors. The method proposed in this paper is not high enough to improve the calibration speed. Optimization of model structure will be considered in the subsequent study to improve the overall speed and effect.

Acknowledgement. First of all, I need to thank my supervisor Liu Pengyu, who provided many constructive suggestions when I encountered difficulties in the research direction of my paper, and put forward many guiding suggestions for revising my paper when writing it, answering my questions in time. At the same time, I am very grateful to the students in the Multimedia Information Processing Laboratory for their help in preparing my thesis. All authors have read and agreed to the published version of the manuscript.

Funding Statement. This paper is supported by the following funds: National Key R&D Program of China (2018YFF01010100), The Beijing Natural Science Foundation (4212001), Basic Research Program of Qinghai Province (2021-ZJ-704) and Advanced information network Beijing laboratory (PXM2019_014204_5000 29).

Conflicts of Interest. The authors declare no conflict of interest.

References

1. Xia, X., Zou, X.: Impacts of AMSU-A inter-sensor calibration and diurnal correction on satellite-derived linear and nonlinear decadal climate trends of atmospheric temperature. Clim. Dyn. **54**(3–4), 1245–1265 (2019). https://doi.org/10.1007/s00382-019-05057-9
2. Hosoda, S., Hirano, M., Hashimukai, T., Asai, S., Kawakami, N.: New method of temperature and conductivity sensor calibration with improved efficiency for screening SBE41 CTD on Argo floats. Prog. Earth Planet. Sci. **6**(1), 1–25 (2019). https://doi.org/10.1186/s40645-019-0310-1
3. Mandal, S., Sairam, N., Sridhar, S., Swaminathan, P.: Nuclear power plant sensor fault detection using singular value decomposition-based method. Sādhanā **42**(9), 1473–1480 (2017). https://doi.org/10.1007/s12046-017-0700-2
4. Yun, Z., Quan, Z., Caixin, S., Shaolan, L., Yuming, L., Yang, S.: RBF neural network and ANFIS-based short-term load forecasting approach in real-time price environment. IEEE Trans. Power Syst. **23**(3), 853–858 (2008)
5. Liang, S., Wang, D., Wu, J., Wang, R., Wang, R.: Method of bidirectional LSTM modelling for the atmospheric temperature. Intell. Autom. Soft Comput. **30**(2), 701–714 (2021)
6. Choi, Y.S.: Development of variable temperature instrument for sensor calibration. J. Mech. Sci. Technol. **28**(2), 747–753 (2014). https://doi.org/10.1007/s12206-013-1140-5
7. Sunny, M.A., Maswood, M.M.S., Alharbi, A.G.: Deep learning-based stock price prediction using LSTM and bi-directional LSTM Model. In: 2020 2nd Novel Intelligent and Leading Emerging Sciences Conference (NILES), vol. 16, pp. 87–92 (2020)
8. Bouktif, S., Fiaz, A., Ouni, A., Serhani, M.A.: Optimal deep learning LSTM model for electric load forecasting using feature selection and genetic algorithm: comparison with machine learning approaches. Energies **11**(7), 1636 (2018)
9. Cao, X., Jiang, L., Wang, X., Jiang, F.: A location prediction method based on GA-LSTM networks and associated movement behavior information. J. Inf. Hiding Priv. Prot. **2**(4), 187–197 (2020)
10. Rodriguez, I.V., Stanchits, S., Burghardt, J.: Relative sensor calibration based on waveform fitting moment tensor inversion. Situ **50**, 891–911 (2017)
11. Liwei, T., Li, F., Yu, S., Yuankai, G.: Forecast of LSTM-XGBoost in stock price based on Bayesian optimization. Intell. Autom. Soft Comput. **29**(3), 855–868 (2021)
12. Fang, W., Zhang, F., Ding, Y., Sheng, J.: A new sequential image prediction method based on LSTM and DCGAN. Comput. Mater. Continua **64**(1), 217–231 (2020)

13. Qian, J., Zhu, M., Zhao, Y., He, X.: Short-term wind speed prediction with a two-layer attention-based LSTM. Comput. Syst. Sci. Eng. **39**(2), 197–209 (2021)
14. Haq, M.A.: CDLSTM: a novel model for climate change forecasting. Comput. Mater. Continua **71**(2), 2363–2381 (2022)
15. Cao, J., Li, Z., Li, J.: Financial time series forecasting model based on CEEMDAN and LSTM. Physica A Stat. Mech. Appl. **5**(19), 127–139 (2019)
16. Feng, R.L., Wang, Z.F., Feng, H.Q.: Comparative study on aerodynamic resistance prediction of low-vacuum pipeline high-speed train based on RBF and BP neural network. J. Vac. Sci. Technol. **40**(9), 827–832 (2020)

A Survey of Traffic Classification Technology for Smart Home Based on Machine Learning

Jie Chen[1] 📖, Yaping Liu[1,2](✉), Shuo Zhang[1,2], Bing Chen[1], and Zhiyu Han[1]

[1] Guangzhou University, Guanzhou 510000, China
ypliu@gzhu.edu.cn
[2] Peng Cheng Laboratory, Shenzhen 518000, China

Abstract. With the wide use of smart home devices and the privacy of their activities, more and more research have focused on the traffic classification for smart home, and traffic classification technology can infer the activity of devices from the encrypted traffic, which is important for the research on smart home privacy leakage, device transparency management, and so on. This paper first introduced the research content and evaluation indicator of smart home traffic classification, and then compared the advantages and disadvantages of different smart home traffic classification approaches in terms of accuracy and real-time performance. Finally, the future research direction is prospected from two aspects: classification algorithm and classification model.

Keywords: Traffic classification · Device identification · Smart home · Machine learning · Privacy

1 Introduction

The field of smart home is booming, and new smart devices bring both convenience and security problem to users, The network traffic generated by smart home devices is usually encrypted [1, 2]. However, even if data encryption technology is adopted, smart homes still have risks. Although encryption protects the semantic information of the data, it is not enough to prevent the user's privacy from leaking. Some or all of the user's activity trajectory can still be obtained through encrypted traffic analysis. The research of smart home traffic classification technology is of great significance for protecting user privacy and security. Different from the extensive research on Internet traffic classification, due to the characteristics of data encryption, smart home traffic classification focuses on the classification of encrypted traffic. The difficulties in the classification of encrypted traffic can be divided into two aspects: one is that the classification algorithm cannot obtain the exact category information from the load, and it is necessary to study which traffic characteristics can characterize different types of traffic; the other is that the traffic classification in the real environment is important for classification. Levels and classification costs have different requirements. The classification algorithm also needs to consider the processing of unknown traffic, the processing of network traffic noise, and so on. According to the different classification methods, the research on smart home traffic classification based on machine learning can be subdivided into four methods based on supervised learning, based on unsupervised learning, based on deep learning, and multi-stage model, which is composed of multiple machine learning methods. In machine learning methods, classification features can affect the accuracy and real-time performance of the algorithm. Many papers studies how to select appropriate traffic features. The selection of features needs to be considered from the four aspects of expressivity, acquisition cost, number of features, and feature classification contribution. There are two main evaluation indicators for the smart home traffic classification methods: classification accuracy (Accuracy, Precision, recall, F1 value) and real-time performance.

In terms of classification accuracy, the definition of each indicator is given according to the confusion matrix, including the following four parts:

Accuracy is defined as the percentage of correct results in the total sample, but when the data set samples are unbalanced, the model performance cannot be measured well. 2) Precision represents the accuracy of the model's prediction of positive samples. 3) The recall rate (recall) represents whether the model's prediction of the positive sample is comprehensive. 4) There is a restrictive relationship between the precision rate and the recall rate. The F1 value (F1-Score) can be combined with the precision rate and the recall rate to give the overall performance of the model.

In terms of real-time performance, Bai Jun et al. [3] gave the real-time performance definition of the classification method of flow-level features in network traffic classification. The (n, m) value of the classification method can be used as an index to judge the real-time performance, n is The number of sub-stream data packets, m is the number of stream characteristics. The source of (n, m) is as follows:

$$nt_0 + mt_1 = t \tag{1}$$

t is the time for real-time traffic identification, t0 is the arrival time interval of data packets, t1 is the time for the classification algorithm to process a feature, n is the number of data packets of the sub-flow that needs to be extracted, and m is the number of features to be extracted by the classification algorithm. In summary, the real-time performance of classification is determined by the time of feature acquisition and algorithm processing of features. For network flow features, the time of collecting features from traffic is much longer than the time of algorithm processing features.

2 Structure

The organization structure of this paper is as follows. Section 1 to 4 respectively introduce the four types of smart home traffic classification algorithms; Sect. 5 compares the advantages and disadvantages of classification algorithms; Sect. 6 is the summarizes and prospects.

3 Methods Based on Supervised Learning

At present, many researches have compared a variety of supervised learning machine learning methods, including: decision trees, random forests, support vector machines (SVM), K nearest neighbor algorithm (KNN), Naive Bayesian, Gradient Boosting Decison Tree, etc. According to the classification method with the highest classification accuracy in the literature, it can be divided into three categories: K nearest neighbor, gradient boosting tree, and random forest.

3.1 Introduction to Methods Based on Supervised Learning

K Nearest Neighbor Algorithm

The KNN algorithm calculates the distance between the instance to be tested and each instance in the training sample set, and selects the class of most instances with the closest distance. The advantages of the KNN algorithm are not easily affected by the outliers in the data set. Since multiple distances need to be calculated for each prediction process, the disadvantage is that the computational complexity and space complexity are relatively high.

In 2017, Noah Apthorpe et al. [4] verified that the use of traffic classification technology can steal user privacy. They uses a third-order K-NN classification model combined with the statistical characteristics of data packets. The disadvantage is that only four devices are used to verify the feasibility, and the classification accuracy under mixed traffic is not discussed. In 2019, Marchal, Samuel, etc. [5] designed an automated network management architecture. The architecture is divided into two parts, IOT Gateway and IOT Cloud Service. The gateway is responsible for extracting device fingerprints, and the server runs KNN algorithm for fingerprint classification. The fingerprint of the device is composed of 33 features related to the flow period. The author uses the discrete Fourier transform to determine the candidate period for a given flow. The advantage is that there is no need for a labeled data set, and the cloud can automatically determine whether a new abstract device category needs to be generated based on the distance between the new device feature and the existing cluster.

Random Forest Algorithm

Random forest is an algorithm that has a better effect in traffic classification. Unlike the gradient boosting tree algorithm, the random forest algorithm is an algorithm based on the Bagging model. In 2017, Sivanathan, Arunan et al. [6] used random forests to classify the traffic of IoT devices in campuses and smart cities, using 13 features such as device sleep time, active volume, and average packet size, and used more features. The advantage is that it can improve the accuracy of classification, but the disadvantage is that it reduces the real-time performance of the algorithm, and some features are more complicated to obtain in reality. In the same year, Markus Miettinen et al. [7] used 23 characteristics of the data packet in the configuration phase of the device (protocol of each layer of the network, packet size, payload data, IP address and port number) to construct the device fingerprint, using the data in the configuration phase packets limit the usage scenarios and cannot perform traffic classification when the device is working normally. Meidan et al. [8] used another set of features to implement device fingerprinting. The author found that the most important features are related to the TTL value in the data packet. The three most important features are ttl_min, ttl_firstQ, and ttl_avg. The author also evaluated The amount of session data required to achieve the best classification effect is 110.

In 2018, Santos et al. [9] calculated the characteristics of data packet size and data volume on two-way streams. They compared the machine learning method with the deep packet inspection technology, and found that the accuracy of those two method has little difference in equipment classification. Shahid et al. [10] narrowed the range of feature extraction, considering the packet size and packet arrival time of the first N packets of bidirectional flow. The disadvantage is that the number of classification devices used in the experiment is too small.

In 2020, Ahmed Alshehri et al. [11] designed a device classification algorithm for smart home device traffic under VPN, using the size of data packets and the sequence of data packets to construct device traffic fingerprints. The selection is based on these two The characteristics will not be concealed by the VPN, and the periodic traffic and active traffic of the device are also considered. The above studies have adopted the classification features of their respective definitions, and the classification accuracy rate is very high, but the basis of the feature definition is not obvious. In response to this problem, TJ OConnor et al. [12] divided the various characteristic values on the traffic into four categories according to the reality: throughput, burstiness, synchronicity, and duration. At the same time, the contribution of these features to the classification accuracy is calculated. The author realized a more detailed device action classification, and realized a smart home data flow control system based on the traffic classification. Batyr Charyyev et al. [13] conducted experiments on device action classification, using the data set published by literature [1] and others. The author focuses on the impact of the following three aspects on the classification accuracy: interaction mode, communication medium, and regional differences. The author finds that the opposite instructions of the same device are easily confused by the classifier.

Unlike most of the smart home devices mentioned above, the traffic information in home cameras is more abundant. In 2016, Hong Li et al. [14] analyzed the characteristics of differential video coding used for camera traffic transmission, and extracted the average and Variance of the data packet size of the traffic segment. They use KNN algorithm identify the daily activities of a limited number of users. In 2019, Jibao Wang et al. [15] improved the handling of I frames in traffic by Hong Li et al., proposed a new user operation flow cutting algorithm, and added more features to achieve fine-grained user activity classification. The influence of light and distance on the classification result is also considered.

3.2 Comparison of Methods Based on Supervised Learning

Table 1 compares the smart home traffic classification methods based on supervised learning. Noah Apthorpe's work [4] and Marchal, Samuel's work [5] both use the KNN classification algorithm. In terms of accuracy, [4] has relatively few experimental equipment, and it is impossible to judge the effectiveness of the large-scale classification of the method used. The accuracy of [5] It is very high. In terms of real-time performance,

[4] does not mention the time to collect data stream data, and [5] takes 30 min to collect data stream data. Among the articles summarized in Table 1, the random forest algorithm has the best effect, and the main difference is the different features used. In the literature that uses the random forest algorithm, the accuracy of Ahmed Alshehri' work [11] is the lowest, because the author can only use two features when the VPN is turned on. Markus Miettinen's work [7] does not have a high recognition accuracy rate for some devices, indicating that only using data packets in the configuration stage can not perform traffic classification well on some devices. In terms of feature selection, Santos's work [9] and Shahid's work [10] is similar, and accuracy is similar. In terms of real-time performance, [9] (N1, 4), [10]is (n, 4) and [10] is a comparison The method in [9] is better in real time performance because it only considers the characteristics of the first N packets on the bidirectional stream. Markus Miettinen's work [7] and TJ Oconnor's work [12] considered extracting features on TCP streams at the same time, [7] considered TTL-related features in data packets, and [12] extracted the rate and data on TCP data streams. For the statistical characteristics of packet size, the process of extracting the characteristics in [7] takes longer, because the corresponding value needs to be extracted from the packet header. Hong Li's work [14] and Jibao Wang's work [15] considers the recognition of encrypted traffic of home cameras, which can recognize limited actions. [15] improves the method of [14], and the accuracy is improved. In summary, the random forest algorithm achieves the best results in most classification scenarios, while the KNN algorithm can handle unlabeled traffic data.

4 Methods Based on Unsupervised Learning

Unsupervised learning is a concept corresponding to supervised learning. Unsupervised learning algorithms do not require labeled data sets. The role of unsupervised learning algorithms is to identify the laws between data, so it has great advantages in dealing with unlabeled data. Clustering algorithm is one of the most commonly used unsupervised ML methods.

In 2019, Thangavelu, Vijayanand et al. [16] proposed a distributed identification fingerprint system. The system is divided into two parts, the controller and the gateway. The gateway uploads the extracted network data packet characteristics to the controller. The supervised learning model which is trained by the controller is sent to the gateway, and the gateway use model classifies IoT data packets. In dealing with unlabel traffic data, the author use an unsupervised algorithm to cluster the traffic characteristics of the new device uploaded by the gateway. When the cluster size of the new category reaches the threshold, the supervised classifier model will be retrained.

In 2020, Trimananda, Rahmadi et al. [17] established a precise signature for each device activity. The signature of each action is a sequence of the size of a set of data packet payloads, and the interaction between the device, cloud, and APP is considered in the direction. The author uses DBSCAN (algorithm based on density clustering) to assist in extracting the stable signature of each function. The advantage is that the signature is very interpretable, but the disadvantage is that the signature library needs to be maintained to eliminate the impact of device software updates.

Table 1. Comparison of methods based on supervised learning.

Method	Goal	feature	Method	Accuracy
Noah Apthorpe [4]	Device	Average and standard deviation of packet size	KNN	94%
Marchal, Samuel [5]	Device	Periodic flows, period accuracy, period duration, period stability	KNN	95%
Sivanathan, A [6]	Device	Device sleep time, active volume, avg packet size, avg rate, peak-to-avg ratio	Random forest	95%
Markus M [7]	Device	Protocols, data packet sizes, payload data, IP addresses and port numbers	Random forest	27devices: 81.5% 17devices: 95%
Meidan [8]	Device	ttl_min, ttl_firstQ, ttl_avg	Random forest	99.49%
Santos [9]	Device	Two direction: total bytes and Maximum packet size	Random forest	98.9%
Shahid [10]	Device	Packets size, arrival time	Random forest	99.9%
Ahmed A [11]	Device	Sequence of N data packets, data packet size	Random forest	83%
TJ Oconnor [12]	Device action	TCP flow, throughput, burstiness, synchronization, and duration	Random forest	99.69%
Batyr Charyyev [13]	Device action	ip.len, tcp.len, ip.ttl, inter arrival time of the frames, common protocols	Random forest	avg Acc:75%
Hong Li [14]	Content	Flow rate	Knn, Dbscan	84%–97%

(continued)

Table 1. (*continued*)

Method	Goal	feature	Method	Accuracy
Jibao Wang [15]	Content	Characteristics related to rate and packet arrival time	Random forest, Alexnet	97.23%

Ortiz, Jorge et al. [18] also focused on the identification of unknown devices, using the LSTM-Autoencoder network to automatically extract features, and output as a fixed-size vector. In the second step, Bayesian modeling was used for the vector to compare with known devices. The TCP flow distribution is used to classify devices. Table 2 compares the smart home traffic classification methods based on unsupervised learning. Unsupervised algorithms are usually used as a pretreatment step in the classification process, which can aggregate device data with similar features or extract features implicit in the traffic data.

Table 2. Comparison of methods based on unsupervised learning.

Method	Goal	Feature	Method	Accuracy
Thangavelu, V [16]	Device	Flow duration and packet size	K-means Random forest	70.55%
Trimananda, R [17]	Device Action	Packet size and direction	DBSCAN	97%
Ortiz, Jorge [18]	Device	TCP packet payload	LSTMAutoencoder, Bayesian Algorith, DBSCAN	F1: 82%, acc 70%

5   Methods Based on Deep Learning Algorithm

In terms of the characteristics, the algorithm in the deep learning framework can be divided into two ways: supervised and unsupervised. In terms of features, deep learning traffic classification models can be divided into two categories [19]. One type needs to extract features from the stream and input them into the network, and the other type uses deep learning methods to automatically learn the hidden features in the data, which will obtain The received data stream is transformed into a suitable form and then input into the network. Recurrent Neural Network (RNN) is a type of recurrent neural network that takes sequence data as input, recursively in the evolution direction of the sequence, and all nodes (recurrent units) are connected in a chain [20], RNN network structure can memorize the historical information of the sequence, which is widely used in the field of natural language processing. The LSTM model is a variant of the RNN network, which improves the gradient disappearance problem of the RNN network when processing long sequences. Some studies apply it in the field of smart home traffic classification. The traffic generated by IoT devices is a series of data packet sequences, which are incremented by timestamp and can be expressed as a time sequence.

5.1 Introduction to Methods Based on Deep Learning Algorithm

In 2018, Bai, Lei et al. [21] used the LSTM-CNN algorithm to capture global and local temporal correlations in a supervised manner. With a time interval of 5 min, 3 features (average packet length, peak packet length, and number of packets) are extracted from user data packets and control data packets. In the experiment, the author observed that the performance decreases as the number of device types increases. Compared with a number of supervised machine learning algorithms, better results have been achieved. In 2020, Shuaike Dong et al. [22] use LSTM network to classifiy smart home device traffic when NAPT and VPN were turned on. For each data packet, extract the binary feature set: <dport, protocol, dir, packetsize, time interval> and enter it into the network. The results show that the two-way LSTM model can achieve high classification accuracy under noisy experimental conditions, which is better than the random forest model. Ortiz, Jorge, etc. [18] used the automatic feature extraction capability of the LSTM network. The author trained a deep LSTM-Autoencoder network, and inputted the payload bytes of 25 tcp packets generated by the device into the network, and output a fixed The size of the vector is different for different devices.

5.2 Comparison of Methods Based on Deep Learning Algorithm

Table 3 summarizes the scheme of using deep learning for traffic classification. In terms of classification features, the Ortiz, Jorge's work [18] uses the LSTM-Autoencoder network to automatically extract the features in the packet payload. For the problem of automatic feature extraction, the Ahmet Aksoy's work [24] uses genetic algorithm to solve the problem, but the they does not compare the advantages of manually defined features, this requires further experimentation. In terms of feature definition, Shuaike Dong's work [22] uses the features in a single data packet, and the feature extraction speed is faster than Bai, Lei's work [21] extracting features from the data stream. In terms of accuracy, [22] performs better than the decision tree model, and the paper [18, 21] does not compare with the traditional model. The advantage of deep learning is that the classification accuracy is relatively high, but the disadvantage is that training the model requires a lot of computational performance. The commonly used LSTM model cannot be parallelized due to the structural characteristics, and the training is relatively slow. At present, there are not many research literatures on the application of deep learning algorithms for smart home traffic classification.

Table 3. Comparison of methods based on supervised learning.

Method	Goal	Feature	Method	Accuracy
Ortiz, Jorge [18]	Device	TCP package length	LSTM Autoencoer, Bayesian, DBSCAN	F1: 82%, acc: 70%
Bai, Lei [21]	Device	Num of packages, Avg package len, Max package len	LSTM-CNN	74.8%–96.7%
Shuaike D [22]	Device	<dport, protocol, dir, packet, size, time interval>	LSTM-RNN	81%–99.2%

6 Methods Based on Multi-stage Prediction Model

The single-stage predictive model mentioned above can realize device activity recognition or device action recognition, but the actual traffic classification requirements are diverse. According to the design goals of the multi-stage predictive model, it can be divided into two categories: classification cost optimization, multiple target recognition.

6.1 Introduction to Methods Based on Multi-stage Prediction Model

The classification method that considers classification cost optimization mainly uses features and algorithms of different classification costs in multiple stages to optimize the time and space overhead in the classification process. In 2019, Sivanathan et al. [23] designed a two-stage prediction model. The first stage uses a bag-of-words model to combine three features (remote port number collection, domain name collection, and encryption suite collection) for classification. The result of input into the second stage. The second stage uses the random forest algorithm to combine features such as the capacity and duration of the data stream. The author also separately considered the time cost of different classification features. The more features used, the higher the classification accuracy.

Ahmet Aksoy et al. [24] considered extracting classification features from a single data packet, and used genetic Algorithm to automatically determine the feature that contributed the most to classification in the packet header field. In order to solve the problem of low classification accuracy between devices of the same brand, the author designed a two-stage classification model. The accuracy is similar to the paper [7], but only uses the features on a single data packet, and the speed is faster.

In 2020, Sivanathan, Arunan, et al. [26] proposed a three-level classification architecture to determine whether the device is an IoT device, the type of the device, and the state of the device according to a progressive relationship. Using the commonly used network protocols (DNS, NTP, SSDP) and remote access addresses for data packets and flow rate characteristics on bidirectional traffic, the author uniquely considers the cost of feature extraction in SDN switches and features for classification Contribution.

In the same year, Abbas Acar et al. [27] proposed a multi-level user activity detection framework. The first three steps implement device identification, device status detection, and device status classification. The last stage combines the status of multiple devices to achieve smart home users. Activity inference. Different from the above research, the author's classification object is the traffic captured in the wireless network.

In 2020, Yinxin Wan et al. [28] designed a two-stage smart home security monitoring model. The first stage uses a supervised algorithm to learn known attack types, and the second stage uses a clustering algorithm to discover other types of traffic. Attack mode. This supervised and unsupervised approach can inspire the design of traffic classification models.

6.2 Comparison of Methods Based on Multi-stage Prediction Model

Table 4 compares the research of multi-stage classification models. Among the classification cost optimization schemes, the classification accuracy of Shuaike Dong's work [22] is the best, but the cost of acquiring features is also the highest, because the information used in stage 1 needs to check the data package The contents of the header. The classification accuracy of Ahmet Aksoy's work [24] and Arman Pashamokhtari's work [25] is similar, but the classification feature cost of [24] is lower.

In the multi-target recognition scheme, attention needs to be paid to the design of the classification target. The Abbas Acar's work [27] extends the classification target to a higher level, and combines the classification results of the previous stages to realize the recognition of user activities. Sivanathan, Arunan's work [26] extends the classification goal to a lower level. Yinxin Wan's work [28] is a research on abnormal traffic detection, using unsupervised algorithms combined with supervised algorithms to deal with

Table 4. Comparison of methods based on multi-stage models.

Method	Goal	feature	Method	Accuracy
Sivanathan [23]	Device	1: Process port number, domain name, encryption suite 2: Duration, data rate; sleep time	1: Bag-of-words 2: Random forest	99%
Ahmet Aksoy [24]	Device	Determined by Genetic Algorithm	Decision tree	90%
Arman P [25]	Device	1: TCP SYN/SYN-ACK 2: DNS name string 3: IP Related features in the data packet	Random forest	1:87% 2:98% 3:99.8%
Sivanathan, A [26]	1: Device 2: Device 3: Device action	avg packet size and avg rate	Random forest	1:96.8% 2:97.4% 3: 90%

unknown traffic. In terms of classification cost, the multi-target recognition scheme is serial, and the overall real-time performance is low.

The advantage of the multi-stage prediction model is to achieve different classification goals or use different performance classification methods at different stages. It is very flexible and is an important research direction in the future.

7   Comparison of Smart Home Traffic Classification Methods

The Table 5 summarizes different traffic classification algorithms and compares them in terms of sample requirements, accuracy, and real-time performance.

In terms of algorithm characteristics, the advantage of supervised algorithms is that they have high classification accuracy and can achieve accurate classification. However, a labeled data set is required. The quality of the training data set can greatly affect the effect of the classification model. The disadvantage is that supervised learning algorithms usually cannot handle unknown traffic.

In terms of real-time performance, the time consumption of deep learning algorithms in the training phase is longer than that of traditional supervised learning algorithms. On the other hand, the time consumption in the test phase mainly depends on the extraction of flow characteristics.

In terms of the characteristics of the algorithm, the unsupervised algorithm mainly solves the problem of unlabeled traffic classification. It can discover the rules in the unknown traffic, can cluster the traffic into abstract categories, and can further integrate the semi-supervised idea to label the clusters. Deep learning algorithms can be applied to automatic feature extraction, and the comparison of their effects with traditional manually defined features requires further experiments. The multi-stage classification model mainly solves the problem of flexibility of the classification model from the aspects of cost and multi-objective.

Table 5. Comparison of smart home traffic classification methods.

Method	Labeled sample	Accuracy	goal
Supervised	Need	High	Accurate traffic
Unsupervised	Not needed	Medium	1. Flow rule extraction 2. Feature validity evaluation
Deep learning	Depends on the algorithm model	High	1. Accurate traffic 2. Auto feature extraction
Multi-stage forecasting model	Depends on the multi-stage algorithm	High	1. Cost flexibility 2. Target flexibility

8 Conclusions and Outlook

At present, there are more and more researches on smart home traffic classification. Combining the advantages and disadvantages mentioned above, the main research directions in the future will be the following two aspects:

8.1 New Classification Algorithm

In terms of machine learning algorithms, deep learning has developed rapidly in the fields of image and natural language processing. Many new designs have been proposed, such as the attention mechanism [29], which has gradually replaced the application of LSTM networks in natural language processing. These new designs need to be explored. The effect of the algorithm design in the field of smart home traffic classification.

8.2 New Classification Model

Both supervised learning algorithms and unsupervised learning algorithms have their limitations. Under realistic conditions, the classification model needs to be accurate, real-time identification, and compatible. It can realize the traffic classification in the following scenarios: 1) It can quickly identify the traffic category that has been learned; 2) It can handle unlabeled traffic data. Designing a multi-stage classification algorithm can achieve the above classification goals, which is a future research direction.

Acknowledgement. We thank anonymous reviewers for their helpful comments in improving the paper. This work is supported in part by Key-Area Research and Development Program of Guangdong Province (No. 2019B010137005).

References

1. Ren, J.J., Dubois, D.J., Choffnes, D., et al.: Information exposure from consumer IoT devices: a multidimensional, network-informed measurement approach. In: Proceedings of the Internet Measurement Conference, 21–23 October 2019, pp. 267–279. Association for Computing Machinery, New York (2019)
2. Hammad, M.M., Shafiq, Z.: Characterizing smart home IoT traffic in the wild. In: 2020 ACM Fifth International Conference on Internet-of-Things Design and Implementation (IoTDI), Sydney, Australia, 21–24 April 2020, pp. 203–215. Association for Computing Machinery, New York (2020)
3. Jun, B., Jingbo, Jixiang, W.: Survey on real-time traffic classification. Comput. Sci. **37**(6), 1402–1412 (2019)
4. Apthorpe, N.J.: Spying on the smart home: privacy attacks and defenses on encrypted IoT traffic. arXiv: 1708.05044 (2017)
5. Marchal, S., Miettinen, M., Nguyen, T.D., et al.: AuDI: toward autonomous IoT device-type identification using periodic communication. IEEE J. Sel. Areas Commun. **37**(6), 1402–1412 (2019)
6. Sivanathan, A., Sherratt, D., Gharakheili, H.H.: Characterizing and classifying IOT traffic in smart cities and campuses. In: IEEE Conference on Computer Communications Workshops (INFOCOM WK- SHPS), pp. 559–564. IEEE (2017)

7. Miettinen, M., Marchal, S., Hafeez, I., et al.: IoT sentinel demo: automated device-type identification for security enforcement in IoT. In: 2017 IEEE 37th International Conference on Distributed Computing Systems (ICDCS), Atlanta, GA, USA, 5–8 June 2017, pp. 2177–2184. IEEE, New York (2017)
8. Meidan, Y.: Detection of unauthorized IOT devices using machine learning techniques. arXiv: 1709.04647 (2017)
9. Santos, M.R.P., Andrade, R.M.C., Gomes, D.G.: An efficient approach for device identification and traffic classification in IoT ecosystems. In: 2018 IEEE Symposium on Computers and Communications (ISCC), pp. 304–309. IEEE (2018)
10. Shahid, M.R, Blanc, G., Zhang, Z.H.: IoT devices recognition through network traffic analysis. In: IEEE International Conference on Big Data (Big Data), pp. 5187–5192. IEEE (2018)
11. Alshehri, A., Granley, J., Yue, C.: Attacking and protecting tunneled traffic of smart home devices. In: Proceedings of the Tenth ACM Conference on Data and Application Security and Privacy, pp. 259–270 (2020)
12. Oconnor, T.J., Mohamed, R., Miettinen, M.: HomeSnitch: behavior transparency and control for smart home IOT devices. In: Proceedings of the 12th Conference on Security and Privacy in Wireless and Mobile Networks, pp. 128–138. ACM (2019)
13. Charyyev, B., Gunes, M.H.: IoT event classification based on network. In: IEEE INFOCOM 2020- IEEE Conference on Computer Communications Workshops (INFOCOM WKSHPS), vol. 2020, pp. 854–859. IEEE (2020)
14. Li, H., He, Y., Sun, L.: Side-channel information leakage of encrypted video stream in video surveillance systems. In: IEEE INFOCOM 2016 - The 35th Annual IEEE International Conference on Computer Communications, pp. 1–9. IEEE (2016)
15. Wang, J., Cao, Z., Kang, C.: User behavior classification in encrypted cloud camera traffic. In: 2019 IEEE Global Communications Conference (GLOBECOM). vol. 2019, pp. 1–6. IEEE (2019)
16. Thangavelu, V., Divakaran, D.M., Sairam, R.: IEEE Internet Things J. 6(1), 940–952 (2019)
17. Trimananda, R., Varmarken, J., Markopoulou, A.: Packet-level signatures for smart home devices. In: Proceedings 2020 Network and Distributed System Security Symposium (2020)
18. Ortiz, J., Crawford, C., Le, F.: DeviceMien: network device behavior modeling for identifying un-known IoT devices. In: Proceedings of the International Conference on Internet of Things Design and Implementation, pp. 106–117. ACM (2019)
19. Zhai, M., Zhang, X., Zhao, B.: Survey of encrypted malicious traffic detectionbased on deep learning. Chin. J. Netw. Inf. Secur. 6(3), 66–77 (2020)
20. Goodfellow, I., Bengio, Y., Courville, A.: Deep Learning. MIT Press, Cambridge, pp. 367–415 (2016)
21. Bai, L., Yao, L.N., Salil, S.: Automatic device classification from network traffic streams of internet of things. In: 2018 IEEE 43rd Conference on Local Computer Networks (LCN), pp. 597–605. IEEE (2018)
22. Dong, S.K., Zhou, L., Tang, D.: Your smart home can't keep a secret: towards automated fingerprinting of IOT traffic with neural networks. In: Proceedings of the 15th ACM Asia Conference on Computer and Communications Security, vol. 2020, pp. 47–59. ACM (2020)
23. Sivanathan, A., Gharakheili, H.H., Loi, F.: Classifying IoT devices in smart environments using network traffic characteristics. IEEE Trans. Mob. Comput. 18, 1745–1759 (2019)
24. Aksoy, A., Gunes, M.H.: Automated IoT Device identification using network traffic. In: IEEE. ICC 2019 - 2019 IEEE International Conference on Communications (ICC), vol. 2019, pp. 1–7. IEEE (2019)
25. Pashamokhtari: Phd forum abstract: Dynamic inference on IoT network traffic using programmable telemetry and machine learning, pp. 371–372 (2020)
26. Sivanathan, A.: IoT behavioral monitoring via network traffic analysis. arXiv:2001.10632 (2020)

27. Acar, A., Fereidooni, H., Abera, T.: Peek-a-Boo: I see your smart home activities. In: Proceedings of the 13th ACM Conference on Security and Privacy in Wireless and Mobile Networks. vol. 2020, pp. 207–218. ACM (2020)

28. Wan, Y., Xu, K., Xue, G.: IoTArgos: a multi-layer security monitoring system for internet-of-things in smart homes. In: IEEE INFOCOM 2020 - IEEE Conference on Computer Communications, vol. 2020, pp. 874–883. IEEE (2020)

29. Vaswani, A., Shazeer, N., Parmar, N.: Attention is all you need. In: Proceedings of the 31st International Conference on Neural Information Processing Systems, pp. 5998–6008. ACM (2017)

30. Bubeck, S.: Introduction to online optimization (2020). https://www.microsoft.com/en-us/research/publication/introduction-online-optimization/

Efficiency Improvement Method of Flyback Switching Power Supply Based on Quasi-Resonance

Jianbin Liu[1]([✉]), Sha Li[1], Zhe Zhang[1], and Jie Zhang[2]

[1] Jiangsu Key Construction Laboratory of IoT Application Technology, Wuxi Taihu University, Wuxi, China
001210@wxu.edu.cn
[2] University of Liverpool, Liverpool L69 3BX, UK

Abstract. Flyback switching power supply is widely used in small to medium power scenarios, such as household appliances. The conversion efficiency is one of the key parameters for evaluating the power characteristics. The switch loss is an important factor affecting the conversion efficiency. Based on quasi resonant technology, ZVS (Zero Voltage Switching) or ZCS (Zero Current Switching) is realized in flyback switching power supply, which can effectively reduce the switch loss and improve the conversion efficiency. The sample test shows that the design in the paper can achieve ZVS through quasi resonance in all kinds of scenarios, effectively improve the conversion efficiency to more than 85%, and the no-load stand-by power consumption is less than 30 mW. The output voltage regulation rate is less than 2%. Moreover, multiple protection functions are included in the design. It is demonstrated that the design indexes are better than the similar products, and meet level VI energy efficiency standard, which has a wide application prospects.

Keywords: Flyback · Quasi-resonance · ZVS · Conversion efficiency

1 Introduction

Among all kinds of common topologies of switching power supply, flyback topology has many advantages, such as simple structure, low cost, high reliability, high conversion efficiency, voltage isolation, wide output voltage range, easy multi-channel output and so on. It is widely used in mobile phone charger, power adapter and other small and medium power supply scenarios [1]. Flyback structure is characterized by the periodic turn-on and cut-off of MOSFET (Metal-Oxide-Semiconductor Field-Effect Transistor). When the switch is on, the input electric energy is converted into magnetic energy and stored in the transformer. When the switch is off, the magnetic energy stored in the transformer is converted into electric energy and released to the load through the rectifier diode. Under the control of the power control unit, MOSFET switches repeatedly, and the transformer stores and releases energy repeatedly, so as to convert the input high-voltage AC (Alternating Current) into the output low-voltage DC (Direct Current).

© The Author(s), under exclusive license to Springer Nature Switzerland AG 2022
X. Sun et al. (Eds.): ICAIS 2022, LNCS 13340, pp. 558–571, 2022.
https://doi.org/10.1007/978-3-031-06791-4_44

The core technical index of switching power supply is conversion efficiency η, which refers to the ratio of output power to input power. The difference between input power and output power is transformed into heat emission. Obviously, the conversion efficiency η is the higher, the better. The most convenient way to improve the conversion efficiency η is to improve the working frequency. With the development of power electronics technology, the working frequency of switching power supply has reached 10 MHz, so that the conversion efficiency can reach more than 95% [2]. With the increase of switching power supply frequency, the loss caused by switching process becomes the main factor to restrain the increase of conversion efficiency. The increase of working frequency also leads to the increase of switch failure rate. In this context, the topology design of flyback switching power supply is optimized, and the soft switching power supply control technology based on quasi-resonance is adopted, which can not only suppress the loss of MOSFET, improve the conversion efficiency of switching power supply, but also reduce the failure rate of switching power supply [3, 4].

2 Working Mode of Flyback

Flyback power supply consists of transformer, control unit and MOSFET, which has double loop feedback control mechanism. One is the output feedback loop, which samples the output current and voltage and feeds back to the control unit, so as to adjust the PWM (Pulse Width Modulation) duty cycle output of the switch, so as to realize constant voltage and constant current output. The other is the input feedback loop, which samples the excitation current of the primary coil and feeds back to the control unit to control the on-off of the switch tube, so as to limit the peak value of the input power. There are three working modes of flyback power supply: CCM (Continuous Conduction Mode), DCM (Discontinuous Conduction Mode) and BCM (Boundary Conduction Mode). The control unit automatically switches these three modes according to the change of power load [5]. Under the control of the power control unit, flyback power supply switches repeatedly, and the transformer stores and releases energy repeatedly, so as to convert the input high-voltage AC into the output low-voltage DC. The process is divided into two stages: energy storage and energy release [6].

2.1 Energy Storage Stage

In the energy storage stage, as shown in Fig. 1, the primary bus voltage V_{bus} is obtained by rectifying the input AC220V voltage and filtering the electrolytic capacitor C_1. When the MOSFET Q_1 is on, the primary current I_P flows through the primary winding N_P, the MOSFET Q_1, the sampling resistance R_{CS} and the primary ground. In this stage, the primary winding N_P of the transformer is equal to the inductance, and the homonymous end of N_P (star in the figure) is negative, so the homonymous ends of the secondary winding N_s and the auxiliary winding N_a of the transformer are also negative, and the secondary rectifier diode D_2 and the auxiliary rectifier diode D_1 are cut off. In this stage, the input electric energy is converted into magnetic energy and stored in the core of the transformer T_1.

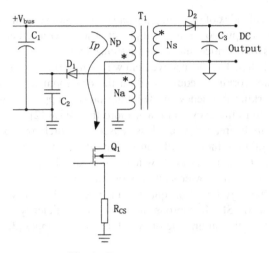

Fig. 1. Energy storage stage.

2.2 Energy Release Stage

As shown in Fig. 2, the MOSFET Q_1 is off. Due to the inductance characteristics of T_1, the current I_P in the primary winding N_P of the transformer needs to maintain the current. At this time, N_P is equivalent to the power supply and releases the current I_P to the outside of the transformer. In this stage, the homonymous end of N_P is positive, the homonymous ends of secondary winding N_s and auxiliary winding N_a are also positive, and the secondary rectifier diode D_2 and auxiliary rectifier diode D_1 are on. In this stage, the magnetic energy stored in the transformer T_1 core is converted into electrical energy, which is released to the output through the T_1 secondary coil.

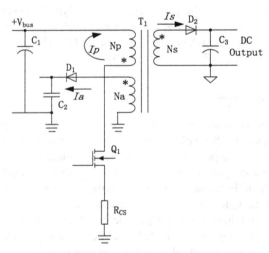

Fig. 2. Energy release stage.

3   Loss Analysis of MOSFET

Driven by the control unit, the high-frequency on-off of MOSFET makes the transformer T_1 high-frequency energy storage and release, so as to realize the energy conversion from high-voltage AC input to low-voltage DC output. The parasitic parameters of MOSFET Q_1 lead to certain delay and lag of current I_P and voltage V_{ds} in the switching process, which is the fundamental reason for the loss of switch and the decrease of power conversion efficiency [7, 8].

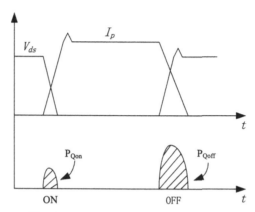

Fig. 3. Waveform of MOSFET switching.

As shown in Fig. 3, when MOSFET is on, it takes a certain time for V_{ds} to drop to 0. During this period, the primary current I_P gradually increases to the peak I_{PK}, and the overlapping area of I_P and V_{ds} is the conduction loss P_{Qon}.

$$P_{Qon} = \frac{2}{3} \times f_{SW} \times C_{Q1} \times V_{bus}^2 \tag{1}$$

When MOSFET is off, the primary current I_P needs a certain time to drop to 0. During this time, the voltage V_{ds} gradually increases, and the overlapping area of I_P and V_{ds} is the cut-off loss P_{Qoff}.

$$P_{Qoff} = \frac{1}{2} \times f_{SW} \times V_{bus} \times I_{PK} \times t_r \tag{2}$$

The loss P_{Qon} and P_{Qoff} together constitute the switch loss P_Q, which is proportional to the working frequency f_{sw} of the power supply, the high voltage V_{bus}, the parasitic capacitance C_{Q1} of MOSFET, the peak value I_{PK} of the primary current, and the rise time t_r of V_{ds}. Obviously, with the development trend of switching power supply, f_{sw} is higher and higher, V_{bus} is determined by the input voltage and can't be changed, C_{Q1} and t_r are related to the characteristics of MOSFET, I_{PK} is determined by the power of the power supply. When the above parameters are limited, the quasi resonant mode can only be used to improve the switching power supply [9, 10].

4 Quasi Resonant Technology

4.1 Design of Quasi Resonant Converter

In order to eliminate the loss of MOSFET, including P_{Qon} and P_{Qoff}, reduce the loss, improve the conversion efficiency η and the electromagnetic compatibility, it is necessary to avoid the overlap of voltage V_{ds} and current I_P. ZVS or ZCS can be used [11–13].

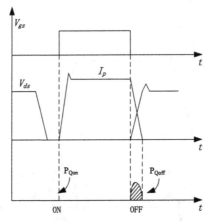

Fig. 4. Waveform of ZVS.

Figure 4 shows ZVS, V_{gs} drives MOSFET to turn on after the voltage V_{ds} drops to zero, so the conduction loss P_{Qon} is 0.

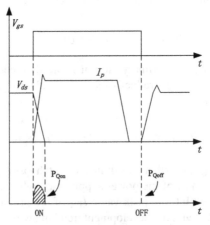

Fig. 5. Waveform of ZCS.

Figure 5 shows the ZCS, V_{gs} drives MOSFET to cut off after the current I_P drops to zero, so the cut-off loss P_{Qoff} is 0.

In order to obtain ZVS or ZCS, the parasitic inductance L_r (mainly determined by the primary excitation inductance L_m) and the resonant capacitance C_r (mainly determined by the parasitic capacitance C_{Q1}) are used to control the switching of MOSFET under ZVS or ZCS. Resonant converters include LRC (Load Resonant Converter), MRC (Multiple Resonant Converter) and QRC (Quasi Resonant Converter), which generally adopt pulse frequency modulation method. LRC has high circulating current energy and is sensitive to load and input voltage. MRC has small switching frequency range and voltage stress of switching devices, but its parameter optimization design is complex and high cost. QRC has stable performance, simple structure and good comprehensive performance, but it needs frequency conversion control, so this design uses QRC [14, 15].

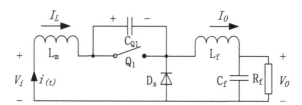

Fig. 6. Circuit diagram of QR-Flyback converter.

QRC is substituted into the flyback power supply circuit to get the QR-Flyback converter shown in Fig. 6. L_m is the primary excitation inductance, C_{Q1} is the parasitic capacitance of MOSFET, D_s is the freewheeling diode, C_f, L_f and R_f are the equivalent parameters of the secondary output winding refracted to the primary input winding.

4.2 Working Process of Quasi Resonant Converter

A working cycle of quasi resonant converter can be divided into four stages: inductor charging stage TM_1, LC resonance stage TM_2, capacitor charging stage TM_3 and freewheeling stage TM_4 [16].

Inductor Charging Stage TM$_1$ [t$_0$, t$_1$]. In the initial state, Q_1 is off and I_L is zero. At t_0, Q_1 is on with zero current, and the current I_L flowing through the excitation inductor L_m increases gradually. At t_1, I_O is equal to I_L, and the output reaches the maximum. In this stage, the equation of state is as follows:

$$\begin{bmatrix} I_L \\ V_O \\ I_O \end{bmatrix} = \begin{bmatrix} 0 & \frac{1}{L_f} & 0 \\ \frac{1}{C_f} & -\frac{1}{R_f C_f} & -\frac{1}{C_f} \\ 0 & \frac{1}{L_m} & 0 \end{bmatrix} \cdot \begin{bmatrix} I_L \\ V_O \\ I_O \end{bmatrix} + \begin{bmatrix} \frac{1}{L_f} \\ 0 \\ 0 \end{bmatrix} \cdot V_i \tag{3}$$

Solving the equation of state, we get the results:

$$TM_1 = \frac{L_m \times I_L}{V_O} \tag{4}$$

LC Resonance Stage TM$_2$ [t$_1$, t$_2$]. At t_1, the excitation inductance L_m and the parasitic capacitor C_{Q1} start to resonate. At t_2, the resonant current returns to zero, MOSFET turns off. In this stage, the equation of state is as follows:

$$
\begin{bmatrix} I_L \\ V_O \\ I_O \\ V_{CQ1} \end{bmatrix} = \begin{bmatrix} 0 & 0 & 0 & \frac{-1}{L_f} \\ 0 & \frac{-1}{R_f C_f} & 0 & 0 \\ 0 & 0 & 0 & \frac{1}{L_m} \\ \frac{1}{C_{Q1}} & 0 & \frac{-1}{C_{Q1}} & 0 \end{bmatrix} \cdot \begin{bmatrix} I_L \\ V_O \\ I_O \\ V_{CQ1} \end{bmatrix} + \begin{bmatrix} \frac{1}{L_f} \\ 0 \\ 0 \\ 0 \end{bmatrix} \cdot V_i \tag{5}
$$

Solving the equation of state, we get the results:

$$
TM_2 = \left[\sin^{-1}\left(-\frac{\sqrt{L_m/C_{Q1}} \times I_L}{V_O} \right) \right] \times \sqrt{L_m \times C_{Q1}} \tag{6}
$$

Capacitor Charging Stage TM$_3$ [t$_2$, t$_3$]. At t_2, the resonant current returns to 0, MOSFET switches off, the resonance ends. Then, the capacitor C_{Q1} starts to charge, the voltage rises, and at t_3, the V_{CQ1} rises to V_O. In this stage, the equation of state is as follows:

$$
\begin{bmatrix} I_L \\ V_O \\ I_O \\ V_{CQ1} \end{bmatrix} = \begin{bmatrix} 0 & 0 & 0 & 0 \\ 0 & \frac{-1}{R_f C_f} & 0 & 0 \\ 0 & 0 & 0 & 0 \\ \frac{1}{C_{Q1}} & 0 & 0 & 0 \end{bmatrix} \cdot \begin{bmatrix} I_L \\ V_O \\ I_O \\ V_{CQ1} \end{bmatrix} + \begin{bmatrix} \frac{1}{L_f} \\ 0 \\ 0 \\ 0 \end{bmatrix} \cdot V_i \tag{7}
$$

Solving the equation of state, we get the results:

$$
TM_3 = \frac{C_{Q1} \times V_O \times (1 - \cos\theta)}{I_L} \tag{8}
$$

Freewheeling Stage TM$_4$ [t$_3$, t$_4$]. At t_3, V_{CQ1} rises to V_O, and the secondary output diode remains on until the next switch on time t_0. In this stage, the equation of state is as follows:

$$
\begin{bmatrix} I_L \\ V_O \\ I_O \end{bmatrix} = \begin{bmatrix} 0 & \frac{1}{L_f} & 0 \\ \frac{1}{C_f} & -\frac{1}{R_f C_f} & 0 \\ 0 & 0 & 0 \end{bmatrix} \cdot \begin{bmatrix} I_L \\ V_O \\ I_O \end{bmatrix} + \begin{bmatrix} \frac{1}{L_f} \\ 0 \\ 0 \end{bmatrix} \cdot V_i \tag{9}
$$

Solving the equation of state, we get the results:

$$
TM_4 = \frac{I_L}{C_f \times V_O} \tag{10}
$$

To sum up, the switching period in quasi resonant mode consists of TM_1–TM_4 stages. The parasitic parameters and output parameters of the circuit have an impact on the oscillation period, and the output parameters have the greatest impact.

5 Circuit Design

According to the design requirements of common chargers and adapters, the input voltage is AC90 ~ 265 V, the output voltage is DC5V and the output current is 2 A. Combining the output feedback loop with the input feedback loop, the primary side feedback technology is obtained. Then, it is fused with the QR-Flyback converter circuit to obtain the quasi resonant primary side feedback flyback converter circuit shown in Fig. 7. The circuit consists control unit, transformer and MOSFET [17–19].

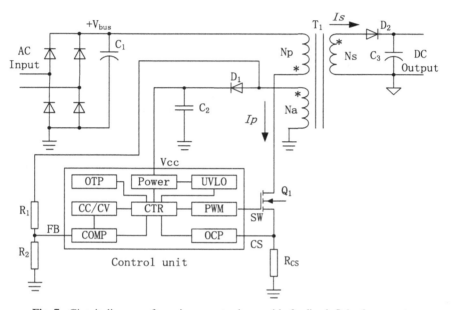

Fig. 7. Circuit diagram of quasi resonant primary side feedback flyback converter.

5.1 Control Unit

The control unit has the following functions:

- Cancel the optocoupler and secondary voltage reference, use the auxiliary winding N_a as the output feedback.
- Through zero voltage detection and zero current detection, control to achieve ZVS or ZCS, so as to reduce the switch loss.
- With the change of output load, it can operate independently in DCM or CCM Switching.
- It can realize constant current output, constant voltage output, over temperature protection, under voltage or over voltage protection, over current protection, open-loop protection and other protection functions.

5.2   Transformer and MOSFET

The design power of transformer T_1 is 12 W, excitation inductance L_m is 2 mH, leakage inductance L_k is 16 uH. Taking the magnetic core and skeleton as the core, N_{P1}, N_s, N_{P2}, and N_a windings are tightly wound in turn by sandwich winding method. The primary winding N_{P1} is 48 turns, the secondary winding N_s is 5 turns, the primary winding N_{P2} is 48 turns, and the auxiliary winding N_a is 11 turns. MOSFET is built in the power chip with parameters of 650 V-1 A. It can save space, improve electromagnetic compatibility and improve reliability.

6   Test Verification

Build the test platform shown in Fig. 8 to test the working condition of quasi resonance and the main performance parameters of power supply. Test instruments include: PF9811 digital intelligent electrical parameter tester, 200 MHz bandwidth and 2 GHz sampling frequency digital storage oscilloscope, 0–200 W power electronic load, 4-bit high precision digital multi-meter [20, 21].

Fig. 8. Diagram of test scheme.

6.1   Working State of Quasi Resonant Converter

The oscilloscope monitors the V_{ds} waveform and observes whether the quasi resonant working state meets the expectation under different output loads.

Figure 9 shows the V_{ds} waveform of output 5 V-1 A (50% load). At the beginning of a cycle, MOSFET is turned on and the transformer stores energy with V_{ds} is zero. When MOSFET is turned off, the transformer releases the stored energy to the secondary for about 15 us, and the leakage inductance L_k oscillates with the parasitic capacitance C_{Q1}. When the primary energy storage is released, the excitation inductance L_m oscillates with the parasitic capacitance C_{Q1}, and the quasi resonant frequency f_s is 350 kHz, and the oscillation period T_s is 45 us. That means one quasi resonant period needs to be completed 16 oscillations. At the beginning of the next cycle, MOSFET turns on at the bottom of the quasi harmonic oscillation. At this time, V_{ds} is the minimum, and the switch loss is the minimum, realizing the quasi resonant ZVS.

Figure 10 shows the V_{ds} waveform of output 5 V-2 A (100% load). The process is similar to that in Fig. 9. The quasi resonant frequency is determined by the excitation inductance L_m and the parasitic capacitance C_{Q1}, and the quasi resonant frequency f_s is maintained at 350 kHz. The oscillation period T_s is determined by the PWM duty cycle of MOSFET, and the increase of the load leads to the increase of the duty cycle, so that

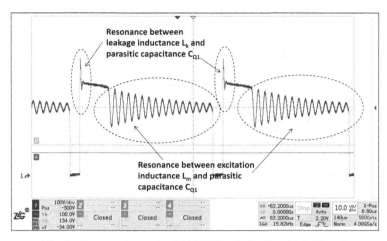

Fig. 9. V_{ds} waveform after MOSFET switch-off under half-load.

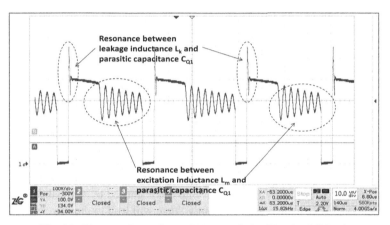

Fig. 10. V_{ds} waveform after MOSFET switch-off under full-load.

the oscillation period T_s is shortened to 18 us. That means one quasi resonant period needs to experience six oscillations. At the beginning of the next cycle, MOSFET is still conducting at the bottom of the quasi harmonic oscillation to realize the quasi resonant ZVS under any output load.

6.2 Power Performance Parameters

In this design, five typical input voltages are selected from the input voltage AC90 ~ 265 V, the output voltage is set to constant voltage 5 V, and the output current is variable in 0–2 A. The conversion efficiency of no-load (5 V/0 A), half-load (5 V/1 A) and full-load (5 V/2 A) is tested. The test data in Table 1 are sorted out and analyzed, which focuses on standby power consumption, output voltage regulation rate and conversion efficiency.

Table 1. Test result.

Input voltage V_{in} (V)	Output current I_o (A)	Output voltage V_o (V)	Input power P_{in} (W)	Output power P_o (W)	Conversion efficiency η(%)
90	0	4.96	0.021	0	–
	1.00	4.87	5.85	4.87	83.3
	2.00	4.85	11.52	9.62	83.5
120	0	4.96	0.024	0	–
	1.00	4.91	5.85	4.91	84.0
	2.00	4.85	11.47	9.66	84.2
170	0	4.96	0.026	0	–
	1.00	4.95	5.85	4.95	84.6
	2.00	4.87	11.57	9.74	84.2
220	0	4.96	0.030	0	–
	1.00	4.95	5.82	4.95	85.1
	2.00	4.90	11.49	9.80	85.3
265	0	4.96	0.031	0	–
	1.00	4.95	5.84	4.95	84.8
	2.00	4.90	11.49	9.80	85.3

6.2.1 Standby Power Consumption

Standby Power Consumption. Figure 11 shows the no-load standby power consumption with I_o is 0, which will gradually increase from 21 mw to 31 mW with the increase of input voltage. The standby power consumption is caused by the leakage current of circuit components. The increase of circuit voltage will lead to the increase of leakage current of circuit components, resulting in the increase of standby power consumption. By increasing the impedance of the device and reducing the capacitive reactance, the standby power consumption can be reduced, but the response speed of the circuit will be reduced, resulting in the output voltage may fluctuate with the change of the load. The standby power consumption required by level 6 energy efficiency standard is not more than 75 mW, this design meets the requirement.

Output Voltage Regulation Rate. Figure 12 shows the variation of output voltage V_o with input voltage V_{in} under three conditions of no-load (5 V-0 A), half load (5 V-1 A) and full load (5 V-2 A). It can be seen that the output voltage V_o decreases with the increase of load and the input voltage V_{in}. This phenomenon is caused by two reasons:

- The heavier the output load, the greater the output current I_o, and the greater the loss of the output circuit including the secondary transformer, secondary rectifier diode, PCB (Printed Circuit Board) wiring, output harness, etc., resulting in the reduction of terminal voltage.

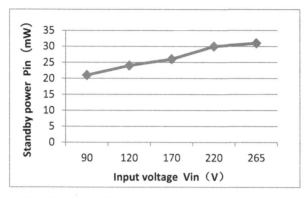

Fig. 11. Curve of no-load standby power consumption.

- The lower the V_{in}, the higher the primary current I_P under the same power, and the easier it is to trigger the primary current limiting peak I_{PK}, resulting in lower output.

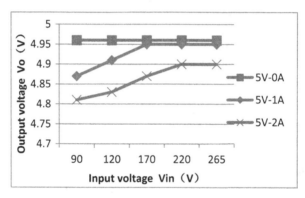

Fig. 12. Curve of output voltage adjustment

Conversion Efficiency. Figure 13 shows the change of conversion efficiency under the condition of half load (5 V-1 A) and full load (5 V-2 A). Compared with level 6 energy efficiency standard (78%) and a well-known charger, this design has certain advantages.

With the increase of input voltage V_{in}, the conversion efficiency η increases slightly and reaches the peak at about 220 V. When V_{in} continues to increase, the conversion efficiency decreases. The reasons are analyzed in several aspects: On the one hand, when V_{in} decreases, the primary current I_P increases, and the loss caused by the current in the input circuit increases, which leads to the decrease of the conversion efficiency. On the other hand, if V_{in} is too high, the leakage current loss will increase and the conversion efficiency will decrease. The two factors lead to the highest conversion efficiency of V_{in} at about 220 V.

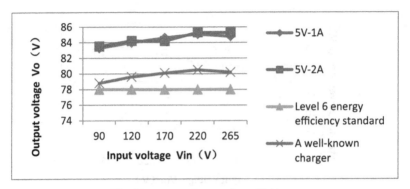

Fig. 13. Curve of conversion efficiency.

7 Conclusions

In order to improve the conversion efficiency of flyback switching power supply and reduce the switch loss, this paper uses quasi resonant technology to realize ZVS or ZCS on flyback switching power supply, and designs a power adapter with input AC90 ~ 265V and output DC5V-2A for verification. After testing, the power supply can achieve ZVS through quasi resonance under different output loads. Its performance meets the most stringent level 6 energy efficiency standard, and is superior to a existing well-known charger in the market. The main indicators include:

- The conversion efficiency η is 83.3%–85.3%, which meets the requirements of level 6 energy efficiency standard higher than 78%.
- The no-load standby power consumption is 21–31 mW, which meets the requirements of level 6 energy efficiency standard lower than 75 mW.
- The output voltage V_o is 4.85–4.96 V, the adjustment rate is less than 2%, and the output is stable.
- With over temperature protection, under voltage or over voltage protection, over current protection and other multiple protection functions.
- The utility model has the advantages of small size, compact structure and low cost.

Acknowledgement. The authors thank all partners in Jiangsu Key Construction Laboratory of IoT Application Technology (Wuxi Taihu University).

Funding Statement. This research was supported in part by the Natural Science Foundation of the Jiangsu Higher Education Institutions of China (Grant No. 18KJB510045), and in part by the Research Foundation of Jiangsu Key Construction Laboratory of IoT Application Technology (Grant No. 18WXWL05).

Conflicts of Interest. The authors declare that they have no conflicts of interest to report regarding the present study.

References

1. Hou, Q.J., Zhang, Li., Xu, D.: The basic principle of switching power supply and development trend of switching power supply. Manuf. Autom. **32**(9), 160–169 (2010)
2. Song, Q., Zhao, B., Liu, W., et al.: Next generation high-frequency-isolation power conversion technology for smart grid. Proc. CSEE **34**(36), 6369–6379 (2014)
3. Park, J., Moom, Y.J., Jeong, M.G.: Quasi-resonant (QR) controller with adaptive switching frequency reduction scheme for flyback converter. IEEE Trans. Industr. Electron **63**(6), 3571–3581 (2016)
4. Han, O., Kim, J.: Uncertainty analysis on electric power consumption. Comput. Mater. Continua **68**(2), 2621–2632 (2021)
5. Murthy-Bellur, D., Kazimierczuk, M.K.: Uncertainty analysis on electric power consumption. Int. J. Circuit Theory Appl. **39**(11), 849–864 (2011)
6. Taha, I.B., Mansour, D.A.: Novel power transformer fault diagnosis using optimized machine learning methods. Intell. Autom. Soft Comput. **28**(3), 739–752 (2021)
7. Chen, Z., Shu, L., Liu, Y., Ge, L.: Analysis of MOSFET loss model based on current source driver. Electr. Power Autom. Equip. **30**(10), 50–53 (2010)
8. Lei, R., Zheng, W., Chunying, G.: Fault feature extraction techniques for power devices in power electronic converters a review. Proc. CSEE **35**(12), 3089–3101 (2015)
9. Kumar, K.S., Paramasivam, K.: Novel power-aware optimization methodology and efficient task scheduling algorithm. Comput. Syst. Sci. Eng. **41**(1), 209–224 (2022)
10. Liu, J., Li, S., Jiang, Y., Cheng, X.: Power line communication technology based on conduction angle modulation in intelligent lighting. Acta Electonica Sinica **49**(7), 1331–1338 (2021)
11. Borage, M., Tiwari, S., Kotaiah, S.: A passive auxiliary circuit achieves zero-voltage-switching in full-bridge converter over entire conversion range. IEEE Power Electron. Lett. **3**(4), 141–143 (2005)
12. Yazdani, M.R., Rahmani, S.: A new zero-current-transition two-switch flyback converter. In: The 5th Annual International Power Electronics, Drive Systems and Technologies Conference (PEDSTC 2014), pp. 390–395. IEEE (2014)
13. Alrajhi, H.: A generalized state space average model for parallel DC-to-DC converters. Comput. Syst. Sci. Eng. **41**(2), 717–734 (2022)
14. Stracquadaini, R.D.: Mixed mode control (fixed off time & quasi resonant) for flyback converter. In: IECON 2010–36th Annual Conference on IEEE Industrial Electronics Society, pp. 556–561. IEEE (2010)
15. Huang, Y., Xu, J., Yin, G., Ma, H.: Quasi-resonant soft-switched two-switch flyback converter. Trans. China Electrotech. Soc. **33**(18), 4313–4322 (2018)
16. Ahmed, E.M., Ahmed, M.A., Ali, Z.M., Khan, I.: Disturbance evaluation in power system based on machine learning. Comput. Mater. Continua **71**(1), 231–254 (2022)
17. Jie, D., Shiwei, Z., Huajie, Y.: A new type of soft switch isolated DC-DC converter with high step-up. Adv. Technol. Electr. Eng. Energy **39**(06), 18–25 (2020)
18. Qiu, J.P., He, L.N., Wang, Y.L.: A multimode digital controller IC for flyback converter with high accuracy primary-side feedback. J. Zhejiang Univ. Sci. C (Comput. Electron.) **14**(8), 652–662 (2013)
19. Park, J., Moom, Y.J., Jeong, M.G.: Quasi-resonant (QR) controller with adaptive switching frequency reduction scheme for flyback converter. IEEE Trans. Industr. Electron. **63**(6), 3571–3581 (2016)
20. El-Zohri, E.H., Rezk, H., Alamri, B., Ziedan, H.A.: Improving the power quality of smart microgrid based solar photovoltaic systems. Intell. Autom. Soft Comput. **30**(1), 201–213 (2021)
21. Liu, J., Jiang, Y., Li, S., et al.: EMC design of electric operating system for miniature circuit breaker. Acta Electron. Sin. **48**(05), 914–921 (2020)

Distributed State Estimation for Topology Random Switching in Sensor Networks

Peng Yan and Yao Xiang[✉]

Jiangsu Key Construction Laboratory of IoT Application Technology, Wuxi Taihu University, Wuxi, China
yx_cathy@qq.com

Abstract. This paper proposes a distributed robust filter design method for sensor networks with sensor saturation nonlinearity and random switching of communication topology. In the sensor network, a large number of sensor nodes are deployed to realize the sensing and measurement of the target system, and transmit it to the remote filter through the network. In filter networks, local estimators not only receive the measurement information of sensor nodes, but also receive and fuse the estimation information of neighboring nodes through random time-varying communication topology to achieve state estimation and trajectory tracking of target objects. The saturation nonlinearity of sensor network is described by Bernoulli binary distribution, the random switching of topology is described by inhomogeneous Markov chain, and the sufficient conditions for the existence of distributed filter are given in the form of linear matrix inequality. Finally, a numerical example is given to illustrate the effectiveness of the proposed design method.

Keywords: Distributed filtering · H_∞ performance · Switching topology · Inhomogeneous Markov chain · Saturation nonlinearity

1 Lead It

Wireless Sensor Network (WSN) is usually composed of a large number of Sensor nodes distributed in space. Wireless sensor networks (WSNS) are widely used in environmental monitoring, industrial automation and military applications, which have attracted more and more scholars' attention [1–5]. In these numerous application fields, the basic problem based on WSN is to design a distributed estimation algorithm for monitoring targets or systems, in order to realize the estimation and tracking of target signals, states or trajectorys. In the past few years, the distributed filtering algorithm based on WSN has made many research achievements [6–9].

Distributed Kalman filter is a common filtering algorithm [10–14]. For example, literature [10] studies the Kalman filter algorithm on peer-to-peer sensor networks, focusing on the network communication transmission mechanism to reduce communication bandwidth, thus improving energy efficiency and extending network life. Literature [12] studies the distributed Kalman filter problem of multi-target tracking system with coupled measurement, and the designed consistent Kalman filter depends on the augmented system of the target. Unfortunately, distributed Kalman filter is no longer applicable when the system model and noise statistics are uncertain. Accordingly, distributed filtering has obtained many research achievements because it does not need accurate system model and noise statistical characteristics H_∞ [15–18]. For example, literature [15] solves the problem of distributed event-triggered filtering in sensor networks affected by measurement saturation network attacks H_∞. In reference [16] and [18], a distributed robust consistency state estimator was designed respectively for channel decay and quantitative measurement in sensor networks H_∞.

Most existing filtering results require strict assumptions about the linearity of sensors. However, wireless sensor networks are usually deployed in harsh environments, such as military battlefields and complex oceans, which include many uncontrollable factors that may lead to sensor random measurement saturation nonlinearity [19–24]. For example, literature [20] studies the finite-time state estimation problem of semi-Markov jump neural networks with sensor nonlinearity. In reference [21], an estimator was designed for A Markov jump system by using partial information of Markov state, transition probability and detection probability, combined with random sensor nonlinearity H_∞. Therefore, it is of practical engineering significance to design a distributed robust filtering method for WSN with random measurement saturation.

It should be pointed out that in many complex network environments, random faults, recovery of communication links, obstructions and uncertain network induced phenomena often lead to changes in sensor network communication topology. Designing distributed filtering algorithm based on fixed network communication topology will be limited in practical application [25–27]. To solve this problem, literature [25] solves the output adjustment problem of linear heterogeneous multi-agent system under switching topology. Literature [26] designed a distributed robust filter based on adaptive event triggering mechanism. However, these research results are based on homogeneous Markov chain to realize the modeling of random changes in communication topology. However, it often takes a lot of time and energy to obtain a complete and accurate transfer probability data of topology change for a complex WSN. At the same time, the law of network topology change may appear nonlinear. Therefore, using non-homogeneous Markov chain to describe the random switching of wireless sensor network communication topology is more in line with the actual demand.

Research, therefore, a kind of sensor under the restriction of saturation with stochastic switching topology design method of distributed state estimation is of great significance, this paper's main contributions are as follows: based on the theory of bounded sector, using Bernoulli random variables to describe random measuring saturated nonlinear wireless sensor network (WSN), the design of the distributed filter has stronger robustness; Based on the inhomogeneous Markov theory, the sufficient conditions for the existence of distributed filter for the random switching of communication topology are obtained, and the desired performance of filtering error dynamic system is guaranteed H_∞.

2 Problem Description

The information exchange between sensor nodes can be represented by a directed graph, where is the node set, is the boundary set and is the adjacency matrix $\mathcal{G}^{r(k)} =$

$(\mathcal{V}, \mathcal{E}, \partial^{r(k)})\mathcal{V} = \{1, 2, \cdots, N\}\mathcal{E} \subseteq \mathcal{V} \times \mathcal{V} \, \partial^{r(k)} = \left[a_{ij}^{r(k)}\right]_{N \times N}$. If a directed graph has a boundary from node to node, then the ordered pair, and the node is called an adjacent node of the node $\mathcal{G}^{r(k)}ji \,\, (i, j) \in \mathcal{E} \, a_{ij}^{r(k)} > 0ji$. The definition matrix is the Laplacian matrix, where $\mathcal{L}^{r(k)} = \left(l_{ij}^{r(k)}\right)_{N \times N} l_{ii}^{r(k)} = \sum_{j \in \mathcal{N}_i^{r(k)}} a_{ij}^{r(k)}, l_{ij}^{r(k)} = -a_{ij}^{r(k)}, \forall i \neq j$. Furthermore, we assume that, for all, $i \in \mathcal{V} a_{ii}^{r(k)} = 0$. The set formed by all adjacent nodes of a node is called the adjacent node set of a node, denoted as $i \, i \mathcal{N}_i^{r(k)} = \{j \in \mathcal{V} : (i, j) \in \mathcal{E}\}$.

Markov chain is used to describe the current communication topology mode and is valued in a finite set, where the time-varying state transition probability matrix is, which represents the probability of sub-topology S jumping to sub-topology T, and satisfies $r(k)\mathcal{S} = \{1, 2, \cdots, n_0\}\Pi(k) = (\pi_{st}(k))_{n_0 \times n_0}\pi_{st}(k)$

$$\pi_{st}(k) = Prob(r(k+1) = t | r(k) = s). \tag{1}$$

$\Pi(k)$ Is a time-varying matrix representing an inhomogeneous Markov chain. Assuming that there is cellular uncertainty, satisfy $\Pi(k)$

$$\Pi(k) = \sum_{m=1}^{m_0} \alpha_m(k)\Pi^{(m)}, \tag{2}$$

Among them

$$\alpha_m(k) > 0, \sum_{m=1}^{m_0} \alpha_m(k) = 1. \tag{3}$$

Here, and for all of them $\pi_{st} \geq 0s, t \in \mathcal{S} \sum_{t=1}^{n_0} \pi_{st} = 1$.
Consider the following discrete time linear time invariant system

$$\begin{cases} x(k+1) = Ax(k) + Bw(k), \\ z(k) = Mx(k), \end{cases} \tag{4}$$

Where is the state vector of the system, is the estimated output vector, is the external interference, and belongs to $x(k) \in \mathbb{R}^{n_x} z(k) \in \mathbb{R}^{n_z} w(k) \in \mathbb{R}^{n_w} l_2 0, \infty)$.

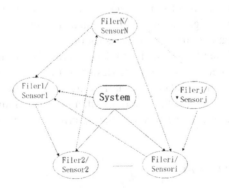

Fig. 1. Distributed filtering system.

The distributed filtering system based on sensor network is shown in Fig. 1. The measurement model of each node in the sensor network is described as

$$\begin{cases} y_i(k) = C_i x(k), \\ y_{\phi,i}(k) = (1 - \theta_i(k))\phi_i(y_i(k)) \\ + \theta_i(k)y_i(k) + D_i v_i(k), \end{cases} \tag{5}$$

where is the measurement vector of node I, is the measurement noise, and belongs to $y_i(k) \in \mathbb{R}^{n_y} v_i(k) l_2 0, \infty)\phi(\cdot)$Phi is the saturation function.

$$\left(\phi_i(y_i(k)) - K_{1,i}y_i(k)\right)^T \left(\phi_i(y_i(k)) - K_{2,i}y_i(k)\right) \le 0. \tag{6}$$

Referring to the processing method in literature [24], nonlinear function can be divided into linear part and nonlinear part $\phi_i(y_i(k)$

$$\phi_i(y_i(k)) = \phi_{sat,i}(y_i(k)) + K_{1,i}y_i(k), \tag{7}$$

Which meet the $\phi_{sat,i}(y_i(k))$

$$\phi_{sat,i}^T(y_i(k))\left(\phi_{sat,i}(y_i(k)) - K_i y_i(k)\right) \le 0, \tag{8}$$

One of them $K_i \triangleq K_{2,i} - K_{1,i}$. In addition, the coefficient matrices all have corresponding dimensions A, B, M, C_i, D_i.

The Bernoulli distribution random white sequence is assumed to be evaluated on, used to describe the saturation nonlinearity of random occurrence, and satisfies $\{\theta_i(k)\}\{0, 1\}$

$$\mathbb{E}\{\theta_i(k)\} = \text{Prob}\{\theta_i(k) = 1\} = \beta_i, \mathbb{E}\{\theta_i(k) = 0\} = 1 - \beta_i,$$
$$\mathbb{E}\{(\theta_i(k) - \beta_i)^2\} = \beta_i(1 - \beta_i) = \alpha_i, \tag{9}$$

And assume that any random variables are independent of each other $1 \le i \le N$ $0 \le k < \infty\theta_i(k)$.

The following filter constrained by random sensor saturation and communication topology switching is constructed

$$\begin{cases} \hat{x}_i(k + 1) = A\hat{x}_i(k) + L_i^s\left(y_{\phi,i}(k) - C_i\hat{x}_i(k)\right) \\ + W_i^s \sum_{j \in \mathcal{N}_i^s} a_{ij}^s\left(\hat{x}_j(k) - \hat{x}_i(k)\right), \\ \hat{z}_i(k) = M\hat{x}_i(k), \end{cases} \tag{10}$$

where is the filter state and is an estimate of the filter pair $\hat{x}_i \in \mathbb{R}^{n_x}\hat{z}_i(k) \in \mathbb{R}^{n_z} iz(k)$. The matrix is the filter parameter that needs to be determined L_i^s, W_i^s — $(I - \beta_i)L_i^s\phi_{sat,i}(y_i(k))e_i(k + 1) = (A + L_i^s C_i)e_i(k) + Bw(k)$. The state estimation error is defined as, then the state error of each node is described as $e_i(k) = x(k) - \hat{x}_i(k)$

$$-L_i^s D_i v_i(k) - W_i^s \sum_{j \in \mathcal{N}_i^s} a_{ij}^s\left(e_i(k) - e_j(k)\right)$$
$$-L_i^s(\theta_i(k) - \beta_i)(C_i - K_{1,i}C_i)x(k)$$
$$-L_i^s(K_{1,i}C_i - \beta_i K_{1,i}C_i + \beta_i C_i - C_i)x(k) \tag{11}$$
$$+L_i^s(\theta_i(k) - \beta_i)\phi_{sat,i}(y_i(k))$$

If the output estimation error is defined as, the output estimation error is described as $\tilde{z}_i(k) = z(k) - \hat{z}_i(k)$

$$\tilde{z}_i(k) = Me_i(k). \tag{12}$$

For the convenience of expression, N nodes are considered at the same time, the estimated error vector system state vector filter state vector output estimated error vector sensor network measurement vector measurement noise vector and system parameter vector.

$$e(k) = \left[e_1^T(k), e_2^T(k), \cdots, e_N^T(k) \right]^T,$$

$$\bar{x}(k) = \left[x^T(k), x^T(k), \cdots, x^T(k) \right]^T,$$

$$\hat{x}(k) = \left[\hat{x}_1^T(k), \hat{x}_2^T(k), \cdots, \hat{x}_N^T(k) \right]^T,$$

$$\tilde{z}(k) = \left[\tilde{z}_1^T(k), \tilde{z}_2^T(k), \cdots, \tilde{z}_N^T(k) \right]^T,$$

$$y(k) = \left[y_1^T(k), y_2^T(k), \cdots, y_N^T(k) \right]^T,$$

$$v(k) = \left[v_1^T(k), v_2^T(k), \cdots, v_N^T(k) \right]^T,$$

$$\bar{A} = diag\{A, A, \cdots, A\}, \bar{B} = \left[B^T, B^T, \cdots, B^T \right]^T,$$

$$\bar{C} = diag\{C_1, C_2, \cdots, C_N\}, D = diag\{D_1, D_2, \cdots, D_N\},$$

$$\bar{M} = diag\{M, M, \cdots, M\}, \beta = diag\{\beta_1, \beta_2, \cdots, \beta_N\},$$

$$\bar{\alpha} = diag\{\alpha_1, \alpha_2, \cdots, \alpha_N\}, \bar{K}_1 = diag\{K_{1,1}, K_{1,2}, \cdots, K_{1,N}\},$$

$$\bar{K}_2 = diag\{K_{2,1}, K_{2,2}, \cdots, K_{2,N}\},$$

$$\bar{\theta}(k) = diag\{\theta_1(k), \theta_2(k), \cdots, \theta_N(k)\},$$

$$\bar{\phi}_{sat}(k) = diag\{\phi_{sat,1}(y_1(k)), \phi_{sat,2}(y_2(k)), \cdots, \phi_{sat,N}(y_N(k))\}. \tag{13}$$

The following filter error system can be obtained

$$\begin{cases} e(k+1) = \left(\bar{A} - \bar{L}^s\bar{C} - \bar{W}^s\mathcal{L}^s \right)e(k) + \bar{B}w(k) - \bar{L}^s\bar{D}v(k) \\ -(I - \bar{\beta})\bar{L}^s\bar{\phi}_{sat}(k) + (\bar{\theta}(k) - \bar{\beta})\bar{L}^s\bar{\phi}_{sat}(k) \\ -\bar{L}^s(\bar{K}_1\bar{C} - \bar{\beta}K_1\bar{C} + \bar{\beta}C - \bar{C})\bar{x}(k) \\ -(\bar{\theta}(k) - \bar{\beta})\bar{L}^s(\bar{C} - \bar{K}_1\bar{C})\bar{x}(k) \\ \tilde{z}(k) = \bar{M}\eta(k) \end{cases} \tag{14}$$

Among them

$$\bar{W}^s = diag\{W_1^s, W_2^s, \cdots W_N^s\}, \bar{L}^s = diag\{L_1^s, L_2^s, \cdots L_N^s\}. \tag{15}$$

According to Eqs. (4), (5) and (14) the following augmented filtering error system can be obtained $\eta(k) = [\bar{x}^T(k)\ e^T(k)]^T$ $\tilde{\phi}_{sat}(k) = \left[0\ \bar{\phi}_{sat}^T(k)\right]^T$

$$
\begin{cases}
\eta(k+1) = \mathcal{A}_1^s \eta(k) + (\bar{\theta}(k) - \bar{\beta})\mathcal{A}_2^s \eta(k) \\
\quad + \mathcal{C}_1^s \tilde{\phi}_{sat}(k) + (\bar{\theta}(k) - \bar{\beta})\mathcal{C}_2^s \tilde{\phi}_{sat}(k) \\
\quad + \mathcal{B}^s \bar{w}(k) \\
\tilde{z}(k) = \mathcal{M}\eta(k)
\end{cases}
\tag{16}
$$

Among them

$$
\mathcal{A}_1^s = \begin{bmatrix} \bar{A} & 0 \\ \Phi_{21}^s & \Phi_{22}^s \end{bmatrix}, \mathcal{A}_2^s = \begin{bmatrix} 0 & 0 \\ \Gamma_{21}^s & 0 \end{bmatrix},
$$

$$
\mathcal{C}_1^s = \begin{bmatrix} 0 & 0 \\ 0 & -(I - \bar{\beta})\bar{L}^s \end{bmatrix} \mathcal{C}_2^s = \begin{bmatrix} 0 & 0 \\ 0 & \bar{L}^s \end{bmatrix},
\tag{17}
$$

$$
\mathcal{B}^s = \begin{bmatrix} \bar{B} & 0 \\ \bar{B} & -\bar{L}^s \bar{D} \end{bmatrix}, \mathcal{M} = \begin{bmatrix} 0 & \bar{M} \end{bmatrix}.
$$

here

$$
\Phi_{21}^s = -\bar{L}^s(\bar{K}_1 \bar{C} - \bar{\beta}\bar{K}_1 \bar{C} + \bar{\beta}\bar{C} - \bar{C}),
$$
$$
\Phi_{22}^s = \bar{A} - \bar{L}^s \bar{C} - \bar{W}^s \mathcal{L}^s, \Gamma_{21}^s = -\bar{L}^s(\bar{C} - \bar{K}_1 \bar{C}).
\tag{18}
$$

Definition 1. Given a disturbance attenuation level. $\gamma > 0$ If there is a positive definite symmetric matrix and the following conditions are satisfied $R^s > 0, s = 1, 2, \cdots n_0$

$$
-\gamma^2 \eta^T(0)R^s \eta(0) < 0. J := \|\tilde{z}(k)\|_{[0,N-1]}^2 - \gamma^2 \|\bar{w}(k)\|_{[0,N-1]}^2
\tag{19}
$$

Then, the augmented filtering error system (16) has robust performance, H_∞.

Lemma 1. If the matrix sum satisfies the following inequality constraints $A, Q = Q^T P > 0$

$$
A^T PA - Q < 0.
\tag{20}
$$

Then, for any matrix G with appropriate dimensions, the following inequality constraints are satisfied

$$
\begin{bmatrix} -Q & * \\ G^T A P - G & - G^T \end{bmatrix} < 0.
\tag{21}
$$

Note 1. Is a random variable subject to Bernoulli distribution and is used to describe a randomly occurring measurement saturation nonlinearity. $\theta_i(k) \in \mathbb{R}\theta_i(k) = 1$, indicating that the sensor works normally at the time, that is, linear measurement; i $k\theta_i(k) = 0$, indicating that saturation nonlinearity occurs at the time of sensor, that is, nonlinear measurement ik.

3 Distributed Filtering Analysis H_∞

Theorem 1. Given a desired level of disturbance attenuation, if there is a positive definite matrix, satisfy, and inequality $\gamma\,(\gamma > 0)P^s > 0\eta^T(0)P^s\eta(0) \leq \gamma^2\eta^T(0)R^s\eta(0), s = 1, 2, \cdots n_0$

$$
\begin{bmatrix}
-P^s & * & * & * & * & * \\
0 & -\gamma^2 I & * & * & * & * \\
\tilde{C}_K & 0 & -2I & * & * & * \\
\overline{P}^s\mathcal{A}_1^s & \overline{P}^s B^s & \overline{P}^s C_1^s & -\overline{P}^s & * & * \\
\sqrt{\overline{\alpha}}\overline{P}^s\mathcal{A}_2^s & 0 & \sqrt{\overline{\alpha}}\overline{P}^s C_2^s & 0 & -\overline{P}^s & * \\
\mathcal{M} & 0 & 0 & 0 & 0 & -I
\end{bmatrix} < 0, \tag{22}
$$

Where, the augmented filter error system (16) has given performance.

$$
\overline{P}^s = \sum_{t=1}^{n_0} \overline{\pi}_{st} P^t, \ \overline{\pi}_{st} = \max_{1 \leq m \leq m_0}\{\pi_{st}^m\}, \ \tilde{C}_K = \begin{bmatrix} 0 & 0 \\ (K_2 - K_1)\overline{C} & 0 \end{bmatrix} H_\infty
$$

Prove, define, and performance analysis functions $\overline{K} = \overline{K}_2 - \overline{K}_1$

$$
J = \eta^T(k+1)P^t\eta(k+1) - \eta^T(k)P^s\eta(k). \tag{23}
$$

According to saturation constraint condition (5), can be obtained

$$
-2\overline{\phi}_{sat}^T(k)\overline{\phi}_{sat}(k) + 2\overline{\phi}_{sat}^T(k)\overline{K}y(k) > 0. \tag{24}
$$

And then you get

$$
\varsigma(k) = -2\tilde{\phi}_{sat}^T(k)\tilde{\phi}_{sat}(k) + 2\tilde{\phi}_{sat}^T(k)\tilde{C}_K\eta(k) > 0. \tag{25}
$$

Introduce the constant zero equation

$$
\tilde{z}^T(k)\tilde{z}(k) - \gamma^2\overline{w}^T(k)\overline{w}(k) - \tilde{z}^T(k)\tilde{z}(k) + \gamma^2\overline{w}^T(k)\overline{w}(k) = 0. \tag{26}
$$

Define the combination of (23) and (25), then $\xi(k) = \left[\eta^T(k)\ \overline{w}^T(k)\ \overline{\phi}_{sat}^T(k)\right]^T$,

$$
\mathbb{E}\{J(k)\} \leq \mathbb{E}\left\{\xi^T(k)\Lambda^s\xi(k) - \tilde{z}^T(k)\tilde{z}(k) + \gamma^2\overline{w}^T(k)\overline{w}(k)\right\}, \tag{27}
$$

Among them

$$
\Lambda^s = \begin{bmatrix} \Lambda_{11}^s & * & * \\ \Lambda_{21}^s & \Lambda_{22}^s & * \\ \Lambda_{31}^s & \Lambda_{32}^s & \Lambda_{33}^s \end{bmatrix},
$$

$$
\Lambda_{11}^s = \mathcal{A}_1^{sT}\overline{P}^s\mathcal{A}_1^s + \overline{\alpha}\mathcal{A}_2^{sT}\overline{P}^s\mathcal{A}_2^s - P^s + \mathcal{M}^T\mathcal{M},
$$

$$
\Lambda_{21}^s = B^{sT}\overline{P}^s\mathcal{A}_1^s, \ \Lambda_{22}^s = B^{sT}\overline{P}^s B^s - \gamma^2 I,
$$

$$\Lambda_{31}^s = \mathcal{C}_1^{sT}\overline{P}^s\mathcal{A}_1^s + \overline{\alpha}\mathcal{C}_2^{sT}\overline{P}^s\mathcal{A}_2^s + \overline{C}_K,$$

$$\Lambda_{32}^s = \mathcal{C}_1^{sT}\overline{P}^s\mathcal{B}^s, \ \Lambda_{33}^s = \mathcal{C}_1^{sT}\overline{P}^s\mathcal{C}_1^s + \overline{\alpha}\mathcal{C}_2^{sT}\overline{P}^s\mathcal{C}_2^s - 2I. \tag{28}$$

$\leq \mathbb{E}\left\{\sum_{k=0}^{N-1}\xi^T(k)\Lambda^s\xi(k)\right\}$ And then, if I add both sides of this inequality from 0 to PI, I get PI $N-1$

$$\sum_{k=0}^{N-1}\mathbb{E}\{J(k)\} \leq \mathbb{E}\left\{\eta^T(N)\overline{P}^s\eta(N)\right\} - \eta^T(0)P^s\eta(0)$$
$$-\mathbb{E}\left\{\sum_{k=0}^{N-1}\left(\tilde{z}^T(k)\tilde{z}(k) - \gamma^2\overline{w}^T(k)\overline{w}(k)\right)\right\}. \tag{29}$$

Then the performance constraints defined in (19) can be further described as $\boldsymbol{H}_\infty$

$$+ \eta^T(0)\left(P^s - \gamma^2 R^s\right)\eta(0). \ J \leq \mathbb{E}\left\{\sum_{k=0}^{N-1}\xi^T(k)\Lambda^s\xi(k)\right\}$$
$$-\mathbb{E}\left\{\eta^T(N)\overline{P}^s\eta(N)\right\} \tag{30}$$

According to Schur's complement lemma, the inequality (22) contains, and notice, the initial conditions $\Lambda^s < 0\overline{P}^s > 0P^s \leq \gamma^2 R^s J < 0$.

4   Distributed Filter Design $\boldsymbol{H}_\infty$

Theorem 2. Given, if there are matrices, and diagonal matrices, satisfy $\gamma > 0P_1^s > 0, P_2^s > 0, V_1^s V_2^s, X^s, Y^s, s = 1, 2, \cdots n_0$

$$\begin{bmatrix}
\Xi_{11}^s & * & * & * & * & * & * & * & * & * & * \\
0 & \Xi_{22}^s & * & * & * & * & * & * & * & * & * \\
0 & 0 & \Xi_{33}^s & * & * & * & * & * & * & * & * \\
0 & 0 & 0 & \Xi_{44}^s & * & * & * & * & * & * & * \\
0 & 0 & 0 & 0 & \Xi_{55}^s & * & * & * & * & * & * \\
\Xi_{61}^s & 0 & 0 & 0 & 0 & \Xi_{66}^s & * & * & * & * & * \\
\Xi_{71}^s & 0 & \Xi_{73}^s & \Xi_{74}^s & 0 & 0 & \Xi_{77}^s & * & * & * & * \\
\Xi_{81}^s & \Xi_{82}^s & \Xi_{83}^s & \Xi_{84}^s & 0 & \Xi_{86}^s & 0 & \Xi_{88}^s & * & * & * \\
0 & 0 & 0 & 0 & 0 & 0 & 0 & 0 & \Xi_{99}^s & * & * \\
\Xi_{101}^s & 0 & 0 & 0 & 0 & \Xi_{106}^s & 0 & 0 & 0 & \Xi_{1010}^s & * \\
0 & \Xi_{112}^s & 0 & 0 & 0 & 0 & 0 & 0 & 0 & 0 & \Xi_{1111}^s
\end{bmatrix} < 0, \tag{31}$$

Among them

$$\bar{P}_i^s = \sum_{t=1}^{n_0} \bar{\pi}_{st} P_i^t, i = 1, 2,$$

$$\Xi_{11}^s = -P_1^s, \Xi_{22}^s = -P_2^s, \Xi_{33}^s = \Xi_{44}^s = -\gamma^2 I,$$
$$\Xi_{55}^s = \Xi_{66}^s - 2I, \Xi_{61}^s = (\bar{K}_2 - \bar{K}_1)\bar{C}, \Xi_{71}^s = V_1^s \bar{A},$$
$$\Xi_{73}^s = V_1^s \bar{B}, \Xi_{74}^s = \Xi_{84}^s = -Y^s \bar{D},$$
$$\Xi_{77}^s = \Xi_{99}^s = \bar{P}_1^s - V_1^s - V_1^{sT},$$
$$\Xi_{81}^s = -Y^s \bar{K}_1 \bar{C} + \bar{\beta} Y^s \bar{K}_1 \bar{C} - \bar{\beta} Y^s \bar{C} + Y^s \bar{C},$$
$$\Xi_{82}^s = V_2^s \bar{A} - Y^s \bar{C} - X^s \mathcal{L}^s, \Xi_{83}^s = V_2 \bar{B},$$
$$\Xi_{86}^s = -Y^s + \bar{\beta} Y^s, \Xi_{88}^s = \Xi_{1010}^s = \bar{P}_2^s - V_2^s - V_2^{sT},$$
$$\Xi_{101}^s = -\sqrt{\bar{\alpha}} Y^s \bar{C} + \sqrt{\bar{\alpha}} Y^s \bar{K}_1 \bar{C},$$

$$\Xi_{106}^s = \sqrt{\bar{\alpha}} Y^s, \Xi_{112}^s = \bar{M}, \Xi_{1111}^s = -I. \tag{32}$$

Then the gain of the filter is

$$\bar{L}^s = (V_2^s)^{-1} Y^s, \overline{W}^s = (V_2^s)^{-1} X^s. \tag{33}$$

Proof selection matrix

$$G^s = diag\{V_1^s, V_2\}, P^s = diag\{P_1^s, P_2^s\},$$
$$\overline{P}^s = diag\{\overline{P}_1^s, \overline{P}_2^s\}, s = 1, 2, \cdots n_0. \tag{34}$$

According to Lemma 1, inequality (22) is equivalent to

$$\begin{bmatrix} -P^s & * & * & * & * & * \\ 0 & -\gamma^2 I & * & * & * & * \\ \tilde{C}_K & 0 & -2I & * & * & * \\ G^s \mathcal{A}_1^s & G^s \mathcal{B}^s & G^s \mathcal{C}_1^s & \overline{P}^s - G^s - G^{sT} & * & * \\ \sqrt{\bar{\alpha}} G^s \mathcal{A}_2^s & 0 & \sqrt{\bar{\alpha}} G^s \mathcal{C}_2^s & 0 & \overline{P}^s - G^s - G^{sT} & * \\ \mathcal{M} & 0 & 0 & 0 & 0 & -I \end{bmatrix} < 0. \tag{35}$$

Considering (13) and (34), it can be calculated

$$\overline{P}^s - G^s - G^{sT} = \begin{bmatrix} \overline{P}_1^s - V_1^s - V_1^{sT} & 0 \\ 0 & \overline{P}_2^s - V_2^s - V_2^{sT} \end{bmatrix},$$

$$G^s \mathcal{A}_1^s = \begin{bmatrix} V_1^s \bar{A} & 0 \\ \psi_{21}^s & \psi_{22}^s \end{bmatrix}, G^s \mathcal{B}^s = \begin{bmatrix} V_1^s \bar{B} & -V_2^s \overline{L}^s \bar{D} \\ V_2^s \bar{B} & -V_2^s \overline{L}^s \bar{D} \end{bmatrix},$$

$$G^s \mathcal{A}_2^s = \begin{bmatrix} 0 & 0 \\ -V_2^s \overline{L}^s \bar{C} + V_2^s \overline{L}^s \bar{K}_1 \bar{C} & 0 \end{bmatrix},$$

$$G^s \mathcal{C}_1^s = \begin{bmatrix} 0 & 0 \\ 0 & -V_2^s \overline{L}^s + \bar{\beta} V_2^s \overline{L}^s \end{bmatrix}, G^s \mathcal{C}_2^s = \begin{bmatrix} 0 & 0 \\ 0 & V_2^s \overline{L}^s \end{bmatrix}, \tag{36}$$

Among them

$$\Psi_{21}^s = -\left(I - \overline{\beta}\right)V_2^s\overline{L}^s\overline{K}_1\overline{C} + \left(I - \overline{\beta}\right)V_2^s\overline{L}^s\overline{C},$$
$$\Psi_{22}^s = V_2^s\overline{A} - V_2^s\overline{L}^s\overline{C} - V_2^s\overline{W}^s\mathcal{L}^s. \tag{37}$$

By substituting Eq. (36) into Eq. (35) and introducing new variables, Theorem 2 can be obtained. $X^s = V_2^s\overline{W}^s$, $Y^s = V_2^s\overline{L}^s$, Never put off till tomorrow what you can.

Note 2. Theorem 2 gives the design method of distributed filter, and the desired distributed filter parameters can be obtained by solving the following convex optimization problem constrained by inequality (31) $H_\infty H_\infty$.

$$\min_{R,Q(s),X^s,Y^s} \gamma^2 \tag{38}$$

5 Simulation Examples

In this section, a numerical simulation example is used to verify the effectiveness of the proposed method.

Consider a sensor network composed of four nodes, and its communication topology is shown in Fig. 2.

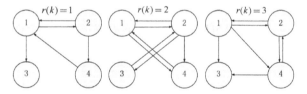

Fig. 2. Sensor network topology.

The corresponding adjacency matrix is

$$\mathcal{A}^1 = \begin{bmatrix} 0 & 1 & 0 & 1 \\ 1 & 0 & 0 & 0 \\ 1 & 0 & 0 & 0 \\ 0 & 1 & 0 & 0 \end{bmatrix}, \mathcal{A}^2 = \begin{bmatrix} 0 & 1 & 0 & 1 \\ 1 & 0 & 1 & 0 \\ 0 & 1 & 0 & 0 \\ 1 & 0 & 0 & 0 \end{bmatrix},$$

$$\mathcal{A}^3 = \begin{bmatrix} 0 & 1 & 0 & 0 \\ 1 & 0 & 0 & 1 \\ 1 & 0 & 0 & 0 \\ 1 & 1 & 0 & 0 \end{bmatrix}.$$

Assuming that topological structure switch has non-homogeneous Markov ran-domness, its transition probability matrix is composed of the following three matrices $\Pi(k)$

$$\Pi^{(1)} = \begin{bmatrix} 0.5 & 0.3 & 0.2 \\ 0.3 & 0.4 & 0.3 \\ 0.2 & 0.3 & 0.5 \end{bmatrix}, \Pi^{(2)} = \begin{bmatrix} 0.3 & 0.3 & 0.4 \\ 0.5 & 0.3 & 0.2 \\ 0.3 & 0.3 & 0.4 \end{bmatrix},$$

$$\Pi^{(3)} = \begin{bmatrix} 0.5 & 0.2 & 0.3 \\ 0.3 & 0.3 & 0.4 \\ 0.3 & 0.4 & 0.3 \end{bmatrix}.$$

The system parameter is

$$A = \begin{bmatrix} 0.3 & 0.1 \\ -1 & 0.2 \end{bmatrix}, B = \begin{bmatrix} 0.3 \\ 0.1 \end{bmatrix}, M = \begin{bmatrix} 2 & 2 \end{bmatrix}.$$

The sensor network measurement parameter is

$$C_1 = \begin{bmatrix} 5 & 4 \end{bmatrix}, C_2 = \begin{bmatrix} 3 & 3 \end{bmatrix}, C_3 = \begin{bmatrix} 4 & 5 \end{bmatrix}, C_4 = \begin{bmatrix} 3 & 4 \end{bmatrix},$$
$$D_1 = 0.3, D_2 = 0.1, D_3 = 0.2, D_4 = 0.1.$$

The saturation nonlinear is described as

$$\phi_{sat,i}(y_i(k)) = 0.5\big(K_{1,i} + K_{2,i}\big)y_i(k)$$
$$+ 0.5\big(K_{2,i} - K_{1,i}\big)\sin(y_i(k))$$

Among them

$$K_{1,1} = K_{1,3} = 0.6, K_{1,2} = K_{1,4} = 0.7,$$
$$K_{2,1} = K_{2,2} = 0.8, K_{2,3} = K_{2,4} = 0.9.$$

In addition, it is assumed that the probability of random nonlinearity occurs in the sensor network, system interference input is, and measurement noise is $\beta_i = 0.8$, $i = 1, 2, 3, 4$ $w(k) = e^{-0.2k}\sin(k)$ $v_i(k) = \frac{1}{k^3}$, $i = 1, 2, 3, 4$. It is assumed that the initial state of the system and the initial state of the filter are zero, and the topology of the initial filter network is $r(0) = 1$.

Matlab Yalmip Toolbox was used to optimize the optimization problem (38), and the optimal $\gamma = 5.0485$. The simulation results are shown in Figs. 3, 4, 5 and 6.

Figure 3 shows the evolution process of a Markov chain $r(k)$. Figure 4 shows the random saturation nonlinear moment of each node in the sensor network. Figure 5 shows the actual output of the system and the estimation of the distributed filter $z(k)$ $\hat{z}_i(k)$, $i = 1, 2, 3, 4$. Figure 6 depicts the comparison curves of filtering network errors when 0, 0.4, 0.8 and 1 are set respectively β_i.

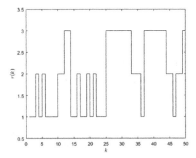

Fig. 3. Markov chain $\{r(k)\}$

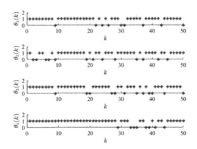

Fig. 4. Random saturation nonlinearity occurrence time.

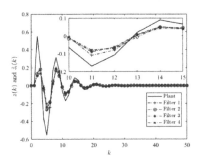

Fig. 5. Estimate of actual output and filter $z(k)$ $\hat{z}_i(k)$, $i = 1, 2, 3, 4$.

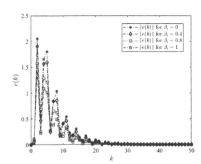

Fig. 6. Filter network estimation error $e_i(k)$, $i = 1, 2, 3, 4$.

Table 1. Different relationship with system robust performance, $\beta_i i = 1, 2, 3, 4$.

β_i	0	0.2	0.4	0.6	0.8	1
γ	5.98	5.84	5.65	5.41	5.04	4.51

In addition, Table 1 shows the influence of different selection on system robustness $\beta_i H_\infty$. It can be seen from Fig. 5 that the filtering method is effective for distributed filter networks whose switching topology meets non-homogeneous Markov characteristics, and the consistency state estimation is finally realized. According to Fig. 6 and Table 1, can be analyzed, the sensor network saturation nonlinearity influence system robust performance, when the sensor network is not measuring saturation nonlinear system robust performance of the best, and when the sensor network fully saturated nonlinear measurement, the robust performance of the system is the worst, compared with the two extreme cases, When the saturation nonlinearity occurs in the sensor network with a certain probability, the system achieves good filtering accuracy while ensuring strong robust performance H_∞.

6 Conclusion

This paper deals with the distributed robust filtering problem in WSN with random measurement saturation nonlinearity and switching topology. Because it is difficult to describe the random change of network communication topology by using a single topological switching probability matrix, this paper uses inhomogeneous Markov to model the topology change of wireless sensor network, and takes the saturation nonlinearity of wireless sensor network into full consideration in the design of distributed filter. Simulation results show that the designed distributed filter method is effective, and the designed distributed filter algorithm has strong robustness against interference, measurement noise and communication topology switching in the network environment.

Acknowledgement. This work was supported by National Key Research and Development Program of China, No. 2018YFD0400902, National Natural Science Foundation of China, No. 61873112, and Natural Science Research Project of Higher Education institutions of Jiangsu Province, No. 18KJB413009.

References

1. Braca, P., Goldhahn, R., Ferri, G., et al.: Distributed information fusion in multistatic sensor networks for underwater surveillance. IEEE Sens. J. **16**(11), 4003–4014 (2015)
2. Ciuonzo, D., Rossi, P.S.: Distributed detection of a non-cooperative target via generalized locally-optimum approaches. Information Fusion **36**, 261–274 (2017)
3. Yang, D., Ma, J., Zhang, H.: Intelligent cooperative industrial wireless sensor network. Acta Electron. Sin. **45**(06), 1537–1544 (2017)
4. Yang, D., Ma, J., Zhang, H.: Smart and cooperative industrial wireless sensor network. Acta Electron. Sin. **6**, 1537–1544 (2017)
5. Susca, S., Bullo, F., Martinez, S.: Monitoring environmental boundaries with a robotic sensor network. IEEE Trans. Control Syst. Technol. **16**(2), 288–296 (2008)
6. Ding, D., Han, Q.L., Wang, Z., et al.: A survey on model-based distributed control and filtering for industrial cyber-physical systems. IEEE Trans. Industr. Inf. **15**(5), 2483–2499 (2019)
7. Xu, H., Chen, X., Feng, M.: Performance analysis and distributed filter design for networked dynamic systems over finite-frequency ranges. Neurocomputing **334**, 143–155 (2019)
8. Chen, W., Ding, D., Dong, H., et al.: Distributed resilient filtering for power systems subject to denial-of-service attacks. IEEE Transactions on Systems, Man, and Cybernetics: Systems **49**(8), 1688–1697 (2019)
9. Li, T., Hlawatsch, F.: A distributed particle-PHD filter using arithmetic-average fusion of Gaussian mixture parameters. Information Fusion **73**, 111–124 (2021)
10. Liu, S., Wang, Z., Wei, G., et al.: Distributed set-membership filtering for multirate systems under the Round-Robin scheduling over sensor networks. IEEE Transactions on Cybernetics **50**(5), 1910–1920 (2019)
11. Battistelli, G., Chisci, L., Selvi, D.: A distributed Kalman filter with event-triggered communication and guaranteed stability. Automatica **93**, 75–82 (2018)
12. Rezaei, H., Mahboobi-Esfanjani, R., Akbari, A., et al.: Event-triggered distributed Kalman filter with consensus on estimation for state-saturated systems. Int. J. Robust Nonlinear Control **30**(18), 8327–8339 (2020)

13. Li, W., Xiong, K., Jia, Y., et al.: Distributed Kalman filter for multitarget tracking systems with coupled measurements. IEEE Transactions on Systems, Man, and Cybernetics: Systems (2020). https://doi.org/10.1109/TSMC.2019.2960081
14. Cheng, Z., Ren, H., Zhang, B., et al.: Distributed kalman filter for large-scale power systems with state inequality constraints. IEEE Trans. Industr. Electron. **68**(7), 6238–6247 (2021)
15. Xie, K., Yang, C., Liu, H., Huang, L.: Packet loss performance analysis and energy optimization of kalman consistency filter. Control Theory Appl. **35**(08), 1177–1185 (2018)
16. Xie, K., Yang, C., Liu, H., Huang, L.: Packet-dropout performance and energy optimization of the distributed Kalman consensus filter. Control Theory Appl. **35**(8), 1177–1185 (2018)
17. Liu, J., Gu, Y., Cao, J., et al.: Distributed event-triggered H_∞ filtering over sensor networks with sensor saturations and cyber-attacks. ISA Trans. **81**, 63–75 (2018)
18. Chen, Y., Wang, Z., Yuan, Y., et al.: Distributed H_∞ filtering for switched stochastic delayed systems over sensor networks with fading measurements. IEEE Transactions on Cybernetics **50**(1), 2–14 (2018)

Blockchain Enable IoT Using Deep Reinforcement Learning: A Novel Architecture to Ensure Security of Data Sharing and Storage

Xuetao Bai[1], Shanshan Tu[1]([✉]), Muhammad Waqas[1,2,3], Aiming Wu[1], Yihe Zhang[1], and Yongjie Yang[1]

[1] Engineering Research Center of Intelligent Perception and Autonomous Control, Faculty of Information Technology, Beijing University of Technology, Beijing 100124, People's Republic of China
sstu@bjut.edu.cn
[2] Faculty of Computer Science and Engineering, GIK Institute of Engineering Sciences and Technology, Topi 23460, Pakistan
[3] School of Engineering, Edith Cowan University, Joondalup Perth, WA 6027, Australia

Abstract. With the continuous development of the Internet of Things, more and more social sectors and smart devices are connected to the Internet of Things. This has led to a spurt of data growth and posed challenges to data security. To solve this problem, the Internet of Things needs a more secure and efficient storage method. Nowadays, one of the most important creative technological advancements that plays a significant role in the professional world is blockchain technology. And Both academia and industry attach great importance to the research of blockchain application technology. Some scholars believe that the blockchain itself is a secure distributed database. So, Blockchain is also considered a safe way to store data. In this paper, we introduce blockchain into the Internet of Things to ensure the security of Internet of Things data. At the same time, we have solved the problem of quantifying the degree of blockchain decentralization, which provides conditions for system optimization. After that, we proposed a system optimization model based on deep reinforcement learning to dynamically adjust system parameters. The simulation results show that the decentralization of the blockchain and the security of the system are guaranteed, and the throughput of the system has been improved.

Keywords: Blockchain · Internet of Things (IoT) · Deep reinforcement learning · Performance optimization

1 Introduction

As a world-connected technology, the Internet of Things plays an important role in industry and commerce, manufacturing and daily life [1]. The Internet of Things technology integrates sensing, storage, computing, application and other technologies and their design ideas. It integrates technologies in the three major fields of electronics, communications, and computers. On the basis of the Internet platform, it uses information technology to establish between objects. A wide range of connections are realized, and an interactive three-dimensional network formed by the communication of things is realized. With the widespread application of IoT technology, more and more smart devices are added to it, and the amount of data generated by these devices in their daily work is extremely large. The traditional way of processing data is to submit the data collected by the sensors of the perception layer to the application layer program through the network layer of IoT. In this process, the data will be temporarily stored on the intermediate node of the Internet of Things, which put forward higher requirements for safety.

In recent years, Blockchain has attracted widespread attention. It is a distributed database and is considered to be one of the important technologies affecting the future. Blockchain uses cryptographic asymmetric encryption and hash functions, which can build a secure data storage and sharing environment. At present, many industries are studying how to introduce blockchain to solve some of their own problems. Shynu et al. researches efficient and safe healthcare services based on blockchain for disease prediction in fog computing [2]. The authors of [3] propose a blockchain-based food supply chain system for audit traceability and quality assurance. It has been proved that blockchain technology can eliminate the potential trust crisis of consumers, especially after the introduction of a new consensus mechanism, it will improve performance while reducing system costs [4]. Zhang [5] describes the construction of a blockchain-based financing system to eliminate investment barriers so that private capital can better support China's infrastructure construction. It can be seen from the above research cases that the blockchain can be integrated with all walks of life, because all industries require data security. The most critical point of blockchain technology is decentralization [6]. Each node is equal and there is no relationship between superiors and subordinates. Therefore, nodes do not need to obey the commands of other nodes, which in a sense also ensures the security of data. In order to ensure the decentralization of the system, the first problem we have to solve is how to evaluate the decentralization level of a system. In addition, a robust blockchain system should also weigh scalability, security and system latency. When the amount of data is large, high latency is intolerable, and when the amount of data is small, the system has more resources to deal with security issues. This article discusses the combination of the blockchain and the Internet of Things, and introduces deep reinforcement learning to dynamically balance the four aspects of the blockchain mentioned above: decentralization, scalability, security, and system delay.

Deep reinforcement learning is a combination of deep learning and reinforcement learning. It not only has the ability of deep learning to analyze high-dimensional data and abstract representation capabilities, but also has the excellent decision-making and control capabilities of reinforcement learning [7]. DRL has broad application potential in robotics, MAV/UAV confrontation, path planning, stock trading and stock price forecasting, and has been applied in some scenarios [8–11]. Sivakumar et al. discussed the combination of deep learning and the IoT [12]. This article applies DRL to the node selection of the blockchain and comprehensively considers the four aspects of the blockchain during the selection process. The simulation results show that the DRL model used in this article has good data analysis and decision-making capabilities. It provides an excellent solution to solve the blockchain application problem.

The main contributions of this paper are listed as follows.

1) Previously, the degree of decentralization of the blockchain was often qualitatively described, and we realized it quantified
2) A system performance optimization model based on deep reinforcement learning is proposed. This model can comprehensively consider the four important aspects of the blockchain: scalability, decentralization, security, latency.
3) The results show that our model can fully guarantee the essential characteristics of the blockchain and effectively improve the throughput.

2 Related Work

Reinforcement learning has shown excellent ability in solving some complex problems. It uses rewards to enable the algorithm to continuously optimize decision-making in the learning process, thereby learning an optimal mapping from state to action [13]. The rewards for performing actions are delayed, that is to say, the pros and cons of the current action cannot be judged immediately. Only after the action has an impact on the state, the cumulative reward obtained from the execution of the action to a certain moment afterwards is calculated. Then the model accomplishes the optimization of the action by reward [14]. Tu et al. propose a reinforcement learning-based attackers identification method, and this method has good performance in terms of false alarm rate, missed detection rate and average error rate [15]. Wan et al. applied reinforcement learning to fog computing and achieved good experimental results [16]. Zhang et al. proposed a novel power allocation strategy in wireless communications [17]. Q-Learning algorithm is a classic algorithm of reinforcement learning, which is the most widely used in reinforcement learning control problems [18]. The basic idea of the Q-Learning algorithm is to store the state and different actions in a table, and then continuously update this table in the iterative process, so a Q value table needs to be maintained during the execution of the Q-Learning algorithm. This brings about a problem. If the state space and action space are very complicated, the system resource overhead of maintaining this table will be huge.

In order to solve the above problem, deep learning and reinforcement learning are combined, and a deep neural network is used to replace this table. The input of the network is the state of the environment, and the output is the action of the agent. This is deep reinforcement learning. DRL has a significant effect in balancing multiple variables to achieve optimization.

Giannopoulos et al. found that DQN-assisted operations can provide enhanced network-wide Energy efficiency (EE), because they balance trade-off between the power consumption and achieved throughput (inMbps/Watt) weigh [19]. Chen et al. proposed a supply chain management (DR-SCM) method based on deep reinforcement learning to make effective decisions on the production and storage of agricultural products to achieve profit optimization [20]. Paeng et al. proposed a scheduling framework based on deep reinforcement learning, which solves the extremely challenging scheduling problem and significantly reduces the total scheduling delay. Meanwhile, they found a trained neural network (NN) can solve the unseen scheduling problems without re-training [21]. Wang et al. proposed a selection algorithm based on deep reinforcement learning (DRL) optimization. From the simulation results of the experiment, it can be seen that the performance of the algorithm is very superior [22]. However, the problems are more complex when DRL is used in the blockchain, because we must weigh in 4 aspects: scalability, decentralization, security and latency.

With the development of science and technology, people are paying more and more attention to the problem of privacy protection, and the blockchain is considered to be an important means to solve the problem of privacy leakage due to its decentralized technical characteristics [23]. Barenji et al. designed a blockchain-based decentralized network structure for cloud manufacturing to solve the security and flexibility problems of centralized industrial networks [6]. Therefore, we believe that decentralization is the key to blockchain technology. Therefore, when deploying the blockchain into a production environment, it has to be ensured that it is decentralized.

Scalability is also an important performance indicator of blockchain. In this regard, researchers have proposed a variety of consensus algorithms to ensure that the blockchain reaches consensus among nodes [24, 25]. Sukhwani et al. studied the impact of PBFT on the performance of the blockchain network and proved that PBFT is a good choice by calculating the average time for the entire network to reach a consensus [26]. Hou et al. applied a private blockchain based on the RAFT consensus algorithm in their research, and the results showed that this method can reduce the system delay while reaching a consensus [27]. The maximum fault-tolerant node supported by the RAFT algorithm is $(N - 1)/2$, where N is the total number of nodes in the cluster. Quorum is considered to be the fastest BFT consensus algorithm [28], thanks to its extremely simple process of reaching a consensus, but it also exposes it to more security risks. The deep reinforcement learning model used in this article will dynamically select one of the three consensus algorithms as the basis to reach consensus based on the current state.

3 System Model

As shown in Fig. 1, The blockchain-enabled IoT system consists of two parts. The IoT part generates data that needs to be stored, and the blockchain system is responsible for processing these data in a safe and reliable manner. The two parts are as follows.

3.1 IoT

There are a large number of devices used to collect and transmit data in the Internet of Things network, such as mobile phones, cameras, sensors, and so on. These data may come from many aspects of modern society, such as green agriculture, industrial control, urban management, medical and health, smart home, smart transportation, environmental monitoring, and so on. Each block on the blockchain consists of two parts, the block header and the block body. The block body contains a data tree. The data in the Internet of Things system needs to be encapsulated into one transaction. Each Transaction constitutes a leaf node of the tree. The intermediate node of the tree stores the hash value calculated by the child nodes.

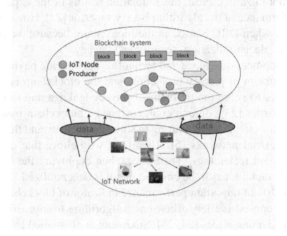

Fig. 1. Illustration of blockchain-enabled IoT systems.

3.2 Blockchain

As the Internet of Things continues to input data to the blockchain system, the producers of the blockchain will continue to pack these data into blocks, this process is divided into two steps:

1) The producer packs the data into a block
2) The block is appended to the end of the blockchain, and a consensus is reached on the entire blockchain network, then other producers will add this block to their own local database.

We assume in this article that there are a total of N IoT nodes, which is denoted as $\{Z_1, Z_2, Z_3, Z_4, \ldots, Z_N\}$, and producers will be selected from these nodes by the DRL model, which we will discuss in detail in the next section. We assign a number to each node that joins the Internet of Things, and the number is related to order of joining. If a node is selected as a producer, it will generate blocks in turn in numbered order and broadcast to the blockchain network to reach a consensus. In this article, considering the system delay and the fault tolerance of the system to malicious nodes, our DRL model will be dynamically adjusted according to the current state of the system in the three consensus algorithms of PBFT, RAFT, and Quorum. The following is a comparison of these three algorithms, in terms of fault tolerance, the time required to reach a consensus, and the complexity of the consensus process.

Table 1. Consensus algorithm comparison

Algorithm	Fault tolerance	Time required	Process complexity
PBFT	N/3	Most	Complex
RAFT	N/2	Medium	Medium
Quorum	0	Least	Simple

As can be seen from the Table 1, the performance of these three aspects cannot be all excellent. When it has excellent performance in one of them. In other respects, it will be inferior to other algorithms. PBFT and RAFT have strong fault tolerance, Quorum is the weakest in this respect. Quorum, thanks to the process of reaching a consensus is simpler than the other two, so it takes the shortest time to reach a consensus. In contrast, the consensus process of PBFT and RAFT is complicated, and it takes longer to reach a consensus in the system. The trained model will know how to weigh these three aspects of the consensus algorithm. Normally, the model will analyze the current state of the system and give a satisfactory selection result.

4 DRL-Based System Optimization Model

In this part, we will quantify the degree of decentralization of the blockchain, and then define the state space of the model input and the action space of the output, and finally give the expression of the model algorithm.

Decentralization is the essential feature of blockchain, and it is also the main reason why blockchain is generally favored by industry and academia. Therefore, we need to evaluate the decentralization of the system, and this requires a quantity to characterize the degree of decentralization. To this end, we introduced the coverage rate in the recommendation system to measure the degree of decentralization. Coverage refers to the proportion of recommended items given by the recommender system to the total item types, and is an important indicator to measure the effectiveness of the recommender system. It is usually calculated according to the following formula:

$$Coverage = \frac{\left| U_{u \in U} R_{(u)} \right|}{|I|} \tag{1}$$

Among them, the user set of the system is U, the item list is I, and the system recommends to each user an item list $R_{(u)}$ of length N. The number of producers in the blockchain network is determined, so the above formula needs to be modified.

In this article, we define the set of IoT nodes as I, and the set of system states as U. $R_{(u)}$ represents the list of producer nodes given by the system in state u, and if the selected producer has been selected in the near future Once selected, the R value will be reduced. If the selected producer has been selected before, the R value will be reduced. The R value will be between 0 and 1. The closer the value is to 0, the lower the decentralization of the system will be if the current node is selected as the producer. 1 is just the opposite, which means that the current choice can effectively ensure the decentralization of the system. We think that the final calculated coverage value is greater than the threshold C_p would be a good choice.

Next, let us discuss in more detail the rationality of choosing coverage as a measure of the level of decentralization. The reason for the disadvantages of the traditional centralized structure model is that the status of each node is unequal, and the central node has more power and needs to complete more work. In this case, the central node has too much pressure, and once the central node has a problem, it will affect all the nodes below it. However, this kind of problem does not exist in a decentralized system. Because there is no superior-subordinate relationship between nodes in a decentralized system, in addition to reaching a consensus, the work of one node is not based on the work done by other nodes. The advantage of this is that the failure of any node will not affect other nodes. In order for the system to have this advantage, we must fairly select nodes as producers. Therefore, the union of several selected nodes should cover the entire IoT node set as much as possible. This coincides with the concept of coverage. It should be noted that in the coverage calculation process, the newly selected node cannot be the same as the node selected for the previous N times. In the simulation experiment, we need to select 21 nodes from 100 IoT nodes as producers. So, we set N to 3. This is a reasonable value. If N is too large, then the union of the nodes selected for the first N times may include all nodes, and subsequent selection work cannot be performed. If N is too small, there may be a situation where two groups of nodes take turns as producers. This situation is like shaking back and forth. Therefore, the determination of the N value requires comprehensive consideration of the actual number of IoT nodes and the number of producers.

4.1 State Space

In order to make the state space design more realistic, we fully consider the quantities involved in the Internet of Things and blockchain systems. And selectively put them into the state space of the model. Specifically, the state space consists of the computing power c of the IoT node, the data transmission rate v, the distance l between any two nodes, the block size x in the blockchain, and the decentralization level d. The set of these quantities is denoted as $S_{(t)} = \{c, v, l, x, d\}_{(t)}$.

4.2 Action Space

In order to ensure the decentralization of the system and to make a good trade-off between throughput and security, the producer p of the blockchain, the consensus algorithm a, and the block size s need to be adjusted. They constitute the action space of the model. The set of action space is denoted as $A_{(t)} = \{p, a, s\}_{(t)}$, where the block producer indicator is $p = \{p_n\}$, $p_n \in \{0, 1\}$, $\sum_{n=1}^{N} p_n = K$, where $p_n = 1$ representing node is chosen as a block producer, while $p_n = 0$ otherwise. In the simulation experiment, we set N to 100 and K to 21. Beside the value of **a** is a set, which is denoted as $a = \{0, 1, 2\}$ representing one of the three consensus algorithms. S represents the block's size, its value set is $S = \{0.2, 0.4, 0.6, 0.8, \ldots, \dot{S}\}$, where $\dot{S}$ represents the maximum value, we set it to 8.

Algorithm1 :

1、 input state from state space.
2、 input action from action space.
3、 pretrain the Q network.
4、 for each epoch do
5、   Based on the $\varepsilon - greedy$ strategy, randomly choose an action A with probability ε or $A^{(t)} = argmax\ Q(S^{(t)}, A^{(t)})$ by the main Q network with probability $1 - \varepsilon$.
6、   Execute action A to select consensus protocol, block size, and producer.
7、   Calculate the reward $R^{(t)}$, Observe the next state $S^{(t+1)}$ of the system.
8、   Store $(S^{(t)}, A^{(t)}, R^{(t)}, S^{(t+1)})$ into memory.
9、   Randomly sample a mini-batch of state $(S^{(i)}, A^{(i)}, R^{(i)}, S^{(i+1)})$ from memory.
10、   Calculate the target Q-value from the target Q network by $y^{(i)} = R^{(i)} + \gamma max_A \cdot Q(S^{(i+1)}, A')$.
11、   Update the target Q network with loss function $L(\theta) = [y^{(i)} - Q(S^{(i)}, A'; \theta)]^2$.
12、   end

4.3 Reward Function

In order to make the model move in the direction of optimizing the system, that is, to increase the throughput under the premise of ensuring decentralization and security.

The model needs to make decisions, and in reinforcement learning is to maximize the Q function:

$$Q(S, A) = E\left[\sum_{t=0}^{\infty} \mu^t R^{(t)}\left(S^{(t)}, A^{(t)}\right) \Big| S^{(0)} = S, A^{(0)} = A\right] \qquad (2)$$

$$C1: \quad Coverage < C_p$$

$$C2: \quad f < \mathcal{F}^\delta, \delta = 0, 1, 2.$$

where $\mu \in (0, 1]$ reflects the tradeoff between the immediate and future rewards, and the R in the Q function is defined as follows:

$$R^{(t)}\left(S^{(t)}, A^{(t)}\right) = \begin{cases} \frac{1}{Coverage}, & \text{if } C1 \text{ and } C2 \text{ are satisfied} \\ 0, & otherwise. \end{cases} \qquad (3)$$

In the previous content, we used a table to summarize the proportion of malicious nodes tolerated by the three consensus algorithms. The model needs to maximize the Q function on the basis of satisfying the above two conditions.

The above are all the quantities involved in the optimization process of the model. Now we can formally give the optimization steps of the model in Algorithm 1.

5   Simulation Results and Analysis

For comparison, we have added two comparison experiments to the simulation experiment.

1) Experiment with a fixed block size.
2) Experiment using the fixed consensus protocol PBFT.
3) Experiment using our standard model.

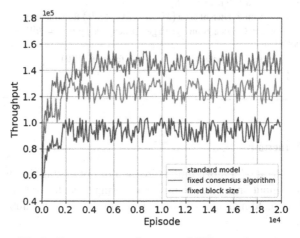

Fig. 2. Convergence performance of different schemes.

Figure 2 shows the performance of our proposed model based on deep reinforcement learning. It can be seen from Fig. 2 that at the beginning of training, the throughput is relatively small. However, as the training continues, the model parameters have been optimized. Therefore, we see that after about 3000 rounds of training, the throughput has reached a fairly high level. And after that, the throughput will fluctuate in a small range. In addition, we can also find from Fig. 2 that our standard model has the best performance in the experiment. The performance of the fixed block size model is the worst, which also tells us that the decision to enter the block size in the action space is correct.

Figure 3 describes the decentralization level of the blockchain system. In the comparative experiment, we set different thresholds to observe the changes in the level of decentralization during the training process. The top line parallel to the x-axis is the ideal curve as close as possible in the experiment. The reason for the value of 0.21 is that we set a total of 100 IoT nodes in the experiment, and select 21 of them as producers each time. The decentralization level at the beginning of the experiment defaults to the optimal situation, and then as the experiment progresses, more and more nodes are constrained and cannot be selected repeatedly, resulting in a decrease in the calculation results. At the same time, because the threshold guarantees that the result will not always drop, the final degree of decentralization will remain around the threshold.

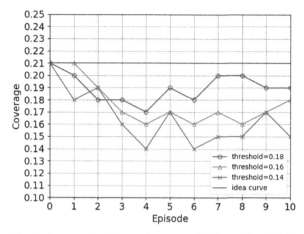

Fig. 3. Decentralization performance of different thresholds.

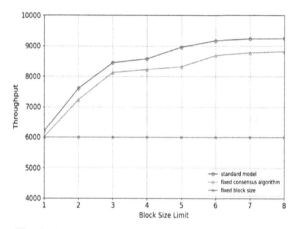

Fig. 4. Convergence performance of different block size.

Figure 4 expresses the effect of block size on performance. In Fig. 4, since Experiment 3 is a comparative experiment with a fixed block size, its performance is unchanged. In the other two cases, the performance will increase with the increase of the block size within a certain range, but there will be no obvious change after increasing to a certain extent, because it is restricted by other attributes of the blockchain. This also shows that we should comprehensively consider all aspects of the blockchain's attributes, and increasing the strength on one side alone cannot increase the performance indefinitely.

6 Conclusion

In this article, we propose an IoT blockchain performance optimization model based on deep reinforcement learning. Since decentralization is the essential feature of the blockchain, we focused on how to ensure the decentralization of the system during the design process. After discussion, we introduced the coverage rate of the recommendation system as a quantity to express the degree of decentralization, which makes the decentralized description of decentralization quantifiable. Secondly, the setting of the threshold requires a trade-off. Although a larger threshold can maintain the level of decentralization at a higher level, the model takes longer to train. Finally, the model is trained to increase throughput while ensuring decentralization and security. In future work, we will consider introducing other more appropriate quantities to indicate the level of decentralization and refine the quantification of the blockchain from other aspects.

References

1. Vijayalakshmi, S.R., Muruganand S.: A survey of internet of things in fire detection and fire industries. In: Proceedings of the I-SMAC, Coimbatore, India, pp. 703–707 (2017)
2. Shynu, P.G., Menno, V.G., Kumar, R.L., Kadry, S., Nam, Y.: Blockchain-based secure healthcare application for diabetic-cardio disease prediction in fog computing. IEEE Access **9**, 45706–45720 (2021)
3. Cocco, L., Mannaro, K., Tonelli, R., Mariani, L., Lodi, M.B.: A blockchain-based trace- ability system in agri-food SME: case study of a traditional bakery. IEEE Access **9**, 62899–62915 (2021)
4. Hu, S., Huang, S., Huang, J., Su, J.F.: Blockchain and edge computing technology enabling organic agricultural supply chain: a framework solution to trust crisis. Comput. Ind. Eng. **153**, 107079 (2021)
5. Zhang, Y., Wang, Z., Deng, J., Gong, Z., Flood, I., Wang, Y.: Framework for a blockchain-based infrastructure project financing system. IEEE Access **9**, 141555–141570 (2021)
6. Barenji, A.V., Guo, H., Tian, Z.G., Li, Z., Wang, W.M., et al.: Blockchain-based cloud manufacturing: decentralization. arXiv:1901.10403 (2019)
7. Jogunola, O., Adebisi, B., Ikpehai, A., Popoola, S.I., Gui, G.: Consensus algorithms and deep reinforcement learning in energy market: a review. IEEE Internet Things **8**(6), 4211–4227 (2021)
8. Yang, L., Zhang, H., Zhu, X., Sheng, X.: Ball motion control in the table tennis robot system using time-series deep reinforcement learning. IEEE Access **9**, 99816–99827 (2021)
9. Li, Y., Han, W., Wang, Y.: Deep reinforcement learning with application to air confrontation intelligent decision-making of manned/unmanned aerial vehicle cooperative system. IEEE Access **8**, 67887–67898 (2020)
10. Luis, S.Y., Reina, D.G., Marín, S.L.T.: A multiagent deep reinforcement learning approach for path planning in autonomous surface vehicles: the Ypacaraí lake patrolling case. IEEE Access **9**, 17084–17099 (2021)
11. Li, Y., Ni, P., Chang, V.: Application of deep reinforcement learning in stock trading strategies and stock forecasting. Computing **102**(6), 1305–1322 (2019). https://doi.org/10.1007/s00607-019-00773-w
12. Sivakumar, N.R., Ibrahim, A.Z.: Deep neural artificial intelligence for IoT based tele health data analytics. Comput. Mater. Continua **70**(3), 4467–4483 (2022)
13. Nian, R., Liu, J.F., Huang, B.: A review on reinforcement learning: Introduction and applications in industrial process control. Comput. Chem. Eng., 139, 106886 (2020)
14. Hatem, M., Foudil, A.: Simulation of the navigation of a mobile robot by the Q-Learning using artificial neuron networks. In: Proceedings of the ICCA, Saida, Algeria (2009)
15. Tu, S., et al.: Reinforcement learning assisted impersonation attack detection in device-to-device communications. IEEE Trans. Veh. Technol. **70**(2), 1474–1479 (2021)

16. Wan, J., Waqas, M., Tu, S., Hussain, S.M., Shah, A.: An efficient impersonation attack detection method in fog computing. Comput. Mater. Continua **68**(1), 267–281 (2021)
17. Zhang, B., Waqas, M., Tu, S., Hussain, S.M., Rehman, S.U.: Power allocation strategy for secret key generation method in wireless communications. Comput. Mater. Continua **2**, 2179–2188 (2021)
18. Karim, O.A., Javaid, N., Sher, A., Wadud, Z., Ahmed, S.: QL-EEBDG: QLearning based energy balanced routing in underwater sensor networks. EAI Endorsed Trans. Energy Web Inf. Technol. **5**(17), e15 (2018)
19. Giannopoulos, A., Spantideas, S., Kapsalis, N., Karkazis, P., Trakadas, P.: Deep reinforcement learning for energy-efficient multi-channel transmissions in 5G cognitive HetNets: centralized, decentralized and transfer learning based solutions. IEEE Access **9**, 129358–129374 (2021)
20. Chen, H., Chen, Z., Lin, F., Zhuang, P.: Effective management for blockchain-based agri-food supply chains using deep reinforcement learning. IEEE Access **9**, 36008–36018 (2021)
21. Paeng, B., Park, I.B., Park, J.: Deep Reinforcement learning for minimizing tardiness in parallel machine scheduling with sequence dependent family setups. IEEE Access **9**, 101390–101401 (2021)
22. Wang, L., Han, D., Zhang, M., Wang, D., Zhang, Z.: Deep reinforcement learning-based adaptive handover mechanism for VLC in a hybrid 6G network architecture. IEEE Access **9**, 87241–87250 (2021)
23. Guidi, B., Michienzi, A.: The decentralization of social media through the blockchain technology. In: Proceedings of the 13th ACM Web Science Conference, WebSci 2021, pp. 138–139 (2021)
24. Kaur, M., Khan, M.Z., Gupta, S., Noorwali, A., Chakraborty, C.: MBCP: performance analysis of large scale mainstream blockchain consensus protocols. IEEE Access **9**, 80931–80944 (2021)
25. Zarrin, J., Wen Phang, H., Babu Saheer, L., Zarrin, B.: Blockchain for decentralization of internet: prospects, trends, and challenges. Clust. Comput. **24**(4), 2841–2866 (2021). https://doi.org/10.1007/s10586-021-03301-8
26. Sukhwani, H., Martínez, J.M., Chang, X., Trivedi, K.S., Rindos, A.: Performance modeling of PBFT consensus process for permissioned blockchain network (hyperledger fabric). In: Proceedings of the 2017 IEEE 36th Symposium on Reliable Distributed Systems (SRDS), pp. 253–255 (2017)
27. Hou, L., Xu, X., Zheng, K., Wang, X.: An intelligent transaction migration scheme for raft-based private blockchain in internet of things applications. IEEE Commun. Lett. **25**(8), 2753–2757 (2021)
28. Guerraoui, R., Knezevic, N., Quema, V., Vukolic, M.: The next 700 BFT protocols. In: Proceedings of the 5th European Conference on Computer Systems, pp. 363–376 (2010)

Mobile Internet Access Control Strategy Based on Trust Perception

Lu Chen[1,2(✉)], Xinjian Zhao[3], Ran Zhao[3], Guoquan Yuan[3], Song Zhang[3], Shi Chen[3], and Fan Wu[4]

[1] Institute of Information and Communication, Global Energy Interconnection Research Institute, Nanjing 210003, China
chenluchina@aliyun.com
[2] State Grid Key Laboratory of Information and Network Security, Nanjing 210003, China
[3] State Grid Jiangsu Electric Power Company, Nanjing 210003, China
[4] Computer Science Department, Tuskegee University, Tuskegee, AL 36088, USA

Abstract. In recent years, the rapid development of mobile Internet services has greatly increased the complexity of network interaction. In the mobile Internet scenario, there are higher requirements for the dynamic and fine-grained access control. However, the existing access control strategy is mainly based on static access control mechanism, which cannot meet its needs. For this reason, this paper proposes a mobile internet access control strategy based on trust perception, which improves the outstanding problems of traditional access control methods such as not supporting dynamic authorization and coarse-grained. This strategy combines the advantages of both the role-based access control (RBAC) model and the attribute-based access control (ABAC) model. And introduce comprehensive trust evaluation to quantify user trust, and realize dynamic authorization and fine-grained access control based on trust perception. User trust consists of two parts: attribute trust and historical trust. Attribute trust is derived based on the user's attributes, and historical trust is calculated based on the user's historical access behavior. Finally, this article simulates the two most common attack methods, bleaching attack and betrayal attack. Comparative experiments show that the method proposed in this paper has better ability to resist bleaching attacks and betrayal attacks.

Keywords: Access control · Mobile internet · Trust perception · RBAC model · ABAC model

1 Introduction

With the advancement of the construction of the Internet and digital transformation services, and the rapid development of mobile Internet services, QuestMobile data shows that as of June 2021, the number of monthly active users of China Mobile Internet reached 1.164 billion, with 26.3 apps per person per month [1]. Especially since the epidemic, the demand for mobile office has increased exponentially, the scope of mobile application business has continued to expand, and mobile internet business has become

X. Sun et al. (Eds.): ICAIS 2022, LNCS 13340, pp. 598–611, 2022.
https://doi.org/10.1007/978-3-031-06791-4_47

an important window for internal and external interaction. As the new working mode of mobile services has greatly increased the complexity of network interactions, security protection objects are no longer limited to dedicated control terminals, business access is no longer restricted by internal and external networks, and various means of breaking through boundary protection and moving laterally are emerging in endlessly. However, the existing authorization method between mobile terminal-mobile platform-back-end services is based on role-based static access control mechanisms, with extensive permission control granularity and solid access control strategies, which can no longer meet the requirements for safe and efficient interaction of mobile Internet services. Traditional access control methods mainly use RBAC [2] and ABAC [3].

RBAC is a widely accepted access control model, which is widely known for its simple policy management. In RBAC, each role has a series of permissions, permissions are associated with users through roles, roles are assigned to users according to certain rules, and users access through roles. However, RBAC cannot specify and implement access control policies based on context information (such as time, location, etc.), and can only achieve static coarse-grained access control. In addition, because RBAC and its extensions grant user permissions through roles, if the organization is large, many roles need to be defined in order to provide fine-grained access, which leads to the problem of role explosion. RBAC and its extensions define permissions based on object identifiers (such as name, id). This does not apply to the situation where there are multiple objects and leads to the problem of permission explosion [4], because different users of the same role may have different permissions.

In order to find an alternative method and solve the limitations of RBAC, the researchers proposed ABAC. ABAC can specify more flexible and dynamic decision-making strategies than RBAC, because it uses the attributes of users (users who can make access requests), objects (objects that need to be protected), and environment (the context in which the access requests are initiated) to define strategies. In recent years, attribute-based access control has been used in various fields [5–7]. However, ABAC also has its own limitations. For example, it increases the complexity of policy review, that is, it is difficult to visualize policy changes. This is because ABAC needs to consider a large number of strategies to view the effect of policy changes or obtain privileges associated with users. If the policy is to be modified, it is difficult to determine which group of users is affected by the policy modification [8].

As mentioned above, RBAC and ABAC have their own advantages and disadvantages [9], and their characteristics can complement each other, so the integration of RBAC and ABAC has become an important research area. Kuhn of the National Institute of Standards and Technology and Coyne, an American scientific application international company, proposed to combine the best features of role-based access control and attribute-based access control [10] to provide effective access control for application systems. Subsequently, Coyne et al. compared role-based access control and attribute-based access control in detail in [11]. He believes that combining the advantages of the two can provide a flexible, extensible, auditable, and understandable access control model.

At present, the three ways of combining attributes and roles are dynamic roles, attribute-centered and role-centered. However, these three methods still have their own problems in large-scale environments. In summary, in order to solve the above problems, this paper proposes a trust-aware mobile internet access control strategy. The main work includes two aspects:

(1) Considering the access control requirements in mobile internet scenarios, we propose an access control strategy that integrates ABAC and RBAC. This strategy integrates ABAC and RBAC models to retain the flexibility provided by ABAC, while keeping RBAC easy to manage and manage. The advantage of easy permission review and strategy analysis.
(2) Introduce trust perception methods, quantify user trust through comprehensive trust evaluation, and realize a dynamic access control strategy based on trust perception to defend against bleaching attacks and betrayal attacks.

2 Related Work

2.1 Access Control Model

With the emergence of new computing environments such as cloud computing, the Internet of Things, and digital transformation services, traditional closed-environment-oriented access control models are difficult to directly apply to the new computing environment. In order to adapt to the new environment, a lot of research has focused on designing a hybrid model of RBAC and ABAC, so as to realize dynamic access control based on RBAC [12]. Jin et al. first proposed the role-centric access control model concept (RABAC) [13], which extended RBAC with user attributes and object attributes. Abhijeet Thakare et al. aimed at the inefficiency of RBAC in the framework of the Internet of Things (IoT) when processing multiple users requesting multiple resources in a dynamic situation. They proposed a priority attribute-based RBAC model (PARBAC) [14]. By adding to the existing RBAC model priority attribute tool. The model classifies policy mechanisms based on priority attributes, which improves flexibility and improves the performance of current access control models. The above research only considered the user-role dynamic allocation, but did not change the static relationship between roles and permissions, and is not suitable for new environments.

To overcome the limitations of ABAC and RBAC, Cai T et al. proposed a combination of roles based on static attributes and rules based on dynamic attributes, and proposed a hybrid attribute-based RBAC (HA-RBAC) model to inherit the advantages of RBAC and ABAC [15]. H. R. Xiong et al. proposed a hybrid extended access control model combining the two, combining attributes with RBAC, and further controlling the effective permissions of session roles by introducing permission filtering strategies [16]. Singh et al. have presented a unified framework that enables specification and enforcement of heterogeneous access control policies (like ABAC, RBAC, etc.) which can have multiple dimensions and multi-level of granularity. In large organizations, the number of users, resources, and operations could be significantly high. As these components in large organizations interact in complex ways; therefore, the administration of heterogeneous access control policies in such organizations is challenging [17]. Accordingly, to effectively handle this, a role-based administrative model is introduced in Singh et al. they present a complete role-based administrative model (named as RAMHAC) for managing heterogeneous access control policies [18].

The above studies retain the role-centered basic ideas in RBAC and combine it with ABAC or attributes to achieve flexible and scalable dynamic access control. However, further research is needed on how to integrate these models with the mobile Internet business environment. Combine and effectively perceive the trust measurement results of mobile terminals and users, and use the trust measurement results to dynamically adjust the authority policy, thereby realizing dynamic and fine-grained access control for mobile Internet services.

2.2 Trust Assessment

Trust evaluation is a relative method to measure the security information, and the trust value is used to express the trustworthiness of the node. With the deepening of the research on the trust model, some scholars have proposed integrating trust into the traditional access control model to achieve dynamic access control [19]. The core of the implementation of dynamic rights management is trust evaluation. The degree of trust is used to indicate the credibility of the access object, which can effectively identify malicious or abnormal access requests. When the credit level reaches the set credit threshold, the access object can obtain matching access rights, thereby realizing dynamic rights management. For example, Chakraborty et al. proposed the TrustBAC model based on the RBAC model [20]. Before the user obtains a role, this model first calculates the user's trust value, and then determines whether the user can obtain the role according to the trust value, that is, the user's trust value determines whether it can obtain the corresponding authority. The TrustBAC model overcomes the shortcomings of the RBAC model's dynamics and insufficient supervision, and can dynamically assign roles. Liu Wu et al. proposed a trust-based access control model TRBAC based on the RBAC model, which enhanced the dynamics and security of authorization, refined the granularity of trust calculation, and controlled the distribution of permissions more accurately [21].

When evaluating the trust value of mobile users, the user's time attribute and location attribute are two important influencing factors.Some scholars have proposed an access control model in mobile scenarios for the evaluation of the credibility of mobile users. For example, J. Y. Shao et al. proposed an access control method suitable for the mobile Internet environment [22]. This method is based on the idea of dynamic trust value, so that the same user corresponds to different roles in different position and time states. Have different access rights. Kang Kai also proposed an access control model in a mobile environment, which divides the influencing factors of user credibility into three categories: time attribute, location attribute and user behavior, and based on this, grants permissions to legitimate users [23].

3   Fusion Access Control Strategy Based on Trust Perception

This paper proposes a trust-aware-based fusion access control strategy. By fusing RBAC model and the ABAC model, the advantages of the RBAC model and the ABAC model complement each other, thereby overcoming RBAC and the limitations of each ABAC.

3.1   Strategic Framework and Process

This paper proposes a trust-aware-based fusion access control strategy. By fusing the role-based access control (RBAC) model and the attribute-based access control (ABAC) model, the advantages of the RBAC model and the ABAC model complement each other, thereby overcoming RBAC and the limitations of each ABAC. This strategy includes 4 parts: ABAC part, RBAC part, trust perception part, access control strategy part. The ABAC part contains the elements of the attribute-based access control model, and access control is performed according to the basic attributes of the user, retaining the flexibility and fine-grained advantages of the ABAC model; the RBAC part contains the elements of the role-based access control model, according to The role and role permissions of the user are used for access control, which retains the advantages of the simple permissions management of the RBAC model; the role of the trust perception part is to evaluate the user's credibility based on specific indicators to achieve more fine-grained access control. Dynamic access control can also be achieved through timely update of user trust values; the access control strategy part contains various strategies, including ABAC allocation strategy, RBAC role permission allocation strategy and control strategy based on trust value, combined into an overall strategy. The fusion strategy is shown in Fig. 1:

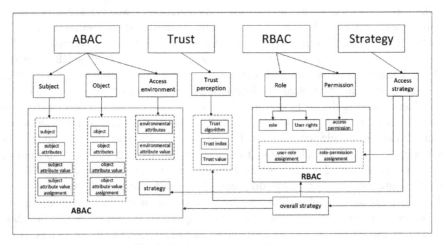

Fig. 1. Fusion access control strategy.

As shown in the diagram, the rectangular box on the left depicts the concept diagram of ABAC, involving subject module, object module and access environment module, mainly including subject attribute, object attribute, environment attribute and subject attribute value, object attribute value, environment attribute Elements such as values and permissions. The subject attribute represents a series of user attributes such as user type, occupation, age, etc., the subject attribute value represents the value of the corresponding user attribute; the object attribute represents a series of access object attributes such as object type, object status, etc., and the object attribute value represents the corresponding Access the numeric value of the object property. The rectangular box on the right depicts the conceptual diagram of RBAC, involving role modules and permission modules, which mainly include roles, user permissions, access permissions, user-role assignment, and role-authority assignment. Among them, user permissions represent the permissions of a user to obtain a certain role, access permissions represent the permissions of a role to access a certain resource, user-role assignment represents a strategy for assigning users to a corresponding role, and role-permission assignment represents a policy for configuring corresponding permissions for a role.

At present, there are three methods for attribute-role fusion access control, namely dynamic role, attribute-centric and role-centric. The method of dynamic roles is that attributes determine which roles a user should be activated. The attribute-centric approach is that roles are no longer associated with permissions, but take roles as a special attribute. The role-centric approach is that roles determine the maximum set of permissions a user has, and attributes are used to limit permissions. All three methods have their own shortcomings. The dynamic role method still has problems in terms of fine-grainedness; the attribute-centered method introduces fine-grained control but also brings the disadvantage of difficulty in auditing; the role-centered method is more difficult to audit. There are still shortcomings in terms of dynamics.

The idea of the integrated access control strategy proposed in this paper is role-centered, using RBAC as the main framework, and at the same time, due to comprehensive consideration of user attributes, object attributes, and environmental attributes as constraints, it enables fine-grained access without role explosion. In addition, dynamic trust values are introduced to overcome the shortcomings of the role-centric access control model's deficiencies in the dynamics.

This strategy will combine user attributes to assign roles to users, and the authority is no longer a single object but a group of objects with the same attributes, composed of object attributes and operations, for example $P_1=$ ((type = confidential $\wedge$ status = active), read), which means that you have read permission for this type of access object. In addition, the constraints composed of environmental attributes and trust values must be bound to permissions to further achieve fine-grained and dynamic access control. For example, permission P_1 is subject to the condition $C=$ (role = administrator $\wedge$ environment $\in E \wedge$ trust value $\geq T$). This condition means that in order to be granted permission P_1, the user must be an administrator and meet the environmental conditions and trust value conditions.

The access control flow of this fusion strategy is shown in the Fig. 2. When a user accesses system resources, firstly, by retrieving the roles owned by the user and querying the permissions of these roles, the user's permission set is obtained. If the corresponding permission is not included in the permission set, the user is denied access. If the permission set contains the corresponding permission, it is judged whether the environment attribute meets the condition, and if the environment attribute does not meet the

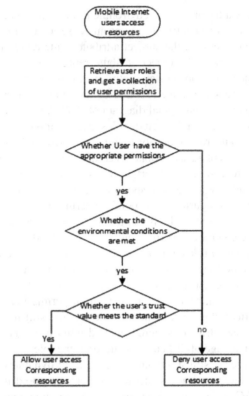

Fig. 2. Access control flow of fusion access control strategy.

condition, the user access is also denied. If the conditions are met, then the trust value is considered to further restrict users. If the trust value meets the requirements, access to the resource is allowed. Otherwise, the access request will be rejected.

3.2   Trust Value Calculation Method

This paper proposes a trust algorithm to solve the problem of trust calculation in access control. The algorithm uses analytic hierarchy process and gray theory to layer various attributes of users, quantifies the attribute trust (AT) of users, and analyzes users through probability statistics. Calculate historical trust (HT) by adding a trust penalty policy to the historical behavior performance of the system.

Attribute Trust. When quantifying the user's attribute trust value, it is necessary to consider the various attributes of the user, and each user attribute is an evaluation index. According to the affiliation of each attribute of each user, all attributes of the user can be abstracted into the form of an attribute tree, which is divided into three levels. The top layer is the target layer, which contains only one root node; the middle layer is the first-level indicators, including subject attributes and environmental attributes, etc.; the bottom layer is the second-level indicators, including various specific attributes, for example, the second-level indicators under the subject attributes can be Is the user type, occupation, age, etc.

In addition, the importance of various attributes possessed by users is definitely different, or the importance of each evaluation index is different. Therefore, each evaluation index should have different weights. Determining the weight of each evaluation index is a kind of affected target evaluation, which belongs to the "multi-index decision-making problem". The principle of Analytic Hierarchy Process (AHP) is to decompose the problem into different components to form a multi-level analysis structure model, and then use the method of solving the eigenvector of the judgment matrix to obtain the weight of each element at each level. Therefore, this article uses the analytic hierarchy process to determine the target weight.

Specific steps are as follows:

(1) Establish an attribute trust judgment matrix. In different application scenarios, the indicators considered in the construction of the judgment matrix are different. This article considers that in the mobile Internet scenario, users have the attributes of time and location, so the first-level indicators include the basic attributes of the subject, environmental attributes, and time-space attributes, and the second-level indicators include household type, occupation, age, network transmission delay, network utilization rate, IP response speed, access time, location, etc. Then through the method of pairwise comparison, the relative importance based on the index of this level is evaluated, and the user's k-th trust attribute judgment matrix A_k is established as

$$A_k = \begin{bmatrix} a_{11}^k & a_{12}^k & \cdots & a_{1j}^k \\ a_{21}^k & a_{22}^k & \cdots & a_{2j}^k \\ \vdots & \vdots & \ddots & \vdots \\ a_{i1}^k & \cdots & \cdots & a_{ij}^k \end{bmatrix} \tag{1}$$

At the same time, the idea of comparing index weights in pairs can greatly reduce the impact of human judgment errors on the evaluation process. When constructing the judgment matrix A_k, a nine-level measurement method is used, and the importance of attributes is represented by numbers 1–9.

(2) Calculate the weight of each indicator according to the judgment matrix.
   ① Calculate the product of the row elements of the judgment matrix

$$w_i^k = \prod_{j=1}^{n} a_{ij}^k, i = 1, 2, \cdots, n \tag{2}$$

② Take the n-th power of the continuous product vector M_i^k

$$M_i^k = \left(m_1^k, m_2^k, \cdots, m_n^k \right)^T m_i^k = \sqrt[n]{M_i^k} \tag{3}$$

③ Normalized processing to get the weight vector W^k

$$W^k = \left(w_1^k, w_2^k, \cdots, w_n^k \right)^T w_i^k = \frac{m_i^k}{\sum_{i=1}^{n} m_i^k}, i = 1, 2, \cdots, n \tag{4}$$

Among them, w_i^k is the weight coefficient of each index of the k-th layer, and W^k is the weight vector.

(3) Consistency inspection. In order to test the coordination between the importance of various indicators, it is necessary to check the consistency of the weight coefficients w_i^k of each layer, and calculate the consistency index CI and the consistency ratio CR. Among them, λ_{max} is the maximum eigenvalue of the judgment matrix A, and RI is the average random consistency index. The smaller the CR, the better the consistency of the judgment matrix. When $CR < 0.1$, it is considered to have satisfactory consistency. Otherwise, the judgment matrix needs to be modified until the test conditions are met before proceeding to the next step.

$$CI = \frac{(\lambda_{max}-n)}{(n-1)} \quad CR = \frac{CI}{RI} \tag{5}$$

Next is the quantification of attribute indicators. The evaluation sample matrix is established according to the expert scores, and each indicator is quantified using the gray function to obtain the user attribute trust value AT. Specific steps are as follows:

(1) Calculate the sample matrix by expert scoring method. The evaluation of the trust value of each indicator is done by experts in the field. Experts score the trust indicators based on their own experience and relevant domain knowledge, and fill in the score sheet.

$$d = \begin{bmatrix} d_{11} & d_{12} & \cdots & d_{1n} \\ d_{21} & d_{22} & \cdots & d_{2n} \\ \vdots & \vdots & \ddots & \vdots \\ d_{m1} & d_{m2} & \cdots & d_{mn} \end{bmatrix} \tag{6}$$

(2) Determine the gray category of the assessment. Determining the evaluation gray class is to determine the number of evaluation gray classes, gray class gray levels and white function f(x), which are divided into 5 Gray classes according to s = {1,2,3,4,5}, using equal scores method.

Calculate the gray evaluation coefficient and construct the gray evaluation weight matrix. For the user's trust evaluation index t_{ij}, the gray evaluation coefficient of the e-th evaluation gray category is $X_{ije} = \sum_{k=1}^{p} f_e(d_{ij})$, and the total gray evaluation coefficient of each evaluation gray category is $X_{ij} = \sum_{e=1}^{5} X_{ije}$. For the evaluation index t_{ij}, the gray evaluation weight value of the evaluation object belonging to the e-th gray class is recorded as r_{ije}, $r_{ije} = \frac{X_{ije}}{X_{ij}}$ can be determined by the gray class weight vector r_{ij} to determine the trust evaluation index t_{ij}, where $r_{ij} = (r_{ij1}, r_{ij2}, \cdots, r_{ije})$. Then, determine the trust evaluation index T (a set of t_{ij}) of the complete matrix R_i of each evaluation gray category gray evaluation.

Calculate the trust value of user attributes. According to the above calculation, the secondary index weight W_i is obtained, and then the secondary index $B_i = W_i \times R_i$ is comprehensively evaluated, and the primary index gray evaluation matrix $R = $

$(B_1, B_2, \cdots, B_i)^T$ is obtained, and the above steps are repeated The first-level comprehensive evaluation is $B = W \times R$, and the user attribute trust value AT is obtained after normalization.

Historical Trust. Historical trust is the credit status of users' historical visit behavior from a macro perspective. If users can maintain good access behavior for a long time, historical trust will have a good accumulation. If malicious access occurs, it will decrease, and the decrease is greater than the increase. In other words, it is easier to destroy historical trust than to establish historical trust. This article adds a punishment strategy to reflect the objective law of the slow increase and decrease of historical trust value in the real environment. The historical trust value algorithm is

$$HT = \begin{cases} \frac{\sum_{i=1}^{n} N_i}{\sum_{i=1}^{n} M_i + \sum_{i=1}^{n} N_i} - \frac{1}{1+e^{\frac{1}{\sum_{i+1}^{n} M_i}}}, & \sum_{i=1}^{n} M_i \leq \sum_{i=1}^{n} N_i \\ 0, & \sum_{i=1}^{n} M_i > \sum_{i=1}^{n} N_i. \end{cases} \quad (7)$$

where N_i is the number of normal operations, and M_i is the number of malicious operations. Due to the existence of the penalty factor $1 + e^{1/\sum_{i+1}^{n} M_i}$, once malicious access occurs, even if $1 + e^{1/\sum_{i+1}^{n} M_i}$, its access history trusts Will be greatly reduced, which will increase the price users pay for malicious access. When malicious access exceeds normal access, the historical trust value is considered to be zero.

4 Experimental Simulation

In general, various attacks against user trust mainly occur during the user's access to resources. The traditional trust attribute value is an inherent characteristic of the user itself and does not change with the access process. The static strategy cannot achieve high-precision access control. The historical trust proposed in this paper is calculated based on the historical access behavior, which can effectively Improve this. When calculating a user's historical trust value, the most vulnerable attack is a bleaching attack and a betrayal attack. A bleaching attack refers to a malicious user's whitewashing behavior and deliberately high credit value, while a betrayal attack refers to a sudden attack by a user who has always performed well. Malicious operation. The following is a comparative analysis of the algorithm's ability to resist bleaching attacks and betrayal attacks with the literature algorithm.

The Fig. 3 shows the comparison of the simulation results of the user behavior historical trust value evaluation algorithm proposed in this paper (blue) and the reputation evaluation algorithm (red) in the reference [24] and the algorithm with the penalty factor removed (green), where malicious access is taken The number of times is 1, and the number of normal visits increases from 0 to 100 times.

It can be seen from the figure that the historical trust value of the user in the algorithm of Reference [24] approaches the extreme value 1 with the continuous accumulation of the number of normal visits, which completely conceals the influence of previous malicious visits on the historical trust value. The objective law of credibility evaluation;

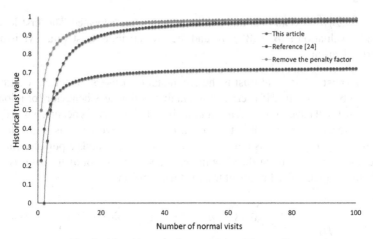

Fig. 3. Bleaching attack test. (Color figure online)

at the same time, the historical trust value in the Reference [24] can increase rapidly with the accumulation of the number of normal visits, which violates the natural law of slow increase in credibility. The algorithm in this paper compares the algorithm with the penalty strategy removed, and it can be seen that the penalty factor greatly enhances the influence of malicious access behavior on the historical trust value. Even if there are multiple normal visits in the follow-up, it is difficult to increase the historical trust value to an ideal level, which reflects the principle of slow increase in trust value. Therefore, the algorithm in this paper has a stronger ability to resist bleaching attacks than the algorithm in the literature.

When the number of normal visits is 300 and the number of malicious visits increases from 0 to 200, the comparison result is shown in the Fig. 4.

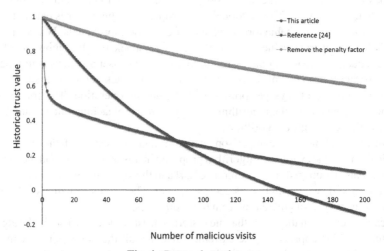

Fig. 4. Betrayal attack test.

It can be seen from the Fig. 4 that the historical trust value of the user when there is no malicious access behavior is 1. Once malicious access behavior occurs, the user historical trust value of the algorithm that removes the penalty factor drops very slowly, indicating that the user is not sensitive to malicious behavior; Reference [24] The user behavior trust value of decreases approximately uniformly with the increase of the number of malicious visits, which cannot highlight the special influence of the initial malicious visit behavior on the historical trust value, and the historical trust value appears negative in the later period, and the measurement index is unreasonable; The historical trust value obtained by the algorithm in this paper decreases exponentially with the occurrence of the first few malicious behaviors. Once a user has malicious access to other users, the user's historical trust value will rapidly decrease, especially when the first malicious access occurs, the decline rate is the fastest, which fully reflects the objective law of the historical trust value plummeting. When the historical trust value drops to a certain level, it begins to slowly decay and stays within the measurement range of [0, 1]. Therefore, the algorithm in this paper has better ability to resist betrayal attacks.

Due to the existence of the punishment factor, the influence of malicious access behavior on the historical trust value is strengthened. Even if there is only one malicious visit, the historical trust value will be reduced to below $1 - \frac{1}{1+e}$, even if there is a large number of normal visits, it cannot be recovered. When users access resources, they need to meet specific trust value conditions. For some particularly important system resources, the trust value requirements can be set to be greater than $1 - \frac{1}{1+e}$. In this way, as long as the user has malicious access behavior, its trust value will not meet the requirements. The system will reject its access request to ensure that important resources are not obtained by malicious users.

5 Conclusion

With the rapid development of mobile Internet services, the complexity of network interaction has greatly increased. The RBAC model and ABAC model proposed in this paper integrate access control strategies, combine trust perception, and use the user's trust value as one of the judgment indicators to achieve dynamic authorization. And finer access granularity. Experiments show that the algorithm also has better resistance to bleaching attacks and betrayal attacks. For future work, our goal is to optimize the trust perception algorithm, and introduce an identity authentication scheme for mobile internet scenarios, to further standardize and expand the current access control strategy.

Funding Statement. This work is supported by the science and technology project of State Grid Corporation of China Funding Item: "Research on Dynamic Access Authentication and Trust Evaluation Technology of Power Mobile Internet Services Based on Zero Trust" (Grand No. 5700-202158183A-0-0-00).

Conflicts of Interest. The authors declare that they have no conflicts of interest to report regarding the present study.

References

1. QuestMobile China Mobile Internet 2021 Semi-Annual Report (2021). https://www.questm obile.com.cn/research/report-new/164. (in Chinese)
2. Ferraiolo, D., Cugini, J., Kuhn, D.R.: Role-based access control (RBAC): features and motivations (1995)
3. Yuan, E., Tong, J.: Attributed based access control (ABAC) for web services. In: IEEE International Conference on Web Services IEEE, pp. 569–572 (2005)
4. Barkha, P., Sahani, G.: Analysis of various RBAC and ABAC based access control models with their extension. Int. J. Eng. Develop. Res **5**(2), 487–492 (2017)
5. Feng, T., Pei, H., Ma, R., Tian, Y., Feng, X.: Blockchain data privacy access control based on searchable attribute encryption. Comput. Mater. Continua **66**(1), 871–890 (2021)
6. Li, L., Xu, C., Yu, X., Dou, B., Zuo, C.: Searchable encryption with access control on keywords in multi-user setting. J. Cyber Secur. **2**(1), 9–23 (2020)
7. Rajkumar, V., Prakash, M., Vennila, V.: Secure data sharing with confidentiality, integrity and access control in cloud environment. Comput. Syst. Sci. Eng. **40**(2), 779–793 (2022)
8. Aftab, M., Qin, Z.: The evaluation and comparative analysis of role based access control and attribute based access control model. In: 15th International Computer Conference on Wavelet Active Media Technology and Information Processing (ICCWAMTIP), pp. 79–81 (2018)
9. Narayana, D.V.S., Kumar, P.V.: Control of data centric through RBAC in clouds. Int. J. Innovat. Eng. Manage. Res. **8**(5), 273–279 (2019)
10. Kuhn, D.: Adding attributes to role-based access control. Computer **43**(6), 79–81 (2010)
11. Coyne, E., Weil, T.R.: ABAC and RBAC: scalable, flexible, and auditable access management. IT Professional **15**, 14–16 (2013)
12. Ullah, I., Zahid, H., Khan, M.A.: An access control scheme using heterogeneous signcryption for IoT environments. Comput. Mater. Continua **70**(3), 4307–4321 (2022)
13. Xin, J., Sandhu, R., Krishnan, R.: RABAC: role-centric attribute-based access control. In: Proceedings of the 6th International Conference on Mathematical Methods, Models and Architectures for Computer Network Security: Computer Network Security, vol. 7531, pp. 84–96 (2012)
14. Thakare, A., Lee, E., Kumar, A., Nikam, V.B., Kim, Y.G.: PARBAC: priority-attribute based RBAC model for azure IoT cloud. IEEE Internet Things J. **7**(4), 2890–2900 (2020)
15. Cai, T., Jian, Z., Xing, D.: A hybrid attribute based RBAC model. Int. J. Secur. Applicat. **9**(7), 317–328 (2015)
16. Xiong, H.R., Chen, X.Y., Fei, X.F., Gui, H.R.: Hybrid extended access control model based on attributes and RBAC. Comput. Applicat. Res. **33**(7), 2162–6169 (2016)
17. Singh, M.P., Sural, S., Vaidya, J., Atluri, V.: Managing attribute-based access control policies in a unified framework using data warehousing and in-memory database. Comput. Secur. **86**, 183–205 (2019)
18. Singh, M.P.: A role-based administrative model for administration of heterogeneous access control policies and its security analysis. Inf. Syst. Front. 1–18 (2021)
19. R, N., Raj, D.P.: Enhanced trust based access control for multi-cloud environment. Comput. Mater. Continua **69**(3), 3079–3093 (2021)
20. Chakraborty, S., Ray, I.: TrustBAC: integrating trust relationships into the RBAC model for access control in open systems. In: Proceedings of the ACM Symposium on Access Control Models & Technologies. lake Tahoe, vol. 18, no. 37, pp. 49–58 (2016)
21. Liu, W., Duan, H.X., Zhang, H., Ren, P., Wu, J.P.: TRBAC: trust-based access control model. Comput. Res. Dev. **48**(8), 1414–1420 (2011)
22. Shao, J.Y., Chen, F.Z., Qin, P.Y., Chen, J.J.: Research on access control method based on dynamic trust value in mobile internet environment. Inf. Netw. Secur. **30**(8), 46–53 (2016)

23. Kang, K.: Research on Access Control Model in Mobile Environment. Xi'an University of Science and Technology, China (2018)
24. Liu, H.Y., Yan, J.Z., Ma, J.F.: A fine-grained RBAC access control model framework based on credibility. J. Communicat. **30**(1), 51–57 (2009)

Fine-Grained Access Control for Power Mobile Service Based on PA Network Under Zero-Trust Framework

Yong Li[1,2(✉)], Lu Chen[1,2], Nige Li[1,2], Ziang Lu[1,2], Zaojian Dai[1,2], and and Fan Wu[3]

[1] Institute of Information and Communication, Global Energy Interconnection Research Institute, Nanjing 210003, China
liyong@geiri.sgcc.com.cn
[2] State Grid Key Laboratory of Information and Network Security, Nanjing 210003, China
[3] Computer Science Department, Tuskegee University, Tuskegee, AL 36088, USA

Abstract. In the power mobile interconnection scenario, the traditional role-based access control (RBAC) is no longer applicable due to the large number of mobile terminals and resource services, complex and diverse access requirements, and data security. In this paper, a fine-grained access control system based on Planner-Analyst network is designed under the framework of Zero Trust, and the hierarchical model that based on perception layer, edge layer, network layer, control layer and application layer is constructed. When the access information is generated, the Planner network classifies the access subject into a role through the control method of role attribute fusion, in which the role has a horizontal permission span, the Analyst network generates the access security probability index according to the access subject information, which has the depth of authority in the vertical sense In the end, the access controller controls the access of the request from the access subject according to the pre-set permission threshold, The contribution of this paper is to propose a new type of zero-trust system architecture based on existing research, which has better stability and higher security in structure and function, but its disadvantage is that the total calculation is large.

Keywords: Fine-grained access control · Zero-trust framework · Power mobile interconnection services · Planner-Analyst network · Variable cache module

1 Introduction

The earliest beginnings of zero trust came in 2004 with the founding of the Yearley Forum, whose mission was to define and find solutions to cybersecurity problems in the borderless trend. In 2010, Forrester analyst John Johan officially used the term zero trust, noting in his research that all network traffic is untrustworthy and needs to be accounted for, security control of any request to a resource.

Software Defined Perimeter (SDP) is the technical framework of zero-trust security. The whole idea of SDP is to build a virtual boundary through Software in the mobile cloud era, identity-based access control (IDACC) is used to solve the problem of coarse granularity and low efficiency of authority control caused by fuzzy boundary, so as to protect the data security of organization. This architecture is widely used and its access control method can be improved continuously.

Access Control Research and development can be divided into four stages: the first stage (1970s) is applied to large scale host systems access control, the representative works are the BLP and BIBA models to ensure confidentiality and integrity, respectively. In phase 2(1980s), access control can be divided into free access control and Mandatory access control, depending on the role of the access administrator. In the third stage (around 2000), with the large-scale application of information system in enterprises and institutions and the increasing prosperity of the internet, role-based access control (RBAC) emerged as an effective solution. Reference [1] presents an Internet of things access control system, Heracles, which can achieve robust, fine-grained access control in the enterprise. A capability-based approach is used to describe the authorization of a principal to an individual or a set of objects in a single or batch operation using a secure, unforgeable token. Add-ons to DAC and Mac. In essence, "Roles" match the organizational structure of enterprises and institutions. In the fourth stage, with the emergence of new computing environments such as cloud computing and Internet of things, some features of the new computing environments have brought huge challenges to the application of access control technology, traditional access control models such as DAC, Mac and RBAC are not suitable for new computing environment. Attribute-based access control (ABAC), based on user, resource, operation and run context attributes, with subject and object attributes as basic decision elements, using the requester's property set to decide whether to grant access pairs or not, it can separate policy management from permission decisions.

Because attribute is inherent in subject and object, it doesn't need to assign by hand, at the same time access control is a many-to-many way, making ABAC management relatively simple. and the attribute can describe the entity from many angles, so can change the policy according to the actual situation. For example, an access control model based on temporal constraints is proposed to introduce temporal constraints into the access control system by analyzing that users may have different identities at different times, the access operation of the user is constrained by the time attribute [2]. Another example is the Usage Control model (UCON) [3], which introduces constraints (such as system load, access time limits, and so on) that must be met to perform access Control. In addition, the strong extensibility of ABAC makes it possible to combine with data privacy protection mechanisms such as encryption mechanism to ensure that user data cannot be analyzed and leaked on the basis of fine-grained access control, ID-based Encryption [4]. Reference [5] based on the concept of dynamic attributes, in order to effectively reduce the key management overhead caused mainly by rekeying, a distributed lightweight group key management architecture for dynamic access control in Internet of Things (IoT) environment is proposed, and a new distributed lightweight group key management architecture is introduced for access control in IoT environment, a new master token management protocol is proposed to manage key propagation for a group of subscribers. The simulation results show that the resource benefit of the scheme is considerable in terms of storage, computation and communication overhead in the fast-growing IoT devices for sensitive data processing. In reference [6], fine-grained access control is proposed to assign unique access rights for specific users to access real-time data directly from nodes in wireless sensor networks (WSNS). The scheme is not very lightweight per se, but resists many active and passive security attacks. In literature [7] an access control scheme based on static and dynamic attributes is proposed for multi-access scenarios. In this scenario, the data owner can combine dynamic attributes with regular attributes maintained by the attribute manager. Including dynamic properties for encryption provides run-time security for data stored in the cloud. Therefore, even if the user has credentials from the attribute authority, the dynamic attribute must be satisfied to decrypt the data in the mobile device. Use Cloud Infrastructure to outsource the heavy computing and communication overhead of mobile users. By adding dynamic attributes to the traditional ID-based encryption, the security is improved and the computing complexity of mobile users is greatly reduced. However, dynamic property based access control is not suitable for secure communication between multiple devices in IoT environment, so in order to achieve secure communication between any two adjacent sensor devices in IoT environment, literature [8] designs a new certificate-based device access control scheme for IoT environment, any two adjacent smart devices first authenticate each other with their preloaded certificates and other secret credentials, and the "Key protocol process" allows authenticated devices to build keys between them, secure data communication. Detailed security analysis using "Informal security analysis and formal security verification under the widely accepted ROR model and the widely used Avispa software verification tool." It is shown that the scheme has lower communication and computing costs and higher security and functional attributes.

Because of the extensive application of RBAC access control model, a lot of research focus on the design of RBAC and ABAC hybrid model, and then realize dynamic permission control based on RBAC. A rule-based RBAC model (RB-RBAC) is proposed by Al-kahtani [9] to solve the problem of user-role assignment, which can automatically assign user roles by obtaining the attribute value of the user, thereby reducing the amount of work to be done manually. In reference [10, 11], the role in RBAC is regarded as a special attribute, and the combination of RBAC and ABAC is used to realize fine-grained authorization and dynamic access control, however, this method greatly weakens or abandons the advantages of the RBAC model, such as easy management, simplicity and convenience. All the above researches keep the basic idea of role-centered in RBAC, and combine it with ABAC or attribute to realize flexible and extensible dynamic access control, however, further research is needed on how to integrate these models into the power mobile interconnection services environment and effectively perceive the trust measurement results of power mobile terminals and users, the result of trust measurement is used to adjust the access policy dynamically, so as to realize the fine-grained access control. A new method of big data security control is introduced in reference [12], that is, zero-trust based user context recognition, fine-grained data access authentication control and network-wide traffic based data access audit to identify and intercept risk data. This method can identify most of the data security risks, but there are still some problems in scheduling. Reference [13] designed a SDN-based fine-grained access control method for IoT devices, which can effectively filter the illegal access of different device sources, request actions, access time and so on. But depending on the SDN network, the extensibility is not strong. In reference [14], the concept of identity-based fine-grained broadcast proxy re-encryption is proposed to solve the problem of fine-grained encrypted micro-video sharing. It also effectively solves some difficult problems in fine-grained access control. In reference [15], Enhanced Trust-Based Access Control System for Multi-Cloud Environments. In reference [16], the article proposes building a blockchain application to implement service-aware access control assisting real-time applications. In reference [17], An access control scheme using heterogeneous signcryption in the Internet of Things environment is proposed to ensure the security of access control.

In the power mobile interconnection scenario, the traditional role-based granular access control (RBAC) is no longer applicable due to the large number of mobile terminals and resource services, complex and diverse access requirements, and data security. Traditional authorization mechanisms are mostly constructed with a single access control model and evaluated once by static access control rules, black-and-white lists, etc., this rigid method lacks the support of continuous measurement of risk and trust, which is difficult to meet the needs of complex business scenarios and is prone to introduce security risks such as over-authorization and resource abuse. Therefore, it is necessary to introduce trust assessment into access control process to realize the dynamic perception of threat risk. However, the traditional role-based authorization management mechanism has the advantages of easy management and easy understanding. How to add dynamic trust perception to traditional role-based access control (RBAC) model and realize the balance between easy operation and dynamic flexibility of authorization management is an urgent problem.

The chapter of this article is arranged as follows. The second section introduces the zero-trust architecture in the electric power mobile service, and analyzes the security hidden trouble of the electric power mobile interconnection service, the PA network structure is proposed to solve this part of the problem. In the third section, based on the traditional access control strategy and combined with the PA network structure proposed in the second chapter, we focus on a zero-trust framework, solution of different granularity access control in power mobile interconnection service. In the fourth section, a storage method is designed to reduce the storage load of the architecture.

2 Zero-Trust Architecture for Power Mobile Interconnection Services

2.1 Security Analysis of Power Mobile Interconnection Services

With the continuous extension of a large number of mobile internet services, mobile office and other services need to be carried out at any time anywhere, the interactive complexity of mobile services has put forward higher requirements for the flexibility, precision and moderation of mobile security protection. In the past, the power mobile service authorization was mainly based on the static role-based access control mechanism, and the business level access control was not flexible enough. Nowadays, the traditional mobile service authorization method is no longer applicable to the risk of massive attack and identity forgery in the power mobile network. How to add trust dynamic evaluation to role-based access control model to balance the operability and security of authorization management is one of the research difficulties.

2.2 Design of Access Control Architecture Based on PA Network

The architecture of Power Mobile interconnection services access control model integrated with Planner network and Analyst network is divided into five layers, which are perception layer, data layer, network layer, control layer and application layer, as shown in Fig. 1.

The sensing layer consists of two parts: the basic sensing devices (such as RFID tag and reader, various kinds of sensors, cameras, GPS, intelligent distribution and transformation terminals, equipment condition monitoring sensors, equipment environment sensors) and the network of sensors (such as RFID network, sensor network). The core technology of this layer includes radio frequency technology, emerging sensor technology, wireless network technology, field bus control technology (FCS), etc.

The edge layer connects the perceptive layer and the network layer, and is mainly responsible for the functions of collecting, transmitting, managing, distributing and processing the edge device data, these include: 1) switches: switches are managed by the control layer, and access rules are defined by the control layer. There are two kinds of switches. One of them is the Software Defined Network (SDN) switch. The other is the SDN access switch. The SDN switch is used to forward data. The SDN controller uses a flow table to configure the SDN switch device and connect it to the communicating device. SDN access switch not only includes the functions of SDN switch, but also can filter the illegal permission data stream when there are illegal permission data stream between IoT devices. One of them is the security manager gateway. The other is the variable cache module. The security manager gateway is used to realize the role-perception fusion information processing. The variable cache module is used to store the fresh data from the perceptive layer and make corresponding requests to the upper layer devices in time. 3) power IoT devices: iot devices including the perceptive layer and other IoT terminal devices.

The network layer consists of internal link state authentication, Gateway Authentication and network authentication, including SSH, flow control, error detection, VPN and so on.

The control layer is the control center of the system. This layer is responsible for generating intra-network exchange paths and boundary business paths, as well as handling network state change events. The policy manager and Bayes controller are the core components of this layer and the core of access control management. The policy manager and Bayes controller are the core components of this layer.

The application layer contains its application interface: an application that reflects the user's intent. These are called collaboration layer applications, and typical applications include OSS (operational support system), Open stack, and so on.

In this paper, the access control of the electric power mobile Internet service lies in the application layer of the above architecture, which will decide the decision-making of the access rights of the data in the electric power mobile internet. There will be other

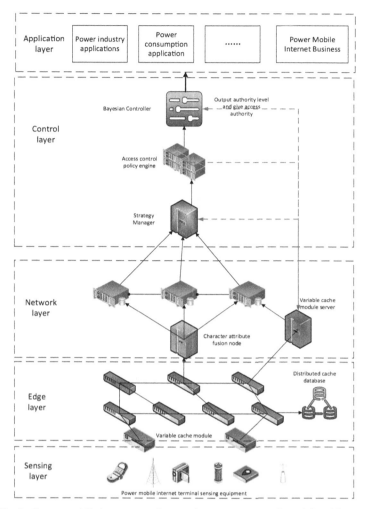

Fig. 1. Power mobile interconnection services access control model architecture.

applications to store, back up, analyze, merge, and mine data streams after access control decisions that meet security requirements.

2.3 An Access Control Flow Design Based on PA Network

The access control model based on the Planner-Analyst network is designed based on the above hierarchy, and the flow of access control is shown in Fig. 2:

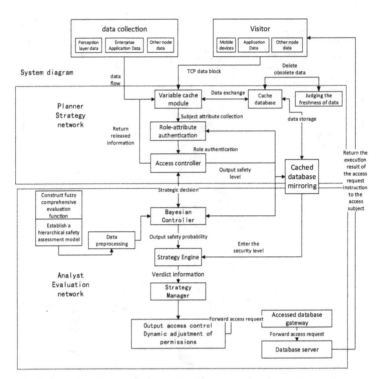

Fig. 2. Power mobile interconnection business access control flow diagram.

The access principal packages the specified information and requests into information blocks and generates them in the form of TCP packets. The access principal sends the TCP packets to the variable cache module and to the switch, at the same time variable cache module for data filtering. The access switch receives the TCP packet sent by the access agent and authenticates the role, such as sending the access information to the access controller of the control layer; The access controller is used as the variable cache module of the Planner policy network request to obtain the attribute information of the access subject and output the permission level according to its role-attribute and so on The access controller handles the access request of the access subject with reference to the Bayes controller, and the Access Controller handles the access request of the access subject with reference to the Bayes controller, the access right, access time and access level are judged by the updated access level. The authorization information is transmitted to the access subject through the gateway.

Under the framework of Zero Trust, the possibility of attack on internal network database is eliminated, the normal access of the source system under the reasonable authority is guaranteed, and the anti-attack performance of the source system under the abnormal condition is guaranteed. When an access subject (mobile device, application data, other nodes, etc.) makes an initial access request, it will be judged according to its environment, subject attributes, subject actions, etc., different access control permissions (time, data level, etc.) are given for different security levels, the variable cache module greatly reduces the data redundancy and data load in the power mobile service, and a memory access control method can also reduce the unbalanced resource utilization in the system.

3 Service Access Control Strategy for Power Mobile Interconnection Based on Planner-Analyst

3.1 Planner Strategy Network

The traditional Role-based access control (RBAC) is a kind of static access control model related to the organization structure of a unit, which greatly reduces the complexity of authorization management, RBAC is a static access control model, once users are assigned roles, it cannot be dynamically adjusted. Attribute-based access control (ABAC) adopts the concept of Attribute-based access control, which can realize context-aware and make full use of the attribute of subject and object and the attribute of environment resource, be able to adapt to more flexible and dynamic delegation. The disadvantage of ABAC is that this model is more complex than RBAC model.

Therefore, this section of the Planner network will combine the two points for an access control strategy based on role-attribute fusion.

Role-Attribute Fusion Access Control Policy

Fig. 3. RBAC schematic.

In RBAC, the role is associated with the user, and the role is associated with the permission indirectly. It increases the role of the link, directly to the role of the allocation of permissions, users only need to bind to a role on it. In RBAC, the system's default user-bound role does not change.

If we need more information for more sophisticated access control to match our complex business scenarios, we also want this new model to be easy to understand and implement, as well as for control and operations, that's what ABAC is trying to solve. In simple terms, for ABAC we determine whether a user has access to a resource by calculating its many different properties.

Thus, by combining the advantages of roles and attributes, we design the following calculation:

First, in the system we stipulate that the different roles have initial access control permissions, which we set to a new concept: access security probability. This probability is a floating-point number from 0 to 1, according to which our system will allocate access time, access data layer, and so on, however, the exact value of this allocation is left to the system administrator. Attribute then uses key-value to store the attributes that access the subject and the information, which are used to represent the subject, object, or environment conditions. We divide it into an n dimensional feature dictionary in the following format: $\{KEY_1 : value_1, KEY_2 : value_2, KEY_3 : value_3, ..., KEY_n : value_n\}$. In these attributes, we extract the feature vector, the format is: $[value_1, value_2, value_3, ..., value_n]$, put it into the MPL for classification, get the weight of the role to which it belongs, according to the maximum weight of the final role classification, and get a permission: access security probability, which is calculated as shown in the Fig. 4.

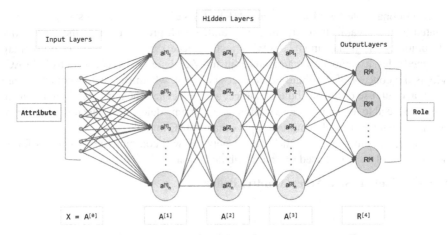

Fig. 4. Schematic of a classified MLP from attribute to role.

3.2 Analyst Evaluation Network

The method based on role-attribute fusion is lightweight and applicable in the non-mobile service network, but it takes into account the complex environment and access situation in the electric power mobile Internet network under the zero-trust framework. We need to take user trust as an attribute, build a dynamic authorization model, avoid premature authorization, continuously collect user trust data, and dynamically control access rights as trust changes. User Trust is continuously evaluated and dynamically changed. A dynamic authorization management method is designed according to the trust degree, and the access authority is dynamically adjusted according to the trust degree of the access subject, adjust or revoke user access.

Therefore, an Analyst evaluation network is proposed, which is a continuous trust evaluation network based on the Planner policy network. The main body of the network is composed of Bayesian network [18], and its flow is as Fig. 5:

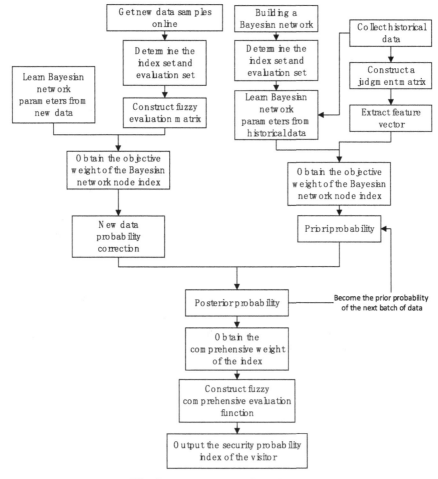

Fig. 5. Analyst network flow diagram.

Firstly, the access agent property information sent by the variable cache module is divided into the access agent role identity, the access agent region security rate, the access agent history behavior information, the access agent request behavior and the property information freshness parameter.

The controller authenticates for the first time according to the two parameters of the role identity and the access behavior. If the access subject conforms to the specified role-attribute authentication, the access controller first releases the access request of the access subject and returns a release message to the variable cache module; The variable cache module stores the authenticated request from the access controller and sends the updated property information again.

Then, a Bayesian network is constructed to collect the historical access data of the subject [19], construct a judgment matrix from the historical data, and extract the feature vectors. Then, the objective weight of the Bayesian network is obtained by combining the Bayesian network parameters obtained from the historical data, and the access security probability is obtained by using the statistical model, which is regarded as a prior probability, among them, access security probability is evaluated by fusing three kinds of information (IoT basic feasibility, device attribute security and access request threat).

Based on the prior probability of the historical data, the new sample data is obtained on-line, the index set and evaluation set of the new sample data are determined, and the fuzzy evaluation matrix is constructed. Then, the objective weight of the Bayesian network is obtained by combining the Bayesian network parameters obtained from the new data. By using Bayes formula to combine the prior probability with the on-line data, the prior probability is modified, and the posterior probability is obtained, which is used as the prior probability corresponding to the next batch of on-line data, a posteriori probability is continuously obtained, and then a fuzzy evaluation function is constructed after the comprehensive weight of the indexes is obtained. The new data are input into the fuzzy evaluation function to obtain the safety probability index in the interval (0,1].

3.3 Access Control for Policy Manager

After obtaining the final security probability index, the administrator first sets the mapping relationship between the security probability index and the security level in the Analyst network, and the content validity of the access is determined by the role, then the security probability is used to get the different levels of permissions that the access request can be allocated.

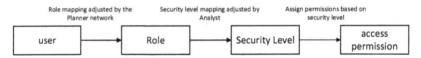

Fig. 6. Permission mapping method for policy manager.

This permission is set by the administrator security level corresponding to different access rights: access time and the level of access data. If the permission is too low, the access will be denied and the connection will be disconnected. If the permission level is within the scope of the mapping set by the administrator, the permission will be granted according to the length of access and the level information, then the policy manager receives the policy engine decision information. If the information is access denied information, the policy manager receives the policy engine decision information, the proxy gateway of the policy execution point is informed to terminate the connection with the access principal, if the information is access permission information, the principal is authorized and the data access request is forwarded to the database gateway The database gateway receives the data access request and forwards the data access request to the database service process, which completes the SQL instruction corresponding operation in the access request in the database, the result of SQL instruction execution is obtained and forwarded to the database server gateway, which sends the result of SQL instruction execution to the user to complete the access control flow.

4 Conclusions

In this paper, an access control method based on Planner-Analyst network is designed for the fine-grained access control of the power mobile interconnection services under the zero-trust framework: combining RBAC and ABAC, the access information generated by the access agent is classified and the initial access security probability is obtained; The Bayesian network is used to evaluate the access request from the access subject in real time, which achieves the goal of continuous trust evaluation and permission dynamic adjustment. This method guarantees the normal access of the source system under the reasonable permission and the anti-attack performance of the source system under the abnormal situation. The limitation of this paper is that the access control method in this paper has a lot of computation and needs to be attached to a better performance computing device, reduce the computational load of the entire network.

Acknowledgement. This work is supported by the science and technology project of State Grid Corporation of China Funding Item: "Research on Dynamic Access Authentication and Trust Evaluation Technology of Power Mobile Internet Services Based on Zero Trust" (Grand No. 5700-202158183A-0–0-00).

Conflicts of Interest. The authors declare that they have no conflicts of interest to report regarding the present study.

References

1. Qian, Z., Elbadry, M., Fan, Y., Yang, Y.: Heracles: scalable, fine-grained access control for internet-of-things in enterprise environments. In: IEEE INFOCOM 2018 - IEEE Conference on Computer Communications, pp. 1772–1780 (2018)
2. Bertino, E., Bonatti, P.A., Ferrari, E.: TRBAC: a temporal role-based access control model. In: Proceedings RBAC, pp. 191–233 (2001)
3. Park, J., Sandhu, R.: Towards usage control models: Beyond traditional access control. In: Proceedings SACMAT, pp. 57–64. Monterey, California, USA (2002)
4. Lewko, A., Okamoto, T., Sahai, A., Takashima, K., Waters, B.: Fully secure functional encryption: Attribute-based encryption and (hierarchical) inner product encryption. In: Annual International Conference on the Theory and Applications of Cryptographic Techniques, pp. 62–91 (2010)
5. Dammak, M., Senouci, S.M., Messous, M.A., Elhdhili, M.H., Gransart, C.: Decentralized lightweight group key management for dynamic access control in IoT environments. IEEE Trans. Netw. Serv. Manage. **17**(3), 1742–1757 (2020)
6. Roy, S., Chatterjee, S.: An efficient fine-grained access control scheme for hierarchical wireless sensor networks. Int. J. Ad Hoc Ubiquitous Comput. **29**(3), 161–180 (2016)
7. Li, F., Rahulamathavan, Y., Rajarajan, M.: LSD-ABAC: lightweight static and dynamic attributes based access control scheme for secure data access in mobile environment. In: 39th Annual IEEE Conference on Local Computer Networks, pp. 354–361 (2014)
8. Das, A.K., Wazid, M., Yannam, A.R., Rodrigues, J.J.P.C., Park, Y.: Provably secure ecc-2526based device access control and key agreement protocol for IoT environment. IEEE Access **7**, 55382–55397 (2019)

9. Al-Kahtani, M.A., Sandhu, R.: A model for attribute-based user-role assignment. In: 18th Annual Computer Security Applications Conference, pp. 353–362. Las Vegas, NV, USA (2002)

10. Chadwick, D.W., Otenko, A., Ball, E.: Implementing role based access controls using X. 509 attribute certificates. NATO Science Series pp. 26–39 (2004)

11. Jin, X., Krishnan, R., Sandhu, R.: A unified attribute-based access control model covering DAC, MAC and RBAC. In: Proceedings of the 26th Annual IFIP International Federation for Information, pp. 41–55 (2012)

12. Yang, T., Zhu, L., Peng, R.: Fine-grained big data security method based on zero trust model. In: 2018 IEEE 24th International Conference on Parallel and Distributed Systems (ICPADS), Singapore, pp. 1040–1045 (2018)

13. Wei, M., Liang, E., Nie, Z.: A SDN-based IoT fine-grained access control method. In: 2020 International Conference on Information Networking (ICOIN), pp. 637–642 (2020)

14. Ge, C., Zhou, L., Xia, J., Szalachowski, P., Su, C.: Secure fine-grained micro-video subscribing system in cloud computing. IEEE Access 7, 137266–137278 (2019)

15. R, N., Raj, D.P.: Enhanced trust based access control for multi-cloud environment. Comput. Mater. Continua **69**(3), 3079–3093 (2021)

16. Almagrabi, A.O., Bashir, A.K.: Service-aware access control procedure for blockchain assisted real-time applications. Comput. Mater. Continua **67**(3), 3649–3667 (2021)

17. Ullah, I., Zahid, H., Khan, M.A.: An access control scheme using heterogeneous signcryption for iot environments. Comput. Mater. Continua **70**(3), 4307–4321 (2022)

18. Albahli, S., Nabi, G.: Defect prediction using Akaike and Bayesian information criterion. Comput. Syst. Sci. Eng. **41**(3), 1117–1127 (2022)

19. Liwei, T., Li, F., Yu, S., Yuankai, G.: Forecast of LSTM-xgboost in stock price based on Bayesian optimization. Intell. Automat. Soft Comput. **29**(3), 855–868 (2021)

Multi-device Continuous Authentication Mechanism Based on Homomorphic Encryption and SVM Algorithm

Wei Gan[1], Xuqiu Chen[2], Wei Wang[2], Lu Chen[3,4(✉)], Jiaxi Wu[2], Xian Wang[2], Xin He[2], and Fan Wu[5]

[1] State Grid Sichuan Electric Power Company, Chengdu 610000, China
[2] State Grid Chengdu Electric Power Supply Company, Chengdu 610000, China
[3] Institute of Information and Communication, Global Energy Interconnection Research Institute, Nanjing 210003, China
chenluchina@aliyun.com
[4] State Grid Key Laboratory of Information and Network Security, Nanjing 210003, China
[5] Computer Science Department, Tuskegee University, Tuskegee, AL 36088, USA

Abstract. In order to meet the higher security requirements of authentication technology under the current mobile Internet background, continuous identity authentication technology based on single authentication improvement came into being. At present, continuous authentication technology has problems such as low security, low efficiency, and lack of a scientific punishment mechanism. How to efficiently, safely and comprehensively evaluate the legal and illegal requests of the terminal is a huge challenge for continuous authentication. The multi-device continuous authentication mechanism based on homomorphic encryption and SVM algorithm can satisfy the server in a sufficiently secure environment to enable the terminal request to be continuously authenticated. Moreover, based on the existing research, this paper designs a new penalty protocol and applies it to the continuous authentication mechanism. For this purpose, an illegal request processing model is constructed, and the penalty protocol designed to cope with the illegal request Further processing solves the problem that the existing continuous authentication mechanism is insufficient to handle illegal requests and is not humane enough. Finally, the experimental results of SVM and convolutional network on a single device and multiple devices are compared from three dimensions. The comparison of the experimental results verifies the effectiveness of the proposed model and protocol.

Keywords: Homomorphic encryption · Continuous authentication · Penalty protocol · SVM

1 Introduction

At present, the mobile Internet has increasingly higher requirements for the security and humanization of identity authentication technology. The traditional identity authentication technology represented by the single identity authentication technology requests

X. Sun et al. (Eds.): ICAIS 2022, LNCS 13340, pp. 625–638, 2022.
https://doi.org/10.1007/978-3-031-06791-4_49

identification and authentication of the terminal based on a password, a password or a token. Continuous identity authentication technology uses an authentication model that is different from single authentication technology. The main manifestation is that the data used is changed from passwords to biometrics. The model built is no longer just to achieve simple information matching, but to use complex machine learning models. Realizing the classification and processing of biometrics. In addition, the certification cycle has changed dramatically, from the traditional single certification to continuous certification. Therefore, the continuous identity authentication mechanism reduces the use of credentials and improves the security level. The existing continuous identity authentication technology is mainly based on the model construction of behavioral biometrics in a given time window. The specific steps of its implementation are mainly divided into three stages. First, the behavioral biometrics are screened by dimensions, data, and characteristics; secondly, based on the screened behavioral biometrics, machine learning or deep learning techniques are used to build models; finally, the continuous authentication mechanism uses the constructed model to process uninterruptedly the new behavioral biometrics are classified and matched to determine whether the request is authenticated.

Existing continuous identity authentication research has implemented the steps mentioned in the background [1, 2] on single terminal devices such as mobile phones and personal computers. However, the continuous identity authentication technology based on a single device lacks performance in terms of equal error rate, accuracy rate, and security, and there are mainly three problems in the following aspects. First, the processed data are all from the same terminal device, which is too single, which makes the safety and accuracy not guaranteed; secondly, the model built under a single device is basically not portable and has low efficiency; finally, the data is basically in plain text Processing in the state, once the data is stolen illegally, the system may face severe security threats. Although the subsequent research on continuous identity authentication with multiple devices has to some extent alleviated the problems in the above-mentioned single device continuous identity authentication, and as mentioned above, continuous authentication technology has many advantages [3, 14, 15] However, there are still many problems in the overall design of the mechanism.

To this end, this paper proposes a multi-device continuous authentication mechanism based on homomorphic encryption and SVM algorithm. The main contributions are as follows. (1) The authentication mechanism proposed in this article collects behavioral biometrics from multiple terminals of mobile phones, personal computers, tablet computers, and desktop computers to ensure multiple levels of data, thereby solving the single problem of data mentioned above. (2) The CSS Conference [13] in 2011 proposed to combine homomorphic encryption with machine learning and apply homomorphic encryption to practice. This paper inherits the advantages of existing research, uses homomorphic encryption to implement data privacy protection, and builds a model with SVM algorithm to solve the problem of illegal data theft mentioned above. (3) In terms of mechanism design, this article innovatively proposes a penalty protocol, combines it with the existing continuous identity authentication mechanism, adds a penalty mechanism, and handles illegal requests more specifically and comprehensively. To a certain extent, it improves the existing the design of the mechanism improves the humanization of the authentication mechanism. (4) Starting from the two categories of single-device and multi-device, SVM and convolutional network algorithms are evaluated in terms of accuracy, recall and f1 score. The experimental results show the feasibility and advantages of this scheme. Under the premise of increasing the penalty mechanism, the performance is not much different from the existing mechanism.

2 Related Work

Literature [4] continuously uses free text-based keystroke dynamics to verify the user's identity in real time, and evaluates it based on the data set collected from the user's daily life when interacting with the mailbox. However, it is based on a homogeneous data set, and experiments have been carried out based on this. The current form of network security is more severe. Therefore, the security of the solution provided by literature [4] needs to be improved. Mohammed Abuhamad [7] and others proposed the AUToSen mechanism, which uses a smart phone sensor based implicit continuous authentication based on deep learning. Similar to the limitations mentioned earlier, on the one hand, it is based on the limitations of a single device. On the other hand, there is no privacy protection mechanism. For the data being processed, attackers are likely to obtain and embezzle it through illegal methods.

Literature [5] proposed a mechanism called SmartCAMPP, which is based on continuous authentication of smart phones and uses motion sensors with privacy protection. It mainly uses acceleration data and gyroscope data from the mobile phone. Compared with non-privacy protection settings, it has made a big breakthrough in privacy security. However, judging from the type of data and the performance shown by SmartCAMPP, there are great limitations. In 2020, Pedro Miguel Sánchez Sánchez et al. [6] proposed another continuous identity authentication mechanism with privacy protection, Auth-CODE. Although certain breakthroughs have been made in data and data processing on the basis of the literature [5], since the user's behavior is evaluated every minute, the attacker can use the device in a short time without being detected. In addition, due to the application of ML/DL classification algorithms, user recognition performance depends on how different each user's behavior is from other users. If the number of users increases too much, there may be a problem with scalability of the model.

Literature [8] proposed a multi-device anonymous authentication. Compared with the continuous authentication scheme, this kind of authentication is easy to be illegally invaded after one verification. Therefore, continuous authentication still has a higher advantage in terms of security. Literature [9] proposed a continuous authentication feature test mobile application based on machine learning. This method can be used in any data-sensitive mobile application, and the data privacy of the device owner can be protected through continuous authentication. The program should expand behavioral characteristics and use other machine learning methods to improve the accuracy of the system and establish advantages in accuracy and privacy. Literature [10] is a review of continuous authentication methods in an IoT environment. It provides an overall view of CA related to users in the IoT environment, and how to use blockchain to enhance the entire CA process. Literature [11] uses soft biometrics based on typing patterns collected in a multi-device environment. The main limitation is that it is difficult to obtain a high-quality data set. Literature [12] proposes context-aware identity verification using co-location equipment. The mechanism verifies the user's identity by detecting data generated by short-range radio signals from nearby devices, and conducts internal experiments by using a bag method involving perceiving contextual data. But it does not enhance the proposed mechanism by combining the dependence on the physical context and providing countermeasures for context replay attacks.

3 Multi-Device Continuous Authentication Mechanism Based on Homomorphic Encryption and SVM Algorithm

3.1 Formalization of the Problem

The formalization of the question includes an overview of the proposed mechanism and a description of the characteristics of the data used. The general scheme is shown in Fig. 1, where U is the user, D is the terminal device, S is the server, and ED is the encrypted data. The authentication decision made by the server is marked as R.

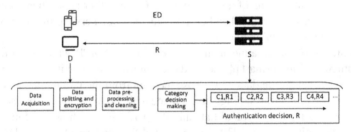

Fig. 1. Overview of the mechanism model.

The input data is obtained from the sensors of the terminal equipment, including gyroscopes and acceleration sensors, etc. The dimension is determined by the sensor data of the largest dimension. In order to ensure the rationality of the data and the accuracy of the model, such data is preprocessed, and large values are compressed to make the data look smoother. At the terminal device, the data is encrypted and preprocessed. After S receives the encrypted data, it analyzes it, generates a decision R and sends it to the terminal device D. The following section provides a more detailed description.

How to judge that multiple devices belong to the same user? When the user registers with the current device for the first time or logs in to the system using this mechanism, the user will be authorized to obtain the unique identifier of the current user device, such as the machine code, and register it with the user information. In the end, all the information of the device used by the current user will be saved under one user information. When these devices are used, the previously recorded identifier will be used to match the user device and this can also be used to attribute multiple devices to the same One user.

3.2 Proposed Model

Collect user U's behavioral biological information for the purpose of identity authentication. Information is collected from terminal device D, especially terminal sensor data, such as accelerometers and gyroscopes.

The server S processes the data received from the terminal D in a continuous manner, first classifies it, and divides it into illegal requests and reasonable requests, and secondly, based on the machine code and punishment protocol, the illegal requests in the classification results are separated from man and machine. Punishment, and finally repeat the encryption classification and punishment operations for new users and authenticated legitimate users to achieve the purpose of continuous authentication.

The degree of model optimization and accuracy on the server side depend on the data transmitted from the terminal, and the selection of various parameters of the data also depends on the processing form of the model.

The following attackers are the main threats to the model:

An external attacker who intends to steal information. It may implant malicious programs in the user's terminal device to collect user behavior information, or hijack the terminal information we collect, or collect data in the process of sending the data to the server.

The server follows the established protocol and learns all possible information from the received message.

End users who are not the user. The user's own terminal is very likely to be lost or lend the terminal to others for use. If someone observing the user's own behavior and habits in advance and imitating the user's own biological behavior to use the terminal without the user's knowledge, it is possible Cause harm.

On the basis of the prevention strategy of the previous authentication model, we provide a new penalty protocol to assist the server in solving the illegal requests that have appeared. Figure 2 is the penalty protocol designed in this paper.

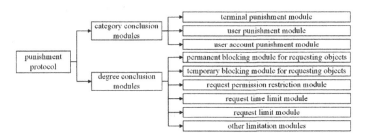

Fig. 2. Penalty protocol.

Among them, the other restriction modules are the extensible modules of the model, which improves the scalability of the penalty protocol. When a new penalty module is needed, the penalty can quickly learn and apply the new penalty module.

As shown in Fig. 2, the punishment protocol consists of several category of conclusion modules: terminal punishment module, user punishment module, user account punishment module. The terminal punishment module is mainly aimed at a series of problems caused by the terminal, such as frequent replacement of unfamiliar terminals to send requests, unsafe terminal environment, terminal loss, terminal data leakage, and low application version. The user punishment module is mainly aimed at a series of problems caused by the user, such as the theft of real names, network attackers, and multiple serious violations. The user account punishment module is mainly aimed at a series of problems caused by the account, such as account misappropriation, illegal operation of the account, and low account safety factor.

The punishment protocol consists of several degree conclusion modules: permanent blocking module for requesting objects, temporary blocking module for requesting objects, request permission restriction module, request time limit module, request limit module, and other limitation modules. Among them, the permanent blocking module for requesting objects mainly involves the excessively high degree of illegality of the request object, which causes excessive harm to the system, including the permanent block of the machine code, ID number, and account number. The temporary blocking module for requesting objects is a blocking module for a certain period of time as opposed to a permanent blocking. After the blocking period has expired, there will be a period of inspection and testing. After passing the system security inspection, the blocking will be completely lifted, and the user will have the initial rights. The request permission restriction module is mainly aimed at illegal requests whose illegality has not reached the banned level. The system will limit the authority of the requested object according to the illegality, generally to reduce user authority and ensure the security of the system. The request time limit module is mainly for illegal requests with abnormal specific characteristics, and the request limit module is mainly for the number of abnormal requests that are too frequent.

The category conclusion module mainly makes the decision on who should be punished, and the degree conclusion module mainly makes the punishment for a certain aspect of the object to be punished.

The overall model architecture includes the following steps. Extract user terminal sensor and application data based on data splitting, and use homomorphic encryption technology to immediately encrypt the split data. Training models and predictions. Finally, the multi-terminal continuous authentication method based on the accurate classification and punishment protocol of illegal requests is used to obtain the judgment results of illegal requests. The three steps are represented by formulas 1, 2 and 3 respectively.

$$x = encrypt(data) \tag{1}$$

$$c = svms(x) \tag{2}$$

$$R = PA(C) \tag{3}$$

Among them, PA represents the penalty agreement, as shown in Fig. 2. SVM boils down to the optimization problem in formula 4, which uses the idea of iteration to find its optimal value. It solves the mean value of the maximum interval of multiple experiments, so as to find the optimal segmentation hyperplane, and finally obtain the model.

$$\min_{w,b} \frac{\sum_{i=1}^{n} \frac{1}{2}\|w_i\|^2}{\sqrt{n^2+1}} \tag{4}$$

$$S \cdot t \cdot 1 - y^{(N)}\left(w_i^T x_i^{(n)} + b\right) \leq 0 \ \forall N \in \{1, \ldots, N+\}. \tag{5}$$

Among them, n is the number of effective experiments, N is each sample, w is the feature weight, x is the feature value, b is the parameter, and y is the classification result of each sample.

The encryption algorithm will be specifically introduced in Sect. 4.1.

3.3 Target

Privacy protection. No one except the user can access the sensor data. Moreover, the user's data is always encrypted from acquisition to the end of use, even when it is being processed.

Efficient. The mechanism will feed back the results of the processing to the user within the time tolerated by the user.

Accuracy. The mechanism will classify user data with high accuracy.

Streamline. For illegal requests, we no longer simply reject them rudely, but give them reasonable punishments, reduce their frequency or even prevent them from appearing again. Moreover, the punishment is carried out based on the designed punishment module, and the punishment operation is refined to make it more targeted, while reducing the possibility of wrong punishment.

Scalability. For new modules that may appear, the mechanism can learn in time and add them to the penalty protocol.

In terms of efficiency, in fact, the performance requirements of homomorphic encryption are very high, but when the model is stable and the data is stable, the current general server performance can meet general needs. If the demand becomes higher, the homomorphic encryption itself is realized with the help of cloud computing, which not only guarantees the performance requirements, but also guarantees the security in the authentication process. Therefore, in terms of efficiency, the current hardware development and the development of the cloud make it possible to meet the basic needs.

3.4 Description

As a whole, the continuous authentication mechanism proposed in this paper, like other identity authentication mechanisms, is a mechanism for continuous interaction between the terminal and the server, as shown in Fig. 3. Their interactive design authenticates and feedbacks sensor data, and these data will be transmitted and processed through the data protection technology of homomorphic encryption.

Before it runs correctly, it is necessary to train the classifier in the server. The classifiers we trained here include SVM and traditional convolutional neural network classifiers. For the latter, in the context of a large amount of data, the data will be better processed and the classification results will be returned.

Data collection. First, the terminal retrieves sensor data from the sensors and stores them for further processing. This step is executed periodically according to the collection rate of the relevant sensor.

Data preprocessing. Each sensor reading consists of a set of characteristics. Therefore, the n features $V = \{v_1, ..., v_n\}$ selected in this step are read every time.

Data encryption. First, define the KG function, that is, the key generation function, which is executed by the terminal and generates the key Key used by the encrypted data *Data*. Among them, there are some public constants PP as needed. Define the EC function, that is, the encryption function, which is run by the terminal and encrypts the characteristic matrix data *Data* with the previously generated *Key* to obtain the ciphertext CT. Define the EL function, that is, the evaluation function [16]. This function is executed by the remote system, and the ciphertext is operated under the data processing method f given by the system, so that the result is equivalent to that the user key *Key* encrypts $f(Data)$. Here f is usually the neural network classifier model trained by the system. Define the DC function, that is, the decryption function. This function is run by the terminal and used to obtain the result $f(Data)$ processed by the system.

Classification. Eliminate the features within the reasonable value range in the illegitimate feature matrix and reduce the dimensionality of the illegitimate feature matrix. Calculate the difference between each feature value in the illegal feature matrix and the normal threshold, remove the feature with too small deviation value, and reduce the dimension of the feature matrix again. Add invalid data to keep the dimensions of each illegal feature matrix the same and use the illegal feature matrix to train a neural network classifier for illegal request classification. The classification result of the classifier is pre-defined, such as the illegal operation of the account itself, the illegal operation of the account by others, the malicious attack by illegal personnel, the low safety factor of the terminal environment, the illegal operation of the terminal by others, the illegal operation of the terminal itself, etc. Use the classifier to classify the illegal feature matrix and use the classification result as the illegal label of the feature matrix. According to the calculated deviation [17] value and the degree of harm caused by the illegal behavior to the system, the feature and its value for recording the degree of illegality are generated data. The degree of illegality is mainly divided into five levels, and the harm gradually increases from small to large, and the most serious can cause the system to be paralyzed and unable to work normally. Combine the two to form a new feature matrix. Taking n users as a unit, the obtained feature matrix is formed into a feature matrix with a dimension of $n * 2$. The penalty protocol analyzes the generated feature matrix and generates corresponding penalty measures. According to the punishment measures generated by the protocol, the system will punish the request object corresponding [18] to the feature. The parameters of the classifier are trained based on the illegal data that may be generated by the power mobile application and belong to a special classifier model. In addition, the penalty protocol used is unique to the continuous identity authentication process of the system.

4   Experimental Evaluation

4.1   Single Device Data Set Experiment

Table 1 shows the characteristics of the acceleration and gyroscope sensor data used in the experiment and some of the experimental data, as well as the encrypted results. The data calculated in the experiment are all encrypted data as shown in the table. The data used in the experiment comes from 124 volunteers. The sensor data of these volunteers when using mobile phones and the biological data when using personal computers are collected. Behavioral data, sensor [19] data when using a tablet computer, and related data when using a desktop computer, etc. These data are divided into multiple features

Table 1. Accelerometer and gyroscope selected features and key encryption.

Feeature Name	Range(Hz)	Example data	key	Encrypted Data
acc_x	0–101.12	61.287	8h0n506duqq32ugqdhuei	48784
acc_y	0–102.25	101.29	Djiejdiejdi9302jidjeidnan	12546998
acc_z	0–253.14	217.58	Djie9jdi019dijidanoa0dii	89646
gyr_x	0–256	12.25	090ajidjiaa1njdnaj29ndai	4328492
gry_y	0–256	144.97	Dodkqokdo5dd8dwdq7dq	3019193
gry_z	0–256	102.254	Dqddq4d7dd4q8273824d	319389189

and encrypted like sample data. That is, $Y = FFX.EncryptK.K.T(X)$, decrypted as $X = FFX.DecryptK.K.T(X)$ [5]. Where K refers to the key, X is the plaintext and a fine-tuning T.

This section describes the accuracy of continuous certification in single-device and multi-device experimental environments. In view of the relatively large amount of data and the characteristics of the data set, it is necessary to preprocess the data. Our first step is data preprocessing, discarding some similar and repeated data, discarding data that deviates too much from the normal value, and using one-hot to encode each classification feature. Next, select SVM and convolutional neural network to perform the initial classification process on the data set collected by a single device. Both of these algorithms provide an estimate of the performance of each feature. In addition, they can manage a large number of features and have better performance in dealing with unbalanced data. The data set is divided into fragments [20] with a fixed time window size, and 20% of the fragments are randomly selected to form the test set. In the process of training the SVM model, this article mainly selects and optimizes the parameters C and gamma, and under the premise that the former remains unchanged, selects and evaluates each kernel function until the optimal training and testing effect is reached. Our performance indicators are mainly FPR, FRR and their combined comprehensive evaluation.

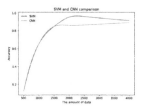

Fig. 3. The performance of SVM and convolutional network on a single device data set.

The abscissa in Fig. 3 represents the data volume of the device sensor data as the test data, and the ordinate represents the accuracy of the model prediction, that is, whether the classification is successful and corresponding punishment. Figure 3 shows the accuracy of the SVM and convolutional neural network in this experiment on single device data. It can be seen that when the amount of data is small, the performance of the traditional machine learning algorithm SVM is better than that of the convolutional neural network.

However, as the amount of data increases, the performance of convolutional neural networks is gradually better than SVM. However, considering the security of encryption, this article chooses SVM, whose performance is basically negligible in terms of high data volume.

According to the actual application scenarios envisioned in this article, this article selects a scale of about 5000 to 20000 data, and further conducts verification experiments. The experimental results show that the performance gap between SVM and convolutional neural networks is not very large. Among them, the accuracy rate, recall rate and f1 score are basically maintained between 80% to 97%.

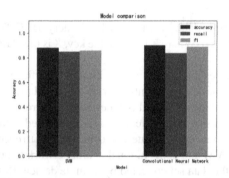

Fig. 4. Display of results in three dimensions on a single device.

The abscissa in Fig. 4 represents two different models, namely SVMS and convolutional neural network, and the ordinate represents the two models with single device sensor data as the test set, and their respective accuracy, recall, and f1 scores Performance.

4.2 Multi-device Data Set Experiment

For the data set on each device, this paper selects the combination of their most discriminating features to ensure the identity verification results obtained during the experiment. Moreover, in the choice of time window, this article reduces the time window to increase the frequency of authentication. In view of the fact that the experiments are all carried out on personal computers, the performance may be severely affected. This article does not consider the size of the computer resources consumed by the experiments. In the multi-device data set, the main cell phone sensor data is mainly used, and the data of other devices are supplemented. If any device is not active in the same time period, their characteristics are set to 0 by default. This article also only generates vectors with activities.

In this paper, the SVM algorithm and the convolutional neural network algorithm are respectively put on the data set suitable for them for experiment, and their respective hyperparameters are optimized.

The abscissa of Fig. 5 represents two different models, namely SVMS and convolutional neural network, and the ordinate represents the two models using multi-device sensor data as the test set, and their respective accuracy, recall, and f1 scores Performance.

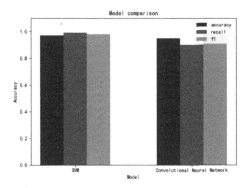

Fig. 5. Display of results in three dimensions on multiple devices.

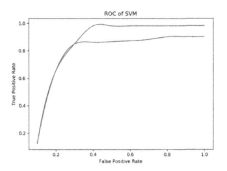

Fig. 6. ROC curves for baseline SVM.

In addition, Fig. 6 shows the relationship between FPR and TPR.

The hardware facility of this experiment is a personal computer, so there is no comparative reference in the performance data. As far as the performance consumption of personal computers is concerned, within an acceptable range, it is expected that the experimental results obtained on better-performing hardware facilities will be even better.

In order to enrich the experimental results, Table 2 shows the performance of the two models in different dimensions in other aspects. It can be seen that according to the needs of this article, the effect of SVM is better than that of CNN.

From the comparison experiment with literature [6], it can be seen that this article has a significant improvement in the training accuracy of the model SVM, but due to the encryption algorithm used, there may be a decrease in time efficiency. In general, the method proposed in this article is better (Table 3).

Table 2. SVM and CNN in other aspects of performance.

Model	Dataset	AVG.Precise	AVG.Recall	AVG.F1	AVG.FPR
SVM	PersonalComputer	0.85	0.84	0.88	0.0098
SVM	Sensors	0.88	0.85	0.86	0.0092
SVM	Muti-device	0.97	0.99	0.98	0.0054
CNN	PersonalComputer	0.86	0.88	0.87	0.0112
CNN	Sensors	0.90	0.84	0.89	0.0214
CNN	Muti-device	0.95	0.90	0.98	0.0094

Table 3. Contrast experiment with literature [6].

Model	Dataset	AVG.Precise	Source
SVM	Single-device	0.86	Literature [6]
SVM	Muti-device	0.96	Literature [6]
SVM	Single-device	0.88	This article
SVM	Muti-device	0.97	This article

5   Conclusions

This article introduces a multi-device continuous authentication mechanism based on homomorphic encryption and SVM algorithm, a multi-device continuous identity authentication architecture for mobile Internet services. It uses machine learning technology and deep learning technology to continuously authenticate users based on their behavior. This mechanism provides a privacy protection function and a punishment mechanism to solve the problem that the processing of illegal requests is not reasonable enough and the punishment protocol is not comprehensive enough in the current continuous identity authentication process. These include: a processing mechanism for classifying encrypted data composed of various terminals based on homomorphic encryption and classifiers; a mechanism for separating illegal requests from the classification results based on machine code and punishment protocol; a punishment mechanism for separating humans and machines; for new users and Authenticated legitimate users repeatedly implement encryption classification and punishment operations to achieve the purpose of continuous authentication. This mechanism can provide a more reasonable identification mechanism and punishment mechanism for illegal requests while improving the security of multi-terminal continuous identity authentication, thereby improving the usability of the system for users and making the processing results of illegal requests more accurate.

Because it may be restricted by the performance of homomorphic encryption, the mechanism designed in this paper may not perform so well in large-scale systems. How to improve the performance needs to be further studied.

As future work, it is planned to experiment and evaluate the performance of this mechanism and the accuracy of identity authentication through more users and on more advanced equipment. It is also possible to test and evaluate the application of the new algorithm in classification operations. In addition, due to the continuous popularity of Internet of Things devices, consider combining this mechanism with the Internet of Things, and expand the realization of use cases in new dimensions. Generate novel and different-dimensional data sets, and continuously improve the problems that arise in the continuous certification process of multiple devices. Finally, look for new evaluation indicators and angles to evaluate the mechanism we designed more comprehensively.

Acknowledgement. This work is supported by the State Grid Sichuan Company Science and Technology Project: "Research and Application of Key Technologies of Network Security Protection System Based on Zero Trust Model" (No. SGSCCD00XTJS2101279).

Conflicts of Interest. The authors declare that they have no conflicts of interest to report regarding the present study.

References

1. Gomi, H., Yamaguchi, S., Tsubouchi, K., Sasaya, N.: Continuous authentication system using online activities. In: 2018 17th IEEE International Conference on Trust, Security and Privacy; in Computing and Communications/12th IEEE International Conference on Big Data Science And Engineering (TrustCom/BigDataSE), pp. 522–532 (2018)
2. Patel, V.M., Chellappa, R., Chandra, D., Barbello, B.: Continuous user authentication on mobile devices: Recent progress and remaining challenges. IEEE Signal Process. Mag. **33**(4), 49–61 (2016)
3. Song, X., Zhao, P., Wang, M., Yan, C.: A continuous identity verification method based on free-text keystroke dynamics. In: 2016 IEEE International Conference on Systems, Man, and Cybernetics (SMC), Budapest, Hungary, pp. 000206–000210 (2016)
4. Messerman, A., Mustafic´, T., Camtepe, S.A., Albayrak, S.: Continuous and non-intrusive identity verification in real-time environments based on free-text keystroke dynamics. In: 2011 International Joint Conference on Biometrics (IJCB), Washington, DC, USA, pp. 1–8 (2011)
5. Hernández-Álvarez, L., Fuentes, J.M.D., González-Manzano, L., Encinas, L.H.: SmartCAMPP-Smartphone-based continuous authentication leveraging motion sensors with privacy preservation. Pattern Recogn. Lett. **147**, 189–196 (2021)
6. Sánchez, P.M.S., Maimó, L.F., Celdrán, A.H., Pérez, G.M.: AuthCODE: A privacy-preserving and multi-device continuous authentication architecture based on machine and deep learning. Comput. Secur. **103**, 102168 (2021)
7. Abuhamad, M., Abuhmed, T., Mohaisen, D., Nyang, D.: AUToSen: Deep-learning-based implicit continuous authentication using smartphone sensors. IEEE Internet Things J. **7**(6), 5008–5020 (2020)
8. Kluczniak, K., Wang, J., Chen, X., Kutyłowski, M.: Multi-device anonymous authentication. Int. J. Inf. Secur. **18**(2), 181–197 (2018). https://doi.org/10.1007/s10207-018-0406-4
9. Samet, S., Ishraque, M.T., Ghadamyari, M., Kakadiya, K., Mistry, Y., Nakkabi, Y.: Touch-Metric: a machine learning based continuous authentication feature testing mobile application. Int. J. Inf. Technol. **11**(4), 625–631 (2019). https://doi.org/10.1007/s41870-019-00306-w
10. Al-Naji, F.H., Zagrouba, R.: A survey on continuous authentication methods in Internet of Things environment. Comput. Commun. **163**, 109–133 (2020)

11. Udandarao, V., Agrawal, M., Kumar, R., Shah, R.R.: On the Inference of Soft Biometrics from Typing Patterns Collected in a Multi-device Environment. In: IEEE Sixth International Conference on Multimedia Big Data (BigMM), New Delhi, India, pp. 76–85 (2020)

12. Gomi, H., Yamaguchi, S., Ogami, W., Teraoka, T., Higurashi, T.: Context-Aware Authentication Using Co-Located Devices. In: 18th IEEE International Conference on Trust, Security and Privacy; In: Computing And Communications/13th IEEE International Conference On Big Data Science And Engineering, Rotorua, New Zealand, pp. 304–311 (2019)

13. Naehrig, M., Lauter, K., Vaikuntanathan, V.: Can homomorphic encryption be practical? In: Proceedings CCSW, pp. 113–124 (2011)

14. Ceccarelli, A., Montecchi, L., Brancati, F., Lollini, P., Marguglio, A.: Continuous and transparent user identity verification for secure internet services. IEEE Transactions on Dependable and Secure Computing 12(3), 270–283 (2014)

15. Leggett, J., Williams, G., Usnick, M., Longnecker, M.: Dynamic identity verification via keystroke characteristics. Int. J. Man Mach. Stud. 35(6), 859–870 (1991)

16. Khan, A.A., Khan, F.A.: A cost-efficient radiation monitoring system for nuclear sites: designing and implementation. Intelligent Automation & Soft Computing 32(3), 1357–1367 (2022)

17. Shao, X.: Accurate multi-site daily-ahead multi-step pm2.5 concentrations forecasting using space-shared cnn-lstm. Computers, Materials & Continua 70(3), 5143–5160 (2022)

18. Malavika, R., Valarmathi, M.L.: Adaptive server load balancing in sdn using pid neural network controller. Comput. Syst. Sci. Eng. 42(1), 229–243 (2022)

19. Alrajhi, H.: A generalized state space average model for parallel dc-to-dc converters. Computer Systems Science and Engineering 41(2), 717–734 (2022)

20. Ju, X.: An Overview of Face Manipulation Detection. Journal of Cyber Security 2(4), 197–207 (2020)

A Binary Code Vulnerability Mining Method Based on Generative Adversarial Networks

Ji Lai[1], Shuo Li[1], and Qigui Yao[2(✉)]

[1] Platform Operation and Security Department, Information and Telecomnunication Company, Beijing 100000, China
[2] State Grid Key Laboratory of Information and Network Security, Global Energy Interconnection Research Institute Co. Ltd., Nanjing 210000, China
yaoqigui@geiri.sgcc.com.cn

Abstract. Generative adversarial networks (GAN) is one of the most promising methods of unsupervised learning in complex distribution in recent years. Gan is widely used to generate data sets for data enhancement. However, the existing binary vulnerability mining methods can be divided into three ways: static analysis, dynamic analysis and dynamic static analysis. The research on the method of fundamentally expanding the data set to achieve vulnerability mining also has strong application value. Therefore, aiming at the problem of too few binary code vulnerability data sets, this paper proposes a binary code vulnerability mining model based on generation countermeasure network. In particular, the proposed system also combines automatic code generation technology, fuzzy testing and symbol execution technology to further optimize and train the generator and discriminator in the generation countermeasure network model to generate high-quality data sets. The experimental results show that, The binary code vulnerability mining model based on generative countermeasure network proposed in this paper can effectively solve the problem of too few data sets.

Keywords: Vulnerability discovery · Generative adversarial networks · Fuzzing · Symbolic execution · Automatic code generation technology

1 Introduction

With the rapid development and advancement of computer technology, software application fields are wider and more diverse, bringing more convenience to people, but at the same time software and device applications also bring many security risks. The Internet of Things technology promotes the continuous transformation of the power system to intelligent, refined, and networked. At the same time, the increasing safety and quality goals are still facing many problems and challenges. At present, the power Internet of Things security threats are endless [1]. Although the introduction of these power grid equipment brings convenience, but they bring more security threats. For example, on May 5, 2020, Venezuela's national power grid was attacked. Except for the capital, Caracas, power outages occurred in 11 state capitals across the country. This is not the first time that a similar power grid attack has hit Venezuela. In March 2019, the Venezuelan

© The Author(s), under exclusive license to Springer Nature Switzerland AG 2022
X. Sun et al. (Eds.): ICAIS 2022, LNCS 13340, pp. 639–650, 2022.
https://doi.org/10.1007/978-3-031-06791-4_50

power system was paralyzed by a cyber attack. Although power supply was restored in some areas after rush repairs, the second round of cyber attacks soon caused the power system to collapse again. Then began the country's longest history of power outages since 2012 and the most extensively affected areas. The longest and most widespread history of power outages in the region. In addition to Venezuela, large-scale power outages in many parts of South America last year also caused widespread concern. In the early morning of June 16, 2019, a large-scale blackout swept through three South American countries: Argentina, Uruguay, and Paraguay. Nearly 50 million people experienced the "dark weekend". The power outage lasted about 14 h, roads were blocked, public facilities were paralyzed, and water supply was in short supply. It was not until the evening that electricity began to recover. It can be seen that the application of smart grid equipment has become more extensive, and the losses brought by it have become more and more huge.

Vulnerabilities in the current cyberspace are getting more and more attention from all parties. At present, more and more software appears in the form of binary code in practical applications. Therefore, the research on binary code vulnerability mining technology has attracted wide attention from researchers. The research on binary code vulnerability mining technology has strong practical value and binary code vulnerability mining is also one of the important technologies to ensure the security of cyberspace. At present, there are three main methods for discovering code vulnerabilities: white box testing, black box testing and gray box testing [2]. Mainstream vulnerability mining trap detection methods include static analysis methods [3] and dynamic analysis methods [4]. At present, common vulnerability mining and analysis techniques also include fuzzing testing, data flow analysis, binary comparison, model checking, pollution analysis and symbolic execution [5, 6]. Among these vulnerabilities, part of them is determined by comparing the vulnerability data sets in the CVE (Common Vulnerabilities & Exposures) library to determine the vulnerabilities and the types of vulnerabilities, but more are uncertain suspected vulnerabilities. Due to the diversification of these vulnerabilities, for these suspected vulnerabilities, the current technology only gives descriptions of the suspected vulnerabilities, but this code still needs to be further distracted; from a certain aspect, these descriptions can provide Help, for security researchers to mine and exploit vulnerabilities more quickly, but in terms of efficiency, when faced with a large number of suspected vulnerabilities detected in a large number of power grid equipment, most security operation and maintenance personnel do not have the ability to manually verify the vulnerabilities The ability of digging binary code vulnerabilities has always plagued power grid companies. In recent years, with the rise of the artificial intelligence industry. A large number of machine learning methods have been tried to solve the problem of software vulnerability mining. Existing binary code vulnerability data sets have incomplete coverage, and artificial binary program vulnerability mining is difficult and inefficient.

The generative adversarial network used in this article can solve the problem of too few vulnerability code data sets. Compared with common binary code vulnerability mining methods, the generative adversarial network (GAN) is a kind of deep learning model, which is a complex distribution in recent years. One of the most promising methods of unsupervised learning, GAN is widely used to generate data sets for data enhancement. The model uses (at least) two modules in the framework: the generator module and the discriminator module to learn from each other to produce quite good output and discriminative results. Combine fuzz testing and symbolic execution to train the generative adversarial network model to effectively expand the binary vulnerabilities Code data set.

The contributions of this work are summarized as follows:

(1) We propose a new binary code vulnerability mining model, which can effectively expand the code vulnerability data set by using the method of generating adversarial networks;
(2) We suggest combining generative confrontation network technology with automatic code generation technology, fuzzing testing and symbolic execution technology to generate code data sets in various forms to achieve the purpose of data set expansion;
(3) We simulated the binary code vulnerability mining model based on the generative confrontation network.

The structure of the article is as follows: Section 2 will outline the previous work; Section 3 will introduce the preliminary research results and the research network model; Sections 4 and 5, the vulnerability code automatic generation module is proposed, which contains Vulnerability detection technology combined with fuzzing testing and symbolic execution and the overall model algorithm flow. Section 6 shows the simulation results of the proposed scheme. Section 7 sets out the conclusions of this article and future research work.

2 Related Work

Generative adversarial networks (GAN) mainly include two model networks, namely generator (G) and discriminator (D). The input of G is a random noise sequence z, and the output is a pseudo-generated image; the input of D is a pseudo-generated image and a real image x, and the output is the judgment result of the pseudo-generated image, that is, the true and false probability value. G and D confront each other and make progress together in competition to reach the Nash equilibrium. But the GAN model has the problem of data collapse. Auxiliary Classifier GAN (ACGAN) was proposed to improve this problem. One use of ACGAN is to generate multi-class enhanced data. This paper proposes to use the generated confrontation network for binary code vulnerability mining.

Various classification methods [6] currently used for binary code vulnerability analysis are: According to different classification standards, we regard different methods that can cover all categories in all classification standards as typical techniques, including fuzzing, symbolic execution and taint analysis., These methods can cover the various ranges of binary vulnerability analysis techniques. According to the exploit theory, taint analysis is effective in principle [7]. Symbolic analysis focuses on control flow, while taint analysis focuses on data flow. These two techniques can complement each other [8]. Fuzzy algorithms are the most widely used because they do not rely on source code and are highly efficient.

For vulnerability analysis, many researchers have proposed several analysis methods, including taint analysis such as Bintaint proposed by Feng Z [9] and symbolic execution such as Anger proposed by Shoshitaishvili [10], but most of them are only applicable to certain Some specific types of vulnerabilities, or improvement of existing methods, these binary vulnerability analysis methods have certain limitations: First, many tasks cannot be reused, cannot be further expanded on the current work, and only one function is available. Re-implemented on the framework of, it is inefficient and time-consuming; secondly, each method has its limitations so far, such as path explosion and excessive computational overhead, which have not been well solved. Another important method of vulnerability detection and mining is the fuzzing technology. In the report of Google Project Zero [11] in 2019, the number of vulnerabilities found through fuzzing was as high as 37%. In the security industry, the research work on fuzzing technology has never stopped from beginning to end. ZHANQICU proposed the coverage-guided symbolic execution of fuzz testing, which is a defect detection method based on the combination of symbolic execution and fuzz testing [12]. This method solves the path coverage and defect detection ability of traditional fuzzing. Low problem. Grieco et al. [13] proposed a vulnerability mining analysis method using machine learning technology. This method uses lightweight static and dynamic features to predict whether a binary program may contain vulnerable memory corruption vulnerabilities. Use linear scan disassembly to extract static features from a series of call sequences of the standard C library in the program, and then extract dynamic features by analyzing the program execution trajectory, but this method still has the problem of not combining static and dynamic features. Many researchers have also proposed new tools. For example, Zenan Feng et al. [14] developed a static stain analysis tool Bintaint with portability and low false alarm rate, and proposed a static stain analysis method customized on demand. With Bintaint, static symbol execution only needs to cover the propagation path of the taint, further reducing the traversal path space, and effectively alleviating the path explosion problem and high false alarm rate. In this research, we propose to use generative adversarial networks for binary code vulnerability mining. Compared with existing solutions, our design mainly solves the problem of too few vulnerability data sets. By increasing the vulnerability data set data, we can determine the vulnerability and the type of vulnerability by comparing the binary code.

3 Binary Code Vulnerability Mining Scheme Based on Generative Confrontation Network

3.1 Scheme Process

In this paper, a binary code vulnerability mining method is designed based on the main frame of ACGAN. On the one hand, the first step is to construct a generator that generates a confrontation network to process random noise, obtain the underlying feature data, send the underlying feature data to the generation confrontation network for training, and generate a pseudo sample composed of an approximate binary code string composed of 0,1. On the other hand, the source code samples are generated through the model-based automatic code generation method, but not limited to this automatic code generation technology, and the source code is monitored for vulnerabilities through fuzzing. A testing method for binary code-oriented fuzz testing is adopted here. Fuzzing is a kind of vulnerability detection technology. By using a random character stream generated for the target code, multiple tests are performed on the target code [15] to detect possible existence vulnerabilities. After fuzzing testing, the generated code is tested for vulnerabilities, the vulnerable code is continued to be compiled into binary code, and the binary sample data, the original binary code data set and the binary code generated by the automatic generation technology are input together to generate a discriminator module trained by the adversarial network. After discrimination by the discriminator, the discrimination result of the new pseudo-binary code sample and whether there are loopholes in the binary code are obtained [16].

The specific flow chart is shown in Fig. 1:

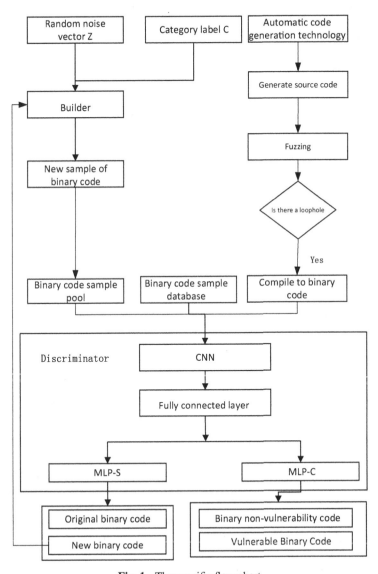

Fig. 1. The specific flow chart.

3.2 Scheme Algorithm Model

Compared with traditional code vulnerability mining methods, the scheme proposed in this article adopts the conditional generative adversarial network (Auxiliary Classifier GAN) method [17]. The generative adversarial network (GAN) provides a way to learn deep representations without extensively annotated training data [18]. Methods. This is achieved by deriving the backpropagation signal through a competition process involving a pair of networks. The representations that can be learned by traditional generative adversarial networks can be used in a variety of applications, including image synthesis, semantic image editing, style conversion, image super-resolution, and classification [19]. The conditional generation confrontation network is a model that contains conditional information, and a well-trained model can generate data based on classification. The random vector is input to the generator with category information, and the discriminator can distinguish the categories of the input data.

The structure diagram is shown in Fig. 2.

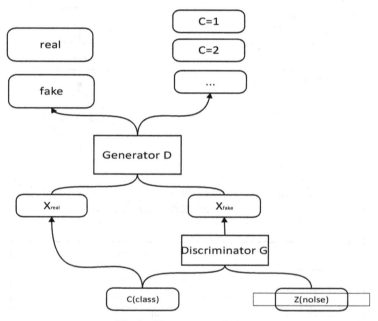

Fig. 2. The structure diagram.

The generator is used to generate binary code samples based on the information of random noise z; The generator is to generate real binary code samples as much as possible, The purpose of the discriminator is to determine whether the output is a newly generated binary code and to determine whether the binary code is vulnerable. Train the generator and the discriminator according to the discriminator's discriminating results, and continue until the generator can generate high-quality binary vulnerable code. The content of training and generating a confrontation network includes: The generator generates pseudo samples, the discriminator distinguishes "true and false", and the classifier performs classification. The generator model G learns a mapping from random noise z to real data x, which can be expressed as $G : z \rightarrow x$. The discriminator needs to judge the probability distribution $F(S|X)$ on the real data and the probability distribution $F(C|X)$ on the class label. First you need to define the loss function. From the perspective of the overall structure of the network, it includes two parts: a generator and a discriminator. The output of the network also has two parts, which are the "true and false" of the code and the judgment of whether the code has loopholes. Where L_S represents the true and false discrimination loss, L_c means classification loss, $X_{new} = G(z, c)$ represents the binary code generated by the generator, $X_{original}$ represents the binary code from the training set. For the loss of the code "true and false", that is, against the loss of discriminating true and false, the loss function is defined as shown in formula (1): The specific calculation methods of the user trust are as follows:

$$L_S = E[\log P(S = original|X_{original})] + E[\log P(S = new|X_{new})] \tag{1}$$

For the category loss of the code, since the category of the invention code has nothing to do with the "true or false" of the code, it is equivalent to the convolutional neural network part of the discriminator and the fully connected classifier at the end to complete an independent classification result. The loss function that defines this classification is shown in formula (2):

$$L_c = F[\log P(C = l|X_{original})] + F[\log P(C = l|X_{new})] \tag{2}$$

For the discriminator, it is hoped that the classification is correct, but also that it can correctly distinguish the true and false of the data. Therefore, the loss function of the discriminator is defined as shown in Eq. (3):

$$L_P = L_S + L_C \tag{3}$$

The true and false judgment loss of the generator, the definition of this loss function is shown in formula (4):

$$L_S = E[\log P(S = original|X_{original})] \tag{4}$$

The classification judgment loss of the generator, the definition of this loss function is shown in formula (5):

$$L_C = E[\log P(C = c|X_{original})] \tag{5}$$

For the generator, it is also hoped that the classification can be correct. At that time, it is hoped that the discriminator cannot correctly distinguish fake data. Therefore, the loss function of the discriminator is defined as shown in Eq. (6):

$$L_P = L_C - L_S \tag{6}$$

4 Experiment

A method for mining binary code vulnerabilities based on Generative Adversarial Networks is proposed, which uses Generative Adversarial Networks to solve the problem of too few binary code vulnerability data sets. First, IDA pro is used to convert the source code data sets downloaded from SARD into hexadecimal data. Set, send the data set to the generative confrontation network for training.

4.1 Experimental Environment

The experimental environment of this experiment is shown in Table 1:

Table 1. Experimental environment parameters.

Category	Parameters
GPU	NVIDA RTX2060S
Operating System	Win 10
CPU	AMD 2700x
CUDA Version	7.5
CuDNN Version	10.5

Table 2. The results of this experiment.

	Precision	Recall	F1-score	Support
No vulnerability	1.0000	0.7727	0.8718	22
With vulnerabilities	0.8276	1.0000	0.9057	24
Accuracy			0.8913	46
Macro avg	0.9138	0.8864	0.8887	46
Weighted avg	0.9100	0.8913	0.8895	46

4.2 Introduction to the Experimental Data Set

This data set contains multiple vulnerable binary files and their source code forms written by developers.Directly use the relevant source code to convert to hexadecimal and then to binary. This method avoids the problem of reduced vulnerability detection accuracy caused by binary code decompilation. The data sets used in the experiment are written in C language, including 330 vulnerable data samples and 300 normal samples.

4.3 Experimental Result

We evaluate the experiment from three aspects:

- Accuracy rate: The accuracy rate is for our prediction results. It indicates how many of the samples whose predictions are positive are truly positive samples. Then there are two possibilities for the prediction to be positive, one is to predict the positive class as a positive class (TP), and the other is to predict the negative class as a positive class (FP)

$$Precision = TP/(TP + FP) \tag{7}$$

- Recall: The recall is based on our original sample. It indicates how many positive examples in the sample are predicted correctly. There are also two possibilities, one is to change the original positive The class is predicted as a positive class (TP), and the other is to predict the original positive class as a negative class (FN).

$$Recall = TP/(TP + FN) \tag{8}$$

- F1-score: F1-score is calculated based on recall rate and precision rate:

$$F1 \text{ - score} = 2 * \Pr ecision * \operatorname{Re}call/(\Pr ecision + \operatorname{Re}call) \tag{9}$$

In the field of machine learning, the confusion matrix is also called the possibility table or error matrix. It is a specific matrix used to visualize the performance of the algorithm. The confusion matrix diagram of this experiment is shown in Fig. 3:

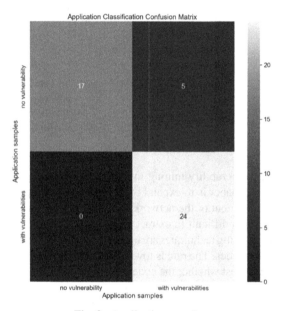

Fig. 3. Application samples.

5 Analysis of Program Advantages

Binary code vulnerability mining technology is divided into static mining and dynamic mining technology. The current vulnerabilities can be divided into known vulnerabilities, suspected vulnerabilities, and new vulnerabilities. New vulnerabilities can be mined based on known vulnerabilities. This type of method can be fast in the early stage of equipment operation. Discover the vulnerabilities in the equipment. However, with the rapid development of the network, the number of existing vulnerability data sets is too small, and it is difficult to extract more vulnerability features. Today, the existing mainstream methods of binary code vulnerability mining, such as taint analysis technology, symbolic execution technology, and fuzzing testing technology, have not started from the expansion of vulnerability data sets, and there are still unresolved problems, as shown in Table 3:

Table 3. Comparison table of technical methods.

Technical method	Advantage	Defect
Stain analysis technology	Dynamic stain analysis technology: higher reliability of detection; Static stain analysis technology: improve analysis accuracy	High false negative rate, low accuracy, and consume more resources
Symbolic execution	This method can make the fuzz test get better coverage, and can go deep into the program to explore the areas where there may be loopholes	Path explosion problem
Fuzzing	Simple design and fast test speed	Test cases are not guaranteed to cover all statement branches, and the degree of automation is not high at present

The binary code vulnerability mining method based on the generative adversarial network adopted in this paper is to expand the vulnerability samples from the data set. Due to the rapid development of the network, the number of existing vulnerability data sets is too small, and it is difficult to extract more vulnerability features. However, the existing vulnerability mining techniques are based on and traditional fuzzing methods are difficult to cover all branches. The rate is low. Effectively improving the problem of low coverage rate can better test whether the code has vulnerabilities, and further expanding the data set of binary code vulnerabilities can effectively improve the accuracy and efficiency of vulnerability mining, and avoid the problems that may be encountered by existing mainstream vulnerability analysis methods.

The advantages of the framework of this thesis are as follows:

(1) The main body of the framework model in this article is a generative model. Compared with other generative models, only back-propagation is used, which can avoid complicated Markov chains and make the model simpler.
(2) Secondly, compared with other existing models, GAN can produce clearer and more realistic samples.
(3) GAN adopts an unsupervised learning method for training, which can be widely used in the fields of unsupervised learning and semi-supervised learning.
(4) If the discriminator is well trained, then the generator can learn the distribution of training samples perfectly.

(5) Using conditional generation of confrontation network, the generated sample code can be directly classified and judged through the label.
(6) Training the network model can generate high-quality samples to achieve the purpose of effectively expanding the data set.

6 Conclusion

As the Internet of Things technology promotes the continuous transformation of the power system to the direction of intelligence, refinement, and networking, the increasing safety and quality goals are still facing many problems and challenges. At present, the security threats of the power Internet of Things are increasing day by day, and effective mining of vulnerabilities can avoid the occurrence of serious security threats as early as possible, and greatly reduce the economic losses caused by malicious code. To this end, this paper proposes a binary code vulnerability mining method based on a generative confrontation network. The method first constructs a generative confrontation network, trains the generator and discriminator of the generative confrontation network, and the generator processes random noise to obtain the underlying feature data. Generate a pseudo sample composed of 0, 1 similar to the binary code. On the other hand, the source code samples are generated through the model-based automatic code generation method, but not limited to this automatic code generation technology, and the source code is monitored for vulnerabilities through fuzzing. Here is a testing method for binary code-oriented fuzzing. Fuzzing is a kind of vulnerability detection technology. By using a random character stream generated for the target code, the target code is tested multiple times to detect possible vulnerabilities. After fuzzing testing, the generated code is tested for vulnerabilities, the vulnerable code is continued to be compiled into binary code, and the binary sample data, the original binary code data set and the binary code generated by the automatic generation technology are input together to generate a discriminator module trained against the network. After the discriminator, the result of the new pseudo-binary code sample and whether the binary code has vulnerabilities can be obtained, which can effectively solve the problem of too few vulnerability data sets to achieve the purpose of vulnerability mining. This method can effectively solve the problem of too few samples of data set, and also can avoid the defects of the current mainstream mining technology.

Acknowledgement. This paper is supported by the project of Lightweight security reinforcement and threat perception technologies for energy Internet-oriented smart terminal equipment (52018E20008K).

References

1. Tang, B., Yang, M.: Research on security protection countermeasures of internet of things. J. Phys: Conf. Ser. **1650**(3), 32098 (2020)
2. Chen, Y.: Advancement of the study on fuzzy testing. Comput. Applicat. Softw. **11**(7), 32098 (2011)

3. Park, J.J.H., Barolli, L., Xhafa, F., Jeong, H.Y. (eds.): Information Technology Convergence. LNEE, vol. 253. Springer, Dordrecht (2013). https://doi.org/10.1007/978-94-007-6996-0

4. Clause, J., Li, W., Orso, A.: Dytan: a generic dynamic taint analysis framework. In: International Symposium on Information Technology Convergence, vol. 11, pp. 196–206 (2017)

5. Hou, J.B., Li, T., Chang, C.: Research for vulnerability detection of embedded system firmware. Proc. Comput. Sci. 107(181), 814–818 (2013)

6. Yan, S., Wang, R., Salls, C.: SOK: (state of) the art of war: offensive techniques in binary analysis. In: Proceedings IEEE Symposium on Security and Privacy (SP), pp. 138–157 (2016)

7. Zhuge, J., Chen, L., Tian, F., Bao, Y., Lu, X.: Type-based dynamic taint analysis technology. J. Tsinghua Univ. 52(10), 1320–1334 (2012)

8. Bai, H., Hu, C.Z., Zhang, G., Jing, X.C., Li, N.: Binary oriented vulnerability analyzer based on hidden markov model. IEICE Trans. Inf. Syst 93(12), 3410–3413 (2010)

9. Feng, Z., Wang, Z., Dong, W.: Bintaint: a static taint analysis method for binary vulnerability mining. In: Proceedings ICCBB, pp. 1–8 (2018)

10. Baldoni, R., Coppa, E., D'elia, D.C., Demetrescu, C., Finocchi, I.: A survey of symbolic execution techniques. ACM Comput. Surv. 51(3), 1–39 (2018)

11. Russell, R., Kim, L., Hamlton, L.: Automated vulnerability detection in source code using deep representation learning. In: The 17th IEEE Int'l Conference on Machine Learning and Applications (ICMLA), pp. 757–762 (2018)

12. Xie, Z., Cui, Z., Zhang, J.: CSEFuzz: fuzz testing based on symbolic execution. IEEE Access 8(8), 187564–187574 (2020)

13. Grieco, G., Grinblat, G.L., Uzal, L.: Toward large-scale vulnerability discovery using machine learning. In: The Sixth ACM Conference on Data and Application Security and Privacy, pp. 85–96 (2016)

14. Du, C., Liu, S., Guo, Y., Si, L., Jin, T.: Detection and information extraction of similar basic blocks used for directed Greybox fuzzing. In: International Conference on Artificial Intelligence and Security, vol. 12240, no. 21, pp. 353–364 (2020)

15. Li, J., Zhao, B., Zhang, C.: Fuzzing: a survey. Cybersecurity 1(1), 1–13 (2018). https://doi.org/10.1186/s42400-018-0002-y

16. Huang, C., Huang, C.: Cvae-gan emotional ai music system for car driving safety. Intell. Automat. Soft Comput. 32(3), 1939–1953 (2022)

17. Luo, Z.: Review of gan-based person re-identification. J. New Media 3(1), 11–17 (2021)

18. Fang, K., Ouyang, J.Q.: Classification algorithm optimization based on Triple-GAN. J. Artif. Intell. 2(1), 1–15 (2020)

19. Liu, X., Chen, X.: A survey of gan-generated fake faces detection method based on deep learning. J. Inf. Hiding Priv. Protect. 2(2), 87–94 (2020)

Simulation Research on Iron Core Air Gap of Energy-Taking Current Transformer (CT) Based on Ansys

Pingping Yu[1], Zihui Xu[1(✉)], Xiaodong Zhao[1], and Eugene Murray[2]

[1] Hebei University of Science and Technology, Shijiazhuang 050000, China
1208222954@qq.com
[2] Russian Institute of Advanced Technologies, Karan 420126, Russia

Abstract. Currently, the development of the power of the Internet of Things brings some challenges to all aspects of power system, one of which is the power supply problem of electric transmission line condition monitoring equipment. Energy-taking current transformer get the favor of the researchers at home and abroad because of its high practical value. Aiming at the existing problems of large starting current, easy saturation of iron core, and inability to adapt to wider electric transmission line current of energy-taking current transformer, many of them pay more attention to the research of post-stage circuit, but neglect the design and improvement of iron core structure. To solve the above problems, this paper mainly work as follows: on the basis of the initial permeability, saturation magnetic flux density and iron core loss and cost to determine the iron core material; Ansys software is used to analyze the iron core air gap shape design and simulation, through the iron core under different shape of air gap magnetic leak situation draw rectangular half opening effect optimal; Control variable method is used to analyze the air gap size simulation experiment, through the iron core of the saturated magnetic induction intensity and size of secondary side power output for the quantitative analysis of the air gap size. For the energy-taking current transformer's iron core structure design and parameters of the actual selection provides a good engineering value.

Keywords: Power Internet of Things · Energy-taking current transformer · Iron core structure · The Ansys simulation

1 Introduction

In the context of rapid social development, smart grid can rely on Internet of Things technology to form a highly safe and reliable power Internet of Things for power generation, transmission, transformation, distribution, electricity consumption and grid asset management. The construction of power Internet of Things must realize the high integration of power flow, information flow and business flow under the overall requirements of strong, reliable and economic efficiency of smart grid. However, the strong, reliable, economical and efficient smart grid poses great challenges to all aspects of the power system [1–4]. Among them, the power supply of electric transmission line condition monitoring equipment will restrict the transformation of power system development. At present, energy supply methods mainly include solar panels, wind, capacitor partial voltage, battery and energy-taking CT, etc. [5–7]. Compared with these energy supply methods, energy-taking CT has higher practical value due to its advantages of high reliability, small volume, long life and simple insulation [8–12]. However, energy-taking CT still has problems like large starting current, easy saturation of iron core, and inability to adapt to the working current of wider transmission lines. Researchers at home and abroad focus on the improvement of post-stage circuits [13–17], while neglect the design of iron core structure. Therefore, this paper analyzes and simulates the material, air gap shape, air gap size and other aspects of the iron core through Ansys software, and makes a detailed analysis of the simulation results and draws a conclusion. This has a good engineering value for the structural design and actual parameter selection of the iron core of energy-taking CT source.

2 Theoretical Analysis of Energy-Taking CT

Because energy-taking CT is mainly used in a high voltage transmission line with a wide range of current fluctuations. The high line current will cause energy-taking CT's iron core into the saturation state, when the iron core work in saturated state, magnetic induction intensity will no longer continue to increase with the increase of magnetic field intensity, and field current will increase rapidly, which leads to secondary side voltage waveform distortion, it seriously affects the transmission capacity of the energy-taking CT and makes the secondary load unable to work normally. At present, the method of adding air gap [18] to the energy-taking CT's iron core can not only effectively delay the saturation of the iron core when the transmission line is in a high current, but also reduce the voltage induced by the secondary side coil, so as to protect the rear stage circuit. Therefore, the magnetic circuit model of energy-taking CT with air gap is analyzed theoretically.

Figure 1(a) is a schematic diagram of iron core with air gap, where R represents the outer radius of the iron core, r represents the inner radius, H represents the thickness of the iron core, and D represents the width of the air gap. Figure 1(b) is the equivalent magnetic circuit diagram of iron core with air gap. Since the iron core opens an air gap, the magnetoresistance is divided into iron core and air gap magnetoresistance, R_c represents iron core magnetoresistance, R_g represents air gap magnetoresistance, and R_l represents power circuit and load. The size of R_l varies according to the purpose of the CT, but the value of R_l is constant for power supply circuits and loads with fixed power.

First of all, according to magnetic circuit Ohm's law,

$$F = \Phi \cdot R_a \tag{1}$$

$$F = N_1 \cdot I \tag{2}$$

In Eqs. (1) and (2), F represents the magnetic potential, Φ represents the magnetic flux through the coil, and R_a represents the total magnetic resistance of the iron core.

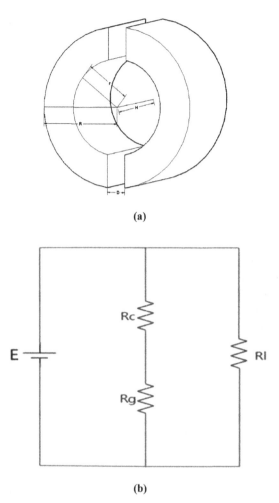

(a)

(b)

Fig. 1 (**a**) Schematic diagram of iron core with air gap (**b**) Equivalent magnetic circuit diagram of iron core with air gap

N_1 is the number of turns of primary side, and the value is 1. I represents the current in the primary side.

And according to the Ampere loop law,

$$H \cdot L = I \tag{3}$$

In Formula (3), I is the primary side current, H is the magnetic field intensity generated by the primary current, and L represents the average magnetic circuit length. Among them, the magnetic circuit is divided into iron core and air gap. L_c and L_g are defined to represent the average magnetic circuit length of iron core and air gap respectively [19]. Define R_c as iron core reluctance, R_g as air gap reluctance,

$$L_c = \pi(R + r) \tag{4}$$

$$L_g = D \tag{5}$$

$$R_c = \frac{L_c}{\mu S} \tag{6}$$

$$R_g = \frac{L_g}{\mu_0 S} \tag{7}$$

In Eqs. (6) and (7), u represents the iron core permeability, and u_0 represents the air permeability.

Finally, according to formula 4.44, the induced voltage of the secondary side is:

$$U = 4.44 f N_2 \Phi_{Max} \tag{8}$$

In Formula (8), N_2 represents the number of turns of the secondary side coil, Φ_{Max} represents the maximum magnetic flux of the iron core, and f represents the frequency of the primary side current.

When the electric transmission line current is determined, the output power of the secondary side of the CT can be deduced according to the above deduction:

$$P = \frac{U^2}{R_1} \tag{9}$$

namely:

$$P = \frac{19.71 f^2 I^2 \mu^2 \mu_0^2 N_2^2 S^2}{[\mu_0 \pi (R + r) + D]^2 \cdot R_1^2} \tag{10}$$

According to the above theoretical deduction, iron core size, air gap width, iron core permeability, secondary side winding turns, secondary side load size and primary side current value will have a certain impact on the secondary side output power. When the electric transmission line current is not enough to saturate the iron core, the iron core will operate in a linear region. In this working state, according to Eq. (10), the output power of the secondary side of the iron core is proportional to the square of the line current. With the increase of transmission line current, the iron core will gradually enter the saturation area. In this state, Eq. (10) will no longer be applicable. The increase of magnetic field intensity will no longer cause the increase of magnetic induction intensity, and the excitation current will also increase rapidly, leading to the distortion of secondary side voltage waveform, thus affecting the transmission capacity of energy-taking CT.

3 Ansys Simulation Analysis of Iron Core Structure

3.1 Selection of Iron Core Materials

In view of the existing problems like large starting current and easy saturation of the iron core, it can be pretreated by selecting iron core materials. In this section, four commonly used like silicon steel sheet, permalloy, iron based nanocrystals and cobalt-based amorphous materials are selected to conduct comparative analysis on their initial permeability, saturation flux density, iron core loss and cost respectively. The results are shown in Table 1.

First of all, when the electric transmission line current is small, the higher the initial permeability of the material, the greater the secondary side induced voltage, the easier it is to meet the normal operation power of the secondary side load (that is, the smaller the starting current of the equipment). Secondly, the saturation flux density of the material indicates the maximum electric transmission line current that can be borne, that is, the critical point of the iron core entering the saturation zone. The larger the saturation flux density is, the wider the range of line current can be borne. The smaller the iron core loss, the higher the transfer efficiency of energy-taking CT. According to Table 1, the initial permeability of permalloy and cobalt-based amorphous materials is higher, but the saturated flux density of permalloy is lower. In addition, cobalt-based amorphous materials are better in terms of iron core loss and price. Therefore, based on the above four main parameters, selecting cobalt-based amorphous as iron core material can further improve the performance of energy-taking CT.

Table 1. Common material parameter list.

The basic parameters	Initial permeability (mH/m)	Saturated flux density (T)	Iron core loss (W/kg)	Price (Yuan /kg)
Silicon steel sheet	1×10^3	2.0	8.14	10
Permalloy	$>1 \times 10^5$	1.0	14	166
Iron based nanocrystals	8×10^4	1.7	30	28.42
Cobalt-based amorphous	1.4×10^5	1.83	4.7	13

3.2 Simulation and Analysis of Iron Core Air Gap Shape

Due to the influence of edge effect on the iron core with air gap added, magnetic leakage will increase, and then reduce the transmission capability of energy-taking CT. In view of the influence caused by edge effect, this paper designs from the shape of air gap, and adopts three air gap shapes as shown in Fig. 2. Among them, rectangular iron core (b) with half-open opening and V-shaped iron core (c) have similar analysis principle to full-open iron core (a), but the calculation method of reluctance is different. The number of magnetic leakage generated in each air gap shape was analyzed by Ansys simulation, and the air gap shape with better effect was selected by comparison.

Firstly, the iron core is modeled, and the thickness and volume of the iron core can be quantitatively calculated in combination with Eq. (3), (4) and (5). Then, the iron core

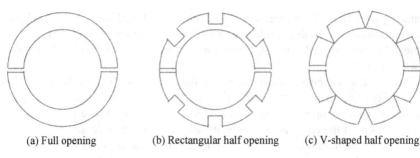

(a) Full opening   (b) Rectangular half opening   (c) V-shaped half opening

Fig. 2. Schematic diagram of three air gap shapes.

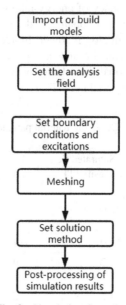

Fig. 3. Simulation flow chart.

size can be determined according to the wire size of the high-voltage transmission line, the output power of the secondary side, the iron core volume, the cross-sectional area, the magnetization curve of the strip and other factors. Then, according to the selection principle of the number of turns of the secondary side coil [20], the voltage input range of the back-end voltage regulator module can be satisfied within a larger current range without making the iron core saturate too fast. The basic parameters of the iron core in this paper are finally determined as follows: R = 142 mm, r = 60 mm, H = 50 mm, N_2 = 130, where R, r and H respectively represent the outer diameter, inner diameter and thickness of the iron core, and N_2 represents the number of turns of secondary side-line. Secondly, Ansys software is used for simulation. The simulation process is shown in Fig. 3.

Under the condition that all parameters except the shape and size of air gap are the same, iron cores with three air gap shapes are simulated to obtain magnetic vector diagrams, as shown in Fig. 4(a), (b) and (c).

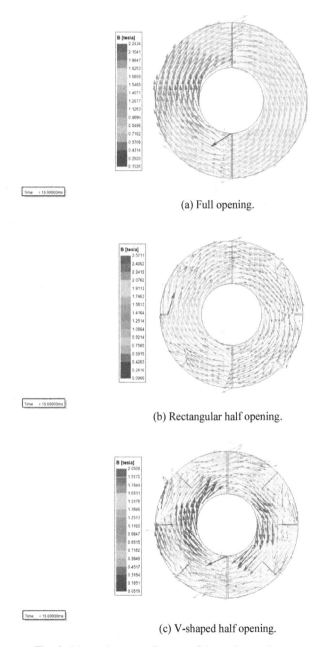

(a) Full opening.

(b) Rectangular half opening.

(c) V-shaped half opening.

Fig. 4. Magnetic vector diagram of three air gap shapes.

As can be seen from the above figure, when the iron core opens the air gap, it can be seen that the magnetic vector will have magnetic leakage of different sizes at the air gap. When the air gap is fully open, there will be large magnetic leakage and low magnetic induction intensity amplitude. The magnetic flux intensity amplitude is similar in the V-shaped air gap and semi-open rectangle, but the magnetic leakage of the latter is obviously smaller than that of the former. Therefore, it can be concluded that there will be less magnetic leakage in the semi-open rectangle air gap, which ensures the transmission capacity of the energy-taking current transformer. At the same time, the higher magnetic induction intensity and amplitude can better delay the saturation of the iron core.

3.3   Simulation and Analysis of Iron Core Air Gap Size

Through the simulation analysis of the air gap shape in the previous section, it can be concluded that under the condition of the same primary side current, the semi-open rectangle air gap produces less magnetic leakage and also plays a certain role in delaying the saturation of the iron core, but the size of the air gap has not been quantitatively analyzed. Therefore, on this basis, this section analyzes the effect performance of the iron core under different air gap widths through Ansys simulation and draws a conclusion. First of all, in the primary side current, secondary side load, ratio of transformation are the same situation, select the iron core of the half-open rectangular air gap, change the vertical width of the rectangular air gap from 0.005 cm to 0.03 cm, take 0.005 cm as step length to simulate different situations. The results are shown in Fig. 5(a)–(f):

Figure 5(a)–(f) are the cloud images of magnetic induction intensity of the iron core. Observe the simulation diagram, with the continuous increase of the vertical width of the rectangular air gap of the iron core, the peak value of magnetic induction intensity will rise first and then fall. The greater the magnetic induction intensity, the greater the primary side current that the iron core can withstand. When the vertical width of the rectangular air gap reaches 0.02 cm, the magnetic induction intensity is the maximum, and the maximum power is obtained by combining the secondary induced electromotive force waveform and load. Therefore, when the vertical width of the rectangular air gap is 0.02 cm, the saturation current of the iron core will be better increased.

Secondly, when the primary side current, secondary side load size and ratio of transformation are the same, and the vertical width of rectangular air gap is 0.02 cm, change the transverse width of the rectangular air gap, ranging from 0.15 cm to 0.4 cm, and take 0.05 cm as a step to simulate different situations. The results are shown in Fig. 6(a)–(f):

Fig. 6(a)–(f) are the cloud images of magnetic induction intensity of the iron core. According to the above simulation figure, when the vertical width of the rectangular air gap is constant, with the increase of the transverse width of the rectangular air gap, the saturation magnetic induction intensity of the iron core will increase first and then decrease. When the transverse width of the rectangular air gap is 0.3 cm, the magnetic induction intensity of the iron core reaches the maximum. Therefore, when the vertical width of the rectangular air gap of the iron core is 0.02 cm and the transverse width is 0.3 cm, the transmission capacity of the energy-taking current transformer can be better guaranteed and the saturation of the iron core can be better delayed.

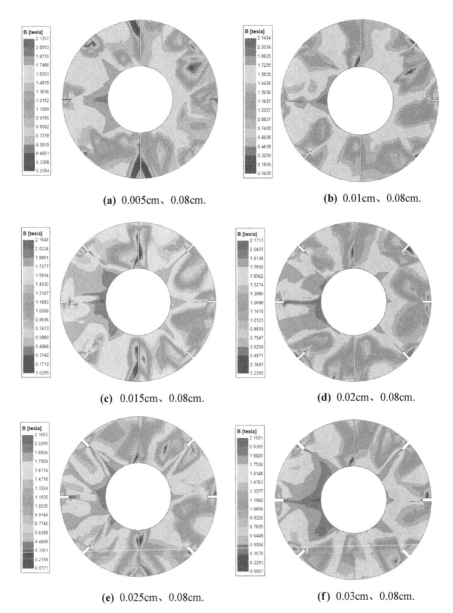

(a) 0.005cm、0.08cm.

(b) 0.01cm、0.08cm.

(c) 0.015cm、0.08cm.

(d) 0.02cm、0.08cm.

(e) 0.025cm、0.08cm.

(f) 0.03cm、0.08cm.

Fig. 5. (a) 0.005 cm, 0.08 cm. (b) 0.01 cm, 0.08 cm. (c) 0.015 cm, 0.08 cm. (d) 0.02 cm, 0.08 cm. (e) 0.025 cm, 0.08 cm. (f) 0.03 cm, 0.08 cm.

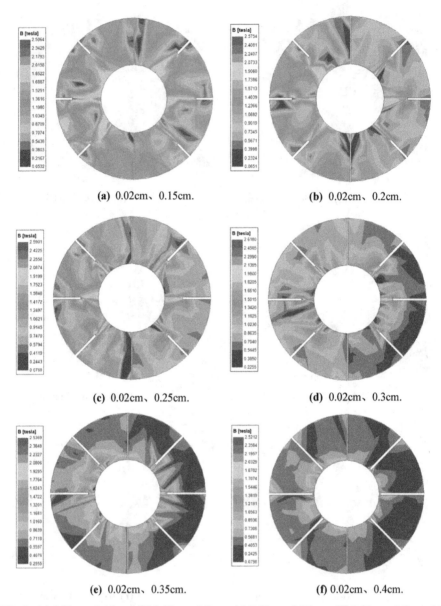

(a) 0.02cm、0.15cm.

(b) 0.02cm、0.2cm.

(c) 0.02cm、0.25cm.

(d) 0.02cm、0.3cm.

(e) 0.02cm、0.35cm.

(f) 0.02cm、0.4cm.

Fig. 6. (a) 0.02 cm, 0.15 cm. (b) 0.02 cm, 0.2 cm. (c) 0.02 cm, 0.25 cm. (d) 0.02 cm, 0.3 cm. (e). 0.02 cm, 0.35 cm. (f) 0.02 cm, 0.4 cm.

4   Conclusion

In this paper, Ansys software is used to simulate the iron core structure of energy-taking CT. Firstly, the iron core materials are determined according to the initial permeability, saturated flux density, iron core loss and cost. Secondly, according to the magnetic leakage of the iron core under different air gap shape, it is concluded that the rectangular half-opening effect is the best. Finally, the air gap size is simulated by using the control variable method, and the air gap size is quantitatively analyzed from the saturation magnetic induction intensity of the iron core and the output power of the secondary side. The conclusions obtained in this paper are of great guiding significance to the analysis of saturation characteristics and output power of iron core in the design of energy- taking CT power supply. It also can be used to guide the design of iron core and power supply parameters.

Funding Statement. This research was funded by the Hebei College and Middle School Students Science and Technology Innovation Ability Cultivation Special Project (Grant No. 2021H011403), and the 2020 Education and Teaching Research Project of Polytechnic College of Hebei University of Science and Technology (Grant No. 2020Y03).

References

1. Zhang, Y., Wang, A.: Overview of smart grid development in China. Electr. Power Syst. Prot. Control **49**(5), 180–187 (2021)
2. Yu, Y.: Smart grid for the 21st century. J. Tianjin Univ. **53**(6), 551–556 (2020)
3. Li, X., Liu, J.: Internet of things technology for smart grid and its application. Telecommun. Technol. **8**(8), 41–45 (2010)
4. Kadhim, M.H., Mardukhi, F.: A novel IoT application recommendation system using metaheuristic multi-criteria analysis. Comput. Syst. Sci. Eng. **37**(2), 149–158 (2021)
5. Alamri, A., Alamri, S.: Live data analytics with IoT intelligence-sensing system in public transportation for covid-19 pandemic. Intell. Autom. Soft Comput. **27**(2), 441–452 (2021)
6. Hsiao, S., Sung, W.: Realization of IoT integration system of led based on particle swarm optimization. Intell. Autom. Soft Comput. **27**(2), 499–517 (2021)
7. Che, B., Liu, L.: KNEMAG: key node estimation mechanism based on attack graph for IOT security. J. Internet Things **2**(4), 145–162 (2020)
8. Gong, X., Zhou, H.: A design of high power supply for transmission line. Power Syst. Prot. Control **40**(3), 124–134 (2012)
9. Xu, C., Mei, L.F.: IoT Services: realizing private real-time detection via authenticated conjunctive searchable encryption. J. Cyber Secur. **3**(1), 55–67 (2021)
10. Zhang, P., Miao, J.: A survey of ubiquitous network. J. Beijing Univ. Posts Telecommun. **33**(5), 1–6 (2010)
11. Zhang, Y., Zhou, Y.: Survey on data security and privacy-preserving for the research of edge computing. J. Commun. **39**(3), 1–21 (2018)
12. Zeng, M., Yang, Y.: Generation-grid-load-storage coordinative optimal operation mode of energy internet and key technologies. Power Syst. Technol. **40**(1), 114–124 (2016)
13. Li, P., Wen, Y.: A high-efficiency management circuit using multiwinding upconversion current transformer for power-line energy harvesting. IEEE Trans. Industr. Electron. **62**(10), 6327–6335 (2015)

14. Badal, F.R., Das, P., Sarker, S.K., Das, S.K.: A survey on control issues in renewable energy integration and microgrid. Prot. Control Mod. Power Syst. **4**(1), 1–27 (2019)
15. Luo, J., Yu, C.: A review on risk assessment of power grid security and stability under natural disasters. Power Syst. Prot. Control **46**(6), 158–170 (2018)
16. Liu, Y., Sheng, G.: Design of current transformer power supply based on power control method. Autom. Electr. Power Syst. **34**(3), 70–73 (2010)
17. Gao, T., Zhang, C.: Finite element analysis of energy absorption current transformer. Water Power Energy Sci. **37**(12), 144–147 (2019)
18. Jiao, B., Fu, W.: Design of CT power supply for high voltage transmission line. Power Supply Technol. **137**(1), 130–132 (2013)
19. Wang, L., Li, H.: New high voltage transmission line low and low limit dead zone high power online energy harvesting device. High Volt. Technol. **37**(12), 344–352 (2014)
20. Guo, S., Wang, P.: Summary of electromagnetic energy collection and storage technologies for high voltage transmission systems. Energy Storage Sci. Technol. **8**(1), 33–46 (2019)

A Rapid Device Type Identification Method Based on Feature Reduction and Dynamical Feature Weights Assignment

Xiuting Wang[1,2], Xiangyang Luo[1,2], Shaoyong Du[1,2,3(✉)], Lingling Li[4], Yang Yang[5], and Fenlin Liu[1,2]

[1] State Key Laboratory of Mathematical Engineering and Advanced Computing, Zhengzhou 450000, China
shaoyong.du.cs@gmail.com
[2] Henan Province Key Laboratory of Cyberspace Situation Awareness, Zhengzhou 450001, China
[3] Institute of Information Engineering, State Key Laboratory of Information Security, Beijing 100093, China
[4] School of Intelligent Engineering, Zhengzhou University of Aeronautics, Zhengzhou 450046, China
[5] School of Computing and Information Systems, Singapore Management University, Singapore 188065, Singapore

Abstract. The network device identification technology refers to using the network detection technology to obtain device data and transform the device data into device fingerprints to identify network devices. Currently, the mainstream network device identification method obtains network traffic data generated in the process of device communication, extract device features, and identify devices based on a variety of machine learning algorithms. However, these methods ignore the impact of redundant features and interference features when analyzing device traffic data, resulting in a high-false positive rate and heavy time cost. In order to identify network devices more efficiently and accurately, we propose a network device recognition method based on feature reduction and dynamical feature weights assignment. Firstly, feature redundancy analysis was carried out based on fast filtering algorithm and redundant features were deleted. Then, each feature is dynamically weighted according to its relevance to the device type. Finally, the target device type is identified by calculating the similarity between the target device and the known device type. Experimental results on existing public data sets show that the proposed method improves the recognition accuracy by 3.5%, 10.8% and reduces the time cost by 80%, 72% in random forest and LightGBM respectively. The proposed method is better than the existing method based on feature reduction for device type recognition.

Keywords: Network device identification · Device identification · Feature reduction · Dynamical feature weights assignment

1 Introduction

With the rapid development of Internet, more and more network devices are connected by the Internet. According to IDC (Internet Data Center) expected, there will be 55.9 billion network devices connected to the Internet in 2025, including cars, smart home devices and wearable devices [1]. Although the massive network device brings convenience to people's life, it also brings various security problems. For example, a massive DDoS attack brought down much of the Internet in the United States, mainly using a botnet of about 1.5 million network devices in October 2016 [2]. Therefore, for the purpose of maintaining network security, it is necessary to identify network devices, and improving the security of network devices is of urgency.

Efficient and accurate identification of network device is the basis for enhancing cyberspace security [3], realizing asset evaluation [4], and carrying out network situation awareness [5]. Network device identification refers to obtaining information such as the operating system, device type, location, and service of the target device through various network detection technologies. Existing network device identification methods are mainly divided into two categories: One is to identify through proprietary cyberspace search engines, such as Shodan [6], Censys [7], ZoomEye [8], etc. These cyberspace search engines can feedback the device required by searchers in a very short time, such as servers and industrial control devices, cameras, smartwatches and other smart home devices; the other is to process the traffic generated by network devices or device identification information to generate device fingerprints and match them with the known device fingerprint database to identify device types. At present, the second type of method is the key research field of network device identification, researchers have conducted a great deal of work around the second type of approach. In order to realize the identification of network devices, A. Cui et al. [9] extract the protocol features of the application layer to construct the fingerprint of fixed devices. Q. Li et al. [10] propose to generate fine-grained fingerprints based on the subtle differences between hardware information of the device, and to process the hardware information of the device using natural language processing technology, and verify the effectiveness of the proposed method through the system. S. Aneja et al. [11] propose to apply deep learning to analyze network traffic to automatically identify network devices. X. M. Guo et al. [12] propose a network device identification method based on MAC boundary inference, which identifies device types by inferring MAC address boundaries corresponding to device types. S. Zande et al. [13] propose to take clock offset information as device identification, and generate device fingerprints by extracting the timestamp difference between detection packets and response packets. The features extracted from the existing network traffic-based device identification often have redundant features and interference features, which increase the time cost of identification and reduce the accuracy of identification.

To solve the above problems, this paper proposes a feasible method for the rapid identification of network device types. This method uses feature reduction strategies and dynamical feature weights assignment mechanisms to reduce the device identification time overhead and improve the identification precision. This method uses a fast filter algorithm in the feature reduction part. Firstly, the features with low device correlation are first analyzed and deleted. Then, this algorithm calculates the correlation between features and the correlation between features and devices, performs feature redundancy analysis and delete. If the two features have a high correlation and both have a high correlation with the device. It means that the two features are redundant with each other, and delete one of the two features that are less relevant to the device. Finally, we will get the optimal feature subset. Since the same feature has different "contributions" to different device types, we assign different weights to this feature when identifying different device types (called dynamic weighting). In the dynamic weighting part, we calculate the correlation between each feature and the device type through mutual information, and assign the corresponding weight to it according to the correlation, so as to achieve dynamic weighting.

The main work of this paper is as follows:

Propose a device identification technology based on feature reduction and dynamic weighting. This method performs redundant analysis and deletion of network traffic features to form an optimal feature space, and dynamically assign weights to features in the optimal feature subset. Compared with existing methods, this method can efficiently and accurately identify network devices.

Propose a feature reduction strategy. In this strategy, redundant features are analyzed and deleted through a fast filter algorithm to reduce the dimension of the feature space and form the optimal feature space. Compared with the existing method, this method can effectively reduce the equipment identification time overhead.

Propose a dynamical feature weights assignment strategy. According to the principle of different importance of device features, the strategy calculates the correlation between each feature and the identification of the different device, and takes it as the weight of features. Compared with the existing methods, this method can effectively improve the accuracy of equipment identification.

We conduct experiments on time cost and accuracy based on different machine learning algorithms. The experimental results on the public data set show that the method in this paper improves the recognition accuracy of the existing method by 3.5% and reduces the time cost by 80% in the random forest; the recognition accuracy of the existing method is improved by 10.8%; time expenditure has been reduced by 72% in LightGBM.

The rest of the paper is organized as follows. Section 2 introduces the related work of network device identification. Section 3 presents the method of this paper in detail. After that, Sect. 4 introduces the experiment of this paper and analyzes the results, and Sect. 5 summarizes the whole paper and looks into the future work.

2   Related Work

In recent years, network device identification has gradually become a research hotspot in cyberspace security. The main identification methods are to identify devices based on network traffic. First, these kinds of methods capture data packets [14] and firmware information [15] of network devices through detection tools. Then they process the captured traffic data and select the best features, which remove interference features and redundant features. Finally, they identify network devices through various learning algorithms. We test and analyze in different shapes of the localization region.

Y. Meidan et al. [16] propose a method to identify network devices through network traffic, which is based on machine learning. This method monitors and obtains the TCP data packets of the device, using the feature extraction tool to convert them into feature vectors and constructing a feature space. In addition, this method uses machine learning algorithms to identify devices and constructs an optimal classifier for each device type. This method has achieved high recognition accuracy. However, a single protocol data packet cannot fulfill the identification of existing devices of various types. In order to solve this problem, A. Sivanathan et al. [17] propose a network identification method based on network traffic profiles. This method not only analyzes the behavior characteristics of the network device, including traffic rate, idle time signal transmission protocol, etc., but also analyzes the traffic profile of the network device, such as the average rate of the network device, the ratio of peak rate to average rate, active time and active traffic, etc. This paper also designs a classification method to learn the behavior of network devices for recognition. J. Martin et al. [18] design a network device traffic monitoring system based on C5.0 decision tree and time series analysis, using the CNN-LSTM model to detect and obtain device traffic to identify network devices. This method avoids manual intervention features and different data types need to train different models, so its model applicability is poor.

D. Bekerman et al. [19] propose a method to identify network devices by analyzing network traffic. This method extracts 972 behavioral features across different protocols and network layers and uses CFS (Correlation features) algorithm to select the most meaningful features, which reduces the data dimension to a manageable size. The experimental results show that the method has good performance, while the method can only identify known devices and cannot detect network devices in an untrained network environment. E. B. Beigi et al. [20] analyze the relative importance of each feature in network traffic to device type recognition, and select the most meaningful feature subset to produce the best classification accuracy, improving the recognition accuracy of network devices. The algorithm uses all the features to calculate the recognition accuracy and uses it as a baseline. It iteratively deletes each feature and observes how the recognition accuracy changes to show the relative importance of each feature attribute. It keeps the accuracy results and gives a ranked list of the importance of features. The experimental results show that multi-dimensional features from different network stream layers can improve the classification accuracy, while the time overhead brought is high for large data sets. J. L. Xu et al. [21] propose a classification method for IoT devices based on network traffic analysis by analyzing and classifying network traffic data. This method trains a multi-stage meta-classifier. In the first stage, the classifier can distinguish the traffic generated by IoT devices and non-IoT devices. In the second stage, a specific classification model is constructed for each IoT device. When entering a piece of sample data, the classifier runs in each classification model and calculates the similarity with each device type until the device type is determined. The results show that this method has high recognition accuracy, but it ignores the time overhead caused by data redundancy. M. B. Umair et al. [22] propose an efficient network device traffic classification system based on multi-layer deep learning. This method preprocesses data, uses deep neural network (DNN) to extract flow features, and uses maximum entropy classifier to classify Internet traffic. The machine learning traffic classification system based on shallow neural network proposed in this paper has achieved very good classification effect and very high recognition accuracy, but the method does not carry out further fine-grained identification of network devices.

According to the results of the existing methods, device identification methods based on network traffic still have shortcomings in the environment with many types and large numbers of device. Since the feature attribute set extracted from the network traffic data packet is multi-dimensional, including features that are not related to the type of identification device and redundant features, these interference features will increase time overhead and even affect the recognition accuracy.

To solve the above problems, this paper proposes a rapid device type identification method based on feature reduction and dynamical feature weights assignment, which improves the efficiency and accuracy by reducing features and assigning weights to each feature. This method calculates the correlation between the feature and the device. It sets a threshold and deletes the features whose correlation is less than the threshold. This method performs redundancy analysis and calculates the correlation between every two features in turn. If two features have a high correlation and have a high correlation with the device, these indicate that the two features are redundant with each other, and the feature having a lower correlation with the device is deleted. Each feature attribute is determined according to the degree of influence of the feature attribute on device recognition. The type of device is determined by calculating the similarity between the device to be identified and the known device. This method reduces the dimensionality of the feature space through feature reduction and dynamically assigning feature weights, which improves the data quality of the feature space and the efficiency of device recognition.

3   Proposed Method

This section presents a network device identification method based on feature reduction and dynamic weighting. We use a fast correlation filtering algorithm to perform feature reduction and dynamical feature weights assignment attributes by calculating mutual information, which realizes fast and efficient identification of network devices.

3.1   Framework of Device Identification Method

Aiming at the problem of high time overhead caused by feature redundancy in the existing device identification methods based on network traffic, this paper proposes a rapid identification method for network devices based on feature reduction and dynamic weighting. The basic idea of this method is as follows: first, we delete the features that have low correlation with the device type and perform feature redundancy analysis, and delete redundant features, thereby reducing the dimensionality of the feature space, improving the data quality of the feature space and the efficiency of device recognition. Then we determine the weight of each feature attribute according to the degree of influence of the feature attribute on the device type. Finally, we calculate the similarity between the devices to be identified and the known device, and determine the type of device to be identified based on the similarity. Figure 1 shows the overall architecture of the network device identification method based on feature reduction and dynamic weighting.

The framework is mainly composed of four parts: data preprocessing, feature reduction, dynamic weighting and, device type discrimination modules.

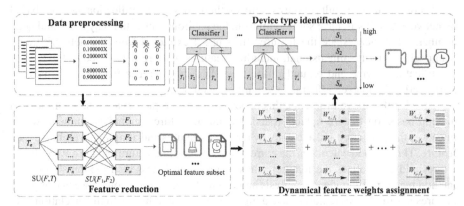

Fig. 1. Network device type recognition framework based on feature reduction and dynamical feature weights assignment.

The specific workflow is as follows:

1. **Data preprocessing:** Normalize the data and perform low-variance filtering to remove features whose attribute values remain basically unchanged. Experimental data shows that these low-variance features carry very little information. Therefore, in this method, a threshold is set in advance, and features whose variance is less than this threshold is deleted.

2. **Feature reduction:** Calculate the correlation between each feature attribute and the correlation between each feature and type, first remove the attribute features that have very little correlation with the device type, that is, useless features; then remove redundant features. If both feature attributes are related to the device type and the two feature attributes also have a high correlation, the one of the two feature attributes that has a smaller impact on the device type is eliminated. By eliminating useless features and interference features, the feature reduction is realized to reduce the dimension of the feature space, and finally the optimal feature space is formed.

3. **Dynamical feature weights assignment:** For the reduced feature space, we use mutual information to calculate the impact of each feature attribute on the device type, and assign weights to each feature attribute according to the degree of impact on the device type, then the characteristic data of different data types are integrated into a file as the sample data of the classifier.

4. **Construct classifiers:** Construct a classifier for each device type, and use dynamically assigned feature data as the input of the classifier to train the optimal classification model. The feature data is divided into two parts, one part is used as training data to construct the classifier, and the other part is used as the verification data set to verify the classification effect of the classifier.

5. **Device type identification:** Input the sample data to the classifier and calculate the similarity of the two groups of features through the similarity measure; and the type

of device is judged based on the similarity to determine the type of device. If two or more classifiers output the same similarity value, the confidence of the two sets of data is calculated to determine which type of device data that the sample data is more similar to, and the type with the highest confidence is taken as the device type.

3.2 Features Reduction

This paper uses the FCBF algorithm (Fast Correlation-Based Filter, fast correlation filter algorithm) to achieve feature reduction, FCBF is a method based on SU (Symmetrical Uncertainty) [23]. In this method, T is the device type, which contains m device types, and denote it as:

$$T_k = [t_1, t_2, \ldots, t_m], k \in \{1, 2, \ldots, m\} \tag{1}$$

Let F be the device feature, which contains n feature attributes, and denote it as:

$$F_i = [f_1, f_2, \ldots, f_n], i \in \{1, 2, \ldots, n\} \tag{2}$$

We in advance set a threshold δ to determine whether there is a high correlation between the feature and the device type. This algorithm first calculates the $SU(f_i, t)$ $SU_{f,t}$ between the feature f_i and the device type t. When $SU(f_i, t) < \delta$ $SU_{f,t} < \delta$ means that the correlation between the feature f_i and the device type t is too low. That is, the "contribution" to the identification device type t is too small, so the feature f is eliminated.

Then, this algorithm calculates the $SU(f_j, t)$ $SU_{f,t}$ between the feature f_j and the device type t, the $SU(f_i, f_j)$ between the feature f_i and f_j. We can know that f_j is a redundant feature and can be deleted from the feature list if and only if $SU(f_i, t) \geq SU(f_j, t)$ and $SU(f_i, f_j) \geq SU(f_j, t)$. This is due to the correlation between feature f_i and f_j is stronger than the correlation between the feature f_j and the device type t. According to Markov Blanket [24], f_j can be represented by f_i, f_j is a redundant feature, so the feature f_j can be deleted from the feature list. Finally, all features in the feature set are computed iteratively until the optimal feature subset is found.

The formula for calculating the SU value between features and device types can be expressed as:

$$SU(F, T) = 2 \left[\frac{IG(F|T)}{H(F) + H(T)} \right] \tag{3}$$

From Eq. (3), it can be seen that SU is a normalized form of IG, which standardizes the correlation of two variables between 0–1. When $SU = 0$, the two variables are independent of each other; when $SU = 1$, the two variables are completely related. And respectively represent the information entropy of features and device types. The formula of SU value between two features is expressed as:

$$SU(f_i, f_j) = 2 \left[\frac{IG(f_i|f_j)}{H(f_i) + H(f_j)} \right] \tag{4}$$

The IG information gain formula can be expressed as:

$$IG(F) = H(T) - H(T|F) \tag{5}$$

The specific feature reduction process is shown in Algorithm 1. The input of algorithm 1 is device type list S_t, the unselected features list S_u and the threshold value δ. The algorithm first traverses S_t and S_u and calculates the SU values between every feature and the device type respectively. Then, the algorithm calculates the SU values between two features and eliminates irrelevant features and redundant features in the unselected features list S_u. Finally, the algorithm output the feature list S_f after feature reduction.

Algorithm 1: Feature reduction algorithm

Input: S_t, S_u, δ

Output: S_f, r_s /* The result of SU calculation */

1: **begin**

2:   $\delta = 0$;

3:   initialize S_f = null;

4: **for** each feature **in** S_u **do:**

5:     calculate r_{s1} for S_t, S_u;   /* Calculates the SU between one feature and the device type */

6:     **if** $r_{s1} \geq \delta$:

7:       insert feature into S_f;

8:     **end if**

9: **end for**

10: **for** each feature **in** S_f **do:**

11:   **while** len(S_f) $\neq$ 0 **do:**

12:       calculate r_{s2} for S_t, S_u;   /* Calculates the SU between another feature and the device type */

13:       calculate r_{s3} for S_u;   /* Calculates the SU between two features */

14:       order S_f in descending;

15:       **if** $r_{s1} \geq r_{s2}$ and $r_{s3} \geq r_{s2}$:

16:         delete another feature from S_f;

17:       **end if**

18:     **end while**

19:   **end for**

20: **end**

3.3 Dynamical Feature Weights Assignment

In this method, we use Eq. (6) to measure the relationship between feature F and device type T. The mutual information of two variables refers to the degree of correlation between the two variables. When the mutual information is 0, it means that the feature and the device type are independent of each other; the larger the mutual information value is, the stronger the dependence between the two is, that is, the correlation is greater.

$$I(T; F) = \int_T \int_F P(T, F) \log \frac{P(T, F)}{P(T)P(F)} = H(T) - H(F|T) \tag{6}$$

where $H(F)$ is the entropy of F, which can be expressed as:

$$H(F) = -\int P(F) \log P(F) \tag{7}$$

The specific feature dynamic weighting process is shown in Algorithm 2. The input of Algorithm 2 is the device list S_t, the selected feature list S_f, and the output is the device feature weight list S_w. This algorithm first traverses S_f and S_t and calculates the mutual information value r_i. Then, the algorithm inputs the mutual information value r_i into the list S_w. That is, each mutual information value r_i is assigned as a weight to the corresponding feature in the feature list S_f. Finally, the algorithm outputs the weights list S_w.

Algorithm 2: Dynamic weighting algorithm

Input: S_t, S_f

Output: S_w, r_i /* The result of mutual information calculation */

1: **begin**
2: initialize S_f = null;
3: **for** each type **in** S_t **do:**
4:     **for** each feature **in** S_f **do:**
5:         calculate $H(T)$ for S_t;   /* Calculate the entropy of the device type */
6:         $H(t) = -\int P(t) \log P(t)$;
7:         calculate $H(T)$ for S_f;   /* Calculate the entropy of the feature*/
8:         $H(f) = -\int P(f) \log P(f)$;
9:         calculate r_i for S_t, S_f;
10:        $r_i = H(T)-H(F|T)$;
11:    **end for**
12:    insert r_i into S_w;   /* Insert the MI of features and devices into the weights list*/
13: **end for**
14: **end**

---

4 Experiment Results and Analysis

In order to evaluate the performance of the device type identification method proposed in Sect. 3, this section carries out real data experimental verification, and compares the rapid identification method proposed in this article with the existing identification methods based on network traffic. The experiment uses the data set of paper [16], and this section conducts comparative experiments in terms of time cost and accuracy.

4.1 Experiment Setup

This experiment uses the data set of paper [16]. In this data set, the network traffic of 10 kinds of devices are collected, which include Baby_monitor, Light, Motion_sensor, Security_camera, Smoke_detector, Socket, Thermostat, TV, Watch, Water sensor. Each instance in the data set represents a session (a TCP connection from a SYN packet to a FIN packet). Each session contains several TCP packets, and each piece of data represents a TCP packet. The total number of the data in this experimental data set is about 390,000. The specific structure of the experimental data set is shown in Table 1.

Table 1. Experimental data set.

Device type	Manufacturer	Device model	Number of items
Baby_monitor	Beseye	Baby Monitor Pro	51377
Lights	Samsung	Samsung	100000
Motion_sensor	Wemo	Wemo F7C028uk	50712
Security_camera	Withings	Withings WBP02/WT9510	14190
Smoke_detector	Nest	Nest Nest_Protect	168
Socket	Efergy	Efergy Ego	100000
Thermostat	Nest	Nest Learning Thermostat 3	18814
TV	Samsung	Samsung UA55J5500AKXXS	59069
Watch	LG	LG Urban	4187
Water_sensor	Waveshare	Waveshare water_sensor	1026

4.2 Time Overhead Experiment

This section compares the time cost required for identification with the recognition method in paper [16]. In this paper, experiments on the recognition methods based on random forest and LightGBM algorithms are carried out on the same data set. We perform the reduction processing in Sect. 3.2 on the feature data in the data set, and the final selected features and their SU values are shown in Table 2. It can be seen from Table 2 that the correlation between different features and devices is different. Among them,

Table 2. Partial features and SU values

Features	Notes	SU
ttl_thirdQ	Third quartile of TCP packet lifetime	0.56360573
B_port_is_8080	The client port number is 8080	0.54843636
ttl_min	Minimum TCP packet survival time	0.54500229
ssl_count_client_ciphersuites	Number of SSL encryption suites supported	0.308317
B_port_is_9543	The client port number is 9543	0.01777781
B_port_is_8280	The client port number is 8280	0.01002722
B_port_is_5228	The client port number is 5228	0.00899002
B_port_is_11095	The client port number is 11095	0.0009748

the survival time and port number of TCP packets have a higher degree of discrimination for identifying device types.

This experiment uses ten-fold cross-validation to calculate the average of the time required for code testing and compare the time required for device identification with different algorithms. Table 3 shows the comparison of the time required for the identification test between the method in this paper and the device identification method without feature selection algorithm under different algorithms. It can be seen from Table 3 that our algorithm is compared with the method in paper [16], in the random forest and LightGBM algorithm, the required time overhead is reduced by 80%, 72% respectively. Therefore, when FCBF is applied to feature reduction, the time overhead required will be significantly reduced.

Table 3. Time overhead (seconds)

Method	RF	LightGBM
Our method	6.22	11.12
In [16] method	36.1	40.3

4.3 Device Identification Precision Experiment

In this section, the accuracy of device type recognition is used to measure the performance of the method in this paper. In this experiment, we use the dynamic weighting method of Sect. 3.3 to assign values to the features left after reduction, and increase the accuracy of the important features that have a higher "contribution" to the recognition device. We calculated the proportions of 8 features in 10 types of equipment, as shown in Fig. 2. It can be seen from Fig. 2 that the important features of different device types are different. For example, the feature f_1 corresponding to the weight w_1 in Lights is more distinguishing than other features, while the feature f_4 corresponding to the weight w_4 in the device type Smoke_detector compared with other characteristics is more distinguishing. Based on this data set, compare the recognition effects of this method and the existing methods on different machine learning algorithms.

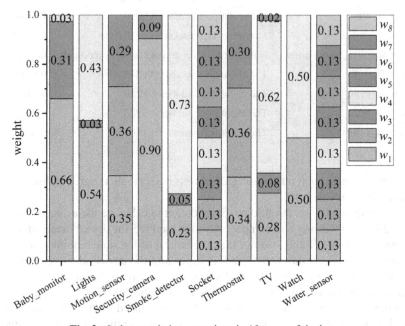

Fig. 2. 8 characteristic proportions in 10 types of device.

This experiment uses four common performance indicators of accuracy, precision, recall, and F1-Score to evaluate the effectiveness of this method in terms of recognition accuracy. Among them, TP refers to the number of samples that are determined to be a certain device type and actually belong to the device type, FP refers to the number of samples that are determined to be a certain device type but do not actually belong to the device type, and TN refers to the number of samples that are determined to be non-existent. The number of samples that belong to a certain equipment type but actually belong to the equipment type. FN refers to the number of samples that do not belong to a certain equipment type in the judgment and in practice.

$$Accuracy = \frac{TP + TN}{TP + TN + FP + FN} \tag{8}$$

$$Precision = \frac{TP}{TP + FP} \tag{9}$$

$$Recall = \frac{TP}{TP + FN} \tag{10}$$

$$F_{Score} = 2\frac{Precision * Recall}{Precision + Recall} \tag{11}$$

Figure 3 shows the comparison of the recognition accuracy under the random forest between the algorithm in this paper and the method in paper [16] after ten-fold cross-validation. It can be seen from Fig. 3 that on the real data set, although the recognition accuracy of the devices Security_camera, Thermostat, TV and Watch decreases slightly, this is due to the fact that after feature reduction and weighting, some have higher recognition of the device. The characteristics of relevance may have information loss, resulting in a slight decrease in recognition accuracy. However, the device identification method based on feature reduction and dynamic weighting in this paper has a slightly higher recognition accuracy than the method proposed in the paper [16], and is relatively stable, with smaller fluctuations.

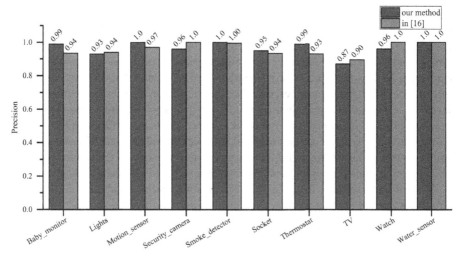

Fig. 3. Comparison of accuracy between this method and the method in paper [16] under RF algorithm.

Table 4 shows the comparison of recognition accuracy, recall rate and F1 value under the random forest and LightGBM algorithms. It can be seen from Table 4 that the use of feature reduction and dynamic weighting algorithms has improved recognition accuracy, recall and F1 value than the method proposed in paper [16]. It further shows that this method can significantly reduce time overhead while ensuring a slight increase in accuracy, and has stronger practicability in large data sets.

Table 4. Performance comparison between RF and LightGBM algorithm.

Method	RF			LightGBM		
	Precision	Recall	F1	Precision	Recall	F1
Our method	96.5%	85%	85%	81%	85%	82%
In [16] method	93%	82%	80%	70.2%	80%	80%

The above experimental results show that the rapid device identification method based on feature reduction and dynamic weighting proposed in this paper can use very few features to achieve better recognition performance and reduce time overhead while improving accuracy. Through the evaluation of the method in this paper on the public data set, the recognition performance of the method in this paper is better than the existing network device type recognition method based on network traffic.

5   Conclusion

The existing device type identification methods based on network traffic often ignore the different effects of the same feature attribute on a specific device type, and fail to fully consider the impact to time overhead and accuracy brought by redundant features. This paper proposes a method to quickly identify device types through feature reduction strategies and feature attribute dynamic weighting. According to the correlation between features and device types, delete the interference features and redundant features. At the same time, At the same time, we consider that the same feature has different degrees of influence on different device types, calculate the correlation between the feature and the device category, and dynamically assign it as a weight to each feature, so as to realize the rapid and efficient identification of network devices. We have performed identification experiments on 10 types of intelligent network devices on real data sets. The experimental results show that the method in this paper can use fewer features, reduce time overhead while ensuring higher accuracy, and has stronger practicality in practical applications.

In the future, we will focus on the identification and applicability of large-scale network devices to achieve accurate identification and improve the security of network devices.

Funding Statement. This work was supported by the National Natural Science Foundation of China (No. U1804263, 61872448, 62172435, and 62002386) and the Zhongyuan Science and Technology Innovation Leading Talent Project (No. 214200510019).

Conflicts of Interest. The authors declare that they have no conflicts of interest to report regarding the present study.

References

1. Gillivray, C.M., Reinsel, D.: IDC worldwide global data sphere IoT device and data forecast. Internet Data Center (2019)
2. Li, Q., Feng, X., Wang, H., Sun, L.: Automatically discovering surveillance devices in the cyberspace. In: Proceedings of MMSys, pp. 331–342 (2017)
3. Zhang, H., Han, W., Lai, X., Lin, D., Ma, J., Li, J.: Survey on cyberspace security. Sci. China Inf. Sci. **58**(11), 1–43 (2015). https://doi.org/10.1007/s11432-015-5433-4
4. Feng, G.D., Zhang, Y., Zhang, Y.Q.: Overview of information security risk assessment. J. China Inst. Commun. **25**(7), 10–18 (2004)
5. Xi, R.G., Yun, X.C., Jin, S.Y.: Research survey of network security situation awareness. Comput. Appl. **32**(1), 1–4 (2012)

6. Bodenheim, R., Butts, J., Dunlap, S., Mullins, B.: Evaluation of the ability of the Shodan search engine to identify internet-facing industrial control devices. Int. J. Crit. Infrastruct. Prot. **7**(2), 114–123 (2014)

7. Durumeric, Z., Adrian, D., Mirian, A.: A search engine backed by internet-wide scanning. In: Proceedings of ACM SIGSAC, pp. 542–553 (2015)

8. Li, R., Shen, M., Yu, H., Li, C., Duan, P., Zhu, L.: A survey on cyberspace search engines. In: Proceedings of CCIS, pp. 206–214 (2020)

9. Cui, A., Stolfo, S.: A quantitative analysis of the insecurity of embedded network devices: results of a wide-area scan. In: Proceedings of ACSAC, pp. 97–106 (2010)

10. Li, Q., Feng, X., Wang, R., Li, Z., Sun, L.: Towards fine-grained fingerprinting of firmware in online embedded devices. In: Proceedings of INFOCOM, pp. 2537–2545 (2018)

11. Kotak, J., Elovici, Y.: IoT device identification using deep learning. In: Herrero, Á., Cambra, C., Urda, D., Sedano, J., Quintián, H., Corchado, E. (eds.) CISIS 2019. AISC, vol. 1267, pp. 76–86. Springer, Cham (2021). https://doi.org/10.1007/978-3-030-57805-3_8

12. Guo, X., Li, X., Li, R., Wang, X., Luo, X.: Network device identification based on MAC boundary inference. In: Sun, X., Zhang, X., Xia, Z., Bertino, E. (eds.) ICAIS 2021. CCIS, vol. 1424, pp. 697–712. Springer, Cham (2021). https://doi.org/10.1007/978-3-030-78621-2_58

13. Zande, S., Murdoch, S.J.: An improved clock-skew measurement technique for revealing hidden services. In: Proceedings of USENIX Security Symposium, pp. 211–226 (2008)

14. Zhu, B.K., et al.: IoT device monitoring system based on C5.0 decision tree and time-series analysis. IEEE Access **10**, 36637–36648 (2021)

15. Gao, K.: A passive approach to wireless device fingerprinting. In: Proceedings of DSN, pp. 383–392 (2010)

16. Meidan, Y., et al.: ProfilIoT: a machine learning approach for IoT device identification based on network traffic analysis. In: Proceedings of SAC, pp. 506–509 (2017)

17. Sivanathan, A., Sherrat, D., Gharakheili, H.H., et al.: Characterizing and classifying IoT traffic in smart cities and campuses. In: Proceedings of INFOCOM WKSHPS, pp. 559–564 (2017)

18. Martin, J., Rye, E., Beverly, R.: Decomposition of MAC address structure for granular device inference. In: Proceedings of ACSAC, pp. 78–88 (2016)

19. Bekerman, D., Shapira, B., Rokach, L., Bar, A.: Unknown malware detection using network traffic classification. In: Proceedings of CNS, pp. 134–142 (2015)

20. Beigi, E.B., Jazi, H.H., Stakhanova, N., Ghorbani, A.A.: Towards effective feature selection in machine learning-based botnet detection approaches. In: Proceedings of IEEE CNS, pp. 247–255 (2014)

21. Sivanathan, A., et al.: Classifying IoT devices in smart environments using network traffic characteristics. IEEE Trans. Mob. Comput. **18**(8), 1745–1759 (2019)

22. Umair, M.B., et al.: An efficient internet traffic classification system using deep learning for IoT. Comput. Mater. Contin. **71**(1), 407–422 (2022)

23. Senliol, B., Gulgezen, G., Yu, L., Cataltepe, Z.: Fast correlation based filter (FCBF) with a different search strategy. In: Proceedings of ISCIS, pp. 1–4 (2008)

24. Xu. H.: Research on Markov blanket discovery algorithm based on Bayesian networks. M. S. Dissertation, University of Electronic Science and Technology of China, Chengdu (2012)

MGDP: Architecture Design of Intelligent Detection Platform for Marine Garbage Based on Intelligent Internet of Things

Ning Cao[1], Yansong Wang[2], Xiaofang Li[3(✉)], Rongning Qu[3], Yuxuan Wang[2], Zhikun Liang[2], Zijian Zhu[2], Chi Zhang[2], and Dongjie Zhu[2]

[1] College of Information Engineering, Sanming University, Sanming 365000, China
[2] School of Computer Science and Technology, Harbin Institute of Technology, Weihai 264209, China
[3] Department of Mathematics, Harbin Institute of Technology, Weihai 264209, China
lixiaofang@hit.edu.cn

Abstract. With the rapid development of global technology and economy, the problem of environmental pollution has become more and more prominent, and people's environmental protection concepts have also been continuously improved. Among them, the treatment of marine garbage is a topic of common concern in the international community nowadays. The advancement of maritime waste management is a rigid need to protect the diversity of the ecological environment. However, there is a large amount of garbage in the sea, which is widely distributed and difficult to deal with. In this context, how to efficiently detect marine garbage and understand the distribution of marine garbage has become a crucial issue. The significance of this system is to effectively integrate and link operators with different responsibilities so that they can effectively integrate their information, understand the distribution of garbage in the sea, and speed up the process of garbage disposal in the sea. This system adopts the B/S architecture, Vue is used in the front-end, and SpringBoot is used in the back-end. The highlight of the technology is that the WebGIS is used to call the map display interface on the front-end, and the pictures taken by the drone can be displayed on the specific location of the map in dots so that it is convenient to check whether there is rubbish or the cleanup of rubbish and then upload it. The picture understands the path taken by the drone and whether the work of the garbage cleaner is effective, which greatly improves the efficiency of garbage treatment.

Keywords: Internet of Things · Network geographic information system · Marine garbage detection · Online target marking

1 Introduction

With the rapid development of global technology and economy, while the industrialization of information, the problem of ecological environmental pollution

X. Sun et al. (Eds.): ICAIS 2022, LNCS 13340, pp. 678–688, 2022.
https://doi.org/10.1007/978-3-031-06791-4_53

has also become prominent [14], and marine pollution bears the brunt. Among them, the treatment of marine garbage is the basis for the treatment of marine pollution, and it is also a topic of common concern in the international community [7,9,13]. Compared with land-based garbage, marine garbage has a high cleaning cost, high activity, and a variety of pollution sources. If the land-based garbage cleaning strategy is imitated to treat marine garbage [6], the efficiency is low and the effect is not obvious. The key to efficient management of marine garbage is accurate positioning and rapid action, so we need to locate garbage through scientific means, speed up the process of garbage cleanup, and reduce the cost of garbage cleanup activities [3,11]. In the system implemented in this paper, we use drones to accurately locate the location of marine garbage [4,5], record the characteristics of garbage through pictures or videos [12], and efficiently display the distribution of garbage through WebGIS [8,15], and make decisions through flexible strategies, you can choose the most cost-effective and effective cleaning method according to the characteristics of garbage in advance [2]. At the same time, the system rationally controls and promotes the entire waste management process through scientific and efficient work processes, and effectively integrates operators with different responsibilities in each link, so that the work progress and information are quickly diffused. And through the garbage information collected to understand and analyze the law of garbage distribution in the sea, speed up the speed of marine pollution control.

2   Related Work

Many countries in the world have implemented garbage classification [1] and recycling very early, and their garbage classification policies have been relatively complete [6]. From the experience provided by these countries, we can sum up several points: First, the economic value of waste sorting and recycling is far greater than the value of simply incineration of waste; secondly, if there is a good waste sorting incentive policy, it can be effectively improve the efficiency of garbage classification; third, the garbage classification system is clear and clear. By doing sufficient work in garbage classification, to ensure that the final value of garbage is also utilized [15].

China's research on garbage classification is mainly based on residents' independent classification. Many community property systems can identify garbage, but these identifications are generated when there is trash bin positioning. The emergence of many smart trash cans has indeed improved our view on garbage classification [4,10]. However, to deal with the garbage in the sea, it is of no value to place multiple trash cans on the sea surface. Because the garbage in the sea is generated with ocean currents, it appears from time to time.

In the classification of garbage, some areas need to be improved. In terms of the accuracy of data acquisition [13], to reduce costs and increase profits, some companies will choose some outsourcing companies to perform garbage labeling tasks for a large number of sea area pictures. These data processed by outsourcing companies will inevitably have a series of accuracy problems. The problems are all that we need to pay attention to [7]. It is essential to ensure the ease of use of software products so that users of any education level can get started after simple learning and training [9].

3   MGDP: Intelligent Detection Platform for Marine Garbage Based on Intelligent Internet of Things

This chapter will introduce in detail the design of our proposed marine garbage intelligent detection platform based on the intelligent Internet of Things. First, give a general introduction to the architecture of the entire system, and then introduce the design of each functional module in the system in detail.

3.1   System Overall Architecture Design

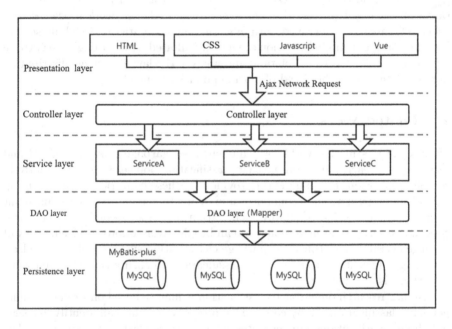

Fig. 1. MGDP system overall architecture diagram.

The whole system adopts B/S architecture, and the main display form is Web page program.

The B/S architecture is composed of a browser and a server. The browser is responsible for data display and user interaction as the front-end, and the server is responsible for logic processing and data persistent storage as the back-end. As long as the developed system is deployed on the server, the user does not need any additional programs and only needs to use the developed product in the browser. The program developed in this way has lower cost and is more user-friendly, which makes the B/S architecture system more popular.

The back-end of the garbage detection platform(MGDP) adopts the Spring-Boot framework, and the software architecture diagram is shown in Fig. 1. The whole platform(MGDP) includes three layers: the presentation layer, business layer, and persistence layer. The main functions of each layer are as follows:

Presentation layer: The presentation layer is mainly the page displayed to the user, including requirements for the interactive response, data display, and complete functions. The issues that need to be considered when implementing a presentation layer page generally include: how to display data, how to use page logic to represent the data processing process, and how to display a beautiful interface when the browser opens the website.

Service layer: The business layer is mainly responsible for the realization of business logic and data processing. All data that needs to be displayed in the presentation layer needs to be obtained by the business layer from the persistence layer, processed in the business layer and passed to the presentation layer. The data passed by the user to the business layer through the presentation layer also needs to be logically processed and then passed to the lower persistence layer for storage.

Persistence layer: The persistence layer is mainly responsible for the persistent storage of the entire system data and directly interacts with the database.

3.2   Modular Design

There are three types of users in the MGDP system. The administrator's responsibility is to assign tasks and create users. Ordinary users (garbage cleaners and drone pilots) are mainly actual workers, and the responsibility of the leader is to check the progress of the work. Among them, only user management is a functional module unique to the role of administrator, while the role of leader can only be viewed in the visual map module in the MGDP system.

1) The main functions of the administrator module are as follows:
   (1) The management of general user information mainly includes basic functions such as modifying basic user information;
   (2) Data upload. The uploaded data types include pictures but are not limited to pictures;
   (3) Data download. The data that can be downloaded include records of garbage found in any area within the monitoring range of the platform, where the attributes of the records include time, location, etc.;
   (4) Upload of garbage cleaning data. The main functions include uploading garbage cleanup records and garbage classification data to the platform;
   (5) Smart labeling. Intelligently label the garbage existing in the sea area pictures uploaded to the platform;
   (6) Check the map;
   (7) Assign tasks and news announcements. The main functions include assigning tasks to users, sending message notifications to designated users, etc.;

2) The main functions of the common user module are as follows:
   (1) The management of general user information mainly includes basic functions such as modifying basic user information;
   (2) View task and message notifications. Ordinary users in the platform can view the specific tasks assigned to them by the platform administrator and the message notifications sent by the platform;
   (3) Upload of garbage cleaning data. The main functions include uploading garbage cleanup records and garbage classification data to the platform;
   (4) Smart labeling. Intelligently label the garbage existing in the sea area pictures uploaded to the platform;
   (5) Check the map;
3) The main functions of leadership are as follows:
   (1) Check the map;
   (2) View the work process. Users with leadership roles in the platform have the right to view the work progress of all ordinary users in the platform;
   (3) Post task reminders. Users with leadership roles in the platform can send reminder messages to user administrators in the platform, prompting them to allocate the backlog of tasks in the platform;

4   Experiments

In this chapter, we will explain in detail the deployment and testing of MGDP.

4.1   Experimental Environment

In order to test the capabilities of MGDP, we built a complete experimental system. The specific configuration of the test environment is as follows: Windows 10 operating system (64-bit), Chrome browser Version 1.32.115 (64 bit), IntelliJ IDEA 2019.2.4 × 64, MySQL Database, Visual Studio Code.

The back-end of the MGDP system uses the SpringBoot framework, the front-end uses the Vue-CLI scaffolding, and the ant-design framework is used for the beautiful interface design. After completing the front-end Vue-CLI scaffolding installation and some simple configurations, you can directly use the npm run serve command to run the developed project. It should be noted that the simple configuration mentioned above refers to the need to install some third-party dependent components for the operation of the platform, such as OSS, ant-design framework, map framework, etc. In terms of the implementation of the persistence layer of this platform, we have added the MyBatis persistence layer framework to the back-end framework SpringBoot used. MyBatis is a Java-based persistence layer framework that provides convenient database operation interfaces including SQL Maps and Data Access Objects (DAOs). The MyBatis framework reads the database-related configuration set by the developer from the application. Properties or application.yaml file, and performs database link creation and data interaction.

4.2   Experimental Results

User Login Module. The user login interface is shown in Fig. 2.

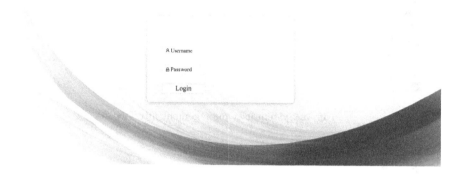

Fig. 2. User login interface.

The user login process is roughly divided into the following simple steps: First, the user needs to enter the user name and password on the login page and click the login button; then, the browser sends a request to the server, and the server will first determine whether the account password is correct; If there is an error that the account password does not correspond to, the server will return a prompt of the wrong password to the browser; When the server confirms that the account password entered by the user is correct by checking the account password stored in the persistence layer, it returns a login success prompt to the browser and returns a unique token string at the same time; The browser can store the token information returned by the server in the local cache, and all subsequent requests initiated carry the token string stored in the local cache.

The system user management interface is shown in Fig. 3.

User Uploads Drone Shooting Data Module. In the file upload interface (as shown in Fig. 4), users can choose to upload pictures, upload videos, or upload picture folders. When the user drags the file or folder to be uploaded to the specified location according to the requirements or selects the file or folder to be uploaded by clicking and selecting in the specified area, the platform will have a detailed prompt of the file upload progress and whether the upload is successful.

The user upload list interface is shown in Fig. 5.

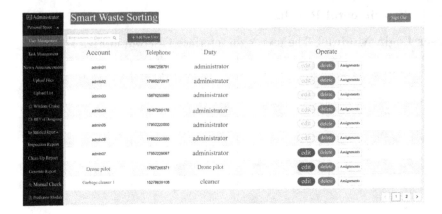

Fig. 3. System user management interface.

Fig. 4. Device management interface diagram.

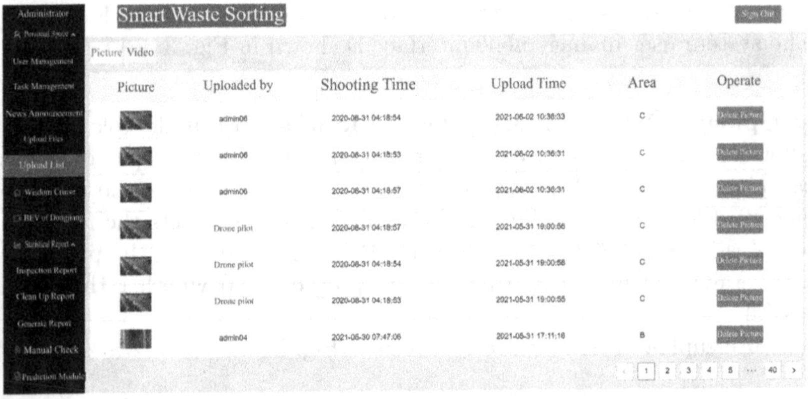

Fig. 5. User upload list interface.

User Picture Annotation Module. In the manual verification interface, users can annotate the uploaded pictures. You can choose to annotate the original icon or continue to annotate the original and annotated pictures. After the annotation is successful, you can submit or cancel the annotation.

The user picture annotation interface is shown in Fig. 6. On the left side of the image annotation work area, users can annotate the uploaded images to be annotated, explicitly annotate the garbage area in the image, and at the same time modify and improve the annotated images. On the right side of the picture labeling work area, users can make macro statistics on the distribution of the trash that has been marked in the current system.

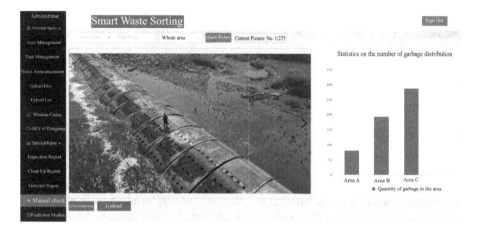

Fig. 6. User picture annotation interface.

User Map Display. Users can view the map pictures and videos previously uploaded to the platform on the bird's-eye view of Dongjiang or Wisdom Seeking Bay interface. At the same time, users can see on the map the distribution of the uploaded pictures in the geographic location where they were taken and the route taken by the video photographer in the uploaded video.

The specific user map display interface is shown in Fig. 7. Among them, the red dot indicates that there are photos taken here on the platform, and the blue line indicates the geographic location of the video shooter. Through the patrol track drawn on the map based on the pictures or videos uploaded by the user, the manager can efficiently summarize the situation of the entire supervision area through the system.

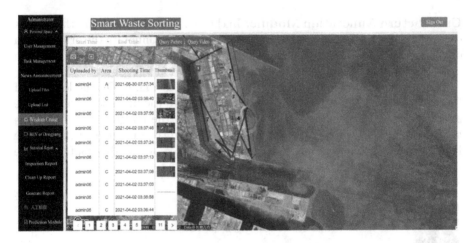

Fig. 7. Map display interface.

5   Conclusions

The MGDP platform uses drones to take pictures or videos of marine garbage characteristics, accurately locate the garbage location, and analyze the nature of the garbage in detail, so that decisions can be made in advance and the most appropriate cleaning plan can be selected, which improves cleaning efficiency and reduces cleaning costs. In addition, the MGDP platform uses a scientific and reliable workflow system to approve and advance the sea area garbage cleanup process, and at the same time efficiently diffuse the work progress and information obtained by different working link staff, thereby ensuring the efficient advancement of the sea area garbage cleanup process. The MGDP platform uses UAV-based Internet of Things technology to combine sea area garbage monitoring with image labeling, geographic information systems and other technologies, and integrates management perspectives to effectively improve the work efficiency of sea area garbage monitoring and garbage cleaning and recycling. The system has effectively improved the marine debris cleanup process, but still has the following problems:

(1) The method of obtaining marine garbage on the MGDP platform is mainly through drones and manual positioning. Due to the priority and high cost (maintenance, repair, marine failure rate) of drones, the garbage involved can only be distributed in the coastal waters. Moreover, the breadth of the coastline coverage is also proportional to the scale of system usage, and the cost will also rise sharply as the scale expands. Therefore, a technical method that compromises cost and efficiency is needed to locate garbage;

(2) Due to natural factors such as tides, sea breeze, extreme weather, and ocean currents at sea, marine garbage will not stand still for a long time. Therefore, if the interval from the positioning display to the cleaning action is too long, the cleaning effect will be affected, and the cleaning scale will also

be affected. Therefore, it is necessary to simulate the movement of garbage on the sea through weather information (wind direction, wind speed) and ocean currents, and other information models, to find the accumulation and temporal rules of garbage, and to improve the cleaning efficiency.

Acknowledgement. The authors would like to thank the associate editor and the reviewers for the time and effort provided to review the manuscript.

Funding Information. This work is supported by the Fundamental Research Funds for the Central Universities (Grant No. HIT. NSRIF.201714), Weihai Science and Technology Development Program (2016DX GJMS15), Weihai Scientific Research and Innovation Fund (2020), the Grant 19YG02, Sanming University and Key Research and Development Program in Shandong Provincial (2017GGX90103).

Conflicts of Interest. The authors declare that they have no conflicts of interest to report regarding the present study.

References

1. Aleem, A., Tehsin, S., Kausar, S., Jameel, A.: Target classification of marine debris using deep learning. Intelligent Automat. Soft Comput. **32**(01), 73–85 (2022)
2. Cancan, W.: Design and Implementation of Urban Community Waste Classification Management System Based on Internet of Things. Master's thesis, Beijing Forestry University (2020)
3. Chengxiu, G.: A Study on the Model of Two Cooperatives in the Sorting and Disposal of Domestic Waste in Shanghai Communities-Taking M Community in Xuhui District as an Example. Master's thesis, Shanghai Normal University (2020)
4. Dexin, L., Zhigang, Y., Jiuyun, S.: Research on classification and detection technology of river floating garbage based on drone vision. Metal Mine **50**(09), 199 (2021)
5. Li, C., Sun, X., Cai, J.: Intelligent mobile drone system based on real-time object detection. J. Artif. Intell. **1**(1), 1 (2019)
6. Ninglai, Z.: A new method for detecting global marine plastic waste. Synthetic Mater. Aging Appl. **49**(06), 177 (2020)
7. Pengyu, H.: Research on the Visualization Design of Garbage Classification and Recycling Information-A Case Study of Beijing. Master's thesis, Beijing Forestry University (2020)
8. Shaohang, L.: Research on Archaeological Information Platform and Key Technologies Based on WebGIS. Master's thesis, Xi'an University of Science and Technology (2020)
9. Shuo, G.: A Practice Report on the Chinese Translation of European Waste Disposal Practice: Problems, Solutions, Prospects. Master's thesis, Harbin Institute of Technology (2020)
10. Sung, W., Devi, I.V., Hsiao, S., Fadillah, F.N.: Smart garbage bin based on AIOT. Intell. Automat. Soft Comput. **32**(03), 1387–1401 (2022)
11. Wang, J., Zhang, T., Cheng, Y., Al-Nabhan, N.: Deep learning for object detection: a survey. Comput. Syst. Sci. Eng. **38**(02), 165–182 (2021)

12. Xu, Z., Zeng, X., Ji, G., Sheng, B.: Improved anomaly detection in surveillance videos with multiple probabilistic models inference. Intelligent Automat. Soft Comput. **31**(3), 1703–1717 (2022)
13. Yanjun, L.: Lessons from the recycling and utilization of packaging waste in developed countries. Guangdong Sci. Technol. **19**, 52–53 (2009)
14. Yazhu, C.: Social Work Involves Residents Participate in Garbage Classification-Take the Garbage Classification Project of Agency X as An Example. Master's thesis, Beijing University of Civil Engineering and Architecture (2020)
15. Yiwen, Y.: Design and implementation of webgis map interface library based on typescript. Geospatial Inf. **19**(05), 72–74+5 (2021)

Dark Chain Detection Based on the IP Address

Jingwen Fang, Qian Shao, Zhongyi Xu, Penghui Li, Baotong Chen,
and Haoliang Lan$^{(\boxtimes)}$

Department of Computer Information and Network Security, Jiangsu Police Institute,
Nanjing 210000, China
lanhaoliang@jspi.cn

Abstract. In recent years, the attack methods of black industry are changing day by day, among which "hidden hyperlink" is a more serious problem, because itself is not much different from ordinary hyperlinks, so the hidden hyperlink in the program is more hidden and difficult to detect. This thesis is mainly concerned with the field of network security, and aims to provide a technique for detecting hidden hyperlinks based on IP addresses. The technique firstly identifies the domain name that needs to be judged, then scans the domain name information of all the links under the website, converts the domain name information into the corresponding IP address, then hands over the IP address information to a third-party threat intelligence agency and the existing malicious IP address database for comparison, and at the same time combines the manual review to identify it as a hidden hyperlink with the title and keywords as the main detection target, and to The data identified as hidden hyperlinks will be extracted and the relevant features will be machine learned, and the data set will be continuously grown to improve the accuracy of machine learning, thus forming a system for automatic detection of hidden hyperlinks in real-world operations.

Keywords: Hidden hyperlink · Detection method · Path splicing · Network crawler · Beautiful soup · Gethostbynam

1 Introduction

"Hidden hyperlink", as the name suggests, are hyperlinks that are invisible or easily ignored on a web page. Although these hyperlinks are "invisible" on the web page, they can still be seen in the source code of the web page. However, what is not visible on the page is often not noticed, so the hidden hyperlinks can even "co-exist and develop" with the website in the long run. Hidden hyperlinks in the website are much hidden and not easily detected by search engines in a short period of time.

In order to make profits, hackers often sell the "hidden hyperlink" of some websites to illegal websites such as "Mark Six" and "cell phone bugging", which are then used to expand their popularity and carry out illegal activities [1]. According to the Changjiang Daily, the statistics of some Chinese government websites "hidden hyperlink attacks" made by Shen Yang, a doctoral supervisor of Wuhan University's School of Information Management, show that, as shown in Fig. 1, of the more than 30 million government web

© The Author(s), under exclusive license to Springer Nature Switzerland AG 2022
X. Sun et al. (Eds.): ICAIS 2022, LNCS 13340, pp. 689–699, 2022.
https://doi.org/10.1007/978-3-031-06791-4_54

pages in China, as many as 10.22% were "hidden hyperlinked" by malicious websites; among them, the most pages with fraudulent information, pornography and gambling information were 3.08 million, accounting for 10.13%.

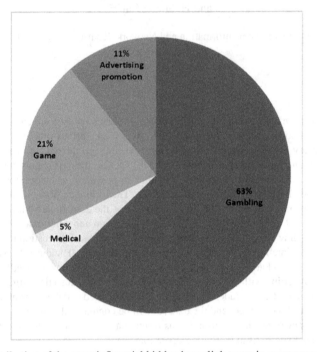

Fig. 1. Distribution of the most influential hidden hyperlink types in government websites.

Hidden hyperlinks mainly use CSS, JS, DIV + JS and other advanced techniques to control the way links are hidden [2]. If a website has hidden hyperlinks, it means that the website has probably been successfully hacked and risks such as leakage of registered user information of the website have occurred. Recently there is a new change in the technique of adding hidden hyperlinks [3]. The attacker no longer simply adds hidden links in the web pages, but directly adds the content that he needs to index and optimize in the web pages, and then identifies the type of browser that accesses the request through a script program placed on the web server, if it is found to be a search engine crawler to access the web pages, then the problematic content is displayed, and vice versa. This new way makes it almost impossible for the user to actively find the abnormality in the web page, even if the web page source code on the browser will not find any abnormality, unless going to the server to analyze the source code of the web page line by line. However, hidden hyperlinks are essentially hyperlinks, which essentially do not pose a substantial threat to users, and security software naturally does not detect hidden hyperlinks, let alone intercept or prompt them.

2   IP Address-Based Hidden Hyperlink Detection

According to the current status of hidden hyperlink detection technology, and the current detection methods for hidden hyperlinks can be divided into two kinds: manual detection and automatic detection by tools [4, 5]. For manual detection, generally through the webmaster often check the source code of web pages at all levels in the website to see whether hidden hyperlinks are inserted, or click to visit all the links in the web pages one by one, if unknown links are found, the web pages are judged to be likely to be inserted with hidden hyperlinks, but the manual detection is time-consuming, labor-intensive and easy to cause misjudgment. In this paper, we mainly crawl web page keywords and titles by IP address as the main entry point, and use web crawlers and multi-threading technology to obtain IP addresses and domain names. The flow of the implementation of the IP address-based hidden hyperlink detection method is shown in the Fig. 2.

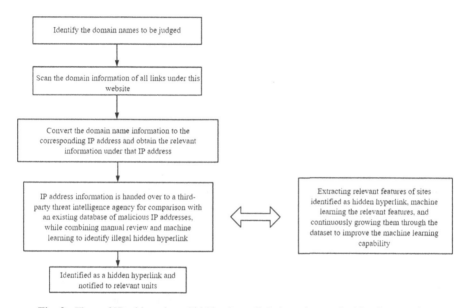

Fig. 2. Flow of IP address based hidden hyperlink detection method implementation.

2.1   Extracting All Domain Links in the Web Page to Be Detected

Open the web page to be detected, and determine the domain names to be scanned and detected by obtaining the web page structure. The web structure is the layout of the web content, and the creation of the web structure is essentially the planning of the layout of the web content. It is one of the important aspects of web page optimization, which affects the overall structure of the website and the number of pages included, as well as the user experience and relevance. "HTML" refers to the standard language for describing web pages. It mainly consists of six elements, such as Fig. 3 is the layout of

HTML5: header element is the page title, header; nav element is the page navigation link part; article element is an article, it is a piece of the page and the context of the independent content; section element is the section of the article; aside element is the sidebar, is with the content of the page The aside element is the sidebar, which is auxiliary information related to the content of the page; the footer element is the bottom, footer of the page [6].

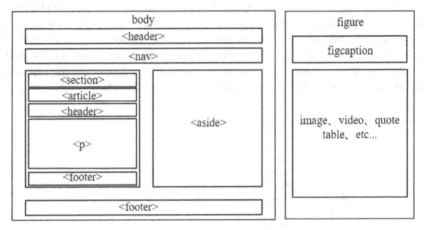

Fig. 3. HTML5 layout diagram.

The current methods of hiding hidden hyperlinks are mainly HTML hidden hyperlinks and JS introduced hidden hyperlinks. Html hidden mainly uses CSS and JS to control how the links are hidden, usually by changing the position attribute to a negative number so that the links cannot be displayed in the visible page; using the marquee attribute to make the links flash quickly so that viewing the page will not be affected; hide hidden hyperlinks using methods such as display: none and visibility: hidden to hide the content in the area; using JS introduction type is mainly through modifying the title of the website and introducing external JavaScript code to implant the hidden hyperlink into the web page, usually by converting the characters through String. Write method to write the hidden hyperlink into the current page; call document.write method in Windows object to introduce the external JS code into the page; use the characteristics of html to change the src in <script> tag to introduce the hidden hyperlink by using decimal Unicode encoding.

Then the crawler gets all the information of the web page and crawls the domain name that needs to be scanned and probed [7]. Figure 4 shows the general workflow of the crawler. Crawler means crawling the data in the web page. First, the web address (URL) of the content is crawled and the source code of the web page is opened. Generally, you can establish a link with the URL through the requests library to get all the html information; then through BeautifulSoup or Xpath, parse the html information obtained through the request function, and go through the attributes and names of the location tags to get the required information; finally, choose to print or download the required information to the local area [8].

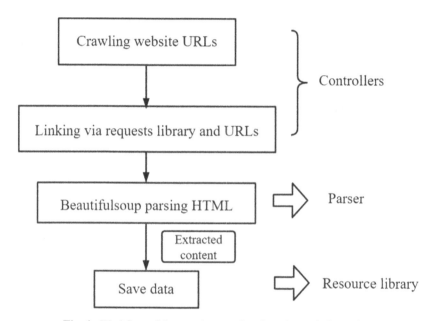

Fig. 4. Workflow of the crawler crawling for relevant information.

Get all the website links under the domain name of the target page, and get the domain name of the website to which the link points from the request information [9]. After crawling all the information, find all the website links and add two protocols to the links respectively to access the web page. These two protocols are http and https. Protocols are designed to enable information interaction between computers consisting of different computers and different operating systems. Http protocol is a request and response based, stateless, application layer protocol where information is transmitted in clear text and most protocols are free so there are certain security issues while being widely used; https protocol is a secure SSL encrypted transmission protocol, compared to the http protocol is more secure, mainly to provide authentication to the web server, while protecting the privacy and integrity of the data exchanged. When using https protocol to access the link, if the decryption is not successful, the web link may have been tampered with and an abnormal interface will appear on the display; conversely, the access link is normal.

2.2 Extract IP Address Information According to Domain Name

Judgment to Obtain Whether the Website URL Structure is Complete and Extract IP address. A complete website URL has five parts: username, password, host, port and path. Because the http protocol is transmitted in clear text when accessing, it is easy for data to be listened to and stolen during transmission, so the https protocol, which uses symmetric and asymmetric encryption to transmit data, is introduced to ensure the security of network communication, so in this paper, we need to try to use a different protocol to access the domain name of the website. When trying to access, we first use the http protocol to request and try to read the server data, as shown in Fig. 5, when using the http protocol to access, we need to enter the URL in the browser first, and let the browser request DNS to resolve the URL into an IP address and return it to the browser. Then the browser establishes a TCP connection with the server and sends the request document GET/index.html to the server. The server returns a status code and a response message to the client after receiving the request. If the value of the returned status code is 200, it means that the client's request is successful and can be accessed using the http protocol. The obtained website home page (index.html) will be sent to the browser and release the TCP connection [10].

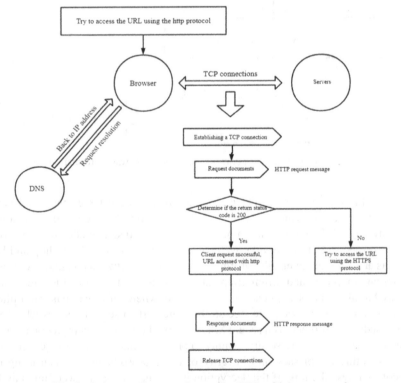

Fig. 5. Judgment diagram of accessing URL with http protocol.

If the http protocol access is not successful, then the https protocol is used again. Https protocol access process is roughly two steps, the first step is the https protocol handshake, and the second step is the information transmission. The former is mainly using asymmetric encryption to obtain the public and private keys and the key for data transmission to establish a data channel for the https protocol. The latter mainly uses symmetric encryption for file encryption transmission [11]. If both are unsuccessful, it means that the server rejects the link or other errors.

Get IP Geographic Address According to Qqwry Library. Qqwry.dat is the file name of Pure IP address database. Pure IP is a database collected, submitted and aggregated by private people spontaneously, which includes a large amount of IP data at home and abroad, and can be regarded as the most authoritative, most accurate address and most IP record IP address database on the current network. Compared with some commercial paid databases, some of the records in the Pure IP database are even more accurate than them, so this paper chooses to query the IP's place of belonging through the Pure IP database and perform the conversion from IP address to geographical area [12].

Qqwry.dat file is structurally divided into 3 blocks: file header, record area, and index area. Generally when we want to find IP, we first look for the record offset in the index area, and then go to the record area to read out the information. Since the records in the record area are of indefinite length, it is impossible to search in the record area directly. Because the number of records is relatively large, if we traverse the index area will also be a bit slow, in general, we can use the dichotomous lookup method to search the index area, which is orders of magnitude faster than traversing the index area.

Preliminary Judgment Based on IP Geographic Address Information. Firstly, we judge the source of IP information and analyze its information: judge the IP address, and if it is a domestic IP, the relevant links within the website are crawled. Then initialize the IP address query related data, set the warning level: 1) crawl the seed website, extract the title, keywords and other domains contained in the website [13]; 2) detect whether each domain name in the website is an abnormal link, extract the main domain name, protocol and IP address of the URL; 3) further in-depth query the IP address belongs to determine whether it is outside the country, if it is, crawl the URL to extract the website decoding, title and keywords, and vice versa, exit the cycle and save the information. Finally, the preliminary judgment process is as shown in Fig. 6.

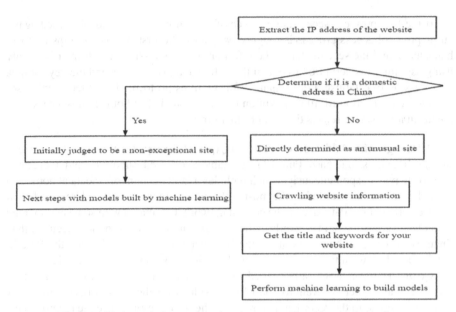

Fig. 6. Preliminary judgment based on ip geographic address information.

2.3 Get the Title and Keywords According to the Domain Name Link and Build a Keyword Database

Crawl the Web Page Information of Domain Links According to the Initial Judgment of Suspicious Domain Links. In this paper, we mainly use regular expressions to crawl web page information. First, we analyze the source code of the web page to get the contents between the tags that appear in pairs, including but not limited to: <td> tag area, <ul> tag area, <tr> tag area and <div> tag area, etc. Then get the links between the hyperlinks <a href =.> </a> between the link text content and the url present in the link, after crawling the url link from the inherent web page, then proceed to the next step of circular crawling or url crawling. The final crawl is usually located in <html><head><title>, which describes the title and keyword information of the page [14].

The format of the crawled data here must be different from the data in the web page, so we also need to parse the data for regularization, get the required data format and save the data.

Extract Domain Titles, Keywords and Other Key Features Based on the Crawled Web Page Information. After crawling the required web page data, the next step is to start analyzing the obtained data, extracting the titles and keywords from the websites, and judging whether they are gambling, pornography and other types of words by manual judgment. Then, based on the manual judgment, a keyword database is constructed, after which the keywords in the obtained web pages can be matched with the keywords in the thesaurus to determine whether the suspicious domain name is a hidden hyperlink address.

2.4 Extracting Relevant Features of Malicious Domain Names for Machine Learning

According to the address that has been identified as a hidden hyperlink, other features such as information, title and keywords in the hidden hyperlink web page are extracted to carry out machine learning and construct a model. Machine learning is a method of receiving a large amount of data, analyzing it automatically, deriving some kind of model and using the model to analyze and predict the unknown data [15]. As shown in Fig. 7, machine learning is similar to human thinking about inductive experience, but machine learning can take into account more complex situations. In general, the more data there is, the more accurate the final model constructed will be in predicting the unknown data.

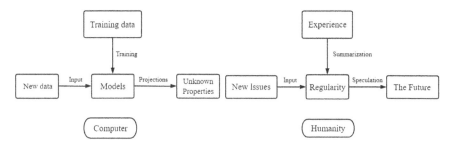

Fig. 7. Comparison of machine learning and human induction.

This paper investigates a statistical machine learning based approach to text classification for hidden hyperlink detection, "training" and constructing a model. The method is based on the unsupervised learning algorithm of clustering, which is used to extract and learn other features such as titles and keywords from web pages, and to analyze their intrinsic patterns [16]. The K-means algorithm is used for clustering. First, a web feature is selected as the centroid of the first cluster; then another web feature with a significant difference from the first centroid is identified as the second centroid, and so on for the remaining features; the distance from each data point to the centroid is calculated, and the data point is placed in that category if it is close to the centroid, and so on. The above steps are repeated to calculate the centre of each cluster, and if the centre converges, the result is output [17]. The algorithm is fast, does not rely on order, and has good clustering results. The algorithm training data is used to infer the labels and build the model. The links that have been made hidden are then judged, and even links without features such as titles and keywords can be predicted by the model built by machine learning, which identifies them as the address of the hidden hyperlink and informs the relevant units. The data captured is shown below in Fig. 8.

3 Model Implementation

rowid	ABNORMAL DOMAIN NETLC	ABNORMAL IP ADDE	ABNORMAL IP REGION	SOURCE DOMAIN TITLE	KEYWORDSOURCE DOMAIN	SOURCE DOMAIN	SOURCE DOMAIN TITLE
1	www.hlbxjj.cn	173.82.250.108	America	Stock large single network	How much is the most suitable stock allocation? Stock return calculation formula	www.valinbl.com	Valin commercial factoring
2	haikou.ssjzw.com	162.159.230.96	America	Haikou part time network	Haikou part time Recruitment . Haikou College Students part time	haikou.tdzyw.com	Haikou Land Resources Network
3	www.lygtour.cn	175.176.195.171	India	Macau Casino Entertainment	Macao casino entertainment website. Macao casino entertainment registration website	www.jltoptour.cn	First tourism network wonderful Jilin
4	www.hrexchange.com.hk	156.253.45.190	South Africa	Special zone Asian Casino - unique home page	Special zone Asian Casino	na.hxrc.com	Nan'an Talent Network
5	www.dbsLs.cn	147.255.178.238	America	Macao liukaicai selected materials 2020 official app	Macao pintebizhong information, lottery history 2020	si.1633.com	Industrial R & D technology and equipment trading platform
6	ncjx.ohqly.com	104.250.144.194	Northern America	Biqu Pavilion Network novel reading network	Biquge reading network	heihe.gongjiao.com	Heihe bus network
7	www.jxvdy.com	91.196.223.88	Ukraine	Golden Elephant micro film network	micro movie, HD free movie, mobile online movie	www.zssqshzyy.com	Basketball live
8	z.xywy.com	202.122.146.91	Malaysia	Medical expert network	Health consultation, appointment experts, professional triage, expert network	www.ys137.com	Health care network
...							

Fig. 8. Technical validation based on IP address hidden hyperlink detection.

4 Conclusions

In this paper, we explain the reasons for the occurrence of hidden hyperlinks in network security threats and the harm they cause to network security from the principle, and systematically propose a solution for hidden hyperlinks from manual identification, feature library construction, and construction system software, and combine the methods of third-party threat intelligence analysis and machine learning to build an identification model for hidden hyperlinks, and on this basis, we extract data from first-line websites to find out the relevant attributes of hidden hyperlinks in order to continuously enhance the identification rate and accuracy of the model. Based on this, we extract data from first-line websites to find out the relevant attributes of the hidden hyperlink addresses, so as to continuously enhance the recognition rate and accuracy rate of the model, and help webmasters automate the hidden hyperlink checking in websites through the combination of different methods. For solving the problem of hidden hyperlinks in websites, it has high guiding significance. The next step will be to improve the efficiency of this algorithm and its reliability and low storage rate on this basis, which can reduce the redundant data and make this algorithm be used reasonably in practical applications.

Acknowledgement. This paper was sponsored by the JSPIGKZ Project (No. 2911121110), Innovative and Entrepreneurial Doctor of Jiangsu Province (No. JSSCBS20210598), Jiangsu Provincial University Nature Science Foundation Project (No. 2020KX007Z), Jiangsu Provincial Science and Technology Research Project (No. 20KJB413002).

References

1. Chen, B., Shi, Y.: Malicious hidden redirect attack web page detection based on css. In: IEEE 4th International Conference on Computer and Communications (ICCC), pp. 1155–1159. IEEE (2018)
2. Liao, K.: New website security risks-dark chain. Int. Technol. **2012**(6), 56–59 (2012)
3. Subroto, A., Apriyana, A.: Cyber risk prediction through social media big data analytics and statistical machine learning. J. Big Data **6**(1), 1–19 (2019). https://doi.org/10.1186/s40537-019-0216-1
4. Sahingoz, O.K., Buber, E., Demir, O.: Machine learning based phishing detection from URLs. Exp. Syst. Appl. **117**, 345–357 (2019)
5. Jain, A.K., Gupta, B.B.: A machine learning based approach for phishing detection using hyperlinks information. J. Ambient. Intell. Humaniz. Comput. **10**(5), 2015–2028 (2018). https://doi.org/10.1007/s12652-018-0798-z
6. Zarrad, R., Doggaz, N., Zagrouba, E.: Wikipedia html structure analysis for ontology construction. Ko Knowl. Organ. **45**, 108–124 (2018)
7. Kaur, S., Singh, A., Geetha, G., Masud, M., Alzain, M.A.: Smartcrawler: a three-stage ranking based web crawler for harvesting hidden web sources. Comput., Mater. Continua **69**(3), 2933–2948 (2021)
8. Hajba, G.: Using Beautiful Soup. Website Scraping with Python. Apress, Berkeley, CA (2018)
9. Thirugnanasambanthan, K.: A new approach to Web Crawling-DHEKTS Crawler in comparison with various Crawlers. Indian J. Sci. Technol. **14**(19), 1580–1586 (2021)
10. Berners-Lee, T., Fielding, R., Frystyk, H.: Hypertext transfer protocol--HTTP/ 1.0 (1996)
11. Yassein, M.B., Aljawarneh, S., Qawasmeh, E.: Comprehensive study of symmetric key and asymmetric key encryption algorithms. In: 2017 international conference on engineering and technology (ICET), pp. 1–7 (2017)
12. Zhang, F., Liu, F., Xu, R., Luo, X., Ding, S.: Street-level IP geolocation algorithm based on landmarks clustering. Comput., Mater. Continua **66**(3), 3345–3361 (2021)
13. Kumar, M., Bhatia, R., Rattan, D.: A survey of Web crawlers for information retrieval. Wiley Interdisc. Rev. Data Mining Knowl. Discovery **7**, 1218 (2017)
14. Wang, X., Xu, Y., Jiang, J., Ormond, O., Liu, B., Wang, X.: StriFA: stride finite automata for high-speed regular expression matching in network intrusion detection systems. IEEE Syst. J. **7**(3), 374–384 (2013)
15. Mubarak, S., Habaebi, M.H., Islam, M.R., Diyana, F., Tahir, M.: Anomaly detection in ics datasets with machine learning algorithms. Comput. Syst. Sci. Eng. **37**(1), 33–46 (2021)
16. Caron, M., Bojanowski, P., Joulin, A.: Deep clustering for unsupervised learning of visual features. In: Proceedings of the European Conference on Computer Vision (ECCV), pp. 132–149 (2018)
17. Puthige, I., Bansal, K., Bindra, C., Kapur, M., Singh, D.: Safest route detection via danger index calculation and k-means clustering. Comput. Mater. Continua **69**(2), 2761–2777 (2021)

High-Reliability Mapping Algorithm Based on Network Topology Characteristics in Network Slicing Environment

Zhonglu Zou[1], Hao Xu[1], and Yin Yuan[2(✉)]

[1] Dongguan Power Supply Bureau of Guangdong, Power Grid Co., Ltd., Dongguan 523120, China
[2] Guangdong Planning and Designing Institute of Telecommunications Co., Ltd., Guangzhou 510630, China
13826243083@139.com

Abstract. In the network slicing environment, in order to solve the problem of low reliability of virtual network resources, this paper proposes a high-reliability mapping algorithm based on network topology characteristics. This algorithm is a heuristic resource allocation algorithm that simultaneously allocates the underlying nodes and the underlying links. The algorithm includes three steps: reliability attribute analysis of underlying network resources, reliability attribute analysis of virtual network resources, and resource allocation for virtual network requests. In order to analyze the reliability attributes of the underlying network resources, this paper calculates the weights and reliability values of the attributes of the underlying nodes and links based on the reliability attribute values of the underlying nodes and links. In the performance analysis link, the algorithm in this paper is compared with the traditional algorithm. From the two dimensions of the impact of the underlying network size on the algorithm performance and the impact of the underlying node failure rate on the algorithm performance, it is verified that the algorithm in this paper improves the reliability of the virtual network.

Keywords: Network slicing · Resource allocation · Reliability · Network topology

1 Introduction

As 5G network technology matures and application scenarios increase, more and more power services are carried in the 5G network environment. The high bandwidth and low latency of 5G networks have led to a rapid increase in the scope and scale of power communication networks built by power companies. In order to reduce the huge investment caused by the rapid construction of power communication network resources, network slicing technology has become a key technology for power companies to build communication networks [1, 2]. In the network slicing environment, the traditional physical network is divided into the underlying network and the virtual network. The underlying network provider is responsible for building the underlying network resources, including the underlying network nodes and underlying network links. The virtual network provider is responsible for creating a virtual network to carry specific power services. The virtual network includes virtual nodes and virtual links. The resources of the virtual node are allocated by the underlying node. The resources of the virtual link are allocated by the underlying link. From the network characteristics after network slicing, it is an important research content to effectively allocate the underlying network resources to the virtual network [3–6]. Therefore, how to improve the utilization of the underlying network resources while meeting the demand for more virtual network resources is an urgent problem to be solved [7].

In order to improve the utilization rate of the underlying network resources, literature [8] proposed a heuristic resource allocation algorithm based on node attribute characteristics, which improved the utilization rate of the underlying network resources. Literature [9] uses a node attribute feature analysis mechanism to propose a multi-attribute sorting resource allocation algorithm, which improves the resource utilization of the underlying network. In order to solve the problem of low security of the underlying network resources in a multi-domain environment, literature [10] based on cryptography technology proposed a multi-role encryption mechanism to realize the safe allocation of resources in a multi-domain environment. In order to solve the problem of high link resource allocation failure rate, literature [11] proposed a resource allocation algorithm based on link resource attribute characteristics, which effectively improved the performance of the virtual network resource allocation algorithm. Literature [12] uses integer programming theory to improve the utilization of underlying network resources. Literature [13] uses convolutional neural network technology to solve the optimal solution of resource allocation, which improves the success rate of resource allocation. Literature [14] uses genetic algorithm to improve the adaptive ability of the algorithm. Literature [15, 16] uses neural network theory to improve the success rate of resource allocation algorithms.

Through the analysis of the existing research, it can be known that the existing research adopts heuristic algorithm, artificial intelligence algorithm and other technologies, which effectively improves the utilization rate of the underlying network resources. However, as the types and numbers of power companies' businesses increase, virtual networks have increasingly higher requirements for the reliability of underlying network resources. To solve this problem, this paper aims to improve the reliability of virtual networks, and proposes a high-reliability mapping algorithm based on network topology characteristics in a network slicing environment.

2 Problem Description

In the network slicing environment, the network topology includes the underlying network and the virtual network. In terms of the underlying network, use $G(N, E)$ to represent the underlying network. Use $n_i \in N$ to represent the underlying node, and $e_{ij} \in E$ to represent the underlying link. In terms of virtual networks, $G^v(N^v, E^v)$ is used to represent a virtual network, $n_i^v \in N^v$ is used to represent a virtual node, and $e_{ij}^v \in E^v$ is used to represent a virtual link with virtual node $n_i^v \in N^v$ and virtual node $n_j^v \in N^v$ as the start and end nodes. In terms of resource allocation, the bottom-layer node allocates computing resources for the virtual node, and the bottom-layer link allocates bandwidth resources for the virtual link. In terms of node resource allocation, use $C(n_i)$ to represent the computing resources of the underlying node $n_i \in N$. Use $C_{re}(n_i^v)$ to represent the computing resources requested by virtual node $n_i^v \in N^v$. Use $B(e_{ij})$ to represent the bandwidth resource of the underlying link $e_{ij} \in E$. Use $B_{re}(e_{ij}^v)$ to represent the bandwidth resource requested by virtual link $e_{ij}^v \in E^v$.

The two bottom nodes that allocate resources to the virtual link start node $n_i^v \in N^v$ and end node $n_j^v \in N^v$ belong to any two bottom nodes that meet their resource requirements. When two bottom-level nodes are not connected by a directly connected bottom-level link, a bottom-level path needs to be allocated for this virtual link, and the start and end bottom-level nodes of the bottom-level path are the bottom-level nodes mapped by the start and end virtual nodes of the virtual link. The path length is the bottom path of the shortest path. For ease of description, the process of allocating resources from the underlying link to the virtual link is denoted as $e_{ij}^v \rightarrow p(e_{ij}^v)$. Among them, $p(e_{ij}^v)$ represents the bottom-level path allocating resources for the virtual link, and $p(e_{ij}^v)$ includes multiple bottom-level links $e_{ij} \in p(e_{ij}^v)$ that are connected end to end.

3   Reliability Attributes of Resources

In order to meet customers' requirements for the reliability of virtual networks, it is necessary to allocate appropriate underlying network resources for them based on the reliability characteristics of the underlying network and virtual network. This paper analyzes the reliability of the underlying network and virtual network based on the network topology characteristics.

3.1   Node Reliability

According to the experience of network operation and maintenance, the factors related to the reliability of network nodes mainly include the degree of the node, the centrality of the node, the replacement of the node, the number of node failures, the resource availability rate of the node, and the number of available resources of the node. They are described separately below. Because the virtual node does not have some attributes of the bottom node, the following takes the bottom node as an example for description.

The degree of a node refers to the number of edges directly connected to the current node. When the degree of the node is large, any directly connected edge fails, and the other edges can quickly replace the failed link, thereby improving the reliability of the virtual network. Use Deg_{n_i} to represent the degree of network node $n_i \in N$. The centrality of a node refers to the distance from the current node to other nodes in the network. The greater the centrality of the node, the smaller the distance between the current node and other nodes in the network. When the bottom node allocates resources to the virtual node, the bottom node with large node centrality can quickly find the shortest path, thereby saving the resources of the bottom link. Use Cor_{n_i} to represent the centrality of the underlying node n_i. Use formula (1) to calculate. hop_{n_i,n_j} represents the distance from the bottom node n_i to the bottom node n_j. This article uses the end-to-end hop count for calculation.

$$Cor_{n_i} = \frac{1}{\sum_{n_j \in N} hop_{n_i, n_j}} \tag{1}$$

The substitutability of a node refers to the ability of a bottom node to be replaced by another bottom node after a failure occurs. When the replaceability of the node is greater, the current bottom node is easier to be replaced by other nodes. Therefore, nodes with large node substitutability have higher reliability. Use $F(n_i^s)$ to represent the substitutability of the underlying node n_i^s, and use formula (2) for calculation.

$$F(n_i^s) = \frac{1}{\sum_{n_{ia}^s, n_{ib}^s \in r(n_i^s)} (1 - R(n_{ia}^s, n_{ib}^s))} \tag{2}$$

Among them, $R(n_{ia}^s, n_{ib}^s)$ represents the relationship between the bottom-level node n_{ia}^s and the bottom-level node n_{ib}^s. Use formula (3) to calculate. $r(n_i^s)$ represents a collection of bottom-level nodes directly connected to bottom-level node n_i^s in the bottom-level network. It can be seen from formula (3) that the closer the relationship between the underlying node n_{ia}^s and the underlying node n_{ib}^s, the larger the value of $R(n_{ia}^s, n_{ib}^s)$. At this time, the more common neighbor nodes of the underlying node n_{ia}^s and the underlying node n_{ib}^s, the greater the probability that these two nodes can be substituted for each other. Therefore, the greater the substitutability of the underlying node n_i^s calculated by formula (2), the greater the reliability of the current node. The larger the value of $F(n_i^s)$ of the bottom node n_i^s, the easier it is for the bottom node n_i^s to find a backup node.

$$R(n_i^s, n_j^s) = \frac{|r(n_i^s) \cap r(n_j^s)|}{|r(n_i^s) \cup r(n_j^s)|} \tag{3}$$

In terms of the number of historical failures, because the greater the number of historical failures, the greater the number of failures of the current node. Therefore, it is necessary to select the bottom node with a smaller number of historical failures to allocate resources to the virtual node. Use FN_{n_i} to represent the reciprocal of the number of failures of the underlying node n_i in a recent period of time. The larger the value, the fewer the number of failures of the current node, and the higher the reliability of the current node. The availability rate of the resources of the underlying nodes refers to the proportion of the remaining available resources of the underlying nodes in the total resources.

Because the higher the resource utilization, the worse the performance of the underlying node. Therefore, the higher the availability of the underlying node resources allocated to the virtual node, the higher the reliability of the current underlying node, and the higher the reliability of the virtual node that obtains the resource. Use RU_{n_i} to represent the resource availability rate of the underlying node n_i.

3.2 Link Reliability

According to network operation and maintenance experience, in order to achieve the goal of the virtual network resource allocation algorithm, this article focuses on the centrality of the link, the number of historical failures of the link, the availability of link resources, and the amount of link resources. The historical link failure times and link resource availability are similar to node attributes, and no detailed description will be given here. The number of historical failures of the link is represented by FN_{e_i}, and the availability of link resources is represented by RU_{e_i}.

The amount of link resources refers to the sum of the amount of available bandwidth of the current link and the amount of computing resources possessed by the two end points of the link. The greater the amount of link resources, it indicates that the current link resources can allocate resources for more virtual links. Use $totRe_{e_i}$ to indicate the amount of link resources. The centrality of the link refers to the connectivity of link resources in the network. The stronger the connectivity of the link, the greater the possibility that the link will be connected to other links in the network. When the link connectivity is strong, resources can be allocated to more virtual links, which effectively avoids the problem of link resource allocation failure due to lack of link resources.

Using $CorLink_{e_{n_i^s n_j^s}}$ to represent the centrality of the underlying link $e_{ij} \in E$, the centrality $CorLink_{e_{n_i^s n_j^s}}$ of the underlying link $e_{ij} \in E$ can be analyzed by analyzing the characteristics of the two underlying nodes n_i^s and n_j^s of the underlying link $e_{ij} \in E$. The calculation method is shown in formula (4). $Cor_{n_i^s}$ represents the centrality of the underlying node n_i^s. $NG_{n_i^s n_j^s} = |r(n_i^s) \cap r(n_j^s)|$ represents the same neighbor set of the bottom node n_i^s and the bottom node n_j^s. $r(n_i^s)$ represents the set of all nodes connected to the underlying node n_i^s. Through the analysis of formula (5), it can be known that the two end points of the underlying link $e_{ij} \in E$ are in the center of the network, and the two end points have more nodes connected in common, at this time the network has strong centrality.

$$CorLink_{e_{n_i^s n_j^s}} = NG_{n_i^s n_j^s} + (Cor_{n_i^s} + Cor_{n_j^s}) \tag{4}$$

3.3 Multi-attribute Weight Calculation

Through the analysis of node reliability and link reliability, it can be seen that there are many reliability factors of the node and link. In order to make full use of the relevant attributes of the network topology and improve the reliability of resource allocation, it is necessary to adopt a strategy of unifying the attribute dimensions and calculating the attribute weights. In terms of the unification of the attribute dimension, the min-max method is used to normalize the attribute value. In terms of attribute weight calculation, the analytic hierarchy process is used to calculate the weight. When using the analytic hierarchy process to calculate the weights, it is necessary to compare the importance of attributes in pairs. Considering that the goal of resource allocation in this paper is to ensure the reliability of virtual network services, the importance of the reliability attributes of the underlying nodes are in order of the number of historical failures, the degree of the node, the centrality of the node, the amount of resources, and the substitutability of the node. The importance of the reliability attribute of the underlying link is in order of the number of historical failures of the link, the centrality of the link, the amount of resources, and the availability rate. When virtual network resources are allocated, the method to improve the reliability of virtual network resources is to ensure that each virtual node and virtual link obtains a highly reliable underlying resource. Therefore, the importance of the reliability attribute of the virtual node is in order of the degree of the node, the centrality of the node, the amount of resources, and the substitutability of the node. According to the importance relationship between the node and link attributes, formula (5) is used to solve the attribute importance matrix W. Among them, i and j represent two attributes of network resources.

$$W = (w_{ij}) = \begin{cases} 1, & \text{i is more important than j} \\ 0.5, & \text{i and j are equally important} \\ 0, & \text{j is more important than i} \end{cases} \tag{5}$$

Based on the value of W, formula (6) can be used to obtain the weighting factor relationship matrix of the attribute. m represents the number of network resource attributes, n represents the number of network resources. $y_{ij} = \frac{y_i - y_j}{2n} + 0.5. y_i = \sum_{j=1}^{m} w_{ij}$.

$$Y = (y_{ij})_{n \times m} = \begin{bmatrix} y_{11} & \cdots & y_{1m} \\ \cdots & \cdots & \cdots \\ y_{n1} & \cdots & y_{nm} \end{bmatrix} \tag{6}$$

According to the analytic hierarchy process, the calculation method of the weight factor of attribute k is shown in formula (7).

$$\eta_k = \frac{\sum_{j=1}^{m} y_{kj}}{\sum_{i=1}^{m} \sum_{j=1}^{m} y_{ij}} \tag{7}$$

4 Mapping Algorithm

In order to improve the reliability of virtual network resources, the high-reliability mapping algorithm based on network topology characteristics (HRMAoNTC) proposed in this paper is a heuristic resource allocation algorithm that simultaneously allocates the underlying nodes and the underlying links. The algorithm includes three steps: reliability attribute analysis of underlying network resources, reliability attribute analysis of virtual network resources, and resource allocation for virtual network requests. In step 1, the main task is to analyze the reliability attributes of the underlying network resources. According to the reliability attribute value of the bottom node and the bottom link, calculate the weight and reliability value of each attribute of the bottom node and the bottom link, and arrange them in descending order. In step 2, the reliability attributes of virtual network resources are analyzed. According to the reliability attribute value of the virtual node, calculate the weight and reliability value of each attribute of the virtual node, and arrange them in descending order. In step 3, resource allocation is performed one by one for the virtual networks in the virtual network request set.

5 Performance Analysis

In order to analyze the performance of the HRMAONTC algorithm in this paper, the GT-ITM tool [17] is used to generate the network topology environment in the experimental link. The network topology includes the underlying network topology and the virtual network topology. The number of underlying nodes of the underlying network topology has been increased from 100 to 600, which is used to simulate the network environment under different network scales. The bottom layer link is generated by connecting any two bottom layer nodes with a probability of 0.2. The resources of the underlying nodes and the underlying links are uniformly distributed from [40,60]. In terms of virtual network topology, the number of virtual nodes obeys the uniform distribution of [2, 6], and the resources of virtual nodes and virtual links obey the uniform distribution of [3, 5].

In terms of algorithm comparison, compare the HRMAONTC algorithm in this paper with the virtual network resource allocation algorithm based on shortest path (VNRAAoSP). The algorithm VNRAAoSP uses the shortest path algorithm to allocate resources for the virtual network. In order to analyze the influence of the algorithm in this paper on the reliability of the network, the analysis is carried out in a network environment where the underlying network node fails. According to operating experience, the probability of failure of the underlying node is low, so the failure probability of the underlying network node is set to obey (0.07%, 0.09%) uniform distribution. At this time, the comparison index of the two algorithms is the reliability of the virtual network. Virtual network reliability refers to the percentage of the total number of paths that have no faults among the end-to-end paths of all virtual networks. The end-to-end path of the virtual network uses 10% of the nodes of the virtual network to send data to the other 10% of the nodes to simulate. According to the number of unavailable paths, the reliability of the virtual network is evaluated.

Figure 1 shows the results of the impact of the underlying network size on the performance of the algorithm when the failure rate of the underlying network node is (0.07%, 0.09%). The X axis in the figure indicates that the number of underlying network nodes has increased from 100 to 600. The Y axis represents the reliability of the virtual network. It can be seen from the figure that the two algorithms have achieved good results under different network scales. It shows that the reliability of the virtual network under the two algorithms tends to converge. In terms of performance comparison of the two algorithms, the reliability of the virtual network under the HRMAONTC algorithm in this paper is maintained at about 72%, and the reliability of the virtual network under the comparison algorithm VNRAAoSP is maintained at about 46%. Through analysis, it can be known that the virtual network under the algorithm of this paper is more reliable. This is because the reliability of the underlying network resources obtained by the virtual network under the algorithm of this paper is higher, which improves the reliability of the virtual network (Fig. 2).

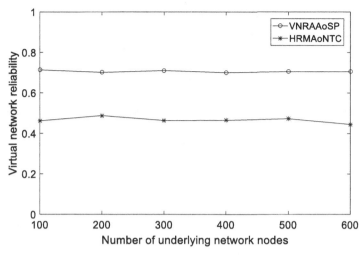

Fig. 1. The impact of the underlying network size on algorithm performance.

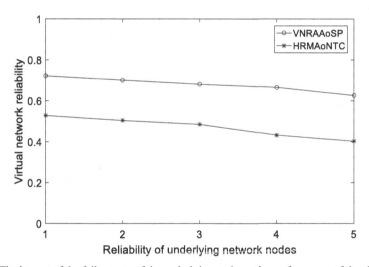

Fig. 2. The impact of the failure rate of the underlying node on the performance of the algorithm.

6 Conclusion

With the rapid construction and application of 5G networks, network slicing technology has become a necessary technology for network construction. In the network slicing environment, how to improve the reliability of virtual network resources has become an urgent problem to be solved. To solve this problem, this paper proposes a high-reliability mapping algorithm based on network topology characteristics. In the performance analysis part, from the two dimensions of the influence of the scale of the underlying network on the performance of the algorithm and the influence of the failure rate of the underlying nodes on the performance of the algorithm, it is verified that the algorithm in this paper improves the reliability of the virtual network. Taking into account that resource redundancy backup is a necessary technology to improve reliability, in the next step, based on the research results of this paper, we will combine resource redundancy backup with the algorithm of this paper to back up key resources with low reliability to further improve this paper. The application value of the algorithm.

Acknowledgement. This work was supported by Installation project of wireless service global access communication network management system of Dongguan Power Supply Bureau of Guangdong Power Grid Co., Ltd. (No. 031900GS62200248).

References

1. Tao, X., Han, Y., Xu, X., Zhang, P., Leung, V.C.M.: Recent advances and future challenges for mobile network virtualization. Sci. China Inf. Sci. **60**(4), 1–12 (2017)
2. Yuan, X.: Research on network resource optimal allocation algorithm based on game theory. Intell. Autom. Soft Comput. **27**(1), 249–257 (2021)
3. Bannour, F., Souihi, S., Mellouk, A.: Distributed sdn control: survey, taxonomy, and challenges. IEEE Cummun. Surv. Tutor. **20**(1), 333–354 (2018)
4. Al-Wesabi, F.N., Khan, I., Alamgeer, M., Al-Sharafi, A.M., Choi, B.J.: A joint algorithm for resource allocation in d2d 5g wireless networks. Comput. Mater. Continua **69**(1), 301–317 (2021)
5. Li, L., Wei, Y., Zhang, L., Wang, X.: Efficient virtual resource allocation in mobile edge networks based on machine learning. J. Cyber Secur. **2**(3), 141–150 (2020)
6. Al-Wesabi, F.N., Khan, I., Mohammed, S.L., Jameel, H.F., Alamgeer, M.: Optimal resource allocation method for device-to-device communication in 5g networks. Comput. Mater. Continua **71**(1), 1–15 (2022)
7. Amaldi, E., Coniglio, S., Koster, A.: On the computational complexity of the virtual network embedding problem. Electron. Notes Discrete Math. **52**, 213–220 (2016)
8. Cao, H., Zhu, Y., Yang, L., Zheng, G.: A efficient mapping algorithm with novel node-ranking approach for embedding virtual networks. IEEE Access **5**(1), 22054–22066 (2017)
9. Cao, H., Yang, L., Zhu, H.: Novel node-ranking approach and multiple topology attributes-based embedding algorithm for single-domain virtual network embedding. IEEE Internet Things J. **5**(1), 108–120 (2018)
10. Mano, T., Inoue, T., Ikarashi, D., Hamada, K., Mizutani, K., Akashi, O.: Efficient virtual network optimization across multiple domains without revealing private information. IEEE Trans. Netw. Serv. Manag. **13**(3), 477–488 (2016)
11. Andreev, S., Galinina, O., Pyattaev, O., et al.: Exploring synergy between communications, caching, and computing in 5g-grade deployments. IEEE Commun. Mag. **54**(8), 60–69 (2016)
12. Chowdhury, S.R., Shahriar, A.R., N: Revine: reallocation of virtual network embedding to eliminate substrate bottlenecks. In: IFIP/IEEE Symposium on Integrated Network and Service Management (IM), pp. 116–124 (2017)
13. Dolati, M., Hassanpour, S.B., Ghaderi, M.: Virtual network embedding with deep reinforcement learning. In: IEEE INFOCOM 2019-IEEE Conference on Computer Communications Workshops (INFOCOM WKSHPS), pp. 879–885 (2019)
14. Jahani, A., Khanli, L.M., Hagh, M.T.: EE-CTA: energy efficient, concurrent and topology-aware virtual network embedding as a multi-objective optimization problem. Comput. Stand. Interfaces 1–17 (2019)

15. Jahani, A., Khanli, L.M., Hagh, M.T.: Green virtual network embedding with supervised self-organizing map. Neurocomputing **351**, 60–76 (2019)
16. Hamid, A.K., Al-Wesabi, F.N., Nemri, N., Zahary, A., Khan, I.: An optimized algorithm for resource allocation for d2d in heterogeneous networks. Comput. Mater. Continua **70**(2), 2923–2936 (2022)
17. Zegura, E.W., Calvert, K.L., Bhattacharjee, S.: How to model an internetwork. In: Proceedings of IEEE INFOCOM'96. Conference on Computer Communications, vol. 2, pp. 594–602 (1996)

New Generation Power System Security Protection Technology Based on Dynamic Defense

Xiaowei Chen[1], Hefang Jiang[1], Shaocheng Wu[1], Tao Liu[1], Tong An[2(✉)],
Zhongwei Xu[2], Man Zhang[3], and Muhammad Shafiq[4]

[1] Shenzhen Power Supply Bureau Co. Ltd., Shenzhen 518001, China
[2] School of Cyberspace Security, Beijing University of Posts and Telecommunications,
Beijing 100876, China
antong@bupt.edu.cn
[3] Peng Cheng Laboratory, Shenzhen 518055, China
[4] Cyberspace Institute of Advanced Technology, Guangzhou University, Guangzhou 510006,
China

Abstract. With the development of power information systems and the evolution of attack means, the traditional security protection scheme is difficult to deal with the increasing network attacks. In order to deal with the increasingly severe security risks, this paper studies dynamic defense technologies such as mimic defense and moving target defense and their applications in power information systems, and proposes a power system security architecture based on dynamic defense. The architecture includes the mimic defense layer, the mimic network switching layer, the mimic service layer, application management layer and dynamic management module. Through the functions of dynamic adjudication, reconstruction, cleaning, and switching, the power system is endowed with dynamic defense capabilities, so that the system has endogenous security attributes. The dynamic protection technology is applied to the access program and computing area of the information management area, and the system can resist unknown attacks by using mimicry and mobile target defense.

Keywords: Dynamic defense · Power information system · Safety protection

1 Introduction

With the development of power information systems, the requirements of data protection and security guarantee for power information systems have been increasing. The current power defense system is a defense-in-depth system composed of multiple lines of defense, including firewalls, intrusion detection systems, and isolation devices. It is reinforced by encryption authentication, access control, virus detection, and other technical means. However, with the continuous disclosure of relevant security incidents in recent years, the shortcomings of traditional defense and defense-in-depth systems have gradually been exposed. Because it is built on a system of known rules and lacks real-time and efficient countermeasures for unknown backdoor vulnerabilities, external defense methods are difficult to meet the security requirements of power information systems. Therefore, improving the active defense capability of electric power information systems is an important way to solve the unknown security risks.

Referring to the current understanding and practice of improving system active defense, this paper introduces the concept of dynamic defense in view of the unknown backdoor vulnerabilities and other risks faced by the current power information system. On this basis, a new generation of power information system security architecture is constructed by combining dynamic defense with existing power information system architecture. It enhances the endogenous security capability of the system while meeting the premise of high system availability.

2 Security Risks of Power Information Systems

In recent years, security and trust problems become a scorching topic, although the power information system is becoming more intelligent and networked, the number of cyber attacks is increasing [1]. There are two main reasons: First, with the continuous development of network attack and defense technology, ransomware, and unknown backdoor vulnerabilities have emerged one after another. Many hacker groups and terrorists have the ability to launch attacks on power information systems and reap huge profits. Second, The component of the power information systems is very complex, covering multiple fields, integrating multiple technologies, and using many kinds of devices to realize the existing functions of the system. And the device boundary is constantly expanding, which increases the attack surface of the system while blurring the security boundary, leading to many information security risks. Since 2020, the power information system has been attacked many times. In February 2020, through an unknown vulnerability, the power information system of the Massachusetts Electric Power Company was hit by a ransomware attack that affected its official website, electricity bill payments, and other operations [2]. In April 2020, Energias de Portugal (EDP), the Portuguese multinational energy giant and one of the largest European operators in the energy and wind sectors, had been hit by the ransomware, Ragnar Locker. After troubleshooting, it was found that the system had been accessed by an unauthorized third party, resulting in the theft of a large amount of sensitive data [3]. In September 2020, K-Electric, the sole electricity provider for Karachi, Pakistan, has suffered a Netwalker ransomware attack that led to the disruption of billing and online services. A large number of unencrypted files were stolen by ransomware organizations [4]. It is clear that the power information system, as a key infrastructure, is concerned with international livelihood. Once breached, the attacker can not only get a large amount of private data but also gain a huge amount of revenue. Therefore, the frequency of attacks on power information systems is increasing, and the security situation of power grid systems should not be underestimated.

By analyzing the above security incidents, the main security risks of power information systems exist in the following two aspects.

The first is the risk of unknown backdoor vulnerabilities. The attacker will try to infiltrate the unknown backdoor vulnerabilities present in the target system before the attack. Due to the lack of monitoring and management of the system for insider behavior, attackers can lurk in the intranet after initially obtaining system privileges. Then gradually rely on system management flaws to obtain higher system privileges and cause damage to the system. The challenge is that these malicious code behaviors are not detectable with the usual detection methods [5]. Therefore, it is highly concealed.

The second is the border security risk, that is, the risk caused by the weakening of the security border. Power information systems have complex components, involve many fields, and are located in a changing environment, so it is difficult to cover the entire system through traditional security defense means. The 5G network provides higher bandwidth and lower latency for edge IoT devices to access the core business network. But at the same time, it also expands the attack surface of the core network [6]. In the IoT network environment anomaly and intrusion detection is a very challenging problem [7]. A large number of devices and systems have brought a wider attack surface to attackers, affecting the overall security of the system.

In view of the above security risks, this paper constructs a dynamic defense-based security architecture for power information systems based on the existing security architecture for power information systems to enhance the endogenous security attributes of power information systems.

3 Research on Dynamic Defense Technology

With the development of power information systems, more and more web application systems are put into use, the security boundary of power system is weakening, and the attack means against the application layer is becoming more and more advanced. Facing the new situation of power system data security protection, the traditional static security protection technologies such as firewall and intrusion detection systems are not enough to deal with the increasing unknown threats. Therefore, dynamic protection technologies such as mobile target defense and mimic defense have become research hotspots, and are more and more applied in practiced projects.

Moving target defense (MTD) is a dynamic defense idea proposed by the national science and Technology Commission to change the asymmetric situation of network attack and defense [8]. The main means is to realize the conversion of attack surface through diversified transformation and random change, to make the system unpredictable and increase the attack cost and difficulty [9]. In 2010, NITRD pointed out the meaning of mobile target defense in "Cybersecurity game-change research & development recommendations" [10]. NITRD believes that the expectation of mobile target defense is to increase the cost and complexity of the attack, reduce the vulnerability exposure of the system and the probability of being attacked, to improve the security elasticity. In order to achieve this expectation, NITRD pointed out that the security mechanisms and policies of the system need to be diverse and change over time. In 2011, Manadhata proposed the concept of attack surface conversion for mobile target defense. The attack surface describes the vulnerability set of the system, that is, the larger the attack surface, the more ways the attacker poses a threat to the system. The attack surface conversion is to change the attack target through the switching of executors and the transformation of IP addresses during the operation of the system, so as to convert the attack surface so that the system presents an unpredictable attack target to the attacker and achieve the effect of mobile target defense [11].

Mimic defense (MD) is an active defense technology proposed by the research team led by Academician Jiangxing Wu. Dynamic heterogeneous redundancy (DHR) is a technical theory proposed by Jiangxing Wu's team in 2008 and is the core method of mimic defense [12]. Dynamic redundancy and heterogeneity mean that multiple executors with equivalent functions and different structures perform the same task, and perform dynamic scheduling among executors, so as to reduce static security defects and avoid the threat caused by common-mode vulnerabilities. Compared with the previous passive defense technology, mimic defense no longer pursues the security protection boundary without loopholes but makes the system unpredictable through the combination of diversity and randomness of actuators. It is an endogenous security mechanism with the ability of autonomy, adaptation, and self-growth.

According to the commonness of the above defense methods, it can be concluded that the core idea of dynamic defense is to increase the attack cost and difficulty and cut off the ongoing attack through unpredictable changes.

At present, the dynamic defense of the power system mainly focuses on mobile target defense and mimic defense. Reference [13] studies a power system defense system for intranet security, formulates the terminal security mechanism, improves the data transmission security protocol, designs the intranet application system model, and uses the idea of dynamic defense to ensure data security from the source. Reference [14] points out that the distribution automation system is an important part of the power system control area. It is considered that whether to identify unknown attacks is the difference between active defense and passive defense. An active defense method is designed for the distribution master station to change the defense mode of the distribution master station into active through trusted computing, active trapping, and other technologies. Reference [15] analyzes the security characteristics and risks of power industry control systems, points out that the existing protection methods of the power system can not find loopholes in time, and believes that mimic security defense can solve the uncertain threat of power industrial control system. Mimic security defense technology makes the system change continuously in the dynamic heterogeneous redundant space through heterogeneous and dynamic scheduling at the levels of platform, software, network, and data, which makes it difficult for attackers to attack.

4   Power System Security Architecture Based on Dynamic Defense

Unlike traditional network security architectures that ignore system endogenous security, the basic idea of dynamic defense is to import elements of diversity, dynamism, and randomness into the dissimilarity redundancy structure in the field of reliability. Based on the adaptive transformation mechanism of the attack surface, it constructs a "dynamic heterogeneous security" system with heterogeneous key service components and polymorphic business applications under the condition of functional semantic equivalence.

It inherits the multimode adjudication-based policy scheduling mechanism of the mimic defense architecture, conducts multidimensional dynamic reconfiguration of the system attack surface, and adds a dynamic security control mechanism based on the closed-loop "detection-response-reconfiguration-recovery". The defense architecture not only blocks vulnerability exploitation attacks against the underlying hardware and software environment but also hinders attacks that leverage internal logic vulnerabilities in the target business system. Therefore, the defense architecture can make the target system have the "endogenous security" attributes of high reliability, high availability, and high persistence [16].

In the face of the current security situation of power information systems, which is characterized by the proliferation of unknown backdoor vulnerabilities and the increasingly urgent need for security protection, this paper uses the idea of dynamic defense on the existing architecture of power grids and combines it with the existing gateways, firewalls, intrusion detection systems and other security devices of power grids to build a logical architecture for power system security based on dynamic defense, as shown in Fig. 1. The logical architecture mainly includes mimic defense layer, mimic network switching layer, mimic service layer, application management layer, and dynamic management module.

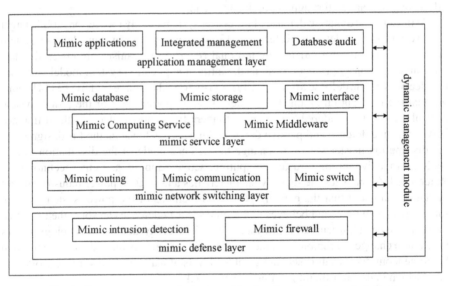

Fig. 1. Power system security logic architecture based on dynamic defense.

4.1   Mimic Defense Layer

The mimic defense layer includes a mimic intrusion detection system, a mimic firewall, a mimic anti-virus gateway, etc. It is responsible for the overall defense of the architecture. Get rid of the traditional defense thinking that relies on prior knowledge, and dynamically heterogeneous original security equipment. To achieve effective defense against unknown backdoor vulnerabilities, and provide a full range of security protection for the entire system.

4.2   Mimic Network Switching Layer

The mimic network switching layer includes mimic communication server, mimic switch, mimic routing, etc. It is responsible for the overall communication of the architecture. Construct a mimic network by mimicking access procedures, network topology, transmission paths, and communication protocols. Thereby enhancing the endogenous security of the architecture at the network level. The mimic network switching layer provides data exchange services for the mimic service layer.

4.3   Mimic Service Layer

The mimic service layer includes mimic storage, mimic database, mimic interface, mimic computing server, mimic middleware, etc. It is responsible for the basic services of the architecture. Construct high-security distributed services by mimicking storage devices, databases, interface programs, and basic servers. Ensure the security and privacy of data while guaranteeing high availability. Enhance the endogenous security of the architecture at the basic service level.

4.4   Application Management Layer

The application management layer includes a mimic application server, a mimic integrated supervision server, a mimic database audit device, etc. It is responsible for the application and comprehensive management of the architecture. By mimicking web applications and management servers, it solves the security threats caused by the upper-layer applications of web services and internal management errors. At the same time, it monitors the overall operation of the architecture for comprehensive management and transmits the results to the dynamic module. Thereby enhancing the endogenous security of the architecture at the application management level. The direct object of the application management layer is the mimic service layer.

4.5   Dynamic Control Module

The dynamic control module dynamically controls the overall architecture, including functions such as dynamic adjudication, dynamic reconstruction, abnormal cleaning, and variant switching. It is responsible for the implementation of dynamic defense of the architecture. Dynamic adjudication votes on the output vectors of multiple variants, generating correct output responses and adjudicating variants with questionable behavior. The suspicious variant behavior is then monitored to detect its possible attack activity, thus converting the attack event into a probabilistically manageable reliability problem for the defender. As a result, the attacker has to face a dynamic target and launch a coordinated and consistent attack under non-cooperative conditions; Dynamic reconfiguration requires the construction of a collection of multiple alternative system variants with functional semantic equivalence. Through the attack surface adaptive transformation mechanism, the correspondence between system functionality and implementation structure is allowed to dynamically transform in time and space. Thus, the attacker loses the grasp of the structure of the target object, the operating environment, making it nonlinearly more difficult to detect perception or predict defensive behavior. In addition, the dynamic control module should metric and evaluate the attack effectiveness in real-time to strategically perform cleaning and software variant switching. It makes the defense scenario observed by the attacker more dynamic and complex. It is impossible to replicate or inherit the attack experience and difficult to accurately detect the target body structure and operating environment, thus making the attack action impossible to produce a plannable and predictable effect [16].

The dynamic control module enables the dynamization of the entire power system by uniting all layers of the architecture. It dramatically increases the difficulty and cost of attackers, improves the system's defense against APT and unknown backdoor vulnerabilities, and fundamentally changes the offensive and defensive pattern that is easy to attack but difficult to defend [16].

5 Typical Application Scenarios of Power Information System

The security area of the power system is mainly divided into generation control area and security management area, in which the information management area is divided into several business security areas. The information management area is located at the master station layer. There are a large number of services in its business security area, such as query service, collection management, data management, operation, and maintenance monitoring, which are vulnerable to DDoS, XSS, CSRF, and other attacks on Web services, and data security is threatened. Aiming at the web service security of the business security area of the information management area, this paper proposes to apply the power system security architecture based on dynamic defense to the dynamic defense transformation of the data management service, including the mimicry transformation of the access program and the mobile target defense transformation of the computing area. Through the mimicry construction of the network access program in the information management region, the access request can be judged in multiple variants to avoid illegal access caused by common-mode vulnerabilities. Through the mobile target defense transformation of the computing area, the concealment and attack surface conversion of a single variant vulnerability is realized, so that the attacker can not grasp the attack targets and vulnerabilities so that the attack behavior is unsustainable.

5.1   Access Program Mimicry

The most important change attribute of the mimic defense system is unpredictability, which needs to be combined with diversity and randomness. Diversity is the basis, which means that a large available configuration space needs to be provided for the system, and randomness is to maximize the use of this configuration space, which is the key to affecting unpredictability. The mimicry construction of the network access program includes two parts. The first is to realize the heterogeneous access program in order to maximize its diversity, and then schedule heterogeneous access programs to maximize their randomness, to maximize the unpredictability of network access programs on the premise of ensuring the quality of service. The access program of the power system production control area provides external access services. In the power system security architecture based on dynamic defense, the mimic access program belongs to the mimic service layer.

The Heterogeneous of Secure Access Program in Information Management Region.
The heterogeneous technology of access programs is the basis of mimicry to construct access programs and the key to realizing diversity. Heterogeneous of the programs is to realize the same function through different programs, which can be regarded as different variants of the same program. To realize the heterogeneous access program, we need to consider how to reproduce the same program in different ways, that is, to realize the same function with different logic. At present, the available methods include code confusion, cyclic multi-version compilation, and so on. By randomizing the layout of the linear region such as heap, stack, and shared library mapping, it is possible to prevent the attacker from directly locating the location of the attack code by increasing the difficulty of the attacker to predict the destination address [17].

Mimic Scheduling Strategy for Heterogeneous Program Variants. The scheduling strategy of program variants plays a decisive role in the effectiveness of mimicry construction, and randomness needs to be realized to make the access program of mimicry construction unpredictable. Therefore, the key of scheduling strategy research is the scheduling algorithm, that is, how to make the variants selected by the algorithm meet three requirements: 1) sufficient randomness; 2) Sufficient heterogeneity; 3) Adequate service quality. To meet the heterogeneity, the algorithm needs to select a heterogeneous variant set; In order to meet the quality of service, the algorithm needs to decide according to the variant quality of service; To meet the randomness, some choices of the algorithm should be random. When receiving the user's access request, first determine the access authentication result. If the authentication passes, select a variant meeting the above three conditions from the program variant resource pool according to the algorithm to provide access services to the user. When the environment meets the variant switching conditions in the scheduling policy, reselect the program variant meeting the above three conditions to continue to provide services. The access and response process is shown in Fig. 2.

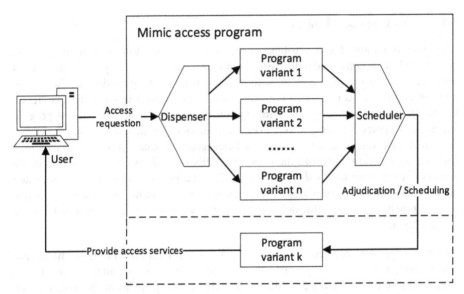

Fig. 2. User's access request and the scheduling procedure for program variants.

5.2 Mobile Target Defense in Computing Area

The attack surface conversion mechanism in mobile target defense actively changes the system information system in a way controllable by the defender and destroys the dependence of the attack chain on the determination of the operating environment and single characteristics by dynamically and randomly changing the system configuration attributes [18]. The system attack surface conversion mechanism can improve the uncertainty of the target system.

Construction of Server Resource Pool and Execution Set. To construct mobile target defense in the computing area, we must first construct multiple heterogeneous redundant computing servers. Different servers are constructed through the combination of different operating systems and different hardware. Then, heterogeneous server sets are selected by the scheduling algorithm to form an execution set, which is used to execute computing services.

Anomaly Adjudication and Attack Surface Conversion Mechanism. Multiple heterogeneous executors are parallel, and the transformation (movement) of all executors has a great impact on the service efficiency of the system. For this reason, the system uses a multi-table decision mechanism to judge the execution of multiple executable bodies. If the most executor is normal and a few executors are abnormal, it is decided that a few executors may be running fault or external penetration, as shown in Fig. 3, and then the scheduling mechanism makes it offline and loading alternative servers. Since the vulnerable server is offline, the attacker cannot continue to exploit the vulnerability or even find the target, and the new server replaces the vulnerable server, as shown in Fig. 4, that is, the process of attack surface conversion is completed. Then, the replaced execution is cleaned and restored, and put back into the resource pool for scheduling.

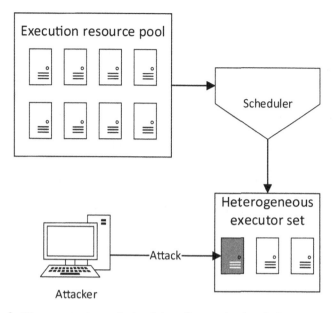

Fig. 3. The executor is attacked and the ruling mechanism finds an exception.

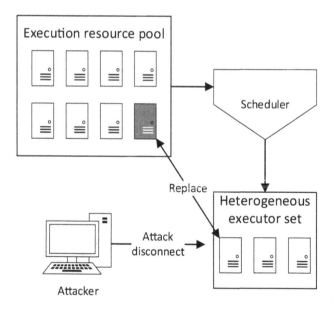

Fig. 4. Attack surface conversion.

6 Epilogue

Aiming at the data security protection of power systems, this paper points out that the traditional static defense strategy gradually does not adapt to the increasing threats in the power information system. Facing the new situation of power information system protection, it is necessary to adopt the idea of dynamic security to make the system have endogenous security capability. This paper studies the mobile target defense and mimic security strategy puts forward the dynamic defense strategy for power systems and designs a new generation of power data security protection architecture based on dynamic defense. The dynamic defense technology is applied to the information management area of the power system, the network access program and computing area are dynamically transformed, and the system can resist unknown attacks through mimic judgment and attack surface conversion. In the aspect of actuator scheduling, we can continue to research algorithm optimization to reduce the switching time and ensure the quality of service of the system.

References

1. Shafiq, M., Tian, Z., Bashir, A.K., Du, X., Guizani, M.: CorrAUC: a malicious bot-IoT traffic detection method in IoT network using machine learning techniques. IEEE Internet Things J. **8**(5), 3242–3254 (2020)
2. RMLD (2020). https://www.rmld.com/sites/g/files/vyhlif1126/f/uploads/rmld_press_rele ase_ransomware_02.24.20_x.pdf
3. Bleeping computer (2020). https://www.bleepingcomputer.com/news/security/edp-energy-giant-confirms-ragnar-locker-ransomware-attack/
4. TechNadu (2020). https://www.technadu.com/pakistans-largest-electric-supplier-crippled-netwalker-ransomware/198606/
5. Lu, H., Jin, C., Helu, X., Zhu, C., Guizani, N., Tian, Z.: AutoD: intelligent blockchain application unpacking based on JNI layer deception call. IEEE Netw. **35**(2), 215–221 (2021)
6. Shafiq, M., Tian, Z., Sun, Y., Du, X., Guizani, M.: Selection of effective machine learning algorithm and Bot-IoT attacks traffic identification for internet of things in smart city. Futur. Gener. Comput. Syst. **107**, 433–442 (2020)
7. Hu, N., Tian, Z., Lu, H., Du, X., Guizani, M.: A multiple-kernel clustering based intrusion detection scheme for 5G and IoT networks. Int. J. Mach. Learn. Cybernet. **12**, 1–16 (2021)
8. Guilin, C., Baosheng, W., Tianzuo, W.: Research and development of moving target defense technology. J. Comput. Res. Dev. **53**(5), 968–987 (2016)
9. Zhou, Y.Y., Cheng, G., Guo, C.S.: Survey on attack surface dynamic transfer technology based on moving target defense. J. Softw. **29**(9), 2799–2820 (2018)
10. Nitrd (2010). https://www.nitrd.gov/pubs/CSIA_IWG_%20Cybersecurity_%20GameCha nge_RD_%20Recommendations_20100513.pdf
11. Manadhata, P.K., Tan, K.M., Maxion, R.A., et al.: An approach to measuring a system's attack surface, pp. 1–29. Carnegie-Mellon Univ Pittsburgh Pa School of Computer Science, Pittsburgh (2007)
12. Wu, J.X.: Cyberspace mimic security defense. Secrecy Sci. Technol. **2014**(10), 4–9 (2014)
13. Chen, Y.F., Li, Q.: Research on security defense system of power system intranet. Modern Ind. Econ. Inf. **2016**(6), 131–132 (2021)
14. Kang, C.Q., Li, E.X., et al.: An active defense structure design method of new generation distribution automation master station. Electr. Power Inf. Commun. Technol. **19**(3), 65–73 (2021)

15. Ying, H., Liu, S.H., Song-Hua, L.: Overview of power industry control system security technology. Electr. Power Inf. Commun. Technol. **16**(3), 56–63 (2018)
16. Ji, X.S., Liang, H., Hongchao, H.U.: New thoughts on security technologies for space-ground integration information network. Telecommun. Sci. **33**(12), 24–35 (2017)
17. Lu, H., et al.: Research on intelligent detection of command level stack pollution for binary program analysis. Mobile Netw. Appl. **26**, 1–10 (2020)
18. Lei, C., Ma, D.H.: Moving target defense technique based on network attack surface self-adaptive mutation. Chin. J. Comput. **41**(05), 1109–1131 (2018)

Author Index